The 1995 Genealogy Annual

The 1995 Genealogy Annual

A Bibliography of Published Sources

Thomas J. Kemp

SR Scholarly Resources Inc.
Wilmington, Delaware

Scholarly Resources Inc.
104 Greenhill Avenue
Wilmington, DE 19805-1897

International Standard Serial Number: 1090-7440
International Standard Book Number: 0-8420-2661-4

⊗The paper used in this publication meets the minimum requirements of the American National Standard for permanence of paper for printed library materials, Z39.48, 1984.

recycled paper

Dedicated to my wife Vi

and children Andrew and Sarah

About the Author

Thomas J. Kemp is the head of the Special Collections Department of the University of South Florida Library in Tampa. He has served as the chair of the Council of National Library and Information Associations, chair of the History Section of the American Library Association, and president of the American Society of Indexers. Prior to his current position, he was the library director of the Historical Society of Pennsylvania. He is the author of numerous books including the *International Vital Records Handbook* and the *Connecticut Researcher's Handbook*.

Contents

Genealogical Sources by State

Introduction

*T*HE *1995 GENEALOGY ANNUAL* is a comprehensive bibliography of genealogies, handbooks, and source materials published in 1995. It is a valuable core reference tool for genealogists and local historians and builds on the traditions of P. William Filby's *American and British Genealogy and Heraldry: A Selected List of Books* (Boston, MA: New England Historic Genealogical Society, 1983), and *A Bibliography of American County Histories* (Baltimore, MD: Genealogical Publishing, 1985); Marion J. Kaminkow's *Genealogies in the Library of Congress* (Baltimore, MD: Magna Charta Books, 1972–1987), and *United States Local Histories in the Library of Congress, a Bibliography* (Baltimore, MD: Magna Charta Books, 1975); and *Genealogies Cataloged by the Library of Congress since 1986* (Washington, DC: Library of Congress, 1992).

The 1995 Genealogy Annual is divided into three sections beginning with FAMILY HISTORIES, which cites American and international single and multifamily genealogies. Each genealogy is listed alphabetically by the major surnames included in each book. The GUIDES AND HANDBOOKS section is subdivided into two parts and contains reference and how-to books for researching specific record groups or areas of this country or the world. The first part, the **United States**, is arranged alphabetically by subject or region. The second part, **International**, arranges entries by country or region of the world. Finally, GENEALOGICAL SOURCES BY STATE includes data on cemetery, census, military, and other useful records. It is organized alphabetically by state and then by city or county.

Although many local libraries have strong genealogy and local history collections, none owns all of the sources listed in *The 1995 Genealogy Annual*. However, they can assist the researcher in locating copies of every book cited here, either within their own collection or by interlibrary loan. It is now much more common for libraries to lend genealogical and local history books. Library regional and statewide online catalogs and OCLC, the international library online catalog, can instantly display which libraries own copies of these materials, thereby bringing the strength of these combined libraries to every local library and personal computer.

In addition, several major U.S. libraries attempt to collect all new genealogical materials. The Library of Congress, the New York Public Library, and the Allen County (Indiana) Public Library, for example, have strong genealogical collections. The largest such collection is at the Family History Library in Salt Lake City, Utah, with its network of over 2,850 Family History Centers located in the United States and sixty-two other countries and territories.

Most Important Books of 1995

O F THE THOUSANDS OF NEW BOOKS published in 1995, the following have been singled out for their insight, usefulness, and permanent value. It is noteworthy that three of our foremost institutions are well documented. James B. Allen's *Hearts Turned to the Fathers, a History of the Genealogical Society of Utah, 1894–1994* (Provo, UT: Brigham Young University), John A. Schutz's *A Nobel Pursuit, the Sesquicentennial of the New England Historic Genealogical Society, 1845–1995* (Boston, MA: New England Historic Genealogical Society), and Robert M. Warner's *Diary of a Dream, a History of the National Archives Independence Movement, 1980–1985* (Metuchen, NJ: Scarecrow Press) are thorough and timely studies that provide important background information and insight into the history and growth of these premier repositories and should be read by every genealogist and local historian.

Robert Charles Anderson's three-volume *The Great Migration Begins, Immigrants to New England, 1620–1633* (Boston, MA: New England Historic Genealogical Society), David W. Hartman and David Coles's *Biographical Rosters of Florida's Confederate and Union Soldiers, 1861–1865* (Wilmington, NC: Broadfoot Pub. Co.), and Frank N. Schubert's *On the Trail of the Buffalo Soldier, Biographies of African Americans in the United States Army, 1866–1917* (Wilmington, DE: Scholarly Resources) are well-produced documented sources that will serve as standard works for years to come.

Paula Kay Byers wrote the *African-American Genealogical Sourcebook*, *Asian-American Genealogical Sourcebook*, *Hispanic-American Genealogical Sourcebook*, and *Native-American Genealogical Sourcebook*, thereby signaling that Gale Research Inc. is again becoming an important genealogical publisher. And Gary Mokotoff continues his strong and authoritative contributions with *How to Document Victims and Locate Survivors of the Holocaust* (Teaneck, NJ: Avotaynu).

Colin D. Rogers's *The Surname Detective, Investigating Surname Distribution in England, 1086–Present Day* (Manchester, England: Manchester University Press) is a welcome sequel to his significant and readable *The Family Tree Detective* (Manchester, England: Manchester University Press, 1983), which was perhaps the finest genealogical how-to book ever published. Raymond S. Wright's *The Genealogist's Handbook, Modern Methods for Researching Family History* (Chicago, IL: American Library Association) is very much in this tradition and will be widely used for personal instruction and as a classroom text.

FAMILY HISTORIES

— A ————————————————————————————

Aaron
Baldree, Garvis Brookshire. *The Baldree Family*. Author, 1995. 212p.

Abbott
Cagle, Ruby Abbott. *The Bishop Family from Manchester, England to Washington County, Maine*. Jasper, TN: Author, 1995. Unpgd.
Hare, Norma Q. *Puritans, Pioneers and Planters, an Ingraham, Abbott, Wardwell, Culver, Burbank Genealogy*. Arroyo Grande, CA: N. L. Enterprises, 1995. 330p.
Koickler, Eloyce Hubbard. *Hiestand, Hestand, Hastings*. Helena, MT: Author, 1995. 127p.

Abrams
McBride, Jean Coleman. *The Colemans of West Alabama and Allied Families*. Aliceville, AL: Author, 1995. 200p.

Acker
Acker, Mary Paschel. *Ackers through the Ages*. Amarillo, TX: Author, 1995. 479p.

Ackerman
McCants, Beaufort Theron. *A Traditional McCants Family History, 1590–1988*. Hemingway, SC: Three Rivers Historical Society, 1995. 291p.

Acland
Beswetherick, Kathleen. *The Aclands and Budehaven: The Story of a Devon Family and a Cornish Town*. Bude, England: Author, 1995. 48p.

Acquisto
La Marca, Jeffrey Peter. *Window to the Past, Door to the Future, a Glimpse at an American Genealogy, Compilation of Data on the Acquisto, Calamera, Carroll, Crowley, Guastaferro, Hawley, La Marca, Lavier, and Steigerwalt Families*. Yorba Linda, CA: Shumway Family History Services, 1995. 214p.

Acuff
McNamara, Billie R. *Abstracts of Military Service Pension Records for the Surname Acuff*. Knoxville, TN: Author, 1995. 43p.

Adair

Adair, Shirley Brown. *Robert Adair (1770–1845c.), an Adair Family History, Reid, Emerson, Hobbs, Worley, Thompson (Related Lines)*. Rockwall, TX: Author, 1995. 146p.

R. E. W. Thompson (1856–1937), Adair, Clark, Carroll, Sellers, Lawson (Related Lines). Rockwall, TX: S. B. Adair, 1995. 133p.

Adams

Ad Infinitum, Stories of the Families of the Sons and Daughters of Glenn and Elizabeth Adams. Decorah, IA: Anundsen Pub. Co., 1995. 292p.

Counce, Oliver Joseph. *The Counce Genealogy, the Descendants of Edward Counce (Counts) and Sarah Adams*. New Orleans, LA: Author, 1995. Unpgd.

Gardner Glynn, Gary. *The Adams Family of Massachusetts*. Needham, MA: Author, 1995. 480p.

Spoden, Muriel Clark. *An American Ancestry of the Clark-Morton and Tyman-Millar-Adams History*. Kingsport, TN: Spoden Associates, 1995. 547p.

Adcock

Adcock, John J., Sr. *Adcock, Nix Genealogy*. Author, 1995. 46p.

Addington

Addington, Jacquelyn Snyder. *Historical Sketches of the Addington and Kindred Families*. Andover, KS: Author, 1995. 101p.

Ader

Ward, Naomi Etta. *The Ward Connections, Nourse, Kimmel, Wood, Babbs, Shelton, Sasubjak, Ader, Guffey, Pontiny, Archibald, Asbell*. Evansville, IN: Author, 1995. 545p.

Admire

Snyder, Ruth Curtis. *Admire Is the Name, George and Margaret (Coon) Admire of Rowan County, North Carolina, and Henry County, Kentucky*. Lincoln, NE: Author, 1995. Unpgd.

Aisenbrey

Myers, JoEllen Aisenbrey. *Aisenbrey-Kreis-Kost-Edelman*. Pleasanton, CA: Author, 1995. Unpgd.

Aizenberg

Aharon Eliyahu Aizenberg, 1864–1932. Israel: Arkhiyon ha-mishpahah, 1995. Unpgd.

Albrecht

Albrecht, Leo J. *Descendants of Peter and Katherine (Peifer) Becker, Becker Family Reunion, Sunday, August 6, 1995, Belle Plaine, Minnesota*. Belle Plaine, MN: Author, 1995. 99p.

Alexander

Cates, Banks R. *The Ancestors of Nancy Davidson Alexander, Wife of Hugh McAulay of Daniel*. Author, 1995. 139p.

Hauk, Carol A. *Descendants of Rice Hooe of Virginia, Ancestor of President James Madison.* 2nd. ed. Anderson, IN: Hauk Data Services, 1995. 93p.

Moore, Freddie Gene. *My Virginia Ancestors and Their Descendants in the Families, Burdett, Alexander, Anderson, King, Boone, Welsh, McHenry, Cornwell, Alford, Coleman, Dixon, Morgan, Jarman, Maugridge.* Author, 1995. 46p.

Smith, Herbert F. *Plummer Ancestry, Including Some Alexander, Erwin, and Flinn Links of Herbert F. Smith.* 2nd. ed. Silver Spring, MD: Author, 1995. Unpgd.

Alford

Moore, Freddie Gene. *My Virginia Ancestors and Their Descendants in the Families, Burdett, Alexander, Anderson, King, Boone, Welsh, McHenry, Cornwell, Alford, Coleman, Dixon, Morgan, Jarman, Maugridge.* Author, 1995. 46p.

Allen

Allen, Granville O'Neal. *Our Allens from Maryland to Muscle Shoals via the Mid-West.* Author, 1995. 439p.

Allen, Hardy Lee Hiram. *The Allens of Little Egypt, Egypt Is That One-Hundred Mile Tip of Southern Illinois, Hemmed in on Three Sides by the Mississippi, Ohio, and Wabash Rivers.* Baltimore, MD: Gateway Press, 1995. 483p.

Allen, Patricia Remmell. *The Remmell and Allen Families of New Castle County, Delaware.* Horsham, PA: Author, 1995. 71p.

Allen, Roy. *Allens of Ulster.* Mississauga, Ontario, Canada: Author, 1995. 65p.

Davis, Walter Goodwin. *Massachusetts and Maine Families in the Ancestry of Walter Goodwin Davis.* Baltimore, MD: Genealogical Publishing Co., 1995. 3 vols.

Gork, Frances Allen. *Ancestors and Descendants of David Allen and Mary Stanley Allen of Dearborn, Michigan.* Jackson, MI: Author, 1995. 132p.

Howe, Jeffrey. *The Block Island Allens.* 1995. 218p.

Roche, Hazel. *A Study of the Gambrells, Allens, Hensleys, Brewers, and Others from Clay and Knox Counties, Kentucky.* Moravian Falls, NC: Author, 1995. 44p.

Sellers, Betty Jane. *Til We Meet Again.* Melber, KY: Simmons Historical Pubs., 1995. 2 vols.

Streeter, Allen Raymond. *Descendants of James and Anna Bella (Sterritt) Allen of County Down, Ireland, Second in Descent from Richard and Martha Allen.* Saginaw, MI: Author, 1995. 5p.

Wicker, Richard Fenton. *The Allen Family of England, Virginia, North Carolina, Tennessee, Mississippi, Texas, and Illinois, 1600–1995, the Descendants of Captain William Allen and His Wives, Hannah Watson and Mary Hunt Minge.* Baltimore, MD: Gateway Press, 1995. 325p.

Alley

Alley, Gene. *Alley-Barnes Connection, an Oxford, Kansas, Family History.* Udall, KS: Author, 1995. 99p.

Cole, Mary. *The Bunyard Family Research and Allied Families, Alley, Fitzwater, Foster, Hughes, Jones, Ledlow, McNeely, Rose.* Kentfield, CA: Author, 1995. 151p.

Allison

Allison, James. *The Allison Family and Related Family Histories.* Oklahoma City, OK: Author, 1995. 2 vols.

Allmand

Allmand, Barbara J. *Three Virginia Families, Allmand, Parker, and Sinclair, Including a Collection of 19th Century Letters and Other Writings.* Overland Park, KS: Author, 1995. 252p.

Almond

Tinley, Ruth. *Dusty Almonds, a History of a Milling Family.* North Hykeham, Lincolnshire: Author, 1995. 24p.

Altomus

Berger, Dale E. *The Descendants of Hans Peter Altomus.* Oreland, PA: Author, 1995. 2 vols.

Ambler

Hauk, Carol A. *Descendants of Richard Ambler of Virginia.* Anderson, IN: Hauk Data Services, 1995. 96p.

Amis

Scott, Billy Dave. *Johnston-Southern of Clairborne County, Tennessee and Parker County, Texas: Isaac McNew Johnston (1838–1918) and His Wife Norvesta Melocky Southern (1841–1929) and Allied Families Amis, Haynes, Huddleston, Seabolt, Southern and Spears.* Maryville, MO: Author, 1995. 215p.

Amos

Koickler, Eloyce Hubbard. *Hiestand, Hestand, Hastings.* Helena, MT: Author, 1995. 127p.

Anctil

Anctil, Marcel. *Les Familles Anctil en Amerique.* Quebec: Author, 1995. 392p.

Anderson

Ancestors and Descendants of William Whitaker Smith, 1860–1944, and Florence Ellen Sullivan, 1875–1926, of Anderson and Greenville Counties, South Carolina. Spartanburg, SC: Reprint Co., 1995. 146p.

Anderson, Melvin Robert. *The Anderson Story.* Raleigh, NC: Lifescapes Corp., 1995. 102p.

Caldwell, Janice. *The Lost Branch of the Anderson Family, Ancestors and Descendants of Thomas Allen Howard Anderson and His Wife Martha Ann Stanley, Including Allied Families.* Helotes, TX: Author, 1995. 438p.

Carter, Park W. *A History of Some Park Families in Jefferson County, Indiana, and Allied Families of Anderson, Mann, Gilchrist and Others.* Eureka, KS: Author, 1995. Unpgd.

Dix, Roberta Cook Jackson. *The First Shall be Last, a Family History.* Author, 1995. 137p.

Moore, Freddie Gene. *My Virginia Ancestors and Their Descendants in the Families, Burdett, Alexander, Anderson, King, Boone, Welsh, McHenry, Cornwell, Alford, Coleman, Dixon, Morgan, Jarman, Maugridge.* Author, 1995. 46p.

Nimmo, Sylvia. *The Descendants and Ancestors of Milo and Dora (Moon) Russell.* Papillion, NE: Author, 1995. 44p.

O'Neal, Marcia Corrigan. *O'Neal Genealogy from the Early 1800s and Including Ancestors Anderson, Childers, Davis, Griffith, Hunt, Savage, Venard, and Willcuts.* Richmond, IN: Author, 1995. 43p.

Pearson, Frederick John. *Anderson*. Houston, TX: Author, 1995. 352p.

Pringle, Sheila. *Pringle-Anderson Family History Book*. Sumter, SC: New Concepts, 1995. Unpgd.

Stene, Charles Sherwin. *The Stene Family, Includes Rohn, Anderson, Bothwell, Davenport, Lloyd*. Decorah, IA: Anundsen Pub. Co., 1995. 385p.

Whitmore, Robert Devore. *Whitmore Family Genealogy*. Steubenville, OH: Public Library of Steubenville and Jefferson County, 1995. 14p.

Wright, Diana. *Robinson Roots*. Author, 1995. Unpgd.

York, Dorothy Anderson. *Our Anderson Family and Their Kin*. Fort Worth, TX: Author, 1995. 307p.

Andrew

Partridge, Craig. *The Descendants of William Andrew of Cambridge, Massachusetts*. Camden, ME: Penobscot Press, 1995. 365p.

Andrews

Avery, Thomas Lynn. *Family Life of John Henry and Ellen (Andrews) Swann*. Chico, CA: Author, 1995. 115p.

Partridge, Craig. *The Descendants of William Andrew of Cambridge, Massachusetts*. Camden, ME: Penobscot Press, 1995. 365p.

Angier

Johnston, Francis Clairborne. *The Angier Family of Orange and Durham Counties, North Carolina, and Allied Families of North Carolina and Virginia*. Richmond, VA: Author, 1995. 329p.

Anson

Igo, Louis M. *The Jacob Igo and Elizabeth Anson Family: Their Roots and Branches*. Georgetown, TX: Author, 1995. 447p.

Sanders, Patrick B. *Genealogies of the Sanders and Watson Families, Examining the Descendants of Henry Sanders of Germany and Donald Watson of Scotland*. Chapel Hill, NC: Professional Press, 1995. 270p.

Apgar

Atteridg, Paul T. *The Attridges of North America*. Granby, CO: Author, 1995. 429p.

Appel

Apple, Slovie Solomon. *They Were Strangers, a Family History*. NY: Vantage Press, 1995. 213p.

Appleton

Karr, Nola M. *Baker Family Record, a Genealogy of Many of the Descendants of John Baker Who Immigrated from England in 1637*. White Plains, MD: Automated Graphic Systems, 1995. 663p.

Aragon

Sanchez, George Abe. *The Gurule/Aragon Family of San Miguel County, New Mexico, a Genealogical Study*. El Paso, TX: Author, 1995. 59p.

Arceneaux

Arceneaux, Julius Charles. *From Where We Came, 1614–1996: The First Family to Settle in South Louisiana*. Greenwell Springs, LA: Author, 1995. 103p.

Archibald

Ward, Naomi Etta. *The Ward Connections, Nourse, Kimmel, Wood, Babbs, Shelton, Sasubjak, Ader, Guffey, Pontiny, Archibald, Asbell*. Evansville, IN: Author, 1995. 545p.

Armbruster

Deiss, Kathryn. *The Family of Joseph and Hilda (Armbruster) Deiss*. Author, 1995. Unpgd.

Armengol

Nelson, Carmen Valls. *Our Family under Seven Flags, an Informal History of the Mendiola and Valls-Armengol Families*. Laredo, TX: Author, 1995. 255p.

Armentrout

Miller, DeWitt Henry. *Ancestors and Descendants of Walter William Wisman and Mary Elizabeth Armentrout*. Roanoke, VA: Author, 1995. 65p.

Armistead

Hauk, Carol A. *Descendants of William Armistead of Virginia*. 4th. ed. Anderson, IN: Hauk Data Services, 1995. 2 vols.

Johnston, Anne Plummer. *The Plummer Lineage of America*. Reston, VA: M. L. Tomaselli, 1995. 56p.

Armitage

Linn, Jo White. *Ancestry of Moore/Rowan Families, with Related Lines of Fleming, Renick, Bosley, Green, Girault, Beatty, Reading, Armitage, Ryerson, Rapelje*. New Orleans, LA: Author, 1995. 186p.

Armstrong

Ziegel, Ruth Turner. *Julius Christy of Virginia and Kentucky, 1730–1808, and Agatha Barnett Christy, 1740–1820, and Related Families of Barnett, Gibbs, Blackburn, Cave, Glass, Kirtley, Bush, Lindsey, Armstrong, Whaley, Davis, and Day*. Cincinnati, OH: Author, 1995. 92p.

Arnesen

Nachman, Rosemary A. *The Families Hansen, Bentsen of Holt Parish, Aust-Agdar County, Norway and Johnsdatter-Arnesen of Valer and Moss, Ostfold County, Norway*. San Diego, CA: Author, 1995. Unpgd.

Arnold

Kaufman, Mary Arnold. *Martin-Arnold and Allied Families, Lanier, Bailey, Swan, Sandidge, Gholston, Morgan, and Born, Migration from Virginia to Tennessee, Georgia, Alabama and Arkansas*. Knoxville, TN: Tennessee Valley Pub., 1995. 212p.

Arthaud

Arthaud, John Bradley. *The Arthaud Family of Bourbonne-les-Bains and Langres, Department of Haute Marne, France, with Related Families of Gascard, Gautherot, Lauzanne, Liegault, Mutinot and Walferdin and One Immigrant Branch in the United States*. Columbia, MO: Author, 1995. 123p.

Asbell

Ward, Naomi Etta. *The Ward Connections, Nourse, Kimmel, Wood, Babbs, Shelton, Sasubjak, Ader, Guffey, Pontiny, Archibald, Asbell*. Evansville, IN: Author, 1995. 545p.

Ashby

Hauk, Carol A. *Descendants of Edmund Ashby of Virginia*. Anderson, IN: Hauk Data Services, 1995. 51p.

Ashpaw

Gardiner Jackson, Ann E. *Roots: Gardiner, Ingram, Grimmeissen, Ashpaw, Thiessen, Jackson, Meeker*. Author, 1995. 35p.

Aslakson

ZumBrunnen, Mary Hanna. *Genealogy, History of the Aslakson, Hana and Related Families, 1550–1995*. DeForest, WI: Hanbrunn House Pubs., 1995. 528p.

Atkinson

Atkinson, Robert Wilmer. *Atkinson Ancestors and Allied Families*. Decorah, IA: Anundsen Pub. Co., 1995. 263p.

Attridge

Atteridg, Paul T. *The Attridges of North America*. Granby, CO: Author, 1995. 429p.

Austin

Carlin, Jim. *Some Descendants of Richard Austin of Charlestown, Massachusetts*. Charlestown, MA: Austin Families Association of America, 1995. 692p.

Carlin, Liz Austin. *The Ancestry of Humilis Owen, Wife of Nathaniel Austin*. West Hills, CA: Author, 1995. 67p.

Ross, Louise. *Jane Austin, Family History*. London: Routledge, 1995. 5 vols.

Sherard, Rodney Merle. *The Descendants of William Henry Hurlbert and Amy Adeline Austin*. Greenwood, IN: Author, 1995. 164p.

Sutherland, Elihu Jasper. *Swindall and Austin Family of Virginia and North Carolina and Related Families*. Clintwood, VA: Author, 1995. 400p.

Auxier

Auxier, Dave. *The Auxier Family*. Memphis, TN: Author, 1995. 686p.

Auzenne

Auzenne, Conrad Andrew. *Auzenne, Donato, Frilot, Lemelle, Meullion, a Genealogical Study of Five Families and Other Allied Families of Southern Louisiana*. Author, 1995. 222p.

Avery

Gelinas, Daisy Frances Avery. *The Avery Trail, Virginia to Georgia.* Author, 1995. 65p.

Axtell

Axtell, William Douglas. *Axtell, 1534–1995.* Author, 1995. Unpgd.

Ayres

Ayres, Thomas D. *Ayres Genealogy, Some of the Descendants of Captain John Ayres of Brooksfield, Massachusetts.* 5th ed. Simsbury, CT: Author, 1995. 66p.

Bostic, Paul Eugene. *Bruce, Maupin, Carr and Some Related Families Including Ballard, Hearn, Ayres, McCubbin, Cloud, Lane, Eveland (Elfland), Graves, Sharp and Willis.* Clinton, TN: Author, 1995. 391p.

Craig, Noreen Ayres. *Papers of Seymour Augustus Ayres, 1875–1959, and His Wife Mabel Rebecca Wells, 1878–1941.* Farmington, NM: Author, 1995. 88p.

–B

Babbitt

McKee, Ruth Vernette. *The Known Ancestry of Prudence May, Daughter of Ezra May and Margaret Lyon, and Wife of Isaac Babbitt.* Minneapolis, MN: Author, 1995. 83p.

———. *The Known Ancestry of Rev. Isaac Babbitt, 1757–1833, Including Cooper, Crane, Ford, Lovell, Morse, Pierce, Tarne, Tisdale, Walker and Whitman Families.* Minneapolis, MN: Author, 1995. 42p.

Babbs

Ward, Naomi Etta. *The Ward Connections, Nourse, Kimmel, Wood, Babbs, Shelton, Sasubjak, Ader, Guffey, Pontiny, Archibald, Asbell.* Evansville, IN: Author, 1995. 545p.

Babitzke

Norquist, Carolyn Brost. *The Legacy of Jakob and Margaretha Brosz, Germans from Russia, Unser Leute.* Baltimore, MD: Gateway Press, 1995. 125p.

Backenstoss

Backensto, Elwood Bruce. *Addendum to Backenstoss-Baggenstoss Family History.* Woodbury, NJ: Author, 1995. 411p.

Bacon

Reynolds, Beatrice Kay. *Thomas Davenport of Dorchester, Massachusetts, His Descendants in Sidney, Maine (1762–1995).* Sidney, ME: Author, 1995. 34p.

Baehr

Boehr, Ewanda Siebert. *From Hemp and Flax Fields to Lands of Wheat and Corn, Baehr, Bohr, Boehr Genealogy, 1700–1995.* Langham, Saskatchewan, Author, 1995. 356p.

Bagley

Breffeilh, Melva Kinch. *The Ancestors and Descendants of Horatio Edmund Needham and Lucina Bagley, Who Married 25 November 1852 in Royalton, Cuyahoga County, Ohio.* Sulphur, LA: Wise Publications, 1995. 307p

Guevarra, Mark Bennett. *A Heritage of Service: Families of Chester County, South Carolina, Lawrence County, Mississippi, Wyoming County, New York, and the Philippines.* Houston, TX: Author, 1995. 611p.

Bahler

Wagner, Betty Marie Daley. *The Schneider Genealogy and Related Families, Ancestors and Descendants of Carl Rudolph Schneider and Elizabeth Lena Bahler, Later Spelled Beller, John G. Bahler (Beller) and Anna Elisabeth Schneider, Samuel Bahler (Beller) and Elisabeth Litzy of Uetendorf, Canton Berne, Switzerland and Green County, Wisconsin, 1765–1995.* Milford, OH: Author, 1995. 201p.

Bailey

Bailey, Rex Franklin. *Baileys from Bute, Featuring the Genealogy of the Two Sons of James Bailey, William Fleming Bailey, Sr., the Revolutionary Soldier and Kennedy Bailey.* Fountain Inn, SC: Author, 1995. 257p.

Batcher, Olive M. *Hill Wallace Family History.* Ames, IA: Author, 1995. 253p.

Howard, David Lane. *The Descendants of Jacob and Sarah (Berry) Bailey of Leeds, Androscoggin, Maine, 1791–1995.* Salt Lake City, UT: Author, 1995. 28p.

Kaufman, Mary Arnold. *Martin-Arnold and Allied Families, Lanier, Bailey, Swan, Sandidge, Gholston, Morgan, and Born, Migration from Virginia to Tennessee, Georgia, Alabama and Arkansas.* Knoxville, TN: Tennessee Valley Pub., 1995. 212p.

Koickler, Eloyce Hubbard. *Hiestand, Hestand, Hastings.* Helena, MT: Author, 1995. 127p.

Baker

Berry, Eddie Clayton. *Berry-Baker Connection.* Houston, TX: Author, 1995. 409p.

Davidson, Betty Baker. *The Descendants of William and Mary Evans Baker, a History of the Baker Family and Related Families of Marion County (1739–1995).* Columbia, SC: Author, 1995. 178p.

Jackson, Betty Hallandsworth. *Charles and Cynthia.* Fresno, CA: Wayland Jackson, 1995. 378p.

Karr, Nola M. *Baker Family Record, a Genealogy of Many of the Descendants of John Baker Who Immigrated from England in 1637.* White Plains, MD: Automated Graphic Systems, 1995. 663p.

Baldree

Baldree, Garvis Brookshire. *The Baldree Family.* Author, 1995. 212p.

Baldwin

Baldwin, George E. *The Descendants of Deacon Aaron Baldwin of North Bradford, Connecticut, 1724–1800, with a Brief Account of His Ancestors.* Bowie, MD: Heritage Books, 1907, 1995. 106p.

Ball

Adair, Shirley Brown. *Descendants of Asher B. Beauchamp and John Casey, Nave, Ball, Bingham (Related Lines).* Rockwall, TX: Author, 1995. 139p.

Hauk, Carol A. *Descendants of William Ball of Virginia*. Anderson, IN: Hauk Data Services, 1995. 229p.

Maerz, Claudette. *Alling Ball of Connecticut*. St. Louis Park, MN: Author, 1995. 22p.

————. *The Ball Families of Maryland*. St. Louis Park, MN: Author, 1995. 27p.

————. *The Ball Families of Pennsylvania*. Bloomington, MN: Author, 1995. 42p.

————. *Valentine Ball and Susannah Lewis, a Study*. St. Louis Park, MN: Author, 1995. 18p.

Ballard

Bostic, Paul Eugene. *Bruce, Maupin, Carr and Some Related Families Including Ballard, Hearn, Ayres, McCubbin, Cloud, Lane, Eveland (Elfland), Graves, Sharp and Willis*. Clinton, TN: Author, 1995. 391p.

Gardner, Oscar William. *Gardner/Ballard and Allied Families, Edmondson, Lee, Daniel, Cauthen, and Starr*. Morrow, GA: Author, 1995. 456p.

Hauk, Carol A. *Descendants of William Cocke of Virginia*. Anderson, IN: Hauk Data Services, 1995. 64p.

Miller, Lynne D. *Ballards of America Marriages*. Lincolnton, NC: Author, 1995. Unpgd.

Banks

King, Kernie L. *Banks Branches, Family Tree of George and Lovdy Banks*. Howell, MI: Author, 1995. 125p.

Banta

Griffiths, George R. *Early Settlers in New York and New Jersey, Banta Family, Benson Family, Staats Family, Mabie Family*. Chandler, AZ: Author, 1995. 21p.

Baptista

Eaton, Mildred E. *The Descendants of Anselmo Silveira Baptista and His Wife Anna Martins (Emigrants from the Azore Islands)*. Seattle, WA: Author, 1995. 36p.

Barber

Barber, Franklin Taylor. *The Barbers and Allied Families*. Plano, TX: Author, 1995. 317p.

Barbour

Hauk, Carol A. *Descendants of James Barbour of Virginia*. Anderson, IN: Hauk Data Services, 1995. 34p.

Barclay

Hauk, Carol A. *Descendants of John Carter of Virginia*. Anderson, IN: Hauk Data Services, 1995. 2 vols.

Barefoot

Barefoot, Michael. *Barefoot Family of the Lower Thames Valley*. England: Author, 1995. 112p.

Bargwannas

Litfin, Lynette. *Please Spell That Name Again, a History of the Bargwannas in Cornwall and Australia*. Northbridge, Western Australia: Access Press, 1995. 226p.

Barker

Covert, Norman M. *Tree of Life, Genealogy of Covert, Goodson, Dey, Barker, Triplett and Allied Families from 1607*. Baltimore, MD: Gateway Press, 1995. 463p.

Barkley

Oates, Nancy Kay. *Beneath the Barkley Branches, Descendants of George Barkley, 1799–1995*. Austin, TX: Nortex Press, 1995. 482p.

Barnes

Alley, Gene. *Alley-Barnes Connection, an Oxford, Kansas, Family History*. Udall, KS: Author, 1995. 99p.

Barnes, Rufus Edward. *A History of Our Barns/Barnes and Martin Families*. Mesa, AZ: F. C. Spidel, 1995. 404p.

Barnett

Barnett, Bobby D. *Tommy Lewis Barnett and Relatives*. Clemson, SC: Author, 1995. 182p.

Brunson, Nolen L. *Barnett-McMakin Union, Ancestors Collateral Relatives and Descendants of John James Barnett and Harriet (Hattie) McMakin*. South Carolina: Author, 1995. 278p.

Ziegel, Ruth Turner. *Julius Christy of Virginia and Kentucky, 1730–1808, and Agatha Barnett Christy, 1740–1820, and Related Families of Barnett, Gibbs, Blackburn, Cave, Glass, Kirtley, Bush, Lindsey, Armstrong, Whaley, Davis, and Day*. Cincinnati, OH: Author, 1995. 92p.

Barnhisle

Boyer, Carol Constance Younker. *Barnhiser/Bernheisel Family Lines*. Rev. ed. Denver, CO: Author, 1995. Unpgd.

Barnhouse

Riley, Jane Barnhouse. *The William Telford Barnhouse Family: Ancestors and Descendants*. Smithville, TX: Author, 1995. 497p.

Barr

Barr, Charles Richard. *A Barr Family History, Descendants of Robert Barr (ca. 1725–1808) and His Wife, Mary Wills, of McAlevys Fort, Pennsylvania*. Baltimore, MD: Gateway Press, 1995. 217p.

Rowland, Joseph S. *Southern Peace Families and the Barr Descendants of Margaret Scott Barr Peace*. Tuscaloosa, AL: Author, 1995. 563p.

Barrett

Barrett, Dan E. *Barrett International Register Index, 1995*. Author, 1995. 95p.

Barrett, James P. *John Barrett of Hall County, Georgia, and His Kin*. Bedford, TX: Author, 1995. 186p.

Barrios

Barrios, Alcide J. *Theophile Barrios Descendants*. Baton Rouge, LA: Author, 1995. 45p.

Barron

Barron, George L. *The Barron Family from Banffshire, Scotland to Moody County, Dakota Territory, USA.* Jamestown, ND: Author, 1995. 341p.

Barrows

Porter, Edward T. *The Barrows Family of East Anglia, 1702–1995: Their Descendants in North America and Some of Their Related British Families.* Tacoma, WA: Author, 1995. 520p.

Barry

Skelton, Isaac Newton. *Ike, This Is You, a History of the Skelton, Boone, Barry, Beach, Blattner, Corum, Hoagland, Lehew, Strode, Wright and Young Families.* Washington, DC: Author, 1995. 223p.

Bartell

Fry, Steven R. *Bartell's in Logan County, Kansas.* Mulvane, KS: Author, 1995. 129p.

Barthelemy

Feasel, Hubert. *A Genealogy and History of Charles Edmond Lambert and Related Families of Barthelemy and Duquaine.* Decatur, IN: H. & L. Feasel, 1995. 120p.

Bartleson

Layman, Marvin Virgil. *Bartlesons of Grand Chain.* Tulsa, OK: True Image Pub., 1995. 396p.

Bartlett

Wakefield, Robert S. *Robert Bartlett of the "Anne" and His Descendants for Four Generations.* Plymouth, MA: General Society of Mayflower Descendants, 1995. 126p.

Barton

Elder, Shirley Bowen. *My Bowen, Barton, Harris, Scott, Hendon, Cranford Family Connections.* 2nd. ed. Raleigh, NC: Author, 1995. 356p.

Hill, George Byron. *The Genealogy of the Hill, Combs, Barton, Starr and Allied Families.* Nashville, TN: Author, 1995. 296p.

Bashelier

Scane, L. Dean. *Genealogy of Bashelier Family, Family Originally Emigrating from Near Saarbrueken, Germany to Fort Wayne, Allen County, Indiana.* Evanston, IL: Author, 1995. 175p.

Basinger

Ritter, Robert P. *The Ancestors and Descendants Including Some of the Relations of Deacon Ulrich Steiner and Elizabeth Basinger of Wilmot Township, Waterloo County, 1720–1995.* Wingham, Ontario: Author, 1995. 212p.

Bassano

Lasocki, David. *The Bassanos, Venetian Musicians and Instrument Makers in England, 1531-1665.* Aldershot, England: Scholars Press, 1995. 288p.

Bassett

Hauk, Carol A. *Descendants of William Bassett of Virginia.* 2nd. ed. Anderson, IN: Hauk Data Services, 1995. 106p.

Bastian

Liston, Lois Jane Breakiron. *The Breakiron Family History Also Including the Bastian, Brecheisen, Casey, Dusenberry, Garlow, Hutchinson, Johnson, McMillen, Miller, Morris, Roderick and Other Families.* Wyandotte, OK: Gregath Pub. Co., 1995. 620p.

Bastron

Walters, Henry. *Bastron.* Lincoln, NE: Author, 1995. 45p.

Batman

Batman, Richard F. *History of the Batman Family.* Newark, DE: Author, 1995. 24p.

Battaile

Hauk, Carol A. *Descendants of John Battaile of Virginia.* Anderson, IN: Hauk Data Services, 1995. 69p.

Battle

Johnston, Anne Plummer. *The Plummer Lineage of America.* Reston, VA: M. L. Tomaselli, 1995. 56p.

Bauchspies

Bauchspies, James Schmauch. *Genealogical Record of the Bauchspies Family, Descendants of Henry and Robert H. Bauchspies, Natives of Germany Who Settled in Carbon County, Pennsylvania, 1855 to 1995.* Baltimore, MD: Gateway Press, 1995. 140p.

Baugher

Putman, Nancy J. *The Baugher Family Heritage, a Celebration of Generations.* Athens, AL: Author, 1995. 191p.

Baum

Ruskay, Joseph A. *Leaves from a Family Tree.* NY: Vantage Press, 1995. 244p.

Bauman

Bowman, Bill. *Ancestors and Descendants of Rev. Henry (Shantz) Bauman, 1867–1935.* Gananoque, Ont.: Author, 1995. 124p.

Baumbarger

Lones, Lela Lillian. *Dawsons (Thomas, John W., Cyrus P.), Baumbarger (Johann Ulrich).* Perry, IA: Author, 1995. 56p.

Bays

Sayre, Rodney Allen. *The Bays Family, Ancestors of Lulu Marie.* Baltimore, MD: Gateway Press, 1995. Unpgd.

Baytop

Hauk, Carol A. *Descendants of Thomas Baytop of Virginia*. Anderson, IN: Hauk Data Services, 1995. 65p.

Beach

Beach, Lois Black. *The Beach Book, Thirteen Generations, 350 Years from John Beach, the Pilgrim*. College Station, TX: Author, 1995. Unpgd.

Skelton, Isaac Newton. *Ike, This Is You, a History of the Skelton, Boone, Barry, Beach, Blattner, Corum, Hoagland, Lehew, Strode, Wright and Young Families*. Washington, DC: Author, 1995. 223p.

Beachy

Beachy, William Vernon. *The Descendants of Abraham B. Beachy and Elizabeth Miller of Holmes County, Ohio*. Baltimore, MD: Author, 1995. 136p.

———. *Strong John Beachy and His Descendants*. Decorah, IA: Anundsen Pub. Co., 1995. 211p.

Yoder, M. Marie. *The Daniel Beachy Family of Aurora, West Virginia, Their Lineage and Life Stories*. Grantsville, MD: Author, 1995. 280p.

Beal

Beal, Charles Lewis. *The Direct Descendants of William Beale, Sr. of York, Maine, to Francis Guy Beal, Sr. of Newton, Massachusetts, Including Other Beal Descendants*. Yorba Linda, CA: Author, 1995. 52p.

Bell, Ernest Elmont, Jr. *One Line of Descent from Our Immigrant, Alexander Bell/Beall of Maryland, a Genealogical History, 1600 AD to 2000 AD, with an Autobiography by Ernest Elmont Bell, Jr. for His Descendants*. Baywood Park, CA: Author, 1995. 508p.

Hauk, Carol A. *Descendants of John Eustace of Virginia*. Anderson, IN: Hauk Data Services, 1995. 43p.

———. *Descendants of Thomas Beale of Virginia*. Anderson, IN: Hauk Data Services, 1995. 211 p.

Beals

Morris, B. A. *One Line of the Beals/Bales*. Chanute, KS: Author, 1995. Unpgd.

Beaman

Parr, Richard Eugene. *Genealogy of Richard Eugene Parr*. Morgan Hill, CA: Author, 1995. 79p.

Bean

Thatcher, Alice Trundy. *Ancestors and Descendants of Alfred Eames Trundy and of His Wife Elizabeth Mehitable Bean*. Baltimore, MD: Gateway Press, 1995. 92p.

Bearss

Van Schoonhoven, Linda. *Our Family Tree*. Tampa, FL: Author, 1995. 354p.

Beatty

Cherry, Lu Ann Kennedy. *The Beatty Book, the Descendants of Samuel Beatty of Armstrong County, Pennsylvania, Including the Families of Guthrie, Sedwick, and Sutton*. Decorah, IA: Anundsen Pub. Co., 1995. 159p.

Linn, Jo White. *Ancestry of Moore/Rowan Families, with Related Lines of Fleming, Renick, Bosley, Green, Girault, Beatty, Reading, Armitage, Ryerson, Rapelje*. New Orleans, LA: Author, 1995. 186p.

Beauchamp
Adair, Shirley Brown. *Descendants of Asher B. Beauchamp and John Casey, Nave, Ball, Bingham (Related Lines)*. Rockwall, TX: Author, 1995. 139p.

Becker
Albrecht, Leo J. *Descendants of Peter and Katherine (Peifer) Becker, Becker Family Reunion, Sunday, August 6, 1995, Belle Plaine, Minnesota*. Belle Plaine, MN: Author, 1995. 99p.
Johnston Fretchel, Sandra. *The Johnston and Becker Family Histories*. Oshkosh, WI: Author, 1995. Unpgd.

Beckner
Moore, Phillip James. *Up and Down Our Family Tree*. Utica, KY: McDowell Pub., 1995. 201p.

Bedell
Carman, Daniel. *The Carman Family of Long Island*. Norfolk, VA: Author, 1995. 69p.
Smith, Carlita Hargrave. *A Tree Planted*. Virginia Beach, VA: Author, 1995. 263p.

Bedenbaugh
Holcomb, Brent. *Bedenbaugh-Betenbaugh Family, Descendants of Johann Michael Bidenbach from Germany to South Carolina, 1752*. Columbia, SC: SCMAR, 1995. 245p.

Beebe
Hunt, Mitchell J. *Supplement to the Early Beebe Families of Vermont*. Willow Grove, PA: Author, 1995. 23p.

Beer
Hochstetler, Irene Steiner. *Peter and Anna Beer Moser*. Orville, OH: Author, 1995. 272p.
Kelly, Michael. T. *The Ancestral Roots of the Case Family of Easton, Pennsylvania, and the Beers Family of Warren County, New Jersey, and Elsewhere*. Oak Park, IL: Author, 1995. 36p.

Beilanski
Beilanski, Phyllis Jean Olin. *The Descendants of Sebastian and Anna Bielanski and Michala and Katarzyna Wegrzyn*. Lakeland, FL: Author, 1995. Unpgd.

Belden
Belden, Evera Kestler. *The Family History of Hattie M. Raymond Belden and Collateral Families*. Racine, WI: Author, 1995. Unpgd.

Belding
Popham, Geraldine E. *Grandma's Ancestors, 1634–1936, Thomas Judd, the Emigrant to Nelson Judd, and Addie (Judd) Dowd*. Lodi, CA: Author, 1995. 148p.

Beling

Beling, Willard A. *Family History, Our Beling and Worner Roots*. Woodland Hills, CA: Author, 1995. Unpgd.

Bell

Bell, Ernest Elmont, Jr. *One Line of Descent from Our Immigrant, Alexander Bell/Beall of Maryland, a Genealogical History, 1600 AD to 2000 AD, with an Autobiography by Ernest Elmont Bell, Jr. for His Descendants*. Baywood Park, CA: Author, 1995. 508p.

Bell, Raymond Martin. *The Family of William Bell of Juniata County, Pennsylvania*. Caralville, IA: Author, 1995. 10p.

Stockslager, Bonnie J. *The Dick, Bell, Cleland Family Book of History and Recipes*. Chantilly, VA: Classic Printing Center, 1995. 125p.

Bellamy

Boney, Leslie N., Jr. *The John Bellamy Family Including John D. Bellamy, MD of Wilmington, North Carolina*. 2nd. ed. Wilmington, NC: Author, 1995. 26p.

Bellemare

Bellemare, Gaetane. *Généalogie de Phidime Bellemare*. Quebec: Author, 1995. 131p.

Beller

Wagner, Betty Marie Daley. *The Schneider Genealogy and Related Families, Ancestors and Descendants of Carl Rudolph Schneider and Elizabeth Lena Bahler, Later Spelled Beller, John G. Bahler (Beller) and Anna Elisabeth Schneider, Samuel Bahler (Beller) and Elisabeth Litzy of Uetendorf, Canton Berne, Switzerland and Green County, Wisconsin, 1765–1995*. Milford, OH: Author, 1995. 201p.

Bellinger

Beling, Willard A. *Family History, Our Beling and Worner Roots*. Woodland Hills, CA: Author, 1995. Unpgd.

Belser

Koickler, Eloyce Hubbard. *Hiestand, Hestand, Hastings*. Helena, MT: Author, 1995. 127p.

Bendall

Bendall, Colin C. *Gloucestershire Bendalls*. Great Sutton, England: Author, 1995. 130p.

Bender

Joseph Jutzi and Marie Bender Family History and Genealogy. Waterloo, Ontario: The Committee, 1995. 184p.

Benighoff

Penticoff, Mary Joyce. *Descendants of Albert Benighoff*. Rockton, IL: Author, 1995. 263p.

Bennett

Guevarra, Mark Bennett. *A Heritage of Service: Families of Chester County, South Carolina, Lawrence County, Mississippi, Wyoming County, New York, and the Philippines*. Houston, TX: Author, 1995. 611p.

Wright, Diana. *Robinson Roots*. Author, 1995. Unpgd.

Benson

Benson, Phillip Leroy. *The Phillip Leroy Benson Roots*. Las Vegas, NV: Southern Nevada Times, 1995. 42p.

Griffiths, George R. *Early Settlers in New York and New Jersey, Banta Family, Benson Family, Staats Family, Mabie Family*. Chandler, AZ: Author, 1995. 21p.

Nachman, Rosemary A. *The Families Hansen, Bentsen of Holt Parish, Aust-Agdar County, Norway and Johnsdatter-Arnsen of Valer and Moss, Ostfold County, Norway*. San Diego, CA: Author, 1995. Unpgd.

Reynolds, Beatrice Kay. *Thomas Davenport of Dorchester, Massachusetts, His Descendants in Sidney, Maine (1762–1995)*. Sidney, ME: Author, 1995. 34p.

Benthiem

Mayer, Marion. *History of a Family Dispersed*. Chicago, IL: Author, 1995. 298p.

Bentley

McLeod, Stephen Archie. *The House of Cantelou & Co., the Story of a Southern Family*. Tallahassee, FL: Author, 1995. 705p.

Benton

McLane, Curren Rogers. *The Rogers Family Genealogy*. Fort Worth, TX: Author, 1995. Unpgd.

Berg

Hougen, Harvey Richard. *The Hougen-Berge Family, Norwegian Pioneers of Manitowoc County*. Valders, WI: Valders Journal, 1995. 73p.

Bergen

Bergen, William Sawyer. *Jacob Milton Bergen, Sr., Family of Long Island, New York, Ancestors & Descendants and Allied Families, Jacob Milton Bergen, Sr., Mary Alice Baylis*. Baltimore, MD: Gateway Press, 1995. 480p.

Bergklint

Koppel, John. *Our Bergklint Ancestry*. Decorah, IA: Anundsen Pub., 1995. 440p.

Bergman

Sand, Vernon Jerome. *The Life and Times of Vernon and Renee Sand and Related Families, Geiselhart, Bittle, Warner, Sand, Vilmo, Bergman, Legrand, Lassauge, Prado, and Carpentier*. Austin, TX: Author, 1995. 501p.

Berkeley

Hauk, Carol A. *Descendants of George Reade of Virginia*. Anderson, IN: Hauk Data Services, 1995. 393p.

————. *Descendants of Thomas Nelson Virginia*. Anderson, IN: Hauk Data Services, 1995. 184p.

Berkey

Berkey, William Albert. *The Berkey Book*. 2nd. ed. Arlington, VA: R. B. Reichley, 1995. 992p.

Bernheisel

Boyer, Carol Constance Younker. *Barnhiser/Bernheisel Family Lines*. Rev. ed. Denver, CO: Author, 1995. 411p.

Berry

Berry, Eddie Clayton. *Berry-Baker Connection*. Houston, TX: Author, 1995. 409p.

Howard, David Lane. *The Descendants of Jacob and Sarah (Berry) Bailey of Leeds, Androscoggin, Maine, 1791–1995*. Salt Lake City, UT: Author, 1995. 28p.

Parr, Richard Eugene. *Genealogy of Richard Eugene Parr*. Morgan Hill, CA: Author, 1995. 79p.

Sheridan, Doris R. *Chase-Berry-Bully Families*. Troy, NY: Author, 1995. 12p.

York, Dorothy Anderson. *Our Anderson Family and Their Kin*. Fort Worth, TX: Author, 1995. 307p.

Bessent

Rowland, Arthur Ray. *The Bessent Family of Georgia: Descendants of Abraham Bessent and Peter Bessent, with Beginnings in North and South Carolina*. Augusta, GA: Author, 1995. 20p.

Best

Eggert, Irving John. *Peter Eggert of Mecklenburg and Related Families in America, Best, Bitz, Broekemeier, Hackbarth, Kane, Meisner, Nellis, Schunk, Strenkowski, Voight, Winston*. Decorah, IA: Anundsen Pub. Co., 1995. 224p.

Betenbaugh

Holcomb, Brent. *Bedenbaugh-Betenbaugh Family, Descendants of Johann Michael Bidenbach from Germany to South Carolina, 1752*. Columbia, SC: SCMAR, 1995. 245p.

Bethells

Garde, Carol. *The Early Bethells and Their Descendants, 1635 to 1994*. Interlaken, NY: Heart of the Lakes Pub., 1995. 690p.

Betts

Auch, Viola. *Jacob Betz and Katherina Pfaff's Ancestors and Descendants*. Freeman, SD: Pine Hill Press, 1995. 166p.

McDonald, David Michael. *Polly's Family, the New England Ancestry and Some Descendants of Polly Putnam (1793–1886) and Her Husband Jonathan Betts (1787–1841)*. Dyer, IN: Author, 1995. 44p.

Beverley

Hauk, Carol A. *Descendants of Robert Beverley of Virginia*. Anderson, IN: Hauk Data Services, 1995. 330p.

Biddle
The Biddle Genealogy. Fremont, OH: L. Murray, 1995. Unpgd.

Bidenbach
Holcomb, Brent. *Bedenbaugh-Betenbaugh Family, Descendants of Johann Michael Bidenbach from Germany to South Carolina, 1752*. Columbia, SC: SCMAR, 1995. 245p.

Bierly
Rice, Suzanne Walkowiak. *The Descendants of Anthony Bierly, 1743–1825, and His Wife Anna Maria Warner, 1752–1841, of Centre County, Pennsylvania*. Madison, WI: Author, 1995. 185p.

Biggar
Biggar, Harold Arthur. *The Biggar Families of Greenwich, Connecticut, and County Tyrone, North Ireland*. Stamford, CT: Author, 1995. Unpgd.

Biggers
Vaughn, Barbara Biggers. *Lick Creek Beckoned, History and Records of the Biggers-Fagan Families Embracing Branches of Allied Families—Dooley, Eads, Grigsby, Harrison, Richardson and Woodward*. Decorah, IA: Anundsen Pub. Co., 1995. 310p.

Billings
Oncley, Lephia French. *Our Weaver Cousins, Ancestry of Samuel Stanton Weaver, 1793–1857, and His Wife, Lucy Billings Palmer, 1798–1851, with Some of Their Descendants and Related Families*. Ann Arbor, MI: Author, 1995. 244p.

Bingham
Adair, Shirley Brown. *Descendants of Asher B. Beauchamp and John Casey, Nave, Ball, Bingham (Related Lines)*. Rockwall, TX: Author, 1995. 139p.
Marsh, Mary Bingham. *Bingham or Bigham, Ancestry and Descendants of James Bingham or Bigham, Sr. of Marion District, South Carolina*. Hemingway, SC: Three Rivers Historical Society, 1995. Unpgd.

Binnington
Irwin, JoAnn . *Descendants of Robert Norris (1774–1858) and Hannah Binnington (1781–1848)*. Richland, MI: Author, 1995. Unpgd.

Birdsong
Birdsong, Dean John. *American Birdsong Ancestry, the Descendants of John and Elizabeth Birdsong (circa 1683–1732) through Five Generations*. San Diego, CA: Goodway Printing & Graphics, 1995. 387p.

Birkett
Davidson, Charlene Gaskill. *Birkett and Pew Families*. Shawnee, KS: Author, 1995. 12p.

Biser
Kiddoo, Nancy Rice. *Jakob Dorner, German Pioneer of Frederick County, Maryland, and Three Generations of Descendants, 1748–1895*. Whippany, NJ: Author, 1995. 140p.

Bish

Jesberger, Sherry. *The Joseph Edward and Susannah (Bennett) Bish Family History*. Kersey, PA: Author, 1995. 68p.

Bishop

Bryson, George Washington, Jr. *John Bishop, the Settler, a Family History*. Author, 1995. Unpgd.

Cagle, Ruby Abbott. *The Bishop Family from Manchester, England to Washington County, Maine*. Jasper, TN: Author, 1995. Unpgd.

Melle, Jane Hentges. *Bishop, Carrick, Hotchkiss, Johnson and Related Families, a Family History as Known in 1994*. Bowling Green, OH: Author, 1995. 2 vols.

Bittinger

Beachy, Betty Kathryn. *Emanuel Bittinger, 1838–1908, and His Descendants*. Decorah, IA: Anundsen Pub. Co., 1995. 149p.

Bittle

Sand, Vernon Jerome. *The Life and Times of Vernon and Renee Sand and Related Families, Geiselhart, Bittle, Warner, Sand, Vilmo, Bergman, Legrand, Lassauge, Prado, and Carpentier*. Austin, TX: Author, 1995. 501p.

Bitz

Eggert, Irving John. *Peter Eggert of Mecklenburg and Related Families in America, Best, Bitz, Broekemeier, Hackbarth, Kane, Meisner, Nellis, Schunk, Strenkowski, Voight, Winston*. Decorah, IA: Anundsen Pub. Co., 1995. 224p.

Bixby

Karr, Nola M. *Baker Family Record, a Genealogy of Many of the Descendants of John Baker Who Immigrated from England in 1637*. White Plains, MD: Automated Graphic Systems, 1995. 663p.

Bjorn

Pearson, Frederick John. *Anderson*. Houston, TX: Author, 1995. 352p.

Black

Black, John Baxter. *A History of the Family of Mr. and Mrs. Frank Blymyer Black of Mansfield, Ohio*. Baltimore, MD: Gateway Press, 1995. 2 vols.

Black, Lewis S. *The Black Family on the Brandywine*. Wilmington, DE: Author, 1995. 135p.

Blackburn

Duxbury, Donald E. *Blackburn/Blackbourn Family Updated Report: Ancestors and Descendants of George and Martha (Nevitt) Blackbourn and Richard and Mary Anne (Houghton) Blackbourn, Lincolnshire, England to Wisconsin Territory (1759–1995)*. Madison, WI: Author, 1995. 615p.

Blackmon

McPhail, John P. *The Blackmon Family of Johnston, Harnett and Sampson Counties*. Author, 1995. 2 vols.

Blackshear

Blackshear Family History, 1505–1995. 1995. 2 vols.

Blackwell

Hauk, Carol A. *Descendants of John Eustace of Virginia.* Anderson, IN: Hauk Data Services, 1995. 43p.

———. *Descendants of Joseph Blackwell of Virginia.* Anderson, IN: Hauk Data Services, 1995. 119p.

Blagrave

Blagrove, Ian S. G. *Blagrave and Blagrove, a History.* Windsor, England: Author, 1995. 48p.

Blagrove

Blagrove, Ian S. G. *Blagrave and Blagrove, a History.* Windsor, England: Author, 1995. 48p.

Blair

Beck, William M. *The Samuel Blair Family.* East Peoria, IL: Author, 1995. 74p.

Blair, Frederick Eugene. *The Descendants of James and Mary Colbert Blair, Bucks County, Pennsylvania, Augusta County, Virginia, Guilford and Caldwell Counties, North Carolina, Thence Nationwide.* St. Simmons Island, GA: Author, 1995. 214p.

Graves, Kenneth Vance. *Deacon George Graves, 1636 Settler of Hartford, Connecticut, and His Descendants.* Wrenthen, MA: Author, 1995. 446p.

Hauk, Carol A. *Descendants of Archibald Blair of Virginia.* Anderson, IN: Hauk Data Services, 1995. 26p.

McBride, Jean Coleman. *The Colemans of West Alabama and Allied Families.* Aliceville, AL: Author, 1995. 200p.

Blaisdell

Reynolds, Beatrice Kay. *Thomas Davenport of Dorchester, Massachusetts, His Descendants in Sidney, Maine (1762–1995).* Sidney, ME: Author, 1995. 34p.

Blanchan

Zuendel, Jean. *Taylor, Blanchan, Cochran, DuBois, Foreman, Hite, Morris, Parker, Van Meteren.* Author, 1995. Unpgd.

Blanding

Blanding, Leonard Clark. *Genealogy of the Blanding Family.* 2nd. ed. Grand Rapids, MI: Author, 1995. 1,091p.

Blattner

Skelton, Isaac Newton. *Ike, This Is You, a History of the Skelton, Boone, Barry, Beach, Blattner, Corum, Hoagland, Lehew, Strode, Wright and Young Families.* Washington, DC: Author, 1995. 223p.

Blauvelt

Griffiths, George R. *A Dutch Cooper Family, and Blauvelt Family.* Chandler, AZ: Author, 1995. 18p.

Blewer

Hughes, Nancy Caroline Phillips. *Hugh Phillips, Some of His Descendants, Including Allied Families of Bolin, Blewer (Bluer), Reidheimer, Salley, Schuler (Shuler) and Winningham.* Columbia, SC: Author, 1995. 46p.

Block

Feder, June Constance. *The Genealogy of the Price and Stull Families of the Town of Rush, Monroe County, New York, the Murrays, Wallings, and Hills of Victor, New York, and the Otto, Block, Hill and Summerhays Families of Rochester, New York.* Fairport, NY: Author, 1995. 75p.

Kruse, Naomi M. *The Blocks' Kin, Descendants of Cord Heinrich Karl Block and Catharina Sophie Bultmann Block.* Author, 1995. 157p.

Blodgett

Koickler, Eloyce Hubbard. *Hiestand, Hestand, Hastings.* Helena, MT: Author, 1995. 127p.

Bloodgood

Carman, Daniel. *The Carman Family of Long Island.* Norfolk, VA: Author, 1995. 69p.

Blumenberg

Bellin, Loretta M. *The Family of Johan Christian Friedrich Blumenberg and Helene Dorothea Matthiansen-Martinsen, 1780–1994.* Oshkosh, WI: Author, 1995. 228p.

Blunden

Newcomb, Viettia Alberta. *Newcomb, Hartt and Slye, Blunden Families.* Ukiah, CA: Author, 1995. 408p.

Blunier

Clegg, Mary Lou. *Blunier Family History.* Fort Wayne, IN: Author, 1995. 82p.

Blythe

Wright, William Blythe. *Some Blythe Families of Pennsylvania.* Woodcliff Lake, NJ: Author, 1995. 142p.

Bobbitt

Kump, Warren Lee. *The Kumps, the Bobbitts and Others.* Minneapolis, MN: Author, 1995. 480p.

Boehm

Koickler, Eloyce Hubbard. *Hiestand, Hestand, Hastings.* Helena, MT: Author, 1995. 127p.

Boehning

Boehning, Ross William. *Johann Bohning and His Descendants, a Family Tree and History of the Boehning/Bohning Family, 1650 to 1995.* Pasadena Hills, MO: Author, 1995. Unpgd.

Boehr

Boehr, Ewanda Siebert. *From Hemp and Flax Fields to Lands of Wheat and Corn, Baehr, Bohr, Boehr Genealogy, 1700–1995.* Langham, Sask.: Author, 1995. 356p.

Bogan

Becknell, Mike. *Family History of Isaac C. Bogan*. Bogansville, SC: Author, 1995. 10p.

Boggess

Rutledge, Fred Alvah. *Some Descendants of Thomas Watts, Jr., 1747 Virginia, 1797 Georgia, and Hannah Rust Boggess, 1753 Virginia, 1836 Alabama*. Baltimore, MD: Author, 1995. Unpgd.

Boians

Edwards, Eva Dean. *Boians of Kentucky and Allied Families*. Irvine, KY: Author, 1995. 763p.

Bolen

Hughes, Nancy Caroline Phillips. *Hugh Phillips, Some of His Descendants, Including Allied Families of Bolin, Blewer (Bluer), Reidheimer, Salley, Schuler (Shuler) and Winningham*. Columbia, SC: Author, 1995. 46p.

Bolling

Brawley, Dorothy Loraine Perry. *The Bolling, Gay, Gaston, Brawley, Paper Trail, with Allied Families and Friends*. Author, 1995. 644p.

Dye, Helen Sides. *The Browder Connection*. Bowie, MD: Heritage Books, 1995. 430p.

Hauk, Carol A. *Descendants of Archibald Blair of Virginia*. Anderson, IN: Hauk Data Services, 1995. 26p.

———. *Descendants of Richard Bolling of Virginia*. Anderson, IN: Hauk Data Services, 1995. 315p.

Bond

Bond, James O. *Friends for 340 Years, the Story of My Quaker Family*. Baltimore, MD: Gateway Press, 1995. 158p.

Boney

Scott, Margaret Scott. *Genealogical Portrait of Joseph Carr and Barbara Gastor Beverett, the Carr Descendants of Duplin County, NC*. Warsaw, NC: Author, 1995. 418p.

Bonner

Hagler, Travis Jackson. *Bonner, Brown, Boswell Family History: Southeastern Alabama Era*. Huntsville, AL: Author, 1995. 370p.

Bonnett

Wagoner, Crystal. *John Waggoner, 1751–1842, Margaret (Bonnett) Waggoner, Ancestors, Families, and Descendants*. Bowie, MD: Heritage Books, 1995. 343p.

Bontrager

Mast, Eli H. *Family History of Noah J. Miller and Elizabeth Bontrager 1849–1994*. Baltic, OH: Author, 1995. 286p.

Boone

Jones, Daniel Wilbur. *Genealogical Memoranda of Daniel Rufus Cable and Georgiana McKinney Cable*. Cary, NC: Author, 1995. 183p.

Moore, Freddie Gene. *My Virginia Ancestors and Their Descendants in the Families, Burdett, Alexander, Anderson, King, Boone, Welsh, McHenry, Cornwell, Alford, Coleman, Dixon, Morgan, Jarman, Maugridge.* Author, 1995. 46p.

Skelton, Isaac Newton. *Ike, This Is You, a History of the Skelton, Boone, Barry, Beach, Blattner, Corum, Hoagland, Lehew, Strode, Wright and Young Families.* Washington, DC: Author, 1995. 223p.

Booth

Booth, John N. *The Booth Family History.* Oklahoma City, OK: Author, 1995. 4 vols.

Hauk, Carol A. *Descendants of Thomas Booth of Virginia.* Anderson, IN: Hauk Data Services, 1995. 115p.

Partridge, Craig. *The Descendants of William Andrew of Cambridge, Massachusetts.* Camden, ME: Penobscot Press, 1995. 365p.

Booty

Jordan, Thomas Franklin. *An American Migration.* Thesis (M.A.), Louisiana State University, 1995. 194p.

Borchert

DeRose, Lucille. *The Borcherts of Nicollet and Brown Counties, Minnesota, a Family History, the Families of Friedland, Mecklenburg, Germany, the Borcherts, the Hackers, the Kleins.* Sacramento, CA: Author, 1995. 99p.

Borden

Batcher, Olive M. *Hill Wallace Family History.* Ames, IA: Author, 1995. 253p.

Boriack

Boriack, David. *Boriack Family Tree, 1995.* Lincoln, TX: Author, 1995. 303p.

Born

Kaufman, Mary Arnold. *Martin-Arnold and Allied Families, Lanier, Bailey, Swan, Sandidge, Gholston, Morgan, and Born, Migration from Virginia to Tennessee, Georgia, Alabama and Arkansas.* Knoxville, TN: Tennessee Valley Pub., 1995. 212p.

Bosley

Linn, Jo White. *Ancestry of Moore/Rowan Families, with Related Lines of Fleming, Renick, Bosley, Green, Girault, Beatty, Reading, Armitage, Ryerson, Rapelje.* New Orleans, LA: Author, 1995. 186p.

Bosse

Barringer, Joyce Eilers. *Bosse Family Tree, Bussa, Bosse, Bussey.* Muskegon, MI: Author, 1995. 114p.

Bossler

Muhlhausen, Marvin David. *Thode, Bossler, a Story of the Ancestors and Descendants of Andreas Thode and Anna Dorothea Bossler.* Ellicott City, MD: Author, 1995. Unpgd.

Bost

Spencer, Mary Ruth. *The Ancestors and Descendants of Charles Albert Cannon and Ruth Louise Coltrane*. Carmel, CA: Author, 1995. Unpgd.

Bostain

Bostain, Addison. *Bostain Family*. Chapin, SC: Author, 1995. 40p.

Boswell

Hagler, Travis Jackson. *Bonner, Brown, Boswell Family History: Southeastern Alabama Era*. Huntsville, AL: Author, 1995. 370p.

Bothwell

Stene, Charles Sherwin. *The Stene Family, Includes Rohn, Anderson, Bothwell, Davenport, Lloyd*. Decorah, IA: Anundsen Pub. Co., 1995. 385p.

Bott

Ratts, Kenneth R. *From Germany to Wherever?*. Sun City Center, FL: Author, 1995. Unpgd.

Bouchard

Fiola-Bouchard, Françoise. *Histoire et Généalogie de Nos Familles, Fiola, Bouchard, Côte, Gagnon*. Ste.-Anne-des-Monts, Quebec: Author, 1995. 129p.

Bouchier

Bradley, John. *Sarah Wallington, 1719–1757, and Her Wallington, Pead, Okes, Fownes, Perry, and Bouchier Ancestors of Wotton-under-Edge*. Devizes, England, Author, 1995. 213p.

Bouma

Lyons, Janet Kay. *The Bouma Story*. Dorr, MI: Author, 1995. 154p.

Bourdon

Bourdon, Frederick Francis. *Jacques Bourdon, 7000 Descendants et/and Ancestors/Ancetres Canada-USA-France*. Pompano Beach, FL: Author, 1995. 322p.

Boven

Boven, John Henry. *Boven Dutch Apple Pie, the Story of Boven Emigration to the United States*. Nipomo, CA: Author, 1995. 206p.

Bowden

Scott, Margaret Scott. *Genealogical Portrait of Joseph Carr and Barbara Gastor Beverett, the Carr Descendants of Duplin County, NC*. Warsaw, NC: Author, 1995. 418p.

Bowen

Elder, Shirley Bowen. *My Bowen, Barton, Harris, Scott, Hendon, Cranford Family Connections*. 2nd. ed. Raleigh, NC: Author, 1995. 356p.

Bower
Teeter, Mary Bowers. *Descendants of Samuel Bower of Perry Co., PA* . Morenci, MI: Author, 1995. 90p.

Bowie
Hauk, Carol A. *Descendants of John Bowie of Virginia.* Anderson, IN: Hauk Data Services, 1995. 38p.

Bowlby
Muessig, Linda Huff. *The Bowlby Family.* Bloomsbury, NJ: Author, 1995. 61p.

Bowles
Powell, Ruth Burr. *Burr-Bowles Genealogy.* Baltimore, MD: Gateway Press, 1995. 278p.

Bowman
Dye, Helen Sides. *The Browder Connection.* Bowie, MD: Heritage Books, 1995. 430p.

Bowyer
Bowyer, L. Ray. *Bowyer-Skavdahl Genealogy.* Randolph, NJ: Author, 1995. 276p.
Moore, Freddie Gene. *My Virginia Ancestors and Their Descendants in the Families, Ratliff, Skidmore, Watson, Hamilton, Wallace, Cahoon, Bowyer, Grimes, Sharp, Meeks.* Author, 1995. 116p.

Boyd
Hargis, Margaret Ann Finley. *Boyd.* Warrenton, VA: Author, 1995. 60p.
Torrens, Frank, Mrs. *William Boyd Family.* Warrenton, VA: M. F. Hargis, 1995. 60p.

Boylston
Boylston, Samuel L. *The Boylstons: a Family History, the James Wyatt and Martha Ann Corbitt Boylston Family.* Raleigh, NC: Boylston Enterprises, 1995. 215p.

Braamharr
Ralph, Charles L. *Genealogy of a Poinsett Family from the Atlantic Seacoast to the Colorado Rockies, with Notes on the Worrell and Braamharr Families.* Ft. Collins, CO: Author, 1995. 84p.

Brace
Opat, Donna Burrough. *A Pearce-Brace Family History.* Lindsborg, KS: Author, 1995. 174p.

Bradley
Hamilton, Robert Bradley. *The Ancestors of the Descendants of Robert Addyman Hamilton and Laura Helen Bradley.* Santa Rosa, CA: Author, 1995. 2 vols.
York, Dorothy Anderson. *Our Anderson Family and Their Kin.* Fort Worth, TX: Author, 1995. 307p.

Bradshaw
York, Dorothy Anderson. *Our Anderson Family and Their Kin.* Fort Worth, TX: Author, 1995. 307p.

Bradt

Hindmarsh, F. I. *Descendants of Claas Frederickse Van Petten (1641–1728) and His Wife Aeffie Arentse Bradt (1649–1728), a Family History Research Project.* Aylmer, Ont: Author, 1995. 281p.

Reamer, Kathleen R. *Descendants of John Reamer and Margaret Schermerhorn, 1758–1995.* Imlay City, MI: Author, 1995. 246p.

Bragg

Reynolds, Beatrice Kay. *Thomas Davenport of Dorchester, Massachusetts, His Descendants in Sidney, Maine (1762–1995).* Sidney, ME: Author, 1995. 34p.

Brake

Jackson, Nancy Ann. *Colonel Edward Jackson, 1759–1828, Revolutionary Soldier, History and Genealogy of the Son of Immigrants John and Elizabeth Cummins Jackson, His Wives and Families of Mary Haddan and Elizabeth W. Brake, Grandparents of General Stonewall Jackson.* Franklin, NC: Genealogy Pub. Service, 1995. 1,135p.

Branberg

Brooks, Shirley A. *Peterson Branberg Family.* Lake Elsinore, CA: Author, 1995. Unpgd.

Branch

Mann, Marion. *The Kigh, Mann, Reagin, and Sykes Families, Including the Branch, Brown, Dean, Fort, Gerran, Leake, Marquis, Moses, Oakes, Powell, Reid, Trammell, Walk, Wilkey, Wingfield, and Woods Families, a Genealogy and Family History.* Baltimore, MD: Gateway Press, 1995. 218p.

Brandon

Brandon, Stephen Arthur. *The Ancestors of Stephen Warren Brandon and Amy Elizabeth Brandon, 1733–1979.* Nashville, TN: Author, 1995. Unpgd.

Brandt

Brandt, Marlin Kent. *An Ancestral Genealogy Record of Brandt, a Chronological Accumulation of the Ancestors of Rachel Ann Brandt and Raymond Alan Brandt with Emphasis on Brandt and Williams.* Riverside, CA: Hondo Pub., 1995. 420p.

Branham

Phillips, Shelby Fleming. *David Branham and His Descendants.* Williamson, WV: Author, 1995. 354p.

Salyers, Brenda Dotson. *Branhams and Kin, the Descendants of Milly Branham.* 5th. ed. Pound, VA: Heritage Nook Book Pub., 1995. 211p.

Branson

Cory Nyblod, Marilou. *Brownson Branches, Including Bronson, Brunson, Branson, and All Spelling Variations.* Sultan, WA: Author, 1995. 41p.

Braun

Braun, Henry J. *Braun Family Tree, Jacob D. Braun, 1826–1919, Katherina (Funk) Braun, 1827- 1920.* 2nd. ed. Steinbach, MB: Braun Family Tree Committee, 1995. 282p.

Brawley

Brawley, Dorothy Loraine Perry. *The Bolling, Gay, Gaston, Brawley, Paper Trail, with Allied Families and Friends*. Author, 1995. 644p.

Braxton

Hauk, Carol A. *Descendants of George Braxton of Virginia*. Anderson, IN: Hauk Data Services, 1995. 111p.

Breakiron

Liston, Lois Jane Breakiron. *The Breakiron Family History Also Including the Bastian, Brecheisen, Casey, Dusenberry, Garlow, Hutchinson, Johnson, McMillen, Miller, Morris, Roderick and Other Families*. Wyandotte, OK: Gregath Pub. Co., 1995. 620p.

Breitenstein

Penn, John Herman. *A Brief Genealogical History of the Ancestors and Descendants of Lawrence Heinauer, Senior and Barbara Breitenstein of the Villages of Schweinheim and Kleigoft, Westhouse Marmoutier, Department Bas Rhin, France and the Families of Joseph Maria Von Keitz and Frederike Dernbach of Robinson, Stowe and Kennedy Townships, McKees Rocks, Allegheny County, Pennsylvania, United States of America*. El Torro, CA: Author, 1995. 125p.

Breland

Breland, Charles Gregory. *The Breland Families of the Southern States, 1755–1875*. Pennington, NJ: Queenstown Press, 1995. 101p.

Bremer

Schnatz, Darlene Becnel. *The Nodell-Bremer Descendants*. Beaumont, TX: Author, 1995. 108p.

Brent

Christoffersen, Dorothy Gray. *Brents, Calverts, Dawkins and Grays*. Lawrenceville, NJ: Author, 1995. 27p.

Brenton

Brenton, Chester Fay. *Descendants of Brentons of Bourbon County, Kentucky*. Spokane, WA: Author, 1995. 145p.

Brewer

Roche, Hazel. *A Study of the Gambrells, Allens, Hensleys, Brewers, and Others from Clay and Knox Counties, Kentucky*. Moravian Falls, NC: Author, 1995. 44p.

Brien

Hanrahan, Patrick Lloyd. *Charlebois (Wood) Family History, and the Allied Families of Brien, Brule, Daudelin, Gagnon, LeBlanc and Riel*. Milwaukie, OR: Author, 1995. 179p.

Brigance

Brigance, Albert Henry. *Brigance Genealogy*. Maryville, TN: Brigance Enterprises, 1995. 2 vols.

Briggs
Udell, Marcia. *Noah Briggs of Allegan County, Michigan, His Ancestors and Descendants.* Marshall, MI: Author, 1995. 75p.

Bringhurst
Johnston, Anne Plummer. *The Plummer Lineage of America.* Reston, VA: M. L. Tomaselli, 1995. 56p.

Brisbin
The Largs Australians. Largs, Scotland: Largs & District Historical Society, 1995. 21p.

Brister
Spencer, Sarah Nell. *Mississippi Bristers, Ancestors and Descendants, Twelve Generations, 1649–1995.* Bogue Chitto, MS: Author, 1995. 350p.

Bristol
Spencer, Sarah Nell. *Mississippi Bristers, Ancestors and Descendants, Twelve Generations, 1649–1995.* Bogue Chitto, MS: Author, 1995. 350p.

Brizendine
Westfall, Dawn Watts. *Spencer, Brizendine, Malone, Families of Trigg County, Kentucky.* High Springs, FL: Author, 1995. 26p.

Broadus
Hauk, Carol A. *Descendants of Edward Broadus of Virginia.* 3rd. ed. Anderson, IN: Hauk Data Services, 1995. 64p.

Brockman
Robertson, Joanna. *A Tree Grows in America: My Family Line.* West Columbia, SC: Author, 1995. 238p.
Stultz, Carolyne. *The Page Family Research Report, Including a Genealogy on Descendants of Robert and Rachel (Brockman) Page, from Virginia to South Carolina, Some of Their Sons Came to Kentucky and Then to Illinois.* Danville, IN: Author, 1995. 123p.

Brodhead
Smith, Jean and Anne Goodwill. *The Brodhead Family. Volume 6. The Story of Captain Daniel Brodhead, His Wife Ann Tye and Their Descendants.* Port Ewin, NY: Author, 1995. 96p.

Brodnax
Ezell, Mildred Seab. *Brodnax.* Starkville, MS: Author, 1995. Unpgd.

Broekemeier
Eggert, Irving John. *Peter Eggert of Mecklenburg and Related Families in America, Best, Bitz, Broekemeier, Hackbarth, Kane, Meisner, Nellis, Schunk, Strenkowski, Voight, Winston.* Decorah, IA: Anundsen Pub. Co., 1995. 224p.

Bronson

Cory Nyblod, Marilou. *Brownson Branches, Including Bronson, Brunson, Branson, and All Spelling Variations*. Sultan, WA: Author, 1995. 41p.

Brook

Hauk, Carol A. *Descendants of Lawrence Smith of Virginia*. 2nd. ed. Anderson, IN: Hauk Data Services, 1995. 287p.

————. *Descendants of Robert Brook of Virginia*. Anderson, IN: Hauk Data Services, 1995. 109p.

Brosz

Norquist, Carolyn Brost. *The Legacy of Jakob and Margaretha Brosz, Germans from Russia, Unser Leute*. Baltimore, MD: Gateway Press, 1995. 125p.

Brotherton

Thrasher, Joel J. *A Brotherton Tree, Some Branches and Many Twigs*. Author, 1995. 151p.

Broughton

Creech, Lillian Broughton. *Kentucky Lineage, Broughton, Slusher, Woolum, Payne and Related Families*. Baltimore, MD: Gateway Press, 1995. 592p.

Fenner, Jim. *Fenner-Broughton Family History, the Family of James Elory Fenner, 1844–1912, and Hester Adamantha (Broughton) Fenner, 1847–1922, of Crawford County, Pennsylvania*. Apollo, PA: Closson Press, 1995. 384p.

Broussard

Broussard, Earl. *Our Ancestors, Gone But Not Forgotten*. Author, 1995. 204p.

Conover, Michael. *Broussard, Descendants of Francois and Nicolas*. Lafayette, LA: Author, 1995. Unpgd.

Browder

Dye, Helen Sides. *The Browder Connection*. Bowie, MD: Heritage Books, 1995. 430p.

Brown

Anderson, Chris. *The Brown Family Book: Genealogy of William Brown and Hannah Taylor: Ireland, Pennsylvania, Ohio*. Lancaster, OH: Golden Crowns Press, 1995. 102p.

Barron, William P. *The Family History of Belva Nevada Woolery, Wife of Bill Schamel and Wyatt McMillan and Her Descendants: With Notes on Related Families Brown, Lockhart, Schaeffer, Wiesman, Williams*. Fairborn, OH: Heritage Family Publications, 1995. Unpgd.

Bennett, Katie Brown. *Soaking the Yule Log: Biographical Sketches of the Brown, Cheshier, Sain, and Allied Families, 1749–1995*. Decorah, IA: Anundsen Pub. Co., 1995. 514p.

Brown, Shirley M. *The Philip Brown Family of Tulpehocken Valley*. Richland, PA: Author, 1995. 715p.

Brown, William Jay, Jr. *The Ancestors and Descendants of William Gage Brown and Harriet Alice Wolfe of Urbana, Illinois*. Wellesley, MA: Author, 1995. Unpgd.

Franklin, Lisa R. *The Family Tree of Alaina Monte Brown, Research and Lineage of Some Autauga, Coosa and Tallapoosa Counties Early Alabama Families*. Montgomery, AL: Author, 1995. 40p.

Hagler, Travis Jackson. *Bonner, Brown, Boswell Family History: Southeastern Alabama Era.* Huntsville, AL: Author, 1995. 370p.

Horned, Joseph. *A Beginner's Guide for Researching Brown in Cherokee Records, Dawes Roll, Guion Miller Roll, Drennen Roll, Chapman Roll.* New Beginnings Pubns., 1995. 61p.

Mann, Marion. *The Kigh, Mann, Reagin, and Sykes Families, Including the Branch, Brown, Dean, Fort, Gerran, Leake, Marquis, Moses, Oakes, Powell, Reid, Trammell, Walk, Wilkey, Wingfield, and Woods Families, a Genealogy and Family History.* Baltimore, MD: Gateway Press, 1995. 218p.

Piepenburg, Betty Lou. *The Descendants of Nathaniel Brown, Sr..* Author, 1995. 294p.

Price, William Spencer. *Wendel Brown (Johan Wendel Braun) and Descendants, General Index to Volumes I through VI.* West Covina, CA: Ewing Genealogical Services, 1995. 76p.

Brownfield

Brownfield, Florence E. *The Brownfields in America, John Brownfield and Mary Lewis Worrell and Their Descendants.* Tustin, CA: Author, 1995. 93p.

Brownlee

Ancestors and Descendants of William Whitaker Smith, 1860–1944, and Florence Ellen Sullivan, 1875–1926, of Anderson and Greenville Counties, South Carolina. Spartanburg, SC: Reprint Co., 1995. 146p.

Brownson

Cory Nyblod, Marilou. *Brownson Branches, Including Bronson, Brunson, Branson, and All Spelling Variations.* Sultan, WA: Author, 1995. 41p.

Brubaker

Smith, Robert Lee. *Ancestors of Thelma Margaret Gander.* Alexandria, VA: Author, 1995. 65p.

Bruce

Bostic, Paul Eugene. *Bruce, Maupin, Carr and Some Related Families Including Ballard, Hearn, Ayres, McCubbin, Cloud, Lane, Eveland (Elfland), Graves, Sharp and Willis.* Clinton, TN: Author, 1995. 391p.

Brugh

Connett, Robert Paul. *Descendants and Ancestors of Charles Louis Brugh and Mollie Bell Snider.* Author, 1995. Unpgd.

Brule

Hanrahan, Patrick Lloyd. *Charlebois (Wood) Family History, and the Allied Families of Brien, Brule, Daudelin, Gagnon, LeBlanc and Riel.* Milwaukie, OR: Author, 1995. 179p.

Brunson

Cory Nyblod, Marilou. *Brownson Branches, Including Bronson, Brunson, Branson, and All Spelling Variations.* Sultan, WA: Author, 1995. 41p.

Martsteller, Charles M. *Brunson Index.* Rev. ed. San Francisco, CA: Author, 1995. 54p.

Brush

Brush, Stuart Camp. *Supplement I & II to the Descendants of Thomas and Richard Brush of Huntington, Long Island*. Baltimore, MD: Gateway Press, 1995. 313p.

Bryan

Bielkiewicz, Julia Bryant. *Lineage of Alexander Bryan, Revolutionary Scout*. Author, 1995. 21p.

Powell, John W. *Ancestors and Descendants of Alvie C. Bryan and His Wife, Martha E. Wallace, Warrick County, Indiana*. Evansville, IN: Author, 1995. 125p.

Buchanan

Bruce, Mary B. *The Buchanans, Some Historical Notes*. Stirling, England: Stirling District Libraries, 1995. 23p.

Buchholtz

Buchholtz, George John. *Backgrounds and Lineages of Some Copley and Buchholtz Families*. Baltimore, MD: Gateway Press, 1995. 301p.

Buckius

Buckius, Bob. *The Bockius/Buckius Family, 10 Generations*. Mineral Wells, WV: Author, 1995. Unpgd.

Buckley

Buckley, Kenneth Welch. *The Descendants of Butler Buckley and Elizabeth Story, 1710–1994*. Baltimore, MD: Gateway Press, 1995. 661p.

Buckmaster

Buckmaster, Rodney Earle. *A History of Descendants of Nathaniel Buckmaster, a Genealogical Account*. Laguna Niguel, CA: Old Glory Pub., 1995. 171p.

Buckwalter

Grove, James Francis. *Bouch Walder, Buckwalter, Buchwalter, Bookwalter*. Hemet, CA: Author, 1995. 3 vols.

Buetow

McMullin, Kathleen Buetow. *The Family History of Levi O. Buetow and Amelia (Stark) Buetow of Chippewa County, Wisconsin*. Rochester, MN: Author, 1995. 93p.

Bufford

Hauk, Carol A. *Descendants of John Early of Virginia*. 2nd. ed. Anderson, IN: Hauk Data Services, 1995. 219p.

———. *Descendants of Richard Bufford of Virginia*. 4th. ed. Anderson, IN: Hauk Data Services, 1995. 216p.

———. *Descendants of Richard Perrott of Virginia*. 2nd. ed. Anderson, IN: Hauk Data Services, 1995. 278p.

Bugg

Brochu, Francis Louis. *The Buggs of Big Albemarle County, Virginia, in Three Parts*. Salem, VA: Author, 1995. 160p.

Bullard

Maxwell, Ruth. *The Alman Carson Bullard Family*. Dallas, TX: Author, 1995. Unpgd.

Bullen

Bullen, William Dean. *Pioneer Reuben R. Bullen of Aurelius Township, Ingham County, Michigan, and Some of His Descendants*. Mason, MI: Author, 1995. 403p.

Bullock

Rowland, Arthur Ray. *Distant Cousins: The Huguenots, Connecting Rowland, Bulloch, de Bourdeaux, de Veaux, and Roosevelt Families of South Carolina, Georgia, North Carolina and New York*. Augusta, GA: RR Books, 1995. 16p.

Bully

Sheridan, Doris R. *Chase-Berry-Bully Families*. Troy, NY: Author, 1995. 12p.

Bunge

Cardenas, Eduardo Jose. *La Familia de Octavio Bunge*. Buenos Aires: Editorial Sudamericana, 1995. Unpgd.

Bunte

Clark, LaVerne Harrell. *The Bunte Family History, Smithville, Texas, 1880–1995, for the Smithville Centennial, 1995: With Histories of the Allied Families-the Garlipps, Lammes and Walls of Texas, c. 1849*. Denton, TX: Texas Women's University Library, 1995. 245p.

Buntin

Buntin, Robert McCollum. *Out of the Past: Buntin and McCollum Ancestors*. Baltimore, MD: Gateway Press, 1995. 302p.

Bunyard

Cole, Mary. *The Bunyard Family Research and Allied Families, Alley, Fitzwater, Foster, Hughes, Jones, Ledlow, McNeely, Rose*. Kentfield, CA: Author, 1995. 151p.

Burbank

Hare, Norma Q. *Puritans, Pioneers and Planters, an Ingraham, Abbott, Wardwell, Culver, Burbank Genealogy*. Arroyo Grande, CA: N. L. Enterprises, 1995. 330p.

Burdett

Moore, Freddie Gene. *My Virginia Ancestors and Their Descendants in the Families, Burdett, Alexander, Anderson, King, Boone, Welsh, McHenry, Cornwell, Alford, Coleman, Dixon, Morgan, Jarman, Maugridge*. Author, 1995. 46p.

Burgett

Burgett, Milbrey Otto. *The Burghardt/Burgett Family in America, 1625–1995*. Fort Lauderdale, FL: Author, 1995. Unpgd.

Burghardt

Burgett, Milbrey Otto. *The Burghardt/Burgett Family in America, 1625–1995*. Fort Lauderdale, FL: Author, 1995. Unpgd.

Burgin

McBride, Jean Coleman. *The Colemans of West Alabama and Allied Families*. Aliceville, AL: Author, 1995. 200p.

Burney

Burney, William P. *Those Horseshoe Swamp Burneys of Bladen County, North Carolina*. Dexter, MI: Thomson-Shore, 1995. 432p.

Sanders, Patrick B. *Genealogies of the Sanders and Watson Families, Examining the Descendants of Henry Sanders of Germany and Donald Watson of Scotland*. Chapel Hill, NC: Professional Press, 1995. 270p.

Burns

The Family of Hal Augustus Burns and Olive May West. Ft. Worth, TX: Author, 1995. 93p.

Burr

Burr, Wesley R. *A History of the Burr Pioneers*. Provo, UT: Author, 1995. Unpgd.

Powell, Ruth Burr. *Burr-Bowles Genealogy*. Baltimore, MD: Gateway Press, 1995. 278p.

Burress

Flanders, Charles M. *The Descendants of Colonel David Hart (1770–1835) and Other Related Families*. Author, 1995. 140p.

Burrier

Harter, Helen Eager. *Ancestors and Descendants of Adam Burrier, 1799–1890*. Palm Desert, CA: Author, 1995. Unpgd.

Burris

Robertson, Joanna. *A Tree Grows in America: My Family Line*. West Columbia, SC: Author, 1995. 238p.

Burrows

Porter, Edward T. *The Barrows Family of East Anglia, 1702–1995, Their Descendants in North America and Some of Their Related British Families*. Tacoma, WA: Author, 1995. 520p.

Burson

Marsteller, Charles M. *Burson Index*. San Francisco, CA: Author, 1995. 54p.

Burt

Crouse, Roger Paul. *Crouse Family History, the Descendants of the New Brunswick Loyalists, Philip and Sarah Crouse, with Allied Burt and Clark Families.* Seattle, WA: Rogue Publishing, 1995. 177p.

Burwell

Hauk, Carol A. *Descendants of Lewis Burwell of Virginia.* Anderson, IN: Hauk Data Services, 1995. 395p.

McLane, Curren Rogers. *The Rogers Family Genealogy.* Fort Worth, TX: Author, 1995. Unpgd.

Bush

Ziegel, Ruth Turner. *Julius Christy of Virginia and Kentucky, 1730–1808, and Agatha Barnett Christy, 1740–1820, and Related Families of Barnett, Gibbs, Blackburn, Cave, Glass, Kirtley, Bush, Lindsey, Armstrong, Whaley, Davis, and Day.* Cincinnati, OH: Author, 1995. 92p.

Bustrak

Gunderson, Marion Abbott. *Gunderson/Bustrak, the Ancestors and Descendants of Gunder Bjornsen Bustrak and His Wife, Marthe Jorgensdatter Boe/Grave.* Rolfe, IA: Author, 1995. 2 vols.

Butler

Kiddoo, Nancy Rice. *Jakob Dorner, German Pioneer of Frederick County, Maryland, and Three Generations of Descendants, 1748–1895.* Whippany, NJ: Author, 1995. 140p.

Butterfield

Sanders, Patrick B. *Genealogies of the Sanders and Watson Families, Examining the Descendants of Henry Sanders of Germany and Donald Watson of Scotland.* Chapel Hill, NC: Professional Press, 1995. 270p.

Bymaster

Bymaster Richards, Willa. *Descendants of Christopher Bymaster.* Carnation, WA: Author, 1995. Unpgd.

Byrd

Hauk, Carol A. *Descendants of William Byrd of Virginia.* Anderson, IN: Hauk Data Services, 1995. 198p.

Cable

Jones, Daniel Wilbur. *Genealogical Memoranda of Daniel Rufus Cable and Georgiana McKinney Cable.* Cary, NC: Author, 1995. 183p.

Rowan, Frances Dugger. *The Dugger Family, Johnson County, Tennessee.* Author, 1995. 331p.

Cade

Johaningsmeir, Henry Marshall. *A Cade Family Story, Some of the Descendants of Phineas Cade and Catherine Alkire of Pickaway County, Ohio.* Western Springs, IL: Author, 1995. 201p.

Cady

Cady, James William. *Supplement to Cady Genealogy, Revised and Updated.* Baltimore, MD: Gateway Press, 1995. Unpgd.

Cagle

Cagle, Ruby Abbott. *The Bishop Family from Manchester, England to Washington County, Maine.* Jasper, TN: Author, 1995. Unpgd.

Cahoon

Moore, Freddie Gene. *My Virginia Ancestors and Their Descendants in the Families, Ratliff, Skidmore, Watson, Hamilton, Wallace, Cahoon, Bowyer, Grimes, Sharp, Meeks.* Author, 1995. 116p.

Cain

Cain, Winton Burell. *A Cain Connection: Maryland to Mississippi and Beyond, 1686–1995.* Warner Robins, GA; Author, 1995. 301p.

Calamera

La Marca, Jeffrey Peter. *Window to the Past, Door to the Future, a Glimpse at an American Genealogy, Compilation of Data on the Acquisto, Calamera, Carroll, Crowley, Guastaferro, Hawley, La Marca, Lavier, and Steigerwalt Families.* Yorba Linda, CA: Shumway Family History Services, 1995. 214p.

Caldwell

Caldwell, Archie. *Caldwells and Their Cousins of Virginia and Southeast Kentucky.* Murfreesboro, TN: Caldwell Genealogical Assn., 1995. 278p.

Hutsell, Virginia D. *Caldwells Galore.* Lewisburg, WV: Author, 1995. 44p.

Terry, Imogene McCreight Fitzgerald. *Caldwell Kith and Kin.* Tyler, TX: Sunshine Press, 1995. 244p.

Calhoun

Camfield, Thomas W. *The Royal and Ancient Heritage of Family Colquhou, Being an Account of the Calhouns and Allied Families from the Dark Ages until the Present Day.* Port Townsend, WA: Ah Tom Pubns., 1995. 336p.

Hamilton, Fred. *The Descendants and Some Ancestors of James Meriwether and Julia Calhoun Hamilton, 1855–1936, 1853–1939.* Ruston, LA: Author, 1995. 104p.

Callan

Callan, James Brady. *The Callans of Winona Boulevard.* Rochester, NY: Corpus Christi Publications, 1995. 121p.

Callaway

Hauk, Carol A. *Descendants of Joseph Callaway of Virginia.* Anderson, IN: Hauk Data Services, 1995. 68p.

Calvert

Christoffersen, Dorothy Gray. *Brents, Calverts, Dawkins and Grays.* Lawrenceville, NJ: Author, 1995. 27p.

Camp

Lineage, the Florida Camps. 1995. 17p.

Campbell

Buchanan, Paul C. *Campbell Immigrants to the Shenandoah.* Springfield, VA: Author, 1995. 46p.

Campbell Craven, Frederick W. *Campbell Family History, Descendants of James Campbell and Amelia Harrison of Harrisonburg, Rockingham County, Virginia.* Placerville, CA: Author, 1995. 68p.

Curtis, Oscar Franklin. *Curtis and Allied Families.* Chelsea, MI: Author, 1995. 241p.

The Family of Hal Augustus Burns and Olive May West. Ft. Worth, TX; Author, 1995. 93p.

Martin, Robert Doud. *The Descendants of John Campbell, 1798–1884: Listing 621 Descendants for 8 Generations.* Eagle River, AK: Bear Toe Publications, 1995. 141p.

Canham

Canham, Alvah Bernard. *The Canham Family, Genealogical Notes.* Vassalboro, ME: Author, 1995. 85p.

Cannon

Spencer, Mary Ruth. *The Ancestors and Descendants of Charles Albert Cannon and Ruth Louise Coltrane.* Carmel, CA: Author, 1995. Unpgd.

Cantelou

McLeod, Stephen Archie. *The House of Cantelou & Co., the Story of a Southern Family.* Tallahassee, FL: Author, 1995. 705p.

Cantrell

Cantrell, Charles Thomas. *The Family of Charles Patterson Cantrell and Cora Gustava Hunt.* Brentwood, TN: Author, 1995. 112p.

Caplinger

Caplinger, Robert D. *Marshall and Anna Caplinger of Greensburg, Kansas.* Baltimore, MD: Gateway Press, 1995. 160p.

Capwell

Capwell, Lois J. *Stephen Capwell, a.k.a. Stephen Cappell-Capel-Capel-Capple of Rhode Island and His Descendants, through the 5th Generation.* South Windsor, CT: Tri-Mar Printers, 1995. 224p.

Carey

Rigsby, Michael Hall. *The Ancestry of Laura Elaine Rigsby*. 5th ed. Houston, TX: Author, 1995. 217p.

Carl

Brooks, Shirley A. *Our Family of Many Names: The Ancestors and Descendants of James Edward Hancock*. Lake Elsinore, CA: Author, 1995. 155p.

Carman

Carman, Daniel. *The Carman Family of Long Island*. Norfolk, VA: Author, 1995. 69p.

Carpenter

Carpenter, Terry Lee. *Carpenter Kinfolks, Descendants of Daniel and Martha (Marlar) Carpenter of Old Tishomingo County, Mississippi*. Version 3.1. Gainesville, FL: Author, 1995. 88p.

Dix, Roberta Cook Jackson. *The First Shall be Last, a Family History*. Author, 1995. 137p.

Carpentier

Sand, Vernon Jerome. *The Life and Times of Vernon and Renee Sand and Related Families, Geiselhart, Bittle, Warner, Sand, Vilmo, Bergman, Legrand, Lassauge, Prado, and Carpentier*. Austin, TX: Author, 1995. 501p.

Carr

Bostic, Paul Eugene. *Bruce, Maupin, Carr and Some Related Families Including Ballard, Hearn, Ayres, McCubbin, Cloud, Lane, Eveland (Elfland), Graves, Sharp and Willis*. Clinton, TN: Author, 1995. 391p.

Scott, Margaret Scott. *Genealogical Portrait of Joseph Carr and Barbara Gastor Beverett, the Carr Descendants of Duplin County, NC*. Warsaw, NC: Author, 1995. 418p.

Carrara

Neidich, Joyce Grill. *The Descendants of the Grill(i) and Carrara Families of Pettorano sul Gizio, Italy*. Franklin, PA: Author, 1995. 3 vols.

Carrick

Melle, Jane Hentges. *Bishop, Carrick, Hotchkiss, Johnson and Related Families, a Family History as Known in 1994*. Bowling Green, OH: Author, 1995. 2 vols.

Carroll

La Marca, Jeffrey Peter. *Window to the Past, Door to the Future, a Glimpse at an American Genealogy, Compilation of Data on the Acquisto, Calamera, Carroll, Crowley, Guastaferro, Hawley, La Marca, Lavier, and Steigerwalt Families*. Yorba Linda, CA: Shumway Family History Services, 1995. 214p.

R. E. W. Thompson (1856–1937), Adair, Clark, Carroll, Sellers, Lawson (Related Lines). Rockwall, TX: S. B. Adair, 1995. 133p.

Carruth

Carson, Arlie Aaron. *Carruth to Carson, a Genealogy*. Author, 1995. 132p.

Carson

Carson, Arlie Aaron. *Carruth to Carson, a Genealogy*. Author, 1995. 132p.

Streeter, Doris. *Descendants of William John and Mary Catherine (Jenereaux) Carson of Norfolk County, Ontario, Canada and Later of Tuscola County, Michigan*. Saginaw, MI: Author, 1995. 11p.

Carter

Barnes, Mary Lee Anderson. *The Carter, Knight, and Foreman Families of Edgecombe County, North Carolina, 1730–1800, Some Ancestors and Descendants*. Athens, TX: Author, 1995. 144p.

Barnum, Charles W. *Carter*. Sparks, NV: Author, 1995. Unpgd.

Griggs, Kendall. *Levi W. and Sarah E. (Carter) Hopkins, Their Ancestors and Descendants*. Hutchinson, KS: Author, 1995. 198p.

Hauk, Carol A. *Descendants of John Carter of Virginia*. Anderson, IN: Hauk Data Services, 1995. 2 vols.

―――. *Descendants of Moore Fauntleroy of Virginia*. Anderson, IN: Hauk Data Services, 1995. 69p.

―――. *Descendants of Thomas Beale of Virginia*. Anderson, IN: Hauk Data Services, 1995. 211p.

―――. *Descendants of Robert Beverley of Virginia*. Anderson, IN: Hauk Data Services, 1995. 330p.

Cary

Hauk, Carol A. *Descendants of Miles Cary of Virginia*. Anderson, IN: Hauk Data Services, 1995. 421p.

―――. *Descendants of William Fitzhugh of Virginia*. 3rd. ed. Anderson, IN: Hauk Data Services, 1995. 138p.

Johnston, Anne Plummer. *The Plummer Lineage of America*. Reston, VA: M. L. Tomaselli, 1995. 56p.

Case

Kelly, Michael. T. *The Ancestral Roots of the Case Family of Easton, Pennsylvania, and the Beers Family of Warren County, New Jersey, and Elsewhere*. Oak Park, IL: Author, 1995. 36p.

Casey

Adair, Shirley Brown. *Descendants of Asher B. Beauchamp and John Casey, Nave, Ball, Bingham (Related Lines)*. Rockwall, TX: Author, 1995. 139p.

Liston, Lois Jane Breakiron. *The Breakiron Family History Also Including the Bastian, Brecheisen, Casey, Dusenberry, Garlow, Hutchinson, Johnson, McMillen, Miller, Morris, Roderick and Other Families*. Wyandotte, OK: Gregath Pub. Co., 1995. 620p.

Thomas, Cecelia E. *The Caseys of the Strand, County Westmeath, Ireland, Canada, and the United States*. Baltimore, MD: Gateway Press, 1995. 147p.

Cash

Miller, Vivian Cash. *The Family of Warren Cash and Allied Lines*. Mulberry Grove, IL: Author, 1995. 182p.

Cast

York, Dorothy Anderson. *Our Anderson Family and Their Kin*. Fort Worth, TX: Author, 1995. 307p.

Casteel

Koickler, Eloyce Hubbard. *Hiestand, Hestand, Hastings*. Helena, MT: Author, 1995. 127p.

Castellani

Ciappelli, Giovanni. *Una Famiglia e le sue Recordanze, i Castellani de Firenze nel tre-quattrocento*. Firenze, Italy: L. S. Olschki, 1995. 251p.

Catlett

Hauk, Carol A. *Descendants of John Catlett of Virginia*. 5th. ed. Anderson, IN: Hauk Data Services, 1995. 216p.

―――. *Descendants of Lawrence Smith of Virginia*. 2nd. ed. Anderson, IN: Hauk Data Services, 1995. 287p.

―――. *Descendants of Robert Taliafero of Virginia*. 6th. ed. Anderson, IN: Hauk Data Services, 1995. 358p.

―――. *Descendants of Thomas Gaines of Virginia, Ancestor of President James Madison and USA Generals Gaines, Patton and Marshall*. Anderson, IN: Hauk Data Services, 1995. 284p.

Scott, Margaret Scott. *Genealogical Portrait of Joseph Carr and Barbara Gastor Beverett, the Carr Descendants of Duplin County, NC*. Warsaw, NC: Author, 1995. 418p.

Catt

Fail Families and Allied Families: Catt, Hensley, Kenyon, Lane and Sprague, 1818–1995, a Work in Progress. Decorah, IA: Anundsen Pub. Co., 1995. 348p.

Cauthen

Gardner, Oscar William. *Gardner/Ballard and Allied Families, Edmondson, Lee, Daniel, Cauthen, and Starr*. Morrow, GA: Author, 1995. 456p.

Chad

Teeter, Mary Bowers. *Descendants of Christ Chad and Anne Hulli of Grand Charmont, France, the Short Families of Williams and Fulton Counties, Ohio*. Rev. Morenci, MI: Author, 1995. 386p.

Chadwick

Templer, Janice Lindley. *George Washington Templer, His Ancestors and Descendants*. Claremore, OK: Author, 1995. 86p.

Chaille

Chaille, Jack Harry. *The Chailles in France and America, the Unique History of the "Famille Chaille" from Its Earliest Beginning in the Poitou Area of France to America in the 21st Century*. Baltimore, MD: Gateway Press, 1995. 451p.

Challeen

Challeen, Gordon Ellis. *A Challeen Family History*. Inver Grove Heights, MN: Author, 1995. 143p.

Chamlee

Brown, Phyllis Lee Barrett. *Index to Jacob Chamlee (1752) and Descendants*. Fayetteville, GA: Author, 1995. 35p.

Charlebois

Hanrahan, Patrick Lloyd. *Charlebois (Wood) Family History, and the Allied Families of Brien, Brule, Daudelin, Gagnon, LeBlanc and Riel*. Milwaukie, OR: Author, 1995. 179p.

Charton

Bymaster Richards, Willa. *Descendants of Eugene Richards and Sabrina Charlton*. Carnation, WA: Author, 1995. Unpgd.

Chase

Sheridan, Doris R. *Chase-Berry-Bully Families*. Troy, NY: Author, 1995. 12p.

Chastain

Pierre Chastain and His Descendants. St. Petersburg, FL: Southern Heritage Press, 1995. Unpgd.

Chaudoin

Smith, Gloria Jean Cowan. *Chaudoins of Virginia, 1750–1900*. Baltimore, MD: Gateway Press, 1995. 219p.

Cheatham

Baldree, Garvis Brookshire. *The Baldree Family*. Author, 1995. 212p.
Berry, Eddie Clayton. *Berry-Baker Connection*. Houston, TX: Author, 1995. 409p.

Chenier

Chenier, Theodore Gilbert Ronald. *The Descendants of Bertrand Chesnay dit Lagarenne, the Chesnays, Chenays, Chaines, Chaineys, Chenes, Cheniers*. Nepean, Ont.: Author, 1995. 365p.

Cherry

Pinkston, Margaret Darracott. *Mosswood Remembered*. Baltimore, MD: Gateway Press, 1995. Unpgd.

Cheshier

Bennett, Katie Brown. *Soaking the Yule Log: Biographical Sketches of the Brown, Cheshier, Sain, and Allied Families, 1749–1995*. Decorah, IA: Anundsen Pub. Co., 1995. 514p.

Chesson

Chesson, Eugene. *Foy and Allied Families of the Eastern Carolinas and New England*. Prescott, AZ: Author, 1995. Unpgd.

Cheston

Cheston, James. *The Cheston Genealogy, Descendants of Richard Cheston.* Albuquerque, NM: Author, 1995. 191p.

Chevry

Chevry, J. *Famille Chevry au Siècle de Saint Louis.* Gigondas, France: Author, 1995. 73p.

Chew

Hauk, Carol A. *Descendants of William Ball of Virginia.* 2nd. ed. Anderson, IN: Hauk Data Services, 1995. 113p.

Chi

Cortez, Constance. *Gaspar Antonio Chi and the Xiu Family Tree.* Dissertation (Ph.D.), University of California, Los Angeles, 1995. 349p.

Chichester

Chichester, James Nathaniel. *Chichester Family.* Lynn Haven, FL: Author, 1995. Unpgd.

Childers

O'Neal, Marcia Corrigan. *O'Neal Genealogy from the Early 1800s and Including Ancestors Anderson, Childers, Davis, Griffith, Hunt, Savage, Venard, and Willcuts.* Richmond, IN: Author, 1995. 43p.

Chitty

Priest, Lyman W. *The Chitty Family: Benjamin and Sarah (Palmer) Chitty and Their Descendants.* Charlottesville, VA: Author, 1995. 228p.

Chouinard

Association des Chouinard d'Amerique du Nord. *The Chouinards, Their Origin in France and Settlement in Canada.* Sillery, Quebec: Author, 1995. 111p.

Chrest

Chrest, Jim. *The History of the Chrest Family, from Norway to North Dakota, Christianson to Chrest.* St. Helens, OR: Paulson Printing, 1995. 102p.

Chrismon

Chrismon, Roger Lee. *Chrismon Family Directory.* 2nd. ed. Charlotte, NC: Author, 1995. 65p.

Christ

Gillespie, William Robert. *Maternal Lineal Genealogy in the Christ Line for William Robert Gillespie Who Is the Son of William Monroe Gillespie and His Wife Eleanor Elizabeth Christ.* Reading, PA: Author, 1995. 32p.

Christenson

Chrest, Jim. *The History of the Chrest Family, from Norway to North Dakota, Christianson to Chrest.* St. Helens, OR: Paulson Printing, 1995. 102p.

Ludvigson, Merrill Talmadge. *The Christensons and the Platsons: Where We Came From, Who We Are*. Decorah, IA: Anundsen Pub. Co., 1995. 459p.

Christiansen

Chrest, Jim. *The History of the Chrest Family, from Norway to North Dakota, Christianson to Chrest*. St. Helens, OR: Paulson Printing, 1995. 102p.

Huckaby, Sheila White. *Frederick Christiansen and Christine Hansen (Hansdatter) and Their Descendants, a Danish Family*. Plano, TX: Author, 1995. 625p.

Christopher

Partin, SheRita Kae. *The Descendants of John Christopher*. Nacogdoches, TX: Partin Publications, 1995. Unpgd.

Christy

Ziegel, Ruth Turner. *Julius Christy of Virginia and Kentucky, 1730–1808, and Agatha Barnett Christy, 1740–1820, and Related Families of Barnett, Gibbs, Blackburn, Cave, Glass, Kirtley, Bush, Lindsey, Armstrong, Whaley, Davis, and Day*. Cincinnati, OH: Author, 1995. 92p.

Churchill

Crosby, Roberta Churchill. *The History of the Churchill Family of Richmond County, Virginia*. Author, 1995. 250p.

Hauk, Carol A. *Descendants of William Churchill of Virginia*. 2nd. ed. Anderson, IN: Hauk Data Services, 1995. 250p.

Cisneros

Cisneros, Cecil Herminio. *Cisneros, Familia del Noble Fuerte de Andalgala*. Tucumán, Argentina: Lucio Piérola Ediciones, 1995. 93p.

Clairborne

Dorman, John Frederick. *Clairborne of Virginia, Descendants of Colonel William Claiborne, the First Eight Generations*. Baltimore, MD: Gateway Press, 1995. 836p.

Clapp

Jones, Daniel Wilbur. *Genealogical Memoranda of Daniel Rufus Cable and Georgiana McKinney Cable*. Cary, NC: Author, 1995. 183p.

Clark

Clark, Olive Eleanor. *Daughter of the Manse*. 1995. 135p.

Crouse, Roger Paul. *Crouse Family History, the Descendants of the New Brunswick Loyalists, Philip and Sarah Crouse, with Allied Burt and Clark Families*. Seattle, WA: Rogue Publishing, 1995. 177p.

Gould, Robert F. *Ezra Thompson Clark's Ancestors and Descendants*. 2nd. ed. Guilford, CT: Gould Books, 1995. 677p.

McCurdy, Mary Ellen Clark. *A Selected History of the McCurdy Family, 1920–1995*. Author, 1995. 86p.

Meigs, Peter Sanford. *Our Meigs and Smith Ancestors, Including the Clarke, Clifford, Eldredge, Fellows, Howe, MacMillan, Mann, Remington, Rice, Robinson, Scadgel, Skillings, and Thing Families.* Danville, NH: Author, 1995. Unpgd.

Partridge, Craig. *The Descendants of William Andrew of Cambridge, Massachusetts.* Camden, ME: Penobscot Press, 1995. 365p.

Phelps, Barbara Barratt. *The Ralph and Olive Clarke Smith of Burlington, New Jersey, Family History, 1694–1994.* Littleton, CO: Author, 1995. 326p.

R. E. W. Thompson (1856–1937), Adair, Clark, Carroll, Sellers, Lawson (Related Lines). Rockwall, TX: S. B. Adair, 1995. 133p.

Spoden, Muriel Clark. *An American Ancestry of the Clark-Morton and Tyman-Millar-Adams Families.* Kingsport, TN: Spoden Associates, 1995. 547p.

Claud

Dobbins, Anne White. *Some Descendants of Phillipe Claud, Huguenot Immigrant to Virginia.* Rockport, TX: Author, 1995. 30p.

Clayton

Green, Virginia Splawn. *The Clayton Clique, the Descendants of George Clayton, 1723–1786.* Tampa, FL: Author, 1995. Unpgd.

Hauk, Carol A. *Descendants of Samuel Clayton of Virginia.* 2nd. ed. Anderson, IN: Hauk Data Services, 1995. 152p.

Cleland

Stockslager, Bonnie J. *The Dick, Bell, Cleland Family Book of History and Recipes.* Chantilly, VA: Classic Printing Center, 1995. 125p.

Clevenger

Groff, Clifford. *The Stairs Families of Westmoreland and Somerset Counties of Pennsylvania and Their Ancestors, Steer, Summy, Monticue, Harshberger, Colborn, Tissue, Kreger and Clevenger.* Arnold, MD: Author, 1995. 147p.

Cline

Schneider, Jerry L. *Cline Family History, the Descendants of John Cline through His Three Sons, John, George and Jacob.* Decorah, IA: Author, 1995. 123p.

Clinkscale

Ancestors and Descendants of William Whitaker Smith, 1860–1944, and Florence Ellen Sullivan, 1875–1926, of Anderson and Greenville Counties, South Carolina. Spartanburg, SC: Reprint Co., 1995. 146p.

Clisby

Swayne, Rosemary Clisby. *Heirs of Our Lineage, Clisby/Swayne.* Bow, WA: Author, 1995. Unpgd.

Clodfelter

Clodfelter, Hubert. *Clodfelter Pioneer Days, a Collection of True Stories and Events about the Descendants of Solomon Clodfelter.* Brownsburg, IN: Malcolm S. Romine, 1995. 190p.

Cloud

Bostic, Paul Eugene. *Bruce, Maupin, Carr and Some Related Families Including Ballard, Hearn, Ayres, McCubbin, Cloud, Lane, Eveland (Elfland), Graves, Sharp and Willis*. Clinton, TN: Author, 1995. 391p.

Clough

Moore, Freddie Gene. *The Descendants of William Horne, Sr. and Jacob H. Horne and Their Descendants in the Families Clough, Ham, Heard, Hull, Varney, Starbuck, Otis, Stoughton, Pitman, Wentworth, Knight, Miller, Nock, Tibbetts, Emery, Simmons*. Spring, TX: Author, 1995. 148p.

Coate

Park, Ernest S. *The Ancestors and Descendants of Marmaduke Coate of South Carolina and Ohio*. Grahanna, OH: Linda Coate Dudick, 1995. 277p.

Coats

Park, Ernest S. *The Ancestors and Descendants of Marmaduke Coate of South Carolina and Ohio*. Grahanna, OH: Linda Coate Dudick, 1995. 277p.

Partin, SheRita Kae. *The Family of John Coats, a Sketch on the Family of John Coats of Nacogdoches County, Texas*. Nacogdoches, TX: Partin Publications, 1995. 14p.

Cobb

Ashford, Adelle Brown. *Kith and Kin, Simmons and Related Families*. Malvern, AR: Author, 1995. 208p.

Holmes, Marguerite. *Holmes from John of England and Plymouth, Massachusetts, to Holmes Brothers William Hudson, Horace William and Rodney Arthur Holmes of Aroostook County, Maine, and Related Families Cobbs, Redman, Libby and Shorey*. San Antonio, TX: Author, 1995. 101p.

Cochran

Zuendel, Jean. *Taylor, Blanchan, Cochran, DuBois, Foreman, Hite, Morris, Parker, Van Meteren*. Author, 1995. Unpgd.

Cocke

Hauk, Carol A. *Descendants of William Cocke of Virginia*. Anderson, IN: Hauk Data Services, 1995. 64p.

Cocking

Collett, Richard Cliff. *The Cocking Family History*. Fremont, CA: Author, 1995. Unpgd.

Coder

Huffman, Richard Glenn. *Coder-Koder Genealogy, 1550–1985, 435 Years, 1995 Supplement, Includes Philip Koder Update*. Whitney, PA: Author, 1995. Unpgd.

Coffey

Vander Wegen, Betty Ann. *Our Family, the Interrelated Coffeys, Graggs, Hollanders, Webbs of Avery County, North Carolina*. Union, WA: Author, 1995. Unpgd.

Coffin

Cagle, Ruby Abbott. *The Bishop Family from Manchester, England to Washington County, Maine*. Jasper, TN: Author, 1995. Unpgd.

Coffman

Smith, Robert Lee. *Ancestors of Thelma Margaret Gander*. Alexandria, VA: Author, 1995. 65p.

Coker

Brown, Gerald Douglas. *Descendants of Daniel and Rebecca McKenzie, Old Williamsburg, Sumter Districts of South Carolina*. Hemingway, SC: Three Rivers Historical Society, 1995. 116p.

Cola

Taylor, Edna M. *History and Memories of the Cola Family*. Sacramento, CA: Author, 1995. Unpgd.

Colbert

Cousineau, Eugena M. *The Colbert Family of Hancock County, Kentucky*. Lincoln Park, MI: Author, 1995. Unpgd.

Colborn

Groff, Clifford. *The Stairs Families of Westmoreland and Somerset Counties of Pennsylvania and Their Ancestors, Steer, Summy, Monticue, Harshberger, Colborn, Tissue, Kreger and Clevenger*. Arnold, MD: Author, 1995. 147p.

Cole

Cole, Wayne S. *A Great Adventure, the Story of the Paternal Ancestry of Thomas Roy Cole*. Silver Spring, MD: Author, 1995. 92p.

Sweet, Joyce Lisle. *A Pike Family History: William and Tryphena (Cole) Pike, Their Descendants and Related Families*. Hendersonville, NC: Author, 1995. 263p.

Coleman

Hauk, Carol A. *Descendants of Robert Coleman of Virginia*. Anderson, IN: Hauk Data Services, 1995. 226p.

McBride, Jean Coleman. *The Colemans of West Alabama and Allied Families*. Aliceville, AL: Author, 1995. 200p.

Moore, Freddie Gene. *My Virginia Ancestors and Their Descendants in the Families, Burdett, Alexander, Anderson, King, Boone, Welsh, McHenry, Cornwell, Alford, Coleman, Dixon, Morgan, Jarman, Maugridge*. Author, 1995. 46p.

Collier

Hauk, Carol A. *Descendants of William Collier*. 2nd. ed. Anderson, IN: Hauk Data Services, 1995. 53p.

Colson

Walters, Rolland K. *Jost Hite and Other Pioneer Ancestors of Buchanan (Hamm) Colson of Urbana, Illinois*. Author, 1995. Unpgd.

Coltrane

Spencer, Mary Ruth. *The Ancestors and Descendants of Charles Albert Cannon and Ruth Louise Coltrane*. Carmel, CA: Author, 1995. Unpgd.

Colvard

Holloman, Ann C. *Colvard Cousins by the Dozens, from John Stokely Colvard and Sarah Gibson*. Albany, GA: Author, 1995. 466p.

Combs

Hill, George Byron. *The Genealogy of the Hill, Combs, Barton, Starr and Allied Families*. Nashville, TN: Author, 1995. 296p.

Koickler, Eloyce Hubbard. *Hiestand, Hestand, Hastings*. Helena, MT: Author, 1995. 127p.

Comingore

Comingore, Betty Ann Terry. *The Comingore and Comingo Family Descended from Hendrick Janse Kamminga*. Sequin, TX: Author, 1995. Unpgd.

Conboy

Conboy, James C. *The Conboys of Susquehanna County, Pennsylvania*. 2nd. ed. Cheboygan, MI: Author, 1995. Unpgd.

Conerly

Sandel, Elias Wesley. *The Descendants of John Peter Sandel and Cullen Conerly*. Roseland, LA: Ara Ann Pubns., 1995. Unpgd.

Conlee

Morgan, Jim. *Conlee Clan, Searching for the Descendants of Isaac and Mary Conlee*. Sun City West, AR: Author, 1995. 173p.

Conn

Conn, Nancy H. *Connecting the Conn, Cowen, Greenaway Families from County Armagh to Upper Canada*. Toronto: Author, 1995. Unpgd.

Converse

Reamer, Kathleen R. *Descendants of John Reamer and Margaret Schermerhorn, 1758–1995*. Imlay City, MI: Author, 1995. 246p.

Conway

Hauk, Carol A. *Descendants of Edwin Conway of Virginia, Ancestor of President James Madison*. 4th. ed. Anderson, IN: Hauk Data Services, 1995. 187p.

———. *Descendants of Thomas Gaines of Virginia, Ancestor of President James Madison and USA Generals Gaines, Patton and Marshall*. Anderson, IN: Hauk Data Services, 1995. 284p.

———. *Descendants of William Fitzhugh of Virginia*. 3rd. ed. Anderson, IN: Hauk Data Services, 1995. 138p.

Conyers

Brown, Gerald Douglas. *A Genealogy of a Locklair Family, Mainly of the Old Sumter District of South Carolina, Present Day Sumter and Lee Counties.* Hemingway, SC: Three Rivers Historical Society, 1995. 102p.

Cook

Bruner, LaWanda Prindle. *William Cook Descendants in Union County, Tennessee, and Davies County, Kentucky.* Old Hickory, TN: Author, 1995. 62p.

Craft, Kenneth F. *Some Branches of the Ward Family of Montgomery County, Maryland, with Earliest Ancestor, Revolutionary War Soldier James White Ward (also Known as James White) Including Some Allied Lines: Fairfax, Thompson, Ray, Cooke and Wylie.* Norcross, GA: Author, 1995. Unpgd.

Hauk, Carol A. *Descendants of Mordecai Cooke of Virginia.* 3rd. ed. Anderson, IN: Hauk Data Services, 1995. 309p.

Cooley

Cooley, Edith Rigby. *The Family of Walter A. and Edith R. Cooley, August 1978.* Logan, UT: Herald Printing, 1995. Unpgd.

Coon

Robertson, Joanna. *A Tree Grows in America: My Family Line.* West Columbia, SC: Author, 1995. 238p.

Snyder, Ruth Curtis. *Admire Is the Name, George and Margaret (Coon) Admire of Rowan County, North Carolina, and Henry County, Kentucky.* Lincoln, NE: Author, 1995. Unpgd.

Cooper

Griffiths, George R. *A Dutch Cooper Family, and Blauvelt Family.* Chandler, AZ: Author, 1995. 18p.

McKee, Ruth Vernette. *Coopers in Virginia.* Minneapolis, MN: Author, 1995. 147p.

———. *The Known Ancestry of Rev. Isaac Babbitt, 1757–1833, Including Cooper, Crane, Ford, Lovell, Morse, Pierce, Tarne, Tisdale, Walker and Whitman Families.* Minneapolis, MN: Author, 1995. 42p.

Miller, Mary Cooper. *Coopers of Izard County, Arkansas.* Batesville, AR: Author, 1995. 475p.

Reamer, Kathleen R. *Descendants of John Reamer and Margaret Schermerhorn, 1758–1995.* Imlay City, MI: Author, 1995. 246p.

Wilson, Gladys Ophelia Mitchell. *Cooper Legacy, 1800s to 1995, a Pictorial Genealogy.* Author, 1995. 312p.

Coote

Coots, Dave. *The Immigrant Ancestors: Thomas and Elizabeth Coote.* Le Roy, NY: Author, 1995. 141p.

Cope

Cope, William DeLoach. *250 Years of the Cope Family in America.* Author, 1995. 138p.

Copeland

Robertson, Joanna. *A Tree Grows in America: My Family Line.* West Columbia, SC: Author, 1995. 238p.

Copley

Buchholtz, George John. *Backgrounds and Lineages of Some Copley and Buchholtz Families.* Baltimore, MD: Gateway Press, 1995. 301p.

Coppinger

Allen, Patricia Remmell. *The Remmell and Allen Families of New Castle County, Delaware.* Horsham, PA: Author, 1995. 71p.

Corben

Chabot, Diana. *The Corbens of Purbeck.* Hove, England: Hemphill Publications, 1995. 35p.

Corbin

Hauk, Carol A. *Descendants of Henry Corbin of Virginia.* 2nd. ed. Anderson, IN: Hauk Data Services, 1995. 312p.

Cornthwaite

Meehan, Wesley. *Edward Cornthwaite, Senior, His Family and Descendants.* Hamilton, OH: Author, 1995. 124p.

Cornwell

Moore, Freddie Gene. *My Virginia Ancestors and Their Descendants in the Families, Burdett, Alexander, Anderson, King, Boone, Welsh, McHenry, Cornwell, Alford, Coleman, Dixon, Morgan, Jarman, Maugridge.* Author, 1995. 46p.

Corrigan

Kennelly, Jack. *The Jim and Margaret Corrigan Family.* West St. Paul, MN: Author, 1995. 150p.

Corum

Skelton, Isaac Newton. *Ike, This Is You, a History of the Skelton, Boone, Barry, Beach, Blattner, Corum, Hoagland, Lehew, Strode, Wright and Young Families.* Washington, DC: Author, 1995. 223p.

Cory

Cory, Michael. *The English Corys, Their History and Distribution.* London: Cory Society, 1995. 223p.

Coslet

Bailey, Chris H. *Coslets and Cosletts in America.* New Haven, CT: Author, 1995. 163p.

Coston

Coston, Dean Walter. *The Coston Genealogy: An Initial Survey.* Falls Church, VA: Author, 1995. 24p.

Côte

Fiola-Bouchard, Françoise. *Histoire et Généalogie de Nos Familles, Fiola, Bouchard, Côte, Gagnon.* Ste.-Anne-des-Monts, Quebec: Author, 1995. 129p.

Counce

Counce, Oliver Joseph. *The Counce Genealogy, the Descendants of Edward Counce (Counts) and Sarah Adams*. New Orleans, LA: Author, 1995. Unpgd.

Counts

Counce, Oliver Joseph. *The Counce Genealogy, the Descendants of Edward Counce (Counts) and Sarah Adams*. New Orleans, LA: Author, 1995. Unpgd.

Courtenay

Courtenay, French Line c.1126-c.1750. Exeter, England: Courtenay Society, 1995. 17p.

Coveney

Dunlay, Margaret Mary. *Descendants of John Gorman and Mary Ann Coveney*. Rochester, NY: Author, 1995. 60p.

Covert

Covert, Norman M. *Tree of Life, Genealogy of Covert, Goodson, Dey, Barker, Triplett and Allied Families from 1607*. Baltimore, MD: Gateway Press, 1995. 463p.

Coward

Scarborough, Eleazer Pate. *A Genealogy of the South Carolina Coward-Cowart Family*. Hemingway, SC: Three Rivers Historical Society, 1995. Unpgd.

Cowen

Conn, Nancy H. *Connecting the Conn, Cowen, Greenaway Families from County Armagh to Upper Canada*. Toronto: Author, 1995. Unpgd.

Cox

Collie, Betty Cox. *The Cox Family from Caswell County*. Elon College, NC: Author, 1995. 473p. *Cox-Wheeler and Related Families*. Hemingway, SC: Three Rivers Historical Society, 1995. 269p.

Elliott, Margaret Coppess. *The Nicholls Family of Jefferson County, Ohio, the Rudd, Cox, Smith, and Related Families Who Came to Berlin Township, Ionia County, Michigan, before 1870*. Ionia, MI: Author, 1995. Unpgd.

Thacker, Jack H. *Some Descendants of John Cox, Sr. and Sarah Nunnally, Born in Halifax County, Virginia, in 1758, Emigrated from Henry County, Virginia, to Logan (Now Warren) County, Kentucky, in 1787*. Fairborn, OH: Author, 1995. Unpgd.

Coxey

Harris, Arlo D. *Family Tree Document for William Lester Harris and Charlotte Augusta Ernst*. 2nd. ed. Dayton, OH: Author, 1995. 109p.

Coyle

Brooks, Shirley A. *Our Family of Many Names: The Ancestors and Descendants of James Edward Hancock*. Lake Elsinore, CA: Author, 1995. 155p.

Gabbard, John E. *Family Links, the Gabbard/Coyle, Eden/Hornsby Connection*. Berea, KY: Author, 1995. 520p.

Craig

Miller, Kimberlee. *Descendants of Captain Jacob Prickett, Sr.*. Fairmont, WV: Jacob's Meadow, Inc., 1995. 178p.

Craigo

Stultz, Carolyne. *The Craigo Family Research Report, Including a Genealogy on Descendants of Eli and Experience (Jones) Craigo, Also Variance of Spelling, Craig, Craigo, and Crago.* Danville, IN: Author, 1995. Unpgd.

Cramer

Aton, Mary Price Creamer. *A Creamer Genealogy, Some Descendants of Daniel Cramer/ Creamer of Jefferson County, West Virginia, 1787–1995.* Sun City Center, FL: Author, 1995. Unpgd.

Kramer, Milton E. *The Kramers, the Next Generation.* NY: Kramer Family Centennial Committee, 1995. 218p.

Crane

McKee, Ruth Vernette. *The Known Ancestry of Rev. Isaac Babbitt, 1757–1833, Including Cooper, Crane, Ford, Lovell, Morse, Pierce, Tarne, Tisdale, Walker and Whitman Families.* Minneapolis, MN: Author, 1995. 42p.

Pelcher, Barbara Jane Tillotson. *Pioneers, Crain, Manning, McKenzie, Stanley and Allied Families.* San Bernardino, CA: Author, 1995. 186p.

Cranford

Elder, Shirley Bowen. *My Bowen, Barton, Harris, Scott, Hendon, Cranford Family Connections.* 2nd. ed. Raleigh, NC: Author, 1995. 356p.

Cratin

Winkler, Margaret Thompson. *The Long Tree and Others: Longs, Davises, Thompsons, Cratins and Slatons.* Montgomery, AL: Uchee Pub., 1995. 347p.

Crawford

Ellis, Ruth. *The Crawford Family, the Family of James Crawford and His Wife, Rachel Benedict.* Woodstock, Ont.: Author, 1995. 133p.

Scholl, Allen W. *The Brothers Crawford, Colonel William, 1722–1782, and Valentine, Jr., 1724-1777.* Bowie, MD: Heritage Books, 1995. 2 vols.

Creamer

Aton, Mary Price Creamer. *A Creamer Genealogy, Some Descendants of Daniel Cramer/ Creamer of Jefferson County, West Virginia, 1787–1995.* Sun City Center, FL: Author, 1995. Unpgd.

Crenshaw

Peden, Henry C. *The Crenshaws of Kentucky, 1800–1995.* Westminster, MD: Family Line Pub., 1995. 202p.

Crerar

Crerar, David Anthony. *Crerar Compendium.* Vancouver, British Columbia: Author, 1995. 259p.

Crocker

Leonard, Andrea. *A Crocker Genealogy*. Bowie, MD: Heritage Books, 1995. 311p.

Weaver, Clyde Richard. *The Descendants of Gurdon II and Delilah Wilber Crocker*. Wooster, OH: Author, 1995. 189p.

Crockett

McGinn, Ann Winston. *A McGinn McCorkle Family History, 1796–1995: With Related Families, Crockett, Dabney, Egnatoff, Fontaine, Freirson, Gillespie, Huddart, Kennemore, O'Donnell, Patton, Ring, Sheppard, Winston, and Others*. Spring Hill, FL: Author, 1995. 313p.

Crohn

Ruskay, Joseph A. *Leaves from a Family Tree*. NY: Vantage Press, 1995. 244p.

Crombach

Vilkaitis, Gregg A. *The Prachel Family of Monroe County, New York*. Charleston, WV: Author, 1995. 56p.

Crosby

Crosby, Eleanor Davis. *Simon Crosby, the Immigrant. His English Ancestry and Some of His American Descendants*. Bowie, MD: Heritage Books, 1914, 1995. 159p.

Cross

Ralston, Harold Alan. *Our Ralston Families: Including Ralston, McAffee, Cross, McMichael, Hanna, and Others*. Rev. Racine, WI: Author, 1995. 134p.

Smith, Edith G. Heflin. *The Descendants of Samuel Cross, Innkeeper of Charleston*. Author, 1995. 67p.

Crouse

Crouse, Roger Paul. *Crouse Family History, the Descendants of the New Brunswick Loyalists, Philip and Sarah Crouse, with Allied Burt and Clark Families*. Seattle, WA: Rogue Publishing, 1995. 177p.

Crowder

Crowder, Norman Kenneth. *John and Margaret (Jaycocks) Crowder, Their Descendants*. Nepean, Ontario: Author, 1995. 76p.

Crowley

Cagle, Ruby Abbott. *The Bishop Family from Manchester, England to Washington County, Maine*. Jasper, TN: Author, 1995. Unpgd.

La Marca, Jeffrey Peter. *Window to the Past, Door to the Future, a Glimpse at an American Genealogy, Compilation of Data on the Acquisto, Calamera, Carroll, Crowley, Guastaferro, Hawley, La Marca, Lavier, and Steigerwalt Families*. Yorba Linda, CA: Shumway Family History Services, 1995. 214p.

Crozier

Crozier, Ida Florence Wright. *The Family History of Lieutenant John Crosier and His Descendants, 1750–1995*. Hamilton, Ontario: GENCO, 1995. Unpgd.

Crumpler

Crum, Raymond. *A De Long Family in Ohio and Illinois, Including Relationships to the Hobaker and Crumpler Families, 1995 Companion Edition, with De Long-Wade Genealogy, Family Memories and Cumulative Name Indexes*. Ventura, CA: Author, 1995. 222p.

Crymes

McLeod, Stephen Archie. *The House of Cantelou & Co., the Story of a Southern Family*. Tallahassee, FL: Author, 1995. 705p.

Cudahy

Kennedy, Joseph. *The Cudahys, an Irish American Success Story*. Callan, Ireland: Author, 1995. 127p.

Cullerton

Naanes, Ted E. *Cullertons, an American Family, 1835–1995*. Chicago, IL: Author, 1995. 222p.

Culman

Bauer, Marguerite Swagler. *The Family History of George Halliwell, Johan George Culman, Joseph Spice*. Seville, OH: Author, 1995. 41p.

Culver

Hare, Norma Q. *Puritans, Pioneers and Planters, an Ingraham, Abbott, Wardwell, Culver, Burbank Genealogy*. Arroyo Grande, CA: N. L. Enterprises, 1995. 330p.

Cummings

Cummings, Jerome Lyons. *Cummings Chronicles*. La Canada, CA: Author, 1995. 104p.

Cummins

Bower, Eugene Elmer. *Joseph Cummins Family, 1793–1995*. Fairfield, CA: Author, 1995. 757p.
Jackson, Nancy Ann. *Colonel Edward Jackson, 1759–1828, Revolutionary Soldier, History and Genealogy of the Son of Immigrants John and Elizabeth Cummins Jackson, His Wives and Families of Mary Haddan and Elizabeth W. Brake, Grandparents of General Stonewall Jackson*. Franklin, NC: Genealogy Pub. Service, 1995. 1,135p.

Cureton

Ancestors and Descendants of William Whitaker Smith, 1860–1944, and Florence Ellen Sullivan, 1875–1926, of Anderson and Greenville Counties, South Carolina. Spartanburg, SC: Reprint Co., 1995. 146p.

Curl

Curl, Clarence Lee. *Curl, May et al., a Compilation of Family Records*. El Paso, TX: High Desert Pub. Co., 1995. 271p.

Current

May, John Russell. *Current Family History and Genealogy*. Fort Wayne, IN: Author, 1995. Unpgd.

Curtin

Curtin, Paul Joseph. *West Limmerick Roots, the Laurence Curtin Family of Knockbrack, County Limmerick, Ireland.* Austin, TX: Author, 1995. 424p.

Curtis

Curtis, Oscar Franklin. *Curtis and Allied Families.* Chelsea, MI: Author, 1995. 241p.

Gorlick, Jeanne. *The Family Tree of Curtis, Francisco, Hayes, Keller, Leavel, and LeRoy, with Procter, Ressequie, Sipperley, Spence and Weaver.* Author, 1995. 345p.

Hamilton, Fred. *The Descendants and Some Ancestors of James Meriwether and Julia Calhoun Hamilton, 1855–1936, 1853–1939.* Ruston, LA: Author, 1995. 104p.

Cuvalier

Hayes, Edward R. *Margaret Elizabeth Ferrel Hayes and Her Ancestors.* Author, 1995. 200p.

Dabney

Hauk, Carol A. *Descendants of Cornelius Dabney of Virginia.* 2nd. ed. Anderson, IN: Hauk Data Services, 1995. 162p.

McGinn, Ann Winston. *A McGinn McCorkle Family History, 1796–1995: With Related Families, Crockett, Dabney, Egnatoff, Fontaine, Freirson, Gillespie, Huddart, Kennemore, O'Donnell, Patton, Ring, Sheppard, Winston, and Others.* Spring Hill, FL: Author, 1995. 313p.

Daebelliehn

Scott County Iowa Genealogical Society. *A Family Tree: Kirk, Johnston, Daebelliehn, Peitscher, Lawrence, Ott, Jarvis, Delzell.* Davenport, IA: Author, 1995. Unpgd.

Dague

Schetter, Carole J. *History and Some Dague Descendants of John and Barbara Waltner Dague, John (1820–1895), Barbara (1816–1900).* Highlands Ranch, CO: Author, 1995. 68p.

Dahl

Peters, Herbert. *A Genealogy of the Jacob Dahl Family.* Saskatoon, Sask.: Author, 1995. 60p.

Daniel

Daniel, Kevin Wayne. *Thomas Daniel of Colonial Virginia and Eight Generations of His Descendants.* Bowie, MD: Heritage Books, 1995. 341p.

Daniel Family History. St. Albans, England: Author, 1995. 310p.

Gardner, Oscar William. *Gardner/Ballard and Allied Families, Edmondson, Lee, Daniel, Cauthen, and Starr.* Morrow, GA: Author, 1995. 456p.

Hauk, Carol A. *Descendants of William Daniel of Virginia*. Anderson, IN: Hauk Data Services, 1995. 40p.

Partridge, Craig. *The Descendants of William Andrew of Cambridge, Massachusetts*. Camden, ME: Penobscot Press, 1995. 365p.

Dapp

Poston, J. Michael. *Dapp Family in America, a Genealogy of the Descendants of Gottlieb Dapp of Stockhausen, Balingen, Kingdom of Wuerttembury*. Rockville, MD: Author, 1995. 54p.

Darby

Irwin, Charles T. *Darby Family History*. Fort Wayne, IN: Author, 1995. 106p.

Darnel

Darnel, Michael R. *Darnel Family Notebooks*. Granger, IN: Author, 1995. 122p.

Darracott

Pinkston, Margaret Darracott. *Mosswood Remembered*. Baltimore, MD: Gateway Press, 1995. Unpgd.

Daudelin

Hanrahan, Patrick Lloyd. *Charlebois (Wood) Family History, and the Allied Families of Brien, Brule, Daudelin, Gagnon, LeBlanc and Riel*. Milwaukie, OR: Author, 1995. 179p.

Davenport

Reynolds, Beatrice Kay. *Thomas Davenport of Dorchester, Massachusetts, His Descendants in Sidney, Maine (1762–1995)*. Sidney, ME: Author, 1995. 34p.

Stene, Charles Sherwin. *The Stene Family, Includes Rohn, Anderson, Bothwell, Davenport, Lloyd*. Decorah, IA: Anundsen Pub. Co., 1995. 385p.

David

Joseph, Anne. *Heritage of a Patriarch, Canada's First Jewish Settlers and the Continuing Story of These Families in Canada*. Sillery, Quebec: Septentrion, 1995. 562p.

Davidow

Boonin, Harry Davidow. *Davidows: The Experiences of an Immigrant Family*. Philadelphia: Author, 1995. 167p.

Davidson

Flanders, Charles M. *The Descendants of Colonel David Hart (1770–1835) and Other Related Families*. Author, 1995. 140p.

Davis

Dietz, Richard R. *Descendants of Samuel Davis, I (c.1610-c.1667)*. 2nd. ed. El Monte, CA: Golden West Marketing, 1995. 293p.

Jackson, Betty Hallandsworth. *Charles and Cynthia*. Fresno, CA: Wayland Jackson, 1995. 378p.

Manning, Marcia McBrayer. *A History of the Davis Family*. Lexington, MO: Author, 1995. Unpgd.

O'Neal, Marcia Corrigan. *O'Neal Genealogy from the Early 1800s and Including Ancestors Anderson, Childers, Davis, Griffith, Hunt, Savage, Venard, and Willcuts*. Richmond, IN: Author, 1995. 43p.

Seward, Kathryn E. *Davis*. Owosso, MI: Author, 1995. 332p.

Tillotson, Olin. *Tillotson of East Montpelier, Vermont: Being an Account of the Ancestors and Descendants of Olin Locke Tillotson (1854–1956) and Susan Dellah Davis (1861–1932) and Their Allied Families*. Surrey, BC: Author, 1995. Unpgd.

Wade, Nancy Banik. *A Davis Family History, The Descendants of Edward Davis of Oxford, England*. Decorah, IA: Author, Anundsen Pub. Co., 1995. 250p.

Winkler, Margaret Thompson. *The Long Tree and Others: Longs, Davises, Thompsons, Cratins and Slatons*. Montgomery, AL: Uchee Pub., 1995. 347p.

Ziegel, Ruth Turner. *Julius Christy of Virginia and Kentucky, 1730–1808, and Agatha Barnett Christy, 1740–1820, and Related Families of Barnett, Gibbs, Blackburn, Cave, Glass, Kirtley, Bush, Lindsey, Armstrong, Whaley, Davis, and Day*. Cincinnati, OH: Author, 1995. 92p.

Davison

Davison, Alexander. *The Davisons of Knockboy, Broughshane, County Antrim*. County Antrim, Ireland: Black Eagle Press, 1995. 109p.

Dawkins

Christoffersen, Dorothy Gray. *Brents, Calverts, Dawkins and Grays*. Lawrenceville, NJ: Author, 1995. 27p.

Dawson

Lones, Lela Lillian. *Dawsons (Thomas, John W., Cyrus P.), Baumbarger (Johann Ulrich)*. Perry, IA: Author, 1995. 56p.

Day

Covert, Norman M. *Tree of Life, Genealogy of Covert, Goodson, Dey, Barker, Triplett and Allied Families from 1607*. Baltimore, MD: Gateway Press, 1995. 463p.

Day, Donald D. *The Day Genealogy*. Scarborough, ME: Author, 1995. 43p.

Ziegel, Ruth Turner. *Julius Christy of Virginia and Kentucky, 1730–1808, and Agatha Barnett Christy, 1740–1820, and Related Families of Barnett, Gibbs, Blackburn, Cave, Glass, Kirtley, Bush, Lindsey, Armstrong, Whaley, Davis, and Day*. Cincinnati, OH: Author, 1995. 92p.

Dean

Mann, Marion. *The Kigh, Mann, Reagin, and Sykes Families, Including the Branch, Brown, Dean, Fort, Gerran, Leake, Marquis, Moses, Oakes, Powell, Reid, Trammell, Walk, Wilkey, Wingfield, and Woods Families, a Genealogy and Family History*. Baltimore, MD: Gateway Press, 1995. 218p.

Deavers

Luntz, Shelia Diann West. *A Deavers Family of Page County, Virginia*. Fairfield, PA: Author, 1995. 147p.

DeCell

DeCell, John Ashland. *The DeCell Families from Mississippi*. Memphis, TN: Author, 1995. 178p.

DeGood

DeGood, Harold B. *The DeGood Family in America ca. 1742 to 1995*. Kansas City, MO: Author, 1995. 390p.

Deiss

Deiss, Kathryn. *The Family of Joseph and Hilda (Armbruster) Deiss*. Author, 1995. Unpgd.

De Kay

De Kay, Eckford J. *The De Kay Family in America*. Rev. ed. San Jose, CA: Acom Press, 1995. 300p.

De la Vergne

Garven, Dorothy. *Descendants of Nicolas de la Vergne of Dutchess County, New York, through His Son Lewis (1738–1805)*. Rev. ed. Los Angeles: Alder Tree Press, 1995. 296p.

Dellinger

Dellinger, Paul H. *Descendants of George and Jacob Dellinger*. Lincolnton, NC: Author, 1995. 374p.

De Long

Crum, Raymond. *A De Long Family in Ohio and Illinois, Including Relationships to the Hobaker and Crumpler Families, 1995 Companion Edition, with De Long-Wade Genealogy, Family Memories and Cumulative Name Indexes*. Ventura, CA: Author, 1995. 222p.

Delzell

Scott County Iowa Genealogical Society. *A Family Tree: Kirk, Johnston, Daebelliehn, Peitscher, Lawrence, Ott, Jarvis, Delzell*. Davenport, IA: Author, 1995. Unpgd.

Demonbreun

DeMunbruna, Weldon. *The Descendants of John Baptiste Demonbreun, 1788–1872*. Louisville, KY: Author, 1995. 277p.

Dennison

Dennison, Allan. *In Service of His Country: a Brief History and Partial List of Descendants of Private Michael Dennison, First Battalion, and Private John Manzer, Third Battalion, General Oliver Delancey's Brigade of Loyalists*. Acton, MA: Author, 1995. Unpgd.

Haught, Betty J. Dennison. *My Branch of the Dennison Family Tree*. Author, 1995. Unpgd.

Derouen

Broussard, Earl. *Our Ancestors, Gone But Not Forgotten*. Author, 1995. 204p.

Derrick

Kilgore, LaVerne Keeler. *Simon Derrick Descendants, with Fox, Fry, Keeler*. Fort Worth, TX: Author, 1995. 400p.

Derryberry

Derryberry, Bob G. *The Derryberry Families in America.* Garland, TX: Author, 1995. 668p.

Dettmer

Dettmer, Clara Berke. *The Dettmer Family. Charles and Catharina Dettmer History and Cookbook.* Kearney, NE: Morris Press, 1995. 198p.

Detty

Detty, Nancy Syphrett. *Detty, Syphrett-Syfrett and Related Families.* Kerrville, TX: Author, 1995. 180p.

Devault

Jones, Daniel Wilbur. *Genealogical Memoranda of Daniel Rufus Cable and Georgiana McKinney Cable.* Cary, NC: Author, 1995. 183p.

DeWald

Beck, William M. *Matthias J. DeWald and Katherine Kauffman.* East Peoria, IL: Author, 1995. 26p.

Dey

Covert, Norman M. *Tree of Life, Genealogy of Covert, Goodson, Dey, Barker, Triplett and Allied Families from 1607.* Baltimore, MD: Gateway Press, 1995. 463p.

Dibble

Taylor-Goins, Elsie. *Naudin-Dibble Family, Selected South Carolina Historic Sites.* Columbia, SC: Author, 1995. 70p.

Dick

Stockslager, Bonnie J. *The Dick, Bell, Cleland Family Book of History and Recipes.* Chantilly, VA: Classic Printing Center, 1995. 125p.

Dickens

Dix, Roberta Cook Jackson. *The First Shall be Last, a Family History.* Author, 1995. 137p.

Diehm

Frappier, Patricia Shaffer. *Ancestors and Descendants of Johan Adam Diehm, the Immigrant of 1754 and Early Settler of Montgomery and Chester Counties, Pennsylvania.* Kettering, OH: Author, 1995. 385p.

Dierschke

Warschak, Carroll E. *Wilde Family History, 1683–1995, a Record of the Wilde Origins in Germany and of the Bernhard Wilde Descendants in America.* Waco, TX: Author, 1995. 323p.

Digges

Hauk, Carol A. *Descendants of Dudley Digges of Virginia.* Anderson, IN: Hauk Data Services, 1995. 32p.

Dillman

Bowen, Liz Dillman. *Dillman Family History, 1811 to 1995, a Heritage of Strength.* Author, 1995. 363p.

Dimond

Dimond, Edmunds Grey. *Patrick Dimon/Diamond/Dimon, Eighteenth Century Migrant, a Survey of His American Descendants.* Kansas City, MO: Diastole Hospital Hill, 1995. 222p.

Dix

Dix, Roberta Cook Jackson. *The First Shall be Last, a Family History.* Author, 1995. 137p.

Popham, Geraldine E. *Grandma's Ancestors, 1634–1936, Thomas Judd, the Emigrant to Nelson Judd, and Addie (Judd) Dowd.* Lodi, CA: Author, 1995. 148p.

Dixon

Moore, Freddie Gene. *My Virginia Ancestors and Their Descendants in the Families, Burdett, Alexander, Anderson, King, Boone, Welsh, McHenry, Cornwell, Alford, Coleman, Dixon, Morgan, Jarman, Maugridge.* Author, 1995. 46p.

Dobbins

Swanson, Thor. *The Descendants of Jacob and Ann (Marshill) Dobbins.* Milwaukee, WI: Author, 1995. Unpgd.

Dodd

Cragg, Michael. *Family History, Dodd Family.* Author, 1995. Unpgd.

Dollar

Johnston, Francis Clairborne. *The Angier Family of Orange and Durham Counties, North Carolina, and Allied Families of North Carolina and Virginia.* Richmond, VA: Author, 1995. 329p.

Donaldson

Holmes, Marguerite. *Warman from George of Canterbury, England, and Kent County, Canada, to George Frederick of Canada and Ludlow, Maine.* San Antonio, TX: Author, 1995. 44p.

Donato

Auzenne, Conrad Andrew. *Auzenne, Donato, Frilot, Lemelle, Meullion, a Genealogical Study of Five Families and Other Allied Families of Southern Louisiana.* Author, 1995. 222p.

Donham

Trimble, Scott T. S. *Donham Family History.* San Rafael, CA: Author, 1995. 249p.

Dooley

Vaughn, Barbara Biggers. *Lick Creek Beckoned, History and Records of the Biggers-Fagan Families Embracing Branches of Allied Families—Dooley, Eads, Grigsby, Harrison, Richardson and Woodward.* Decorah, IA: Anundsen Pub. Co., 1995. 310p.

Doolittle

Bielanski, Phyllis Jean Olin. *Andrew Powell Family Tree, Including Powell, Farr, Ten Brock Branches and Wolcott, Stiles, Doolittle, Kelch, Eldridge Branches.* Lakeland, FL: Author, 1995. Unpgd.

Dorchester

Swanson, Earle S. *The Dorchester Family Chronicles.* Fort Wayne, IN: Author, 1995. 89p.

Dorner

Kiddoo, Nancy Rice. *Jakob Dorner, German Pioneer of Frederick County, Maryland, and Three Generations of Descendants, 1748–1895.* Whippany, NJ: Author, 1995. 140p.

Douglas

Douglas, William H. *Douglass, Milam, Guess Family Tree.* Bowling Green, KY: N. G. Hudnall, 1995. 30p.

Douglass

White, Woodrow Wilson. *Douglass Woofter Union, Updated Family Tree of Alvin and Dora (Woofter) Douglass, 1813–1995.* Orlando, FL: Author, 1995. 74p.

Dover

Garreans, Martha Dover. *Dover Family.* Travelers Rest, SC: Author, 1995. 20p.

Dowling

Dowling, Enos E. *Dowlings of Southern Indiana, with Allied Families, Particularly in Washington, Lawrence and Jackson Counties.* Lincoln, IL: Author, 1995. 389p.

Drendel

Drendel, Gilbert Xavier. *Harvest of the Ages, the Xavier Drendel and Therese Roth Family.* Decorah, IA: Anundsen Pub. Co., 1995. 558p.

Driver

Kapas, Margery Ann. *Spanning the Ocean.* New Westminster, BC: Author, 1995. Unpgd.
McBride, Jean Coleman. *The Colemans of West Alabama and Allied Families.* Aliceville, AL: Author, 1995. 200p.

Drumheiser

Coxe, Myron. *The Drumheiser (Trommershaeuser) Family in the United States, 1849–1995.* Leetsdale, PA: Author, 1995. 78p.

Drummond

Suman, Estaleene Nash. *Drummond, Harvey, Suman and Other Allied Families.* Buffton, IN: Author, 1995. 1,063p.

DuBois

Zuendel, Jean. *Taylor, Blanchan, Cochran, DuBois, Foreman, Hite, Morris, Parker, Van Meteren.* Author, 1995. Unpgd.

Du Breuil

Stewart, John Manning. *The Dubreuil Families of Early Illinois and St. Louis*. Port Republic, MD: Author, 1995. 34p.

Dudenhefner

Schneider, Joseph J. *Family History of John L. and Margaretha (Dudenhefner) Schneider*. Dickinson, ND: Author, 1995. Unpgd.

Duggan

Anderson, Arthur Grant. *From Enniskillen, Ireland to Grand Forks, North Dakota: The Dr. Frederick Joseph Duggan, Mary Ann O'Reilly Family Biography*. Author, 1995. Unpgd.

Dugger

Rowan, Frances Dugger. *The Dugger Family, Johnson County, Tennessee*. Author, 1995. 331p.

Duhamel

Thompson, Laura Jones. *Jones, Richardson, Duhamel, and Allied Families of Maryland*. Nutley, NJ: M. A. Hook, 1995. 511p.

Duke

Johnston, Francis Clairborne. *The Angier Family of Orange and Durham Counties, North Carolina, and Allied Families of North Carolina and Virginia*. Richmond, VA: Author, 1995. 329p.

Duncan

Ancestors and Descendants of William Whitaker Smith, 1860–1944, and Florence Ellen Sullivan, 1875–1926, of Anderson and Greenville Counties, South Carolina. Spartanburg, SC: Reprint Co., 1995. 146p.

Cousineau, Eugena M. *The Duncan Family from Frederick County, Virginia, to LaRue County, Kentucky*. Lincoln Park, MI: Author, 1995. Unpgd.

McKechnie, Evelyn Duncan. *Dear Grandchildren, As the Chips Fell*. Author, 1995. 376p.

Rowe, Howard Morrison. *Our Heritage, a Story of Twenty Families*. San Diego, CA: Author, 1995. 524p.

Dunham

Trimble, Scott T. S. *Donham Family History*. San Rafael, CA: Author, 1995. 249p.

Dunkum

York, Dorothy Anderson. *Our Anderson Family and Their Kin*. Fort Worth, TX: Author, 1995. 307p.

Dunn

Peck, Patricia Dunn. *Jones Family Genealogy, a History of the Christopher M. Jones Family of Philadelphia with Emphasis on the Descendants of His Son, Levi Taylor Jones of Philadelphia and Trenton and Related Thropp, Yetter, Dunn and Steele Families*. Saratoga Springs, NY: Peckhaven Pub., 1995. 98p.

Duppa

Evans, Elwyn. *Hollingbourne and the Duppa Family.* Hollingbourne, England: All Saint's Church and the Hollingbourne Society, 1995. 28p.

Duprey

Davila Valldjuli, José. *Genealogía Valldejuli, Duprey y Roque de Puerto Rico.* Lubbock, TX: Author, 1995. 145p.

Duquaine

Feasel, Hubert. *A Genealogy and History of Charles Edmond Lambert and Related Families of Barthelemy and Duquaine.* Decatur, IN: H. & L. Feasel, 1995. 120p.

Durbin

Carson, Betty Jewell Durbin. *The Durbin and Logsdon Genealogy with Related Families, 1626-1994.* Rev. ed. Bowie, MD: Heritage Books, 1995. 2 vols.

Durrett

Robertson, Joanna. *A Tree Grows in America: My Family Line.* West Columbia, SC: Author, 1995. 238p.

Dusenberry

Liston, Lois Jane Breakiron. *The Breakiron Family History Also Including the Bastian, Brecheisen, Casey, Dusenberry, Garlow, Hutchinson, Johnson, McMillen, Miller, Morris, Roderick and Other Families.* Wyandotte, OK: Gregath Pub. Co., 1995. 620p.

Dutt

Dutt, Haradhan. *Dutt Family of Wellington Square.* Calcutta: Author, 1995. 123p.

Dvorak

Billingsley, Lorraine. *History and Genealogy of Frank and Frances Jukl Dvorak in Bohemia and Nebraska.* Topeka, KS: Author, 1995. 204p.

Dyer

Reynolds, Beatrice Kay. *Thomas Davenport of Dorchester, Massachusetts, His Descendants in Sidney, Maine (1762–1995).* Sidney, ME: Author, 1995. 34p.

—E—

Eades

Vaughn, Barbara Biggers. *Lick Creek Beckoned, History and Records of the Biggers-Fagan Families Embracing Branches of Allied Families—Dooley, Eads, Grigsby, Harrison, Richardson and Woodward.* Decorah, IA: Anundsen Pub. Co., 1995. 310p.

Eaker

Acker, Mary Paschel. *Ackers through the Ages*. Amarillo, TX: Author, 1995. 479p.

Poling, Virginia S. *The Family of John Ecker and Elizabeth Engle Ecker*. Hagerstown, MD: Author, 1995. 53p.

Earl

Reamer, Kathleen R. *Descendants of John Reamer and Margaret Schermerhorn, 1758–1995*. Imlay City, MI: Author, 1995. 246p.

Earle

Moore, William B. *Letters to Rebecca*. Bowie, MD: Heritage Books, 1995. 368p.

Earling

Earling, L. E. *The Earlings of Indians and Their Ancestors*. Old Lake, IN: Author, 1995. 2 vols.

Early

Hauk, Carol A. *Descendants of John Early of Virginia*. 2nd. ed. Anderson, IN: Hauk Data Services, 1995. 219p.

———. *Descendants of Richard Perrott of Virginia*. 2nd. ed. Anderson, IN: Hauk Data Services, 1995. 278p.

Earnhardt

Earnhardt, Ralph. *Paul Adolphus Earnhardt Genealogy*. Kannapolis, NC: Author, 1995. Unpgd.

Easton

Canfield, Rosemary. *Some Rhode Island Descendants of Nicholas Easton*. Pacific Grove, CA: Author, 1995. 40p.

Eastwood

Mallard, Shirley Jones. *Keeping Up with the Joneses, a Book about the Rafe Jones Family of Granville, North Carolina*. Chapel Hill, NC: Author, 1995. 244p.

Eaton

Eaton, Ralph R. *Eaton*. Lyons, IL: Author, 1995. Unpgd.

Eberhart

Barnhart, Shawn. *Eberhart/Everhart Ancestry in the United States of America, a Comprehensive Manual, 1727–1995*. Bowie, MD: Heritage Books, 1995. 148p.

Eberhart, Leona. *History of the John Gottlieb and Sophia (Wiesner) Eberhardt Family, 1770-1995, Germany and USA, Primarily in Portage, Outagamie, Ozaukee and Wood Counties*. Wisconsin Rapids, WI: Author, 1995. 123p.

Ebersole

Ebersole, Patricia Smith. *Ebersole-Robinson Family History*. Chesterville, OH: Author, 1995. 273p.

Ecker

Poling, Virginia S. *The Family of John Ecker and Elizabeth Engle Ecker*. Hagerstown, MD: Author, 1995. 53p.

Eckhardt

Eckhardt Evans, Doris. *Descendants of Johann Jakob Eckhardt, Born 15 August 1743, Nidda, Hesse, Holy Roman Empire*. Almira, WA: Author, 1995. 558p.

Ed

Ed, Robert Calhoun. *Wretman Roots, the Genealogy and History of the Wretman Families Who Emigrated from Ostergorland Lan, Sweden to Moline, Illinois, 1880–1891, Including Chapters on the Nymans and the Juthes*. Livingston, TX: Author, 1995. 295p.

Eddington

Bartram, Chester E. *The George Washington McCoy Family of Mason County, West Virginia, Prominent Related Families Eddington, Ferrell, Hoschar, Jividen, King, Sayre, Strait*. Knoxville, TN: Author, 1995. 187p.

Edelman

Myers, JoEllen Aisenbrey. *Aisenbrey-Kreis-Kost-Edelman*. Pleasanton, CA: Author, 1995. Unpgd.

Eden

Gabbard, John E. *Family Links, the Gabbard/Coyle, Eden/Hornsby Connection*. Berea, KY: Author, 1995. 520p.

Edgerly

Edgerly, Dorthea Roach. *Jared Rundle (Rundell), Jr. of Sullivan County, Indiana, His Ancestors and Descendants*. Oceanside, CA: Author, 1995. 484p.

Edmonds

Camp, Helen Moore. *Forging Our Families, Moore, Edmonds and Mayberry Connection*. Mooresville, NC: J. M. Leonard, 1995. 222p.

Moore, Selah Elizabeth. *The Edmonds' Epic*. Mt. Vernon, IN: Windmill Publications, 1995. 428p.

Edmondson

Gardner, Oscar William. *Gardner/Ballard and Allied Families, Edmondson, Lee, Daniel, Cauthen, and Starr*. Morrow, GA: Author, 1995. 456p.

Edwards

Cottrell, Richard Gary. *The Tyler-Fruhauf Family History, and Genealogical Record of Associated Edwards, Ellis, Helme, Mason, Pritchard, Seymour, Sherrerd, and Whiting Families*. Parma, MI: Author, 1995. 2 vols.

West, Donal S. *Hannah West and Elisha Edwards, Their Family*. Fort Wayne, IN: Author, 1995. 2 vols.

Eggert

Eggert, Irving John. *Peter Eggert of Mecklenburg and Related Families in America, Best, Bitz, Broekemeier, Hackbarth, Kane, Meisner, Nellis, Schunk, Strenkowski, Voight, Winston.* Decorah, IA: Anundsen Pub. Co., 1995. 224p.

Eggleston

Eggleston, Gene E. *Powhatan Revisited, 1611–1994, Joseph, Richard, Benjamin Eggleston.* Author, 1995. Unpgd.

Egnatoff

McGinn, Ann Winston. *A McGinn McCorkle Family History, 1796–1995: With Related Families, Crockett, Dabney, Egnatoff, Fontaine, Freirson, Gillespie, Huddart, Kennemore, O'Donnell, Patton, Ring, Sheppard, Winston, and Others.* Spring Hill, FL: Author, 1995. 313p.

Eiler

Carrico, Jane Barnett. *The Descendants of Martin Weddle and Johan Eiler.* Hilton Head, SC: Author, 1995. 239p.

Eip

Savage, Earl Roland and William Henry Kiblinger. *The American Descendants of Peter Kublinger, Germany, 1705 circa 1748.* Richmond, VA: Author, 1995. 143p.

Eitelbuss

Steffey, Dale E. *Genealogy of Andreas Rempp and His Wife Anna Eitelbuss, Oschelbronn, Germany.* El Cajon, CA: Author, 1995. 74p.

Elam

Neill, Norma C. *Elam Family, Quaker Merchants of England and America.* Doncaster, South Yorkshire: Author, 1995. 108p.

Elder

The Largs Australians. Largs, Scotland: Largs & District Historical Society, 1995. 21p.

Eldridge

Bielanski, Phyllis Jean Olin. *Andrew Powell Family Tree, Including Powell, Farr, Ten Brock Branches and Wolcott, Stiles, Doolittle, Kelch, Eldridge Branches.* Lakeland, FL: Author, 1995. Unpgd.

Meigs, Peter Sanford. *Our Meigs and Smith Ancestors, Including the Clarke, Clifford, Eldredge, Fellows, Howe, MacMillan, Mann, Remington, Rice, Robinson, Scadgel, Skillings, and Thing Families.* Danville, NH: Author, 1995. Unpgd.

Elkins

Stultz, Carolyne J. *Our Elkins Family.* Danville, IN: Author, 1995. 2 vols.

Wright, Diana. *Robinson Roots.* Author, 1995. Unpgd.

Elliott

Allen, Patricia Remmell. *The Remmell and Allen Families of New Castle County, Delaware.* Horsham, PA: Author, 1995. 71p.

Beck, William M. *Elliott/Elliot.* East Peoria, IL: Author, 1995. 52p.

Ellis

Bodishbaugh, Sue W. *The Jacob, Philipp, and Adam Erion Family Letters.* Tampa, FL: Author, 1995. Unpgd.

Boles, Harold W. *The Lineage of Reason Cary Ellis (1853–1937), Hensley Township, Johnson County, Indiana.* Kalamazoo, MI: Author, 1995. 45p.

Cottrell, Richard Gary. *The Tyler-Fruhauf Family History, and Genealogical Record of Associated Edwards, Ellis, Helme, Mason, Pritchard, Seymour, Sherrerd, and Whiting Families.* Parma, MI: Author, 1995. 2 vols.

Ellis, Lois A. *Genealogy of an Ellis Family of Michigan, Part II, the Goodwin Family.* Warren, MI: Author, 1995. 41p.

Ericson, Carolyn Reeves. *Cousins by the Dozens, Descendants of James and Sarah (Riggs) Ellis, 1758–1995.* Bowie, MD: Heritage Books, 1995. 2 vols.

Rusinak, Rick. *The Ellis Family, an Incomplete Genealogy.* Maplewood, MN: Author, 1995. 36p.

Ellison

Hayes, Edward R. *Margaret Elizabeth Ferrel Hayes and Her Ancestors.* Author, 1995. 200p.

Ely

Bell, Raymond Martin. *The Ely-Ealy Families, of Washington County, Pennsylvania, and Knox County, Ohio.* Coralville, IA: Author, 1995. 11p.

Emerson

Adair, Shirley Brown. *Robert Adair (1770–1845c.), an Adair Family History, Reid, Emerson, Hobbs, Worley, Thompson (Related Lines).* Rockwall, TX: Author, 1995. 146p.

Emmons

Emmons, Donald LaVern. *Emmons History, 1797–1995.* El Monte, CA: Author, 1995. Unpgd.

Empie

Chamberlain, Merle. *On the Trail of Zebulon Latimer and His Family.* Wilmington, DE: Lower Cape Fear Historical Society, 1995. Unpgd.

Engel

Engel, Jan Marcin. *Engel Family.* San Jose, CA: Genealogical Data Systems, 1995. 324p.

Enns

Enns, Edward. *In Search of Abraham Ens (1789-?), Abraham Ens (1826–1913), Abraham Ens (1861–1935).* Winnipeg: Author, 1995. Unpgd.

Erdmann

Erdmann Morrison, Kathleen. *Erdmann, Zastrow, Morrison.* Beaverton, OR: Author, 1995. Unpgd.

Erickson

Beguhn, Janice Mae Larson. *The Family of Ole and Kari Erickson, 1790–1995*. Minnesota, MN: Author, 1995. 681p.

Gunderson, Oddvin Archie. *Gunderson, Groth, Everson, Erickson, and Fossay, Ancestors and and Descendants in Norway and America, 1560–1994*. Issaquah, WA: Author, 1995. Unpgd.

Erion

Bodishbaugh, Sue W. *The Jacob, Philipp, and Adam Erion Family Letters*. Tampa, FL: Author, 1995. Unpgd.

Ernsberger

Hostetler, Bette Jane Smith. *Marryin-in, the Ernsberger Family That Married into the Amos L. Hochstetler #6281 Family*. Clearwater, FL: Sunshine Manuscripts, 1995. Unpgd.

Ernst

Harris, Arlo D. *Family Tree Document for William Lester Harris and Charlotte Augusta Ernst*. 2nd. ed. Dayton, OH: Author, 1995. 109p.

Levi, Arthur. *Genealogy and Family History: Maurice Pappenheim and Margit Ernst*. Longmeadow, MA: Author, 1995. 101p.

Erskine

Ralston, Raymond, Mrs. *Our Hamiltons and Erskines, Two Noble Families of Scotland*. Slippery Rock, PA: Author, 1995. 211p.

Erwin

Smith, Herbert F. *Plummer Ancestry, Including Some Alexander, Erwin, and Flinn Links of Herbert F. Smith*. 2nd. ed. Silver Spring, MD: Author, 1995. Unpgd.

Eshleman

Eshleman, Grace Nolt Rissler. *Ancestors and Related Families of Jacob L. Eshelman and Adaline Shelly*. Lancaster, PA: Author, 1995. Unpgd.

———. *The Family of Samuel Cassel Eshleman, 1862–1940, and Emma Jane Harnish*. Lancaster, PA: Author, 1995. 23p.

Etherton

Leake, Preston H. *The Descendants of Anderson Etherton and Millicent Hall*. Hopewell, VA: Author, 1995. 20p.

Eubank

Eubank, Roger Tate. *The Eubank Family of England, an Historical Perspective*. Singapore: Author, 1995. 87p.

———. *George Eubank, a Virginian of the War of the Revolution, His Descendants*. Singapore: Author, 1995. 29p.

Eudy

Hinson, William Ashley. *Geottfried Uhde and His Descendants, a History of the Eudys of Cabarrus and Stanley Counties, North Carolina*. Kernersville, NC: Author, 1995. 215p.

Eustace

Hauk, Carol A. *Descendants of John Eustace of Virginia*. Anderson, IN: Hauk Data Services, 1995. 43p.

Evans

Anderson, Eric. *Genealogy of Martha Ellen Tupper, the First Caucasian Girl Born in Petaluma and Descendants, 1620–1995*. Dillon Beach, CA: Author, 1995. 63p.

Eveland

Bostic, Paul Eugene. *Bruce, Maupin, Carr and Some Related Families Including Ballard, Hearn, Ayres, McCubbin, Cloud, Lane, Eveland (Elfland), Graves, Sharp and Willis*. Clinton, TN: Author, 1995. 391p.

Evers

Gunderson, Oddvin Archie. *Gunderson, Groth, Everson, Erickson, and Fossay, Ancestors and and Descendants in Norway and America, 1560–1994*. Issaquah, WA: Author, 1995. Unpgd.

Ewing

Carson, Betty Jewell Durbin. *Our Ewing Heritage with Related Families*. Bowie, MD: Heritage Books, 1995. 2 vols.

—F—

Fabian

Fabian, Merrill Horace. *Fabian Families of Bucks County, Pennsylvania*. Port Orange, FL: Author, 1995. 487p.

Fagan

Vaughn, Barbara Biggers. *Lick Creek Beckoned, History and Records of the Biggers-Fagan Families Embracing Branches of Allied Families—Dooley, Eads, Grigsby, Harrison, Richardson and Woodward*. Decorah, IA: Anundsen Pub. Co., 1995. 310p.

Fair

Parr, Richard Eugene. *Genealogy of Richard Eugene Parr*. Morgan Hill, CA: Author, 1995. 79p.

Fairfax

Craft, Kenneth F. *Some Branches of the Ward Family of Montgomery County, Maryland, with Earliest Ancestor, Revolutionary War Soldier James White Ward (also known as James White) Including Some Allied Lines: Fairfax, Thompson, Ray, Cooke and Wylie*. Norcross, GA: Author, 1995. Unpgd.

Fales

Fail Families and Allied Families: Catt, Hensley, Kenyon, Lane and Sprague, 1818–1995, a Work in Progress. Decorah, IA: Anundsen Pub. Co., 1995. 348p.

Fallis

May, John Russell. *Vaughn-Fallis Family History and Genealogy.* Fort Wayne, IN: Author, 1995. Unpgd.

Farias

Farias, George. *The Farias Chronicles, a History and Genealogy of a Portuguese/Spanish Family.* Edinburg, TX: New Santander Press, 1995. 294p.

Farmer

Guinn, Hazel Simmons. *Descendants of Kass and Ellen Farmer.* Author, 1995. 244p.

Farney

Farney, Charles Edward. *The Revised Farney Family Tree.* Gilbert, AZ: Hampton and Associates Research and Publication, 1995. 46p.

Farnham

Stepanek, Antoinette Farnham. *Farnham Families in England.* Bowie, MD: Heritage Books, 1995. 776p.

Farr

Bielanski, Phyllis Jean Olin. *Andrew Powell Family Tree, Including Powell, Farr, Ten Brock Branches and Wolcott, Stiles, Doolittle, Kelch, Eldridge Branches.* Lakeland, FL: Author, 1995. Unpgd.
Turner, Richard J. *The Farrs of Grant County, Indiana.* Author, 1995. Unpgd.

Farrell

Brand, Barbara Farrell. *Farrell: Descendants of Patrick Farrell and Elizabeth Welliver Farrell, Bellevue, Iowa.* Shingletown, CA: Author, 1995. 42p.

Farrington

White, Mary Hamilton. *William Lomax and His Descendants.* Author, 1995. 452p.

Faulk

Fowlkes, Eugene Franklin. *Our Folks, a Genealogy.* Fort Worth, TX: Author, 1995. 134p.

Fauntleroy

Hauk, Carol A. *Descendants of Moore Fauntleroy of Virginia.* Anderson, IN: Hauk Data Services, 1995. 69p.

Fehder

Sedgwick, Barbara Merle Fader. *Johann Henrich Fehder and His Descendants, 1752–1952, a Two Hundred Year History of the Fader Family, Descendants of the First Fehder Settler in Nova Scotia.* Needham, MA: Author, 1995. 285p.

Feitler

Mayer, Marion. *History of a Family Dispersed.* Chicago, IL: Author, 1995. 298p.

Fellows

Davis, Lana DeLong. *Zebina's Kin, the Descendancy of a Puritan People, Jael Fellows (1789–1822) and Zebina Rice (1787–1873), Narrative, Letters and Charts.* Bowie, MD: Heritage Books, 1995. 171p.

Meigs, Peter Sanford. *Our Meigs and Smith Ancestors, Including the Clarke, Clifford, Eldredge, Fellows, Howe, MacMillan, Mann, Remington, Rice, Robinson, Scadgel, Skillings, and Thing Families.* Danville, NH: Author, 1995. Unpgd.

Fenner

Fenner, Jim. *Fenner-Broughton Family History, the Family of James Elory Fenner, 1844–1912, and Hester Adamantha (Broughton) Fenner, 1847–1922, of Crawford County, Pennsylvania.* Apollo, PA: Closson Press, 1995. 384p.

Ferguson

FitzSimons, Marion Ferguson. *The Ferguson Family, from St. Fillans, Perthshire, Scotland to Ontario, Canada.* Toronto: Pro Familia Pub., 1995. 40p.

Stallard, Christine. *Ferguson Connection: Russell County, Virginia, 1775–1994: A Family History.* Ormond Beach, FL: Author, 1995. 586p.

Trimble, Scott T. S. *Donham Family History.* San Rafael, CA: Author, 1995. 249p.

Ferrell

Bartram, Chester E. *The George Washington McCoy Family of Mason County, West Virginia, Prominent Related Families Edington, Ferrell, Hoschar, Jividen, King, Sayre, Strait.* Knoxville, TN: Author, 1995. 187p.

Hayes, Edward R. *Margaret Elizabeth Ferrel Hayes and Her Ancestors.* Author, 1995. 200p.

Ferril

Best Strange, Norma. *Descendants of Henry Ott/Utt and Margaret Ferril.* Chilhowee, MO: Author, 1995. 100p.

Ferris

Ferris, James G. *A Ferris Family Tree.* Brownsboro, AL: Author, 1995. Unpgd.

Grossman, Annetta. *History of Donal George Young and Barbara Maxine Ferris and Allied Families.* Wabash, IN: Author, 1995. 74p.

Ferry

Ferry, Walker D. *Ferry Forebears.* Utica, KY: McDowell Pub., 1995. 202p.

Field

Reynolds, Beatrice Kay. *Thomas Davenport of Dorchester, Massachusetts, His Descendants in Sidney, Maine (1762–1995).* Sidney, ME: Author, 1995. 34p.

Findeisen

Schaefer, Jeanette Kriegel. *Family Trees for Descendants of Carl Christoph Findeisen, Sr. and Johanna Dorothea Hetzel.* Austin, TX: Author, 1995. 120p.

Finley

Weber, Verlene Vaughn. *Sherman, Olney, Finley Families*. Bath, MI: Author, 1995. 54p.

Fiola

Fiola-Bouchard, Françoise. *Histoire et Généalogie de Nos Familles, Fiola, Bouchard, Côte, Gagnon*. Ste.-Anne-des-Monts, Quebec: Author, 1995. 129p.

Firth

Firth, Richard Allan. *Firth Family, the Study of John and Mary Firth and Associated Families*. Sun City, AZ: Author, 1995. Unpgd.

Fisher

Dosch, Alice. *The Fisher's from Strassburg, Russia*. Ipswich, SD: Author, 1995. 191p.
Gallipeau, Beatrice. *Addendum to Fisher Genealogy*. Author, 1995. 37p.

Fitch

Burkhart, Steve. *Fitch Family*. Orlando, FL: Mary Jane Knisely, 1995. Unpgd.

Fitzherbert

Smith, Barbara M. *A History of the Fitzherbert Family*. Montreux, England: Minerva Press, 1995. 48p.

Fitzhugh

Hauk, Carol A. *Descendants of Anthony Savage of Virginia*. Anderson, IN: Hauk Data Services, 1995. 276p.
———. *Descendants of Edwin Conway of Virginia, Ancestor of President James Madison*. 4th. ed. Anderson, IN: Hauk Data Services, 1995. 187p.
———. *Descendants of John Battaile of Virginia*. Anderson, IN: Hauk Data Services, 1995. 69p.
———. *Descendants of John Catlett of Virginia*. 5th. ed. Anderson, IN: Hauk Data Services, 1995. 216p.
———. *Descendants of Lawrence Smith of Virginia*. 2nd. ed. Anderson, IN: Hauk Data Services, 1995. 287p.
———. *Descendants of Mordecai Cooke of Virginia*. 3rd. ed. Anderson, IN: Hauk Data Services, 1995. 309p.
———. *Descendants of Robert Taliafero of Virginia*. 6th. ed. Anderson, IN: Hauk Data Services, 1995. 358p.
———. *Descendants of Thomas Gaines of Virginia, Ancestor of President James Madison and USA Generals Gaines, Patton and Marshall*. Anderson, IN: Hauk Data Services, 1995. 284p.
———. *Descendants of William Fitzhugh of Virginia*. 3rd. ed. Anderson, IN: Hauk Data Services, 1995. 138p.
———. *Descendants of William Thornton of Virginia*. Anderson, IN: Hauk Data Services, 1995. 361p.
Lee, Elizabeth Nuckols. *The Fitzhugh Family of King George County, Virginia, the Daniel McCarty Fitzhugh Family, 1763–1823*. King George, VA: Author, 1995. 112p.

Fitzpatrick

Fuller, Donald Mitchell. *Our Family: A Composition Comprised of Histories, Biographical Sketches, Vignettes, Pictures and the Author's Recollections.* Author, 1995. 123p.

Fitzwater

Cole, Mary. *The Bunyard Family Research and Allied Families, Alley, Fitzwater, Foster, Hughes, Jones, Ledlow, McNeely, Rose.* Kentfield, CA: Author, 1995. 151p.

Flaming

Flaming, Harvey D. *The History and Members of the Andreas and Helena (Unruh) Flaming Family.* Yukon, OK: Author, 1995. 161p.

Flansburgh

Reamer, Kathleen R. *Descendants of John Reamer and Margaret Schermerhorn, 1758–1995.* Imlay City, MI: Author, 1995. 246p.

Fleming

Linn, Jo White. *Ancestry of Moore/Rowan Families, with Related Lines of Fleming, Renick, Bosley, Green, Girault, Beatty, Reading, Armitage, Ryerson, Rapelje.* New Orleans, LA: Author, 1995. 186p.

Fleshman

Shuck, Larry Gorden. *Our Families, Shuck, Fleshman, Sydenstricker, Smith, Lewis, Kincaid, Keister et al. of West Virginia.* Baltimore, MD: Gateway Press, 1995. 565p.

Fletcher

Wilson, Gladys Ophelia Mitchell. *Cooper Legacy, 1800s to 1995, a Pictorial Genealogy.* Author, 1995. 312p.

Flinn

Smith, Herbert F. *Plummer Ancestry, Including Some Alexander, Erwin, and Flinn Links of Herbert F. Smith.* 2nd. ed. Silver Spring, MD: Author, 1995. Unpgd.

Flitcraft

Eberhart, Edith Whitcraft. *A Branch of the Flitcraft, Whitcraft, Witcraft and Allied Families Who Came to America during the Colonial Period.* Baltimore, MD: Gateway Press, 1995. 176p.

Flora

Donson, Gladys Walters. *The Thomas Flora Family of London, Maryland, and Virginia.* Houston, TX: Donath Pub., 1995. 79p.

Floyd

Brown, Gerald Douglas. *Descendants of Daniel and Rebecca McKenzie, Old Williamsburg, Sumter Districts of South Carolina.* Hemingway, SC: Three Rivers Historical Society, 1995. 116p.

———. *A Genealogy of a Lee Family, Mainly of Old Williamsburg District, Present Day Florence County, South Carolina.* Hemingway, SC: Three Rivers Historical Society, 1995. 143p.

Miller, Martha Floyd. *Floyd Roots, Limbs, and Leaves (Twigs Included), the Family of Ervin Anse Floyd of Smith County, Mississippi.* Huntsville, AL: Author, 1995. 154p.

Fogo

Basgall, Winifred F. *Descendants of John Fogo and Mary Lambie.* Emporia, KS: Author, 1995. Unpgd.

Fontaine

McGinn, Ann Winston. *A McGinn McCorkle Family History, 1796–1995: With Related Families, Crockett, Dabney, Egnatoff, Fontaine, Freirson, Gillespie, Huddart, Kennemore, O'Donnell, Patton, Ring, Sheppard, Winston, and Others.* Spring Hill, FL: Author, 1995. 313p.

Foote

Allen, Patricia Remmell. *The Remmell and Allen Families of New Castle County, Delaware.* Horsham, PA: Author, 1995. 71p.

Popham, Geraldine E. *Grandma's Ancestors, 1634–1936, Thomas Judd, the Emigrant to Nelson Judd, and Addie (Judd) Dowd.* Lodi, CA: Author, 1995. 148p.

Forbes

Dix, Roberta Cook Jackson. *The First Shall be Last, a Family History.* Author, 1995. 137p.

Ford

Ford, Jo Ann. *Descendants of William Ford I and Harriet Thompson Ford, Also Some Related Families, 1800–1995.* IL: Author, 1995. 360p.

McKee, Ruth Vernette. *The Known Ancestry of Rev. Isaac Babbitt, 1757–1833, Including Cooper, Crane, Ford, Lovell, Morse, Pierce, Tarne, Tisdale, Walker and Whitman Families.* Minneapolis, MN: Author, 1995. 42p.

Foreman

Zuendel, Jean. *Taylor, Blanchan, Cochran, DuBois, Foreman, Hite, Morris, Parker, Van Meteren.* Author, 1995. Unpgd.

Forman

Barnes, Mary Lee Anderson. *The Carter, Knight, and Foreman Families of Edgecombe County, North Carolina, 1730–1800, Some Ancestors and Descendants.* Athens, TX: Author, 1995. 144p.

Forman, Everett W. *More Formans of New York and Descendants.* Bradenton, FL: Author, 1995. 179p.

Formy-Duval

Formy-Duval, Michael. *The Formy-Duvals, Descendants of Dr. Jean Prosper Formy-Duval, 1789–1996.* Author, 1995. 114p.

Forsthoff

Watson, Lyle Brooks. *The Forsthoff (Vorsthoven) Families, 1825–1994, and Their Connections*. Bentleyville, PA: Author, 1995. 257p.

Forsythe

Mallard, Shirley Jones. *Keeping Up with the Joneses, a Book about the Rafe Jones Family of
Granville, North Carolina*. Chapel Hill, NC: Author, 1995. 244p.

Fort

Mann, Marion. *The Kigh, Mann, Reagin, and Sykes Families, Including the Branch, Brown,
Dean, Fort, Gerran, Leake, Marquis, Moses, Oakes, Powell, Reid, Trammell, Walk, Wilkey,
Wingfield, and Woods Families, a Genealogy and Family History*. Baltimore, MD: Gate-
way Press, 1995. 218p.

Foshee

Foshee, Velma Lowman. *Foshee, Foushee Families, South Carolina*. Platteville, CO: Author,
1995. 700p.

Fossay

Gunderson, Oddvin Archie. *Gunderson, Groth, Everson, Erickson, and Fossay, Ancestors and
and Descendants in Norway and America, 1560–1994*. Issaquah, WA: Author, 1995. Unpgd.

Foster

Cole, Mary. *The Bunyard Family Research and Allied Families, Alley, Fitzwater, Foster, Hughes,
Jones, Ledlow, McNeely, Rose*. Kentfield, CA: Author, 1995. 151p.

Fovargue

Grant, Ian C. *Fovargue Family Indented Pedigree*. Nottingham, England: Author, 1995. 110p.

Fowler

Rolfe, Frederick G. *Early Rolfe Settlers of New England*. Baltimore, MD: Gateway Press,
1995. 2 vols.

Fownes

Bradley, John. *Sarah Wallington, 1719–1757, and Her Wallington, Pead, Oakes, Fownes, Perry,
and Bouchier Ancestors of Wotton-Under-Edge*. Devizes, England, Author, 1995. 213p.

Fox

Grant, Mary F. *Our Heinrich, the Ancestry, Life and Some Descendants of Henrich/Henry Fox
(1818–1898) of Earl and Ephrata Townships, Lancaster County, Pennsylvania*. Morgantown,
PA: Masthof Press, 1995. 168p.

Kilgore, LaVerne Keeler. *Simon Derrick Descendants, with Fox, Fry, Keeler*. Fort Worth, TX:
Author, 1995. 400p.

Foxon

Adams, Hebron E. *The Foxons of Leicestershire and Wisconsin*. Reston, VA: Foxon Press,
1995.

Foy
Chesson, Eugene. *Foy and Allied Families of the Eastern Carolinas and New England*. Prescott, AZ: Author, 1995. Unpgd.

Fradette
Proulx, Antonin. *Recueil des Familles Frechette et Fradette, les Descendants de Mes Arrière-Grands-Parents (Côte Maternel)*. Ottawa, Ontario: Author, 1995. 143p.

Frakes
Frakes, Joseph I. *Early Frakes Records with Frigg, Freke, Frake and Other Variants, 1490–1820*. Crescent City, FL: Author, 1995. 192p.

Francis
Ambro, Martha Ann Francis Roy. *Precious Loving Memories of Edd and Eva Francis and Their Family from 1910 to 1982 with Some Data on Edd and Eva's Younger Years*. Author, 1995. 331p.

Francisco
Gorlick, Jeanne. *The Family Tree of Curtis, Francisco, Hayes, Keller, Leavel, and LeRoy, with Procter, Ressequie, Sipperley, Spence and Weaver*. Author, 1995. 345p.

Frank
Joseph, Anne. *Heritage of a Patriarch, Canada's First Jewish Settlers and the Continuing Story of These Families in Canada*. Sillery, Quebec: Septentrion, 1995. 562p.

Frechette
Proulx, Antonin. *Recueil des Familles Frechette et Fradette, les Descendants de Mes Arrière-Grands-Parents (Côte Maternel)*. Ottawa, Ontario: Author, 1995. 143p.

Freedle
Freedle, Peggy McCrary. *Freedle Family History*. Lexington, NC: Author, 1995. 44p.

Freeman
Meyers, Patty Barthell. *Ancestors and Descendants of Lewis Ross Freeman with Related Families, Based Partially on the Work of Freeman Worth Gardner and Willis Freeman*. San Antonio, TX: Author, 1995. 938p.

Freeny
Freeny, Ellis. *Peter Freeny and His Descendants in America*. Oklahoma City, OK: Author, 1995. 400p.

Freitag
Freitag, Duane H. *John Jacob and Maria Freitag, the Life and Times of Our Pioneer Immigrant Ancestors*. Greendale, WI: Author, 1995. 15p.

French
Moore, Freddie Gene. *The Descendants of Thomas Moore, Sr. of Suffolk County, England and the Related Families, Youngs, Landon, Spencer, French, Norris, Simmons, Ratliff, Slaughter*. Author, 1995. Unpgd.

Freytag

Freitag, Duane H. *John Jacob and Maria Freitag, the Life and Times of Our Pioneer Immigrant Ancestors*. Greendale, WI: Author, 1995. 15p.

Frierson

McGinn, Ann Winston. *A McGinn McCorkle Family History, 1796–1995: With Related Families, Crockett, Dabney, Egnatoff, Fontaine, Freirson, Gillespie, Huddart, Kennemore, O'Donnell, Patton, Ring, Sheppard, Winston, and Others*. Spring Hill, FL: Author, 1995. 313p.

Friesen

Klippenstein, Bernard D. *Genealogy of Heinrich Klippenstein, 1849–1977*. Manitou, Manitoba: Western Canadian, 1995. 104p.

Frilot

Auzenne, Conrad Andrew. *Auzenne, Donato, Frilot, Lemelle, Meullion, a Genealogical Study of Five Families and Other Allied Families of Southern Louisiana*. Author, 1995. 222p.

Frink

Chesson, Eugene. *Foy and Allied Families of the Eastern Carolinas and New England*. Prescott, AZ: Author, 1995. Unpgd.

Fritsche

Boriack, David. *Boriack Family Tree, 1995*. Lincoln, TX: Author, 1995. 303p.

Fritz

Fritz, Jacob Otto. *The Fritz Family History*. Sun Prairie, WI: Author, 1995. 263p.

Frohmann

Mayer, Marion. *History of a Family Dispersed*. Chicago, IL: Author, 1995. 298p.

Fry

Hauk, Carol A. *Descendants of Joshua Fry of Virginia*. Anderson, IN: Hauk Data Services, 1995. 56p.

———. *Descendants of Robert Taliafero of Virginia*. 6th. ed. Anderson, IN: Hauk Data Services, 1995. 358p.

Kilgore, LaVerne Keeler. *Simon Derrick Descendants, with Fox, Fry, Keeler*. Fort Worth, TX: Author, 1995. 400p.

Fuchs

Fuchs, M. Tharsilla. *Christoph Fuchs, Sr. Family, Roots and Memories*. San Antonio, TX: Author, 1995. 327p.

Grant, Mary F. *Our Heinrich, the Ancestry, Life and Some Descendants of Henrich/Henry Fox (1818–1898) of Earl and Ephrata Townships, Lancaster County, Pennsylvania*. Morgantown, PA: Masthof Press, 1995. 168p.

Fuhrwerk

Holzmann, Herbert A. *Descendants of Ernst Wilhelm Raba, 1874–1951, and Maria Margareta Fuhrwerk, 1875–1965*. San Antonio, TX: Author, 1995. Unpgd.

Fullenkamp

O'Reilly, Dolores Brokamp. *Documentary of the Fullenkamp Ancestry*. Sidney, OH: Author, 1995. 87p.

Fullenwider

Wood, Thomas Fullenwider. *Connections, the Wood and Fullenwider Families in America*. Author, 1995. 130p.

Fuller

Dearing, William C., Mrs. *Elkanah "F" Gustin, Descendants of Mayflower Passenger Edward Fuller*. Anderson, IN: Author, 1995. 53p.

Fuller, Donald Mitchell. *Our Family: A Composition Comprised of Histories, Biographical Sketches, Vignettes, Pictures and the Author's Recollections*. Author, 1995. 123p.

Fuller, Samuel S. *Breaking Away*. Suffield, CT: Author, 1995. 310p.

MacGunnigle, Bruce Campbell. *Mayflower Families Through Five Generations, Descendants of the Pilgrims Who Landed at Plymouth, Massachusetts, December 1620. The Family of Edward Fuller*. 2nd. ed. Plymouth, MA: General Society of Mayflower Descendants, 1995. Unpgd.

Oncley, Lephia French. *Our Weaver Cousins, Ancestry of Samuel Stanton Weaver, 1793–1857, and His Wife, Lucy Billings Palmer, 1798–1851, with Some of Their Descendants and Related Families*. Ann Arbor, MI: Author, 1995. 244p.

Smith, Edith G. Heflin. *The Descendants of Ezekiel Fuller, Isle of Wight, Virginia*. Author, 1995. 191p.

Fullerton

Fullerton, Gordon W. *The Fullertons, Fullingtons, Fullartons, Fulletons, Fullitons of North America*. 7th. ed. Honolulu, HI: Polynesian Dynamics, 1995. Unpgd.

Funk

Funk, Eunice M. *Our Tree Grew in Beverly (Illinois, That Is)*. Author, 1995. 153p.

Furey

Hughes, Richard B. *The Hughes, Furey and Gast Genealogies*. Author, 1995. 27p.

–G

Gabbard

Gabbard, John E. *Family Links, the Gabbard/Coyle, Eden/Hornsby Connection*. Berea, KY: Author, 1995. 520p.

Gage

Gage-Gagne, Lynn. *The Gage Family History, 1696–1995*. Manchester, NH: Author, 1995. 198p.

Gagnon

Fiola-Bouchard, Françoise. *Histoire et Généalogie de Nos Familles, Fiola, Bouchard, Côte, Gagnon*. Ste.-Anne-des-Monts, Quebec: Author, 1995. 129p.

Hanrahan, Patrick Lloyd. *Charlebois (Wood) Family History, and the Allied Families of Brien, Brule, Daudelin, Gagnon, LeBlanc and Riel*. Milwaukie, OR: Author, 1995. 179p.

Gailey

White, Mary Hamilton. *William Lomax and His Descendants*. Author, 1995. 452p.

Gaines

Hauk, Carol A. *Descendants of Anthony Savage of Virginia*. Anderson, IN: Hauk Data Services, 1995. 276p.

———. *Descendants of Cornelius Dabney of Virginia*. 2nd. ed. Anderson, IN: Hauk Data Services, 1995. 162p.

———. *Descendants of Edward Broadus of Virginia*. 3rd. ed. Anderson, IN: Hauk Data Services, 1995. 64p.

———. *Descendants of Philip Pendleton of Virginia*. 6th.ed. Anderson, IN: Hauk Data Services, 1995. 287p.

———. *Descendants of Thomas Gaines of Virginia, Ancestor of President James Madison and USA Generals Gaines, Patton and Marshall*. Anderson, IN: Hauk Data Services, 1995. 284p.

———. *Descendants of William Strother of Virginia*. 4th. ed. Anderson, IN: Hauk Data Services, 1995. 130p.

———. *Descendants of William Thornton of Virginia*. Anderson, IN: Hauk Data Services, 1995. 361p.

Galiano

Oster, Brian J. *Descendants of Salvador Galiano and His Brother Yldefonso Galiano*. Tampa, FL: Author, 1995. 158p.

Gallaher

Golding, Joyce Buttner. *Empire of Cousins or the Gallaher Trail*. Bend, OR: Maverick Pub., 1995. 376p.

Gallop

Moore, Donald W. *Some Descendants of Patrick Gallop in North Carolina and Virginia*. Virginia Beach, VA: Pungo Press, 1995. 22p.

Gamble

Rowe, Howard Morrison. *Our Heritage, a Story of Twenty Families*. San Diego, CA: Author, 1995. 524p.

Gambrell

Roche, Hazel. *A Study of the Gambrells, Allens, Hensleys, Brewers, and Others from Clay and Knox Counties, Kentucky*. Moravian Falls, NC: Author, 1995. 44p.

Gander

Smith, Robert Lee. *Ancestors of Thelma Margaret Gander*. Alexandria, VA: Author, 1995. 65p.

Gann

Dryden, Marie Gann. *Ganns in Tennessee, a Collection of Source Material for Study*. Author, 1995. 180p.

Gardiner

Gardiner Jackson, Ann E. *Roots: Gardiner, Ingram, Grimmeissen, Ashpaw, Thiessen, Jackson, Meeker*. Author, 1995. 35p.

Gardner

Gardner, Oscar William. *Gardner/Ballard and Allied Families, Edmondson, Lee, Daniel, Cauthen, and Starr*. Morrow, GA: Author, 1995. 456p.

Gardner, Robert Arthur. *Gardiner-Gardner Genealogy, Descendants of George Gardiner, First Generation in America*. East Farmingdale, NY: Author, 1995. 25p.

Lide, Neoma Lawhon. *The Lawhons of Texas, Direct Family Connections of J. C. Lawhon and His Wife, Judith Ellen (Gardner) Lawhon*. Texas: Author, 1995. 61p.

Scarborough, Eleazer Pate. *A Genealogy of the South Carolina Coward-Cowart Family*. Hemingway, SC: Three Rivers Historical Society, 1995. Unpgd.

Garland

Smith, Thomas Russell. *Hello Choctaw, Meet Your Garland Ancestors*. Ventura, CA: Teesmith, 1995. Unpgd.

Garlipps

Clark, LaVerne Harrell. *The Bunte Family History, Smithville, Texas, 1880–1995, for the Smithville Centennial, 1995: With Histories of the Allied Families-the Garlipps, Lammes and Walls of Texas, c. 1849*. Denton, TX: Texas Women's University Library, 1995. 245p.

Garlow

Liston, Lois Jane Breakiron. *The Breakiron Family History Also Including the Bastian, Brecheisen, Casey, Dusenberry, Garlow, Hutchinson, Johnson, McMillen, Miller, Morris, Roderick and Other Families*. Wyandotte, OK: Gregath Pub. Co., 1995. 620p.

Garnsey

Card, Eva Louise Garnsey. *The Garnsey-Guernsey Genealogy. 1995 Supplement*. Hampton, VA: J. L. Young-Thayer, 1995. 130p.

Garrick

Miller, Gayla. *South Carolina Garick/Garrick Family Roots, 1752–1995*. Coalgate, OK: Author, 1995. 355p.

Garrison

Scott, Margaret Scott. *Genealogical Portrait of Joseph Carr and Barbara Gastor Beverett, the Carr Descendants of Duplin County, NC*. Warsaw, NC: Author, 1995. 418p.

Gascard

Arthaud, John Bradley. *The Arthaud Family of Bourbonne-les-Bains and Langres, Department of Haute Marne, France with Related Families of Gascard, Gautherot, Lauzanne, Liegault, Mutinot and Walferdin and One Immigrant Branch in the United States*. Columbia, MO: Author, 1995. 123p.

Gaskins

Wright, Diana. *Robinson Roots*. Author, 1995. Unpgd.

Gast

Hughes, Richard B. *The Hughes, Furey and Gast Genealogies*. Author, 1995. 27p.

Gaston

Brawley, Dorothy Loraine Perry. *The Bolling, Gay, Gaston, Brawley, Paper Trail, with Allied Families and Friends*. Author, 1995. 644p.

Dearing, William C., Mrs. *Elkanah "F" Gustin, Descendants of Mayflower Passenger Edward Fuller*. Anderson, IN: Author, 1995. 53p.

Gastor

Scott, Margaret Scott. *Genealogical Portrait of Joseph Carr and Barbara Gastor Beverett, the Carr Descendants of Duplin County, NC*. Warsaw, NC: Author, 1995. 418p.

Gatchell

Bell, Ernest Elmont, Jr. *One Line of Descent from Our Immigrant, Alexander Bell/Beall of Maryland, a Genealogical History, 1600 AD to 2000 AD, with an Autobiography by Ernest Elmont Bell, Jr. for His Descendants*. Baywood Park, CA: Author, 1995. 508p.

Gates

Nimmo, Sylvia. *The Descendants and Ancestors of Milo and Dora (Moon) Russell*. Papillion, NE: Author, 1995. 44p.

Gattis

Jones, Jeanenne Gattis. *Sifting Sanders*. Sayre, OK: Author, 1995. 59p.

Gaudart

Place, Agnès de. *Histoire et Généalogies de la Famille Gaudart*. Versailles, France: Author, 1995. 513p.

Gause

Chesson, Eugene. *Foy and Allied Families of the Eastern Carolinas and New England*. Prescott, AZ: Author, 1995. Unpgd.

Gautherot

Arthaud, John Bradley. *The Arthaud Family of Bourbonne-les-Bains and Langres, Department of Haute Marne, France with Related Families of Gascard, Gautherot, Lauzanne, Liegault, Mutinot and Walferdin and One Immigrant Branch in the United States*. Columbia, MO: Author, 1995. 123p.

Gawthrop

Gawthrop, Philip E. *A Genealogical Record of the Descendants in the Male Line of Thomas Gawthrop, an Early Traveling Friend (Quaker)*. Bowie, MD: Heritage Books, 1995. 256p.

Gay

Brawley, Dorothy Loraine Perry. *The Bolling, Gay, Gaston, Brawley, Paper Trail, with Allied Families and Friends*. Author, 1995. 644p.

Geiger

Herrington, Ilene Elma. *Schultheis, Geiger Families*. Norwich, NY: Author, 1995. 58p.

Geiselhart

Sand, Vernon Jerome. *The Life and Times of Vernon and Renee Sand and Related Families, Geiselhart, Bittle, Warner, Sand, Vilmo, Bergman, Legrand, Lassauge, Prado, and Carpentier*. Austin, TX: Author, 1995. 501p.

George

Sandifer, Wilma R. *Smith Family Tree*. East Windsor, NJ: Author, 1995. 144p.

Gerig

Roth, Reuben E. *The John Gerig Family Record, 1806–1953*. Grabill, IN: Author, 1995. 37p.

Gerran

Mann, Marion. *The Kigh, Mann, Reagin, and Sykes Families, Including the Branch, Brown, Dean, Fort, Gerran, Leake, Marquis, Moses, Oakes, Powell, Reid, Trammell, Walk, Wilkey, Wingfield, and Woods Families, a Genealogy and Family History*. Baltimore, MD: Gateway Press, 1995. 218p.

Gholston

Kaufman, Mary Arnold. *Martin-Arnold and Allied Families, Lanier, Bailey, Swan, Sandidge, Gholston, Morgan, and Born, Migration from Virginia to Tennessee, Georgia, Alabama and Arkansas*. Knoxville, TN: Tennessee Valley Pub., 1995. 212p.

Gibbel

Gibbel, Ira William. *The Descendants of Henry Gibbel*. Author, 1995. 596p.

Gibbon

Nelson, Eleanor G. *Benjamin and Mary Gibbon Family*. Dodgeville, WI: Author, 1995. 60p.

Gibbs

Ziegel, Ruth Turner. *Julius Christy of Virginia and Kentucky, 1730–1808, and Agatha Barnett Christy, 1740–1820, and Related Families of Barnett, Gibbs, Blackburn, Cave, Glass, Kirtley, Bush, Lindsey, Armstrong, Whaley, Davis, and Day*. Cincinnati, OH: Author, 1995. 92p.

Gibson

Moore, Phillip James. *Up and Down Our Family Tree*. Utica, KY: McDowell Pub., 1995. 201p.

Gilbert

Berry, Eddie Clayton. *Berry-Baker Connection*. Houston, TX: Author, 1995. 409p.

Gilchrist

Carter, Park W. *A History of Some Park Families in Jefferson County, Indiana, and Allied Families of Anderson, Mann, Gilchrist and Others*. Eureka, KS: Author, 1995. Unpgd.

Finegan, James A. *History and Legends of Clan MacLachlan*. Research Triangle Park, NC: Clan MacLachlan Assn., 1995. 128p.

Gilky

Ancestors and Descendants of William Whitaker Smith, 1860–1944, and Florence Ellen Sullivan, 1875–1926, of Anderson and Greenville Counties, South Carolina. Spartanburg, SC: Reprint Co., 1995. 146p.

Gillespie

Gillespie, William Robert. *Maternal Lineal Genealogy in the Christ Line for William Robert Gillespie Who Is the Son of William Monroe Gillespie and His Wife Eleanor Elizabeth Christ*. Reading, PA: Author, 1995. 32p.

McGinn, Ann Winston. *A McGinn McCorkle Family History, 1796–1995: With Related Families, Crockett, Dabney, Egnatoff, Fontaine, Freirson, Gillespie, Huddart, Kennemore, O'Donnell, Patton, Ring, Sheppard, Winston, and Others*. Spring Hill, FL: Author, 1995. 313p.

Gillman

Berry, Eddie Clayton. *Berry-Baker Connection*. Houston, TX: Author, 1995. 409p.

Gingrich

Holthouse, Marilyn Lucile Lipsett. *John Gingrich Descendants*. Camarillo, CA: Author, 1995. 52p.

Gipson

Phillips, Judy Henley. *The Gipson Family of Franklin County, Tennessee: Their Ancestors and Descendants*. Tullahoma, TN: Author, 1995. 304p.

Girault

Linn, Jo White. *Ancestry of Moore/Rowan Families, with Related Lines of Fleming, Renick, Bosley, Green, Girault, Beatty, Reading, Armitage, Ryerson, Rapelje*. New Orleans, LA: Author, 1995. 186p.

Glaradon

Powell, John W. *Ancestors and Descendants of William Powell and His Wife, Elizabeth Glaradon, Warrick County, Indiana*. Evansville, IN: Author, 1995. 162p.

Glasco

Boucher, Jessie Faye Glasco. *From the Root of Jesse: The Biography of Jesse Martin Glasco, 1818–1886*. Quitman, TX: Author, 1995. Unpgd.

Glass

Ziegel, Ruth Turner. *Julius Christy of Virginia and Kentucky, 1730–1808, and Agatha Barnett Christy, 1740–1820, and Related Families of Barnett, Gibbs, Blackburn, Cave, Glass, Kirtley, Bush, Lindsey, Armstrong, Whaley, Davis, and Day*. Cincinnati, OH: Author, 1995. 92p.

Glattfelder

Regan, Randy. *The Descendants of Adam Glattfelder (1547–)*. Norfolk, VA: Author, 1995. 4 vols.

Glatz

Skillings, Dorothy M. *The Christian Frederick Glatz and Christopher Glatz Lines in the United States*. Lansing, MI: Author, 1995. 63p.

Gleason

Quick, Robert V. *A Genealogy of the Family of Gleason*. Memphis, TN: Author, 1995. 60p.

Glen

Glen, Bob. *History of the Scottish Family Glen*. Edinburgh: Cuescot Press, 1995. 31p.

Glendening

White, Madalene Bowler. *Descendants of Immigrants, Glendening, Mason, Watson*. Centerville, IN: Author, 1995. 61p.

York, Dorothy Anderson. *Our Anderson Family and Their Kin*. Fort Worth, TX: Author, 1995. 307p.

Glenn

These are the Larsens, Brief Histories of the Larsen, Kanouse, Glenn, McClelland and McMeans Families. Loveland, CO: Author, 1995. 32p.

Glosemeyer

Paulochik, Paul M. *Roots and Branches, Paulochik, Gosemeyer, Yanik, Lonergan, and Related Families*. O'Fallon, IL: Author, 1995. 489p.

Glover

Roher, Celeste Glover. *One Glover Family*. North Potomac, MD: Author, 1995. 390p.

Goad

Haas, Kenneth F. *The Goads, a Frontier Family*. 2nd ed. Ozark, MO: Dogwood Printing, 1995. 148p.

Gochenour

Smith, Robert Lee. *Ancestors of Thelma Margaret Gander*. Alexandria, VA: Author, 1995. 65p.

Gochnauer

Gochnauer, Lena Sue. *John Abraham and Margaret Gochnauer Descendants*. Apple Creek, OH: Author, 1995. 125p.

Goetz

Adams, Kathleen Carmichael. *The Descendants of Joseph Goetz, 1811–1872*. Cold Springs, KY: Author, 1995. 485p.

Golden

Dubel, Zelda. *Golden, Hildreth and Replogle Genealogy*. Fresno, CA: Author, 1995. 29p.

Golladay

Golladay, Walter D. *The Golladay Family in America: Joseph Golladay, Sybilla Kneisley, Oldest Known Descendants through German Ancestors*. Loveland, OH: Author, 1995. Unpgd.

Gomezjurado

Gomezjurado Zevallos, Javier. *Los Gomezjurado en Ecuador y Colombia, 1570–1995*. Quito: Delta, 1995. 302p.

Gonnella

One Man's Family, from Italy to Occidental, the History and Heritage of an Italian Immigrant Family, As Seen and Heard through Eight Generations of One Man. Occidental, CA: Gonnella Family Assn., 1995. 476p.

Good

Weber, Dale K. *The Good Book*. Bath, MI: Author, 1995. 93p.

Goodman

Andrus, Gloria Ruth Goodman. *To Hannah and Will with Love, a History of Hannah McNeil and William Ezra Goodman*. Rexburg, ID: Author, 1995. 700p.

Goodner

Lacey, Hubert Wesley. *The Goodner Family, a Genealogical History, with a Brief History of the Family of Jacob Daniel Scherrer, and Notes on Other Allied Families*. Cullman, AL: Gregath Pub. Co., 1995. 2 vols.

Goodson

Covert, Norman M. *Tree of Life, Genealogy of Covert, Goodson, Dey, Barker, Triplett and Allied Families from 1607*. Baltimore, MD: Gateway Press, 1995. 463p.

Goodwin

Ellis, Lois A. *Genealogy of an Ellis Family of Michigan, Part II, the Goodwin Family*. Warren, MI: Author, 1995. 41p.

Gorman

Dunlay, Margaret Mary. *Descendants of John Gorman and Mary Ann Coveney*. Rochester, NY: Author, 1995. 60p.

Gosner

Rehm, Jeffrey Charles. *Genealogy of Moses Gonser and Louisa Wright of Hudson, Indiana*. Fort Wayne, IN: Author, 1995. 64p.

Gossett

Jones, Dorothy Gossett. *Elijah Gossett, Texas Pioneer*. Houston, TX: D. Armstrong Co., 1995. 460p.

Gossom

Gossom, James Hubert. *The Gossom Family of Missouri*. St. Louis, MO: Author, 1995. 60p.

Gott

Vilkaitis, Gregg A. *The Prachel Family of Monroe County, New York*. Charleston, WV: Author, 1995. 56p.

Gould

Karr, Nola M. *Baker Family Record, a Genealogy of Many of the Descendants of John Baker Who Immigrated from England in 1637*. White Plains, MD: Automated Graphic Systems, 1995. 663p.

Gourdin

Gourdin, John Raymond. *Gourdin, the History and Genealogy of a French-African-American Family from Georgetown County, South Carolina, 1830–1994*. Baltimore, MD: Gateway Press, 1995. 300p.

Gove

Smith, Robert Lee. *Ancestors of Thelma Margaret Gander*. Alexandria, VA: Author, 1995. 65p.

Graadt

Graadt van Roggen, August Harmen Freddy. *Genealogy of the Families Van Roggen, Graadt van Roggen, and Graadt*. Kennett Square, PA: Author, 1995. 547p.

Graadt van Roggen

Graadt van Roggen, August Harmen Freddy. *Genealogy of the Families Van Roggen, Graadt van Roggen, and Graadt*. Kennett Square, PA: Author, 1995. 547p.

Gragg

Vander Wegen, Betty Ann. *Our Family, the Interrelated Coffeys, Graggs, Hollanders, Webbs of Avery County, North Carolina*. Union, WA: Author, 1995. Unpgd.

Graham

DeMarce, Virginia Easley. *Sorting Out the Family of Edward Graham and Green Graham of Warren and Allen Counties, Kentucky*. Arlington, VA: Author, 1995. 107p.

Gramm

Savage, Earl Roland and William Henry Kiblinger. *The American Descendants of Peter Kublinger, Germany, 1705 circa 1748*. Richmond, VA: Author, 1995. 143p.

Granberry

Williams, Carl Clifford. *The Williams and Granberry Families*. Midland, TX: Author, 1995. 287p.

Graubard

Wenger, Irving. *Wenger and Graubard Genealogy*. Long Beach, CA: Author, 1995. Unpgd.

Graves

Bostic, Paul Eugene. *Bruce, Maupin, Carr and Some Related Families Including Ballard, Hearn, Ayres, McCubbin, Cloud, Lane, Eveland (Elfland), Graves, Sharp and Willis*. Clinton, TN: Author, 1995. 391p.

Graves, Kenneth Vance. *Deacon George Graves, 1636 Settler of Hartford, Connecticut, and His Descendants*. Wrenthen, MA: Author, 1995. 446p.

Robertson, Joanna. *A Tree Grows in America: My Family Line*. West Columbia, SC: Author, 1995. 238p.

Gray

Christoffersen, Dorothy Gray. *Brents, Calverts, Dawkins and Grays*. Lawrenceville, NJ: Author, 1995. 27p.

Grayson

Hauk, Carol A. *Descendants of John Grayson of Virginia*. 2nd. ed. Anderson, IN: Hauk Data Services, 1995. 65p.

Greely

Middleton, Edith S. *Marion Thomas Whitney: The Story of His Predecessors and Descendants, Parker, Greely, Tufts*. Portland, OR: Author, 1995. 45p.

Green

Aldridge, Bryan Keith. *The Green Family, Descendants of George Washington Green, Sr. and Nancy Gasperson Green*. Marion, NC: Author, 1995. 453p.

Hauk, Carol A. *Descendants of William Green of Virginia*. 4th. ed. Anderson, IN: Hauk Data Services, 1995. 69p.

Holmes, Marguerite. *Warman from George of Canterbury, England, and Kent County, Canada to George Frederick of Canada and Ludlow, Maine*. San Antonio, TX: Author, 1995. 44p.

Linn, Jo White. *Ancestry of Moore/Rowan Families, with Related Lines of Fleming, Renick, Bosley, Green, Girault, Beatty, Reading, Armitage, Ryerson, Rapelje*. New Orleans, LA: Author, 1995. 186p.

Mallard, Shirley Jones. *Keeping Up with the Joneses, a Book about the Rafe Jones Family of Granville, North Carolina*. Chapel Hill, NC: Author, 1995. 244p.

Whitmore, Robert Devore. *Whitmore Family Genealogy*. Steubenville, OH: Public Library of Steubenville and Jefferson County, 1995. 14p.

Greenaway

Conn, Nancy H. *Connecting the Conn, Cowen, Greenaway Families from County Armagh to Upper Canada*. Toronto: Author, 1995. Unpgd.

Greenlee

McBride, Jean Coleman. *The Colemans of West Alabama and Allied Families*. Aliceville, AL: Author, 1995. 200p.

Greenville

Parsley, Linda Flathers. *Descendants of Peter and Jane Greenville, Eight Generations in America*. Stephens City, VA: Commercial Press, 1995. 402p.

Greenwell

Rowan, Frances Dugger. *The Dugger Family, Johnson County, Tennessee.* Author, 1995. 331p.

Greer

Scott, Margaret Scott. *Genealogical Portrait of Joseph Carr and Barbara Gastor Beverett, the Carr Descendants of Duplin County, NC.* Warsaw, NC: Author, 1995. 418p.

Grier

Grier, William Milton. *Grier and Allied Families Directory, 1995.* Denver, CO: Grier and Co., 1995. Unpgd.

Griffin

Griffin, Alvis Ray. *Jerome Griffith Family of Northampton County, Virginia, 1644–1727, Supplement Number One to along the Neuse, the Craven Bryan Griffin Family, 1728–1992.* Danville, VA: Author, 1995. 20p.

Griffin, John Raymond. *Griffin Families from the United Kingdom to the New World.* Grants Pass, OR: Author, 1995. Unpgd.

Griffith

Griffin, Alvis Ray. *Jerome Griffith Family of Northampton County, Virginia, 1644–1727, Supplement Number One to along the Neuse, the Craven Bryan Griffin Family, 1728- 1992.* Danville, VA: Author, 1995. 20p.

Griffiths, Bernard Stockman. *In Search of My Ancestors.* Alresford, England: Author, 1995, 48p.

O'Neal, Marcia Corrigan. *O'Neal Genealogy from the Early 1800s and Including Ancestors Anderson, Childers, Davis, Griffith, Hunt, Savage, Venard, and Willcuts.* Richmond, IN: Author, 1995. 43p.

Robertson, James Miller. *A Tale of Two Families, Robertson and Griffith.* Corpus Christi, TX: Author, 1995. 412p.

Windland, Harry K. *Benjamin Griffith, His Progeny and Allied Families.* Glen Carbon, IL: Author, 1995. Unpgd.

Griggs

Griggs, Dan. *It's Written in Stone, a Collection of Genealogies from Griggs and Wolford Family Research.* Anchorage, AK: Author, 1995. Unpgd.

Grigsby

Pulleine, Imogene Hamilton. *The Ancestors and Descendants of John William Truett and Priscilla Grigsby.* Author, 1995. 123p.

Grill

Neidich, Joyce Grill. *The Descendants of the Grill(i) and Carrara Families of Pettorano sul Gizio, Italy.* Franklin, PA: Author, 1995. 3 vols.

Grillot

Grillot, R. E. *Grillot and Ancestors.* Author, 1995. 831p.

Grimes

Moore, Freddie Gene. *My Virginia Ancestors and Their Descendants in the Families, Ratliff, Skidmore, Watson, Hamilton, Wallace, Cahoon, Bowyer, Grimes, Sharp, Meeks.* Author, 1995. 116p.

Grimmeissen

Gardiner Jackson, Ann E. *Roots: Gardiner, Ingram, Grimmeissen, Ashpaw, Thiessen, Jackson, Meeker.* Author, 1995. 35p.

Grindberg

Grindberg, Alan. *A Compilation of Information about Earl and Grethe Grindberg and Their Children.* Bismarck, ND: Author, 1995. Unpgd.

Grisham

Grisham, Violet. *My Williamson County Pioneer Kin Folks and Their Descendants.* Marion, IL: Author, 1995. 139p.

Gross

Gross, Grace Dickinson. *Gross Family History: Includes Leier Family.* Orrin, ND: Author, 1995. Unpgd.

Yamanaka, Evalyn. *Gross Families of Hamilton County, Tennessee.* San Jose, CA: Author, 1995. Unpgd.

Grossman, Annetta. *History of Homer Harold Grossman and Annetta Mae Pinkerton and Allied Families.* Wabash, IN: Author, 1995. 626p.

Grosvenor

King, Margaret Ann Scott. *Homestead of the Free, the Jefferies Heritage.* 2nd. ed. Salt Lake City, UT: King-Scott Heritage Foundation, 1995. 647p.

Groth

Gunderson, Oddvin Archie. *Gunderson, Groth, Everson, Erickson, and Fossay, Ancestors and and Descendants in Norway and America, 1560–1994.* Issaquah, WA: Author, 1995. Unpgd.

Groves

Wilson, Robert E. *Groves and Huston and Other Families from Pennsylvania to Ohio.* Taftsville, VT: Author, 1995. Unpgd.

Grymes

Hauk, Carol A. *Descendants of Charles Grymes of Virginia.* Anderson, IN: Hauk Data Services, 1995. 244p.

Guastaferro

La Marca, Jeffrey Peter. *Window to the Past, Door to the Future, a Glimpse at an American Genealogy, Compilation of Data on the Acquisto, Calamera, Carroll, Crowley, Guastaferro, Hawley, La Marca, Lavier, and Steigerwalt Families.* Yorba Linda, CA: Shumway Family History Services, 1995. 214p.

Guernsey

Card, Eva Louise Garnsey. *The Garnsey-Guernsey Genealogy. 1995 Supplement*. Hampton, VA: J. L. Young-Thayer, 1995. 130p.

Guerra

Pena, José F. de la. *Los Guerra de Coahuila, Nuevo León, Tamaulipas, y Texas*. 2nd. ed. Ventura, CA: Author, 1995. 25p.

Guerrero

Pena, José F. de la. *Los Guerra de Coahuila, Nuevo León, Tamaulipas, y Texas*. 2nd. ed. Ventura, CA: Author, 1995. 25p.

Guess

Douglas, William H. *Douglass, Milam, Guess Family Tree*. Bowling Green, KY: N. G. Hudnall, 1995. 30p.

Guest

Douglas, William H. *Douglass, Milam, Guess Family Tree*. Bowling Green, KY: N. G. Hudnall, 1995. 30p.

Guevarra

Guevarra, Mark Bennett. *A Heritage of Service: Families of Chester County, South Carolina, Lawrence County, Mississippi, Wyoming County, New York, and the Philippines*. Houston, TX: Author, 1995. 611p.

Guffey

Ward, Naomi Etta. *The Ward Connections, Nourse, Kimmel, Wood, Babbs, Shelton, Sasubjak, Ader, Guffey, Pontiny, Archibald, Asbell*. Evansville, IN: Author, 1995. 545p.

Gunderson

Gunderson, Marion Abbott. *Gunderson, Bustrak, the Ancestors and Descendants of Gunder Bjornsen Bustrak and His Wife, Marthe Jorgensdatter Boe, Grave*. Rolfe, IA: Author, 1995. 2 vols.

Gunderson, Oddvin Archie. *Gunderson, Groth, Everson, Erickson, and Fossay, Ancestors and and Descendants in Norway and America, 1560–1994*. Issaquah, WA: Author, 1995. Unpgd.

Gunzenhauser

Hackman, Esther Gunzenhauser. *Gunzenhauser Family History, Leonard and Anna (Kauffman) Gunzenhauser, Max and Josephine (Reis) Gunzenhauser, from Wurttemberg, Germany to Lancaster, Pennsylvania, Baker, Proprietor, Candymaker, Grocer, Glue Maker, Symphony Conductor*. Author, 1995. 35p.

Gurley

Cockman, William Curtis. *The Descendants of Jacob Gurley, 1750–1820*. Knoxville, TN: Tennessee Valley Pub., 1995. 190p.

Gurule

Sanchez, George Abe. *The Gurule/Aragon Family of San Miguel County, New Mexico, a Genealogical Study*. El Paso, TX: Author, 1995. 59p.

Gussie

Gussie Nolan, Joyce. *Gussie Family, Gussie Family Reunion, August 1995*. Manitoba: Author, 1995. 130p.

Guth

Roth, Donald Wayne. *The Families of Anna (Guth) and Rediger Roth*. Fort Wayne, IN: Author, 1995. 168p.

Guthmiller

McGovern, Albert. *From Alsace to Dakota, with a Stop along the Way*. Atlanta, GA; Author, 1995. Unpgd.

Guyton

Ancestors and Descendants of William Whitaker Smith, 1860–1944, and Florence Ellen Sullivan, 1875–1926, of Anderson and Greenville Counties, South Carolina. Spartanburg, SC: Reprint Co., 1995. 146p.

Guziak

Guziak, Betty Jean Arnold. *The Guziak Family History*. Waterford, MI: Author, 1995. 67p.

Hackbarth

Eggert, Irving John. *Peter Eggert of Mecklenburg and Related Families in America, Best, Bitz, Broekemeier, Hackbarth, Kane, Meisner, Nellis, Schunk, Strenkowski, Voight, Winston*. Decorah, IA: Anundsen Pub. Co., 1995. 224p.

Hacker

DeRose, Lucille. *The Borcherts of Nicollet and Brown Counties, Minnesota, a Family History, the Families of Friedland, Mecklenburg, Germany, the Borcherts, the Hackers, the Kleins*. Sacramento, CA: Author, 1995. 99p.

Haddan

Jackson, Nancy Ann. *Colonel Edward Jackson, 1759–1828, Revolutionary Soldier, History and Genealogy of the Son of Immigrants John and Elizabeth Cummins Jackson, His Wives and Families of Mary Haddan and Elizabeth W. Brake, Grandparents of General Stonewall Jackson*. Franklin, NC: Genealogy Pub. Service, 1995. 1,135p.

Hafter

Hafter, Ruth. *Linking the Lineage, a Documentary of the Hafter Family, 1780–1995*. West Palm Beach, FL: Author, 1995. 381p.

Hager

Punches, James E. *The Descendants of Peter Punches and Margaret Hager, with Entries for (1761–1994)*. Green River, WY: Author, 1995. 41p.

Hagerman

Whitmore, Robert Devore. *Whitmore Family Genealogy*. Steubenville, OH: Public Library of Steubenville and Jefferson County, 1995. 14p.

Haines

Weller, Christine Rossetti. *Haines Genealogy, Ancestors and Descendants, Zimri & Elizabeth Compton Haines, 1682–1995*. Unpgd.

Hale

Graves, Kenneth Vance. *Deacon George Graves, 1636 Settler of Hartford, Connecticut, and His Descendants*. Wrenthen, MA: Author, 1995. 446p.

Hales

Hales, Kenneth Glyn. *The Hales Chronicles*. Tucson, AZ: Author, 1995. 3 vols.

Halfmann

Warschak, Carroll E. *Wilde Family History, 1683–1995, a Record of the Wilde Origins in Germany and of the Bernhard Wilde Descendants in America*. Waco, TX: Author, 1995. 323p.

Hall

Grubbs, Nancy Carole Early. *The Descendants of James and Elizabeth Joseph Lewis*. Houston, TX: Author, 1995. 71p.

Hall, Alice R. *The Hall Tree, One Line of Direct Descendants from Richard Hall of Bradford, Massachusetts with Allied Families in Direct Descent from Charlemagne and Alfred the Great*. Wasceca, MN: Author, 1995. 260p.

Hall, Floyd M. *Descendants of Thomas and Hannah Hall*. Tolono, IL: Author, 1995. Unpgd.

Hall, John Raymond. *The Halls of Swansea, the Origins of the Hall Family and Its Early Experiences in Swansea*. Fall River, MA: Modern Print Co., 1995. 189p.

Krueger, Maurice. *The Descendants of Kruegers and Halls*. Mina, SD: Author, 1995. 162p.

Leake, Preston H. *The Descendants of Anderson Etherton and Millicent Hall*. Hopewell, VA: Author, 1995. 20p.

Hallenbeck

Reamer, Kathleen R. *Descendants of John Reamer and Margaret Schermerhorn, 1758–1995*. Imlay City, MI: Author, 1995. 246p.

Hallgarth

Davis, Evelyn L. *Hallgarth Genealogy*. Oshkosh, WI: Author, 1995. 28p.

Halliwell

Bauer, Marguerite Swagler. *The Family History of George Halliwell, Johan George Culman, Joseph Spice*. Seville, OH: Author, 1995. 41p.

Hallmark

Henderson, Paul Whit. *Hallmark, 1995*. Fort Worth, TX: Author, 1995. Unpgd.

Halsey

Halsey, David. *Halsey Genealogy since 1395 AD*. Bowie, MD: Author, 1995. 451p.
Wheeler, Raymond David. *The English Ancestry of Thomas Halsey of Southampton, Long Island*. Southampton, NY: Thomas Halsey Family Association, 1995. 28p.

Halstead

Cady, James William. *Supplement to Cady Genealogy, Revised and Updated*. Baltimore, MD: Gateway Press, 1995. Unpgd.
Carman, Daniel. *The Carman Family of Long Island*. Norfolk, VA: Author, 1995. 69p.

Halvorson

Madson, Richard C. *Gjerpen to Gjerpen, the Madson Families Who Came to Wisconsin, Also Mason, Larson, Pedersen, Holm, Halvorson, Simonsen, and Hoen Families*. Mesa, AZ: Author, 1995. 284p.

Hamilton

Hamilton, Fred. *The Descendants and Some Ancestors of James Meriwether and Julia Calhoun Hamilton, 1855–1936, 1853–1939*. Ruston, LA: Author, 1995. 104p.
Hamilton, Robert Bradley. *The Ancestors of the Descendants of Robert Addyman Hamilton and Laura Helen Bradley*. Santa Rosa, CA: Author, 1995. 2 vols.
Hamilton, William R. *Hamilton, James and Manning, William Genealogies, with Emphasis on the Branch of Each Family Which Lived North of Ann Arbor, Michigan*. Saline, MI: Author, 1995. 30p.
Moore, Freddie Gene. *My Virginia Ancestors and Their Descendants in the Families, Ratliff, Skidmore, Watson, Hamilton, Wallace, Cahoon, Bowyer, Grimes, Sharp, Meeks*. Author, 1995. 116p.
Ralston, Raymond, Mrs. *Our Hamiltons and Erskines, Two Noble Families of Scotland*. Slippery Rock, PA: Author, 1995. 211p.

Hamke

Knotts, Margaret Held. *The Hamke Family Tree*. Clinton, IN: Author, 1995. 57p.

Hamm

Moore, Freddie Gene. *The Descendants of William Horne, Sr. and Jacob H. Horne and Their Descendants in the Families Clough, Ham, Heard, Hull, Varney, Starbuck, Otis, Stoughton, Pitman, Wentworth, Knight, Miller, Nock, Tibbetts, Emery, Simmons*. Spring, TX: Author, 1995. 148p.

Hammond

Roe, Nancy Clapp. *The Descendants of George Edgar Ladd (1864–1940) and Mary Hammond Ladd (1864–1959): Where Are They, What Are They Doing in 1995?*. Presque Isle, ME: Author, 1995. 190p.

Hanbury
Tennison, Richard Hanbury. *The Hanburys of Monmouthshire*. Author, 1995. 383p.

Hancock
Ash, Edith Watkins Worley. *The Reynolds Pioneering Chronicles, New York and Southern Michigan Sojourn*. Osseo, MI: Author, 1995. 573p.
Brooks, Shirley A. *Our Family of Many Names: The Ancestors and Descendants of James Edward Hancock*. Lake Elsinore, CA: Author, 1995. 155p.
Harts, Stanley Harold. *The Hancock, Luther, and Luck Family Directory*. Wilmington, NC: Author, 1995. 568p.

Hanks
Hanks, Dale. *Hanks Connections, Westward from Virginia, 1840–1995, a Genealogy with Brief Historical Notes*. Montpelier, VA: Author, 1995. 97p.

Hanna
Perry, Max. *Descendants of John Workman, Captain James Hanna and Captain John E. McConnell of York County, South Carolina*. Greenville, SC: A Press, 1995. 161p.
Ralston, Harold Alan. *Our Ralston Families: Including Ralston, McAffee, Cross, McMichael, Hanna, and Others*. Rev. Racine, WI: Author, 1995. 134p.
ZumBrunnen, Mary Hanna. *Genealogy, History of the Aslakson, Hanna and Related Families, 1550–1995*. DeForest, WI: Hanbrunn House Pubs., 1995. 528p.

Hansen
Hansen, Nikolas Forbes. *A History of the Hansen and Lindsay Families in America, Our Danish and Scotch Heritage*. Indianapolis, IN: Author, 1995. 2 vols.
Huckaby, Sheila White. *Frederick Christiansen and Christine Hansen (Hansdatter) and Their Descendants, a Danish Family*. Plano, TX: Author, 1995. 625p.
Miner, Ethel Nerim. *Hanson, Henson, Hinson, Hynson and Allied Family Names*. Bowie, MD: Heritage Books, 1995. 174p.
Nachman, Rosemary A. *The Families Hansen, Bentsen of Holt Parish, Aust-Agdar County, Norway and Johnsdatter-Arnsen of Valer and Moss, Ostfold County, Norway*. San Diego, CA: Author, 1995. Unpgd.
Peterson, Allen Dean. *Our Father's Family*. St. Augustine, FL: Author, 1995. 57p.
Prigge, Barbara Joan. *Hold the Lutefisk, Please, or, Our Norwegian Heritage, Families of Hansen, Johnson and Schiller*. Summer 1995 ed. Madison, WI: Author, 1995. 55p.

Happel
Happel, Anita J. *Genealogies of the Happel Family and the Mesker Family of Evansville, Indiana*. Author, 1995. 32p.

Hardwick
Hornbeck, Shirley Elro. *Ancestors, Descendants and Siblings of Jesse Orville Hornbeck, 1901–1985, and Lettie Waneta Hardwick, 1906–1995*. Livingston, TX: Author, 1995. 278p.

Haresnape
Haresnape, Robert. *Haresnape, a Family History*. England: Author, 1995. 130p.

Hargis

Hargis, Margaret Finley. *Our Hargis Family*. Warrenton, VA: Author, 1995. Unpgd.

Harlow

Wright, Diana. *Robinson Roots*. Author, 1995. Unpgd.

Harman

Nuckols, Ashley Kay. *Harman-Harmon Family Marriage Records, 1800–1993, Tazewell County, Virginia*. Tazewell, VA: Author, 1995. Unpgd.

Harmon

Nuckols, Ashley Kay. *Harman-Harmon Family Marriage Records, 1800–1993, Tazewell County, Virginia*. Tazewell, VA: Author, 1995. Unpgd.

Harnsberger

Smith, Robert Lee. *Ancestors of Thelma Margaret Gander*. Alexandria, VA: Author, 1995. 65p.

Harp

Binns, Gwendolyn. *Sidener/Harp Family*. Independence, MO: Author, 1995. Unpgd.

Harpst

French, Kenneth. *The Harpst Family of Hancock County, Ohio*. Austin, TX: Author, 1995. 14p.

Harrell

May, John Russell. *Harrell Family History and Genealogy*. Fort Wayne, IN: Author, 1995. Unpgd.

Harris

Brayton, John Anderson. *The Five Thomas Harrises of Isle of Wight County, Virginia*. Winston-Salem, NC: Author, 1995. 190p.

Elder, Shirley Bowen. *My Bowen, Barton, Harris, Scott, Hendon, Cranford Family Connections*. 2nd. ed. Raleigh, NC: Author, 1995. 356p.

Harris, Arlo D. *Family Tree Document for William Lester Harris and Charlotte Augusta Ernst*. 2nd. ed. Dayton, OH: Author, 1995. 109p.

Johnson, Libba Moore. *My Darling Daughters*. Author, 1995. 109p.

McLane, Curren Rogers. *The Rogers Family Genealogy*. Fort Worth, TX: Author, 1995. Unpgd.

Stover, Margaret Harris. *Ely Harris and Lucretia Ransom of Connecticut, New York, and Ontario, Supplement*. Punta Gorda, FL: Author, 1995. 221p.

Waters, Gerald. *The Harris Family*. Markle, IN: Author, 1995. 454p.

Whiteman, Jane. *Three Books in One*. Stuttgart, AR: Author, 1995. Unpgd.

Harrison

Harrison, Bill. *The Harrisons of Gisburn Forest, a Register of the Descendants of Stephen Harrison (1685–1747)*. Settle, England: Owlshaw, 1995. 386p.

Hauk, Carol A. *Descendants of Benjamin Harrison of Virginia.* 4th. ed. Anderson, IN: Hauk Data Services, 1995. 365p.

———. *Descendants of Lewis Burwell of Virginia.* Anderson, IN: Hauk Data Services, 1995. 395p.

———. *Descendants of Miles Cary of Virginia.* Anderson, IN: Hauk Data Services, 1995. 421p.

———. *Descendants of Richard Bolling of Virginia.* Anderson, IN: Hauk Data Services, 1995. 315p.

———. *Descendants of William Churchill of Virginia.* 2nd. ed. Anderson, IN: Hauk Data Services, 1995. 250p.

———. *Descendants of William Randolph of Virginia.* Anderson, IN: Hauk Data Services, 1995. 461p.

Hills, Iva Flo Jackson. *As the West Was Won, History Genealogy.* Springfield, MO: Author, 1995. 311p.

Trimble, Scott T. S. *Donham Family History.* San Rafael, CA: Author, 1995. 249p.

Harsdorf

Saunders, Jo Ann Muenzler. *Christoph Friedrich Munzler and His Descendants.* Austin, TX: Author, 1995. 76p.

Harshner

Waters, Gerald. *The Harshner Family.* Markle, IN: Author, 1995. 846p.

Hart

Flanders, Charles M. *The Descendants of Colonel David Hart (1770–1835) and Other Related Families.* Author, 1995. 140p.

Joseph, Anne. *Heritage of a Patriarch, Canada's First Jewish Settlers and the Continuing Story of These Families in Canada.* Sillery, Quebec: Septentrion, 1995. 562p.

Newcomb, Viettia Alberta. *Newcomb, Hartt and Slye, Blunden Families.* Ukiah, CA: Author, 1995. 408p.

Harvey

Suman, Estaleene Nash. *Drummond, Harvey, Suman and Other Allied Families.* Buffton, IN: Author, 1995. 1,063p.

Hash

Alsip, Steven H. *Hash, from Virginia to Kentucky and California, a Genealogy of My Hash Family, a Research Document.* Corbin, KY: Author, 1995. Unpgd.

Hastings

Koickler, Eloyce Hubbard. *Hiestand, Hestand, Hastings.* Helena, MT: Author, 1995. 127p.

Reynolds, Beatrice Kay. *John Hastings of Cambridge, Massachusetts (1643), Six Generations of His Descendants from Matthew and (Mary Battelle) Hastings, Early Settlers of Maine.* Sidney, ME: Author, 1995. 90p.

Hatfield

Sellards, Harry Leon. *Hatfield Family History.* Deland, FL: Author, 1995. 954p.

Haugen

Haugen, Arnold Otto. *Life of the Norse Haugen Families on Canoe Creek*. Decorah, IA: Anundsen Pub. Co., 1995. 69p.

Haven

Popham, Geraldine E. *Grandma's Ancestors, 1634–1936, Thomas Judd, the Emigrant to Nelson Judd, and Addie (Judd) Dowd*. Lodi, CA: Author, 1995. 148p.

Weir, Lida Haven. *My Haven Ancestors, from Richard, 1620–1703, to Clyde, 1886–1973, and Related Lines*. Geneva, NY: Author, 1995. 232p.

Hawken

Scott, Glenn Robert. *History of the Hachen (Hawken) Family in Switzerland and America, 1565- 1994*. Lakewood, CO: Author, 1995. 129p.

Hawkins

Wyche, Terence. *Say, Our Beginning, a History of the Black Hawkins' Family of Halifax County, North Carolina*. Roanoke Rapids, NC: Author, 1995. 219p.

Hawley

La Marca, Jeffrey Peter. *Window to the Past, Door to the Future, a Glimpse at an American Genealogy, Compilation of Data on the Acquisto, Calamera, Carroll, Crowley, Guastaferro, Hawley, La Marca, Lavier, and Steigerwalt Families*. Yorba Linda, CA: Shumway Family History Services, 1995. 214p.

Hayburn

Mulock, Lenora. *The Hayburn Family*. Menomonee Falls, WI: Author, 1995. 103p.

Hayden

Bock, Margaret Buckridge. *The Hayden Family of Potapaug, Connecticut*. Westbrook, CT: Author, 1995. 55p.

Hayden, Thomas Clay. *The Haydens in England and America from 1185 AD to 1995 AD, a Genealogy of Thomas Clay Hayden, Jr.*. Lewisville, TX: Author, 1995. 127p.

Haydon, Robert. *Thomas Haydon, England to Virginia, 1657*. Little Rock, AR: Author, 1995. 99p.

Lampman, Doris. *Descendants of Richard Lyons and Anne (Hayden) Moran*. Rev. ed. Mercer Island, WA: Author, 1995. 279p.

Hayes

Gorlick, Jeanne. *The Family Tree of Curtis, Francisco, Hayes, Keller, Leavel, and LeRoy, with Procter, Ressequie, Sipperley, Spence and Weaver*. Author, 1995. 345p.

Johnston, Anne Plummer. *The Plummer Lineage of America*. Reston, VA: M. L. Tomaselli, 1995. 56p.

Normandin, Michael A. *The Journey of Life, a History of Benjamin I. Hayes and His Family between 1791 and 1871*. 2nd. ed. San Diego, CA: Author, 1995. 161p.

Haynes

Haynes, John Lanier. *Haynes-McDonald Heritage Quest*. Anchorage, AK: Author, 1995. 514p.

Scott, Billy Dave. *Johnston-Southern of Clairborne County, Tennessee, and Parker County, Texas: Isaac McNew Johnston (1838–1918) and His Wife Norvesta Melocky Southern (1841–1929) and Allied Families Amis, Haynes, Huddleston, Seabolt, Southern and Spears.* Maryville, MO: Author, 1995. 215p.

Hayter
Howell, Danny. *The Hayters and Slades of Boreham and Bishopstrow.* Warminster, England: Bedeguar Books, 1995. 4p.

Hazelton
Hazelton, George Francis. *A Genealogy of Hazelton and Stygles Families.* Baltimore, MD: Gateway Press, 1995. 263p.

Head
Koickler, Eloyce Hubbard. *Hiestand, Hestand, Hastings.* Helena, MT: Author, 1995. 127p.

Heady
Martin, William Albert. *The Heady Family of Hamilton County, Indiana, 1820 to 1900.* Yorba Linda, CA: Author, 1995. 221p.

Healey
Beach, Sue. *The Ancestors and Family of Vera Voynne Healey (1898–1975).* Muncie, IN: Author, 1995. Unpgd.

Hearn
Bostic, Paul Eugene. *Bruce, Maupin, Carr and Some Related Families Including Ballard, Hearn, Ayres, McCubbin, Cloud, Lane, Eveland (Elfland), Graves, Sharp and Willis.* Clinton, TN: Author, 1995. 391p.

Heath
Anderson, David Mowat. *Some Heath Families of Southeastern Erie County, Pennsylvania, circa 1840 to circa 1920.* Lake Havasu City, AZ: Author, 1995. 91p.

Hebert
Broussard, Earl. *Our Ancestors, Gone But Not Forgotten.* Author, 1995. 204p.

Heiken
Bymaster Richards, Willa. *Descendants of Harms Beherns Heiken.* Carnation, WA: Author, 1995. Unpgd.

Heinauer
Penn, John Herman. *A Brief Genealogical History of the Ancestors and Descendants of Lawrence Heinauer, Senior and Barbara Breitenstein of the Villages of Schweinheim and Kleigoft, Westhouse Marmoutier, Department Bas Rhin, France and the Families of Joseph Maria Von Keitz and Frederike Dernbach of Robinson, Stowe and Kennedy Townships, McKees Rocks, Allegheny County, Pennsylvania, United States of America.* El Torro, CA: Author, 1995. 125p.

Helme

Cottrell, Richard Gary. *The Tyler-Fruhauf Family History, and Genealogical Record of Associated Edwards, Ellis, Helme, Mason, Pritchard, Seymour, Sherrerd, and Whiting Families*. Parma, MI: Author, 1995. 2 vols.

Helms

Byard, Richard B. *O'Daniel, Matthews, Mitchem, Helms and Their Relatives in Maryland, Kentucky, Indiana, Alabama and Other States*. Ellicott City, MD: Author, 1995. 88p.
Law, Bobby Cornwell. *Moses Helm*. Nashville, TN: Author, 1995. 489p.

Hemingway

Popham, Geraldine E. *Grandma's Ancestors, 1634–1936, Thomas Judd, the Emigrant to Nelson Judd, and Addie (Judd) Dowd*. Lodi, CA: Author, 1995. 148p.

Hemphill

Johnson, Libba Moore. *My Darling Daughters*. Author, 1995. 109p.

Henderson

Henderson, Robert H. *Hendersons of Early North Carolina: A Beginning Survey of the People Using the Henderson Name from the North Carolina Census and Other Records*. Greer, SC; Author, 1995. Unpgd.

Hendricks

Hendricks, Charles H. *A Swedish Family Odyssey*. Chapel Hill, NC: Hendricks Family Press, 1995. 394p.
Hendricks, Herbert D. *Major, Majors, Mager, Majers, Maoir Family Information*. Poquoson, VA: Author, 1995. Unpgd.

Hendrix

Hendricks, Herbert D. *Major, Majors, Mager, Majers, Maoir Family Information*. Poquoson, VA: Author, 1995. Unpgd.
Hendrix, Janet H. *A Reunion of the Descendants of William J. Hendrix, October 21, 1995, Anson, Texas*. Center Point, TX: Author. 1995. 21p.

Henford

Elder, Shirley Bowen. *My Bowen, Barton, Harris, Scott, Hendon, Cranford Family Connections*. 2nd. ed. Raleigh, NC: Author, 1995. 356p.

Henley

Vollenweider, Betty Ann Henley. *Memories Revisited, the Life and Family of W. W. "Bill" Henley, 1905–1982, and Reba Miars Henley, 1905–1994, Their Lives, Descendants and Ancestors*. Baltimore, MD: Gateway Press, 1995. 665p.

Henninger

Carvill, Kathleen. *Oswald-Henninger*. Author, 1995. 46p.

Henshaw

Atteridg, Paul T. *The Attridges of North America*. Granby, CO: Author, 1995. 429p.

Hensley

Fail Families and Allied Families: Catt, Hensley, Kenyon, Lane and Sprague, 1818–1995, a Work in Progress. Decorah, IA: Anundsen Pub. Co., 1995. 348p.

Roche, Hazel. *A Study of the Gambrells, Allens, Hensleys, Brewers, and Others from Clay and Knox Counties, Kentucky*. Moravian Falls, NC: Author, 1995. 44p.

Herbert

Herbert, John Emery. *Herbert Family Journeys to Oregon in 1845*. Salem, OR: Author, 1995. 211p.

Herbrig

Saunders, Jo Ann Muenzler. *Herbrig Family*. Austin, TX: Author, 1995. 131p.

Herold

Barnard, Kay Michaels. *Herold History, Jacob Herold's Descendants*. Herold, WI: Herold Cemetery Association, 1995. 88p.

Hershberger

Smith, Robert Lee. *Ancestors of Thelma Margaret Gander*. Alexandria, VA: Author, 1995. 65p.

Hertzler

Hertzler, Emmanuel C. *The Other Hertzler-Hartzlers*. Goshen, IN: Author, 1995. 590p.

Hestand

Koickler, Eloyce Hubbard. *Hiestand, Hestand, Hastings*. Helena, MT: Author, 1995. 127p.

Hetzel

Schaefer, Jeanette Kriegel. *Family Trees for Descendants of Carl Christoph Findeisen, Sr. and Johanna Dorothea Hetzel*. Austin, TX: Author, 1995. 120p.

Heumphreus

Bymaster Richards, Willa. *Descendants of Joseph John Wesley Heumphreus*. Carnation, WA: Author, 1995. Unpgd.

Hewey

McKinnon, Donna L. *Hewey Family of Maine and Vermont, with Appendix of Unlinked Families*. Bath, ME: Author, 1995. 108p.

Heyka

Doctor, Marjorie E. *Heyka, USA Descendants, 1888–1995, the Slupske, Heyka and Related Families*. Phoenix, AZ: Author, 1995. 427p.

Hickey

Woodruff, Mark J. *Patrick Hickey of Madison, the Biography of a Famine Emigrant and His Family*. Madison, NJ: Author, 1995. 53p.

Hicks

Cagle, Ruby Abbott. *The Bishop Family from Manchester, England to Washington County, Maine*. Jasper, TN: Author, 1995. Unpgd.

Gifford, Gailen R. *Family History, Hicks Family*. Author, 1995. Unpgd.

Johnston, Anne Plummer. *The Plummer Lineage of America*. Reston, VA: M. L. Tomaselli, 1995. 56p.

Hiestand

Koickler, Eloyce Hubbard. *Hiestand, Hestand, Hastings*. Helena, MT: Author, 1995. 127p.

Hightower

A Compilation of Stories about the Hightower Family. Terre Haute, IN: Author, 1995. Unpgd.

Higley

Byard, Richard B. *O'Daniel, Matthews, Mitchem, Helms and Their Relatives in Maryland, Kentucky, Indiana, Alabama and Other States*. Ellicott City, MD: Author, 1995. 88p.

Hilbrich

Hilbrich, James M. *A Hilbrich Family Tree and History*. Author, 1995. 99p.

Hildebrand

Berzonsky, Patricia L. *Abraham Hildebrand and Related Families*. Mineral Point, PA: Author, 1995. 2 vols.

Hildreth

Dubel, Zelda. *Golden, Hildreth and Replogle Genealogy*. Fresno, CA: Author, 1995. 29p.

Hill

Batcher, Olive M. *Hill Wallace Family History*. Ames, IA: Author, 1995. 253p.

Feder, June Constance. *The Genealogy of the Price and Stull Families of the Town of Rush, Monroe County, New York, the Murrays, Wallings, and Hills of Victor, New York, and the Otto, Block, Hill and Summerhays Families of Rochester, New York*. Fairport, NY: Author, 1995. 75p.

Hill, George Byron. *The Genealogy of the Hill, Combs, Barton, Starr and Allied Families*. Nashville, TN: Author, 1995. 296p.

Hill, Paul L. *One Hill of a Family*. Columbus, NJ: Author, 1995. 32p.

Hill, William. *History of the Hill Family, 1859*. Author, 1995. Unpgd.

Pasay, Marcella Houle. *Hill Family Genealogy and Vitals from Hill Diaries and Patient Records*. Danielson, CT: Killingly Historical Society, 1995. 421p.

Hinchee

Funk, Eunice M. *Our Tree Grew in Beverly (Illinois, That Is)*. Author, 1995. 153p.

Hinchman

Hinchman, Mary. *The Hinchman Family in America*. Allen, KY: Author, 1995. 220p.

Hinde

Lomon, Shirley Newton. *Edward J. Hinde of Erie County, Ohio, and His Descendants*. Mesa, AZ: Author, 1995. 20p.

Hines

Hurley, William Neal. *John William Hines, Born c. 1600 in Londonderry, Ireland, His Descendants, Principally of North Carolina and Virginia and Their Associated Families*. Rev. ed. Bowie, MD: Heritage Books, 1995. 532p.

Jones, Daniel Wilbur. *Genealogical Memoranda of Daniel Rufus Cable and Georgiana McKinney Cable*. Cary, NC: Author, 1995. 183p.

Hinesley

Doris, Neta Jane. *Our Grand Sire, John Jefferson Hinesley, 1822–1910, and His Descendants*. Author, 1995. 56p.

Hinrichs

Buhr, Wilma. *Hinrichs Family*. St. Joseph, IL: Author, 1995. Unpgd.

Hinton

Hinton, Leroy C. *Family Record of Hynton, Hinton, England, Hinton, Stevens of America, 1050 to 1994*. Morehead, KY: Author, 1995. Unpgd.

Hipps

Charley, Janie M. *Hipps Family Reunion*. West Columbia, SC: Author, 1995. Unpgd.

Hite

Hauk, Carol A. *Descendants of Yost Hite of Virginia*. 4th ed. Anderson, IN: Hauk Data Services, 1995. 147p.

Smith, Robert Lee. *Ancestors of Thelma Margaret Gander*. Alexandria, VA: Author, 1995. 65p.

Walters, Rolland K. *Jost Hite and Other Pioneer Ancestors of Buchanan (Hamm) Colson of Urbana, Illinois*. Author, 1995. Unpgd.

Zuendel, Jean. *Taylor, Blanchan, Cochran, DuBois, Foreman, Hite, Morris, Parker, Van Meteren*. Author, 1995. Unpgd.

Hoagland

Blake, Marcelline Abrego. *The Saga of Stanley-Hoagland and Allied Families in America from New England to California, 1600 to 1900s*. Santa Rosa, CA: Author, 1995. Unpgd.

Skelton, Isaac Newton. *Ike, This Is You, a History of the Skelton, Boone, Barry, Beach, Blattner, Corum, Hoagland, Lehew, Strode, Wright and Young Families*. Washington, DC: Author, 1995. 223p.

Hobaker

Crum, Raymond. *A De Long Family in Ohio and Illinois, Including Relationships to the Hobaker and Crumpler Families, 1995 Companion Edition, with De Long-Wade Genealogy, Family Memories and Cumulative Name Indexes*. Ventura, CA: Author, 1995. 222p.

Hobbs

Adair, Shirley Brown. *Robert Adair (1770–1845c.): An Adair Family History, Reid, Emerson, Hobbs, Worley, Thompson (Related Lines)*. Rockwall, TX: Author, 1995. 146p.

Hochstetler

Hochstetler, Daniel Elmer. *Descendants of David J. and Magdalena Hochstetler*. 3rd. ed. Goshen, IN: Author, 1995. 441p.

Schmucker, Daniel M. *The Descendants of Andrew N. Hochstetler and Elizabeth Lehman: Also Includes the Descendants of Elias A. Miller*. Franklin, KY: Author, 1995. 133p.

Hockett

Carroll, Joseph Carlos. *Hockett History, a History of John V. Hockett and His Descendants*. Cedar Park, TX: Author, 1995. 225p.

Hodges

Some Descendants of Thomas Hodges of Hodges Gap, Watauga County, North Carolina. Author, 1995. Unpgd.

Hodgins

Lewis, Allen Roy. *Two Hundred Year History and Genealogy of the Isaac Lewis Family from Cloughjordan (Tipperary), Ireland to Canada and the United States, Including Intermarriages with Hodgins, Myers, Rapley, Slack, Williams, and Many Other Families*. Ver. 1.5. Syracuse, NY: Author, 1995. 215p.

Hodgson

Hodgson, Gordon. *What Name Did You Get? The Thing about Hodgsons*. Calgary, Alberta: Career Seven, 1995. 352p.

Hoen

Madson, Richard C. *Gjerpen to Gjerpen, the Madson Families Who Came to Wisconsin, Also Mason, Larson, Pedersen, Holm, Halvorson, Simonsen, and Hoen Families*. Mesa, AZ: Author, 1995. 284p.

Hoffman

Wells, Lois Jackson. *Huffman, Hoffman, Hoofman Genealogy, Includes Jesse Huffman, Germanna Colony Descendant*. Cullman, AL: Gregath Pub. Co., 1995. 110p.

Hogan

Grillot, R. E. *Grillot and Ancestors*. Author, 1995. 831p.

Hohl

Hull, Phyllis Scott. *Peter Thomas Hohl, 1706–1975*. Rev. Columbia City, IN: P. Shoda, 1995. 80p.

Holland

Hook, John H. *Hook-White Notebook, a Family History and Genealogy for the Descendants of Charles and Mabel Hook*. St. Petersburg, FL: Author, 1995. Unpgd.

Vander Wegen, Betty Ann. *Our Family, the Interrelated Coffeys, Graggs, Hollanders, Webbs of Avery County, North Carolina*. Union, WA: Author, 1995. Unpgd.

Hollcroft

Hollcroft, Donald. *Bible Records and Group Sheets of James McCreary m. Mary Doughty*. Morgantown, IN: Author, 1995. 54p.

Holliday

Hauk, Carol A. *Descendants of John Holladay of Virginia*. Anderson, IN: Hauk Data Services, 1995. 42p.

————. *Descendants of Zachary and Henry Lewis of Virginia*. 4th. ed. Anderson, IN: Hauk Data Services, 1995. 115p.

Hollingsworth

Darrah, Earl L. *Hollingsworth, Westward Migration and Settlement of the Valentine Hollingsworth Family*. 2nd. ed. Tampa, FL: Author, 1995. 260p.

Page, Robert E. *Wilson and Hollingsworth Family*. Indian Rocks Beach, FL: Author, 1995. 37p.

Holloway

York, Dorothy Anderson. *Our Anderson Family and Their Kin*. Fort Worth, TX: Author, 1995. 307p.

Young, Cindy Henson. *The Youngs and Holloways of Randolph County, Alabama, a Family History*. Newville, AL; Author, 1995. 309p.

Holly

Voight, Diane D. *Holly/Holley Family*. Darien, CT: Author, 1995. 19p.

Holm

Madson, Richard C. *Gjerpen to Gjerpen, the Madson Families Who Came to Wisconsin, Also Mason, Larson, Pedersen, Holm, Halvorson, Simonsen, and Hoen Families*. Mesa, AZ: Author, 1995. 284p.

Holmes

Holmes, Marguerite. *Holmes from John of England and Plymouth, Massachusetts, to Holmes Brothers William Hudson, Horace William and Rodney Arthur Holmes of Aroostook County, Maine, and Related Families Cobbs, Redman, Libby and Shorey*. San Antonio, TX: Author, 1995. 101p.

Holsapple

Wright, Diana. *Robinson Roots*. Author, 1995. Unpgd.

Holt

Orton, June P. *Family of Benjamin Holt and Sarah Little Holt of Wilkes County, North Carolina, and Adair and Russell Counties, Kentucky*. Yukon, OK: Author, 1995. 108p.

Holtz

Holtz, Marie Strippgen. *Our Holtz Family Then and Now*. St. Louis, MO: Author, 1995. 93p.

Hooe

Hauk, Carol A. *Descendants of Rice Hooe of Virginia, Ancestor of President James Madison*. 2nd. ed. Anderson, IN: Hauk Data Services, 1995. 93p.

Hoogeboom

Hogoboom, Sarah Davies. *The Hoogeboom Family in America, a Genealogical Journey*. Madison, WI: Author, 1995. 213p.

Hooghteeling

Kassak, Marian and Joseph Kassak. *Descendants of Mathys Coenratsen Hooghteeling*. Reedsburg, WI: Author, 1995. 592p.

Hook

Hook, John H. *Hook-White Notebook, a Family History and Genealogy for the Descendants of Charles and Mabel Hook*. St. Petersburg, FL: Author, 1995. Unpgd.

Hoover

Hoover, Lester M. *Ancestors and Descendants of Henry M. Hoover and Barbara W. Nolt*. Lititz, PA: Author, 1995. 165p.

McLean, Hulda Hoover. *Genealogy of the Herbert Hoover Family*. Revised and expanded ed. West Branch, IA: Herbert Hoover Presidential Library Association, 1995. 486p.

Hopkins

Griggs, Kendall. *Levi W. and Sarah E. (Carter) Hopkins, Their Ancestors and Descendants*. Hutchinson, KS: Author, 1995. 198p.

Phillips, Claris Conner. *Are You Our Cousin?* Garland, TX: Author, 1995. 145p.

Hornbeck

Hornbeck, Shirley Elro. *Ancestors, Descendants and Siblings of Jesse Orville Hornbeck, 1901–1985, and Lettie Waneta Hardwick, 1906–1995*. Livingston, TX: Author, 1995. 278p.

Horne

Allen, Patricia Remmell. *The Remmell and Allen Families of New Castle County, Delaware*. Horsham, PA: Author, 1995. 71p.

Moore, Freddie Gene. *The Descendants of William Horne, Sr. and Jacob H. Horne and Their Descendants in the Families Clough, Ham, Heard, Hull, Varney, Starbuck, Otis, Stoughton, Pitman, Wentworth, Knight, Miller, Nock, Tibbetts, Emery, Simmons*. Spring, TX: Author, 1995. 148p.

Hornsby

Gabbard, John E. *Family Links, the Gabbard/Coyle, Eden/Hornsby Connection*. Berea, KY: Author, 1995. 520p.

Horst

Horst, Florine Gettman. *Family Genealogy*. Loveland, CO: Author, 1995. 151p.

Hoschar

Bartram, Chester E. *The George Washington McCoy Family of Mason County, West Virginia, Prominent Related Families Edington, Ferrell, Hoschar, Jividen, King, Sayre, Strait*. Knoxville, TN: Author, 1995. 187p.

Hostetler

Hostetler, Bette Jane Smith. *Marryin-in, the Ernsberger Family That Married into the Amos L. Hochstetler #6281 Family*. Clearwater, FL: Sunshine Manuscripts, 1995. Unpgd.

Hostetter

McRobie, Raymond Irvin. *The McRobie, McCrobie, Cuppett, Peck, Hostetter, Weimer, Smith, Wilt and Merrill Families of Garrett County*. Fairfax, VA: Author, 1995. 471p.

Hotchkin

Hotchkin, Edgar Elwyn. *Descendants of John Hotchkin of Guilford, Connecticut*. Baltimore, MD: Gateway Press, 1995. 631p.

Hotchkiss

Melle, Jane Hentges. *Bishop, Carrick, Hotchkiss, Johnson and Related Families, a Family History as Known in 1994*. Bowling Green, OH: Author, 1995. 2 vols.

Hottel

Smith, Robert Lee. *Ancestors of Thelma Margaret Gander*. Alexandria, VA: Author, 1995. 65p.

Hougen

Hougen, Harvey Richard. *The Hougen-Berge Family, Norwegian Pioneers of Manitowoc County*. Valders, WI: Valders Journal, 1995. 73p.

Houghton

Houghton, Howard. *Our Houghton Heritage*. Portage, WI: Author, 1995. 206p.

House

Mitchell, Mary Ann. *The Descendants of John House of Edgecomb County, North Carolina*. Jackson, TN: Author, 1995. 187p.

Houston

Cornish, Grace H. *Houston Family History*. Author, 1995. 126p.

Houy

Houy, Edward M. *The Family of Ernst Houy and Dorothea Menges Married in Germany on November 15, 1845, the Story from Europe to Texas and Beyond*. Sunrise Beach, TX: Houy Heritage Club, 1995. Unpgd.

Howard

Scott, Margaret Scott. *Genealogical Portrait of Joseph Carr and Barbara Gastor Beverett, the Carr Descendants of Duplin County, NC*. Warsaw, NC: Author, 1995. 418p.

Howe

Meigs, Peter Sanford. *Our Meigs and Smith Ancestors, Including the Clarke, Clifford, Eldredge, Fellows, Howe, MacMillan, Mann, Remington, Rice, Robinson, Scadgel, Skillings, and Thing Families*. Danville, NH: Author, 1995. Unpgd.

Merfeld, Eunice. *The Howe Book*. Author, 1995. 318p.

Petersen, Bradner. *Sally Tooker and Her Ancestry, a Recent Breakthrough*. Palisade, CO: Tapirback Enterprises, 1995. 14p.

Hsieh

Hunan Liu-Yang Hsieh Shih Tsu Pu. Taiwan, 1995. 245p.

Hubbard

Koickler, Eloyce Hubbard. *Hiestand, Hestand, Hastings*. Helena, MT: Author, 1995. 127p.

Huckel

Buchanan, Merwyn Russell. *Descendants of William and Maria Susannah (Uhle) Huckel*. Blue Bell, PA: Author, 1995. 137p.

Huddart

McGinn, Ann Winston. *A McGinn McCorkle Family History, 1796–1995: With Related Families, Crockett, Dabney, Egnatoff, Fontaine, Freirson, Gillespie, Huddart, Kennemore, O'Donnell, Patton, Ring, Sheppard, Winston, and Others*. Spring Hill, FL: Author, 1995. 313p.

Huddleston

Scott, Billy Dave. *Johnston-Southern of Clairborne County, Tennessee, and Parker County, Texas: Isaac McNew Johnston (1838–1918) and His Wife Norvesta Melocky Southern (1841–1929) and Allied Families Amis, Haynes, Huddleston, Seabolt, Southern and Spears*. Maryville, MO: Author, 1995. 215p.

Hudec

Hudec, Edward Joseph Roy. *The Joseph Barbara Hudec Family Book, 1790 to 1995*. South Euclid, OH: Author, 1995. 531p.

Hudson

Bryant, Cindy. *The Descendants of William and Jennie Hudson*. Benton Harbor, MI: Author, 1995. 27p.

Hughes

Cole, Mary. *The Bunyard Family Research and Allied Families, Alley, Fitzwater, Foster, Hughes, Jones, Ledlow, McNeely, Rose*. Kentfield, CA: Author, 1995. 151p.

Hughes, Bernard Lee. *The Hughes Family, from John in Windham, NH, to Bernard Lee in Ashland, NH*. Ashland, NH: Author, 1995. 20p.

Hughes, Maxine E. *Stories, Pictures, Genealogy: The John Wesley Hughes, Jr. and Martha Anna Van Hyning Hughes Family to 1984*. Keosauqua, IA: Author, 1995. 149p.

Hughes, Richard B. *The Hughes, Furey and Gast Genealogies*. Author, 1995. 27p.

Popham, Geraldine E. *Grandma's Ancestors, 1634–1936, Thomas Judd, the Emigrant to Nelson Judd, and Addie (Judd) Dowd*. Lodi, CA: Author, 1995. 148p.

Huie

Descendants of James and Mary Huie. Forest Park, GA: Old Huie Philadelphia Community Cemetery Association, 1995. Unpgd.

Hull

Hull, Phyllis Scott. *Peter Thomas Hohl, 1706–1975*. Rev. ed. Columbia City, IN: P. Shoda, 1995. 80p.

Hulse

Alderson, Joy. *The Hulse Hatchments*. Poole, England: West Mount, 1995. 24p.

Hunsberger

Hunsberger, George S. *The Hunsbergers*. Baltimore, MD: Gateway Press, 1995. 3 vols.

Hunt

Cantrell, Charles Thomas. *The Family of Charles Patterson Cantrell and Cora Gustava Hunt*. Brentwood, TN: Author, 1995. 112p.

Hunt, Elmer Gay. *The Hunt Family*. Author, 1995. 51p.

Hunt, Stephen D. *Hunt Family, 1799–1995 (200 Years)*. Author, 1995. 164p.

Moore, Roger K. *The Descendants of Nathaniel and Hannah (Hunt) Moore of Chester County, Pennsylvania*. Rock Falls, IL: Author, 1995. 186p.

O'Neal, Marcia Corrigan. *O'Neal Genealogy from the Early 1800s and Including Ancestors Anderson, Childers, Davis, Griffith, Hunt, Savage, Venard, and Willcuts*. Richmond, IN: Author, 1995. 43p.

Hurd

Moore, Freddie Gene. *The Descendants of William Horne, Sr. and Jacob H. Horne and Their Descendants in the Families Clough, Ham, Heard, Hull, Varney, Starbuck, Otis, Stoughton, Pitman, Wentworth, Knight, Miller, Nock, Tibbetts, Emery, Simmons*. Spring, TX: Author, 1995. 148p.

Hurlbert

Sherard, Rodney Merle. *The Descendants of William Henry Hurlbert and Amy Adeline Austin*. Greenwood, IN: Author, 1995. 164p.

Hurley

Hurley, Lucius M. *Thomas Andrew Hurley, His Descendants and the Related Families of Metzger and Stout*. Newton, KS: Author, 1995. 139p.

Hurley, William Neal. *Hurley Families in America*. Bowie, MD: Heritage Books, 1995. 2 vols.

Hurlock

Burch, Dorothy. *Hurlocks of London, 17th to 20th Centuries*. Leicester, England: Author, 1995. 86p.

Husen

Secrist, C. Robert. *Husens, Iowa and Points West, Descendants of Hinrich Husen and Lena Loppentien/Loptien of Scott County, Iowa*. Battle Creek, MI: Progeny Family History Services, 1995. 116p.

Huston

Wilson, Robert E. *Groves and Huston and Other Families from Pennsylvania to Ohio*. Taftsville, VT: Author, 1995. Unpgd.

Hutchins

Hutchins, Jack Randolph. *William Hutchins of Carolina*. Baltimore, MD: Gateway Press, 1995. 655p.

Hutchinson

Liston, Lois Jane Breakiron. *The Breakiron Family History Also Including the Bastian, Brecheisen, Casey, Dusenberry, Garlow, Hutchinson, Johnson, McMillen, Miller, Morris, Roderick and Other Families*. Wyandotte, OK: Gregath Pub. Co., 1995. 620p.

Huyard

Huyard, David E. *A Journal of Bygone Years, History of the Huyards*. Lititz, PA: David Y. Smucker, 1995. 51p.

Huyck

Manfrina, Myra. *Huyck Cousins, 1995 Supplement*. Lompoc, CA: Author, 1995. Unpgd.

Hybarger

Boyd, Joseph Ray. *John and Abraham Hybarger, Early Pioneers*. Lafayette, IN: Author, 1995. 73p.

— I —

Ickes

Jennings, Ruth. *Some Descendants of Jacob Waltz, Great Grandson of Frederick Reinhart Waltz, 1731–1995*. Bluffton, OH: Author, 1995. 346p.

Ingraham

Gardiner Jackson, Ann E. *Roots: Gardiner, Ingram, Grimmeissen, Ashpaw, Thiessen, Jackson, Meeker*. Author, 1995. 35p.

Hare, Norma Q. *Puritans, Pioneers and Planters, an Ingraham, Abbott, Wardwell, Culver, Burbank Genealogy*. Arroyo Grande, CA: N. L. Enterprises, 1995. 330p.

Injaian

Kapeghian, Katchadoor. *The Kapeghian, Jamgochian, Injaian Family Reunion*. Philadelphia, PA: The Reunion, 1995. 148p.

Irwin

Neher, Leslie I. *The Irwin Family of Salamonie Township, Huntington County, Indiana*. Gas City, IN: Author, 1995. 2 vols.

Rigsby, Michael Hall. *The Ancestry of Laura Elaine Rigsby*. 5th ed. Houston, TX: Author, 1995. 217p.

Isaacs

Rowan, Frances Dugger. *The Dugger Family, Johnson County, Tennessee.* Author, 1995. 331p.

Ives

Van Cleve, Edmund C. *The Ives-Van Cleve Family History, the Tie That Binds.* Author, 1995. 52p.

–J

Jacklin

Josey, Jesse Edward. *Jacklin to Jackson, Descendants of John Freeman Jacklin, Loyalist.* Author, 1995. 373p.

Jackson

Dix, Roberta Cook Jackson. *The First Shall be Last, a Family History.* Author, 1995. 137p.

Fahey, Catherine R. *Jonathan Jackson, 1781–1872, with Some of His Descendants and His Possible Lineage from Henry Jackson of Fairfield, Connecticut.* Wheaton, IL: Author, 1995. 74p.

Gardiner Jackson, Ann E. *Roots: Gardiner, Ingram, Grimmeissen, Ashpaw, Thiessen, Jackson, Meeker.* Author, 1995. 35p.

Jackson, Nancy Ann. *Colonel Edward Jackson, 1759–1828, Revolutionary Soldier, History and Genealogy of the Son of Immigrants John and Elizabeth Cummins Jackson, His Wives and Families of Mary Haddan and Elizabeth W. Brake, Grandparents of General Stonewall Jackson.* Franklin, NC: Genealogy Pub. Service, 1995. 1,135p.

Josey, Jesse Edward. *Jacklin to Jackson, Descendants of John Freeman Jacklin, Loyalist.* Author, 1995. 373p.

Marks, Arthur Lee. *Scott Family Journal.* Troy, MI: Author, 1995. 313p.

Smith, Burta B. *Jackson Family Book, a Book of Memories and Other Compiled Material of the Jackson Family.* Antwerp, OH: Author, 1995. 272p.

Jacob

Bodishbaugh, Sue W. *The Jacob, Philipp, and Adam Erion Family Letters.* Tampa, FL: Author, 1995. Unpgd.

James

Simpson, R. Elaine. *James and Parsons: Descendants and Related Families.* Little Rock, AR: Author, 1995. 146p.

Jamgochian

Kapeghian, Katchadoor. *The Kapeghian, Jamgochian, Injaian Family Reunion.* Philadelphia, PA: The Reunion, 1995. 148p.

Janzen

Suderman, Joel. *David P. Schroeder, Sara (Janzen) Schroeder Family History and Genealogy, Including Information About Peter Schroeder, David & Ana (Tiart) Schroeder, Peter & Susanna (Reimer) Schroeder, David P. & Sara (Janzen) Schroeder.* Marion, KS: Author, 1995. 65p.

Jaques

Jaques, Roger A. *Jaques Family Genealogy.* Durham, NH: Author, 1995. 944p.

Jarman

Daniel Beverly, Patteann. *The Spence Family Saga, the Ancestors and Descendants of John and Roxie Ann Jarman Spence.* Midland, TX; Author, 1995. Unpgd.

Moore, Freddie Gene. *My Virginia Ancestors and Their Descendants in the Families, Burdett, Alexander, Anderson, King, Boone, Welsh, McHenry, Cornwell, Alford, Coleman, Dixon, Morgan, Jarman, Maugridge.* Author, 1995. 46p.

Jarvis

Scott County Iowa Genealogical Society. *A Family Tree: Kirk, Johnston, Daebelliehn, Peitscher, Lawrence, Ott, Jarvis, Delzell.* Davenport, IA: Author, 1995. Unpgd.

Jasinska

Zaleski, Dolores Piotrowski. *Nowakowski-Jasinska Family History.* PA: Author, 1995. 118p.

Jasper

Moore, William T. *Jasper and Related Lines.* Somerset, KY: Author, 1995. Unpgd.

Jay

Robb, Arlene Jay. *A Jay Family History, Beginning with Thomas Jay (1610–1678) through the Lineage of Joshua Jay (1762–1841).* Urbana, IL: Author, 1995. 142p.

Jedlicka

Hansen, Henrietta. *Branches of Our Jedlicka Tree.* Woodbury, MN: Author, 1995. 149p.

Jefferson

Barger, Evelyn. *The Jefferson Family of Virginia.* Fort Washington, MD: Author, 1995. Unpgd.

Hauk, Carol A. *Descendants of Thomas Jefferson of Virginia.* Anderson, IN: Hauk Data Services, 1995. 87p.

Jefferies

King, Margaret Ann Scott. *Homestead of the Free, the Jefferies Heritage.* 2nd. ed. Salt Lake City, UT: King-Scott Heritage Foundation, 1995. 647p.

Jenkins

York, Dorothy Anderson. *Our Anderson Family and Their Kin.* Fort Worth, TX: Author, 1995. 307p.

Jernigan

Johnson, Libba Moore. *My Darling Daughters.* Author, 1995. 109p.

Jesse

Jesse, Bev. *William Morgan Jesse and His Descendants*. Baltimore, MD: Gateway Press, 1995. 712p.

Jewell

Immel, Mary Blair. *A Jewell Family Resource Book*. Author, 1995. 125p.

Jewett

Hermann, Theodore Victor. *History and Genealogy of the Jewetts of America*. Rowley, MA: Jewett Family of America, 1995. 2 vols.

Jividen

Bartram, Chester E. *The George Washington McCoy Family of Mason County, West Virginia, Prominent Related Families Edington, Ferrell, Hoschar, Jividen, King, Sayre, Strait*. Knoxville, TN: Author, 1995. 187p.

Job

Nimmo, Sylvia. *The Descendants and Ancestors of Milo and Dora (Moon) Russell*. Papillion, NE: Author, 1995. 44p.

Johaningsmeier

Cady, James William. *Supplement to Cady Genealogy, Revised and Updated*. Baltimore, MD: Gateway Press, 1995. Unpgd.

Johnsdatter

Nachman, Rosemary A. *The Families Hansen, Bentsen of Holt Parish, Aust-Agdar County, Norway and Johnsdatter-Arnsen of Valer and Moss, Ostfold County, Norway*. San Diego, CA: Author, 1995. Unpgd.

Johnson

Hamilton, Fred. *The Descendants and Some Ancestors of James Meriwether and Julia Calhoun Hamilton, 1855–1936, 1853–1939*. Ruston, LA: Author, 1995. 104p.

Horned, Joseph. *A Guide for Researching Johnson/Johnston/Johnstone in Cherokee Records, Dawes Roll, Guion Miller Roll, Drennen Roll, Chapman Roll*. Author, 1995. 77p.

The Johan Petersen (Johnsen/Johnson) Family. Manitowoc, WI: Hansen, 1995. Unpgd.

Johnson, Arthur. *A Record of the William H. Johnson Family with Allied Lines*. Tacoma, WA: M. Lorenzo, 1995. 142p.

Johnson, Charles Glen. *The Ancestors of Charles Glen Johnson of Texas*. Decorah, IA: Anundsen Pub. Co., 1995. 354p.

Johnson, Lynn. *Johnson Family Album*. St. Paul, MN: Author, 1995. 200p.

Johnson, Robert Leland. *The Ancestry of Anthony Morris Johnson*. Denver, CO: Robela Pub., 1995. 2,202-2,726p.

Johnston Fretchel, Sandra. *The Johnston and Becker Family Histories*. Oshkosh, WI: Author, 1995. Unpgd.

Liston, Lois Jane Breakiron. *The Breakiron Family History Also Including the Bastian, Brecheisen, Casey, Dusenberry, Garlow, Hutchinson, Johnson, McMillen, Miller, Morris, Roderick and Other Families*. Wyandotte, OK: Gregath Pub. Co., 1995. 620p.

Melle, Jane Hentges. *Bishop, Carrick, Hotchkiss, Johnson and Related Families, a Family History as Known in 1994.* Bowling Green, OH: Author, 1995. 2 vols.

Prigge, Barbara Joan. *Hold the Lutefisk, Please, or, Our Norwegian Heritage, Families of Hansen, Johnson and Schiller.* Summer 1995 Ed. Madison, WI: Author, 1995. 55p.

Scott, Billy Dave. *Johnston-Southern of Clairborne County, Tennessee, and Parker County, Texas: Isaac McNew Johnston (1838–1918) and His Wife Norvesta Melocky Southern (1841–1929) and Allied Families Amis, Haynes, Huddleston, Seabolt, Southern and Spears.* Maryville, MO: Author, 1995. 215p.

Scott County Iowa Genealogical Society. *A Family Tree: Kirk, Johnston, Daebelliehn, Peitscher, Lawrence, Ott, Jarvis, Delzell.* Davenport, IA: Author, 1995. Unpgd.

Sluby, Paul E. *A Lineal Perspective of John Anderson Lankford and Bishop Henry McNeal Turner, Two Key Figures in the Maternal Lineage of Sara (Johnson) Bumbary.* 1995. Unpgd.

Sowers, William R. *A Pollock Family History, a Listing of Some of the Descendants of John Pollock and Sarah Smith Who Came to America in 1800.* Topeka, KS: Author, 1995. Unpgd.

Wallace, Rachel Rowland. *William Rowland and Nancy Frances Johnson, Their Ancestors and Descendants.* Rev. Lexington, KY: Author, 1995. 105p.

Jonas

Popp, Tony. *Popp, Kemper, Kammerer, Tungate, Wiwi, Jonas and Other Ancestors and Relations.* Florence, KY: Author, 1995. 226p.

Jones

Cole, Mary. *The Bunyard Family Research and Allied Families, Alley, Fitzwater, Foster, Hughes, Jones, Ledlow, McNeely, Rose.* Kentfield, CA: Author, 1995. 151p.

Cox, Mary Joan Tucker. *Breezing through the Jones Tree: John Paul Jones and I.* Knoxville, TN: Author, 1995. 168p.

Harrison, Jerry Norman. *A Few More Descendants of Lewis Jones, 1603–1684.* Bowie, MD: Heritage Books, 1995. 256p.

Hauk, Carol A. *Descendants of John Carter of Virginia.* Anderson, IN: Hauk Data Services, 1995. 2 vols.

———. *Descendants of Robert Taliafero of Virginia.* 6th. ed. Anderson, IN: Hauk Data Services, 1995. 358p.

———. *Descendants of Roger Jones of Virginia.* Anderson, IN: Hauk Data Services, 1995. 38p.

———. *Descendants of William Cocke of Virginia.* Anderson, IN: Hauk Data Services, 1995. 64p.

Johnston, Francis Clairborne. *The Angier Family of Orange and Durham Counties, North Carolina, and Allied Families of North Carolina and Virginia.* Richmond, VA: Author, 1995. 329p.

Jones, Jean Patricia Stack. *The Bruce DesBrisay Jones and Jean Patricia Stack Jones.* Arlington, VA: Author, 1995. 194p.

Jones, Jeanenne Gattis. *Sifting Sanders.* Sayre, OK: Author, 1995. 59p.

Koickler, Eloyce Hubbard. *Hiestand, Hestand, Hastings.* Helena, MT: Author, 1995. 127p.

Lowe, Anthony M. *Three Hundred Years in Eastern Virginia, Descendants of Arthur Jones (1630–1692).* Virginia Beach, VA: Donning Co., 1995. 336p.

Mallard, Shirley Jones. *Keeping Up with the Joneses, a Book about the Rafe Jones Family of Granville, North Carolina.* Chapel Hill, NC: Author, 1995. 244p.

Peck, Patricia Dunn. *Jones Family Genealogy, a History of the Christopher M. Jones Family of Philadelphia with Emphasis on the Descendants of His Son, Levi Taylor Jones of Phila-*

delphia and Trenton and Related Thropp, Yetter, Dunn and Steele Families. Saratoga Springs, NY: Peckhaven Pub., 1995. 98p.

Robertson, Joanna. *A Tree Grows in America: My Family Line*. West Columbia, SC: Author, 1995. 238p.

Stultz, Carolyne. *The Craigo Family Research Report, Including a Genealogy on Descendants of Eli and Experience (Jones) Craigo, also Variance of Spelling, Craig, Craigo, and Crago*. Danville, IN: Author, 1995. Unpgd.

————. *The Jones Family Research Report, Including a Genealogy on Descendants of Jacob and Mary Jane (Yeatton) Jones from Kennebec, Maine, to Edgar County, Illinois*. Danville, IN: Author, 1995. Unpgd.

Thompson, Laura Jones. *Jones, Richardson, Duhamel, and Allied Families of Maryland*. Nutley, NJ: M. A. Hook, 1995. 511p.

Jonville

Jonville, Michel. *Généalogie Chaillon de Jonville, Guyenne, Ile-de-France*. Paris, France: Author, 1995. 126p.

Jordan

Jordan, Mollie. *Aunt Mollie's Diary, the Jordan's of Carpenter's Grove*. Rensselaer, IN: Rose Klaus Nesius, 1995. 170p.

Jordan, Thomas Franklin. *An American Migration*. Thesis (M.A.), Louisiana State University, 1995. 194p.

Jose

Adams, Corlyn Holbrook. *The Jose Family, Utah by Way of Australia*. Wolfe City, TX: Hennington Pub. Co., 1995. 203p.

Joseph

Grubbs, Nancy Carole Early. *The Descendants of James and Elizabeth Joseph Lewis*. Houston, TX: Author, 1995. 71p.

Joseph, Anne. *Heritage of a Patriarch*. Sillery, Quebec: Septentrion, 1995. Unpgd.

Josey

Josey, Jesse Edward. *House of Jossey, Josey*. Author, 1995. Unpgd.

Judd

Popham, Geraldine E. *Grandma's Ancestors, 1634–1936, Thomas Judd, the Emigrant to Nelson Judd, and Addie (Judd) Dowd*. Lodi, CA: Author, 1995. 148p.

Reamer, Kathleen R. *Descendants of John Reamer and Margaret Schermerhorn, 1758–1995*. Imlay City, MI: Author, 1995. 246p.

Juhnke

Juhnke, Jerry. *The Carl F. W. Juhnke and Frances Kaufman Family Record, 1841 to 1995*. Wichita, KS: Author, 1995. 85p.

Jung

Liang Hsi Jung Shih Chia Tsu Shih. Beijing, China: Chung Yang Pien I Chu Pan She, 1995. 308p.

Jungen

Jungen, Paul William. *Addendum II to the Genealogy of the John Jungen and Maria Elizabeth Schneider Family, ca. 1700–1994*. Asheville, NC: Author, 1995. 44p.

Juthe

Ed, Robert Calhoun. *Wretman Roots, the Genealogy and History of the Wretman Families Who Emigrated from Ostergorland Lan, Sweden to Moline, Illinois, 1880–1891, Including Chapters on the Nymans and the Juthes*. Livingston, TX: Author, 1995. 295p.

Jutzi

Joseph Jutzi and Marie Bender Family History and Genealogy. Waterloo, Ontario: The Committee, 1995. 184p.

–K

Kabrick

Kabrick, Walter Eugene. *The Kabrick Families from Germany to Virginia to Missouri*. 2nd. ed. Author, 1995. 155p.

Kader

Kader Keaton Family. Columbus, GA: R. L. Miskelley, 1995. 125p.

Kahler

Kahler, William M. *Kahler Genealogy*. Westbrook, ME: Author, 1995. 34p.

Kairoch

Margolis, Abby Mindelle. *The Zafran Genealogy, Including the Morozowitz, Melnick, and Kairoch Families*. Daly City, CA: 1995. 75p.

Kalsch

Atteridg, Paul T. *The Attridges of North America*. Granby, CO: Author, 1995. 429p.

Kammerer

Popp, Tony. *Popp, Kemper, Kammerer, Tungate, Wiwi, Jonas and Other Ancestors and Relations*. Florence, KY: Author, 1995. 226p.

Kane

Biggar, Harold Arthur. *The Biggar Families of Greenwich, Connecticut, and County Tyrone, North Ireland*. Stamford, CT: Author, 1995. unpgd.

Eggert, Irving John. *Peter Eggert of Mecklenburg and Related Families in America, Best, Bitz, Broekemeier, Hackbarth, Kane, Meisner, Nellis, Schunk, Strenkowski, Voight, Winston*. Decorah, IA: Anundsen Pub. Co., 1995. 224p.

Kanouse

These are the Larsens, Brief Histories of the Larsen, Kanouse, Glenn, McClelland and McMeans Families. Loveland, CO: Author, 1995. 32p.

Kapeghian

Kapeghian, Katchadoor. *The Kapeghian, Jamgochian, Injaian Family Reunion*. Philadelphia, PA: The Reunion, 1995. 148p.

Karch

Bernard, Allen William. *The Bavarian Connection: The George and Walburga Karch Family and Their Descendants*. Newport, KY: Otto Zimmerman & Son, 1995. 263p.

Karg

Bernard, Allen William. *The Bavarian Connection: The George and Walburga Karch Family and Their Descendants*. Newport, KY: Otto Zimmerman & Son, 1995. 263p.

Kargey

Smith, Robert Lee. *Ancestors of Thelma Margaret Gander*. Alexandria, VA: Author, 1995. 65p.

Karr

Karr, Nola M. *Baker Family Record, a Genealogy of Many of the Descendants of John Baker Who Immigrated from England in 1637*. White Plains, MD: Automated Graphic Systems, 1995. 663p.

Kast

Starks, Virginia. *The Kosht-Kost-Kast Genealogy*. 2nd. ed. Ponca City, OK: Author, 1995. 210p.

Kasubjak

Ward, Naomi Etta. *The Ward Connections, Nourse, Kimmel, Wood, Babbs, Shelton, Sasubjak, Ader, Guffey, Pontiny, Archibald, Asbell*. Evansville, IN: Author, 1995. 545p.

Katzbach

Babitzke, Edward B. *Katzbach, Bessarabia*. Tucson, AZ: Author, 1995. Unpgd.

Kauffman

Beck, William M. *Matthias J. DeWald and Katherine Kauffman*. East Peoria, IL: Author, 1995. 26p.

Kauffman, Ivan. *The Family and Descendants of Christian Kauffmann, 1859–1942, and Barbara Nafziger, 1864–1951, Who Were Married in 1883*. Goshen, IN: Author, 1995. 19p.

Smith, Robert Lee. *Ancestors of Thelma Margaret Gander*. Alexandria, VA: Author, 1995. 65p.

Keating

Kader Keaton Family. Columbus, GA: R. L. Miskelley, 1995. 125p.

Keaton

Kader Keaton Family. Columbus, GA: R. L. Miskelley, 1995. 125p.

Keeler

Kilgore, LaVerne Keeler. *Simon Derrick Descendants, with Fox, Fry, Keeler*. Fort Worth, TX: Author, 1995. 400p.

Keen

Keen, Robert Roger. *A Keen Insight, a Genealogical Trace of a Keen Family of Massachusetts and Maine*. Dayton, OH: Author, 1995. 198p.

Keesaman

Crozier, E. Wanda Sloan. *Keesaman-Wolf Families and Allied Families*. Author, 1995. Unpgd.

Keister

Shuck, Larry Gorden. *Our Families, Shuck, Fleshman, Sydenstricker, Smith, Lewis, Kincaid, Keister et al. of West Virginia*. Baltimore, MD: Gateway Press, 1995. 565p.

Kelch

Bielanski, Phyllis Jean Olin. *Andrew Powell Family Tree, Including Powell, Farr, Ten Brock Branches and Wolcott, Stiles, Doolittle, Kelch, Eldridge Branches*. Lakeland, FL: Author, 1995. Unpgd.

Kellars

Dix, Roberta Cook Jackson. *The First Shall be Last, a Family History*. Author, 1995. 137p.

Keller

Bellin, Loretta M. *The Family of Jacob Keller and Rosina Cathrina Maechtle and Sophia Meins, 1700–1994*. Oshkosh, WI: Author, 1995. 237p.

Gorlick, Jeanne. *The Family Tree of Curtis, Francisco, Hayes, Keller, Leavel, and LeRoy, with Procter, Ressequie, Sipperley, Spence and Weaver*. Author, 1995. 345p.

Spease, Rachel Keller. *A Keller History, Descendants of Hans Jacob Keller and Elizabeth Keller of the Cocalico Valley, Lancaster County, Pennsylvania*. Lewiston, PA: Author, 1995. 2 vols.

Kelly

Truche, Jean Loup. *The Descendants of James Kelly and Mary Finlay*. Midland, MI: Author, 1995. 307p.

Kelso

Kelso, Douglas. *Immigrant John Kelso of Pennsylvania and Virginia, His Ancestors and Descendants*. Memphis, TN: Author, 1995. 179p.

Kemer

Flanders, Charles M. *The Descendants of Colonel David Hart (1770–1835) and Other Related Families*. Author, 1995. 140p.

Kemp

Hall, Margaret Veronica. *Kemps of the Borders*. South Africa: Barkley East Reporter, 1995. 239p.

Johnston, Anne Plummer. *The Plummer Lineage of America*. Reston, VA: M. L. Tomaselli, 1995. 56p.

Kemper

Popp, Tony. *Popp, Kemper, Kammerer, Tungate, Wiwi, Jonas and Other Ancestors and Relations*. Florence, KY: Author, 1995. 226p.

Kennelly

Kennelly, Jack. *The Walter and Sarah Kennelly Family*. West St. Paul, MN: Author, 1995. 154p.

Kennedy

Kennedy, Ron. *Glimpses II: A Further Look into a Family Past*. Rio Verde, AZ: Green Desert Pub., 1995. 221p.

Kennemore

McGinn, Ann Winston. *A McGinn McCorkle Family History, 1796–1995: With Related Families, Crockett, Dabney, Egnatoff, Fontaine, Freirson, Gillespie, Huddart, Kennemore, O'Donnell, Patton, Ring, Sheppard, Winston, and Others*. Spring Hill, FL: Author, 1995. 313p.

Kennett

Kennett, Donald Arthur. *Genealogy of the Family of John and Catherine Payne Kennett, in the United States and Canada, 1760–1990*. Kelowana, BC: Author, 1995. 293p.

Kent

Kent, Barrie. *George Kent and His Family*. Petersfield, England: Queenswood Press, 1995. 277p.

Kent, Doris Bankes. *Thomas Kent (1784–1835) and His Descendants*. Baltimore, MD: Gateway Press, 1995. 425p.

Kenyon

Fail Families and Allied Families: Catt, Hensley, Kenyon, Lane and Sprague, 1818–1995, a Work in Progress. Decorah, IA: Anundsen Pub. Co., 1995. 348p.

Kerr

Davis, Hope Willard. *The Descendants of Alexander Kerr of Tyrone County, Northern Ireland, Mid-1700s through 1994*. Salisbury, NC: Author, 1995. 364p.

Smith, Ruth Wiley. *Ancestors and Descendants of John Nelson Sibcy, Who Came to Hamilton County, Ohio, in the Early 1800*. Oxford, OH: Author, 1995. 131p.

Ketchersid

Ketchersid, Burrell Monroe. *Thomas Ketchersid and His Descendants, 1745–1995*. Maryville, TN: Author, 1995. 468p.

Kevil

Evans, Ronald. *The Descendants of Uriah Stevens and Nancy Kevil*. Independence, LA: Author, 1995. 373p.

Keyes

Avery, Thomas Lynn. *Family Life of John Henry and Ellen (Andrews) Swann*. Chico, CA: Author, 1995. 115p.

Wynn, Louise Tompkins. *A Family History of the Tompkins and Keas of North Carolina, South Carolina, and Georgia and Other Related Lines*. Panama City Beach, FL: Author, 1995. 416p.

Keyton

Kader Keaton Family. Columbus, GA: R. L. Miskelley, 1995. 125p.

Kiblinger

Savage, Earl Roland and William Henry Kiblinger. *The American Descendants of Peter Kublinger, Germany, 1705 circa 1748*. Richmond, VA: Author, 1995. 143p.

Kigh

Mann, Marion. *The Kigh, Mann, Reagin, and Sykes Families, Including the Branch, Brown, Dean, Fort, Gerran, Leake, Marquis, Moses, Oakes, Powell, Reid, Trammell, Walk, Wilkey, Wingfield, and Woods Families, a Genealogy and Family History*. Baltimore, MD: Gateway Press, 1995. 218p.

Kimmel

Ward, Naomi Etta. *The Ward Connections, Nourse, Kimmel, Wood, Babbs, Shelton, Sasubjak, Ader, Guffey, Pontiny, Archibald, Asbell*. Evansville, IN: Author, 1995. 545p.

Kincaid

Shuck, Larry Gorden. *Our Families, Shuck, Fleshman, Sydenstricker, Smith, Lewis, Kincaid, Keister et al. of West Virginia*. Baltimore, MD: Gateway Press, 1995. 565p.

King

Bartram, Chester E. *The George Washington McCoy Family of Mason County, West Virginia, Prominent Related Families Edington, Ferrell, Hoschar, Jividen, King, Sayre, Strait*. Knoxville, TN: Author, 1995. 187p.

King, Kenneth R. *Some of the Descendants of John Wesley King*. Flower Mound, TX: Author, 1995. Unpgd.

King, Robert O. *The King Family, New Jersey, North Carolina, Tennessee, Missouri and Texas*. Greenville, SC: Author, 1995. 35p.

Moore, Freddie Gene. *My Virginia Ancestors and Their Descendants in the Families, Burdett, Alexander, Anderson, King, Boone, Welsh, McHenry, Cornwell, Alford, Coleman, Dixon, Morgan, Jarman, Maugridge*. Author, 1995. 46p.

Partin, Sherita Kae. *The Descendants of Nancy Partin and Charles King*. Nacogdoches, TX: Partin Publications, 1995. Unpgd.

Thomas, Theodore. *History of the King, Thomas, and Thompkins Families, Family History*. Denver, CO: Author, 1995. Unpgd.

Tucker, Franklin Bennett. *The King Genealogy: A Morris County, New Jersey, Family*. Seven Lakes, NC: Author, 1995. 45p.

Kingsley

Serre, Robert. *Les Ancêtres Paternels de Wilfred Kingsley (1884–1948) et Blanche Goyette (1886–1975)*. Ottawa, Ontario: Author, 1995. 40p.

Kinnard

Arnold, Bonny Riddle. *Descendants of Joseph Kinnard, Madison County, Kentucky*. Anaheim, CA: Author, 1995. 5p.

Kinser

Kinser, Robert C. *Kinser, Kinzer, Kincer, Kinsar, Kinsor, Kintzer, Kuntzer, Kuentzer, One Immigrant Family*. Asheville, NC: Author, 1995. 32p.

Kinsman

Younglove, James N. *The Descendants of Samuel and Margaret Younglove*. Houston, TX: Author, 1995. 200p.

Kinzalow

Kinzalow, Jayne Baxter. *Kinzalow Pathways: Pioneers of East Tennessee, 1670–1995*. Knoxville, TN: Tennessee Valley Pub., 1995. 159p.

Kirk

Bowyer, L. Ray. *Bowyer-Skavdahl Genealogy*. Randolph, NJ: Author, 1995. 276p.
The Largs Australians. Largs, Scotland: Largs & District Historical Society, 1995. 21p.
Scott County Iowa Genealogical Society. *A Family Tree: Kirk, Johnston, Daebelliehn, Peitscher, Lawrence, Ott, Jarvis, Delzell*. Davenport, IA: Author, 1995. Unpgd.

Kirkland

Corbari, Shirley Kirkland Guio. *The Kirkland Mathews Family*. Campbell, CA: Author, 1995. 796p.

Kirkpatrick

Kirkpatrick, Melvin Eugene. *A Kirkpatrick Genealogy: Being an Account of the Descendants of the Family of James Kirkpatrick of South Carolina, ca. 1715–1786*. 2nd. ed. Coralville, IA: D. Hudson, 1995. 516p.

Kirtley

Ziegel, Ruth Turner. *Julius Christy of Virginia and Kentucky, 1730–1808, and Agatha Barnett Christy, 1740–1820, and Related Families of Barnett, Gibbs, Blackburn, Cave, Glass, Kirtley, Bush, Lindsey, Armstrong, Whaley, Davis, and Day*. Cincinnati, OH: Author, 1995. 92p.

Kittrell

Witt, Mary Emily Smith. *Kittrells in America*. 2nd. ed. Dallas, TX: Mew, 1995. 169p.

Klawitter

Draeger, Ronald. *Family History of Martin Klawitter, 1815–1905, with Additions of the Herman Becker Family*. Spencer, WI: Author, 1995. Unpgd.

Klein

DeRose, Lucille. *The Borcherts of Nicollet and Brown Counties, Minnesota, a Family History, the Families of Friedland, Mecklenburg, Germany, the Borcherts, the Hackers, the Kleins*. Sacramento, CA: Author, 1995. 99p.

Kling

Kling, John Luther. *Descendants of Johan Ludwig Kling*. Author, 1995. 84p.

Klippenstein

Klippenstein, Bernard D. *Genealogy of Heinrich Klippenstein, 1849–1977*. Manitou, Manitoba: Western Canadian, 1995. 104p.

Klotz

Klotz, George David. *Klotz-Zerbe Family History and Genealogy, 1530–1995, Indiana Branches*. Cicero, IN: Author, 1995. Unpgd.

Knapp

Derbyshire, Janet H. *Knapp Cousins, Descendants of Enos Knapp and His Wife Phoebe and His Brother Elijah Knapp and His Wife Dorothy Crawford*. Wyantskill, NY: Author, 1995. 77p.

Knight

Barnes, Mary Lee Anderson. *The Carter, Knight, and Foreman Families of Edgecombe County, North Carolina, 1730–1800, Some Ancestors and Descendants*. Athens, TX: Author, 1995. 144p.

Thomson, Donald Claire. *William Knight and His Descendants*. Stevensville, MD: Author, 1995. 269p.

Knowlton

Bell, George Edward. *The Jackson Knowlton Family*. Ontario, NY: Bell & Hatch Pub., 1995. 122p.

Kock

Osborn, Will E. *Oatman: Some of the Descendants of Johannes Outman, 1654–1716, and His Wife Femmetje Kock, 1654–1732*. Hansen, ID: L. M. Oatman, 1995. 356p.

Kockler

Koickler, Eloyce Hubbard. *Hiestand, Hestand, Hastings*. Helena, MT: Author, 1995. 127p.

Koehler

Winkelman, Philip M. *The Reineke Family History, the Descendants of Johann Heinrich Conrad Reineke and Caroline W. Koehler*. Fegus Falls, MN: Author, 1995. 275p.

Koenig

Houy, Edward W. *The Family of Ludwig Koenig and Sophia Beyer, Married in Germany, Their Son August Koening and Sophia Weber, Married on November 7, 1872 in Texas and the Eleven Children of August and Sophia.* Sunrise Beach, TX: Koenig Klub, 1995. Unpgd.

Kohlhagen

Shreve, Sue Ann Gardner. *Kohlhagen Family Genealogy.* West Bay Shore, NY: Author, 1995. 174p.

Koontz

Smith, Robert Lee. *Ancestors of Thelma Margaret Gander.* Alexandria, VA: Author, 1995. 65p.

Kosht

Starks, Virginia. *The Kosht-Kost-Kast Genealogy.* 2nd. ed. Ponca City, OK: Author, 1995. 210p.

Kost

Myers, Jo Ellen Aisenbrey. *Aisenbrey-Kreis-Kost-Edelman.* Pleasanton, CA: Author, 1995. Unpgd.

Starks, Virginia. *The Kosht-Kost-Kast Genealogy.* 2nd. ed. Ponca City, OK: Author, 1995. 210p.

Kothmann

Kothmann, Forrestine Haney. *The Kothmanns of Texas, 1845–1991.* 4th. ed. San Angelo, TX: Anchor Pub. Co., 1995. 932p.

Krahenbuhl

Krijbolder, Bernard J. J. *Genealogie van het geslacht Crebolder, Krijbolder, Crebolder meergenaamd Krijbolder (ex Krahenbuhl van Bern).* Barneveld, Netherlands: Familievereniging Crebolder-Krijbolder, 1995. 111p.

Kramer

Kramer, Milton E. *The Kramers, the Next Generation.* NY: Kramer Family Centennial Committee, 1995. 218p.

Kratzer

Dailey, Richard Edward. *Walter Lee and Rilma Ione Kratzer.* Newnan, GA: Author, 1995. Unpgd.

Kreger

Groff, Clifford. *The Stairs Families of Westmoreland and Somerset Counties of Pennsylvania and Their Ancestors, Steer, Summy, Monticue, Harshberger, Colborn, Tissue, Kreger and Clevenger.* Arnold, MD: Author, 1995. 147p.

Kreis

Myers, JoEllen Aisenbrey. *Aisenbrey-Kreis-Kost-Edelman.* Pleasanton, CA: Author, 1995. Unpgd.

Krickel

Flanders, Charles M. *The Descendants of Colonel David Hart (1770–1835) and Other Related Families*. Author, 1995. 140p.

Kriegel

Schaefer, Jeanette Kriegel. *A Family History of Karl Kriegel and Sons Fred Kriegel, Paul Kriegel, Gus Kriegel*. Austin, TX: Author, 1995. Unpgd.

Krueger

Krueger, Maurice. *The Descendants of Kruegers and Halls*. Mina, SD: Author, 1995. 162p.

Krug

Wilson, Mary Louise. *The Peter Krug Family, from East Prussia to the United States, a History Anthology*. Piedmont, SD: Author, 1995. 288p.

Kruse

Seebach, Don. *1845–1995, One Hundred Fifty Years in America, Ancestors and Descendants of Ehrenfried Seebach, 1808–1897, and His Wife Maria Kruz, 1815–1887*. Hillsboro, OR: Author, 1995. 329p.

Kublinger

Savage, Earl Roland and William Henry Kiblinger. *The American Descendants of Peter Kublinger, Germany, 1705 circa 1748*. Richmond, VA: Author, 1995. 143p.

Kucas

Anspauch, Donald Jones, Jr. *One Hundred Year History of the Family of Joseph Philip Kucas and Barbara Grace Yakich Kucas, 1884–1984*. West Hollywood, CA: Author, 1995. Unpgd.

Kucherer

Kucherer, Harvey David. *The 8 Generations Wintermyer Family Lineage with Allied Families, and the 8 Generation Ahnentafel Kucherer Family Lineage with Allied Families*. Monroeville, PA: Author, 1995. Unpgd.

Kump

Kump, Warren Lee. *The Kumps, the Bobbitts and Others*. Minneapolis, MN: Author, 1995. 480p.

Kunz

Kunz Family History. Cedar City, UT, 1995. 65p.

Kutschke

Schaefer, Jeanette Kriegel. *A Family History of Karl Kriegel and Sons Fred Kriegel, Paul Kriegel, Gus Kriegel*. Austin, TX: Author, 1995. Unpgd.

– L

Lacefield

Lacefield, William Bryant. *Lacefields of Butler County, Kentucky, and Their Descendants.* Indianapolis, IN: Author, 1995. 185p.

Lacey

Lacey, Garland Howard. *Ancestors and Descendants of Hiram G. Lacey and Sophia Sell.* Washington, IL: Author, 1995. 604p.

Ladd

Roe, Nancy Clapp. *The Descendants of George Edgar Ladd (1864–1940) and Mary Hammond Ladd (1864–1959): Where Are They, What Are They Doing in 1995?.* Presque Isle, ME: Author, 1995. 190p.

Ladenson

The Ganze Mishpoche, a Chronicle of the Ladenson Family. Author, 1995. 84p.

Ladson

Fishburne, Henry Gordon. *The Ladson Family of South Carolina and Georgia, 1678–1900.* Spartanburg, SC: Reprint Co., 1995. 195p.

Lafferty

Wilson, Mary Lafferty. *Lafferty: Genealogy, History, Legend, Myth: Including Many Allied Lines:* Slidell, LA: Author, 1995. 520p.

Lafnear

Lafnear, Joseph Paul. *Relative of Joseph Paul Lafnear.* Rev. ed. Author, 1995. Unpgd.

La Marca

La Marca, Jeffrey Peter. *Window to the Past, Door to the Future, a Glimpse at an American Genealogy, Compilation of Data on the Acquisto, Calamera, Carroll, Crowley, Guastaferro, Hawley, La Marca, Lavier, and Steigerwalt Families.* Yorba Linda, CA: Shumway Family History Services, 1995. 214p.

Lambert

Feasel, Hubert. *A Genealogy and History of Charles Edmond Lambert and Related Families of Barthelemy and Duquaine.* Decatur, IN: H. & L. Feasel, 1995. 120p.

Henley, Lucille Lambert. *History of Robert P. and Caroline Harding Lambert Family in Wells County, Indiana, 1850–1995.* Blackford County, IN: Author, 1995. 70p.

Lamboley

Grillot, R. E. *Grillot and Ancestors.* Author, 1995. 831p.

Lammes

Clark, LaVerne Harrell. *The Bunte Family History, Smithville, Texas, 1880–1995, for the Smithville Centennial, 1995: With Histories of the Allied Families-the Garlipps, Lammes and Walls of Texas, c. 1849.* Denton, TX: Texas Women's University Library, 1995. 245p.

Lamson

Karr, Nola M. *Baker Family Record, a Genealogy of Many of the Descendants of John Baker Who Immigrated from England in 1637.* White Plains, MD: Automated Graphic Systems, 1995. 663p.

Land

Pickard, Frank C. *Some Descendants of Curtis Land of Charles City County, Virginia.* Wyomissing, PA: Author, 1995. Unpgd.

Landon

Moore, Freddie Gene. *The Descendants of Thomas Moore, Sr. of Suffolk County, England and the Related Families, Youngs, Landon, Spencer, French, Norris, Simmons, Ratliff, Slaughter.* Author, 1995. Unpgd.

Landreth

Bell, Ernest Elmont, Jr. *One Line of Descent from Our Immigrant, Alexander Bell/Beall of Maryland, a Genealogical History, 1600 AD to 2000 AD, with an Autobiography by Ernest Elmont Bell, Jr. for His Descendants.* Baywood Park, CA: Author, 1995. 508p.

Landry

Broussard, Earl. *Our Ancestors, Gone But Not Forgotten.* Author, 1995. 204p.

Lane

Fail Families and Allied Families: Catt, Hensley, Kenyon, Lane and Sprague, 1818–1995, a Work in Progress. Decorah, IA: Anundsen Pub. Co., 1995. 348p.

Lane, Christopher W. *The Family Tree of Warren W. Lane.* Philadelphia, PA: Author, 1995. 112p.

Lang

The Largs Australians. Largs, Scotland: Largs & District Historical Society, 1995. 21p.

Long, Michael G. *One of the Lang Families from Germany to the United States.* Frankfort, KY: Author, 1995. 29p.

McLeod, Stephen Archie. *The House of Cantelou & Co., the Story of a Southern Family.* Tallahassee, FL: Author, 1995. 705p.

Lanham

Lanham, William Joseph. *Wonderful Pilgrimage, a Lanham Family History and Personal Journey.* Clemson, SC: Author, 1995. 343p.

Lannom, Douglas Vaughan. *From Longan to Lannom, My Family's Journey from Ireland to Tennessee.* Antioch, TN: Author, 1995. 112p.

Lanier

Kaufman, Mary Arnold. *Martin-Arnold and Allied Families, Lanier, Bailey, Swan, Sandidge, Gholston, Morgan, and Born, Migration from Virginia to Tennessee, Georgia, Alabama and Arkansas.* Knoxville, TN: Tennessee Valley Pub., 1995. 212p.

Lankford

Sluby, Paul E. *A Lineal Perspective of John Anderson Lankford and Bishop Henry McNeal Turner, Two Key Figures in the Maternal Lineage of Sara (Johnson) Bumbary.* 1995. Unpgd.

Larder

Paulson, Louis. *A Larder-Terry Ancestry.* Author, 1995. 72p.

Larsen

Beatt, Irene I. *North Dakota Family.* St. Paul, MN: Author, 1995. 32p.
These are the Larsens, Brief Histories of the Larsen, Kanouse, Glenn, McClelland and McMeans Families. Loveland, CO: Author, 1995. 32p.

Larson

Madson, Richard C. *Gjerpen to Gjerpen, the Madson Families Who Came to Wisconsin, Also Mason, Larson, Pedersen, Holm, Halvorson, Simonsen, and Hoen Families.* Mesa, AZ: Author, 1995. 284p.

LaRue

Carman, Daniel. *The Carman Family of Long Island.* Norfolk, VA: Author, 1995. 69p.

Lasater

Olsen, Lucinda. *A Collection of Lasater Marriages.* Kent, WA; Author, 1995. Unpgd.

Lassauge

Sand, Vernon Jerome. *The Life and Times of Vernon and Renee Sand and Related Families, Geiselhart, Bittle, Warner, Sand, Vilmo, Bergman, Legrand, Lassauge, Prado, and Carpentier.* Austin, TX: Author, 1995. 501p.

Latimer

Chamberlain, Merle. *On the Trail of Zebulon Latimer and His Family.* Wilmington, DE: Lower Cape Fear Historical Society, 1995. Unpgd.
Sayford, Nancy McKinney. *The Latimer Legacy.* 2nd. ed. Greenwood Village, 1995. 214p.

Lautner

Schrader, Robert Ellis. *The Lautner Addition.* Los Angeles, CA: Author, 1995. Unpgd.

Lauzanne

Arthaud, John Bradley. *The Arthaud Family of Bourbonne-les-Bains and Langres, Department of Haute Marne, France with Related Families of Gascard, Gautherot, Lauzanne, Liegault, Mutinot and Walferdin and One Immigrant Branch in the United States.* Columbia, MO: Author, 1995. 123p.

Lavier

La Marca, Jeffrey Peter. *Window to the Past, Door to the Future, a Glimpse at an American Genealogy, Compilation of Data on the Acquisto, Calamera, Carroll, Crowley, Guastaferro, Hawley, La Marca, Lavier, and Steigerwalt Families*. Yorba Linda, CA: Shumway Family History Services, 1995. 214p.

Lawhon

Lide, Neoma Lawhon. *The Lawhons of Texas, Direct Family Connections of J. C. Lawhon and His Wife, Judith Ellen (Gardner) Lawhon*. Texas: Author, 1995. 61p.

Lawrence

McColman, Ora Belle Mayberry. *Descendants of Elder John Lawrence of Southwest Virginia and New England*. Roanoke, VA: Author, 1995. 254p.

Scott County Iowa Genealogical Society. *A Family Tree: Kirk, Johnston, Daebelliehn, Peitscher, Lawrence, Ott, Jarvis, Delzell*. Davenport, IA: Author, 1995. Unpgd.

Lawson

Lewallen, Blanche Sims. *Sims-Marcus-Lawson Connections*. Toccoa, GA: Author, 1995. Unpgd.

R. E. W. Thompson (1856–1937), Adair, Clark, Carroll, Sellers, Lawson (Related Lines). Rockwall, TX: S. B. Adair, 1995. 133p.

Lay

Webster, Carolyn Lay. *Family History: John Lay, Sr. (1610–1674/5)*. Author, 1995. Unpgd.

Layton

Archer, John Harold. *Layton Families of Monmouth County, New Jersey, Descendants of Allen Layton and Annay Foster*. Hightstown, NJ: Author, 1995. Unpgd.

Lea

Lea, Martha. *How I'm Kin to Whom, the Leas in America*. Author, 1995. 209p.

Rose, Ben Lacy. *Report on the Research on the Lea Family in Virginia and North Carolina before 1800*. Decorah, IA: Anundsen Pub., 1995. 172p.

Leake

Mann, Marion. *The Kigh, Mann, Reagin, and Sykes Families, Including the Branch, Brown, Dean, Fort, Gerran, Leake, Marquis, Moses, Oakes, Powell, Reid, Trammell, Walk, Wilkey, Wingfield, and Woods Families, a Genealogy and Family History*. Baltimore, MD: Gateway Press, 1995. 218p.

Leath

Waltman, Leslie Ray. *The Leath Family History*. Dothan, AL: Dothan Print, 1995. Unpgd.

Leavel

Gorlick, Jeanne. *The Family Tree of Curtis, Francisco, Hayes, Keller, Leavel, and LeRoy, with Procter, Ressequie, Sipperley, Spence and Weaver*. Author, 1995. 345p.

LeBel

LeBel, Gilles. *Dictionnaire des LeBel*. Lac St. Augustin, Quebec: Author, 1995. 384p.

LeBlanc

Hanrahan, Patrick Lloyd. *Charlebois (Wood) Family History, and the Allied Families of Brien, Brule, Daudelin, Gagnon, LeBlanc and Riel.* Milwaukie, OR: Author, 1995. 179p.

Ledet

Oster, Brian J. *Descendants of Martial Pierre Ledet and Ursule Marie Duhe.* Tampa, FL: Author, 1995. 217p.

Ledlow

Cole, Mary. *The Bunyard Family Research and Allied Families, Alley, Fitzwater, Foster, Hughes, Jones, Ledlow, McNeely, Rose.* Kentfield, CA: Author, 1995. 151p.

LeDuc

LeDuc, Susan Sparks. *LeDuc/Piedanna Chronicle, France to America.* Fort Wayne, IN: Author, 1995. Unpgd.

Lee

Brown, Gerald Douglas. *A Genealogy of a Lee Family, Mainly of Old Williamsburg District, Present Day Florence County, South Carolina.* Hemingway, SC: Three Rivers Historical Society, 1995. 143p.

———. *A Genealogy of a Locklair Family, Mainly of the Old Sumter District of South Carolina, Present Day Sumter and Lee Counties.* Hemingway, SC: Three Rivers Historical Society, 1995. 102p.

Gardner, Oscar William. *Gardner/Ballard and Allied Families, Edmondson, Lee, Daniel, Cauthen, and Starr.* Morrow, GA: Author, 1995. 456p.

Hauk, Carol A. *Descendants of Benjamin Harrison of Virginia.* 4th. ed. Anderson, IN: Hauk Data Services, 1995. 365p.

———. *Descendants of Richard Lee of Virginia.* 2nd. ed. Anderson, IN: Hauk Data Services, 1995. 202p.

———. *Descendants of William Randolph of Virginia.* Anderson, IN: Hauk Data Services, 1995. 461p.

Lee, Victor Lavon. *The Lees of Bertie County, North Carolina.* Roswell, GA: Hendershot Davis Group, 195. 132p.

Lesser, Robert E. *Lee, Descendants of David Lee of Somerset County, New Jersey.* Loveland, CO: Author, 1995. 59p.

Wadleigh, Robert Lee. *Descendants of Abraham Lee of Franklin County, Indiana.* Hamilton, OH: Author, 1995. 68p.

Leggatt

Younglove, James N. *The Descendants of Samuel and Margaret Younglove.* Houston, TX: Author, 1995. 200p.

LeGrand

LeGrand, Louis Everett. *Pierre in Virginia, 1700.* Baltimore, MD: Gateway Press, 1995. 360p.

Sand, Vernon Jerome. *The Life and Times of Vernon and Renee Sand and Related Families, Geiselhart, Bittle, Warner, Sand, Vilmo, Bergman, LeGrand, Lassauge, Prado, and Carpentier.* Austin, TX: Author, 1995. 501p.

Lehew

Skelton, Isaac Newton. *Ike, This Is You, a History of the Skelton, Boone, Barry, Beach, Blattner, Corum, Hoagland, Lehew, Strode, Wright and Young Families*. Washington, DC: Author, 1995. 223p.

Lehman

Holzmann, Herbert A. *Descendants of Ernst Wilhelm Raba, 1874–1951, and Maria Margareta Fuhrwerk, 1875–1965*. San Antonio, TX: Author, 1995. Unpgd.

Schmucker, Daniel M. *The Descendants of Andrew N. Hochstetler and Elizabeth Lehman: Also Includes the Descendants of Elias A. Miller*. Franklin, KY: Author, 1995. 133p.

Leier

Gross, Grace Dickinson. *Gross Family History: Includes Leier Family*. Orrin, ND: Author, 1995. Unpgd.

Lemelle

Auzenne, Conrad Andrew. *Auzenne, Donato, Frilot, Lemelle, Meullion, a Genealogical Study of Five Families and Other Allied Families of Southern Louisiana*. Author, 1995. 222p.

Lemon

Koickler, Eloyce Hubbard. *Hiestand, Hestand, Hastings*. Helena, MT: Author, 1995. 127p.

Lenzi

Lantzy, Charles A. *Genealogy on the First Known Ancestor Lenzi, 1638–1713, Down to Present Generation Bernard A. Lantzy, 1878–1962*. Mechanicsburg, PA: Author, 1995. 230p.

Leonard

Leonard, Mary E. *Our Leonard Family History, Constantine Leonard, Revolutionary Soldier, and His Descendants, 1775–1995*. Decorah, IA: Anundsen Pub. Co., 1995. Unpgd.

Leonhard

Riley, David Joseph. *Descendants of Theodor Leonhard and Verena Setz of Passaic County, New Jersey*. New Brunswick, NJ: Author, 1995. Unpgd.

Leontev

Narbut, Andrei Nikolaevich. *Leontevy*. Moscow, Russia: Author, 1995. 68p.

Le Quesne

Le Quesne, Walter John. *The Le Quesne of Jersey*. Jersey, England: Channel Islands Family History Society, 1995. 144p.

LeRoy

Gorlick, Jeanne. *The Family Tree of Curtis, Francisco, Hayes, Keller, Leavel, and LeRoy, with Procter, Ressequie, Sipperley, Spence and Weaver*. Author, 1995. 345p.

Lester

Lester, Robert. *Descendants of John Lester, Sr. and Catherine Plickenstalver*. Lincoln University, PA: Author, 1995. 70p.

LeSueur
Daisley, Ellen Niles. *The LeSueur Family*. Guerneville, CA: Author, 1995. 117p.

Letourneau
Proulx, Antonin. *Recueil des Familles Proulx et Letourneau: Les Descendants de Mes Arrière-Grands-Parents (Côte paternel)*. Ottawa, Ontario: Author, 1995. 213p.

Levesque
Boileau, Pierre. *Précis de Généalogie, le Temple des Ancêtres de René Levesque*. Montreal: Guerin, 1995. 112p.

Levin
Pearson, Frederick John. *Anderson*. Houston, TX: Author, 1995. 352p.

Lewis
Grubbs, Nancy Carole Early. *The Descendants of James and Elizabeth Joseph Lewis*. Houston, TX: Author, 1995. 71p.
Hauk, Carol A. *Descendants of George Reade of Virginia*. Anderson, IN: Hauk Data Services, 1995. 393p.
———. *Descendants of John Early of Virginia*. 2nd. ed. Anderson, IN: Hauk Data Services, 1995. 219p.
———. *Descendants of John Waller of Virginia*. Anderson, IN: Hauk Data Services, 1995. 87p.
———. *Descendants of Richard Bufford of Virginia*. 4th. ed. Anderson, IN: Hauk Data Services, 1995. 216p.
———. *Descendants of Richard Perrott of Virginia*. 2nd. ed. Anderson, IN: Hauk Data Services, 1995. 278p.
———. *Descendants of Robert Coleman of Virginia*. Anderson, IN: Hauk Data Services, 1995. 226p.
———. *Descendants of Robert Taliafero of Virginia*. 6th. ed. Anderson, IN: Hauk Data Services, 1995. 358p.
———. *Descendants of William Ball of Virginia*. Anderson, IN: Hauk Data Services, 1995. 229p.
———. *Descendants of William Thornton of Virginia*. Anderson, IN: Hauk Data Services, 1995. 361p.
———. *Descendants of Zachary and Henry Lewis of Virginia*. 4th. ed. Anderson, IN: Hauk Data Services, 1995. 115p.
Lewis, Allen Roy. *Two Hundred Year History and Genealogy of the Isaac Lewis Family from Cloughjordan (Tipperary), Ireland to the Canadas and the United States, Including Intermarriages with Hodgins, Myers, Rapley, Slack, Williams, and Many Other Families*. Ver. 1.5. Syracuse, NY: Author, 1995. 215p.
Robertson, Joanna. *A Tree Grows in America: My Family Line*. West Columbia, SC: Author, 1995. 238p.
Shuck, Larry Gorden. *Our Families, Shuck, Fleshman, Sydenstricker, Smith, Lewis, Kincaid, Keister et al. of West Virginia*. Baltimore, MD: Gateway Press, 1995. 565p.

Libby
Holmes, Marguerite. *Holmes from John of England and Plymouth, Massachusetts, to Holmes Brothers William Hudson, Horace William and Rodney Arthur Holmes of Aroostook County,*

Maine, and Related Families Cobbs, Redman, Libby and Shorey. San Antonio, TX: Author, 1995. 101p.

Liegault

Arthaud, John Bradley. *The Arthaud Family of Bourbonne-les-Bains and Langres, Department of Haute Marne, France with Related Families of Gascard, Gautherot, Lauzanne, Liegault, Mutinot and Walferdin and One Immigrant Branch in the United States*. Columbia, MO: Author, 1995. 123p.

Lightfoot

Hauk, Carol A. *Descendants of William Ball of Virginia*. Anderson, IN: Hauk Data Services, 1995. 229p.

Likes

Likes, William C. *Connections to the Likes Family, 1790–1994*. Denver, CO: Author, 1995. 136p.
———. *The Lykes Family, 1790 to 1994, Supplement 1995*. Denver, CO: Author, 1995. Unpgd.

Lindbeck

Williams, Luella R. *My Father's People: Paulsen/Thoreesen Slekt from Norway, Lindack Slakt from Sweden, Descendants Found in Australia, Canada, Denmark, Norway, Sweden and United States of America*. Iron River, MI: Author, 1995. 475p.

Lindley

Gravlee, Diane Druin. *The Descendants of John Lindley, Including the Rev. Jacob Lindley, First President of Ohio University*. Delmar, NY: Author, 1995. 80p.

Lindquist

Bymaster Richards, Willa. *Descendants of William Anders Lindquist and Mary Nuquist*. Carnation, WA: Author, 1995. Unpgd.

Lindsay

Hansen, Nikolas Forbes. *A History of the Hansen and Lindsay Families in America, Our Danish and Scotch Heritage*. Indianapolis, IN: Author, 1995. 2 vols.
Ziegel, Ruth Turner. *Julius Christy of Virginia and Kentucky, 1730–1808, and Agatha Barnett Christy, 1740–1820, and Related Families of Barnett, Gibbs, Blackburn, Cave, Glass, Kirtley, Bush, Lindsey, Armstrong, Whaley, Davis, and Day*. Cincinnati, OH: Author, 1995. 92p.

Line

Line, Felix G. *The Line Families of East Tennessee*. 2nd. ed. Author, 1995. 250p.

Lipe

McCamon, Jessie Ruddle. *Henry Lipe Family, a Working Draft for Sharing Information*. Wichita, KS: Author, 1995. 51p.

Litton

Lytton, Eugene. *The Ancestry and Progeny of Aker E. Litton, the Final Chapter*. Copperhill, TN: Author, 1995. Unpgd.

Litzenberg

Litzenberg, Homer Laurence. *Litzenberger and Litzenberg, Origins of the Names and the Families*. Author, 1995. 1.007p.

Litzler

Litzler, Andrew August. *The Litzler Journal: The Ancestry and Descendants of John and Sarah Elizabeth Miller Litzler, a Family History*. Fort Worth, TX: Author, 1995. 264p.

Litzy

Wagner, Betty Marie Daley. *The Schneider Genealogy and Related Families, Ancestors and Descendants of Carl Rudolph Schneider and Elizabeth Lena Bahler, Later Spelled Beller, John G. Bahler (Beller) and Anna Elisabeth Schneider, Samuel Bahler (Beller) and Elisabeth Litzy of Uetendorf, Canton Berne, Switzerland and Green County, Wisconsin, 1765–1995*. Milford, OH: Author, 1995. 201p.

Livingston

Davis, Howland. *A Livingston Genealogical Register*. Rhinebeck, NY: Kinship, 1995. Unpgd.

Lloyd

Lloyd, Richard Douglas. *Pride, Prejudice and Politics, a History of the Lloyd Family in Wales, Pennsylvania and Ontario*. Rev. ed. Toronto: Author, 1995. 3 vols.

Stene, Charles Sherwin. *The Stene Family, Includes Rohn, Anderson, Bothwell, Davenport, Lloyd*. Decorah, IA: Anundsen Pub. Co., 1995. 385p.

Lockhart

Barron, William P. *The Family History of Belva Nevada Woolery, Wife of Bill Schamel and Wyatt McMillan and Her Descendants: With Notes on Related Families Brown, Lockhart, Schaeffer, Wiesman, Williams*. Fairborn, OH: Heritage Family Publications, 1995. Unpgd.

Locklair

Brown, Gerald Douglas. *A Genealogy of a Locklair Family, Mainly of the Old Sumter District of South Carolina, Present Day Sumter and Lee Counties*. Hemingway, SC: Three Rivers Historical Society, 1995. 102p.

Lockridge

Walters, Robert Benjamin. *Descendants of James and William Lockridge, Pioneer Brothers of Early Augusta County, Virginia*. Cary, NC: Author, 1995. 561p.

Logan

Chabot, Diana. *The Logans of Portsea*. Hove, England: Hemphill Pubns., 1995. 39p.

Logsdon

Carson, Betty Jewell Durbin. *The Durbin and Logsdon Genealogy with Related Families, 1626-1994*. Rev. ed. Bowie, MD: Heritage Books, 1995. 2 vols.

Logues

Neathery, Milton White. *Logues of Marshall County, Tennessee*. Athens, GA: Georgia Southern Press, 1995. 79p.

Lomax

Lomax, John Benjamin. *Thomas Lomax and His Descendants*. Menlo Park, CA: Author, 1995. 178p.

White, Mary Hamilton. *William Lomax and His Descendants*. Author, 1995. 452p.

London

Vandlen, Geraldine Williams London. *Pifer-Schlosser Ancestry of Geraldine Williams Vandlen, Ancestry of the Londons of Lakeview, Michigan*. Author, 1995. 190p.

Lonergan

Lonergan, James Barry. *The Lonergan Family Saga, the Story of Six Generations of the Lonergan Family*. NY: Author, 1995. Unpgd.

Paulochik, Paul M. *Roots and Branches, Paulochik, Gosemeyer, Yanik, Lonergan, and Related Families*. O'Fallon, IL: Author, 1995. 489p.

Long

David, Johanna Josey. *From Coosawhatchie to Liberty, the Descendants of Reverend James Smart and Levi Long*. Knoxville, TN: Tennessee Valley Pub., 1995. 373p.

Long, Michael G. *One of the Lang Families from Germany to the United States*. Frankfort, KY: Author, 1995. 29p.

Smith, Robert Lee. *Ancestors of Thelma Margaret Gander*. Alexandria, VA: Author, 1995. 65p.

Winkler, Margaret Thompson. *The Long Tree and Others: Longs, Davises, Thompsons, Cratins and Slatons*. Montgomery, AL: Uchee Pub., 1995. 347p.

Longley

Johnston, Anne Plummer. *The Plummer Lineage of America*. Reston, VA: M. L. Tomaselli, 1995. 56p.

Loppentien

Secrist, C. Robert. *Husens, Iowa and Points West, Descendants of Hinrich Husen and Lena Loppentien/Loptien of Scott County, Iowa*. Battle Creek, MI: Progeny Family History Services, 1995. 116p.

Loucks

Restad, Elaine Loucks. *The Adam and Jane Loucks Family, Our Iowa Pioneers*. Author, 1995. 34p.

Louviere

Broussard, Earl. *Our Ancestors, Gone But Not Forgotten*. Author, 1995. 204p.

Love

Johnston, Anne Plummer. *The Plummer Lineage of America*. Reston, VA: M. L. Tomaselli, 1995. 56p.

The Love Families, Robert and Jane of Maryland and Robert and Keziah of Ohio. Lancaster, OH: Author, 1995. 148p.

Lovell

McKee, Ruth Vernette. *The Known Ancestry of Rev. Isaac Babbitt, 1757–1833, Including Cooper, Crane, Ford, Lovell, Morse, Pierce, Tarne, Tisdale, Walker and Whitman Families.* Minneapolis, MN: Author, 1995. 42p.

Lowdermilk

Blankenship, Juanita. *History of the Lowdermilk Family, the Name of Lautermilche.* Mt. Vernon, IN: Windmill Pub., 1995. 398p.

———. *Supplement to the Lowdermilk Family.* Author, 1995. Unpgd.

Lowell

Gower, Janice D. *Tallman Bradbury Lowell, 1805–1870, and His Descendants.* Raymond, ME: Author, 1995. 132p.

Lubenow

Beling, Willard A. *Family History, Our Beling and Worner Roots.* Woodland Hills, CA: Author, 1995. Unpgd.

Lucas

Genealogy of the Descendants of Steven Lucas, 1794–1995, for Nine Generations. 5th. ed. Michigan, 1995. 192p.

Luck

Harts, Stanley Harold. *The Hancock, Luther, and Luck Family Directory.* Wilmington, NC: Author, 1995. 568p.

Ray, Maxine. *Maxine's and Bob's Genealogy of William Stamey Luck, Sr. of North Carolina, 1889–1995.* Columbia, SC: R. W. Streeter, 1995. 32p.

Ludovissy

Putzier, Berdina Ludovissy. *The Ludovissy Family from Clemency, Capellen, Luxembourg to Clayton County, Iowa, United States of America.* Knoxville, TN: Author, 1995. 161p.

Lujan

Lujan, Ernesto Gilberto. *Lujan Family History, The Descendants of Francisco Lujan (Serrano), Juana Trujillo, Charles Asa Williams (Starkweather), Francisca Guillerma Lefebre, Manuel Lefebre Teodora Lopez, Jose Ignacio Pacheco, Maria Severiana Montano, c.1700–1995.* Salt Lake City, UT: Publishers Press, 1995. 287p.

Maes, Arthur F. *Following in the Footsteps of Our Ancestors From "Santa Fe to Maes Creek".* Colorado Springs, CO: Author, 1995. 157p.

Luke

Reamer, Kathleen R. *Descendants of John Reamer and Margaret Schermerhorn, 1758–1995.* Imlay City, MI: Author, 1995. 246p.

Lumière

Lumière, l'Album de Famille. Lyon, France: Archives Municipales, 1995. 162p.

Lush

Lush, Gordon John. *Lush of Hazelbury Bryan*. Ferndown, England: Author, 1995. 87p.

Lusk

Fleetwood, Chester Leroy. *William and Charity (Runyon) Lusk Family, an Auglaize County, Ohio, Pioneer*. Fort Wayne, IN: Author, 1995. 13p.

Luther

Harts, Stanley Harold. *The Hancock, Luther, and Luck Family Directory*. Wilmington, NC: Author, 1995. 568p.

Lykes

Likes, William C. *Connections to the Likes Family, 1790–1994*. Denver, CO: Author, 1995. 136p.

———. *The Lykes Family, 1790 to 1994, Supplement 1995*. Denver, CO: Author, 1995. Unpgd.

Lyle

Waldroop, John Lyle. *Samuel Lyle of Jefferson County, Tennessee*. Author, 1995. Unpgd.

Lynn

Rabold, Mary Moltenberry. *Motley, Willoughby and Lynn Families of Virginia, North Carolina and Kentucky*. Bowling Green, KY: Author, 1995. 250p.

Lyons

Huber, Joan M. *Gone But Not Forgotten, a Book of Remembrance of Charles Roy Lyons and His Ancestors*. 2nd. ed. Fort Wayne, IN: Author, 1995. Unpgd.

– M

Mabie

Griffiths, George R. *Early Settlers in New York and New Jersey, Banta Family, Benson Family, Staats Family, Mabie Family*. Chandler, AZ: Author, 1995. 21p.

Mabry

Tyson, Martha H. *William Spark Mabry, His Life, His Home, His Ancestors*. Houston, TX: Author, 1995. 106p.

McAffee

Ralston, Harold Alan. *Our Ralston Families: Including Ralston, McAffee, Cross, McMichael, Hanna, and Others*. Rev. Racine, WI: Author, 1995. 134p.

McBride

D'Arezzo, Catherine McBride. *Recollections about the McBride Family*. Austin, TX: Author, 1995. 39p.

McCain

McKeehan, Wallace Clark. *The McKeehan Story*. Fort Worth, TX: Author, 1995. 42p.

Maynard, Lawrence W. *Jane McCain of Shelby County, Alabama, and Her Known Descendants*. Fort Worth, TX: Author, 1995. 267p.

McCann

Moore, Phillip James. *Up and Down Our Family Tree*. Utica, KY: McDowell Pub., 1995. 201p.

Scott, Margaret Scott. *Genealogical Portrait of Joseph Carr and Barbara Gastor Beverett, the Carr Descendants of Duplin County, NC*. Warsaw, NC: Author, 1995. 418p.

McCants

McCants, Beaufort Theron. *A Traditional McCants Family History, 1590–1988*. Hemingway, SC: Three Rivers Historical Society, 1995. 291p.

McCarty

Hauk, Carol A. *Descendants of Dennis McCarty of Virginia*. Anderson, IN: Hauk Data Services, 1995. 54p.

McClard

Peters, James Robert. *McClard and Related Families, 1767–1995*. 5th ed. DeSoto, MO: Author, 1995. 638p.

McClarin

Koickler, Eloyce Hubbard. *Hiestand, Hestand, Hastings*. Helena, MT: Author, 1995. 127p.

McClelland

These are the Larsens, Brief Histories of the Larsen, Kanouse, Glenn, McClelland and McMeans Families. Loveland, CO: Author, 1995. 32p.

McClinchey

Peterson, Marion Plath. *Peck, McClinchey, Rouatt Saga*. Decorah, IA: Anundsen Pub. Co., 1995. Unpgd.

McCollum

Buntin, Robert McCollum. *Out of the Past: Buntin and McCollum Ancestors*. Baltimore, MD: Gateway Press, 1995. 302p.

McCollum, J. Kinloch. *The Family of Peter McCollum of Camden, Arkansas*. Orange Park, FL: Author, 1995. 31p.

McConnell

Perry, Max. *Descendants of John Workman, Captain James Hanna and Captain John E. McConnell of York County, South Carolina*. Greenville, SC: A Press, 1995. 161p.

McCoy

Bartram, Chester E. *The George Washington McCoy Family of Mason County, West Virginia, Prominent Related Families Edington, Ferrell, Hoschar, Jividen, King, Sayre, Strait.* Knoxville, TN: Author, 1995. 187p.

McCracken

Ronemous, Hulda Williamson. *Rob and Joe, McCracken and Williamson Ancestors in Eighteenth Century South Carolina.* Baltimore, MD: Gateway Press, 1995. 211p.

McCreary

Hollcroft, Donald. *Bible Records and Group Sheets of James McCreary m. Mary Doughty.* Morgantown, IN: Author, 1995. 54p.

McCubbin

Bostic, Paul Eugene. *Bruce, Maupin, Carr and Some Related Families Including Ballard, Hearn, Ayres, McCubbin, Cloud, Lane, Eveland (Elfland), Graves, Sharp and Willis.* Clinton, TN: Author, 1995. 391p.

McCullough

Anderson, Jerome E. *The American Ancestry of David G. McCullough.* Boston, MA: New England Historic Genealogical Society, 1995. 114p.

Derbes, Marie McCullough. *David Shields McCullough and Anna Jane Smith, Their Ancestors and Descendants.* Covington, LA: Author, 1995. Unpgd.

McCurdy

McCurdy, Mary Ellen Clark. *A Selected History of the McCurdy Family, 1920–1995.* Author, 1995. 86p.

McDonald

Haynes, John Lanier. *Haynes-McDonald Heritage Quest.* Anchorage, AK: Author, 1995. 514p.

Litke, Ruth McDonald. *Goderich to Gardner, the McDonald Family and Other Cass County Pioneers.* St. Cloud, MN: Author, 1995. 222p.

MacDonald, Darby. *The Genealogy of Clan Donald, Addendum, Supplement No. 1.* Brockville, Ontario: MacDonald Research Centre, 1995. 146p.

———. *The Genealogy of Clan Donald, Addendum, Supplement No. 2.* Brockville, Ontario: MacDonald Research Centre, 1995. 50p.

———. *The Genealogy of Clan Donald, Addendum, Supplement No. 3.* Brockville, Ontario: MacDonald Research Centre, 1995. 239p.

MacDonald, Norman H. *The Clan Ranald of Knoydart and Glengarry, a History of the MacDonalds or MacDonells of Glengarry.* 2nd. ed. Edinburgh: N. H. MacDonald, 1995. 195p.

McDonnell

McDonnell, Frank Edward. *The McDonnell Family History, an Unfinished Journey.* Lansdale, PA: Author, 1995. 329p.

McDowell

Adams, Margaret Bickel. *Family Connections along the Blue Ridge, the Ancestry and Close Descendants of Margaret Erwin McDowell and James Thomas Walton.* Alexander, NC: World Comm, 1995. 102p.

Murphy, Nancy McDowell. *McDowells of Ligonier Valley.* Roswell, GA: Author, 1995. 202p.

McElmurray

Rouse, Norma Uldine Smith. *The Descendants of James McElmurray, through Son Patrick, 1745–1818.* Albany, GA: Author, 1995. 161p.

McElwee

Parr, Richard Eugene. *Genealogy of Richard Eugene Parr.* Morgan Hill, CA: Author, 1995. 79p.

McEwan

Finegan, James A. *History and Legends of Clan MacLachlan.* Research Triangle Park, NC: Clan MacLachlan Assn., 1995. 128p.

McFarland

Koickler, Eloyce Hubbard. *Hiestand, Hestand, Hastings.* Helena, MT: Author, 1995. 127p.

Mallard, Shirley Jones. *Keeping Up with the Joneses, a Book about the Rafe Jones Family of Granville, North Carolina.* Chapel Hill, NC: Author, 1995. 244p.

McGainey

Allen, Patricia Remmell. *The Remmell and Allen Families of New Castle County, Delaware.* Horsham, PA: Author, 1995. 71p.

McGinn

McGinn, Ann Winston. *A McGinn McCorkle Family History, 1796–1995: With Related Families, Crockett, Dabney, Egnatoff, Fontaine, Freirson, Gillespie, Huddart, Kennemore, O'Donnell, Patton, Ring, Sheppard, Winston, and Others.* Spring Hill, FL: Author, 1995. 313p.

McGrath

McGrath, John H. *McGrath History, Late 1700s to Present.* Moline, IL: Author, 1995. Unpgd.

McHenry

Moore, Freddie Gene. *My Virginia Ancestors and Their Descendants in the Families, Burdett, Alexander, Anderson, King, Boone, Welsh, McHenry, Cornwell, Alford, Coleman, Dixon, Morgan, Jarman, Maugridge.* Author, 1995. 46p.

McInerny

McInerny, Raymond T., Sr. *A McInerny Family in the Americas since the 1860s.* New Berlin, WI: Author, 1995. 92p.

Mack

Schmidt, Mildred H. *I Remember Grandfather, the Story of Eugene Mack*. Leonard, MI: BMS
    Pub. Co., 1995. Unpgd.

McKay

Swan, Judy Gail. *The Alasdair McKay Family, from Scots to Canadians*. Calgary, Alberta:
    Prairie House Books, 1995. 179p.

McKeehan

McKeehan, Wallace Clark. *The McKeehan Story*. Fort Worth, TX: Author, 1995. 42p.

McKenney

McKenney, Ora Herbert. *A Story of Many Maine McKenney Families*. New Smyrna Beach,
    FL: Author, 1995. 539p.

McKenzie

Brown, Gerald Douglas. *Descendants of Daniel and Rebecca McKenzie, Old Williamsburg,
    Sumter Districts of South Caroliana*. Hemingway, SC: Three Rivers Historical Society,
    1995. 116p.
McKenzie, Gerald Wildrey. *The Genealogy and Family History of William Alexander McKenzie
    from Riviere du Loup*. Wilmington, NC: Author, 1995. Unpgd.
Pelcher, Barbara Jane Tillotson. *Pioneers, Crain, Manning, McKenzie, Stanley and Allied Fami-
    lies*. San Bernardino, CA: Author, 1995. 186p.

McKinney

Jones, Daniel Wilbur. *Genealogical Memoranda of Daniel Rufus Cable and Georgiana
    McKinney Cable*. Cary, NC: Author, 1995. 183p.
McKenney, Ora Herbert. *A Story of Many Maine McKenney Families*. New Smyrna Beach,
    FL: Author, 1995. 539p.

McLaughlin

Finegan, James A. *History and Legends of Clan MacLachlan*. Research Triangle Park, NC:
    Clan MacLachlan Assn., 1995. 128p.
McCurley, James B. *McLaughlin of Maryland (1847)*. Baltimore, MD: Author, 1995. Unpgd.

MacLeod

McLeod, Jean. *The 'Dunosdale' Story*. London: Milieu Press, 1995. 32p.

McMakin

Brunson, Nolen L. *Barnett-McMakin Union, Ancestors Collateral Relatives and Descendants
    of John James Barnett and Harriet (Hattie) McMakin*. South Carolina: Author, 1995. 278p.

McManus

Allen, Patricia Remmell. *The Remmell and Allen Families of New Castle County, Delaware*.
    Horsham, PA: Author, 1995. 71p.

McMaster

Sprott, Nelle McMaster. *The Family History of Hugh Buchanan McMaster (1820–1873) and Elizabeth Boatwright Fleming McMaster (1825–1897), Their Forebears and Their Descendants.* Winnsboro, SC: Author, 1995. 80p.

McMeans

These are the Larsens, Brief Histories of the Larsen, Kanouse, Glenn, McClelland and McMeans Families. Loveland, CO: Author, 1995. 32p.

McMichael

Kapas, Margery Ann. *Spanning the Ocean.* New Westminster, BC: Author, 1995. Unpgd.
Ralston, Harold Alan. *Our Ralston Families: Including Ralston, McAffee, Cross, McMichael, Hanna, and Others.* Rev. Racine, WI: Author, 1995. 134p.

McMillan

Barron, William P. *The Family History of Belva Nevada Woolery, Wife of Bill Schamel and Wyatt McMillan and Her Descendants: With Notes on Related Families Brown, Lockhart, Schaeffer, Wiesman, Williams.* Fairborn, OH: Heritage Family Publications, 1995. Unpgd.
Meigs, Peter Sanford. *Our Meigs and Smith Ancestors, Including the Clarke, Clifford, Eldredge, Fellows, Howe, MacMillan, Mann, Remington, Rice, Robinson, Scadgel, Skillings, and Thing Families.* Danville, NH: Author, 1995. Unpgd.

McMillen

Darnel, Michael R. *Descendants of John Alfred McMillen and Susan Melvina Stone.* Granger, IN: Author, 1995. 16p.
Liston, Lois Jane Breakiron. *The Breakiron Family History Also Including the Bastian, Brecheisen, Casey, Dusenberry, Garlow, Hutchinson, Johnson, McMillen, Miller, Morris, Roderick and Other Families.* Wyandotte, OK: Gregath Pub. Co., 1995. 620p.

McMurray

Hamilton, Fred. *The Descendants and Some Ancestors of James Meriwether and Julia Calhoun Hamilton, 1855–1936, 1853–1939.* Ruston, LA: Author, 1995. 104p.

McNamee

McNamee, Grover Cleveland. *The Descendants of Newa Hugh McNamee Who Was Born in Wales, 1740, and Who Settled at Hagerstown, Washington County, Maryland, and Many of Whose Descendants Were Early Settlers of Fairfield County, Ohio.* Lancaster, OH: Author, 1995. Unpgd.

McNatt

McCornack, John C. *The McNatt Families of America.* 12th. ed. Peoria, IL: Author, 1995. Unpgd.

McNeal

Andrus, Gloria Ruth Goodman. *To Hannah and Will with Love, a History of Hannah McNeil and William Ezra Goodman.* Rexburg, ID: Author, 1995. 700p.

Hamilton, Fred. *The Descendants and Some Ancestors of James Meriwether and Julia Calhoun Hamilton, 1855–1936, 1853–1939.* Ruston, LA: Author, 1995. 104p.

McNeely

Cole, Mary. *The Bunyard Family Research and Allied Families, Alley, Fitzwater, Foster, Hughes, Jones, Ledlow, McNeely, Rose.* Kentfield, CA: Author, 1995. 151p.

McNutt

Nichols, Barbara. *Our Nichols Family History.* Baltimore, MD: Gateway Press, 1995. 162p.

Macon

Johnston, Anne Plummer. *The Plummer Lineage of America.* Reston, VA: M. L. Tomaselli, 1995. 56p.

McPherson

Norcross, Gertrude. *Our McPherson Family History, Pieces of the Past.* San Diego, CA: Author, 1995. 62p.

Trimble, David B. *McPherson of Virginia and North Carolina.* Austin, TX: Author, 1995. 393p.

McQuown

McQuown Family, Three Hundred Years in America, New Jersey, Pennsylvania, New York, Maryland, Virginia, Kentucky, Texas, California. 1995. Unpgd.

McRoberts

McAnna, James. *The McRoberts.* Shotts, England: Author, 1995. 32p.

McRobie

McRobie, Raymond Irvin. *The McRobie, McCrobie, Cuppett, Peck, Hostetler, Weimer, Smith, Wilt and Merrill Families of Garrett County.* Fairfax, VA: Author, 1995. 471p.

McVea

Chambliss, Bena McVea. *The Arch of the Rainbow, Letters of Charles and Lucy McVea, 1866-1875.* Author, 1995. 142p.

Madison

Hauk, Carol A. *Descendants of Isaac Madison of Virginia.* 2nd. ed. Anderson, IN: Hauk Data Services, 1995. 105p.

———. *Descendants of James Taylor of Virginia, (Ancestor of Presidents Taylor and Madison).* 9th. ed. Anderson, IN: Hauk Data Services, 1995. 328p.

———. *Descendants of Thomas Gaines of Virginia, Ancestor of President James Madison and USA Generals Gaines, Patton and Marshall.* Anderson, IN: Hauk Data Services, 1995. 284p.

Madson

Madson, Richard C. *Gjerpen to Gjerpen, the Madson Families Who Came to Wisconsin, Also Mason, Larson, Pedersen, Holm, Halvorson, Simonsen, and Hoen Families.* Mesa, AZ: Author, 1995. 284p.

Maechtle

Bellin, Loretta M. *The Family of Jacob Keller and Rosina Cathrina Maechtle and Sophia Meins, 1700–1994*. Oshkosh, WI: Author, 1995. 237p.

Maes

Maes, Arthur F. *Following in the Footsteps of our Ancestors from "Santa Fe to Maes Creek"*. Colorado Springs, CO: Author, 1995. 157p.

Maggart

Smith, Robert Lee. *Ancestors of Thelma Margaret Gander*. Alexandria, VA: Author, 1995. 65p.

Magie

A Genealogical Record of the Magie Family. Villa Rica, CA: Author, 1995. 135p.

Maginis

Whitmore, Robert Devore. *Whitmore Family Genealogy*. Steubenville, OH: Public Library of Steubenville and Jefferson County, 1995. 14p.

Main

Childress, Nancy. *The Main Tree II, the Descendants of John Main of North Yarmouth, Maine, Sometimes Called Casco Bay, on the West Side of the Wescustogo River*. 2nd. ed. Phoenix, AZ: Author, 1995. 640p.

Major

Hendricks, Herbert D. *Major, Majors, Mager, Majers, Maoir Family Information*. Poquoson, VA: Author, 1995. Unpgd.

Mallard

Scott, Margaret Scott. *Genealogical Portrait of Joseph Carr and Barbara Gastor Beverett, the Carr Descendants of Duplin County, NC*. Warsaw, NC: Author, 1995. 418p.

Malone

Westfall, Dawn Watts. *Spencer, Brizendine, Malone, Families of Trigg County, Kentucky*. High Springs, FL: Author, 1995. 26p.

Malpass

Galmore, Alice Ann. *William Ellis Malpass (Alice Ann Round) Family, Book II*. Detroit, MI: Author, 1995. 42p.

Mann

Carter, Park W. *A History of Some Park Families in Jefferson County, Indiana, and Allied Families of Anderson, Mann, Gilchrist and Others*. Eureka, KS: Author, 1995. Unpgd.

Mann, Marion. *The Kigh, Mann, Reagin, and Sykes Families, Including the Branch, Brown, Dean, Fort, Gerran, Leake, Marquis, Moses, Oakes, Powell, Reid, Trammell, Walk, Wilkey, Wingfield, and Woods Families, a Genealogy and Family History*. Baltimore, MD: Gateway Press, 1995. 218p.

Meigs, Peter Sanford. *Our Meigs and Smith Ancestors, Including the Clarke, Clifford, Eldredge, Fellows, Howe, MacMillan, Mann, Remington, Rice, Robinson, Scadgel, Skillings, and Thing Families.* Danville, NH: Author, 1995. Unpgd.

Manning

Hamilton, William R. *Hamilton, James and Manning, William Genealogies, with Emphasis on the Branch of Each Family Which Lived North of Ann Arbor, Michigan.* Saline, MI: Author, 1995. 30p.

Manrow

Younglove, James N. *The Descendants of Samuel and Margaret Younglove.* Houston, TX: Author, 1995. 200p.

Manuel

Greene, Bob. *Maine Roots, the Manuel, Mathews, Ruby Family.* Brooklyn, NY: Family Affair Production, 1995. 84p.

Manzer

Dennison, Allan. *In Service of His Country: a Brief History and Partial List of Descendants of Private Michael Dennison, First Battalion, and Private John Manzer, Third Battalion, General Oliver Delancey's Brigade of Loyalists.* Acton, MA: Author, 1995. Unpgd.

Marchant

Rentmeester, Jeanne. *Our Marchant Relatives.* Wisconsin: Author, 1995. 377p.

Marcus

Lewallen, Blanche Sims. *Sims-Marcus-Lawson Connections.* Toccoa, GA: Author, 1995. Unpgd.

Marker

Grillot, Nellie Marker. *A Genealogy of the Descendants of Peter Marker (1797–1881) and Mary Polly Warrenfeltz (1809–1879) of Frederick County, Maryland.* Port Tobacco, MD: S. M. Andrusko, 1995. 102p.

Markley

Smith, Ruth Wiley. *Descendants of John Jacob Markley, Who Came to Hamilton County, Ohio, in 1804.* Oxford, OH: Author, 1995. 128p.

Marks

Biggar, Harold Arthur. *The Biggar Families of Greenwich, Connecticut, and County Tyrone, North Ireland.* Stamford, CT: Author, 1995. unpgd.

Marois

Foster, Bernice Sevigny. *The Marois Family.* Baltimore, MD: Gateway Press, 1995. 149p.

Maroney

Partin, Sherita Kae. *The Descendants of Nancy Partin and Charles King.* Nacogdoches, TX: Partin Publications, 1995. Unpgd.

Marquis

Mann, Marion. *The Kigh, Mann, Reagin, and Sykes Families, Including the Branch, Brown, Dean, Fort, Gerran, Leake, Marquis, Moses, Oakes, Powell, Reid, Trammell, Walk, Wilkey, Wingfield, and Woods Families, a Genealogy and Family History*. Baltimore, MD: Gateway Press, 1995. 218p.

Marr

Bodishbaugh, Sue W. *The Jacob, Philipp, and Adam Erion Family Letters*. Tampa, FL: Author, 1995. Unpgd.

Descendants of Ransom T. Marr. 1995. 58p.

Marsh

Marsh, Louise Dollison. *Our Marsh Family in America, 1635–1995*. Madison, WI: Author, 1995. 297p.

Marsh, Virginia Peterman. *The Marsh Family, Cape Fear to Columbia*. Georgetown, FL: Author, 1995. 63p.

Marshall

Hauk, Carol A. *Descendants of Anthony Steptoe of Virginia*. Anderson, IN: Hauk Data Services, 1995. 147p.

———. *Descendants of Augustine Warner of Virginia*. Anderson, IN: Hauk Data Services, 1995. 461p.

———. *Descendants of Francis Willis of Virginia*. Anderson, IN: Hauk Data Services, 1995. 154p.

———. *Descendants of George Nicholas of Virginia*. Anderson, IN: Hauk Data Services, 1995. 130p.

———. *Descendants of George Reade of Virginia*. Anderson, IN: Hauk Data Services, 1995. 393p.

———. *Descendants of Henry Pickett of Virginia*. 5th. ed. Anderson, IN: Hauk Data Services, 1995. 97p.

———. *Descendants of John Marshall of Virginia*. 2nd. ed. Anderson, IN: Hauk Data Services, 1995. 118p.

———. *Descendants of John Norton of Virginia*. 2nd. ed. Anderson, IN: Hauk Data Services, 1995. 202p.

———. *Descendants of Lewis Burwell of Virginia*. Anderson, IN: Hauk Data Services, 1995. 395p.

———. *Descendants of Mordecai Cooke of Virginia*. 3rd. ed. Anderson, IN: Hauk Data Services, 1995. 309p.

———. *Descendants of Richard Ambler of Virginia*. Anderson, IN: Hauk Data Services, 1995. 96p.

———. *Descendants of Thomas Gaines of Virginia, Ancestor of President James Madison and USA Generals Gaines, Patton and Marshall*. Anderson, IN: Hauk Data Services, 1995. 284p.

Marshall, Frank W. *The History of the Marshalls and Allied Family in the USA, 1670–1995*. Seattle, WA: Author, 1995. Unpgd.

Martell

Martell, John Drewett. *A Martell Family History*. Ramsgate, Kent, England: Martell Press, 1995. 159p.

Martin

Barnes, Rufus Edward. *A History of Our Barns/Barnes and Martin Families*. Mesa, AZ: F. C. Spidel, 1995. 404p.

Kaufman, Mary Arnold. *Martin-Arnold and Allied Families, Lanier, Bailey, Swan, Sandidge, Gholston, Morgan, and Born, Migration from Virginia to Tennessee, Georgia, Alabama and Arkansas*. Knoxville, TN: Tennessee Valley Pub., 1995. 212p.

Maes, Arthur F. *Following in the Footsteps of Our Ancestors from "Santa Fe to Maes Creek"*. Colorado Springs, CO: Author, 1995. 157p.

Martin, William Allan. *A Martin Genealogy Tied to the History of Germanna, Virginia*. Bowie, MD: Heritage Books, 1995. 382p.

Snedeker, Lenora A. *Memories at Willowbrook: A History of the Throop-Martin Families of Auburn, New York*. Oxford, NY: Author, 1995. Unpgd.

Martinez

Moraga-Martinez Reunion, March 18–19, 1995, Phoenix-Tempe. 1995. 82p.

Martins

Eaton, Mildred E. *The Descendants of Anselmo Silveira Baptista and His Wife Anna Martins (Emigrants from the Azore Islands)*. Seattle, WA: Author, 1995. 36p.

Martinsen

Bellin, Loretta M. *The Family of Johan Christian Friedrich Blumenberg and Helene Dorothea Matthiansen-Martinsen, 1780–1994*. Oshkosh, WI: Author, 1995. 228p.

Marye

Eberhart, Edith Whitcraft. *The Maryes of Virginia, 1730–1985, 1995 Supplement*. Baltimore, MD: Gateway Press, 1995. 132p.

Hauk, Carol A. *Descendants of James Marye of Virginia*. Anderson, IN: Hauk Data Services, 1995. 35p.

Mason

Cottrell, Richard Gary. *The Tyler-Fruhauf Family History, and Genealogical Record of Associated Edwards, Ellis, Helme, Mason, Pritchard, Seymour, Sherrerd, and Whiting Families*. Parma, MI: Author, 1995. 2 vols.

Madson, Richard C. *Gjerpen to Gjerpen, the Madson Families Who Came to Wisconsin, Also Mason, Larson, Pedersen, Holm, Halvorson, Simonsen, and Hoen Families*. Mesa, AZ: Author, 1995. 284p.

White, Madalene Bowler. *Descendants of Immigrants, Glendening, Mason, Watson*. Centerville, IN: Author, 1995. 61p.

Massey

Horsman, Barbara Massey. *The Massey Family of Worcester County, Maryland*. Baltimore, MD: Heritage Press, 1995. 594p.

Massey, Martha Couch. *Descendants of Oliver Massey, Perry County, Alabama, 1820*. Demopolis, AL: Author, 1995. 426p.

Mathers

Fehr, Martha Robinson. *Descendants of Gavin Mathers (1785–1869), a Supplement to the Mathers-Nesbit Genealogy by Lura B. Mitchell Emery*. Gulf Breeze, FL: Author, 1995. 288p.

Matheson

Wannamaker, William Whetstone. *Descendants of Donald Matheson of Marlboro County, South Carolina*. Orangeburg, SC: Author, 1995. Unpgd.

Mathias

Reamer, Kathleen R. *Descendants of John Reamer and Margaret Schermerhorn, 1758–1995*. Imlay City, MI: Author, 1995. 246p.

Matthews

Byard, Richard B. *O'Daniel, Matthews, Mitchem, Helms and Their Relatives in Maryland, Kentucky, Indiana, Alabama and Other States*. Ellicott City, MD: Author, 1995. 88p.

Corbari, Shirley Kirkland Guio. *The Kirkland Mathews Family*. Campbell, CA: Author, 1995. 796p.

Greene, Bob. *Maine Roots, the Manuel, Mathews, Ruby Family*. Brooklyn, NY: Family Affair Production, 1995. 84p.

Matthew, Ralph. *A History of the Matthew Family*. Moline, IL: Dean Matthew Daniels, 1995. Unpgd.

Scarborough, Eleazer Pate. *A Genealogy of the South Carolina Coward-Cowart Family*. Hemingway, SC: Three Rivers Historical Society, 1995. Unpgd.

Matthiansen

Bellin, Loretta M. *The Family of Johan Christian Friedrich Blumenberg and Helene Dorothea Matthiansen-Martinsen, 1780–1994*. Oshkosh, WI: Author, 1995. 228p.

Mattison

Ancestors and Descendants of William Whitaker Smith, 1860–1944, and Florence Ellen Sullivan, 1875–1926, of Anderson and Greenville Counties, South Carolina. Spartanburg, SC: Reprint Co., 1995. 146p.

Mauck

Smith, Robert Lee. *Ancestors of Thelma Margaret Gander*. Alexandria, VA: Author, 1995. 65p.

Mauldin

Paget, James Suddath. *Ancestors and Descendants of Mary Elise Mauldin Paget and Eilleen Reed Mauldin Mattison*. Greer, SC: Author, 1995. 248p.

Maupin

Bostic, Paul Eugene. *Bruce, Maupin, Carr and Some Related Families Including Ballard, Hearn, Ayres, McCubbin, Cloud, Lane, Eveland (Elfland), Graves, Sharp and Willis*. Clinton, TN: Author, 1995. 391p.

Maxson

Maxson, Gayle. *Our Maxson Heritage*. Denton, TX: Author, 1995. 43p.

Maxwell

Best Strange, Norma. *Descendants of Samuel Maxwell, Sr. and Elizabeth Work*. Chilhowee,
    MO: Author, 1995. 61p.

May

Curl, Clarence Lee. *Curl, May et al., a Compilation of Family Records*. El Paso, TX: High
    Desert Pub., Co., 1995. 271p.

Jones, Daniel Wilbur. *Genealogical Memoranda of Daniel Rufus Cable and Georgiana
    McKinney Cable*. Cary, NC: Author, 1995. 183p.

McKee, Ruth Vernette. *The Known Ancestry of Prudence May, Daughter of Ezra May and
    Margaret Lyon, and Wife of Isaac Babbitt*. Minneapolis, MN: Author, 1995. 83p.

May, John Russell. *Charles May Family History and Genealogy*. Fort Wayne, IN: Author,
    1995. Unpgd.

———. *Kraft May Family, History and Genealogy*. Fort Wayne, IN: Author, 1995. Unpgd.

Snow, Donald R. *The Descendants of David May of Ashe County, North Carolina*. Charleston,
    SC: Author, 1995. Unpgd.

Mayberry

Camp, Helen Moore. *Forging Our Families, Moore, Edmonds and Mayberry Connection*.
    Mooresville, NC: J. M. Leonard, 1995. 222p.

Mayfield

Grubbs, Nancy Carole Early. *The Descendants of James and Elizabeth Joseph Lewis*. Houston,
    TX: Author, 1995. 71p.

Mayrhofen

Saunders, Jo Ann Muenzler. *Christoph Friedrich Munzler and His Descendants*. Austin, TX:
    Author, 1995. 76p.

Mazerolle

Mazerolle, Rodrigue. *Les Mazerolle en Amérique, 1661–1994*. Montreal: Author, 1995. 542p.

Mead

Hauk, Carol A. *Descendants of Andrew Meade of Virginia*. Anderson, IN: Hauk Data Services,
    1995. 81p.

———. *Descendants of Richard Lee of Virginia*. 2nd. ed. Anderson, IN: Hauk Data Services,
    1995. 202p.

———. *Descendants of William Randolph of Virginia*. Anderson, IN: Hauk Data Services,
    1995. 461p.

Mead, John Howard. *The Mead or Meade Family*. Rev. ed. Hampton, VA: Avatar Press, 1995.
    60p.

Mears

Brooks, Shirley A. *Our Family of Many Names: The Ancestors and Descendants of James
    Edward Hancock*. Lake Elsinore, CA: Author, 1995. 155p.

Chamberlain, Merle. *On the Trail of Zebulon Latimer and His Family*. Wilmington, DE: Lower Cape Fear Historical Society, 1995. Unpgd.

Meaut

Lepre, Jerome. *Meaut Family History*. New Orleans, LA: Author, 1995. 274p.

Meeker

Gardiner Jackson, Ann E. *Roots: Gardiner, Ingram, Grimmeissen, Ashpaw, Thiessen, Jackson, Meeker*. Author, 1995. 35p.

Meeks

Moore, Freddie Gene. *My Virginia Ancestors and Their Descendants in the Families, Ratliff, Skidmore, Watson, Hamilton, Wallace, Cahoon, Bowyer, Grimes, Sharp, Meeks*. Author, 1995. 116p.

Meigs

Meigs, Peter Sanford. *Our Meigs and Smith Ancestors, Including the Clarke, Clifford, Eldredge, Fellows, Howe, MacMillan, Mann, Remington, Rice, Robinson, Scadgel, Skillings, and Thing Families*. Danville, NH: Author, 1995. Unpgd.

Meins

Bellin, Loretta M. *The Family of Jacob Keller and Rosina Cathrina Maechtle and Sophia Meins, 1700–1994*. Oshkosh, WI: Author, 1995. 237p.

Meisner

Eggert, Irving John. *Peter Eggert of Mecklenburg and Related Families in America, Best, Bitz, Broekemeier, Hackbarth, Kane, Meisner, Nellis, Schunk, Strenkowski, Voight, Winston*. Decorah, IA: Anundsen Pub. Co., 1995. 224p.

Melgers

Hayes, Edward R. *Margaret Elizabeth Ferrel Hayes and Her Ancestors*. Author, 1995. 200p.

Mellin

McGarvie, Grace. *The Mellin Family Reunion, July 9, 1995*. Plymouth, MN: Author, 1995. 192p.

Mellish

MacDonald, Douglas B. *Thomas Mellish of Prince Edward Island, a Genealogy of Many of His Descendants*. Napean, Ontario: Bayside Pub., 1995. 324p.

Melnick

Margolis, Abby Mindelle. *The Zafran Genealogy, Including the Morozowitz, Melnick, and Kairoch Families*. Daly City, CA: 1995. 75p.

Mendiola

Nelson, Carmen Valls. *Our Family under Seven Flags, an Informal History of the Mendiola and Valls-Armengol Families*. Laredo, TX: Author, 1995. 255p.

Meriwether

Hauk, Carol A. *Descendants of William Thornton of Virginia*. Anderson, IN: Hauk Data Services, 1995. 361p.

Merwin

Buchanan, Merwyn Russell. *The English Ancestry of Miles and Elizabeth (Powell) Merwin*. Blue Bell, PA: Miles (1623–1697) Merwin Association, 1995. 47p.

Mesker

Happel, Anita J. *Genealogies of the Happel Family and the Mesker Family of Evansville, Indiana*. Author, 1995. 32p.

Methot

Methot, Pauline L. *Methot and Related Families*. Manchester, NH: Author, 1995. 2 vols.

Metzger

Hurley, Lucius M. *Thomas Andrew Hurley, His Descendants and the Related Families of Metzger and Stout*. Newton, KS: Author, 1995. 139p.

Mayer, Marion. *History of a Family Dispersed*. Chicago, IL: Author, 1995. 298p.

Meullion

Auzenne, Conrad Andrew. *Auzenne, Donato, Frilot, Lemelle, Meullion, a Genealogical Study of Five Families and Other Allied Families of Southern Louisiana*. Author, 1995. 222p.

Meux

Meux, William L. *A Meux Lineage*. Author, 1995. Unpgd.

Mihindukulasurya

Pranandu, Mihindukulasurya. *Halavata urumaya, Mihindukulasurya rajavamsa kathava*. Kolamba, Sri Lanka: Author, 1995. 186p.

Milam

Douglas, William H. *Douglass, Milam, Guess Family Tree*. Bowling Green, KY: N. G. Hudnall, 1995. 30p.

Miles

Brown, Gerald Douglas. *Descendants of Daniel and Rebecca McKenzie, Old Williamsburg, Sumter Districts of South Carolina*. Hemingway, SC: Three Rivers Historical Society, 1995. 116p.

———. *A Genealogy of a Lee Family, Mainly of Old Williamsburg District, Present Day Florence County, South Carolina*. Hemingway, SC: Three Rivers Historical Society, 1995. 143p.

Miller

Benoit, Julia Ann Crum. *The Millers of Sand Mountain and Allied Families*. Fernandina Beach, FL: Wolfe Pub., 1995. 613p.

Ellingham, Lewis. *The Ancestries of David Miller and Clarissa Moore of Torringford, Connecticut*. San Francisco, CA: Author, 1995. 2 vols.

Graham, Connie Thompson. *Miller Family History*. Fairview Park, OH: Author, 1995. 146p.

Hovemeyer, Eric E. *Miller Genealogy Update*. Author, 1995. 44p.

Liston, Lois Jane Breakiron. *The Breakiron Family History Also Including the Bastian, Brecheisen, Casey, Dusenberry, Garlow, Hutchinson, Johnson, McMillen, Miller, Morris, Roderick and Other Families*. Wyandotte, OK: Gregath Pub. Co., 1995. 620p.

Litzler, Andrew August. *The Litzler Journal: The Ancestry and Descendants of John and Sarah Elizabeth Miller Litzler, a Family History*. Fort Worth, TX: Author, 1995. 264p.

Mast, Eli H. *Family History of Noah J. Miller and Elizabeth Bontrager, 1849–1994*. Baltic, OH: Author, 1995. 286p.

Miller, Mary. *Millers of Feds Creek*. Pikeville, KY: Pikeville College, 1995. 166p.

Perguson, Dee Carl, Jr. *Descendant Families of William Makel Miller and Mary Mitchell Miller of Ohio County, Kentucky, with a Short Biography*. Seattle, WA: Author, 1995. 53p.

Schmucker, Daniel M. *The Descendants of Andrew N. Hochstetler and Elizabeth Lehman: Also Includes the Descendants of Elias A. Miller*. Franklin, KY: Author, 1995. 133p.

Spoden, Muriel Clark. *An American Ancestry of the Clark-Morton and Tyman-Millar-Adams Families*. Kingsport, TN: Spoden Associates, 1995. 547p.

A Treasured Heritage, Ezra J. And Susie (Weaver) Miller Family. Middlebury, IN: The Miller Girls, 1995. 291p.

Whitt, Aileen M. *Miller-Newkirk Family History, Ancestors and Descendants of Ben Miller and Sally (Newkirk) Miller with Related Families*. New Richmond, OH: Author, 1995. 192p.

Yoder, Christian T. *Yoder History, 1700–1970, and Family Record of Abraham A. Yoder and Lydia Miller, 1871–1993*. 1995. 344p.

Yoder, Rebecca Bontrager. *Memories and Family Record of the John D. Miller and Rosina Zehr Family, 1916–1995*. Goshen, IN: Author, 1995. 58p.

Millwee

Millwee, Robert A. *John Wesley Millwee, His Ancestors and Descendants*. Fort Worth, TX: Author, 1995. 169p.

Minor

Hauk, Carol A. *Descendants of Doodes Minor of Virginia*. 2nd. ed. Anderson, IN: Hauk Data Services, 1995. 109p.

———. *Descendants of Robert Taliafero of Virginia*. 6th. ed. Anderson, IN: Hauk Data Services, 1995. 358p.

Miner, John A. *The Ancestral Heritage of Descendants of Thomas Minor, c.1450-c.1700*. Trevett, MA: Thomas Minor Society, 1995. 61p.

Mitchell

Fuller, Donald Mitchell. *Our Family: A Composition Comprised of Histories, Biographical Sketches, Vignettes, Pictures and the Author's Recollections*. Author, 1995. 123p.

Griggs, Kendall. *Levi W. and Sarah E. (Carter) Hopkins, Their Ancestors and Descendants*. Hutchinson, KS: Author, 1995. 198p.

Horne, Ann Mitchell. *Descendants of Jeremiah Mitchell of North Carolina (c.1770-c.1835) and Allied Families*. Decorah, IA: Anundsen Pub. Co., 1995. 427p.

Howe, Jeffrey. *The Block Island Allens*. 1995. 218p.

Mitchell, George Duncan. *Our Kindred Spirits, Some Family Histories*. Ottawa: Author, 1995. Unpgd.

Montgomery, Emma Mitchell. *Mitchell Memories, William Mitchell, Sr., William Mitchell, Jr. and Abigail (Wheeler) Mitchell and Their Descendants 1728–1995*. Dogwood, MO: Dogwood Printing, 1995. 371p.

Perguson, Dee Carl, Jr. *Descendant Families of William Makel Miller and Mary Mitchell Miller of Ohio County, Kentucky, with a Short Biography*. Seattle, WA: Author, 1995. 53p.

Mitchem

Byard, Richard B. *O'Daniel, Matthews, Mitchem, Helms and Their Relatives in Maryland, Kentucky, Indiana, Alabama and Other States*. Ellicott City, MD: Author, 1995. 88p.

Moncure

Hauk, Carol A. *Descendants of Edwin Conway of Virginia, Ancestor of President James Madison*. 4th. ed. Anderson, IN: Hauk Data Services, 1995. 187p.

———. *Descendants of John Moncure of Virginia*. Anderson, IN: Hauk Data Services, 1995. 70p.

———. *Descendants of William Ball of Virginia*. Anderson, IN: Hauk Data Services, 1995. 229p.

Montgomery

Davis, Arnold Isaiah Bell. *The Ancestors and Descendants of Elton Melville Montgomery and Mary Mabel Watson*. Ocala, FL: Author, 1995. 122p.

Monticue

Groff, Clifford. *The Stairs Families of Westmoreland and Somerset Counties of Pennsylvania and Their Ancestors, Steer, Summy, Monticue, Harshberger, Colborn, Tissue, Kreger and Clevenger*. Arnold, MD: Author, 1995. 147p.

Moon

Nimmo, Sylvia. *The Descendants and Ancestors of Milo and Dora (Moon) Russell*. Papillion, NE: Author, 1995. 44p.

Moore

Camp, Helen Moore. *Forging Our Families, Moore, Edmonds and Mayberry Connection*. Mooresville, NC: J.M. Leonard, 1995. 222p.

Ellingham, Lewis. *The Ancestries of David Miller and Clarissa Moore of Torringford, Connecticut*. San Francisco, CA: Author, 1995. 2 vols.

Hauk, Carol A. *Descendants of John Moore of Virginia*. Anderson, IN: Hauk Data Services, 1995. 132p.

Koickler, Eloyce Hubbard. *Hiestand, Hestand, Hastings*. Helena, MT: Author, 1995. 127p.

Linn, Jo White. *Ancestry of Moore/Rowan Families, with Related Lines of Fleming, Renick, Bosley, Green, Girault, Beatty, Reading, Armitage, Ryerson, Rapelje*. New Orleans, LA: Author, 1995. 186p.

McCants, Beaufort Theron. *A Traditional McCants Family History, 1590–1988*. Hemingway, SC: Three Rivers Historical Society, 1995. 291p.

Moor, Ted E. *Moor and Moore*. Beaumont, TX: Author, 1995. 125p.

Moore, Freddie Gene. *The Descendants of Thomas Moore, Sr. of Suffolk County, England and the Related Families, Youngs, Landon, Spencer, French, Norris, Simmons, Ratliff, Slaughter*. Author, 1995. Unpgd.

Moore, Herman J. *The Moores of Hopkins County, Kentucky: Two Hundred Years of Family History*. Louisville, KY: Author, 1995. 27p.

———. *The Moores of Hopkins County, Kentucky: A Supplement*. Louisville, KY: Author, 1995. 14p.

Moore, Mack Arthur. *Descendants of John Moore (Revolutionary War Soldier) and Mary Keller Moore: An Economic Genealogy*. Roswell, GA: Wolfe Pub., 1995. 995p.

Moore, Phillip James. *Up and Down Our Family Tree*. Utica, KY: McDowell Pub., 1995. 201p.

Moore, Roger K. *The Descendants of Nathaniel and Hannah (Hunt) Moore of Chester County, Pennsylvania*. Rock Falls, IL: Author, 1995. 186p.

Nepp, Carol McLean. *Leaves from the Family Tree, or, Moore, Tadlock, Ancestors and Some Descendants*. Tea, SD: Author, 1995. Unpgd.

Moose

Moose, Carl T. *Moose Family, USA, Vol. 8*. Concord, NC: Author, 1995. 178p.

Moraga

Moraga-Martinez Reunion, March 18–19, 1995, Phoenix-Tempe. 1995. 82p.

Moran

Lampman, Doris. *Descendants of Richard Lyons and Anne (Hayden) Moran*. Rev. Mercer Island, WA: Author, 1995. 279p.

Moran, Patrick Edward. *Moran Exodus from Offaly*. Decorah, IA: Anundsen Pub., 1995. 691p.

Morehart

Jaynes, Joretta. *Morehart, 1758–1995*. Columbus, OH: Author, 1995. Unpgd.

Morell

Morell Muñoz, Pedro A. *El Solar Morell de Camuy, Sus Ascendientes y Descendientes*. San Juan, PR: Author, 1995. 670p.

Morgan

Collins, Gerald Edward. *Jonathan Morgan, 1792–1858, His Ancestors and Descendants*. Silver Spring, MD: Author, 1995. 61p.

———. *Ralph Morgan, 1789–1869, His Ancestors and Descendants*. Silver Spring, MD: Author, 1995. 83p.

———. *Ruth Morgan, 1787–186?, Her Ancestors and Descendants*. Silver Spring, MD: Author, 1995. 43p.

———. *Thomas Morgan, 1773–1858, His Ancestors and Descendants*. Silver Spring, MD: Author, 1995. 65p.

———. *William S. Morgan, 1784–1866, His Ancestors and Descendants*. Silver Spring, MD: Author, 1995. 54p.

Halmhuber, Virginia Ackman. *The Descendants of Jeremiah Morgan and Related Families.* Lawrenceburg, KY: Author, 1995. 194p.

Hills, Iva Flo Jackson. *As the West Was Won, History Genealogy.* Springfield, MO: Author, 1995. 311p.

Jones, J. Gwynfor. *The Morgan Family of Tredegar, Its Origins, Growth and Advancement, c.1340–1674.* Newport, Gwent., England: Newport Local History Society, 1995. 29p.

Kaufman, Mary Arnold. *Martin-Arnold and Allied Families, Lanier, Bailey, Swan, Sandidge, Gholston, Morgan, and Born, Migration from Virginia to Tennessee, Georgia, Alabama and Arkansas.* Knoxville, TN: Tennessee Valley Pub., 1995. 212p.

Moore, Freddie Gene. *My Virginia Ancestors and Their Descendants in the Families, Burdett, Alexander, Anderson, King, Boone, Welsh, McHenry, Cornwell, Alford, Coleman, Dixon, Morgan, Jarman, Maugridge.* Author, 1995. 46p.

Morgan, Janet. *North Carolina Tracings.* Jefferson City, MO: Connections, 1995. 436p.

Morgan, Nathaniel Harris. *James Morgan and His Descendants.* Charlottesville, VA: Priscilla D. Kingston, 1995. Unpgd.

Morozowitz

Margolis, Abby Mindelle. *The Zafran Genealogy, Including the Morozowitz, Melnick, and Kairoch Families.* Daly City, CA: 1995. 75p.

Morris

Liston, Lois Jane Breakiron. *The Breakiron Family History Also Including the Bastian, Brecheisen, Casey, Dusenberry, Garlow, Hutchinson, Johnson, McMillen, Miller, Morris, Roderick and Other Families.* Wyandotte, OK: Gregath Pub. Co., 1995. 620p.

Morris, B. A. *Descendants of Levin Windwright Morris.* Chanute, KS: Author, 1995. Unpgd.

Zuendel, Jean. *Taylor, Blanchan, Cochran, DuBois, Foreman, Hite, Morris, Parker, Van Meteren.* Author, 1995. Unpgd.

Morrison

Erdmann Morrison, Kathleen. *Erdmann, Zastrow, Morrison.* Beaverton, OR: Author, 1995. Unpgd.

Morse

Kalbfleisch, Raymond W. *The Stow and Morse Families and Their Connection to the Alexander Smith Family of West Montrose, Ontario and Courtland, Michigan.* Sarasota, FL: Author, 1995. 40p.

McKee, Ruth Vernette. *The Known Ancestry of Rev. Isaac Babbitt, 1757–1833, Including Cooper, Crane, Ford, Lovell, Morse, Pierce, Tarne, Tisdale, Walker and Whitman Families.* Minneapolis, MN: Author, 1995. 42p.

Mortensen

Whetten, Viva Cluff. *The Morten P. Mortensen Family.* Portal, AZ: Author, 1995. 520p.

Mortimer

Remfry, Paul Martin. *The Mortimers of Wigmore.* Worcester, England: SCS Publishing, 1995. Unpgd.

Morton

Spoden, Muriel Clark. *An American Ancestry of the Clark-Morton and Tyman-Millar-Adams Families*. Kingsport, TN: Spoden Associates, 1995. 547p.

Moser

Beddingfield, James. *The Ancestors of Claude Rankin Moser, Pioneers of Catawba County, North Carolina*. Birmingham, AL: Author, 1995. 475p.

Hochstetler, Irene Steiner. *Peter and Anna Beer Moser*. Orrville, OH: Author, 1995. 272p.

Moses

Mann, Marion. *The Kigh, Mann, Reagin, and Sykes Families, Including the Branch, Brown, Dean, Fort, Gerran, Leake, Marquis, Moses, Oakes, Powell, Reid, Trammell, Walk, Wilkey, Wingfield, and Woods Families, a Genealogy and Family History*. Baltimore, MD: Gateway Press, 1995. 218p.

Ward, Edith Croft. *The Moses Families of Big Creek, the Family Pages of Joshua and Sarah Samples Moses and Related Families, Monroe County, Tennessee*. Clinton, TN: Author, 1995. 486p.

Mosier

Koickler, Eloyce Hubbard. *Hiestand, Hestand, Hastings*. Helena, MT: Author, 1995. 127p.

Mostoller

Mostoller, Ralph Vickroy. *Ancestors and Descendants of David Mostoller*. Johnston, PA: Author, 1995. 17p.

Motley

Rabold, Mary Moltenberry. *Motley, Willoughby and Lynn Families of Virginia, North Carolina and Kentucky*. Bowling Green, KY: Author, 1995. 250p.

Moule

Moule, James C. *John Moule and Katie Scanlan*. Albuquerque, NM: Author, 1995. 172p.

Mowes

Widmer, Elmer Andreas. *Genealogical Data on the Relatives of Andreas and Magdalena (Mowes) Widmer Residing in the Kulm/Merricourt and Monango/Forbes, North Dakota Areas from 1900–1950*. Lakeport, CA: Author, 1995. 23p.

Moyer

Moyer, Edith Rodgers. *Moyer-Rodgers Genealogy*. Allentown, PA: Author, 1995. Unpgd.

Moyers

Williams, Jack J. *Meyers from Moyers*. Torrance, CA: Author, 1995. 41p.

Muckleroy

Muckleroy, David V. *Index Guide to Muckleroy Archives and History Library, Owned by David V. Muckleroy*. Nacogdoches, TX: Author, 1995. 96p.

Mullins

Justice, Marie R. *One Mullins Family*. Baltimore, MD: Gateway Press, 1995. 179p.

Mullen, Robert. *Mullen/Mullins Family of Randolph, Grant, Fayette, and Rush Counties, Indiana, and Beard Family of Rush County, Indiana*. Annapolis, MD: Author, 1995. Unpgd.

Mumaw

Mumaw, Virgil R. *From Pequea Creek to Wayne County, a History of the Amos Mumaw Family*. Richmond, VA: Author, 1995. 111p.

Munzler

Saunders, Jo Ann Muenzler. *Christoph Friedrich Munzler and His Descendants*. Austin, TX: Author, 1995. 76p.

Murff

Goodwin, Dorothy Smith. *Smith-Murph Family History*. Author, 1995. 126p.

Murphy

Adkinson, John William. *Murphy Family of Bibb County, Alabama, and Choctaw County, Mississippi*. Author, 1995. 71p.

Murphy, Kevin. *The Sons of Thomas Murphy, and Other Murphys from South Carolina*. St. Louis, MO: Author, 1995. 120p.

Murray

Feder, June Constance. *The Genealogy of the Price and Stull Families of the Town of Rush, Monroe County, New York, the Murrays, Wallings, and Hills of Victor, New York, and the Otto, Block, Hill and Summerhays Families of Rochester, New York*. Fairport, NY: Author, 1995. 75p.

Rivenbark, Audrey Frady. *Murrays of Eastern North Carolina*. 3rd. ed. Charlotte, NC: Author, 1995. 166p.

Musgrave

Shartle, Stanley Musgrave. *A History of a Quaker Branch of the Musgrave Family, of the North of Ireland, Pennsylvania, North Carolina, Illinois, and Elsewhere, with Selected Papers Relating to the Ancient and Landed Musgraves of England*. 2nd. ed. Danville, IN: Author, 1995. 253p.

Musgrove

Jordan, Janie Moseley Garraghty. *The Descendants of Joseph Wilkerson (12 May 1729–15 March 1829), and Allied Families of Bedford County, Virginia*. Lynchburg, VA: Warwick House Pub., 1995. 227p.

Musser

Musser, Charles D. *The Ancestors of Robert Sturgeon Musser, 1842–1888*. Author, 1995. 18p.

Mutinot

Arthaud, John Bradley. *The Arthaud Family of Bourbonne-les-Bains and Langres, Department of Haute Marne, France with Related Families of Gascard, Gautherot, Lauzanne, Liegault, Mutinot and Walferdin and One Immigrant Branch in the United States*. Columbia, MO: Author, 1995. 123p.

Muxlow

Muxlow, Robert Lewis. *Muxlow*. Kirkland, WA: Author, 1995. Unpgd.

Myers

Lewis, Allen Roy. *Two Hundred Year History and Genealogy of the Isaac Lewis Family from Cloughjordan (Tipperary), Ireland to the Canadas and the United States, Including Intermarriages with Hodgins, Myers, Rapley, Slack, Williams, and Many Other Families*. Ver. 1.5. Syracuse, NY: Author, 1995. 215p.

Williams, Jack J. *Meyers from Moyers*. Torrance, CA: Author, 1995. 41p.

Myhre

Russell, Carol. *Sigrid, Sigrid Tufte Myhre Ostrom and Her Ancestors and Descendants, the History of an American Pioneer Woman with Roots in Hallingdal and Aurland, Norway*. Annandale, VA: Author, 1995. Unpgd.

Myren

Myren, Richard A. *Norwegian-American, the Lineage of Richard Albert Myren*. 2nd. ed. Mount Dora, FL: Author, 1995. 225p.

–N

Nader

Beck, William M. *The Joseph Nader Family*. East Peoria, IL: Author, 1995. 52p.

Nagel

Horst, Florine Gettman. *Family Genealogy*. Loveland, CO: Author, 1995. 151p.

Nail

Nail, William Reilly. *Per Stirpes, the John M. Nail Family in Texas, 1839–1995*. Author, 1995. 356p.

Nakamura

Kyu Tama-gun Aburadai-mura Nanushi Nakamura-ke Monjo. Tokyo: Tokyo-to Kyoiku Iinkai, 1995. 219p.

Narbut

Narbut, Andrei Nikolaevich. *Narbuty Chernigoskoi i Vitebskoi Gubernii*. Moscow, Russia: Author, 1995. 56p.

Nash

Carlin, Liz Austin. *The Ancestry of Humilis Owen, Wife of Nathaniel Austin*. West Hills, CA: Author, 1995. 67p.

Naudin

Taylor-Goins, Elsie. *Naudin-Dibble Family, Selected South Carolina Historic Sites.* Columbia, SC: Author, 1995. 70p.

Nave

Adair, Shirley Brown. *Descendants of Asher B. Beauchamp and John Casey, Nave, Ball, Bingham (Related Lines).* Rockwall, TX: Author, 1995. 139p.

Nedham

Allen, Patricia Remmell. *The Remmell and Allen Families of New Castle County, Delaware.* Horsham, PA: Author, 1995. 71p.

Needham

Breffeilh, Melva Kinch. *The Ancestors and Descendants of Horatio Edmund Needham and Lucina Bagley, Who Married 25 November 1852 in Royalton, Cuyahoga County, Ohio.* Sulphur, LA: Wise Publications, 1995. 307p.

Neeley

Koickler, Eloyce Hubbard. *Hiestand, Hestand, Hastings.* Helena, MT: Author, 1995. 127p.

Neely

Carlin, Jim. *Some Descendants of Richard Austin of Charlestown, Massachusetts.* Charlestown, MA: Austin Families Association of America, 1995. 692p.

Jordan, Thomas Franklin. *An American Migration.* Thesis (M.A.), Louisiana State University, 1995. 194p.

Neff

Smith, Robert Lee. *Ancestors of Thelma Margaret Gander.* Alexandria, VA: Author, 1995. 65p.

Neisler

Hargis, Margaret Ann Finley. *A Glimpse at Some of the Descendants of Hans Adam Neuscheler.* Warrenton, WA: Author, 1995. Unpgd.

———. *Our Neisler Family.* Warrenton, WA: Author, 1995. Unpgd.

Nellis

Eggert, Irving John. *Peter Eggert of Mecklenburg and Related Families in America, Best, Bitz, Broekemeier, Hackbarth, Kane, Meisner, Nellis, Schunk, Strenkowski, Voight, Winston.* Decorah, IA: Anundsen Pub. Co., 1995. 224p.

Nelson

Hauk, Carol A. *Descendants of Benjamin Harrison of Virginia.* 4th. ed. Anderson, IN: Hauk Data Services, 1995. 365p.

————. *Descendants of Charles Grymes of Virginia*. Anderson, IN: Hauk Data Services, 1995. 244p.

————. *Descendants of George Reade of Virginia*. Anderson, IN: Hauk Data Services, 1995. 393p.

————. *Descendants of John Page of Virginia*. Anderson, IN: Hauk Data Services, 1995. 243p.

————. *Descendants of Lewis Burwell of Virginia*. Anderson, IN: Hauk Data Services, 1995. 395p.

————. *Descendants of Robert Beverley of Virginia*. Anderson, IN: Hauk Data Services, 1995. 330p.

————. *Descendants of Robert Taliafero of Virginia*. 6th. ed. Anderson, IN: Hauk Data Services, 1995. 358p.

————. *Descendants of Thomas Nelson Virginia*. Anderson, IN: Hauk Data Services, 1995. 184p.

————. *Descendants of William Randolph of Virginia*. Anderson, IN: Hauk Data Services, 1995. 461p.

Nelson, Gary S. *Carl Johan (Nilson) Nelson (1822–1888) and Kerstin (Christina Persdotter (1832–1904)*. Stanley, ND: Author, 1995. 16p.

Nelson, Lyle Edgar. *Nelson Farm, Reminiscences*. Starkville, MS: Author, 1995. 129p.

Usher, Candace. *Peterson, Nelson, Wedien, and Willing Families*. Powell, OH: Author, 1995. 79p.

Nesbitt

Fehr, Martha Robinson. *Descendants of Gavin Mathers (1785–1869), a Supplement to the Mathers-Nesbit Genealogy by Lura B. Mitchell Emery*. Gulf Breeze, FL: Author, 1995. 288p.

Neser

Neser, John Michael. *Nesers in South Africa, 1787–1994*. Cramerview, South Africa: Author, 1995. 190p.

Neufeldt

Enns, Katharine. *Harvest of New Fields, or the I. P. Neufeld Story*. Inman, KS: Author, 1995. 242p.

Wiese, Luella Toevs. *The Neufeldts, Descendants of Gerhard and Oelsie Neufeldt, from Prussia to Russia and on to America, 1758–1995*. Knoxville, Tennessee Valley Pub., 1995. 159p.

Neuscheler

Hargis, Margaret Ann Finley. *A Glimpse at Some of the Descendants of Hans Adam Neuscheler*. Warrenton, WA: Author, 1995. Unpgd.

Neustifter

Neustifter, Rita M. *The Neustifter Family Story*. Jackson, MI: Author, 1995. 55p.

Neville

Mapes, Olin V. *Westmoreland nee Neville*. Rev. ed. Bowie, MD: Heritage Books, 1995. 221p.

Newcomb

Newcomb, Viettia Alberta. *Newcomb, Hartt and Slye, Blunden Families*. Ukiah, CA: Author, 1995. 408p.

Newell

Popham, Geraldine E. *Grandma's Ancestors, 1634–1936, Thomas Judd, the Emigrant to Nelson Judd, and Addie (Judd) Dowd*. Lodi, CA: Author, 1995. 148p.

Newkirk

Whitt, Aileen M. *Miller-Newkirk Family History, Ancestors and Descendants of Ben Miller and Sally (Newkirk) Miller with Related Families*. New Richmond, OH: Author, 1995. 192p.

Newman

Doss, Brenda Collier. *Isaac Newman, with Some of His Ancestors and Descendants*. Author, 1995. 201p.

Newman, Preston Earl. *Thomas Newman, 1620–1700, Original Immigrant to Richmond County, Virginia, and Some of His Descendants*. Atlanta, GA: Author, 1995. 168p.

Nicholas

Hauk, Carol A. *Descendants of George Nicholas of Virginia*. Anderson, IN: Hauk Data Services, 1995. 130p.

Nichols

Chesson, Eugene. *Foy and Allied Families of the Eastern Carolinas and New England*. Prescott, AZ: Author, 1995. Unpgd.

Elliott, Margaret Coppess. *The Nicholls Family of Jefferson County, Ohio, the Rudd, Cox, Smith, and Related Families Who Came to Berlin Township, Ionia County, Michigan, before 1870*. Ionia, MI: Author, 1995. Unpgd.

Hauk, Carol A. *Descendants of George Nicholas of Virginia*. Anderson, IN: Hauk Data Services, 1995. 130p.

Nichols, Barbara. *Our Nichols Family History*. Baltimore, MD: Gateway Press, 1995. 162p.

Partin, Sherita Kae. *Four Generations of the Family of Kindred Allison Partin*. Nacogdoches, TX: Partin Publications, 1995. Unpgd.

Nicholson

Grubbs, Nancy Carole Early. *The Descendants of James and Elizabeth Joseph Lewis*. Houston, TX: Author, 1995. 71p.

Niedenthal

Niedenthal, Corrine. *A Niedenthal Family History*. Kansas: Author, 1995. 175p.

Nix

Adcock, John J., Sr. *Adcock, Nix Genealogy*. Author, 1995. 46p.

Nodell

Schnatz, Darlene Becnel. *The Nodell-Bremer Descendants.* Beaumont, TX: Author, 1995. 108p.

Noel

Carpenter, Wayne. *Noel Family.* Fostoria, OH: Author, 1995. 43p.

Nolt

Hoover, Lester M. *Ancestors and Descendants of Henry M. Hoover and Barbara W. Nolt.* Lititz, PA: Author, 1995. 165p.

Norfleet

Crockett, Evelyn Gurley. *The Family Norfleet: Trailblazers of Tate County, Mississippi.* Oxford, MS: Author, 1995. 249p.

Norris

Irwin, JoAnn G. *Descendants of Robert Norris, Sr. (1800–1884).* Richland, MI: Author, 1995. 128p.
―――. *Descendants of Robert Norris (1774–1858) and Hannah Binnington (1781–1848).* Richland, MI: Author, 1995. Unpgd.
Mallard, Shirley Jones. *Keeping Up with the Joneses, a Book about the Rafe Jones Family of Granville, North Carolina.* Chapel Hill, NC: Author, 1995. 244p.

North

Popham, Geraldine E. *Grandma's Ancestors, 1634–1936, Thomas Judd, the Emigrant to Nelson Judd, and Addie (Judd) Dowd.* Lodi, CA: Author, 1995. 148p.

Norton

Hauk, Carol A. *Descendants of John Norton of Virginia.* 2nd. ed. Anderson, IN: Hauk Data Services, 1995. 202p.

Nourse

Ward, Naomi Etta. *The Ward Connections, Nourse, Kimmel, Wood, Babbs, Shelton, Sasubjak, Ader, Guffey, Pontiny, Archibald, Asbell.* Evansville, IN: Author, 1995. 545p.

Nowakowski

Zaleski, Dolores Piotrowski. *Nowakowski-Jasinska Family History.* PA: Author, 1995. 118p.

Nuquist

Bymaster Richards, Willa. *Descendants of William Anders Lindquist and Mary Nuquist.* Carnation, WA: Author, 1995. Unpgd.

Nyman

Ed, Robert Calhoun. *Wretman Roots, the Genealogy and History of the Wretman Families Who Emigrated from Ostergorland Lan, Sweden to Moline, Illinois, 1880–1891, Including Chapters on the Nymans and the Juthes.* Livingston, TX: Author, 1995. 295p.

O

Oakes

Bradley, John. *Sarah Wallington, 1719–1757, and her Wallington, Pead, Okes, Fownes, Perry, and Bouchier Ancestors of Wotton-under-Edge.* Devizes, England, Author, 1995. 213p.

Mann, Marion. *The Kigh, Mann, Reagin, and Sykes Families, Including the Branch, Brown, Dean, Fort, Gerran, Leake, Marquis, Moses, Oakes, Powell, Reid, Trammell, Walk, Wilkey, Wingfield, and Woods Families, a Genealogy and Family History.* Baltimore, MD: Gateway Press, 1995. 218p.

Oakley

Koickler, Eloyce Hubbard. *Hiestand, Hestand, Hastings.* Helena, MT: Author, 1995. 127p.

Oatman

Osborn, Will E. *Oatman: Some of the Descendants of Johannes Outman, 1654–1716, and His Wife Femmetje Kock, 1654–1732.* Hansen, ID: L. M. Oatman, 1995. 356p.

Obern

Obern, A. Gaylord. *The Saga of the Oberns-Orbens, a Journey from the Palatinate to California.* Naples, FL: Author, 1995. 43p.

Ockey

Young, Audrey Ockey. *A History and Genealogy of the Ockey Family: England, New Zealand and America.* Fresno, CA: Author, 1995. Unpgd.

O'Daniel

Byard, Richard B. *O'Daniel, Matthews, Mitchem, Helms and Their Relatives in Maryland, Kentucky, Indiana, Alabama and Other States.* Ellicott City, MD: Author, 1995. 88p.

O'Donnell

McGinn, Ann Winston. *A McGinn McCorkle Family History, 1796–1995: With Related Families, Crockett, Dabney, Egnatoff, Fontaine, Freirson, Gillespie, Huddart, Kennemore, O'Donnell, Patton, Ring, Sheppard, Winston, and Others.* Spring Hill, FL: Author, 1995. 313p.

O'Ferrall

Odendahl, Paul E. *The O'Ferrall Legacy.* New Orleans, LA: Royal Archivists, 1995. 233p.

Offley

Offley, John Brockenbrough. *Offley Family Papers.* Williamsburg, VA: Author, 1995. 41p.

Ogden

Clark, Harman Reed. *Ogden.* Dunellen, NJ: Author, 1995. 129p.

Ohl

Ohl, Jane P. *Some Surnames in the Genealogical Background of Michael Ohl and Jane Ann Pollock Ohl.* Lakewood, CO: Author, 1995. 41p.

Oien

Hagen, Genevieve K. *The Solem-Oien Connection, the Story of the Ancestors and Descendants of Anders P. Solem, Marit L. Oien and Their Siblings.* Eau Claire, WI: Author, 1995. 329p.

Okes

Bradley, John. *Sarah Wallington, 1719–1757, and her Wallington, Pead, Okes, Fownes, Perry, and Bouchier Ancestors of Wotton-under-Edge.* Devizes, England, Author, 1995. 213p.

Oldham

Randall, Betty. *Oldham Families of Shelby County, Indiana, from Sevier County, Tennessee.* Hope, IN: Author, 1995. 95p.

Oliphant

Oliphant, James A. *The Oliphant Family.* Bossier City, LA: Author, 1995. Unpgd.

Oliver

Butcher, Diana Gale Eaton. *The Known Descendants of David Oliver and His Wife, Mary (Flood) Oliver of Boston, Suffolk County, Massachusetts, for the Years ca. 1700–1995 through Twelve Generations, Comprising the Descendants of Their Grandson, Stephen Oliver, Born Boston, Mass., 1752, and His Wife, Mercy (Griffin) Oliver.* Midland, MI: Author, 1995. 140p.

Hockett, Thomas Jack. *Ancestors and Descendants of Benjamin Snead and Felicia Oliver.* St. David's, PA: Author, 1995. 283p.

Olney

Slocum, Vivian. *Olney Family.* MI: Author, 1995. 51p.

Weber, Verlene Vaughn. *Sherman, Olney, Finley Families.* Bath, MI: Author, 1995. 54p.

Olson

Olson, Scott L. *Olson Family History.* Grand Forks, NC: Author, 1995. 105p.

O'Neal

O'Neal, Marcia Corrigan. *O'Neal Genealogy from the Early 1800s and Including Ancestors Anderson, Childers, Davis, Griffith, Hunt, Savage, Venard, and Willcuts.* Richmond, IN: Author, 1995. 43p.

Oosthuyzen

Oosthuizen, Abrie V. *Wessel Johannes Oosthuyzen van Vogel Vlei, Mosselbaai, n Familie Geskiedenis.* Aliwal Noord, South Africa, 1995. 116p.

Oppenheim

Oppenheim, Bert. *The Oppenheim Family History, 1750–1995.* San Francisco, CA: Robert Reed Pub., 1995. Unpgd.

Orben

Obern, A. Gaylord. *The Saga of the Oberns-Orbens, a Journey from the Palatinate to California*. Naples, FL: Author, 1995. 43p.

O'Reilly

Anderson, Arthur Grant. *From Enniskillen, Ireland to Grand Forks, North Dakota: The Dr. Frederick Joseph Duggan, Mary Ann O'Reilly Family Biography*. Author, 1995. Unpgd.

Orloff

An Orloff Family Tree: Descendants of Simcha and Yenta Orloff. NY: Periodical Studies Service, 1995. 46p.

Ormsby

Rines, Marjorie J. *One Small Branch of the Ormsby Family Tree*. Author, 1995. 76p.

Orrell

Orrell, Reverdy Lewin. *Ancestors and Relatives of Reverdy Lewin Orrell IV*. Catonsville, MD: Author, 1995. 520p.

Ostrander

Van Nostrand, Jacqueline Joslin. *The Ancestors and Descendants of Frederick Van Norstrand and Elizabeth Harris of Cayuga County, New York*. Evart, MI: Family History Publishers, 1995. 388p.

Ostrom

Russell, Carol. *Sigrid, Sigrid Tufte Myhre Ostrom and Her Ancestors and Descendants, the History of an American Pioneer Woman with Roots in Hallingdal and Aurland, Norway*. Annandale, VA: Author, 1995. Unpgd.

Oswalt

Carvill, Kathleen. *Oswald-Henninger*. Author, 1995. 46p.
Roth, Marolyn Oswalt. *Oswalt Family History, 1722–1995*. Bluffton, IN: Author, 1995. 167p.

Ott

Best Strange, Norma. *Descendants of Henry Ott/Utt and Margaret Ferril*. Chilhowee, MO: Author, 1995. 100p.
Scott County Iowa Genealogical Society. *A Family Tree: Kirk, Johnston, Daebelliehn, Peitscher, Lawrence, Ott, Jarvis, Delzell*. Davenport, IA: Author, 1995. Unpgd.

Otto

Feder, June Constance. *The Genealogy of the Price and Stull Families of the Town of Rush, Monroe County, New York, the Murrays, Wallings, and Hills of Victor, New York, and the Otto, Block, Hill and Summerhays Families of Rochester, New York*. Fairport, NY: Author, 1995. 75p.

Overstreet

Windland, Harry K. *James Overstreet, His Progeny and Allied Families*. Glen Carbon, IL: Author, 1995. Unpgd.

Owen

Carlin, Liz Austin. *The Ancestry of Humilis Owen, Wife of Nathaniel Austin.* West Hills, CA: Author, 1995. 67p.

Owens

Owens, Claude M. *William Owens, Sr. (ca. 1725–ca. 1793), His Father and Grandfather.* South Laguna, CA: Author, 1995. 133p.

Owsley

Bodine, Ronny O. *The Ancestry of Dorothea Poyntz, Wife of Reverend John Owsley, Generations 1–12.* Fort Meade, MD: Author, 1995. 162p.

–P

Pace

Hubbard, Terry Lynn. *The Pace Family of Martin's Creek: Lest We Forget.* Mt. Carmel, TN: Author, 1995. 132p.

Jones, Annie Bell. *History of the Pace Family.* Roswell, GA: Author, 1995. 257p.

True, Edward Keene. *Ancestors and Descendants of Edward True, Jr. (1799–1871) and of His Wife Olive King Payson True (1871–1886) of Hope, Maine.* Searsport, ME: Author, 1995. 432p.

Pacheco

Jory, Guadalupe Pacheco. *This Is a True Story of the Melchor Pacheco Family.* San Antonio, TX: Author, 1995. 62p.

Padilla

Sanchez, George Abe. *The Sanchez/Padilla Family of Lincoln County, New Mexico, a Genealogical Study.* El Paso, TX: Author, 1995. 59p.

Page

Bymaster Richards, Willa. *Descendants of Francis Marion Page.* Carnation, WA: Author, 1995. Unpgd.

Hauk, Carol A. *Descendants of Benjamin Harrison of Virginia.* 4th. ed. Anderson, IN: Hauk Data Services, 1995. 365p.

———. *Descendants of Charles Grymes of Virginia.* Anderson, IN: Hauk Data Services, 1995. 244p.

———. *Descendants of George Reade of Virginia.* Anderson, IN: Hauk Data Services, 1995. 393p.

———. *Descendants of John Page of Virginia.* Anderson, IN: Hauk Data Services, 1995. 243p.

———. *Descendants of Robert Beverley of Virginia.* Anderson, IN: Hauk Data Services, 1995. 330p.

———. *Descendants of Thomas Nelson of Virginia.* Anderson, IN: Hauk Data Services, 1995. 184p.

———. *Descendants of William Byrd of Virginia.* Anderson, IN: Hauk Data Services, 1995. 198p.

———. *Descendants of William Randolph of Virginia.* Anderson, IN: Hauk Data Services, 1995. 461p.

Stultz, Carolyne. *The Page Family Research Report, Including a Genealogy on Descendants of Robert and Rachel (Brockman) Page, from Virginia to South Carolina, Some of Their Sons Came to Kentucky and Then to Illinois.* Danville, IN: Author, 1995. 123p.

Paine

Payne, John C. *The Family of Robert Paine/Payne (1791–1859) of North Carolina and Tennessee.* 1995. Unpgd.

Palmer

Oncley, Lephia French. *Our Weaver Cousins, Ancestry of Samuel Stanton Weaver, 1793–1857, and His Wife, Lucy Billings Palmer, 1798–1851, with Some of Their Descendants and Related Families.* Ann Arbor, MI: Author, 1995. 244p.

Palmer, Hollis Arthur. *Deep Roots, Humble Lives, the Story of Our Family in America.* Author, 1995. 209p.

Pappenheim

Levi, Arthur. *Genealogy and Family History: Maurice Pappenheim and Margit Ernst.* Longmeadow, MA: Author, 1995. 101p.

Parent

Galeener-Moore, Laverne. *Parent/Parrent Biographical Dictionary.* Bowie, MD: Heritage Books, 1995. 267p.

Pargeon

John, Lurene. *The Pargeon Family, Our Midwestern Roots.* Portland, OR: Author, 1995. 34p.

Park

Carter, Park W. *A History of Some Park Families in Jefferson County, Indiana, and Allied Families of Anderson, Mann, Gilchrist and Others.* Eureka, KS: Author, 1995. Unpgd.

Park, Percival David. *George Park (d. 1782) and Agness Nichols Park of Rowan (Davidson) County, North Carolina, and Some of Their Descendants.* Charlottesville, VA: Author, 1995. 188p.

Parker

Allmand, Barbara J. *Three Virginia Families, Allmand, Parker, and Sinclair, Including a Collection of 19th Century Letters and Other Writings.* Overland Park, KS: Author, 1995. 252p.

Brown, Gerald Douglas. *Descendants of Daniel and Rebecca McKenzie, Old Williamsburg, Sumter Districts of South Carolina.* Hemingway, SC: Three Rivers Historical Society, 1995. 116p.

Hinson, William Ashley. *Richard Park I and His Descendants, a History of the Parkers of Rowan County and Stanley County, North Carolina.* Kernersville, NC: Author, 1995. 206p.

Middleton, Edith S. *Marion Thomas Whitney: The Story of His Predecessors and Descendants, Parker, Greely, Tufts*. Portland, OR: Author, 1995. 45p.

Parker, Alton W. *History of the Parker Family of Hertford and Northampton Counties, North Carolina, and Related Families*. North Carolina: Author, 1995. Unpgd.

Zuendel, Jean. *Taylor, Blanchan, Cochran, DuBois, Foreman, Hite, Morris, Parker, Van Meteren*. Author, 1995. Unpgd.

Parkhurst

Parkhurst, Peter G. *George Parkhurst Increasings, for Nine Generations*. Los Altos Hills, CA: Author, 1995. 2 vols.

Parks

McLeod, Stephen Archie. *The House of Cantelou & Co., the Story of a Southern Family*. Tallahassee, FL: Author, 1995. 705p.

Parnell

Koickler, Eloyce Hubbard. *Hiestand, Hestand, Hastings*. Helena, MT: Author, 1995. 127p.

Parr

Parr, Richard Eugene. *Genealogy of Richard Eugene Parr*. Morgan Hill, CA: Author, 1995. 79p.

Parsons

Simpson, R. Elaine. *James and Parsons: Descendants and Related Families*. Little Rock, AR: Author, 1995. 146p.

Partin

Partin, Sherita Kae. *Four Generations of the Family of Kindred Allison Partin*. Nacogdoches, TX: Partin Publications, 1995. Unpgd.

————. *The Descendants of Nancy Partin and Charles King*. Nacogdoches, TX: Partin Publications, 1995. Unpgd.

Parton

Hembree, Fred. *Parton*. Kingsport, TN: Author, 1995. Unpgd.

Passons

Makris, Patricia Short. *Passons' Family Connections*. Belleville, IL: Author, 1995. 651p.

Patrick

Price, Patsy Patrick. *Descendants of Robert Patrick of South Carolina, an Historical Account of the Scotch-Irish with Biographical Sketches of Some of the Descendants of Robert Patrick*. Rushton, LA: Author, 1995. 148p.

Patterson

Barger, Herbert. *The Patterson Family, Scotland to Texas*. Ft. Washington, MD: Author, 1995. 147p.

Patton

Hauk, Carol A. *Descendants of Thomas Gaines of Virginia, Ancestor of President James Madison and USA Generals Gaines, Patton and Marshall.* Anderson, IN: Hauk Data Services, 1995. 284p.

McGinn, Ann Winston. *A McGinn McCorkle Family History, 1796–1995: With Related Families, Crockett, Dabney, Egnatoff, Fontaine, Freirson, Gillespie, Huddart, Kennemore, O'Donnell, Patton, Ring, Sheppard, Winston, and Others.* Spring Hill, FL: Author, 1995. 313p.

Paulochik

Paulochik, Paul M. *Roots and Branches, Paulochik, Gosemeyer, Yanik, Lonergan, and Related Families.* O'Fallon, IL: Author, 1995. 489p.

Paulsen

Williams, Luella R. *My Father's People: Paulsen/Thoreesen Slekt from Norway, Lindack Slakt from Sweden, Descendants Found in Australia, Canada, Denmark, Norway, Sweden and United States of America.* Iron River, MI: Author, 1995. 475p.

Payne

Creech, Lillian Broughton. *Kentucky Lineage, Broughton, Slusher, Woolum, Payne and Related Families.* Baltimore, MD: Gateway Press, 1995. 592p.

Payne, John C. *The Family of Robert Paine/Payne (1791–1859) of North Carolina and Tennessee.* 1995. Unpgd.

Peace

Rowland, Joseph S., Jr. *Southern Peace Families and the Barr Descendants of Margaret Scott Barr Peace.* Tuscaloosa, AL: Author, 1995. 563p.

Pead

Bradley, John. *Sarah Wallington, 1719–1757, and Her Wallington, Pead, Okes, Fownes, Perry, and Bouchier Ancestors of Wotton-under-Edge.* Devizes, England, Author, 1995. 213p.

Pearce

Opat, Donna Burrough. *A Pearce-Brace Family History.* Lindsborg, KS: Author, 1995. 174p.

Rothenberger, Delana Pearce. *Descendants of William Robert Pearce.* Author, 1995. 19p.

Pearsall

Scott, Margaret Scott. *Genealogical Portrait of Joseph Carr and Barbara Gastor Beverett, the Carr Descendants of Duplin County, North Carolina.* Warsaw, NC: Author, 1995. 418p.

Pearson

Johnston, Francis Clairborne. *The Angier Family of Orange and Durham Counties, North Carolina, and Allied Families of North Carolina and Virginia.* Richmond, VA: Author, 1995. 329p.

Peck

McRobie, Raymond Irvin. *The McRobie, McCrobie, Cuppett, Peck, Hostetler, Weimer, Smith, Wilt and Merrill Families of Garrett County.* Fairfax, VA: Author, 1995. 471p.

Peterson, Marion Plath. *Peck, McClinchey, Rouatt Saga*. Decorah, IA: Anundsen Pub. Co., 1995. Unpgd.

Pedersen
Madson, Richard C. *Gjerpen to Gjerpen, the Madson Families Who Came to Wisconsin, Also Mason, Larson, Pedersen, Holm, Halvorson, Simonsen, and Hoen Families*. Mesa, AZ: Author, 1995. 284p.

Peifer
Albrecht, Leo J. *Descendants of Peter and Katherine (Peifer) Becker, Becker Family Reunion, Sunday, August 6, 1995, Belle Plaine, Minnesota*. Belle Plaine, MN: Author, 1995. 99p.

Peitscher
Scott County Iowa Genealogical Society. *A Family Tree: Kirk, Johnston, Daebelliehn, Peitscher, Lawrence, Ott, Jarvis, Delzell*. Davenport, IA: Author, 1995. Unpgd.

Peladeau
Peladeau, Suzanne Jacques. *Famille Peladeau*. Author, 1995. 110p.

Pelham
Standen, Jack. *The Standen Book, the Standen Families that Settled in the Lorain County Area of Ohio, Their Ancestors and Descendants, the Descendants of Timothy Standen and Ann Pelham, 1775–1995*. State College, PA: Author, 1995. 400p.

Pelot
Colket, Meredith Bright. *Pelot Family Genealogy, Including Appendices and Allied Families*. Bradenton, FL: William Currie Colket, 1995. 479p.

Pelzel
Pelzel, Michael J. *Pelzl, Pelzel, Pelcl, Past and Present*. Baltimore, MD: Gateway Press, 1995. 2 vols.

Pendleton
Hauk, Carol A. *Descendants of Philip Pendleton of Virginia*. 6th. ed. Anderson, IN: Hauk Data Services, 1995. 287p.

Pépin
Pépin, Jean Pierre Yves. *Pépin and Papin (et Variantes) au Travers le Parchemin et sa Banque de Données Notariales, 1635–1765*. Sherbrooke, Quebec: Association des Familles Pépin, 1995. 107p.
———. *Robert Pépin et sa Descendance au Travers le Parchemin et sa Banque de Données Notariales, 1635–1765*. Sherbrooke, Quebec: Association des Familles Pépin, 1995. 75p.

Percival
Percival, Benjamin. *Benjamin Percival Diary, 1777–1817*. Denton, TX: F. R. Barrow, 1995. 431p.

Perkins

Carlin, Jim. *Some Descendants of Richard Austin of Charlestown, Massachusetts*. Charlestown, MA: Austin Families Association of America, 1995. 692p.

Ra, Isa. *Some Descendants of Rosann and William Perkins*. Olney, IL: Author, 1995. 20p.

Perrott

Hauk, Carol A. *Descendants of Richard Perrott of Virginia*. 2nd. ed. Anderson, IN: Hauk Data Services, 1995. 278p.

Perry

Bradley, John. *Sarah Wallington, 1719–1757, and her Wallington, Pead, Okes, Fownes, Perry, and Bouchier Ancestors of Wotton-under-Edge*. Devizes, England, Author, 1995. 213p.

Carroll, Thelma Ellen Young. *A Source Book for Five Generations of Family History*. Virginia Beach, VA: Merrit Press, 1995. Unpgd.

Petering

Petering, Dorothy Evelyn Kulp. *The Anton Wilhelm Petering Family Genealogy*. Columbus, IN: Author, 1995. 228p.

Peterson

Brooks, Shirley A. *Peterson Branberg Family*. Lake Elsinore, CA: Author, 1995. Unpgd.

The Johan Petersen (Johnsen/Johnson) Family. Manitowoc, WI: Hansen, 1995. Unpgd.

Lawrence, Ardelle L. *Family History of Maren (Mary) Jacobsen and Peter Christian Petersen (Pedersen)*. Las Vegas, NV: Author, 1995. 163p.

Peterson, Allen Dean. *Our Father's Family*. St. Augustine, FL: Author, 1995. 57p.

Usher, Candace. *Peterson, Nelson, Wedien, and Willing Families*. Powell, OH: Author, 1995. 79p.

Pew

Davidson, Charlene Gaskill. *Birkett and Pew Families*. Shawnee, KS: Author, 1995. 12p.

Peyton

Hauk, Carol A. *Descendants of Rice Hooe of Virginia, Ancestor of President James Madison*. 2nd. ed. Anderson, IN: Hauk Data Services, 1995. 93p.

———. *Descendants of Virginia Peyton of Virginia*. Anderson, IN: Hauk Data Services, 1995. Unpgd.

Scarborough, Eleazer Pate. *A Genealogy of the South Carolina Coward-Cowart Family*. Hemingway, SC: Three Rivers Historical Society, 1995. Unpgd.

Pfaff

Auch, Viola. *Jacob Betz and Katherina Pfaff's Ancestors and Descendants*. Freeman, SD: Pine Hill Press, 1995. 166p.

Pflueger

Henderson, Beverly Pflueger. *Pflueger, 1585–1994, a Family Chronicle*. Chicago: Adams Press, 1995. 69p.

Phelps

Heinbuch, Susan Elise. *Micajah Phelps, Sr. of North Carolina Born before 1760 Died 1816.* NY: Author, 1995. 17p.

Phelps, Asa Gray. *A Genealogy of and by Asa Gray Phelps of Bertie County, North Carolina, (b. 1892-d. after 1954), Emphasis on Descendants of John Phelps and Mary (Gill) Phelps.* NY: S. E. Heinbuch, 1995. 57p.

Phillips

Geary, Patricia Little. *Some of the Descendants of Solomon Phillips, a Revolutionary War Soldier, 1760–1839.* Harrisonburg, VA: Author, 1995. 66p.

Hughes, Nancy Caroline Phillips. *Hugh Phillips, Some of His Descendants, Including Allied Families of Bolin, Blewer (Bluer), Reidheimer, Salley, Schuler (Shuler) and Winningham.* Columbia, SC: Author, 1995. 46p.

Kerr, Richard Homer. *Phillips Ancestors and Descendants.* Knoxville, TN: Tennessee Valley Pub., 1995. Austin, TX: Author, 1995. 314p.

Neal, Clarice G. *David Young and Sarah Phillips Descendants, Wilson County, Tennessee, 1796- 1994.* Austin, TX: Author, 1995. 356p.

Phillips, John Wesley. *Descendants of Reuben Phillips.* Bowie, MD: Heritage Books, 1995. 419p.

Philpott

Philpott, John P. *The Descendants of Josiah Philpott (1860–1949) and Emma Zetta Smith (1869-1924).* Grand Prairie, TX: Author, 1995. 22p.

———. *The Four Sons of John William Philpott (1853–1928) and Mary Angelina Hardy (1857-1943).* Grand Prairie, TX: Author, 1995. 58p.

Pickett

Hauk, Carol A. *Descendants of Henry Pickett of Virginia.* 5th. ed. Anderson, IN: Hauk Data Services, 1995. 97p.

Piedanna

LeDuc, Susan Sparks. *LeDuc/Piedanna Chronicle, France to America.* Fort Wayne, IN: Author, 1995. Unpgd.

Pier

Pierre, Joseph H. *The Descendants of Thomas Pier, a Record of the Descendants of Thomas Pier, a Late 17th Century Inhabitant of Lyme, Connecticut.* Bowie, MD: Heritage Books, 1995. 318p.

Pierce

McKee, Ruth Vernette. *The Known Ancestry of Rev. Isaac Babbitt, 1757–1833, Including Cooper, Crane, Ford, Lovell, Morse, Pierce, Tarne, Tisdale, Walker and Whitman Families.* Minneapolis, MN: Author, 1995. 42p.

Pike

Sweet, Joyce Lisle. *A Pike Family History: William and Tryphena (Cole) Pike, Their Descendants and Related Families.* Hendersonville, NC: Author, 1995. 263p.

Pinkston

Pinkston, Margaret Darracott. *Mosswood Remembered*. Baltimore, MD: Gateway Press, 1995. Unpgd.

Pitt

Pitt, Norman E. *Pitt Families, 1477–1995*. Logan, IA: Author, 1995. 612p.

Plano

Bell, George Edward. *The Planos from Piedmont, the Plano Family History*. Ontario, NY: Wayne & Ridge Pub., 1995. 432p.

Platson

Ludvigson, Merrill Talmadge. *The Christensons and the Platsons: Where We Came from, Who We Are*. Decorah, IA: Anundsen Pub. Co., 1995. 459p.

Platter

LeRoy Ladurie, Emanuel. *Le Siècle des Platter, 1499–1628*. Paris: Fayard, 1995. Unpgd.

Playter

Playter, Wesley B. *The Playter Family of Whitchurch Township, York County, Ontario, the Descendants of Watson Playter (b.1766-d.1834) of Pine Orchard*. Newmarket, ON: Author, 1995. 907p.

Plum

Weber, Dale K. *The Good Book*. Bath, MI: Author, 1995. 93p.

Plummer

Johnston, Anne Plummer. *The Plummer Lineage of America*. Reston, VA: M. L. Tomaselli, 1995. 56p.

Smith, Herbert F. *Plummer Ancestry, Including Some Alexander, Erwin, and Flinn Links of Herbert F. Smith*. 2nd. ed. Silver Spring, MD: Author, 1995. Unpgd.

Poeppelman

O'Reilly, Dolores Brokamp. *Documentary of the Poeppelman Ancestry*. Sidney, OH: Author, 1995. 70p.

Poffenberger

Poffenberger, Thomas. *From Germany to Antietam, the Earliest History of the Poffenberger Family*. Ann Arbor, MI: Author, 1995. 59p.

Poindexter

Agee, Nealon Rhea. *Poindexters in America with Related Families*. Nashville, TN: Author, 1995. Unpgd.

Poinsett

Ralph, Charles L. *Genealogy of a Poinsett Family from the Atlantic Seacoast to the Colorado Rockies, with Notes on the Worrell and Braamharr Families*. Ft. Collins, CO: Author, 1995. 84p.

Pollard

Pollard, Una. *Pollard Descendants of John M., Sr.* Piggott, AR: Author, 1995. 703p.

Pollock

Sowers, William R. *A Pollock Family History, a Listing of Some of the Descendants of John Pollock and Sarah Smith Who Came to America in 1800.* Topeka, KS: Author, 1995. Unpgd.

Polzin

Scholla, Kara Polzin. *Polzin, the Descendants of Peter and Charlotte Polzin, 1803–1994.* Minnesota: Author, 1995. 652p.

Pontiny

Ward, Naomi Etta. *The Ward Connections, Nourse, Kimmel, Wood, Babbs, Shelton, Sasubjak, Ader, Guffey, Pontiny, Archibald, Asbell.* Evansville, IN: Author, 1995. 545p.

Pontious

Punches, James E. *The Descendants of Peter Punches and Margaret Hager, with Entries for (1761–1994).* Green River, WY: Author, 1995. 41p.

Poole

Sheridan, Doris R. *The Poole Family.* Troy, NY: Author, 1995. 6p.

Popp

Popp, Tony. *Popp, Kemper, Kammerer, Tungate, Wiwi, Jonas and Other Ancestors and Relations.* Florence, KY: Author, 1995. 226p.

Porter

Hills, Iva Flo Jackson. *As the West Was Won, History Genealogy.* Springfield, MO: Author, 1995. 311p.
Younglove, James N. *The Descendants of Samuel and Margaret Younglove.* Houston, TX: Author, 1995. 200p.

Poston

May, John Russell. *Poston History and Genealogy.* Fort Wayne, IN: Author, 1995. Unpgd.

Pothier

Pothier, Gisèle. *Viens et Suis-moi chez les Pothier.* Saint Hubert, Quebec: Author, 1995. 323p.

Potter

Pothier, Gisèle. *Viens et Suis-moi chez les Pothier.* Saint Hubert, Quebec: Author, 1995. 323p.

Powell

Bielanski, Phyllis Jean Olin. *Andrew Powell Family Tree, Including Powell, Farr, Ten Brock Branches and Wolcott, Stiles, Doolittle, Kelch, Eldridge Branches.* Lakeland, FL: Author, 1995. Unpgd.

Ealy, Arthur R. *Descendants of Joseph Powell, Family Born in Maryland and Pennsylvania, Moving to Ohio*. St. Louis, MO: Author, 1995. Unpgd.

Mann, Marion. *The Kigh, Mann, Reagin, and Sykes Families, Including the Branch, Brown, Dean, Fort, Gerran, Leake, Marquis, Moses, Oakes, Powell, Reid, Trammell, Walk, Wilkey, Wingfield, and Woods Families, a Genealogy and Family History*. Baltimore, MD: Gateway Press, 1995. 218p.

Powell, John W. *Ancestors and Descendants of William Powell and His Wife, Elizabeth Glaradon, Warrick County, Indiana*. Evansville, IN: Author, 1995. 162p.

Power

Partin, Sherita Kae. *Power Family of Nacogdoches County, Texas, a Genealogical Report on the Power Family Ancestors and Descendants of Nacogdoches County, Texas*. Nacogdoches, TX: Partin Pubs., 1995. 16p.

Poyntz

Bodine, Ronny O. *The Ancestry of Dorothea Poyntz, Wife of Reverend John Owsley, Generations 1–12*. Fort Meade, MD: Author, 1995. 162p.

Prachel

Vilkaitis, Gregg A. *The Prachel Family of Monroe County, New York*. Charleston, WV: Author, 1995. 56p.

Prado

Sand, Vernon Jerome. *The Life and Times of Vernon and Renee Sand and Related Families, Geiselhart, Bittle, Warner, Sand, Vilmo, Bergman, Le Grand, Lassauge, Prado, and Carpentier*. Austin, TX: Author, 1995. 501p.

Prettyman

Hills, Iva Flo Jackson. *As the West Was Won, History Genealogy*. Springfield, MO: Author, 1995. 311p.

Price

Feder, June Constance. *The Genealogy of the Price and Stull Families of the Town of Rush, Monroe County, New York, the Murrays, Wallings, and Hills of Victor, New York and the Otto, Block, Hill and Summerhays Families of Rochester, New York*. Fairport, NY: Author, 1995. 75p.

Price, Grant J. *Families of Gideon M. and Pearlillian H. Price: Early North Carolina*. Ogden, UT: Author, 1995. 634p.

Prickett

Miller, Kimberlee. *Descendants of Captain Jacob Prickett, Sr.*. Fairmont, WV: Jacob's Meadow, Inc., 1995. 178p.

Primm

Ponder, Pearlie. *Links to Ancestral Ties, George Primm, Sr. Family*. Sacramento, CA: Ponder Publications, 1995. 200p.

Prindle

Prindle, Franklin Cogswell. *Prindle-Pringle Genealogy*. Bowie, MD: Heritage Books, 1995. 170p.

Pringle

Prindle, Franklin Cogswell. *Prindle-Pringle Genealogy*. Bowie, MD: Heritage Books, 1995. 170p.

Pringle, Sheila. *Pringle-Anderson Family History Book*. Sumter, SC: New Concepts, 1995. Unpgd.

Pritchard

Cottrell, Richard Gary. *The Tyler-Fruhauf Family History, and Genealogical Record of Associated Edwards, Ellis, Helme, Mason, Pritchard, Seymour, Sherrerd, and Whiting Families*. Parma, MI: Author, 1995. 2 vols.

Privat

Privat, John Pierre. *The Privats, Lore, Legends, and Facts, 1600–1995*. Woodinville, WA: Vanderloop Communications, 1995. 255p.

Proctor

Moore, Thomas R. *Plantagenet Desent, 31 Generations from William the Conqueror to Today*. Baltimore, MD: Gateway, 1995. 242p.

Proulx

Proulx, Antonin. *Recueil des Familles Proulx et Letourneau: Les Descendants de Mes Arrière-Grands-Parents (Côte paternel)*. Ottawa, Ontario: Author, 1995. 213p.

Pryor

Pryor, John Gatewood. *A Pryor Family Narrative, Ancestors, Descendants and Related Lineages*. Atlanta, GA: Author, 1995. 298p.

Punches

Punches, James E. *The Descendants of Peter Punches and Margaret Hager, with Entries for (1761–1994)*. Green River, WY: Author, 1995. 41p.

Purdy

Purdy, Clayton C. *Francis Purdy, Seventh Son of Joseph, Phebe Purdy, One of Joseph's Four Daughters*. St. George, UT: Author, 1995. Unpgd.

Pursell

Winchester, Warren. *Benjamin Pursley (Pursell)*. Purcellville, VA: Author, 1995. 248p.

Putnam

McDonald, David Michael. *Polly's Family, the New England Ancestry and Some Descendants of Polly Putnam (1793–1886) and Her Husband Jonathan Betts (1787–1841)*. Dyer, IN: Author, 1995. 44p.

Mize, Joel Sanford. *Putnam-Ramsey Family Genealogy*. Lakewood, CO: Author, 1995. 239p.

Pyle

Sepp, Ferne Whitmore. *My Pile, Sharpe, Ward, Whitmore Family*. Rantoul, IL: Author, 1995. Unpgd.

–Q

Quick

Quick, Robert V. *A Genealogy of the Family of Quick*. Memphis, TN: Author, 1995. 52p.

Quigley

Wolff, Warren. *The Quigley Family*. Worthington, PA: Author, 1995. Unpgd.

–R

Raba

Holzmann, Herbert A. *Descendants of Ernst Wilhelm Raba, 1874–1951, and Maria Margareta Fuhrwerk, 1875–1965*. San Antonio, TX: Author, 1995. Unpgd.

Race

Race, William Benton. *The Rees/Race Family in America, Descendants of Andries (Race) Rees and Celitje Jans*. Santa Rosa, CA: Author, 1995. 110p.

Radford

Harvill, Ruth Radford. *Radford Ramblings, a Family History of the Descendants of William and Mary Milton Radford, Including Some of the Families Which Connect by Marriage*. Cartersville, GA: Author, 1995. 240p.

Ragan

Ragan, Robert Allison. *The Ragans of Gastonia, 1790–1995, George Washington Ragan and Caldwell Ragan, Builders and Pioneers in Southern Textiles*. Charlotte, NC: R. A. Ragan & Co., 1995. 568p.

Rahjes

Rahjes, William. *Herman H. Rahjes Family History, 1895–1995*. Osborne, KS: Osborne Publishing Co., 1995. 184p.

Ralston

Ralston, Harold Alan. *Our Ralston Families: Including Ralston, McAffee, Cross, McMichael, Hanna, and Others*. Rev. Racine, WI: Author, 1995. 134p.

Ramirez

Pena, José F. de la. *Los Ramirez de Revilla Ciudad Guerro, 1712–1900*. Ventura, CA: Author, 1995. 50p.

Ramsey

Mize, Joel Sanford. *Putnam-Ramsey Family Genealogy*. Lakewood, CO: Author, 1995. 239p.

Randall

Randall, Marjorie. *Six Generations of the Edward Randall Family*. Sheboygan, WI: Franzen Litho Screen, 1995. 406p.

Randolph

Hauk, Carol A. *Descendants of Benjamin Harrison of Virginia*. 4th. ed. Anderson, IN: Hauk Data Services, 1995. 365p.
————. *Descendants of Lewis Burwell of Virginia*. Anderson, IN: Hauk Data Services, 1995. 395p.
————. *Descendants of Miles Cary of Virginia*. Anderson, IN: Hauk Data Services, 1995. 421p.
————. *Descendants of Richard Bolling of Virginia*. Anderson, IN: Hauk Data Services, 1995. 315p.
————. *Descendants of Robert and Charles Rose of Virginia*. Anderson, IN: Hauk Data Services, 1995. 51p.
————. *Descendants of Robert Beverley of Virginia*. Anderson, IN: Hauk Data Services, 1995. 330p.
————. *Descendants of William Churchill of Virginia*. 2nd. ed. Anderson, IN: Hauk Data Services, 1995. 250p.
————. *Descendants of William Randolph of Virginia*. Anderson, IN: Hauk Data Services, 1995. 461p.

Ransom

Johnston, Anne Plummer. *The Plummer Lineage of America*. Reston, VA: M. L. Tomaselli, 1995. 56p.
Stover, Margaret Harris. *Ely Harris and Lucretia Ransom of Connecticut, New York, and Ontario, Supplement*. Punta Gorda, FL: Author, 1995. 221p.

Rapelje

Linn, Jo White. *Ancestry of Moore/Rowan Families, with Related Lines of Fleming, Renick, Bosley, Green, Girault, Beatty, Reading, Armitage, Ryerson, Rapelje*. New Orleans, LA: Author, 1995. 186p.

Rapley

Lewis, Allen Roy. *Two Hundred Year History and Genealogy of the Isaac Lewis Family from Cloughjordan (Tipperary), Ireland to the Canadas and the United States, Including*

Intermarriages with Hodgins, Myers, Rapley, Slack, Williams, and Many Other Families. Ver. 1.5. Syracuse, NY: Author, 1995. 215p.

Ratliff

Moore, Freddie Gene. *The Descendants of Thomas Moore, Sr. of Suffolk County, England and the Related Families, Youngs, Landon, Spencer, French, Norris, Simmons, Ratliff, Slaughter.* Author, 1995. Unpgd.

———. *My Virginia Ancestors and Their Descendants in the Families, Ratliff, Skidmore, Watson, Hamilton, Wallace, Cahoon, Bowyer, Grimes, Sharp, Meeks.* Author, 1995. 116p.

Ratts

Ratts, Kenneth R. *From Germany to Wherever?.* Sun City Center, FL: Author, 1995. Unpgd.

———. *Relationship Chart.* Sun City Center, FL: Author, 1995. 83p.

Rawson

A Rawson Family Genealogy. 1995. 214p.

Ray

Craft, Kenneth F. *Some Branches of the Ward Family of Montgomery County, Maryland, with Earliest Ancestor, Revolutionary War Soldier James White Ward (also Known as James White) Including Some Allied Lines: Fairfax, Thompson, Ray, Cooke and Wylie.* Norcross, GA: Author, 1995. Unpgd.

Raymaker

Giroux, Amy Larner. *The Descendants of Adrian and Susanna Raymakers of Belgium and New York, 1691–1994.* Orlando, FL: Author, 1995. 386p.

Rayson

Allen, Mary Barnes. *The Immigrants, George Read/Reed and Sarah Rayson, the Pioneers, Thomas Law Reed and Amantha Ann Smith, with Ancestors and Descendants.* Sonora, CA: Author, 1995. 117p.

Reade

Hauk, Carol A. *Descendants of George Reade of Virginia.* Anderson, IN: Hauk Data Services, 1995. 393p.

Reading

Linn, Jo White. *Ancestry of Moore/Rowan Families, with Related Lines of Fleming, Renick, Bosley, Green, Girault, Beatty, Reading, Armitage, Ryerson, Rapelje.* New Orleans, LA: Author, 1995. 186p.

Reagin

Mann, Marion. *The Kigh, Mann, Reagin, and Sykes Families, Including the Branch, Brown, Dean, Fort, Gerran, Leake, Marquis, Moses, Oakes, Powell, Reid, Trammell, Walk, Wilkey, Wingfield, and Woods Families, a Genealogy and Family History.* Baltimore, MD: Gateway Press, 1995. 218p.

Reamer

Reamer, Kathleen R. *Descendants of John Reamer and Margaret Schermerhorn, 1758–1995.* Imlay City, MI: Author, 1995. 246p.

Redd

Redd, Bryan Lafayette. *Family of James and Martha Red.* Greenville, SC; Southern Historical Press, 1995. 734p.

Redden

The Redden Family Chronicles of Worcester County, Maryland. Author, 1995. Unpgd.

Redfield

Graves, Kenneth Vance. *Deacon George Graves, 1636 Settler of Hartford, Connecticut, and His Descendants.* Wrenthen, MA: Author, 1995. 446p.

Rediger

Roth, Donald Wayne. *The Families of Anna (Guth) and Rediger Roth.* Fort Wayne, IN: Author, 1995. 168p.

Redman

Holmes, Marguerite. *Holmes from John of England and Plymouth, Massachusetts, to Holmes Brothers William Hudson, Horace William and Rodney Arthur Holmes of Aroostook County, Maine and Related Families Cobbs, Redman, Libby and Shorey.* San Antonio, TX: Author, 1995. 101p.

Reecer

Koickler, Eloyce Hubbard. *Hiestand, Hestand, Hastings.* Helena, MT: Author, 1995. 127p.

Reed

Allen, Mary Barnes. *The Immigrants, George Read/Reed and Sarah Rayson, the Pioneers, Thomas Law Reed and Amantha Ann Smith, with Ancestors and Descendants.* Sonora, CA: Author, 1995. 117p.

Ardinger, Dennis B. *Descendants of the Revolutionary War Family of Lieutenant Thomas Reed and Charity Newkirk of Allegheny, Beaver and Washington Counties, Pennsylvania, 1750-1900.* Rev. Bridgeville, PA: Author, 1995. 163p.

Kercheval, Beverly Marie. *The Reed and Stanphill Families.* Slaton, TX: Author, 1995. 533p.

Paget, James Suddath. *Ancestors and Descendants of Mary Elise Mauldin Paget and Eilleen Reed Mauldin Mattison.* Greer, SC: Author, 1995. 248p.

Reed Family of Casey County and Beyond. 1995. 292p.

Rees

Race, William Benton. *The Rees/Race Family in America, Descendants of Andries (Race) Rees and Celitje Jans.* Santa Rosa, CA: Author, 1995. 110p.

Reeve

Reeve, Bert S. *Memoirs of a Thatching Family, 1860–1968.* Dereham, England.: Larks Press, 1995. 73p.

Regan

Jordan, Thomas Franklin. *An American Migration*. Thesis (M.A.), Louisiana State University, 1995. 194p.

Regier

Pearson, Elizabeth Regier. *Abraham-Elizabeth Froese Regier Family History*. Author, 1995. Unpgd.

Reid

Adair, Shirley Brown. *Robert Adair (1770–1845c.), an Adair Family History, Reid, Emerson, Hobbs, Worley, Thompson (Related Lines)*. Rockwall, TX: Author, 1995. 146p.

Mann, Marion. *The Kigh, Mann, Reagin, and Sykes Families, Including the Branch, Brown, Dean, Fort, Gerran, Leake, Marquis, Moses, Oakes, Powell, Reid, Trammell, Walk, Wilkey, Wingfield, and Woods Families, a Genealogy and Family History*. Baltimore, MD: Gateway Press, 1995. 218p.

Reidheimer

Hughes, Nancy Caroline Phillips. *Hugh Phillips, Some of His Descendants, Including Allied Families of Bolin, Blewer (Bluer), Reidheimer, Salley, Schuler (Shuler) and Winningham*. Columbia, SC: Author, 1995. 46p.

Reimer

Suderman, Joel. *David P. Schroeder, Sara (Janzen) Schroeder Family History and Genealogy, Including Information about Peter Schroeder, David & Ana (Tiart) Schroeder, Peter & Susanna (Reimer) Schroeder, David P. & Sara (Janzen) Schroeder*. Marion, KS: Author, 1995. 65p.

Reiner

Zeiszler, Ernest Erwin. *Reiner* Author, 1995. Unpgd.

Reinhart

Beck, William M. *The Nicholas Reinhart Family*. East Peoria, IL: Author, 1995. 54p.

Reinke

Reinke, George F. *The Reinke Family Tree*. Wisconsin: Author, 1995. Unpgd.

Winkelman, Philip M. *The Reineke Family History, the Descendants of Johann Heinrich Conrad Reineke and Caroline W. Koehler*. Fergus Falls, MN: Author, 1995. 275p.

Remington

Meigs, Peter Sanford. *Our Meigs and Smith Ancestors, Including the Clarke, Clifford, Eldredge, Fellows, Howe, MacMillan, Mann, Remington, Rice, Robinson, Scadgel, Skillings, and Thing Families*. Danville, NH: Author, 1995. Unpgd.

Remmell

Allen, Patricia Remmell. *The Remmell and Allen Families of New Castle County, Delaware*. Horsham, PA: Author, 1995. 71p.

Remmler

Saunders, Jo Ann Muenzler. *Christoph Friedrich Munzler and His Descendants*. Austin, TX: Author, 1995. 76p.

Rempel

A History of the Peter F. Rempel Family. Beaverton, OR: A. Dale Aufrecht, 1995. 71p.

Rempp

Steffey, Dale E. *Genealogy of Andreas Rempp and His Wife Anna Eitelbuss, Oschelbronn, Germany*. El Cajon, CA: Author, 1995. 74p.

Renninger

Weaver, Clyde Richard. *The Descendants of Daniel E. and Rebecca Renninger Weaver*. Wooster, OH: Author, 1995. 120p.

Replogle

Dubel, Zelda. *Golden, Hildreth and Replogle Genealogy*. Fresno, CA: Author, 1995. 29p.

Raymond, Edith Madeline Replogle. *The Replogle, Reprogle Genealogy*. 2nd ed. Battle Creek, MI: Author, 1995. 821p.

Repp

Repp, Glenn Arthur. *The History of Glenn A. Repp, the Genealogy and Family History of Glenn A. Repp (1894–1970)*. Duncanville, TX: Author, 1995. 138p.

Reuter

Biggar, Harold Arthur. *The Biggar Families of Greenwich, Connecticut, and County Tyrone, North Ireland*. Stamford, CT: Author, 1995. unpgd.

Rexer

Bell, Ernest Elmont, Jr. *One Line of Descent from Our Immigrant, Alexander Bell/Beall of Maryland, a Genealogical History, 1600 AD to 2000 AD, with an Autobiography by Ernest Elmont Bell, Jr. for His Descendants*. Baywood Park, CA: Author, 1995. 508p.

Reynolds

Ash, Edith Watkins Worley. *The Reynolds Pioneering Chronicles, New York and Southern Michigan Sojourn*. Osseo, MI: Author, 1995. 573p.

Reynolds, Beatrice Kay. *Nathaniel and Mary (Tolman) Reynolds, IV of Bridgewater, Massachusetts, Early Descendants in Sidney, Maine (1780)*. Sidney, ME: Author, 1995. 106p.

———. *Thomas Davenport of Dorchester, Massachusetts, His Descendants in Sidney, Maine (1762–1995)*. Sidney, ME: Author, 1995. 34p.

Reznor

Smith, Jack Edward. *The Reznors of Mercer County, Pennsylvania, Ancestors and Descendants, 1774–1995*. Hermitage, PA: Author, 1995. 269p.

Rhodes

York, Dorothy Anderson. *Our Anderson Family and Their Kin*. Fort Worth, TX: Author, 1995. 307p.

Rice

Davis, Lana DeLong. *Zebina's Kin, the Descendancy of a Puritan People, Jael Fellows (1789-1822) and Zebina Rice (1787–1873), Narrative, Letters and Charts*. Bowie, MD: Heritage Books, 1995. 171p.

Meigs, Peter Sanford. *Our Meigs and Smith Ancestors, Including the Clarke, Clifford, Eldredge, Fellows, Howe, MacMillan, Mann, Remington, Rice, Robinson, Scadgel, Skillings, and Thing Families*. Danville, NH: Author, 1995. Unpgd.

Rice, Frank. *Descendants of William Rice*. Diana, TX: Author, 1995. 67p.

Rich

Koickler, Eloyce Hubbard. *Hiestand, Hestand, Hastings*. Helena, MT: Author, 1995. 127p.

Richards

Bymaster Richards, Willa. *Descendants of Eugene Richards and Sabrina Charlton*. Carnation, WA: Author, 1995. Unpgd.

Richardson

Cooper, Jane Hamer. *A History of John Brown Richardson (1823–1897) and Mary Ann Wagner (1827–1905) of Shade Township, Somerset County, Pennsylvania*. Pittsburgh, PA: Author, 1995. 235p.

Thompson, Laura Jones. *Jones, Richardson, Duhamel, and Allied Families of Maryland*. Nutley, NJ: M. A. Hook, 1995. 511p.

Rick

Rick, Rosemary Ruth. *John Rick (1852–1924), Wausau, Wisconsin, and His Family*. Irving, TX: Author, 1995. 67p.

Rider

Ryder, Dana. *Rider to Ryder, the Descendants of Ebenezer Rider of New Canaan, New Brunswick, Canada (1771–1853)*. Standish, ME: Author, 1995. 229p.

Riedel

Bernard, Allen William. *The Bavarian Connection: the George and Walburga Karch Family and Their Descendants*. Newport, KY: Otto Zimmerman & Son, 1995. 263p.

Riegel

Riegel, Samuel Andrew. *Riegel Family History*. Author, 1995. 214p.

Riggenbach

Clegg, Mary Lou. *Blunier Family History*. Fort Wayne, IN: Author, 1995. 82p.

Riggins

Pinkston, Margaret Darracott. *Mosswood Remembered*. Baltimore, MD: Gateway Press, 1995. Unpgd.

Rigsby

Rigsby, Michael Hall. *The Ancestry of Laura Elaine Rigsby*. 5th ed. Houston, TX: Author, 1995. 217p.

Riley

Givens, Dorothy Bess Riley. *Thomas Butler Riley, Descendants, 1814–1995.* Purcellville, VA: Author, 1995. 58p.

York, Dorothy Anderson. *Our Anderson Family and Their Kin.* Fort Worth, TX: Author, 1995. 307p.

Ring

McGinn, Ann Winston. *A McGinn McCorkle Family History, 1796–1995: With Related Families, Crockett, Dabney, Egnatoff, Fontaine, Freirson, Gillespie, Huddart, Kennemore, O'Donnell, Patton, Ring, Sheppard, Winston, and Others.* Spring Hill, FL: Author, 1995. 313p.

Rinker

Supplee, Marcia Y. *Amy's Family: Descendants of Casper Rinker.* Stephens City, VA; Commercial Press, 1995. 117p.

Rising

Bunner, Gale Joseph. *Rising Genealogy, Descendants of Aaron Rising of Suffield, Connecticut.* Randolph, MA: Rising Family Association, 1995. 521p.

Risley

Bymaster Richards, Willa. *Descendants of Enoch Risley.* Carnation, WA: Author, 1995. Unpgd.

Ritter

Ritter, Victor H. *Ancestors and Descendants of John Monroe Ritter and Susan Matilda Caldwell, Pioneers of Sabine Parish, Louisiana.* Austin, TX; Author, 1995. 78p.

Runner, Ruth Ritter. *Paul Hugo Ritter and Related Families, Rottweil, Germany to Cumberland, Maryland.* Morgantown, WV: Morgantown Printing, 1995. 421p.

Ritterhoff

Harris, Arlo D. *Family Tree Document for William Lester Harris and Charlotte Augusta Ernst.* 2nd. ed. Dayton, OH: Author, 1995. 109p.

Ritz

Olson, Scott L. *Ritz Family History.* Grand Forks, ND: Author, 1995. 27p.

Roark

Hackler, Sarah Katherine Smith. *Rowark, Roark and Related Families of Elk Creek, Grayson County, Virginia.* Galax, VA: Author, 1995. 183p.

Robards

Horned, Joseph. *A Guide for Researching Robards/Roberts/Robertson in Cherokee Records, Dawes Roll, Guion Miller Roll, Drennen Roll, Chapman Roll.* Author, 1995. 30p.

Robbins

Willis, Dorothy Burrows. *Across the Continent with the Ancestors and Descendants of Abner Willis and Martha Robbins.* Oak Harbor, WA: Heritage Cascade, 1995. 300p.

Wrenn, Gladys Robbins Guins. *The Robbins Family, from Virginia to Texas.* Cleveland, TX: Author, 1995. 70p.

Robenhagen
Jordan, Wallace Thomas. *The Robenhagen Chronicles*. Milwaukee, WI: Author, 1995. 127p.

Roberts
Horned, Joseph. *A Guide for Researching Robards/Roberts/Robertson in Cherokee Records, Dawes Roll, Guion Miller Roll, Drennen Roll, Chapman Roll*. Author, 1995. 30p.
Jacobsen, Thomas Andrew. *Robertses of Northern New England*. Bowie, MD: Heritage Books, 1995. 456p.
Mallard, Shirley Jones. *Keeping Up with the Joneses, a Book about the Rafe Jones Family of Granville, North Carolina*. Chapel Hill, NC: Author, 1995. 244p.
Roberts, Theodore Russell. *John Roberts Family of Pensacola, Florida*. Author, 1995. 2 vols.

Robertson
Brayton, John A. *The Ancestry of General James Robertson "Father of Tennessee," Addendum to the Complete Ancestry of Tennessee Williams*. Winston-Salem, NC: Author, 1995. 60p.
Horned, Joseph. *A Guide For Researching Robards/Roberts/Robertson in Cherokee Records, Dawes Roll, Guion Miller Roll, Drennen Roll, Chapman Roll*. Author, 1995. 30p.
Robertson, James Miller. *A Tale of Two Families, Robertson and Griffith*. Corpus Christi, TX: Author, 1995. 412p.

Robinson
Bunnell, Paul Joseph. *The House of Robinson, the Robinsons of Rhode Island, Their Genealogy and Letters and the History of the Robinson & Son Oil Company of Baltimore, Maryland*. Bowie, MD: Heritage Books, 1995. 226p.
Ebersole, Patricia Smith. *Ebersole-Robinson Family History*. Chesterville, OH: Author, 1995. 273p.
Fehr, Martha Robinson. *Descendants of Gavin Mathers (1785–1869), a Supplement to the Mathers-Nesbit Genealogy by Lura B. Mitchell Emery*. Gulf Breeze, FL: Author, 1995. 288p.
Hauk, Carol A. *Descendants of Robinson Families of Virginia*. Anderson, IN: Hauk Data Services, 1995. 106p.
Meigs, Peter Sanford. *Our Meigs and Smith Ancestors, Including the Clarke, Clifford, Eldredge, Fellows, Howe, MacMillan, Mann, Remington, Rice, Robinson, Scadgel, Skillings, and Thing Families*. Danville, NH: Author, 1995. Unpgd.
Wright, Diana. *Robinson Roots*. Author, 1995. Unpgd.

Rochester
Sheriff, Anne. *Rochester Family History*. Central, SC: Author, 1995. 202p.

Roderick
Liston, Lois Jane Breakiron. *The Breakiron Family History Also Including the Bastian, Brecheisen, Casey, Dusenberry, Garlow, Hutchinson, Johnson, McMillen, Miller, Morris, Roderick and Other Families*. Wyandotte, OK: Gregath Pub. Co., 1995. 620p.

Rodgers
Zollars, Constance M. *Snouffer and Rodgers Family Records*. Fort Wayne, IN: Author, 1995. 88p.

Rogers

Crosby, Eleanor Davis. *Simon Crosby, the Immigrant. His English Ancestry and Some of His American Descendants*. Bowie, MD: Heritage Books, 1914, 1995. 159p.

McLane, Curren Rogers. *The Rogers Family Genealogy*. Fort Worth, TX: Author, 1995. Unpgd.

Zollars, Constance M. *Snouffer and Rodgers Family Records*. Fort Wayne, IN: Author, 1995. 88p.

Rogillio

Rogillio, Joseph Griffin. *Rogillio, A Family Record*. Zachary, LA: Author, 1995. 285p.

Rohn

Stene, Charles Sherwin. *The Stene Family, Includes Rohn, Anderson, Bothwell, Davenport, Lloyd*. Decorah, IA: Anundsen Pub. Co., 1995. 385p.

Rolfe

Rolfe, Frederick G. *Early Rolfe Settlers of New England*. Baltimore, MD: Gateway Press, 1995. 2 vols.

Romer

Reamer, Kathleen R. *Descendants of John Reamer and Margaret Schermerhorn, 1758–1995*. Imlay City, MI: Author, 1995. 246p.

Romine

Miller, Kimberlee. *Descendants of Captain Jacob Prickett, Sr.*. Fairmont, WV: Jacob's Meadow, Inc., 1995. 178p.

Roose

Evans, Aleene. *It's All Crystal Clear*. Columbus, GA: Quill Pub., 1995. 94p.

Roose, Kenneth D. *Frederick and Christina Roose, European Origins and Family Heritage in America, 1600–1995*. Boynton Beach, FL: Author, 1995. 69p.

Roosevelt

Rowland, Arthur Ray. *Distant Cousins: The Huguenots, Connecting Rowland, Bulloch, de Bourdeaux, de Veaux, and Roosevelt Families of South Carolina, Georgia, North Carolina and New York*. Augusta, GA: RR Books, 1995. 16p.

Root

Hauk, Carol A. *Descendants of Philip Rootes of Virginia*. Anderson, IN: Hauk Data Services, 1995. 32p.

Roque

Davila Valldjuli, José. *Genealogía Valldejuli, Duprey y Roque de Puerto Rico*. Lubbock, TX: Author, 1995. 145p.

Rose

Cole, Mary. *The Bunyard Family Research and Allied Families, Alley, Fitzwater, Foster, Hughes, Jones, Ledlow, McNeely, Rose*. Kentfield, CA: Author, 1995. 151p.

Hauk, Carol A. *Descendants of Mordecai Cooke of Virginia*. 3rd. ed. Anderson, IN: Hauk Data Services, 1995. 309p.

———. *Descendants of Robert and Charles Rose of Virginia*. Anderson, IN: Hauk Data Services, 1995. 51p.

Roose, Kenneth D. *Frederick and Christina Roose, European Origins and Family Heritage in America, 1600–1995*. Boynton Beach, FL: Author, 1995. 69p.

Welch, Glorya E. *Rose and Wyn Families of Muskegon, Michigan*. La Mirada, CA: Author, 1995. 18p.

Ross

Johnson, Janet Ross. *Ross Genealogy: Pennsylvania, Ohio and Kentucky, 1754–1976*. Bellevue, KY: Author, 1995. 25p.

Roth

Drendel, Gilbert Xavier. *Harvest of the Ages, the Xavier Drendel and Therese Roth Family*. Decorah, IA: Anundsen Pub. Co., 1995. 558p.

Roth, Donald Wayne. *The Families of Anna (Guth) and Rediger Roth*. Fort Wayne, IN: Author, 1995. 168p.

Rouatt

Peterson, Marion Plath. *Peck, McClinchey, Rouatt Saga*. Decorah, IA: Anundsen Pub. Co., 1995. Unpgd.

Rountree

Hall, Clyde W. *The Life and Times and Ancestry of John Willis Rountree and Emma Jane Rountree*. Savannah, GA: Author, 1995. 44p.

Rowe

Rowe, Howard Morrison. *Our Heritage, a Story of Twenty Families*. San Diego, CA: Author, 1995. 524p.

Rowland

Rowland, Arthur Ray. *Distant Cousins: The Huguenots, Connecting Rowland, Bulloch, de Bourdeaux, de Veaux, and Roosevelt Families of South Carolina, Georgia, North Carolina and New York*. Augusta, GA: RR Books, 1995. 16p.

Wallace, Rachel Rowland. *William Rowland and Nancy Frances Johnson, Their Ancestors and Descendants*. Rev. ed. Lexington, KY: Author, 1995. 105p.

Roy

Levesque Babin, Olivette. *Mâture, Voilure et Souvenance, Histoire et Généalogie des Familles Roy et Tremblay (Pascal)*. Ville de la Baie, Quebec: Author, 1995. 342p.

Ruby

Greene, Bob. *Maine Roots, the Manuel, Mathews, Ruby Family*. Brooklyn, NY: Family Affair Production, 1995. 84p.

Woodard, Lucile Ruby. *Ruby Families in America*. Author, 1995. Unpgd.

Rudd

Elliott, Margaret Coppess. *The Nicholls Family of Jefferson County, Ohio, the Rudd, Cox, Smith, and Related Families Who Came to Berlin Township, Ionia County, Michigan before 1870*. Ionia, MI: Author, 1995. Unpgd.

Rudisill

Rudisill, Edward L. *The Rudisill Genealogy, the American Descendants of Hans Rudisuli of Frumsen, Kanton St. Gallen, Switzerland, with an Introduction of the Swiss Families Preceding Our Common Progenitor to circa 1580*. Elverson, PA: Olde Springfield Shoppe, 1995. 1,104p.

Ruffcorn

Ruffcorn Cousins Associated. *Ruffcorn, an All American Family: A True Genealogy*. Freeman, SD: Pine Hill Press, 1995. 285p.

Ruhl

Garbrick, Harry. *Ruhl Family*. Author, 1995. 277p.

Rundell

Edgerly, Dorthea Roach. *Jared Rundle (Rundell), Jr. of Sullivan County, Indiana, His Ancestors and Descendants*. Oceanside, CA: Author, 1995. 484p.

Rupe

McGrew, Everette L. *My Mother Was a Rupe*. Dallas, TX: Author, 1995. 78p.

Rusch

Brombal, Mildred Kist. *The Rusch-Schnell Families*. Santa Barbara, CA: KISTCO, 1995. 212p.

Rushing

Jones, Helen Lyndola Rushing. *Matthew Rushing Descendants in South Mississippi, 1810–1995*. Houston, TX: Armstrong Book Printers & Publishers, 1995. 941p.

Russell

Deems, M. Electa. *History of the Russell Family*. Austin, TX: Author, 1995. 1995. 48p.

Nimmo, Sylvia. *The Descendants and Ancestors of Milo and Dora (Moon) Russell*. Papillion, NE: Author, 1995. 44p.

Our Scottish Russells and Their Descendants in America, a Genealogy and Memoirs of the Families of John Russell and Alexander C. Russell of Marshall County, Illinois. 1995. 309p.

Pierce, Donald Ray. *Russell Pictorial Family History*. Mt. Vernon, IN: Author, 1995. Unpgd.

Rust

Rust, John Howard. *My Life and Times as I Remember Them*. Chicago, IL: Author, 1995. 597p.

Rutledge, Fred Alvah. *Some Descendants of Thomas Watts, Jr., 1747 Virginia, 1797 Georgia, and Hannah Rust Boggess, 1753 Virginia, 1836 Alabama*. Baltimore, MD: Author, 1995. Unpgd.

Ryan

Krohn, Darlene. *The Descendants of Jerome Ryan*. Ocean Springs, MS: Author, 1995. 80p.

Ryder

Ryder, Dana. *Rider to Ryder, the Descendants of Ebenezer Rider of New Canaan, New Brunswick, Canada (1771–1853)*. Standish, ME: Author, 1995. 229p.

Ryerson

Linn, Jo White. *Ancestry of Moore/Rowan Families, with Related Lines of Fleming, Renick, Bosley, Green, Girault, Beatty, Reading, Armitage, Ryerson, Rapelje*. New Orleans, LA: Author, 1995. 186p.

– S

Sabin

Settles, Mary Sullivan. *Saebo Sabin, a Family History*. Napa, CA: Author, 1995. 267p.

Saez

Saez, Florencio. *Guayanilla, Barrio Pasto, Genealogia del Apellido Saez*. Puerto Rico: Editorial Palma Real, 1995. 151p.

Safford

Karr, Nola M. *Baker Family Record, a Genealogy of Many of the Descendants of John Baker Who Immigrated from England in 1637*. White Plains, MD: Automated Graphic Systems, 1995. 663p.

Saile

Lombus, William. *Saile in Hohenberg and Columbus, a Family History, 1590–1990*. Park Hills, KY: Author, 1995. 208p.

Sain

Bennett, Katie Brown. *Soaking the Yule Log: Biographical Sketches of the Brown, Cheshier, Sain, and Allied Families, 1749–1995*. Decorah, IA: Anundsen Pub. Co., 1995. 514p.

Salley

Hughes, Nancy Caroline Phillips. *Hugh Phillips, Some of His Descendants, Including Allied Families of Bolin, Blewer (Bluer), Reidheimer, Salley, Schuler (Shuler) and Winningham*. Columbia, SC: Author, 1995. 46p.

Same

Vilkaitis, Gregg A. *The Prachel Family of Monroe County, New York*. Charleston, WV: Author, 1995. 56p.

Samson

Sherman, Robert Moody. *Henry Samson of the Mayflower and His Descendants for Four Generations*. 2nd ed. Plymouth, MA: General Society of Mayflower Descendants, 1995. 158p.

Sanchez

Maes, Arthur F. *Following in the Footsteps of Our Ancestors from "Santa Fe to Maes Creek."* Colorado Springs, CO: Author, 1995. 157p.

Sanchez, George Abe. *The Sanchez/Padilla Family of Lincoln County, New Mexico, a Genealogical Study*. El Paso, TX: Author, 1995. 59p.

Sand

Sand, Vernon Jerome. *The Life and Times of Vernon and Renee Sand and Related Families, Geiselhart, Bittle, Warner, Sand, Vilmo, Bergman, Le Grand, Lassauge, Prado, and Carpentier*. Austin, TX: Author, 1995. 501p.

Sandel

Sandel, Elias Wesley. *The Descendants of John Peter Sandel and Cullen Conerly*. Roseland, LA: Ara Ann Pubns., 1995. Unpgd.

Sanders

Jones, Jeanenne Gattis. *Sifting Sanders*. Sayre, OK: Author, 1995. 59p.

Robertson, Joanna. *A Tree Grows in America: My Family Line*. West Columbia, SC: Author, 1995. 238p.

Sanders, Patrick B. *Genealogies of the Sanders and Watson Families, Examining the Descendants of Henry Sanders of Germany and Donald Watson of Scotland*. Chapel Hill, NC: Professional Press, 1995. 270p.

Sanders, Ralph A. *Sanders Family Genealogy*. Manlius, NY: Author, 1995. 55p.

———. *Sanders Family Genealogy: A Companion Piece to Sanders Family Genealogy*. Manlius, NY: Author, 1995. 48p.

Sandidge

Kaufman, Mary Arnold. *Martin-Arnold and Allied Families, Lanier, Bailey, Swan, Sandidge, Gholston, Morgan, and Born, Migration from Virginia to Tennessee, Georgia, Alabama and Arkansas*. Knoxville, TN: Tennessee Valley Pub., 1995. 212p.

Santistevan

Santistevan, Donna J. Kargo. *The Joe D. Santistevan Family Tree*. Englewood, CO: Author, 1995. Unpgd.

Sauder

Hershey, J. Eby. *Family Record of Bishop John M. and Susanna G. Sauder*. Author, 1995. 32p.

Sauer

Sowers, Betty. *The Descendants of Philip Sauer/Sowers*. Norfolk, VA: Author, 1995. 2 vols.

Saunders

Crandall, Earl P. *Old Tobe, Some Lines of Descent of Tobias Saunders of Westerly, Rhode Island*. Catskill, NY: Author, 1995. 320p.

Hanna, William Lee. *The Saunders Family of Indiana and Ohio*. Columbia City, IN: Joy Earling, 1995. Unpgd.

Saunders, Edward E. *The Saunders Family from Colonial Virginia to Pioneers Out West*. Riverton, WY: Author, 1995. 61p.

Savage

Chamberlain, Merle. *On the Trail of Zebulon Latimer and His Family*. Wilmington, DE: Lower Cape Fear Historical Society, 1995. Unpgd.

Hauk, Carol A. *Descendants of Anthony Savage of Virginia*. Anderson, IN: Hauk Data Services, 1995. 276p.

O'Neal, Marcia Corrigan. *O'Neal Genealogy from the Early 1800s and Including Ancestors Anderson, Childers, Davis, Griffith, Hunt, Savage, Venard, and Willcuts*. Richmond, IN: Author, 1995. 43p.

Savage, Russell Blair. *Savage Is My Name, a History of Thirteen Generations of a Savage Family in America*. Aurora, OH: Buffalo Run Pub. Co., 1995. 307p.

Sawyer

Sawyer, Eleanor Grace. *Sawyer Families of New England, 1636–1900*. Camden, ME: Penobscot Press, 1995. 718p.

Saxon

Saxon, Jackie. *Saxon and Allied Families*. Author, 1995. 414p.

Sayre

Bartram, Chester E. *The George Washington McCoy Family of Mason County, West Virginia, Prominent Related Families Edington, Ferrell, Hoschar, Jividen, King, Sayre, Strait*. Knoxville, TN: Author, 1995. 187p.

Scadgel

Meigs, Peter Sanford. *Our Meigs and Smith Ancestors, Including the Clarke, Clifford, Eldredge, Fellows, Howe, MacMillan, Mann, Remington, Rice, Robinson, Scadgel, Skillings, and Thing Families*. Danville, NH: Author, 1995. Unpgd.

Scanlon

Moule, James C. *John Moule and Katie Scanlan*. Albuquerque, NM: Author, 1995. 172p.

Schaeffer

Barron, William P. *The Family History of Belva Nevada Woolery, Wife of Bill Schamel and Wyatt McMillan and Her Descendants: With Notes on Related Families Brown, Lockhart, Schaeffer, Wiesman, Williams*. Fairborn, OH: Heritage Family Publications, 1995. Unpgd.

Schaible

Sprenger, Ernest H. *Roots and Relatives*. Ritzville, WA: Author, 1995. 676p.

Schamel

Barron, William P. *The Family History of Belva Nevada Woolery, Wife of Bill Schamel and Wyatt McMillan and Her Descendants: With Notes on Related Families Brown, Lockhart, Schaeffer, Wiesman, Williams*. Fairborn, OH: Heritage Family Publications, 1995. Unpgd.

Scheid

Miller, Marilyn Isabel. *The Winner and Scheid Families*. Cullman, AL: Gregath Pub. Co., 1995. 227p.

Schellenberg

Dueck, Benjamin. *The Descendants of Paul Schellenberg, 1634–1995*. Steinbach, Manitoba: Author, 1995. 82p.

Schellens

Giroux, Amy Lamer. *The Descendants of Adrian and Susanna Raymakers Schellens of Belgium and New York, 1691–1994*. Author, 1995. 386p.

Schenck

Smith, Robert Lee. *Ancestors of Thelma Margaret Gander*. Alexandria, VA: Author, 1995. 65p.

Schermerhorn

Reamer, Kathleen R. *Descendants of John Reamer and Margaret Schermerhorn, 1758–1995*. Imlay City, MI: Author, 1995. 246p.

Scherrer

Lacey, Hubert Wesley. *The Goodner Family, a Genealogical History, with a Brief History of the Family of Jacob Daniel Scherrer, and Notes on Other Allied Families*. Cullman, AL: Gregath Pub. Co., 1995. 2 vols.

Schiller

Prigge, Barbara Joan. *Hold the Lutefisk, Please, or, Our Norwegian Heritage, Families of Hansen, Johnson and Schiller*. Summer 1995 Ed. Madison, WI: Author, 1995. 55p.

Schimank

Boriack, David. *Boriack Family Tree, 1995*. Lincoln, TX: Author, 1995. 303p.

Schlabach

Schlabach, Oma. *History and Genealogy of the Jacob C. and Sadie (Tice) Schlabach Family from 1735 to 1994*. Millersburg, OH: Author, 1995. 131p.

Schleich

Gray, John. *A History and Genealogy of the Schleich/Slyh/Sly Family, J. Frederich Schleich/Slyh, d. 1800, His Wife Christiana, and Their Descendants*. Columbus, OH: Author, 1995. Unpgd.

Schlosser

Schlosser Research Associates. *A Genealogy of the Schlosser, Slusser and Slusher Families of America, 1605–1994*. Kettering, OH: Author, 1995. 527p.

Schmeltz

Fisher, Robert G. *The Descendants of Andreas Schmeltz, 1751–1834*. Decorah, IA: Author, 1995. 402p.

Schmitthaussler

Schmitthausler, Carl M. *An American Melting Pot Saga, a Compilation of Information about a German Immigrant Family, Its Progress in the New World, and Its Network of Alliances.* Lincoln, NE: Alpha & Omega Pub., 1995. 78p.

Schneider

Jungen, Paul William. *Addendum II to the Genealogy of the John Jungen and Maria Elizabeth Schneider Family, ca. 1700–1994.* Asheville, NC: Author, 1995. 44p.

Schneider, Joseph J. *Family History of John L. and Margaretha (Dudenhefner) Schneider.* Dickinson, ND: Author, 1995. Unpgd.

Wagner, Betty Marie Daley. *The Schneider Genealogy and Related Families, Ancestors and Descendants of Carl Rudolph Schneider and Elizabeth Lena Bahler, Later Spelled Beller, John G. Bahler (Beller) and Anna Elisabeth Schneider, Samuel Bahler (Beller) and Elisabeth Litzy of Uetendorf, Canton Berne, Switzerland and Green County, Wisconsin, 1765–1995.* Milford, OH: Author, 1995. 201p.

Schnell

Brombal, Mildred Kist. *The Rusch-Schnell Families.* Santa Barbara, CA: KISTCO, 1995. 212p.

Schoellkopf

Glynn, Diane. *Schoellkopfs, 1842–1994, a Family History.* Niagara Falls, NY: Niagara Falls Memorial Medical Center Foundation, 1995. 285p.

Schroeder

Suderman, Joel. *David P. Schroeder, Sara (Janzen) Schroeder Family History and Genealogy, Including Information About Peter Schroeder, David & Ana (Tiart) Schroeder, Peter & Susanna (Reimer) Schroeder, David P. & Sara (Janzen) Schroeder.* Marion, KS: Author, 1995. 65p.

Schultheis

Herrington, Ilene Elma. *Schultheis, Geiger Families.* Norwich, NY: Author, 1995. 58p.

Schunk

Eggert, Irving John. *Peter Eggert of Mecklenburg and Related Families in America, Best, Bitz, Broekemeier, Hackbarth, Kane, Meisner, Nellis, Schunk, Strenkowski, Voight, Winston.* Decorah, IA: Anundsen Pub. Co., 1995. 224p.

Schunk, John F. *The Descendants of John Schunk, 1851–1907, of Webenheim, Germany, and Tazewell County, Illinois.* Wichita, KS: Author, 1995. 50p.

Schwab

Niedenthal, Corrine. *A Niedenthal Family History.* Kansas: Author, 1995. 175p.

Schwartztrauber

Schwartztrauber, Sayre Archie. *Schwartztrauber, Stewart, and Related Families.* Baltimore, MD: Gateway Press, 1995. 1,000 p.

Schweissguth

Ratts, Kenneth R. *From Germany to Wherever?.* Sun City Center, FL: Author, 1995. Unpgd.

Scott

Elder, Shirley Bowen. *My Bowen, Barton, Harris, Scott, Hendon, Cranford Family Connections*. 2nd. ed. Raleigh, NC: Author, 1995. 356p.

King, Margaret Ann Scott. *Homestead of the Free, the Jefferies Heritage*. 2nd. ed. Salt Lake City, UT: King-Scott Heritage Foundation, 1995. 647p.

Lough, Jeanne Trevillian. *A Genealogical History of the Scott Family Descendants of Alexander Scott, Pioneer Settler of Augusta County, Virginia, c. 1750 and a History of Allied Families in Western Virginia*. Morgantown, WV: George David Hott Memorial Foundation, 1995. 236p.

Marks, Arthur Lee. *Scott Family Journal*. Troy, MI: Author, 1995. 313p.

Scott, Edith Hall. *Scotts of Morgan and Noble Counties, Ohio, 1818–1910*. Austin, TX: Author, 1995. Unpgd.

Seabolt

Scott, Billy Dave. *Johnston-Southern of Clairborne County, Tennessee, and Parker County, Texas: Isaac McNew Johnston (1838–1918) and His Wife Norvesta Melocky Southern (1841–1929) and Allied Families Amis, Haynes, Huddleston, Seabolt, Southern and Spears*. Maryville, MO: Author, 1995. 215p.

Sealock

Durbin, Sue Tucker. *Sealock, Selock, 1763–1995*. Sullivan, IL: Author, 1995. 114p.

Searl

Graves, Kenneth Vance. *Deacon George Graves, 1636 Settler of Hartford, Connecticut, and His Descendants*. Wrenthen, MA: Author, 1995. 446p.

Sedgwick

Sedgwick, Robert P. *A Joseph Sedgwick Lineage*. Bountiful, UT: Family History Pub., 1995. 45p.

See

Hayes, Edward R. *Margaret Elizabeth Ferrel Hayes and Her Ancestors*. Author, 1995. 200p.

See, Lisa. *On Gold Mountain*. New York: St. Martin's Press, 1995. 394p.

Seebach

Seebach, Don. *1845–1995, One Hundred Fifty Years in America, Ancestors and Descendants of Ehrenfried Seebach, 1808–1897, and His Wife Maria Kruz, 1815–1887*. Hillsboro, OR: Author, 1995. 329p.

Seeley

Mills, Madeline M. *Robert Seeley (1602–1666) Descendants, the Sixth Generation Families*. Salt Lake City, UT: Seeley Genealogical Society, 1995. 156p.

Seelinger

Sellinger, Mary. *Seelinger, Selinger, Sellinger, 1632–1995, Family Tree*. Regina, Saskatchewan: Author, 1995. 261p.

Sell

Lacey, Garland Howard. *Ancestors and Descendants of Hiram G. Lacey and Sophia Sell*. Washington, IL: Author, 1995. 604p.

Sellers

R. E. W. Thompson (1856–1937), Adair, Clark, Carroll, Sellers, Lawson (Related Lines). Rockwall, TX: S. B. Adair, 1995. 133p.

Sellers, Harold E. *The John R. Sellers Family and Descendants*. Springfield, VA: Author, 1995. 151p.

Setz

Riley, David Joseph. *Descendants of Theodor Leonhard and Verena Setz of Passaic County, New Jersey*. New Brunswick, NJ: Author, 1995. Unpgd.

Severance

Dewsnap, David C. *The Severance Genealogy*. Bowie, MD: Heritage Books, 1995. 516p.

Sewall

Maule, Elizabeth Singer. *Inventory for Manuscript Collection MS-22. Sewall Family Papers, 1761–1965*. 3rd ed. Bath, ME: Maine Maritime Museum Library, 1995. 553p.

Seymour

Cottrell, Richard Gary. *The Tyler-Fruhauf Family History, and Genealogical Record of Associated Edwards, Ellis, Helme, Mason, Pritchard, Seymour, Sherrerd, and Whiting Families*. Parma, MI: Author, 1995. 2 vols.

Shade

Shade, Janet. *The Shade Family*. West Covina, CA: Forrest DeLoss Shade, Jr., 1995. 148p.

Shahan

Shahan, Elizabeth. *An Early History of the Shahan Family, 1678–1920*. Gaithersburg, MD: Author, 1995. 196p.

Shaklee

Shaklee, William Eugene. *Supplement #1 to Peter Shaklee Genealogy, 1766–1990*. Oklahoma City, OK: Author, 1995. 73p.

Shallenberger

Shallenberger, Martin J. *Shallenbergers of Echo Mountain*. Author, 1995. Unpgd.

Shanks

Baldree, Garvis Brookshire. *The Baldree Family*. Author, 1995. 212p.

Shanor

Ealy, Arthur R. *Descendants of Mathias Shanor, Revolutionary War Veteran and Frontiersman of Southwestern Pennsylvania*. St. Louis, MO: Author, 1995. 41p.

Sharp

Bostic, Paul Eugene. *Bruce, Maupin, Carr and Some Related Families Including Ballard, Hearn, Ayres, McCubbin, Cloud, Lane, Eveland (Elfland), Graves, Sharp and Willis.* Clinton, TN: Author, 1995. 391p.

Moore, Freddie Gene. *My Virginia Ancestors and Their Descendants in the Families, Ratliff, Skidmore, Watson, Hamilton, Wallace, Cahoon, Bowyer, Grimes, Sharp, Meeks.* Author, 1995. 116p.

Sepp, Ferne Whitmore. *My Pile, Sharpe, Ward, Whitmore Family.* Rantoul, IL: Author, 1995. Unpgd.

Sharpe, William Carvosso. *The Sharps of Chester County, Pennsylvania, and Abstracts of Records in Great Britain.* Rutland, VT: Tuttle Antiquarian Books, 1995. 36p.

Shedd

Shade, Janet. *The Shade Family.* West Covina, CA: Forrest DeLoss Shade, Jr., 1995. 148p.

Sheehan

Shahan, Elizabeth. *An Early History of the Shahan Family, 1678–1920.* Gaithersburg, MD: Author, 1995. 196p.

Shelton

Ward, Naomi Etta. *The Ward Connections, Nourse, Kimmel, Wood, Babbs, Shelton, Sasubjak, Ader, Guffey, Pontiny, Archibald, Asbell.* Evansville, IN: Author, 1995. 545p.

Shepard

Crosby, Eleanor Davis. *Simon Crosby, the Immigrant. His English Ancestry and Some of His American Descendants.* Bowie, MD: Heritage Books, 1914, 1995. 159p.

Sheppard

McGinn, Ann Winston. *A McGinn McCorkle Family History, 1796–1995: With Related Families, Crockett, Dabney, Egnatoff, Fontaine, Freirson, Gillespie, Huddart, Kennemore, O'Donnell, Patton, Ring, Sheppard, Winston, and Others.* Spring Hill, FL: Author, 1995. 313p.

Sheridan

Roberts, George Livingston. *The Sheridan Story, This Family History Covers All Known Descendants of James Sheridan.* Scottsdale, AZ: Author, 1995. 59p.

Sherman

Weber, Verlene Vaughn. *Sherman, Olney, Finley Families.* Bath, MI: Author, 1995. 54p.

Sherrerd

Cottrell, Richard Gary. *The Tyler-Fruhauf Family History, and Genealogical Record of Associated Edwards, Ellis, Helme, Mason, Pritchard, Seymour, Sherrerd, and Whiting Families.* Parma, MI: Author, 1995. 2 vols.

Shields

Hauk, Carol A. *Descendants of James Shields of Virginia.* Anderson, IN: Hauk Data Services, 1995. 69p.

Shipp

Robertson, Joanna. *A Tree Grows in America: My Family Line*. West Columbia, SC: Author, 1995. 238p.

Shipsey

Cummings, Jerome L. *The Shipsey Chronicles*. La Canada, CA: Feast of St. Joseph, 1995. 27p.

Shirley

Smith, Robert Lee. *Ancestors of Thelma Margaret Gander*. Alexandria, VA: Author, 1995. 65p.

Shoemaker

Lockhart, George W. *The Who's Who in the Shoemaker Family*. Pacific, MO: Author, 1995. 64p.

Shorey

Holmes, Marguerite. *Holmes from John of England and Plymouth, Massachusetts, to Holmes Brothers William Hudson, Horace William and Rodney Arthur Holmes of Aroostook County, Maine, and Related Families Cobbs, Redman, Libby and Shorey*. San Antonio, TX: Author, 1995. 101p.

Short

Teeter, Mary Bowers. *Descendants of Christ Chad and Anne Hulli of Grand Charmont, France, the Short Families of Williams and Fulton Counties, Ohio*. Rev. Morenci, MI: Author, 1995. 386p.

Shuck

Shuck, Larry Gorden. *Our Families, Shuck, Fleshman, Sydenstricker, Smith, Lewis, Kincaid, Keister et al. of West Virginia*. Baltimore, MD: Gateway Press, 1995. 565p.

Shufelt

Bergdall, Bernese Willis. *Shufelt Family, Palatinate to Hudson Valley to Eastern Shore, 1630-1995*. Pawleys Island, SC: Author, 1995. 147p.

Shull

Johnston, Anne Plummer. *The Plummer Lineage of America*. Reston, VA: M. L. Tomaselli, 1995. 56p.

Shumate

Barbare, C. Richard. *The South Carolina Shumates. Southern Huguenot Heritage and the War between the States*. Edgefield, SC: Author, 1995. 23p.
Shumate, John James. *From Whence We Came, A History of the Shumates of Henry/Pittsylvania Counties, Virginia*. Lynchburg, VA: Author, 1995. 245p.

Shumway

Griggs, Kendall. *Levi W. and Sarah E. (Carter) Hopkins, Their Ancestors and Descendants*. Hutchinson, KS: Author, 1995. 198p.

Shupp

Shupp, Atwood James. *Early German American Schupp/Shupp Families and Their Descendants from the 1600s to the Present*. Glendora, NJ: Author, 1995. Unpgd.

Shute

Shute, Alan Henry. *Richard Shute of Boston, Massachusetts, 1631–1703, and Selected Progeny, with a Brief Discussion of His Brother William Shute, Also of Boston*. Bowie, MD: Heritage Books, 1995. 152p.

Sibcy

Smith, Ruth Wiley. *Ancestors and Descendants of John Nelson Sibcy, Who Came to Hamilton County, Ohio, in the Early 1800s*. Oxford, OH: Author, 1995. 131p.

———. *Descendants of John Jacob Markley, Who Came to Hamilton County, Ohio, in 1804*. Oxford, OH: Author, 1995. 128p.

Sidener

Binns, Gwendolyn. *Sidener/Harp Family*. Independence, MO: Author, 1995. Unpgd.

Silver

Silver, Samuel F. *Silver Notes from South Jersey*. Parker, CO: E. D. Newman, 1995. Unpgd.

Simmons

Ashford, Adelle Brown. *Kith and Kin, Simmons and Related Families*. Malvern, AR: Author, 1995. 208p.

Nolan, Dennis C. *The Simmons Family History*. Boonville, IN: Author, 1995. 95p.

Roberts, Theodore Russell. *Simmons Family History*. FL: Author, 1995. Unpgd.

Simon

Melancon, Mertie Simon. *Simon and Ancestors*. Eunice, LA: Author, 1995. 218p.

Simon, Stephen Eric. *The Descendants of Charles Simon of Hessen-Darmstadt, Germany and New Haven, Connecticut*. Windsor, CT: Author, 1995. 34p.

Simonsen

Madson, Richard C. *Gjerpen to Gjerpen, the Madson Families Who Came to Wisconsin, Also Mason, Larson, Pedersen, Holm, Halvorson, Simonsen, and Hoen Families*. Mesa, AZ: Author, 1995. 284p.

Simonton

Roth, Marolyn Oswalt. *Oswalt Family History, 1722–1995*. Bluffton, IN: Author, 1995. 167p.

Simpson

Heavrin, Charles A. *Simon's Sons, Some Simpson Family Ancestors*. Bountiful, UT: Family History Pub., 1995. 191p.

Noble, Robert Cusick. *Simpson Notes: Sussex County, New Jersey, Persons Named Simpson, Their Ancestors and Descendants*. Philadelphia, PA: Author, 1995. 155p.

York, Dorothy Anderson. *Our Anderson Family and Their Kin*. Fort Worth, TX: Author, 1995. 307p.

Sims

Lewallen, Blanche Sims. *Sims-Marcus-Lawson Connections*. Toccoa, GA: Author, 1995. Unpgd.

Sinclair

Allmand, Barbara J. *Three Virginia Families, Allmand, Parker, and Sinclair, Including a Collection of 19th Century Letters and Other Writings*. Overland Park, KS: Author, 1995. 252p.

Grigsby, Jean. *Sinkler, Sinclair and St. Clair Update, 1995*. Beeville, TX: Family Enterprises, 1995. 154p.

Siner

Quick, Robert V. *A Genealogy of the Family of Siner*. Memphis, TN: Author, 1995. 39p.

Skaggs

Lancaster, Ida M. *Skaggs, the Long Hunter*. Amarillo, TX: Author, 1995. Unpgd.
————. *Thomas Skaggs and His Children*. Amarillo, TX: Author, 1995. 268p.
Toliver, Annabelle. *Skaggs-Wadsworth Family History*. Indianapolis: Author, 1995. 214p.

Skane

Scane, L. Dean. *Genealogy of Bashelier Family, Family Originally Emigrating from Near Saarbrueken, Germany to Fort Wayne, Allen County, Indiana*. Evanston, IL: Author, 1995. 175p.

Skelton

Skelton, Isaac Newton. *Ike, This Is You, a History of the Skelton, Boone, Barry, Beach, Blattner, Corum, Hoagland, Lehew, Strode, Wright and Young Families*. Washington, DC: Author, 1995. 223p.

Skidmore

Moore, Freddie Gene. *My Virginia Ancestors and Their Descendants in the Families, Ratliff, Skidmore, Watson, Hamilton, Wallace, Cahoon, Bowyer, Grimes, Sharp, Meeks*. Author, 1995. 116p.

Hauk, Carol A. *Descendants of Robert Taliafero of Virginia*. 6th. ed. Anderson, IN: Hauk Data Services, 1995. 358p.

Skillings

Meigs, Peter Sanford. *Our Meigs and Smith Ancestors, Including the Clarke, Clifford, Eldredge, Fellows, Howe, MacMillan, Mann, Remington, Rice, Robinson, Scadgel, Skillings, and Thing Families*. Danville, NH: Author, 1995. Unpgd.

Slack

Lewis, Allen Roy. *Two Hundred Year History and Genealogy of the Isaac Lewis Family from Cloughjordan (Tipperary), Ireland to the Canadas and the United States, Including Intermarriages with Hodgins, Myers, Rapley, Slack, Williams, and Many Other Families*. Ver. 1.5. Syracuse, NY: Author, 1995. 215p.

Slade

Howell, Danny. *The Hayters and Slades of Boreham and Bishopstrow*. Warminster, England: Bedeguar Books, 1995. 4p.

Slaton

Winkler, Margaret Thompson. *The Long Tree and Others: Longs, Davises, Thompsons, Cratins and Slatons*. Montgomery, AL: Uchee Pub., 1995. 347p.

Slaughter

Hauk, Carol A. *Descendants of Francis Slaughter of Virginia*. 5th. ed. Anderson, IN: Hauk Data Services, 1995. 118p.

———. *Descendants of Robert Coleman of Virginia*. Anderson, IN: Hauk Data Services, 1995. 226p.

Moore, Freddie Gene. *The Descendants of Thomas Moore, Sr. of Suffolk County, England and the Related Families, Youngs, Landon, Spencer, French, Norris, Simmons, Ratliff, Slaughter*. Author, 1995. Unpgd.

Sloan

Scott, Margaret Scott. *Genealogical Portrait of Joseph Carr and Barbara Gastor Beverett, the Carr Descendants of Duplin County, NC*. Warsaw, NC: Author, 1995. 418p.

Slupske

Doctor, Marjorie E. *Heyka, USA Descendants, 1888–1995, the Slupske, Heyka and Related Families*. Phoenix, AZ: Author, 1995. 427p.

Slusher

Creech, Lillian Broughton. *Kentucky Lineage, Broughton, Slusher, Woolum, Payne and Related Families*. Baltimore, MD: Gateway Press, 1995. 592p.

Schlosser Research Associates. *A Genealogy of the Schlosser, Slusser and Slusher Families of America, 1605–1994*. Kettering, OH: Author, 1995. 527p.

Slusser

Schlosser Research Associates. *A Genealogy of the Schlosser, Slusser and Slusher Families of America, 1605–1994*. Kettering, OH: Author, 1995. 527p.

Sly

Gray, John R. *A History and Genealogy of the Schleich/Slyh/Sly Family, J. Frederich Schleich/Slyh, d. 1800, His Wife Christiana, and Their Descendants*. Columbus, OH: Author, 1995. Unpgd.

Slye

Newcomb, Viettia Alberta. *Newcomb, Hartt and Slye, Blunden Families*. Ukiah, CA: Author, 1995. 408p.

Small

Parr, Richard Eugene. *Genealogy of Richard Eugene Parr*. Morgan Hill, CA: Author, 1995. 79p.

Smart

David, Johanna Josey. *From Coosawhatchie to Liberty the Descendants of Reverend James Smart and Levi Long*. Knoxville, TN: Tennessee Valley Pub., 1995. 373p.

Leslie, H. B. *John Smart of Exeter, NH and Seven Generations*. Rev. ed. Bristol, RI: Author, 1995. Unpgd.

Smeenk

Smeenk, J. H. *De Groote Sande te Hummelo*. Voorburg, Netherlands: Author, 1995. 314p.

Smith

Allen, Mary Barnes. *The Immigrants, George Read/Reed and Sarah Rayson, the Pioneers, Thomas Law Reed and Amantha Ann Smith, with Ancestors and Descendants*. Sonora, CA: Author, 1995. 117p.

Ancestors and Descendants of William Whitaker Smith, 1860–1944, and Florence Ellen Sullivan, 1875–1926, of Anderson and Greenville Counties, South Carolina. Spartanburg, SC: Reprint Co., 1995. 146p.

Depke, Jodie L. M. *Smiths of Smithfield, Jefferson County, Virginia, More of the Story Now, West Virginia*. Loveland, OH: Author, 1995. Unpgd.

Derbes, Marie McCullough. *David Shields McCullough and Anna Jane Smith, Their Ancestors and Descendants*. Covington, LA: Author, 1995. Unpgd.

Diemer, Darryl J. *The Descendants of Richard Smith of Northumberland County, Virginia*. Louisville, KY: Author, 1995. 436p.

Elliott, Margaret Coppess. *The Nicholls Family of Jefferson County, Ohio, the Rudd, Cox, Smith, and Related Families Who Came to Berlin Township, Ionia County, Michigan before 1870*. Ionia, MI: Author, 1995. Unpgd.

Goodwin, Dorothy Smith. *Smith-Murph Family History*. Author, 1995. 126p.

Graves, Kenneth Vance. *Deacon George Graves, 1636 Settler of Hartford, Connecticut and His Descendants*. Wrenthen, MA: Author, 1995. 446p.

Hauk, Carol A. *Descendants of Augustine Warner of Virginia*. Anderson, IN: Hauk Data Services, 1995. 461p.

———. *Descendants of Lawrence Smith of Virginia*. 2nd. ed. Anderson, IN: Hauk Data Services, 1995. 287p.

———. *Descendants of Thomas Smith of Virginia*. Anderson, IN: Hauk Data Services, 1995. 95p.

Horned, Joseph. *A Beginner's Guide for Researching Smith in Cherokee Records, Dawes Roll, Guion Miller Roll, Drennen Roll, Chapman Roll*. New Beginnings Pubns., 1995. 76p.

Kalbfleisch, Raymond W. *Captain Thomas Smith, Born 1767, Died 1850, and Descendants*. Petoskey, MI: Author, 1995. 174p.

———. *The Stow and Morse Families and Their Connection to the Alexander Smith Family of West Montrose, Ontario and Courtland, Michigan*. Sarasota, FL: Author, 1995. 40p.

Koickler, Eloyce Hubbard. *Hiestand, Hestand, Hastings*. Helena, MT: Author, 1995. 127p.

McKinley, Ruth Carter. *Supplement to Smith Family Ties, Descendants of Frederick George Schmidt (Smith) and Caroline Matilda Beadle*. Cullman, AL: Gregrath Pub. Co., 1995. 65p.

Meigs, Peter Sanford. *Our Meigs and Smith Ancestors, Including the Clarke, Clifford, Eldredge, Fellows, Howe, MacMillan, Mann, Remington, Rice, Robinson, Scadgel, Skillings, and Thing Families*. Danville, NH: Author, 1995. Unpgd.

Phelps, Barbara Barratt. *The Ralph and Olive Clarke Smith of Burlington, New Jersey, Family History, 1694–1994*. Littleton, CO: Author, 1995. 326p.

Robertson, Joanna. *A Tree Grows in America: My Family Line*. West Columbia, SC: Author, 1995. 238p.

Sandifer, Wilma R. *Smith Family Tree*. East Windsor, NJ: Author, 1995. 144p.

Shuck, Larry Gorden. *Our Families, Shuck, Fleshman, Sydenstricker, Smith, Lewis, Kincaid, Keister et al. of West Virginia.* Baltimore, MD: Gateway Press, 1995. 565p.

Smith, Carlita Hargrave. *A Tree Planted.* Virginia Beach, VA: Author, 1995. 263p.

Smith, Charles. *Smiths of Marshall County, Kentucky.* Melber, KY: Simmons Historical Publications, 1995. 128p.

Smith, Edmund Burton. *Edmund B. Smith Family History.* Massillon, OH: Author, 1995. Unpgd.

Smith Family Letters, Walden's Ridge, Tennessee, 1926–1977. Rocky Face, GA: Back Door Press, 1995. 253p.

Smith, Walter G. *Genealogy of Eleazer Smith of Grafton, New Hampshire.* Manchester, NH: Author, 1995. 22p.

Smith, William Woodrow. *An Album of Smith History, from Shelby County, Illinois, and Fairfield County, Ohio.* Opdyke, IL: Author, 1995. 31p.

Special Collections Department, Harold B. Lee Library. *Joseph Smith, Sr. Family Collection.* Provo, UT: Brigham Young University, 1995. 19p.

Smyer

Bryant, Neva N. Smyer. *The Smyer Families of Texas County, Missouri.* Mountain Grove, MO: Author, 1995. 100p.

Snead

Hockett, Thomas Jack. *Ancestors and Descendants of Benjamin Snead and Felicia Oliver.* St. David's, PA: Author, 1995. 283p.

Sneeden

Blake, Dorothy Sneeden. *North Carolina Sneedens, 1800–1995.* Wilmington, NC: Author, 1995. 127p.

Snellenbarger

Davis, Emma-Jo Levey. *John Snellenbarger (Schnellenbarger, Shellaberger, Snellen), 1768–1837, and His Descendants.* Williamsburg, VA: Author, 1995. 96p.

Snouffer

Zollars, Constance M. *Snouffer and Rodgers Family Records.* Fort Wayne, IN: Author, 1995. 88p.

Snyder

Smith, Ruth Wiley. *Ancestors and Descendants of John Nelson Sibcy, Who Came to Hamilton County, Ohio, in the Early 1800s.* Oxford, OH: Author, 1995. 131p.

Wagner, Betty Marie Daley. *The Schneider Genealogy and Related Families, Ancestors and Descendants of Carl Rudolph Schneider and Elizabeth Lena Bahler, Later Spelled Beller, John G. Bahler (Beller) and Anna Elisabeth Schneider, Samuel Bahler (Beller) and Elisabeth Litzy of Uetendorf, Canton Berne, Switzerland and Green County, Wisconsin, 1765–1995.* Milford, OH: Author, 1995. 201p.

Sohns

Boriack, David. *Boriack Family Tree, 1995.* Lincoln, TX: Author, 1995. 303p.

Solem

Hagen, Genevieve K. *The Solem-Oien Connection, the Story of the Ancestors and Descendants of Anders P. Solem, Marit L. Oien and Their Siblings.* Eau Claire, WI: Author, 1995. 329p.

Soloveitchik

Meiselman, Shulamit Soloveitchik. *The Soloveitchik Heritage, a Daughter's Memoir.* Hoboken, NJ: KTAV Pub., 1995. 260p.

Sommers

Graham, Connie Thompson. *Miller Family History.* Fairview Park, OH: Author, 1995. 146p.

Sorzano

Allen, Patricia Remmell. *The Remmell and Allen Families of New Castle County, Delaware.* Horsham, PA: Author, 1995. 71p.

Souder

Souder, Tressie Grimsley. *The Anthony Souder History, 1750–1989.* Broadway, VA: Author, 1995. 566p.

Soule

Soule, John E. *George Soule of the Mayflower and His Descendants for Four Generations.* 2nd ed. Plymouth, MA: General Society of Mayflower Descendants, 1995. 157p.

Southern

Scott, Billy Dave. *Johnston-Southern of Clairborne County, Tennessee, and Parker County, Texas: Isaac McNew Johnston (1838–1918) and His Wife Norvesta Melocky Southern (1841–1929) and Allied Families Amis, Haynes, Huddleston, Seabolt, Southern and Spears.* Maryville, MO: Author, 1995. 215p.

Sowers

Sowers, Betty. *The Descendants of Philip Sauer/Sowers.* Norfolk, VA: Author, 1995. 2 vols.

Soza

Soza, Edward. *New World Odyssey, a Search for Roots, the Sosa, Soza Families of Arizona.* Altadena, CA: Author, 1995. 41p.

Sparmann

Spahr, Max. *Sparn, Sparneck, Sparmann, Sparr, Family Data of Germany and Switzerland.* Pocatello, ID: Author, 1995. Unpgd.

Sparn

Spahr, Max. *Sparn, Sparneck, Sparmann, Sparr, Family Data of Germany and Switzerland.* Pocatello, ID: Author, 1995. Unpgd.

Sparneck

Spahr, Max. *Sparn, Sparneck, Sparmann, Sparr, Family Data of Germany and Switzerland.* Pocatello, ID: Author, 1995. Unpgd.

Sparr

Spahr, Max. *Sparn, Sparneck, Sparmann, Sparr, Family Data of Germany and Switzerland.* Pocatello, ID: Author, 1995. Unpgd.

Spears

Scott, Billy Dave. *Johnston-Southern of Clairborne County, Tennessee, and Parker County, Texas: Isaac McNew Johnston (1838–1918) and His Wife Norvesta Melocky Southern (1841–1929) and Allied Families Amis, Haynes, Huddleston, Seabolt, Southern and Spears.* Maryville, MO: Author, 1995. 215p.

Speers

Koickler, Eloyce Hubbard. *Hiestand, Hestand, Hastings.* Helena, MT: Author, 1995. 127p.

Spelbrink

Spelbring, Pamela Criss. *Descendants of Johann Heinrich Spelbrink and His Son George Henry Spelbring (Jorgen Henrich Spelbrink).* Evansville, IL: Author, 1995. 49p.

Spence

Daniel Beverly, Patteann. *The Spence Family Saga, the Ancestors and Descendants of John and Roxie Ann Jarman Spence.* Midland, TX; Author, 1995. Unpgd.

Spencer

Fussell, Lynn Edward. *The Descendants of Samuel Spencer (c. 1774–1835).* Richardson, TX: Author, 1995. 286p.

Westfall, Dawn Watts. *Spencer, Brizendine, Malone, Families of Trigg County, Kentucky.* High Springs, FL: Author, 1995. 26p.

Spice

Bauer, Marguerite Swagler. *The Family History of George Halliwell, Johan George Culman, Joseph Spice.* Seville, OH: Author, 1995. 41p.

Spitler

Smith, Robert Lee. *Ancestors of Thelma Margaret Gander.* Alexandria, VA: Author, 1995. 65p.

Splittorf

McGuire, George. *Splittorf Genealogy.* Author, 1995. Unpgd.

Spomer

Spomer, Roy. *The Spomers, 1994.* Author, 1995. 40p.

Sprague

Fail Families and Allied Families: Catt, Hensley, Kenyon, Lane and Sprague, 1818–1995, a Work in Progress. Decorah, IA: Anundsen Pub. Co., 1995. 348p.

Howe, Jeffrey. *The Block Island Allens.* Author, 1995. 218p.

Sprenger

Sprenger, Ernest H. *Roots and Relatives.* Ritzville, WA: Author, 1995. 676p.

Spring

Spring, Ira. *The Spring Family Adventure*. Edmonds, WA: ABCD Printing, 1995. 348p.

Springer

Miller, Kimberlee. *Descendants of Captain Jacob Prickett, Sr.*. Fairmont, WV: Jacob's Meadow, Inc., 1995. 178p.

Staats

Griffiths, George R. *Early Settlers in New York and New Jersey, Banta Family, Benson Family, Staats Family, Mabie Family*. Chandler, AZ: Author, 1995. 21p.

Stafford

Love, Terry M. *The Descendants of James Stafford of Eccels, England*. Lakeville, MN: Author, 1995. 94p.

Stahl

Stahl, Harriet K. *The Family of Johann Jacob Stahl, Sr., of Lehigh County, Pennsylvania*. Mt. Vernon, IN: Windmill Pub., 1995. 549p.

Stairs

Groff, Clifford. *The Stairs Families of Westmoreland and Somerset Counties of Pennsylvania and Their Ancestors, Steer, Summy, Monticue, Harshberger, Colborn, Tissue, Kreger and Clevenger*. Arnold, MD: Author, 1995. 147p.

Stallings

Chappelear, Patsy Stallings. *Name Index for Stallings Family Records*. 2nd. ed. Houston, TX: Author, 1995. 158p.

Stamper

Latham, Betty Stamper. *Stamper Footprints, Eleven Generations*. Bowie, MD: Heritage Books, 1995. 154p.

Stanard

Hauk, Carol A. *Descendants of William Stanard of Virginia*. Anderson, IN: Hauk Data Services, 1995. 34p.

Stafford, Gail Akins. *Alexander H. Stafford and Some of His Descendants*. Capshaw, AL: Author, 1995. 106p.

Stanclift

Stancliff, Sherry Smith. *The Descendants of James Stanclift of Middleton, Connecticut, and Allied Families*. Cincinnati, OH: S. S. Research, 1995. 548p.

Standen

Standen, Jack. *The Standen Book, the Standen Families that Settled in the Lorain County Area of Ohio, Their Ancestors and Descendants, the Descendants of Timothy Standen and Ann Pelham, 1775–1995*. State College, PA: Author, 1995. 400p.

Standridge

Boyd, C. L. *Standridge*. Dover, AR: Author, 1995. 991p.

Stang

Descendants of Adam (Stang) Stong in America. Little Rock, AR: Betty Cripe Bobo, 1995. Unpgd.

Stanley

Blake, Marcelline Abrego. *The Saga of Stanley-Hoagland and Allied Families in America from New England to California, 1600 to 1900s*. Santa Rosa, CA: Author, 1995. Unpgd.

Caldwell, Janice. *The Lost Branch of the Anderson Family, Ancestors and Descendants of Thomas Allen Howard Anderson and His Wife Martha Ann Stanley, Including Allied Families*. Helotes, TX: Author, 1995. 438p.

Pelcher, Barbara Jane Tillotson. *Pioneers, Crain, Manning, McKenzie, Stanley and Allied Families*. San Bernardino, CA: Author, 1995. 186p.

Stanphill

Kercheval, Beverly Marie. *The Reed and Stanphill Families*. Slaton, TX: Author, 1995. 533p.

Stantial

Gray, Effie Stantial. *The Ancestry of the Maine Stantial/Vaughan Connection and Related Families*. Thomaston, ME: Author, 1995. 460p.

Stark

McMullin, Kathleen Buetow. *The Family History of Levi O. Buetow and Amelia (Stark) Buetow of Chippewa County, Wisconsin*. Rochester, MN: Author, 1995. 93p.

Starkweather

Titsworth, Judy Starkweather. *Starkweather Family*. Robinson, IL: Author, 1995. 45p.

Starr

Gardner, Oscar William. *Gardner/Ballard and Allied Families, Edmondson, Lee, Daniel, Cauthen, and Starr*. Morrow, GA: Author, 1995. 456p.

Harris, Lillie Alberson. *Starr, the Five Sons of John and Mary Starr Who Came to Chester County, Pennsylvania, in the Early 1700s and Their Descendants*. Keystone, IN: Author, 1995. Unpgd.

Hill, George Byron. *The Genealogy of the Hill, Combs, Barton, Starr and Allied Families*. Nashville, TN: Author, 1995. 296p.

Stearns

Stearns, Howard Oliver. *A Geographical Index to "Genealogy and Memoirs of Isaac Stearns and His Descendants" by Avis Stearns Van Wagenen, Published in 1901*. Burlington, VT: Author, 1995. 148p.

Steed

Steed, Paul P. *A Line of Steeds*. Dallas, TX: Author, 1995. 76p.

Steele

Hargis, Margaret Finley. *Our Steele Family*. Warrenton, VA: Author, 1995. Unpgd.

Peck, Patricia Dunn. *Jones Family Genealogy, a History of the Christopher M. Jones Family of Philadelphia with Emphasis on the Descendants of His Son, Levi Taylor Jones of Philadelphia and Trenton and Related Thropp, Yetter, Dunn and Steele Families*. Saratoga Springs, NY: Peckhaven Pub., 1995. 98p.

Steer

Groff, Clifford. *The Stairs Families of Westmoreland and Somerset Counties of Pennsylvania and Their Ancestors, Steer, Summy, Monticue, Harshberger, Colborn, Tissue, Kreger and Clevenger*. Arnold, MD: Author, 1995. 147p.

Steffey

Steffey, Dale E. *Genealogy of Andreas Rempp and His Wife Anna Eitelbuss, Oschelbronn, Germany*. El Cajon, CA: Author, 1995. 74p.

Steiermann

Mayer, Marion. *History of a Family Dispersed*. Chicago, IL: Author, 1995. 298p.

Steigerwalt

La Marca, Jeffrey Peter. *Window to the Past, Door to the Future, a Glimpse at an American Genealogy, Compilation of Data on the Acquisto, Calamera, Carroll, Crowley, Guastaferro, Hawley, La Marca, Lavier, and Steigerwalt Families*. Yorba Linda, CA: Shumway Family History Services, 1995. 214p.

Steiner

Ritter, Robert P. *The Ancestors and Descendants Including Some of the Relations of Deacon Ulrich Steiner and Elizabeth Basinger of Wilmot Township, Waterloo County, 1720–1995*. Wingham, Ontario: Author, 1995. 212p.

Steingart

Penner, Peter. *A Brief History of the Steingart Family*. 2nd. ed. Calgary, Alberta: Author, 1995. 1995. 13p.

Stene

Stene, Charles Sherwin. *The Stene Family, Includes Rohn, Anderson, Bothwell, Davenport, Lloyd*. Decorah, IA: Anundsen Pub. Co., 1995. 385p.

Steptoe

Hauk, Carol A. *Descendants of Anthony Steptoe of Virginia*. Anderson, IN: Hauk Data Services, 1995. 147p.

Stevens

Evans, Ronald. *The Descendants of Uriah Stevens and Nancy Kevil*. Independence, LA: Author, 1995. 373p.

Hinton, Leroy C. *Family Record of Hynton, Hinton, England, Hinton, Stevens of America, 1050 to 1994*. Morehead, KY: Author, 1995. Unpgd.

Kinnersley, William. *The Woolford Family of Dorchester County, Maryland, Ancestors and Descendants of Thomas Woolford and Sarah Stevens.* Lawrence, KS: Author, 1995. 25p.

Stewart

The Descendants of Cornelius Stewart, 1995 Prototype. Author, 1995. 213p.

Gates, Robert Cady. *The Ancestry and World War I Letters of William Galbraith Stewart, Jr. (1896–1935) of Wilkinsburg, Allegheny County, Pennsylvania.* Springfield, MO: Author, 1995. 158p.

Schwartztrauber, Sayre Archie. *Schwartztrauber, Stewart, and Related Families.* Baltimore, MD: Gateway Press, 1995. 1,000p

Stickel

Hazelton, George Francis. *A Genealogy of Hazelton and Stygles Families.* Baltimore, MD: Gateway Press, 1995. 263p.

Stierheim

Brainard, Richard David. *The Stierheim Family in America.* Rev. Portland, OR: Author, 1995. 144p.

Stiles

Bielanski, Phyllis Jean Olin. *Andrew Powell Family Tree, Including Powell, Farr, Ten Brock Branches and Wolcott, Stiles, Doolittle, Kelch, Eldridge Branches.* Lakeland, FL: Author, 1995. Unpgd.

Reamer, Kathleen R. *Descendants of John Reamer and Margaret Schermerhorn, 1758–1995.* Imlay City, MI: Author, 1995. 246p.

Still

Lehmann, Joy Deal. *Still Family History, Six Generations of Descendants of Ebenezer and Susanna Still of Wayne County, New York.* Novato, CA: Author, 1995. 141p.

Stiteler

Bitting, Frederick E. *The Stiteler Family, 1764–1987.* Fair Haven, VT: Author, 1995. Unpgd.

Stocking

Chamberlain, Merle. *On the Trail of Zebulon Latimer and His Family.* Wilmington, DE: Lower Cape Fear Historical Society, 1995. Unpgd.

Stockton

Koickler, Eloyce Hubbard. *Hiestand, Hestand, Hastings.* Helena, MT: Author, 1995. 127p.

Stoddard

Stoddard, Sharlene Ida. *Family of Wells and Eunice Stoddard.* Northwood, IA: Author, 1995. 746p.

Stoll

Feder, June Constance. *The Genealogy of the Price and Stull Families of the Town of Rush, Monroe County, New York, the Murrays, Wallings, and Hills of Victor, New York and the Otto, Block, Hill and Summerhays Families of Rochester, New York.* Fairport, NY: Author, 1995. 75p.

Stone

Stone, Robert H. *Stone Connections: A More Complete Genealogy of the Stone Family*. Updated Version. Springfield, MO: Author, 1995. 450p.

Stong

Descendants of Adam (Stang) Stong in America. Little Rock, AR: Betty Cripe Bobo, 1995. Unpgd.

Story

Buckley, Kenneth Welch. *The Descendants of Butler Buckley and Elizabeth Story, 1710–1994*. Baltimore, MD: Gateway Press, 1995. 661p.

McLeod, Stephen Archie. *The House of Cantelou & Co., the Story of a Southern Family*. Tallahassee, FL: Author, 1995. 705p.

Stout

Hurley, Lucius M. *Thomas Andrew Hurley, His Descendants and the Related Families of Metzger and Stout*. Newton, KS: Author, 1995. 139p.

Stowe

Kalbfleisch, Raymond W. *The Stow and Morse Families and Their Connection to the Alexander Smith Family of West Montrose, Ontario and Courtland, Michigan*. Sarasota, FL: Author, 1995. 40p.

Straight

Bartram, Chester E. *The George Washington McCoy Family of Mason County, West Virginia, Prominent Related Families Edington, Ferrell, Hoschar, Jividen, King, Sayre, Strait*. Knoxville, TN: Author, 1995. 187p.

Berry, Eddie Clayton. *Berry-Baker Connection*. Houston, TX: Author, 1995. 409p.

Strale

Strale, Homer Plumton. *Generation to Generation of the Strale Family, U.S.A., 1850–1994*. Grosse Pointe, MI: Author, 1995. 48p.

Streeter

Streeter, Doris. *Descendants of Frank Raymond and Mary Louise (Moulton) Streeter of Springfield, Massachusetts, Eighth in Descent from Stephen and Ursula (Adams) Streeter of Gloucester, Massachusetts*. Saginaw, MI: Author, 1995. 23p.

Strenkowski

Eggert, Irving John. *Peter Eggert of Mecklenburg and Related Families in America, Best, Bitz, Broekemeier, Hackbarth, Kane, Meisner, Nellis, Schunk, Strenkowski, Voight, Winston*. Decorah, IA: Anundsen Pub. Co., 1995. 224p.

Stricker

Smith, Robert Lee. *Ancestors of Thelma Margaret Gander*. Alexandria, VA: Author, 1995. 65p.

Stringer

Wilson, James O. *Stringer Families of Kentucky*. Lakeland, FL: Author, 1995. Unpgd.

Strode

Skelton, Isaac Newton. *Ike, This Is You, a History of the Skelton, Boone, Barry, Beach, Blattner, Corum, Hoagland, Lehew, Strode, Wright and Young Families*. Washington, DC: Author, 1995. 223p.

Strong

Graves, James Merritt. *A Few Strong Men and Women*. Nashville, TN: Graves Pub. Co., 1995. 136p.

Strother

Hauk, Carol A. *Descendants of Anthony Savage of Virginia*. Anderson, IN: Hauk Data Services, 1995. 276p.
———. *Descendants of Cornelius Dabney of Virginia*. 2nd. ed. Anderson, IN: Hauk Data Services, 1995. 162p.
———. *Descendants of William Strother of Virginia*. 4th. ed. Anderson, IN: Hauk Data Services, 1995. 130p.
McLeod, Stephen Archie. *The House of Cantelou & Co., the Story of a Southern Family*. Tallahassee, FL: Author, 1995. 705p.

Stroud

Stroud, Roger Dean. *From Old Dominion to Volunteer and Pioneer, the Archibald Stroud Family of Wilson County, Tennessee*. Murray, UT: Author, 1995. Unpgd.

Stuart

Carroll, Thelma Ellen Young. *A Source Book for Five Generations of Family History*. Virginia Beach, VA: Merrit Press, 1995. Unpgd.
Hauk, Carol A. *Descendants of David Stuart of Virginia*. Anderson, IN: Hauk Data Services, 1995. 53p.

Stuber

May, John Russell. *Stuber Family History and Genealogy*. Fort Wayne, IN: Author, 1995. Unpgd.

Struble

Struble, Harry Philip. *From Whence We Came: Johann Dietrich Strubel*. Author, 1995. Unpgd.
Struble, Robert M. *Conrad Struble Line, Vol. 1, the Jacob Struble Family of Center County, Pennsylvania*. Author, 1995. 406p.

Study

White, Mary Hamilton. *William Lomax and His Descendants*. Author, 1995. 452p.

Stultz

Stultz, Lowell C. *Stultz Family from Germany to Ohio, Descendants of the Three Stultz Brothers from Nassau, Germany in America, John Henry Stultz, Jacob Stultz, Michael Stultz*. Portage, MI: Author, 1995. 270p.

Sturdza

Popisteanu, Cristian. *Sturdzestii, Din Cronica Unei Familii Istoric.* Bucharest, Romania: Fundatia Culturala Magazin Istoric, 1995. 310p.

Sturgis

Pruett, Dorothy Sturgis. *Thrasher-Sturgis, Descendants of Ernest Blasingame Thrasher and Martha Rouse Carlton.* Montgomery, AL: Author, 1995. 60p.

Sudermann

Willms, Peter A. *Peter Jacob and Katharina (Sudermann) Willms, Their Ancestors, Lives, and Descendants.* Author, 1995. 69p.

Suit

Mallard, Shirley Jones. *Keeping Up with the Joneses, a Book about the Rafe Jones Family of Granville, North Carolina.* Chapel Hill, NC: Author, 1995. 244p.

Sullivan

Ancestors and Descendants of William Whitaker Smith, 1860–1944, and Florence Ellen Sullivan, 1875–1926, of Anderson and Greenville Counties, South Carolina. Spartanburg, SC: Reprint Co., 1995. 146p.

Suman

Suman, Estaleene Nash. *Drummond, Harvey, Suman and Other Allied Families.* Buffton, IN: Author, 1995. 1,063p.

Summerhays

Feder, June Constance. *The Genealogy of the Price and Stull Families of the Town of Rush, Monroe County, New York, the Murrays, Wallings, and Hills of Victor, New York and the Otto, Block, Hill and Summerhays Families of Rochester, New York.* Fairport, NY: Author, 1995. 75p.

Summy

Groff, Clifford. *The Stairs Families of Westmoreland and Somerset Counties of Pennsylvania and Their Ancestors, Steer, Summy, Monticue, Harshberger, Colborn, Tissue, Kreger and Clevenger.* Arnold, MD: Author, 1995. 147p.

Sussman

Mayer, Marion. *History of a Family Dispersed.* Chicago, IL: Author, 1995. 298p.

Sutton

Frazier, Gloria Shipp. *The Descendants of John Wesley Sutton, 1837–1900.* West Plains, MO: G. S. Frazier, 1995. 260p.

Hamilton, Fred. *The Descendants and Some Ancestors of James Meriwether and Julia Calhoun Hamilton, 1855–1936, 1853–1939.* Ruston, LA: Author, 1995. 104p.

Swacina

Swacina, Douglas. *Svacina-Swacina Genealogical Record: Ancestors, Descendants, Relatives.* Springdale, AR: Author, 1995. 93p.

Swann

Avery, Thomas Lynn. *Family Life of John Henry and Ellen (Andrews) Swann*. Chico, CA: Author, 1995. 115p.

Kaufman, Mary Arnold. *Martin-Arnold and Allied Families, Lanier, Bailey, Swan, Sandidge, Gholston, Morgan, and Born, Migration from Virginia to Tennessee, Georgia, Alabama and Arkansas*. Knoxville, TN: Tennessee Valley Pub., 1995. 212p.

Swan, James. *A Heritage Of Love: The Descendants of Walter and Deloris (Robinson) Swan*. Author, 1995. 133p.

Swartzendruber

Glick, Esther Swartzendruber. *Descendants of Frederick Swartzendruber, 1825–1895, and Sarah Yoder, 1829–1867*. Nappanee, IN: Evangel Press, 1995. 459p.

Swayne

Swayne, Rosemary Clisby. *Heirs of Our Lineage, Clisby/Swayne*. Bow, WA: Author, 1995. Unpgd.

Swearington

Oldham, Helen G. *Some Descendants of Garrett and Barbara De Barrette Van Sweringen, 1659- 1995*. Rev. ed. State College, PA: Author, 1995. 507p.

Winkler, Ruth Swearington. *Ancestors and Descendants of Zacharias van Swerington, 1636-1995*. Author, 1995. 149p.

Sweeney

Sweeney, Marvin. *The Sweeney Connection, a Family History and Genealogy*. Vincennes, IN: Author, 1995. 233p.

Swindall

Sutherland, Elihu Jasper. *Swindall and Austin Family of Virginia and North Carolina and Related Families*. Clintwood, VA: Author, 1995. 400p.

Sydenstricker

Shuck, Larry Gorden. *Our Families, Shuck, Fleshman, Sydenstricker, Smith, Lewis, Kincaid, Keister et al. of West Virginia*. Baltimore, MD: Gateway Press, 1995. 565p.

Sykes

Mann, Marion. *The Kigh, Mann, Reagin, and Sykes Families, Including the Branch, Brown, Dean, Fort, Gerran, Leake, Marquis, Moses, Oakes, Powell, Reid, Trammell, Walk, Wilkey, Wingfield, and Woods Families, a Genealogy and Family History*. Baltimore, MD: Gateway Press, 1995. 218p.

Syphrett

Detty, Nancy Syphrett. *Detty, Syphrett-Syfrett and Related Families*. Kerrville, TX: Author, 1995. 180p.

Syverson

Nelson, Gary S. *Eberhard Syverson (1829–1903) and Martha Amundsdatter (1834–1914)*. Stanley, ND: Author, 1995. 20p.

–T

Tackaberry

Whitmore, Robert Devore. *Whitmore Family Genealogy*. Steubenville, OH: Public Library of
    Steubenville and Jefferson County, 1995. 14p.

Tadlock

Nepp, Carol McLean. *Leaves from the Family Tree, or, Moore, Tadlock, Ancestors and Some
    Descendants*. Tea, SD: Author, 1995. Unpgd.

Talbot

Littrell, George Washington. *James Talbott, 1758–1855, and Some of His Descendants*. Winter
    Park, FL: Author, 1995. 111p.
Martin, Shirley A. *Talbot and Talyor i.e. Taylor Families*. Tregaron, Wales: Author, 1995. 61p.

Taliaferro

Hauk, Carol A. *Descendants of Anthony Savage of Virginia*. Anderson, IN: Hauk Data Ser-
    vices, 1995. 276p.
———. *Descendants of Lawrence Smith of Virginia*. 2nd. ed. Anderson, IN: Hauk Data Ser-
    vices, 1995. 287p.
———. *Descendants of Robert Taliafero of Virginia*. 6th. ed. Anderson, IN: Hauk Data Ser-
    vices, 1995. 358p.
———. *Descendants of William Thornton of Virginia*. Anderson, IN: Hauk Data Services,
    1995. 361p.

Talmadge

Schefer, Barbara Jean Connolly. *Talmadge Family Sixth Century, Twentieth Century*. Santa
    Rosa, CA: Author, 1995. 78p.

Tandy

Robertson, Joanna. *A Tree Grows in America: My Family Line*. West Columbia, SC: Author,
    1995. 238p.

Tanghe

Tanghe, Jo. *De Jean Marc à Charlemagne, une Approche Humoristique de la Généalogie, des
    Tableaux d'Ascendance sur Quinze Siècles, Essai*. Paris, France: GabriAndré, 1995. 286p.

Tanguay

Tanguay, Dany. *Les Tanguay, l'histoire de la Famille Tanguay depuis 1692*. Thetford Mines,
    Quebec: Author, 1995. 268p.

Tappy

Roth, Marolyn Oswalt. *Oswalt Family History, 1722–1995*. Bluffton, IN: Author, 1995. 167p.

Tarne

McKee, Ruth Vernette. *The Known Ancestry of Rev. Isaac Babbitt, 1757–1833, Including Cooper, Crane, Ford, Lovell, Morse, Pierce, Tarne, Tisdale, Walker and Whitman Families.* Minneapolis, MN: Author, 1995. 42p.

Tate

Kindred, Kathy Tate. *Tate Family Genealogy.* Carencro, LA: Author, 1995. Unpgd.

Taylor

Ashford, Adelle Brown. *Kith and Kin, Simmons and Related Families.* Malvern, AR: Author, 1995. 208p.

Hauk, Carol A. *Descendants of James Taylor of Virginia, (Ancestor of Presidents Taylor and Madison).* 9th. ed. Anderson, IN: Hauk Data Services, 1995. 328p.

———. *Descendants of Miles Cary of Virginia.* Anderson, IN: Hauk Data Services, 1995. 421p.

———. *Descendants of Philip Pendleton of Virginia.* 6th. ed. Anderson, IN: Hauk Data Services, 1995. 287p.

———. *Descendants of Richard Lee of Virginia.* 2nd. ed. Anderson, IN: Hauk Data Services, 1995. 202p.

———. *Descendants of William Churchill of Virginia.* 2nd. ed. Anderson, IN: Hauk Data Services, 1995. 250p.

———. *Descendants of William Taylor of Virginia.* 2nd. ed. Anderson, IN: Hauk Data Services, 1995. 136p.

Jump, Shirley Taylor. *The Taylor Family.* Corbin, KY: Author, 1995. 103p.

Martin, Shirley A. *Talbot and Talyor i.e. Taylor Families.* Tregaron, Wales: Author, 1995. 61p.

Miller, Kimberlee. *Descendants of Captain Jacob Prickett, Sr..* Fairmont, WV: Jacob's Meadow, Inc., 1995. 178p.

Mortensen, Alice Paula Perkins. *The Family of John Henry Taylor, Jr., Featuring Family Letters Written during and after the Civil War.* Baltimore, MD: Gateway Press, 1995. 136p.

Taylor, Ralph A. *From Sea to Shining Sea, a Taylor Family Saga.* Rev. ed. Wichita, KS: Author, 1995. 854p.

Zuendel, Jean. *Taylor, Blanchan, Cochran, DuBois, Foreman, Hite, Morris, Parker, Van Meteren.* Author, 1995. Unpgd.

Tayman

Spoden, Muriel Clark. *An American Ancestry of the Clark-Morton and Tyman-Millar-Adams Families.* Kingsport, TN: Spoden Associates, 1995. 547p.

Telian

Telian, Margaret Anderson. *Margaret Anderson Telian and Her Golden Jubilee.* Painted Post, NY: Painted Post Press, 1995. 59p.

Templer

Templer, Janice Lindley. *George Washington Templer, His Ancestors and Descendants.* Claremore, OK: Author, 1995. 86p.

Tepolt

Tepolt, Jerry. *The Tepolts of Wisconsin, New York, and Oregon.* Apache Junction, AZ: Author, 1995. Unpgd.

Terry

Paulson, Louis. *A Larder-Terry Ancestry*. Author, 1995. 72p.

Terry, Earnest L. *Terry Family Census, 1790–1920*. Meridian, MS: Author, 1995. 2 vols.

Tester

Rowan, Frances Dugger. *The Dugger Family Johnson County, Tennessee*. Author, 1995. 331p.

Théberge

Théberge, Camille. *Généalogie des Familles Théberge*. Author, 1995. 162p.

Thériot

Thériot-Méaux, Aline. *Petit Historique d'une Famille Theriot*. Author, 1995. 25p.

Thevenet

O'Quinn, Frank Morat. *Thevenets of St. Martin Parish, Louisiana*. Baton Rouge, LA: Author, 1995. 240p.

Thiessen

Gardiner Jackson, Ann E. *Roots: Gardiner, Ingram, Grimmeissen, Ashpaw, Thiessen, Jackson, Meeker*. Author, 1995. 35p.

Thing

Meigs, Peter Sanford. *Our Meigs and Smith Ancestors, Including the Clarke, Clifford, Eldredge, Fellows, Howe, MacMillan, Mann, Remington, Rice, Robinson, Scadgel, Skillings, and Thing Families*. Danville, NH: Author, 1995. Unpgd.

Thode

Muhlhausen, Marvin David. *Thode, Bossler, a Story of the Ancestors and Descendants of Andreas Thode and Anna Dorothea Bossler*. Ellicott City, MD: Author, 1995. Unpgd.

Thomas

Thomas, Theodore. *History of the King, Thomas, and Thompkins Families, Family History*. Denver, CO: Author, 1995. Unpgd.

Thompkins

Thomas, Theodore. *History of the King, Thomas, and Thompkins Families, Family History*. Denver, CO: Author, 1995. Unpgd.

Thompson

Adair, Shirley Brown. *Robert Adair (1770–1845c), an Adair Family History, Reid, Emerson, Hobbs, Worley, Thompson (Related Lines)*. Rockwall, TX: Author, 1995. 146p.

Craft, Kenneth F. *Some Branches of the Ward Family of Montgomery County, Maryland, with Earliest Ancestor, Revolutionary War Soldier James White Ward (also Known as James White) Including Some Allied Lines: Fairfax, Thompson, Ray, Cooke and Wylie*. Norcross, GA: Author, 1995. Unpgd.

McBride, Jean Coleman. *The Colemans of West Alabama and Allied Families*. Aliceville, AL: Author, 1995. 200p.

R. E. W. Thompson (1856–1937), Adair, Clark, Carroll, Sellers, Lawson (Related Lines). Rockwall, TX: S. B. Adair, 1995. 133p.

Winkler, Margaret Thompson. *The Long Tree and Others: Longs, Davises, Thompsons, Cratins and Slatons.* Montgomery, AL: Uchee Pub., 1995. 347p.

York, Dorothy Anderson. *Our Anderson Family and Their Kin.* Fort Worth, TX: Author, 1995. 307p.

Thornbury

Hill, Clara M. *John Thornbury in Tennessee and Alabama.* Author, 1995. 263p.

Thornton

Hauk, Carol A. *Descendants of Anthony Savage of Virginia.* Anderson, IN: Hauk Data Services, 1995. 276p.

———. *Descendants of Robert Taliafero of Virginia.* 6th. ed. Anderson, IN: Hauk Data Services, 1995. 358p.

———. *Descendants of William Thornton of Virginia.* Anderson, IN: Hauk Data Services, 1995. 361p.

The Thornton Legacy. Tuscaloosa, AL: Author, 1995. 125p.

Thorsen

Williams, Luella R. *My Father's People: Paulsen/Thoreesen Slekt from Norway, Lindack Slakt from Sweden, Descendants Found in Australia, Canada, Denmark, Norway, Sweden and United States of America.* Iron River, MI: Author, 1995. 475p.

Thrasher

Pruett, Dorothy Sturgis. *Thrasher-Sturgis, Descendants of Ernest Blasingame Thrasher and Martha Rouse Carlton.* Montgomery, AL: Author, 1995. 60p.

Threadgill

Threadgill, Harvey Edwin. *Threadgills Book III, a Presentation of the Descendants of John Threadgill, Circa 1700.* El Paso, TX: Author, 1995. 341p.

Throckmorton

Hauk, Carol A. *Descendants of John Throckmorton of Virginia.* Anderson, IN: Hauk Data Services, 1995. 38p.

Thropp

Peck, Patricia Dunn. *Jones Family Genealogy, a History of the Christopher M. Jones Family of Philadelphia with Emphasis on the Descendants of His Son, Levi Taylor Jones of Philadelphia and Trenton and Related Thropp, Yetter, Dunn and Steele Families.* Saratoga Springs, NY: Peckhaven Pub., 1995. 98p.

Snedeker, Lenora A. *Memories at Willowbrook: A History of the Throop-Martin Families of Auburn, New York.* Oxford, NY: Author, 1995. Unpgd.

Thruston

Hauk, Carol A. *Descendants of Edward Thruston of Virginia.* Anderson, IN: Hauk Data Services, 1995. 35p.

Tiart

Suderman, Joel. *David P. Schroeder, Sara (Janzen) Schroeder Family History and Genealogy, Including Information about, Peter Schroeder, David & Ana (Tiart) Schroeder, Peter & Susanna (Reimer) Schroeder, David P. & Sara (Janzen) Schroeder*. Marion, KS: Author, 1995. 65p.

Tibbetts

Cagle, Ruby Abbott. *The Bishop Family from Manchester, England to Washington County, Maine*. Jasper, TN: Author, 1995. Unpgd.

Tice

Schlabach, Oma. *History and Genealogy of the Jacob C. and Sadie (Tice) Schlabach Family from 1735 to 1994*. Millersburg, OH: Author, 1995. 131p.

Tichenor

Titchenal, Oliver Ray. *The Titchenal Saga: 350 Years of Faith and Hope and Family Life in America: The Genealogy and History of Thirteen Generations of the Tichenor and Titchenal Families Coupled with American Local History*. North Ridgeville, OH: Author, 1995. Unpgd.

Tidwell

Roberts, Theodore Russell. *B. F. Tidwell Family of Pensacola, Florida, and Southern Alabama*. Author, 1995. Unpgd.

Tillotson

Tillotson, Olin. *Tillotson of East Montpelier, Vermont: Being an Account of the Ancestors and Descendants of Olin Locke Tillotson (1854–1956) and Susan Dellah Davis (1861–1932) and Their Allied Families*. Surrey, BC: Author, 1995. Unpgd.

Tiner

York, Dorothy Anderson. *Our Anderson Family and Their Kin*. Fort Worth, TX: Author, 1995. 307p.

Tinsley

Wilkinson, Sue Tinsley. *John Tinsley Is My Name*. Wills Point, TX: Author, 1995. Unpgd.

Tisdale

McKee, Ruth Vernette. *The Known Ancestry of Rev. Isaac Babbitt, 1757–1833, Including Cooper, Crane, Ford, Lovell, Morse, Pierce, Tarne, Tisdale, Walker and Whitman Families*. Minneapolis, MN: Author, 1995. 42p.

Tissue

Groff, Clifford. *The Stairs Families of Westmoreland and Somerset Counties of Pennsylvania and Their Ancestors, Steer, Summy, Monticue, Harshberger, Colborn, Tissue, Kreger and Clevenger*. Arnold, MD: Author, 1995. 147p.

Titchenal

Titchenal, Oliver Ray. *The Titchenal Saga: 350 Years of Faith and Hope and Family Life in America: The Genealogy and History of Thirteen Generations of the Tichenor and Titchenal Families Coupled with American Local History*. North Ridgeville, OH: Author, 1995. Unpgd.

Titford

Titford, Donald. *Moonrakers in My Family*. Bath, England: Author, 1995. 284p.

Tolman

Reynolds, Beatrice Kay. *Nathaniel and Mary (Tolman) Reynolds, IV of Bridgewater, Massachusetts, Early Descendants in Sidney, Maine (1780)*. Sidney, ME: Author, 1995. 106p.

Tomberlin

Wall, Martha Tomberlin. *Our Tomberlin Heritage*. Baltimore, MD: Gateway Press, 1995. 1,112p.

Tomlinson

Tomlinson, Robert Edward. *The Tomlinson Family from Cheshire in Australia, 1856–1994*. Weston Creek, ACT, Australia: Author, 1995. Unpgd.

Tompkins

Wynn, Louise Tompkins. *A Family History of the Tompkins and Keas of North Carolina, South Carolina, and Georgia and Other Related Lines*. Panama City Beach, FL: Author, 1995. 416p.

Tooker

Petersen, Bradner. *Sally Tooker and Her Ancestry, a Recent Breakthrough*. Palisade, CO: Tapirback Enterprises, 1995. 14p.

Tornblom

Pearson, Frederick John. *Anderson*. Houston, TX: Author, 1995. 352p.

Towle

Jones, William H. *Phillip Towle, Hampton, New Hampshire, His English Origins and Some American Descendants*. Bowie, MD: Heritage Books, 1995. 101p.

Towner

Quick, Robert V. *A Genealogy of the Family of Towner*. Memphis, TN: Author, 1995. 66p.

Townsend

Reynolds, Beatrice Kay. *Daniel Townsend, Sr., Early Settler of Sidney, Maine (1764)*. Sidney, ME: Author, 1995. 35p.

Trammell

Mann, Marion. *The Kigh, Mann, Reagin, and Sykes Families, Including the Branch, Brown, Dean, Fort, Gerran, Leake, Marquis, Moses, Oakes, Powell, Reid, Trammell, Walk, Wilkey, Wingfield, and Woods Families, a Genealogy and Family History*. Baltimore, MD: Gateway Press, 1995. 218p.

Travers

Hauk, Carol A. *Descendants of Rawleigh Travers of Virginia*. Anderson, IN: Hauk Data Services, 1995. 36p.

Tremblay

Levesque Babin, Olivette. *Mâture, Voilure et Souvenance, Histoire et Généalogie des Familles Roy et Tremblay (Pascal)*. Ville de la Baie, Quebec: Author, 1995. 342p.

Trevino

Pena, José F. de la. *Los Trevino de Revilla Ciudad Guerrero, 1757–1920*. Ventura, CA: Author, 1995. 52p.

Trice

Carroll, Thelma Ellen Young. *A Source Book For Five Generations of Family History*. Virginia Beach, VA: Merrit Press, 1995. Unpgd.

Johnston, Francis Clairborne. *The Angier Family of Orange and Durham Counties, North Carolina, and Allied Families of North Carolina and Virginia*. Richmond, VA: Author, 1995. 329p.

Triplett

Covert, Norman M. *Tree of Life, Genealogy of Covert, Goodson, Dey, Barker, Triplett and Allied Families from 1607*. Baltimore, MD: Gateway Press, 1995. 463p.

Troudt

Kaufman, Ervin D. *A Genealogy of Conrad and Magdalena Troudt, Germans from Russia, the Volga Colony of Norka, Russia*. Colorado: Author, 1995. 127p.

Troutman

Troutman, Steve Earl. *The Troutman Trautman Family History, Every Name Index, 1995*. Klingerstown, PA: Author, 1995. 36p.

Trowbridge

Atteridg, Paul T. *The Attridges of North America*. Granby, CO: Author, 1995. 429p.

Troxel

Shriver, Richard Alan. *Troxel Family Data*. Fort Wayne, IN: Author, 1995. 125p.

Troxler

Shriver, Richard Alan. *Troxel Family Data*. Fort Wayne, IN: Author, 1995. 125p.

Trubetskoi

Trubetskoi, Sergei Grigorevich. *Our Family's Album: A Genealogical and Photographic Chronicle of the Descendants of Prince Nikolai Petrovich Troubetzkoy*. Sea Cliff, NY: Author, 1995. 284p.

True

True, Edward Keene. *Ancestors and Descendants of Edward True, Jr. (1799–1871) and of His Wife Olive King Payson True (1871–1886) of Hope, Maine*. Searsport, ME: Author, 1995. 432p.

Truett

Pulleine, Imogene Hamilton. *The Ancestors and Descendants of John William Truett and Priscilla Grigsby*. Author, 1995. 123p.

Trundy

Thatcher, Alice Trundy. *Ancestors and Descendants of Alfred Eames Trundy and of His Wife Elizabeth Mehitable Bean*. Baltimore, MD: Gateway Press, 1995. 92p.

Tschudi

Hayes, Edward R. *Margaret Elizabeth Ferrel Hayes and Her Ancestors*. Author, 1995. 200p.

Tucker

Hamilton, Phillip Forrest. *The Tucker Family and the Dynamics of Generational Change in Jeffersonian, Va., 1775–1830*. Dissertation (Ph.D.), Washington University, 1995. 730p.

Tucker, Franklin Bennett. *The Tooker/Tucker Family from Long Island, New York to New Jersey, a Search for the True Facts, the Period from 1639 to 1800*. Seven Lakes, NC: Author, 1995. 92p.

———. *The Tucker Family of Morris County, New Jersey, in the Area of Pequannock, Rockaway Valley, Montville, and Boonton, Genealogy and History*. Seven Lakes, NC: Author, 1995. 141p.

Tufts

Middleton, Edith S. *Marion Thomas Whitney: The Story of His Predecessors and Descendants, Parker, Greely, Tufts*. Portland, OR: Author, 1995. 45p.

Russell, Carol. *Sigrid, Sigrid Tufte Myhre Ostrom and Her Ancestors and Descendants, the History of an American Pioneer Woman with Roots in Hallingdal and Aurland, Norway*. Annandale, VA: Author, 1995. Unpgd.

Tungate

Popp, Tony. *Popp, Kemper, Kammerer, Tungate, Wiwi, Jonas and Other Ancestors and Relations*. Florence, KY: Author, 1995. 226p.

Tupper

Anderson, Eric. *Genealogy of Martha Ellen Tupper, the First Caucasian Girl Born in Petaluma and Descendants, 1620–1995*. Dillon Beach, CA: Author, 1995. 63p.

Emerson, Ralph Barclay Tupper. *The Tupper Family in the United States and Canada, 1631-1995: One of the Ten Founding Families of Sandwich, Massachusetts, a Genealogy and History of Thomas Tupper (1578–1676) and His Wife, Anne Hodgson (or Hudson) (1598-1676) and Their Descendants*. Baltimore, MD: Gateway Press, 1995. 2 vols.

Turner

Hauk, Carol A. *Descendants of Richard Bolling of Virginia*. Anderson, IN: Hauk Data Services, 1995. 315p.

———. *Descendants of William Randolph of Virginia*. Anderson, IN: Hauk Data Services, 1995. 461p.

Sluby, Paul E. *A Lineal Perspective of John Anderson Lankford and Bishop Henry McNeal Turner, Two Key Figures in the Maternal Lineage of Sara (Johnson) Bumbary*. 1995. Unpgd.

Turniansky

Johnson, Robert L. *The Turniansky Legacy, a Family History*. Michigan: Author, 1995. 186p.

Tuttle

Tuttle, Alva M. *Peter Tuttle, b. 1660, Ancestor of Some Southern Tuttles, from Tuttle-Tuthill Lines in America*. Keno, OR: Solo Press, 1995. 89p.

Tye

Smith, Jean and Anne Goodwill. *The Brodhead Family. Volume 6. The Story of Captain Daniel Brodhead, His Wife Ann Tye and Their Descendants*. Port Ewin, NY: Author, 1995. 96p.

Tyler

Beaman, Chester E. *The Tyler Family of Virginia and Missouri (1690–1995)*. Rev. Alexandria, VA: Author, 1995. Unpgd.

Cottrell, Richard Gary. *The Tyler-Fruhauf Family History, and Genealogical Record of Associated Edwards, Ellis, Helme, Mason, Pritchard, Seymour, Sherrerd, and Whiting Families*. Parma, MI: Author, 1995. 2 vols.

Tyman

Spoden, Muriel Clark. *An American Ancestry of the Clark-Morton and Tyman-Millar-Adams Families*. Kingsport, TN: Spoden Associates, 1995. 547p.

–U

Uhle

Buchanan, Merwyn Russell. *Descendants of William and Maria Susannah (Uhle) Huckel*. Blue Bell, PA: Author, 1995. 137p.

Ulli

Gochnauer, Lena Sue. *John and Mary Ann Ulli Family*. Apple Creek, OH: Author, 1995. 172p.

Upcapher

McCormick, Greg L. *An Index to the Book, the Genealogy of the Uncapher and Unkefer Families, Descendants of Martin Ungefehr by Russell Harris Butler*. Author, 1995. 129p.

Upham

Upham, James Robert. *The Descendants of Henry Clinton Upham, Sr. and Charlotte Hart Peppard Upham*. Hot Springs, AR: Author, 1995. Unpgd.

Urquhart

Holmes, Marguerite. *Warman from George of Canterbury, England, and Kent County, Canada to George Frederick of Canada and Ludlow, Maine*. San Antonio, TX: Author, 1995. 44p.

Utt

Best Strange, Norma. *Descendants of Henry Ott/Utt and Margaret Ferril.* Chilhowee, MO: Author, 1995. 100p.

–V

Valldejuli

Davila Valldjuli, José. *Genealogía Valldejuli, Duprey y Roque de Puerto Rico.* Lubbock, TX: Author, 1995. 145p.

Valls

Nelson, Carmen Valls. *Our Family under Seven Flags, an Informal History of the Mendiola and Valls-Armengol Families.* Laredo, TX: Author, 1995. 255p.

Valois

Valois, Jack. *A Franco American Chronicle, 1666–1995.* Pembroke Pines, FL: Leist & Boullier Publications, 1995. 1,005p.

Van Auken

Van Auken, Robert A. *Index to Individuals and Families Names Van Auken and Van Aken.* North Olmsted, OH: Author, 1995. Unpgd.

Van Buskirk

Phelps, Barbara Barratt. *The Ralph and Olive Clarke Smith of Burlington, New Jersey, Family History, 1694–1994.* Littleton, CO: Author, 1995. 326p.

Van Cleve

Van Cleve, Edmund C. *The Ives-Van Cleve Family History, the Tie That Binds.* Author, 1995. 52p.

Van Culen

White, David E. *The Ancestors and Descendants of Carolus (Charles) White and Margareta Van Culen.* Marlborough, NH: Author, 1995. 458p.

Vande Berg

Vande Berg, Wilma Joyce Hoekstra. *Vanden Berg, Vande Berg Family History, 1500–1995, Includes Surname Variations Vanden Berg.* Sioux Center, IA: Author, 1995. 614p.

Van den Bosch

Bos, Maarten. *Het Stichts-Hollands Geslacht Van den Bosch: Voorlopig Verslag Van een onderzoek naar Persoon en Voorgeslacht Van Cornelis Jacobsz (ca. 1500-ca. 1580) te Waddinxveen.* Hilversum, Netherlands: Verloren, 1995. 256p.

Vanderpool

Hayes, Edward R. *Margaret Elizabeth Ferrel Hayes and Her Ancestors*. Author, 1995. 200p.

Vandlen

Vandlen, Geraldine Williams London. *Pifer-Schlosser Ancestry of Geraldine Williams Vandlen, Ancestry of the Londons of Lakeview, Michigan*. Author, 1995. 190p.

Vane

Vane, Floie Marie. *A Family History, James and Maren Vane of Dawson, Minnesota*. 2nd. ed. Cliffside Park, NJ: Author, 1995. 55p.

Van Meteren

Zuendel, Jean. *Taylor, Blanchan, Cochran, DuBois, Foreman, Hite, Morris, Parker, Van Meteren*. Author, 1995. Unpgd.

Van Nostrand

Van Nostrand, Jacqueline Joslin. *The Ancestors and Descendants of Frederick van Norstrand and Elizabeth Harris of Cayuga County, New York*. Evart, MI: Family History Publishers, 1995. 388p.

Van Orne

Fowlkes, Eugene Franklin. *Our Folks, a Genealogy*. Fort Worth, TX: Author, 1995. 134p.

Van Patten

Hindmarsh, F. I. *Descendants of Claas Frederickse Van Petten (1641–1728) and His Wife Aeffie Arentse Bradt (1649–1728), a Family History Research Project*. Aylmer, Ontario: Author, 1995. 281p.

————. *Descendants of Claas Frederickse Van Petten (1641–1728) and His Wife Aeffie Arentse Bradt (1649–1728), a Family History Research Project*. Rev. Aylmer, Ontario: Author, 1995. 293p.

Van Planck

Hayes, Edward R. *Margaret Elizabeth Ferrel Hayes and Her Ancestors*. Author, 1995. 200p.

Van Roggen

Graadt van Roggen, August Harmen Freddy. *Genealogy of the Families Van Roggen, Graadt van Roggen, and Graadt*. Kennett Square, PA: Author, 1995. 547p.

Van Voorhees

Griffiths, George R. *Van Voorhees Family in Early New York/New Jersey*. Chandler, AZ: Author, 1995. 17p.

Van Wyke

Van Wyke, Millie. *A Dutch Romance, an American Dream, the True Story of Jan Van Wijke and Neeltje Van't Sant, 1887–1937, Their Ancestors and Their Descendants*. Denver, CO: Author, 1995. 349p.

————. *Genealogy, AD 1350–1995, Ancestral Line for Family of Van Wijk, a.k.a. Van Wyke.* Denver, CO: Author, 1995. 21p.

Varner

Crozier, Micki. *The Varner Family: Descendants of Adam and Christina Varner of the Shenandoah Valley in Virginia.* Sedgwick, KS: Author, 1995. Unpgd.

Palmer, Janice Blankenship. *Varner, Verner, Werner Families of America.* Pensacola, FL: Kissing Cousins, 1995. 714p.

Vaughn

Gray, Effie Stantial. *The Ancestry of the Maine Stantial/Vaughan Connection and Related Families.* Thomaston, ME: Author, 1995. 460p.

Johnson, Pamela Call. *More Vaughn Settlers of Erie, Pennsylvania, and Nearby Areas.* Shelley, ID: Author, 1995. 51p.

May, John Russell. *Vaughn-Fallis Family History and Genealogy.* Fort Wayne, IN: Author, 1995. Unpgd.

Venard

O'Neal, Marcia Corrigan. *O'Neal Genealogy from the Early 1800s and Including Ancestors Anderson, Childers, Davis, Griffith, Hunt, Savage, Venard, and Willcuts.* Richmond, IN: Author, 1995. 43p.

Vestromhagen

Jacobson, Cora Gunderson. *Vestromhagen, from the Mountains to the Prairies.* Tower, MN: Tribune Graphic Arts, 1995. 398p.

Vidaurri

Pena, José F. de la. *Los Vidaurri de Coahuila, Nuevo León, Tamaulipas, y Texas, 1740–1920.* Ventura, CA: Author, 1995. 26p.

Vigne

Hayes, Edward R. *Margaret Elizabeth Ferrel Hayes and Her Ancestors.* Author, 1995. 200p.

Villarreal

Pena, José F. de la. *Los Villarreal de Revilla, Ciudad Guerrero, 1757–1900.* Ventura, CA: Author, 1995. 45p.

Vilmo

Sand, Vernon Jerome. *The Life and Times of Vernon and Renee Sand and Related Families, Geiselhart, Bittle, Warner, Sand, Vilmo, Bergman, Le Grand, Lassauge, Prado, and Carpentier.* Austin, TX: Author, 1995. 501p.

Vincent

Vincent, Sheridan Eugene. *The Descendants of Dr. Michael Vincent, Born 1784, Columbia Co., New York.* Rochester, NY: Author, 1995. 76p.

Vliet

Vliet, James. *A Genealogy of the "Van Der" Vliet Family in America.* NY: Author, 1995. Unpgd.

Voight

Eggert, Irving John. *Peter Eggert of Mecklenburg and Related Families in America, Best, Bitz, Broekemeier, Hackbarth, Kane, Meisner, Nellis, Schunk, Strenkowski, Voight, Winston.* Decorah, IA: Anundsen Pub. Co., 1995. 224p.

Volhard

Klebenow, Jean. *The Ancestors of Henry Peter Volhard of Marathon County, Wisconsin.* Reno, NV: Author, 1995. Unpgd.

Volozhiner

Meiselman, Shulamit Soloveitchik. *The Soloveitchik Heritage, A Daughter's Memoir.* Hoboken, NJ: KTAV Pub., 1995. 260p.

Votapka

Hansen, Henrietta. *Branches of Our Jedlicka Tree.* Woodbury, MN: Author, 1995. 149p.

—W—

Wachs

Wax, Charlotte Maris. *History and Genealogy of the Wax (Wachs) Family, 1745–1995, Johann Phillipus Wachs, Henry (Wachs) Wax, Jacob Wax, Nicholas F. Wax, William Caldwell Wax.* Newman, IL: Author, 1995. 216p.

Wade

Crum, Raymond. *A De Long Family in Ohio and Illinois, Including Relationships to the Hobaker and Crumpler Families, 1995 Companion Edition, with De Long-Wade Genealogy, Family Memories and Cumulative Name Indexes.* Ventura, CA: Author, 1995. 222p.

Wadleigh

Wadleigh, Robert Lee. *The Wadley's Wadleighs of Oxford, Ohio.* Hamilton, OH: Author, 1995. Unpgd.

Wadsworth

Toliver, Annabelle. *Skaggs-Wadsworth Family History.* Indianapolis: Author, 1995. 214p.

Waggoner

Waggoner, Walter S. *I Can, Shall and Will Not Stop, a History of the Waggoner Family from North Carolina to Illinois from Samuel Waggoner to Jesse Waggoner (1753–1861).* Quincy, IL: Author, 1995. Unpgd.

Wagoner, Crystal. *John Waggoner, 1751–1842, Margaret (Bonnett) Waggoner, Ancestors, Families, and Descendants.* Bowie, MD: Heritage Books, 1995. 343p.

Walferdin

Arthaud, John Bradley. *The Arthaud Family of Bourbonne-les-Bains and Langres, Department of Haute Marne, France with Related Families of Gascard, Gautherot, Lauzanne, Liegault, Mutinot and Walferdin and One Immigrant Branch in the United States.* Columbia, MO: Author, 1995. 123p.

Walk

Mann, Marion. *The Kigh, Mann, Reagin, and Sykes Families, Including the Branch, Brown, Dean, Fort, Gerran, Leake, Marquis, Moses, Oakes, Powell, Reid, Trammell, Walk, Wilkey, Wingfield, and Woods Families, a Genealogy and Family History.* Baltimore, MD: Gateway Press, 1995. 218p.

Walker

McKee, Ruth Vernette. *The Known Ancestry of Rev. Isaac Babbitt, 1757–1833, Including Cooper, Crane, Ford, Lovell, Morse, Pierce, Tarne, Tisdale, Walker and Whitman Families.* Minneapolis, MN: Author, 1995. 42p.

Mitchell, George Duncan. *Our Kindred Spirits, Some Family Histories.* Ottawa: Author, 1995. Unpgd.

Walker, Norman Lamont. *Our Walker Ancestry, A Genealogical Record of the Walker Family: Descendants of James Walker of Clarke County, Kentucky.* Norwalk, CA: Author, 1995. Unpgd.

Walker, Tony. *The History of the George and Margaret Cheshire Walker Family.* Kansas City, MO: Author, 1995. 89p.

Wallace

Batcher, Olive M. *Hill Wallace Family History.* Ames, IA: Author, 1995. 253p.

Hauk, Carol A. *Descendants of Rice Hooe of Virginia, Ancestor of President James Madison.* 2nd. ed. Anderson, IN: Hauk Data Services, 1995. 93p.

Moore, Freddie Gene. *My Virginia Ancestors and Their Descendants in the Families, Ratliff, Skidmore, Watson, Hamilton, Wallace, Cahoon, Bowyer, Grimes, Sharp, Meeks.* Author, 1995. 116p.

Powell, John W. *Ancestors and Descendants of Alvie C. Bryan and His Wife, Martha E. Wallace, Warrick County, Indiana.* Evansville, IN: Author, 1995. 125p.

Wallen

Feder, June Constance. *The Genealogy of the Price and Stull Families of the Town of Rush, Monroe County, New York, the Murrays, Wallings, and Hills of Victor, New York and the Otto, Block, Hill and Summerhays Families of Rochester, New York.* Fairport, NY: Author, 1995. 75p.

Waller

Hauk, Carol A. *Descendants of John Waller of Virginia.* Anderson, IN: Hauk Data Services, 1995. 87p.

Wallington

Bradley, John. *Sarah Wallington, 1719–1757, and Her Wallington, Pead, Okes, Fownes, Perry, and Bouchier Ancestors of Wotton-under-Edge.* Devizes, England, Author, 1995. 213p.

Walls

Clark, LaVerne Harrell. *The Bunte Family History, Smithville, Texas, 1880–1995, for the Smithville Centennial, 1995: With Histories of the Allied Families-the Garlipps, Lammes and Walls of Texas, c.1849.* Denton, TX: Texas Women's University Library, 1995. 245p.

Walsleben

Huffman, Peggy Walsleben. *The Family History of Frederick William Herman Walsleben and Augusta Jechow Walsleben.* Fort Worth, TX: Author, 1995. 48p.

Walter

Starr, Loren L. *The Walter Way.* Veneta, OR: Author, 1995. 40p.

Walton

Adams, Margaret Bickel. *Family Connections along the Blue Ridge, the Ancestry and Close Descendants of Margaret Erwin McDowell and James Thomas Walton.* Alexander, NC: World Comm, 1995. 102p.

Waltz

Jennings, Ruth. *Some Descendants of Jacob Waltz, Great Grandson of Frederick Reinhart Waltz, 1731–1995.* Bluffton, OH: Author, 1995. 346p.

Wanamaker

Kunz, Carol Wanamaker. *Johann "John" Wannemacher Family Tree: Joseph, Peter, Timothy, Charles, Ferdinand, Benedict, 1798–1995.* Delphos, OH: Author, 1995. 804p.

Wanzek

Wanzek, Brian P. *Wanzek Family History.* North Dakota: Author, 1995. 205p.

Ward

Craft, Kenneth F. *Some Branches of the Ward Family of Montgomery County, Maryland, with Earliest Ancestor, Revolutionary War Soldier James White Ward (also Known as James White) Including Some Allied Lines: Fairfax, Thompson, Ray, Cooke and Wylie.* Norcross, GA: Author, 1995. Unpgd.

Chesson, Eugene. *Foy and Allied Families of the Eastern Carolinas and New England.* Prescott, AZ: Author, 1995. Unpgd.

Jackson, Norris Wayne. *Our Ward Family, a Genealogical History of a Family Bloodline Basically Developed down through Many Generations in the Present Day West Virginia, Ohio, Kentucky Area around Huntington, West Virginia.* Salt Lake City, UT: Author, 1995. 1,111p.

May, John Russell. *Charles May Family History and Genealogy.* Fort Wayne, IN: Author, 1995. Unpgd.

———. *Ward Family History and Genealogy.* Fort Wayne, IN: Author, 1995. Unpgd.

Sepp, Ferne Whitmore. *My Pile, Sharpe, Ward, Whitmore Family.* Rantoul, IL: Author, 1995. Unpgd.

Ward, Naomi Etta. *The Ward Connections, Nourse, Kimmel, Wood, Babbs, Shelton, Sasubjak, Ader, Guffey, Pontiny, Archibald, Asbell.* Evansville, IN: Author, 1995. 545p.

Wardwell

Hare, Norma Q. *Puritans, Pioneers and Planters, an Ingraham, Abbott, Wardwell, Culver, Burbank Genealogy.* Arroyo Grande, CA: N. L. Enterprises, 1995. 330p.

Waring

Johnson, Libba Moore. *My Darling Daughters*. Author, 1995. 109p.

Warling

Warling, Kenneth E. *One Warling's Journey*. Baltimore, OH: Author, 1995. Unpgd.

Warman

Holmes, Marguerite. *Warman from George of Canterbury, England, and Kent County, Canada to George Frederick of Canada and Ludlow, Maine*. San Antonio, TX: Author, 1995. 44p.

Warner

Beling, Willard A. *Family History, Our Beling and Worner Roots*. Woodland Hills, CA: Author, 1995. Unpgd.

English, Carolyn P. *Warner-Werner-Woerner*. Shelbyville, IN: Author, 1995. 363p.

Hauk, Carol A. *Descendants of Augustine Warner of Virginia*. Anderson, IN: Hauk Data Services, 1995. 461p.

Warren

Boyer, Carol Constance Younker. *Warren Family Descendants in Pennsylvania/Indiana*. Rev. Denver, CO: Author, 1995. 181p.

Wakefield, Robert S. *Richard Warren of the Mayflower and His Descendants for Four Generations*. 5th ed. Plymouth, MA: General Society of Mayflower Descendants, 1995. 170p.

Warrenfeltz

Grillot, Nellie Marker. *A Genealogy of the Descendants of Peter Marker (1797–1881) and Mary Polly Warrenfeltz (1809–1879) of Frederick County, Maryland*. Port Tobacco, MD: S. M. Andrusko, 1995. 102p.

Wasey

Collins, Rae P. *Forward to the Past, Another Journey in Ancestry*. Stroud, Gloucestershire, England: A. Sutton, 1995. 156p.

Washington

Hauk, Carol A. *Descendants of Augustine Warner of Virginia*. Anderson, IN: Hauk Data Services, 1995. 461p.

———. *Descendants of George Reade of Virginia*. Anderson, IN: Hauk Data Services, 1995. 393p.

———. *Descendants of Lawrence and John Washington of Virginia*. Anderson, IN: Hauk Data Services, 1995. 173p.

———. *Descendants of Richard Lee of Virginia*. 2nd. ed. Anderson, IN: Hauk Data Services, 1995. 202p.

———. *Descendants of William Ball of Virginia*. Anderson, IN: Hauk Data Services, 1995. 229p.

———. *Descendants of William Randolph of Virginia*. Anderson, IN: Hauk Data Services, 1995. 461p.

Mallard, Shirley Jones. *Keeping Up with the Joneses, a Book about the Rafe Jones Family of Granville, North Carolina*. Chapel Hill, NC: Author, 1995. 244p.

Wass

Cagle, Ruby Abbott. *The Bishop Family from Manchester, England to Washington County, Maine*. Jasper, TN: Author, 1995. Unpgd.

Watkins

Ash, Edith Watkins Worley. *The Reynolds Pioneering Chronicles, New York and Southern Michigan Sojourn*. Osseo, MI: Author, 1995. 573p.

Watson

Davis, Arnold Isaiah Bell. *The Ancestors and Descendants of Elton Melville Montgomery and Mary Mabel Watson*. Ocala, FL: Author, 1995. 122p.

Moore, Freddie Gene. *My Virginia Ancestors and Their Descendants in the Families, Ratliff, Skidmore, Watson, Hamilton, Wallace, Cahoon, Bowyer, Grimes, Sharp, Meeks*. Author, 1995. 116p.

Sanders, Patrick B. *Genealogies of the Sanders and Watson Families, Examining the Descendants of Henry Sanders of Germany and Donald Watson of Scotland*. Chapel Hill, NC: Professional Press, 1995. 270p.

White, Madalene Bowler. *Descendants of Immigrants, Glendening, Mason, Watson*. Centerville, IN: Author, 1995. 61p.

Watts

Hauk, Carol A. *Descendants of Richard Watts of Virginia*. Anderson, IN: Hauk Data Services, 1995. 38p.

Rutledge, Fred Alvah. *Some Descendants of Thomas Watts, Jr., 1747 Virginia, 1797 Georgia, and Hannah Rust Boggess, 1753 Virginia, 1836 Alabama*. Baltimore, MD: Author, 1995. Unpgd.

Wax

Wax, Charlotte Maris. *History and Genealogy of the Wax (Wachs) Family, 1745–1995, Johann Phillipus Wachs, Henry (Wachs) Wax, Jacob Wax, Nicholas F. Wax, William Caldwell Wax*. Newman, IL: Author, 1995. 216p.

Waxler

Saunders, Jo Ann Muenzler. *Christoph Friedrich Munzler and His Descendants*. Austin, TX: Author, 1995. 76p.

Weaver

Jennings, Ruth. *Some Descendants of Jacob Waltz, Great Grandson of Frederick Reinhart Waltz, 1731–1995*. Bluffton, OH: Author, 1995. 346p.

Oncley, Lephia French. *Our Weaver Cousins, Ancestry of Samuel Stanton Weaver, 1793–1857, and His Wife, Lucy Billings Palmer, 1798–1851, with Some of Their Descendants and Related Families*. Ann Arbor, MI: Author, 1995. 244p.

Reed, Anna Weaver. *History and Descendants of the William H. And Lydia G. Weaver Family*. Ephrata, PA: Author, 1995. 141p.

Weaver, Clyde Richard. *The Descendants of Daniel E. and Rebecca Renninger Weaver*. Wooster, OH: Author, 1995. 120p.

Webb

Vander Wegen, Betty Ann. *Our Family, the Interrelated Coffeys, Graggs, Hollanders, Webbs of Avery County, North Carolina*. Union, WA: Author, 1995. Unpgd.

Weber

Weber, Doreen. *The Weber Family, a Genealogy of 2 of the Original 15 Settlers of Frankenmuth, Michigan in 1845*. Frankenmuth, MI: Author, 1995. 305p.

Webler

Webler, Robert Martin. *History of the Martin Webler Family*. Palmyra, PA: Author, 1995. Unpgd.

Webster

Bernhardt, Marcia A. *Webster Family Roots and Branches (through Sherman T. Webster), Ingham County, Michigan*. Iron River, MI: Author, 1995. 39p.

King, Mary Becker. *History of the Descendants of Moses Webster*. Author, 1995. 115p.

Ruskay, Joseph A. *Leaves from a Family Tree*. NY: Vantage Press, 1995. 244p.

Weddle

Carrico, Jane Barnett. *The Descendants of Martin Weddle and Johan Eiler*. Hilton Head, SC: Author, 1995. 239p.

Wedien

Usher, Candace. *Peterson, Nelson, Wedien, and Willing Families*. Powell, OH: Author, 1995. 79p.

Weigum

Zeiszler, Ernest Erwin. *Weigum*. Author, 1995. Unpgd.

Weimer

McRobie, Raymond Irvin. *The McRobie, McCrobie, Cuppett, Peck, Hostetler, Weimer, Smith, Wilt and Merrill Families of Garrett County*. Fairfax, VA: Author, 1995. 471p.

Weiss

Weiss, Joe. *From Dorrenbach, Germany to Indiana and Beyond, the Weiss Family, 1735–1995*. Indianapolis, IN: Author, 1995. 13p.

Welch

Brown, Gerald Douglas. *A Genealogy of a Locklair Family, Mainly of the Old Sumter District of South Carolina, Present Day Sumter and Lee Counties*. Hemingway, SC: Three Rivers Historical Society, 1995. 102p.

Welsh

Moore, Freddie Gene. *My Virginia Ancestors and Their Descendants in the Families, Burdett, Alexander, Anderson, King, Boone, Welsh, McHenry, Cornwell, Alford, Coleman, Dixon, Morgan, Jarman, Maugridge*. Author, 1995. 46p.

Welton

Fredrickson, Carrol. *The Ancestors of John Welton (1605–1995)*. Kenosha, WI: Author, 1995. 131p.

Wenger

Wenger, Irving. *Wenger and Graubard Genealogy*. Long Beach, CA: Author, 1995. Unpgd.

West

The Family of Hal Augustus Burns and Olive May West. Ft. Worth, TX; Author, 1995. 93p.

West, Donal S. *Hannah West and Elisha Edwards, Their Family*. Fort Wayne, IN: Author, 1995. 2 vols.

Westmoreland

Mapes, Olin V. *Westmoreland nee Neville*. Rev. ed. Bowie, MD: Heritage Books, 1995. 221p.

Whaley

Ziegel, Ruth Turner. *Julius Christy of Virginia and Kentucky, 1730–1808, and Agatha Barnett Christy, 1740–1820, and Related Families of Barnett, Gibbs, Blackburn, Cave, Glass, Kirtley, Bush, Lindsey, Armstrong, Whaley, Davis, and Day*. Cincinnati, OH: Author, 1995. 92p.

Wheeler

Cox-Wheeler and Related Families. Hemingway, SC: Three Rivers Historical Society, 1995. 269p.

Mallard, Shirley Jones. *Keeping Up with the Joneses, a Book about the Rafe Jones Family of Granville, North Carolina*. Chapel Hill, NC: Author, 1995. 244p.

Montgomery, Emma Mitchell. *Mitchell Memories, William Mitchell, Sr., William Mitchell, Jr. and Abigail (Wheeler) Mitchell and Their Descendents, 1728–1995*. Dogwood, MO: Dogwood Printing, 1995. 371p.

Wheeler, Frances. *The Wheelers of Granville County, North Carolina, Their Antecedents and Descendants*. Rev. ed. Okeechobee, FL: Author, 1995. 353p.

Whitcraft

Eberhart, Edith Whitcraft. *A Branch of the Flitcraft, Whitcraft, Witcraft and Allied Families Who Came to America during the Colonial Period*. Baltimore, MD: Gateway Press, 1995. 176p.

White

Dennis, Kenneth A. *David White, Kentucky Pioneer*. Louisville, KY: Author, 1995. 9p.

Hook, John H. *Hook-White Notebook, a Family History and Genealogy for the Descendants of Charles and Mabel Hook*. St. Petersburg, FL: Author, 1995. Unpgd.

White, Beatrice. *The Descendants of Wesley Willis White (1812–1886)*. Warrenton, VA; Author, 1995. 52p.

White, David E. *The Ancestors and Descendants of Carolus (Charles) White and Margareta Van Culen*. Marlborough, NH: Author, 1995. 458p.

White, Mary Hamilton. *William Lomax and His Descendants*. Author, 1995. 452p.

White, Winifred. *The White Family: the Descendants of Jesse White and Elizabeth Wells From 1762*. Augusta, GA: Author, 1995. 165p.

Willey, Eula Elizabeth White. *Ancestors and Descendants of J. Thomas White and Allie B. Lane of Perquimans County, North Carolina*. Author, 1995. Unpgd.

Whited

Whited, Barbara Craig. *William Whitehead and His Whited Descendants*. Author, 1995. 112p.

Whitehead

Whited, Barbara Craig. *William Whitehead and His Whited Descendants*. Author, 1995. 112p.

Whiting

Hauk, Carol A. *Descendants of Henry Whiting of Virginia*. Anderson, IN: Hauk Data Services, 1995. 64p.

Whitman

McKee, Ruth Vernette. *The Known Ancestry of Rev. Isaac Babbitt, 1757–1833, Including Cooper, Crane, Ford, Lovell, Morse, Pierce, Tarne, Tisdale, Walker and Whitman Families*. Minneapolis, MN: Author, 1995. 42p.

Whitmore

Sepp, Ferne Whitmore. *My Pile, Sharpe, Ward, Whitmore Family*. Rantoul, IL: Author, 1995. Unpgd.

Whitmore, Robert Devore. *Whitmore Family Genealogy*. Steubenville, OH: Public Library of Steubenville and Jefferson County, 1995. 14p.

Whittemore, Grace Kilmer. *Descendants of Jacob O. Whitmore*. Denver, CO: Author, 1995. 428p.

Whitney

Middleton, Edith S. *Marion Thomas Whitney: The Story of His Predecessors and Descendants, Parker, Greely, Tufts*. Portland, OR: Author, 1995. 45p.

Whitsill

Jones, Daniel Wilbur. *Genealogical Memoranda of Daniel Rufus Cable and Georgiana McKinney Cable*. Cary, NC: Author, 1995. 183p.

Whitsitt

Whitsitt, William. *Annals of Scotch-Irish Family, the Whitsitts of Nashville, Tennessee*. Nashville, TN: Friends of Mill Creek Baptist Church Graveyard, 1995. 45p.

Whitten

McBride, Jean Coleman. *The Colemans of West Alabama and Allied Families*. Aliceville, AL: Author, 1995. 200p.

Moore, William B. *Letters to Rebecca*. Bowie, MD: Heritage Books, 1995. 368p.

Whonstetler

Graham, Connie Thompson. *Miller Family History*. Fairview Park, OH: Author, 1995. 146p.

Wichelns

Wichelns, Maureen Butterfield. *The Wichelns Family in America.* Albuquerque, NM: Author, 1995. 128p.

Wicks

Koickler, Eloyce Hubbard. *Hiestand, Hestand, Hastings.* Helena, MT: Author, 1995. 127p.

Widmer

Widmer, Elmer Andreas. *Genealogical Data on the Relatives of Andreas and Magdalena (Mowes) Widmer Residing in the Kulm/Merricourt and Monango/Forbes, North Dakota Areas from 1900–1950.* Lakeport, CA: Author, 1995. 23p.

Wiebe

Hildebrand, Marjorie. *The Oak Tree: The Story of the Ancestors and Descendants of Peter and Margaretha Wiebe, 1797–1945.* Steinbach, Manitoba: Author, 1995. 85p.

Wiesman

Barron, William P. *The Family History of Belva Nevada Woolery, Wife of Bill Schamel and Wyatt McMillan and Her Descendants: With Notes on Related Families Brown, Lockhart, Schaeffer, Wiesman, Williams.* Fairborn, OH: Heritage Family Publications, 1995. Unpgd.

Wiesner

Eberhart, Leona. *History of the John Gottlieb and Sophia (Wiesner) Eberhardt Family, 1770-1995, Germany and USA, Primarily in Portage, Outagamie, Ozaukee and Wood Counties.* Wisconsin Rapids, WI: Author, 1995. 123p.

Wilcox

Wilcox, Richard Frederick. *Willcock to Wilcock to Wilcox, Daniel Willcock, the First of Our Family to Come to America.* Marmora, NJ: Author, 1995. 12p.

Wilde

Warschak, Carroll E. *Wilde Family History, 1683–1995, a Record of the Wilde Origins in Germany and of the Bernhard Wilde Descendants in America.* Waco, TX: Author, 1995. 323p.

Wilder

Tallent, Othar Kimmer. *Wilder Family History, a Brief History of Joe and Gertrude Wilder, Their Ancestors and Descendants.* Oak Ridge, TN: Author, 1995. 146p.

True, Edward Keene. *Ancestors and Descendants of Edward True, Jr. (1799–1871) and of His Wife Olive King Payson True (1871–1886) of Hope, Maine.* Searsport, ME: Author, 1995. 432p.

Wildey

Reamer, Kathleen R. *Descendants of John Reamer and Margaret Schermerhorn, 1758–1995.* Imlay City, MI: Author, 1995. 246p.

Wiley

Jones, Jean Patricia Stack. *The Bruce DesBrisay Jones and Jean Patricia Stack Jones.* Arlington, VA: Author, 1995. 194p.

Smith, Ruth Wiley. *Ancestors and Descendants of John Nelson Sibcy, Who Came to Hamilton County, Ohio, in the Early 1800s.* Oxford, OH: Author, 1995. 131p.

———. *Descendants of John Jacob Markley, Who Came to Hamilton County, Ohio, in 1804.* Oxford, OH: Author, 1995. 128p.

Wilhoit

Jones, Charles P. *A History of the Wilhoit Family of Central North Carolina, 1700s-1900s.* 2nd ed. Lawrenceville, GA: Author, 1995. 310p.

Wilkerson

Jordan, Janie Moseley Garraghty. *The Descendants of Joseph Wilkerson (12 May 1729–15 March 1829), and Allied Families of Bedford County, Virginia.* Lynchburg, VA: Warwick House Pub., 1995. 227p.

Wilkey

Mann, Marion. *The Kigh, Mann, Reagin, and Sykes Families, Including the Branch, Brown, Dean, Fort, Gerran, Leake, Marquis, Moses, Oakes, Powell, Reid, Trammell, Walk, Wilkey, Wingfield, and Woods Families, a Genealogy and Family History.* Baltimore, MD: Gateway Press, 1995. 218p.

Wilkins

Wikins, Muriel A. *Wilkins Family: 300 Years in America!.* Lincoln, NE: Author, 1995. 90p.

Wilkinson

D'Arezzo, Catherine McBride. *Recollections about the McBride Family.* Austin, TX: Author, 1995. 39p.

Willcuts

O'Neal, Marcia Corrigan. *O'Neal Genealogy from the Early 1800s and Including Ancestors Anderson, Childers, Davis, Griffith, Hunt, Savage, Venard, and Willcuts.* Richmond, IN: Author, 1995. 43p.

Williams

Barron, William P. *The Family History of Belva Nevada Woolery, Wife of Bill Schamel and Wyatt McMillan and Her Descendants: With Notes on Related Families Brown, Lockhart, Schaeffer, Wiesman, Williams.* Fairborn, OH: Heritage Family Publications, 1995. Unpgd.

Brayton, John A. *The Ancestry of General James Robertson "Father of Tennessee," Addendum to the Complete Ancestry of Tennessee Williams.* Winston-Salem, NC: Author, 1995. 60p.

———. *The Ancestry of Tennessee Williams, "Father of Tennessee," Addendum to the Complete Ancestry of Tennessee Williams.* Winston-Salem, NC: Author, 1995. 60p.

Hauk, Carol A. *Descendants of Benjamin Harrison of Virginia.* 4th. ed. Anderson, IN: Hauk Data Services, 1995. 365p.

———. *Descendants of James Williams of Virginia.* 2nd. ed. Anderson, IN: Hauk Data Services, 1995. 47p.

———. *Descendants of Miles Cary of Virginia.* Anderson, IN: Hauk Data Services, 1995. 421p.

————. *Descendants of Philip Pendleton of Virginia.* 6th. ed. Anderson, IN: Hauk Data Services, 1995. 287p.

————. *Descendants of Robert Coleman of Virginia.* Anderson, IN: Hauk Data Services, 1995. 226p.

————. *Descendants of William Randolph of Virginia.* Anderson, IN: Hauk Data Services, 1995. 461p.

Heritage of the Williams Family of Chatham County, North Carolina, the First Centennial Commemorating 100 Years of Family Reunions, 1895–1995. Chatham County, NC: Williams Family Circle, 1995. 196p.

Horned, Joseph. *A Guide for Researching Williams/Williamson in Cherokee Records, Dawes Roll, Guion Miller Roll, Drennen Roll, Chapman Roll.* Author, 1995. 62p.

Lewis, Allen Roy. *Two Hundred Year History and Genealogy of the Isaac Lewis Family from Cloughjordan (Tipperary), Ireland to the Canadas and the United States, Including Intermarriages with Hodgins, Myers, Rapley, Slack, Williams, and Many Other Families.* Ver. 1.5. Syracuse, NY: Author, 1995. 215p.

McBride, Jean Coleman. *The Colemans of West Alabama and Allied Families.* Aliceville, AL: Author, 1995. 200p.

McLeod, Stephen Archie. *The House of Cantelou & Co., the Story of a Southern Family.* Tallahassee, FL: Author, 1995. 705p.

Partin, Sherita Kae. *Four Generations of the Family of Kindred Allison Partin.* Nacogdoches, TX: Partin Publications, 1995. Unpgd.

Prokopowicz, A. John. *Descendants of Roger Williams, a Descendancy List of His Son Daniel Williams.* Author, 1995. 383p.

Williams, Carl Clifford. *The Williams and Granberry Families.* Midland, TX: Author, 1995. 287p.

Williams, Curtis C. *The Williams Family.* Seminole, FL: Author, 1995. 13p.

Williamson

Horned, Joseph. *A Guide For Researching Williams/Williamson in Cherokee Records, Dawes Roll, Guion Miller Roll, Drennen Roll, Chapman Roll.* Author, 1995. 62p.

Ronemous, Hulda Williamson. *Rob and Joe, McCracken and Williamson Ancestors in Eighteenth Century South Carolina.* Baltimore, MD: Gateway Press, 1995. 211p.

Willing

Usher, Candace. *Peterson, Nelson, Wedien, and Willing Families.* Powell, OH: Author, 1995. 79p.

Willis

Barber, Franklin Taylor. *The Barbers and Allied Families.* Plano, TX: Author, 1995. 317p.

Bergdall, Bernese Willis. *Shufelt Family, Palatinate to Hudson Valley to Eastern Shore, 1630–1995.* Pawleys Island, SC: Author, 1995. 147p.

Bostic, Paul Eugene. *Bruce, Maupin, Carr and Some Related Families Including Ballard, Hearn, Ayres, McCubbin, Cloud, Lane, Eveland (Elfland), Graves, Sharp and Willis.* Clinton, TN: Author, 1995. 391p.

Hauk, Carol A. *Descendants of Augustine Warner of Virginia.* Anderson, IN: Hauk Data Services, 1995. 461p.

————. *Descendants of Francis Willis of Virginia.* Anderson, IN: Hauk Data Services, 1995. 154p.

Willis, Dorothy Burrows. *Across the Continent with the Ancestors and Descendants of Abner Willis and Martha Robbins.* Oak Harbor, WA: Heritage Cascade, 1995. 300p.

Willms

Willms, Peter A. *Peter Jacob and Katharina (Sudermann) Willms, Their Ancestors, Lives, and Descendants.* Author, 1995. 69p.

Willoughby

Rabold, Mary Moltenberry. *Motley, Willoughby and Lynn Families of Virginia, North Carolina and Kentucky.* Bowling Green, KY: Author, 1995. 250p.

Wilson

Bymaster Richards, Willa. *Descendants of Nathaniel Wilson.* Carnation, WA: Author, 1995. Unpgd.

Dix, Roberta Cook Jackson. *The First Shall be Last, a Family History.* Author, 1995. 137p.

Kline, Lucile. *Wilson Family History, 1739–1995.* Peru, IN: Author, 1995. 114p.

Lyon, Randolph W. *The Wilson Family History, 75th Anniversary Edition, 1921–1995.* Traer, IA: Author, 1995. 287p.

Page, Robert E. *Wilson and Hollingsworth Family.* Indian Rocks Beach, FL: Author, 1995. 37p.

Stevens, Ken. *The New England Wilson Index.* Author, 1995. 358p.

Thornton, Mary Ann. *The Wilson Family from South Carolina to Texas.* Santa Fe, NM: Author, 1995. 200p.

Wilson, Robert E. *The Wilson and Related Families.* Taftsville, VT: Author, 1995. 2 vols.

Wine

Wine, Norman F. *Descendants of Jesse Wine.* Lebanon, PA: Author, 1995. 69p.

Wing

Moulton, Virginia Plaisted. *Reunions of the Wing Family of Phillips, Maine, 1893–1994.* Jay, ME: Author, 1995. 153p.

Wingfield

Mann, Marion. *The Kigh, Mann, Reagin, and Sykes Families, Including the Branch, Brown, Dean, Fort, Gerran, Leake, Marquis, Moses, Oakes, Powell, Reid, Trammell, Walk, Wilkey, Wingfield, and Woods Families, a Genealogy and Family History.* Baltimore, MD: Gateway Press, 1995. 218p.

Winkler

Ratts, Kenneth R. *From Germany to Wherever?.* Sun City Center, FL: Author, 1995. Unpgd.

Winner

Miller, Marilyn Isabel. *The Winner and Scheid Families.* Cullman, AL: Gregath Pub. Co., 1995. 227p.

Winningham

Hughes, Nancy Caroline Phillips. *Hugh Phillips, Some of His Descendants, Including Allied Families of Bolin, Blewer (Bluer), Reidheimer, Salley, Schuler (Shuler) and Winningham.* Columbia, SC: Author, 1995. 46p.

Winstead

Winstead, Martha. *The Winsteads, Descendants of Samuel Winstead, 1701–1774, Branch Three, Samuel Winstead.* South Bend, IN: Author, 1995. 740p.

Winston

Eggert, Irving John. *Peter Eggert of Mecklenburg and Related Families in America, Best, Bitz, Broekemeier, Hackbarth, Kane, Meisner, Nellis, Schunk, Strenkowski, Voight, Winston.* Decorah, IA: Anundsen Pub. Co., 1995. 224p.

McGinn, Ann Winston. *A McGinn McCorkle Family History, 1796–1995: With Related Families, Crockett, Dabney, Egnatoff, Fontaine, Freirson, Gillespie, Huddart, Kennemore, O'Donnell, Patton, Ring, Sheppard, Winston, and Others.* Spring Hill, FL: Author, 1995. 313p.

Whitmore, Robert Devore. *Whitmore Family Genealogy.* Steubenville, OH: Public Library of Steubenville and Jefferson County, 1995. 14p.

Winterhalder

Dunn, Geoffrey. *Pioneer Spirit, a History of the Winterhalder Family in Santa Cruz County.* Capitola, CA: Capitola Book Co., 1995. 12p.

Wintermyer

Kucherer, Harvey David. *The 8 Generations Wintermyer Family Lineage with Allied Families, and the 8 Generation Ahnentafel Kucherer Family Lineage with Allied Families.* Monroeville, PA: Author, 1995. Unpgd.

Winterringer

Carey, Patricia Winterringer. *Bernard Wintringer and His Descendants.* Le Mars, IA: Red's Printing Co., 1995. 250p.

Wise

Wise, Erbon W. *Wise Footsteps from England and Ireland, an Ancestral Study of Wise and Allied Families.* Sulphur, LA: Author, 1995. 298p.

Wisman

Miller, DeWitt Henry. *Ancestors and Descendants of Walter William Wisman and Mary Elizabeth Armentrout.* Roanoke, VA: Author, 1995. 65p.

Withers

Johnston, Francis Clairborne. *The Angier Family of Orange and Durham Counties, North Carolina, and Allied Families of North Carolina and Virginia.* Richmond, VA: Author, 1995. 329p.

Wiwi

Popp, Tony. *Popp, Kemper, Kammerer, Tungate, Wiwi, Jonas and Other Ancestors and Relations.* Florence, KY: Author, 1995. 226p.

Wolcott

Bielanski, Phyllis Jean Olin. *Andrew Powell Family Tree, Including Powell, Farr, Ten Brock Branches and Wolcott, Stiles, Doolittle, Kelch, Eldridge Branches.* Lakeland, FL: Author, 1995. Unpgd.

Wolfe

Baldree, Garvis Brookshire. *The Baldree Family*. Author, 1995. 212p.

Brown, William Jay, Jr. *The Ancestors and Descendants of William Gage Brown and Harriet Alice Wolfe of Urbana, Illinois*. Wellesley, MA: Author, 1995. Unpgd.

Crozier, E. Wanda Sloan. *Keesaman-Wolf Families and Allied Families*. Author, 1995. Unpgd.

Wood

Hanrahan, Patrick Lloyd. *Charlebois (Wood) Family History, and the Allied Families of Brien, Brule, Daudelin, Gagnon, LeBlanc and Riel*. Milwaukie, OR: Author, 1995. 179p.

Ward, Naomi Etta. *The Ward Connections, Nourse, Kimmel, Wood, Babbs, Shelton, Sasubjak, Ader, Guffey, Pontiny, Archibald, Asbell*. Evansville, IN: Author, 1995. 545p.

Wood, Gary Edward. *John Wood of Wayne County, Illinois, and Descendants, 1817–1878*. Baltimore, MD: Gateway Press, 1995. 197p.

Wood, Thomas Fullenwider. *Connections, the Wood and Fullenwider Families in America*. Author, 1995. 130p.

Woodbridge

Coldwell, Mary Kathryn Woodbridge. *The Forefathers and Descendants of Mark Judson Woodbridge, a Continuation of the Woodbridge Record Being an Account of the Descendants of the Rev. John Woodbridge of Newbury, Massachusetts*. Broken Arrow, OK: C. A. C. Arledge, 1995. 143p.

Woodhouse

Chesson, Eugene. *Foy and Allied Families of the Eastern Carolinas and New England*. Prescott, AZ: Author, 1995. Unpgd.

Woodman

Woodman, John A. *Genealogy and History of the Descendants of Mr. Edward Woodman, Who Settled at "Ould Newbury," Province of Massachusetts Bay in 1635*. Ocala, FL: Author, 1995. 808p.

Woodruff

Popham, Geraldine E. *Grandma's Ancestors, 1634–1936, Thomas Judd, the Emigrant to Nelson Judd, and Addie (Judd) Dowd*. Lodi, CA: Author, 1995. 148p

Woodrum

Woodrum, Lawrence E. *A Small Segment of Woodrum Family History*. Fort Wayne, IN: Author, 1995. 92p.

Woods

Mann, Marion. *The Kigh, Mann, Reagin, and Sykes Families, Including the Branch, Brown, Dean, Fort, Gerran, Leake, Marquis, Moses, Oakes, Powell, Reid, Trammell, Walk, Wilkey, Wingfield, and Woods Families, a Genealogy and Family History*. Baltimore, MD: Gateway Press, 1995. 218p.

Woodward

Reeks, Lindsay S. *Woodward/Woodard Ancestors of New England*. Baltimore, MD: Gateway Press, 1995. 232p.

Woodworth

Dix, Roberta Cook Jackson. *The First Shall be Last, a Family History*. Author, 1995. 137p.

Woody

Smith, James Everett. *Woody Cousins, Originating in Laclede and Pulaski Counties, Missouri and Elsewhere*. Springfield, MO: Author, 1995. 269p.

Woofter

White, Woodrow Wilson. *Douglass Woofter Union, Updated Family Tree of Alvin and Dora (Woofter) Douglass, 1813–1995*. Orlando, FL: Author, 1995. 74p.

Woolery

Barron, William P. *The Family History of Belva Nevada Woolery, Wife of Bill Schamel and Wyatt McMillan and Her Descendants: With Notes on Related Families Brown, Lockhart, Schaeffer, Wiesman, Williams*. Fairborn, OH: Heritage Family Publications, 1995. Unpgd.

Woolford

Kinnersley, William. *The Woolford Family of Dorchester County, Maryland, Ancestors and Descendants of Thomas Woolford and Sarah Stevens*. Lawrence, KS: Author, 1995. 25p.

Woolum

Creech, Lillian Broughton. *Kentucky Lineage, Broughton, Slusher, Woolum, Payne and Related Families*. Baltimore, MD: Gateway Press, 1995. 592p.

Work

Best Strange, Norma. *Descendants of Samuel Maxwell, Sr. and Elizabeth Work*. Chilhowee, MO: Author, 1995. 61p.

Workman

Perry, Max. *Descendants of John Workman, Captain James Hanna and Captain John E. McConnell of York County, South Carolina*. Greenville, SC: A Press, 1995. 161p.

Worley

Adair, Shirley Brown. *Robert Adair (1770–1845c.), an Adair Family History, Reid, Emerson, Hobbs, Worley, Thompson (Related Lines)*. Rockwall, TX: Author, 1995. 146p.

Wormer

Reamer, Kathleen R. *Descendants of John Reamer and Margaret Schermerhorn, 1758–1995*. Imlay City, MI: Author, 1995. 246p.

Worner

Beling, Willard A. *Family History, Our Beling and Worner Roots*. Woodland Hills, CA: Author, 1995. Unpgd.

Worrell

Brownfield, Florence E. *The Brownfields in America, John Brownfield and Mary Lewis Worrell and Their Descendants*. Tustin, CA: Author, 1995. 93p.

Ralph, Charles L. *Genealogy of a Poinsett Family from the Atlantic Seacoast to the Colorado Rockies, with Notes on the Worrell and Braamharr Families.* Ft. Collins, CO: Author, 1995. 84p.

Wren

Hook, John H. *Hook-White Notebook, a Family History and Genealogy for the Descendants of Charles and Mabel Hook.* St. Petersburg, FL: Author, 1995. Unpgd.

Wretman

Ed, Robert Calhoun. *Wretman Roots, the Genealogy and History of the Wretman Families Who Emigrated from Ostergorland Lan, Sweden to Moline, Illinois, 1880–1891, Including Chapters on the Nymans and the Juthes.* Livingston, TX: Author, 1995. 295p.

Wright

Biggar, Harold Arthur. *The Biggar Families of Greenwich, Connecticut, and County Tyrone, North Ireland.* Stamford, CT: Author, 1995. unpgd.

Rehm, Jeffrey Charles. *Genealogy of Moses Gonser and Louisa Wright of Hudson, Indiana.* Fort Wayne, IN: Author, 1995. 64p.

Skelton, Isaac Newton. *Ike, This Is You, a History of the Skelton, Boone, Barry, Beach, Blattner, Corum, Hoagland, Lehew, Strode, Wright and Young Families.* Washington, DC: Author, 1995. 223p.

Wright, Robert Daniel. *Daniel Peyton Wright, Jr. and Amanda Amber (Evans) Wright, Their Ancestors and Their Descendants.* Wichita, KS: Author, 1995. 451p.

Wright, Sharon Theresa. *Job Wright, Nine Generations.* Jacksonville, FL: Author, 1995. 171p.

Wright, William Henry, Gertrude Wright Ketcham, and Marie L. Wright. *History of the Wright Family.* Bowie, MD: Heritage Books, 1913, 1995. 235p.

Wright-Alford, Evelyn Geraldine. *I'm Always Wright.* Greenfield, IN: Author, 1995. 1995. 178p.

Wyatt

Ancestors and Descendants of William Whitaker Smith, 1860–1944, and Florence Ellen Sullivan, 1875–1926, of Anderson and Greenville Counties, South Carolina. Spartanburg, SC: Reprint Co., 1995. 146p.

Hauk, Carol A. *Descendants of Francis and Haute Wyatt of Virginia.* 2nd. ed. Anderson, IN: Hauk Data Services, 1995. 56p.

Wylie

Craft, Kenneth F. *Some Branches of the Ward Family of Montgomery County, Maryland, with Earliest Ancestor, Revolutionary War Soldier James White Ward (Also Known as James White) Including Some Allied Lines: Fairfax, Thompson, Ray, Cooke and Wylie.* Norcross, GA: Author, 1995. Unpgd.

Wyn

Welch, Glorya E. *Rose and Wyn Families of Muskegon, Michigan.* La Mirada, CA: Author, 1995. 18p.

Wyrick

Jones, Daniel Wilbur. *Genealogical Memoranda of Daniel Rufus Cable and Georgiana McKinney Cable.* Cary, NC: Author, 1995. 183p.

Xui

Cortez, Constance. *Gaspar Antonio Chi and the Xiu Family Tree*. Dissertation (Ph.D.), University of California, Los Angeles, 1995. 349p.

Yager

Reamer, Kathleen R. *Descendants of John Reamer and Margaret Schermerhorn, 1758–1995*. Imlay City, MI: Author, 1995. 246p.

Yancey

Johnston, Francis Clairborne. *The Angier Family of Orange and Durham Counties, North Carolina, and Allied Families of North Carolina and Virginia*. Richmond, VA: Author, 1995. 329p.

Yanik

Paulochik, Paul M. *Roots and Branches, Paulochik, Gosemeyer, Yanik, Lonergan, and Related Families*. O'Fallon, IL: Author, 1995. 489p.

Yarborough

Ratts, Kenneth R. *From Germany to Wherever?*. Sun City Center, FL: Author, 1995. Unpgd.

Yeager

Johnson, Elizabeth Yates. *The Family of Daniel Wayne Yeager, 1835–1910, His Ancestors and Descendants*. Houston, TX: Clear Lake Secretarial, 1995. 202p.

Yearick

Garbrick, Harry. *Yearick Family*. Author, 1995. 118p.

Yeatton

Stultz, Carolyne. *The Jones Family Research Report, Including a Genealogy on Descendants of Jacob and Mary Jane (Yeatton) Jones from Kennebec, Maine, to Edgar County, Illinois*. Danville, IN: Author, 1995. Unpgd.

Yetter

Peck, Patricia Dunn. *Jones Family Genealogy, a History of the Christopher M. Jones Family of Philadelphia with Emphasis on the Descendants of His Son, Levi Taylor Jones of Phila-*

delphia and Trenton and Related Thropp, Yetter, Dunn and Steele Families. Saratoga Springs, NY: Peckhaven Pub., 1995. 98p.

Yoder

The Descendants of Benjamin J. Yoder and Fannie I. Yoder, 1880–1995. Sugarcreek, OH: Carlisle Printing, 1995. 52p.

Yoder, Christian T. *Yoder History, 1700–1970, and Family Record of Abraham A. Yoder and Lydia Miller, 1871–1993*. 1995. 344p.

Yoder, Ernest. *The Moses H. Yoder Family History*. Kokomo, IN: Selby Pub., 1995. 340p.

Yoder, Orley W. *The Family Book of Joseph J. Yoder and Lydia C. (Yoder)*. Goshen, IN: Author, 1995. 101p.

Yoder Memoirs: Noah and Mattie Yoder's Family Line: How Love Reigned through Hardships. Goshen, IN: GET Printing, 1995. 136p.

Yorke

McCready, Harriet Yorke. *The Descendants of Captain Edward Yorke, a New England Planter in Nova Scotia*. Parrsboro, Nova Scotia: Author, 1995. Unpgd.

Young

Bell, Ernest Elmont, Jr. *One Line of Descent from Our Immigrant, Alexander Bell/Beall of Maryland, a Genealogical History, 1600 AD to 2000 AD, with an Autobiography by Ernest Elmont Bell, Jr. for His Descendants*. Baywood Park, CA: Author, 1995. 508p.

Carroll, Thelma Ellen Young. *A Source Book for Five Generations of Family History*. Virginia Beach, VA: Merrit Press, 1995. Unpgd.

Fetters, William B. *Baltzer Young (1760–1845) and Mary Elizabeth Buss, Ancestors and Descendants*. Bowie, MD: Author, 1995. 247p.

Grossman, Annetta. *History of Donal George Young and Barbara Maxine Ferris and Allied Families*. Wabash, IN: Author, 1995. 74p.

Neal, Clarice G. *David Young and Sarah Phillips Descendants, Wilson County, Tennessee, 1796- 1994*. Austin, TX: Author, 1995. 356p.

Skelton, Isaac Newton. *Ike, This Is You, a History of the Skelton, Boone, Barry, Beach, Blattner, Corum, Hoagland, Lehew, Strode, Wright and Young Families*. Washington, DC: Author, 1995. 223p.

Young, Cindy Henson. *The Youngs and Holloways of Randolph County, Alabama, a Family History*. Newville, AL; Author, 1995. 309p.

Younglove

Younglove, James N. *The Descendants of Samuel and Margaret Younglove*. Houston, TX: Author, 1995. 200p.

Youngs

Moore, Freddie Gene. *The Descendants of Thomas Moore, Sr. of Suffolk County, England and the Related Families, Youngs, Landon, Spencer, French, Norris, Simmons, Ratliff, Slaughter*. Author, 1995. Unpgd.

Yulga

Grillot, R. E. *Grillot and Ancestors*. Author, 1995. 831p.

Yuncker

Yuncker, David Bernard. *The Yuncker Family of Baerendorf, Their History, Culture and Impact.* Author, 1995. 116p.

–Z

Zafran

Margolis, Abby Mindelle. *The Zafran Genealogy, Including the Morozowitz, Melnick, and Kairoch Families.* Daly City, CA: 1995. 75p.

Zaring

Zaring, Wilson M. *The Descendants of Ludwig Zehrung, Mathias Zehrung, Anna Elizabeth Zehrung and Philip Zehring.* Champaign, IL: Author, 1995. 848p.

Zastrow

Erdmann Morrison, Kathleen. *Erdmann, Zastrow, Morrison.* Beaverton, OR: Author, 1995. Unpgd.

Zehr

Yoder, Rebecca Bontrager. *Memories and Family Record of the John D. Miller and Rosina Zehr Family, 1916–1995.* Goshen, IN: Author, 1995. 58p.

Zerbe

Klotz, George David. *Klotz-Zerbe Family History and Genealogy, 1530–1995, Indiana Branches.* Cicero, IN: Author, 1995. Unpgd.

Zoch

Boriack, David. *Boriack Family Tree, 1995.* Lincoln, TX: Author, 1995. 303p.

Zosa

Soza, Edward. *New World Odyssey, a Search for Roots, the Sosa, Soza Families of Arizona.* Altadena, CA: Author, 1995. 41p.

Zumwalt

Carrier, Helynn Marie. *One Zumwalt Family, Zumalt, Zeumalt, Zum Wald, Zumwault, Sommalt, Its Many, Varied, and Interwoven Branches, a Study Paper.* San Jose, CA: Author, 1995. 389p.

Zwick

Henscheid, Eckhard. *Die Zwicks, Fronvogte, Zwingherrn und Vasallen: Die Geschichte Einer Bedeutenden Familie.* Zurich: Haffmans Verlag, 1995. 213p.

GUIDES AND HANDBOOKS

United States

General and How-to Books

Allen, Desmond Walls. *Social Security Applications, a Genealogical Resource*. Conway, AR: Research Associates, 1995. 18p.

Bentley, Elizabeth Petty. *County Courthouse Book*. 2nd ed. Baltimore, MD: Genealogical Publishing Co., 1995. 405p.

―――. *Genealogist's Address Book*. 3rd ed. Baltimore, MD: Genealogical Publishing Co., 1995. 653p.

Bilgrad, Robert. *National Death Index User's Manual*. Rev. ed. Hyattsville, MD: U.S. Department of Health and Human Services, Public Health Service, 1995. Unpgd.

Bonsey, Lynn. *Memories and Memorabilia: More Than 600 Easy Ways to Preserve Them*. Bowie, MD: Heritage Books, 1995. 203p.

Boyer, Carl, 3rd. *Index to Genealogical Periodicals by Donald Lines Jacobus*. Rev. ed. Santa Clarita, CA: Author, 1995. 373p.

Boy Scouts of America. *Genealogy (Merit Badge Book)*. Irving, TX: Author, 1995. 72p.

Brigham Young University's Annual Genealogy and Family History Conference. Provo, UT: Brigham Young University, 1995. 918p.

Cemetery Recording Instruction Booklet. 3rd. ed. Richmond, British Columbia: British Columbia Genealogical Society, 1995. Unpgd.

City Directories III, Guide to the Microfilm Collection. (1882–1901, City Directories of the United States). Woodbridge, CT: Research Publications, 1995. 29p.

Clunies, Sandra MacLean. *Creating Genealogy Booklets on a Laser or Inkjet Printer*. Boston, MA: New England Historic Genealogical Society, 1995. 49p.

Croom, Emily Anne. *Unpuzzling Your Past: A Basic Guide to Genealogy*. 3rd. ed. Cincinnati, OH: Betterway Books, 1995. 180p.

Dieterle, Diane. *Successful Genealogy*. Bountiful, UT: AGLL, 1995. 84p.

Dollarhide, William. *Managing a Genealogical Project*. Rev. ed. Baltimore, MD: Gateway Press, 1995. 71p.

Evans, Barbara Jean. *A to Zax. A Comprehensive Dictionary for Genealogists and Historians*. Alexandria, VA: Hearthside Press, 1995. 300p.

Frontier Genealogy: Special Sources and Techniques for Tracing Your Pioneer Ancestors. Topeka, KS; Topeka Genealogical Society, 1995. 76p.

Heisey, John W. *Genealogy Helps, Hints, and Hope.* Morgantown, PA: Masthof Press, 1995. 147p.

Homberger, Eric. *The Penguin Historical Atlas of North America.* NY: Penguin, 1995. 144p.

Increasing the Utility of the Criminal History Record: Report of the National Task Force. Washington, DC: National Task Force on Increasing the Utility of the Criminal History Record, U.S. Department of Justice, 1995.

Jacobson, Judy. *A Genealogist's Refresher Course.* Baltimore, MD: Clearfield, 1995. 84p.

Jerger, Jeanette L. *A Medical Miscellany for Genealogists.* Bowie, MD: Heritage Books, 1995. 178p.

Kirkpatrick, Kathy. *Basic Genealogy, Including Steps Sometimes Forgotten by the Pros.* Bountiful, UT: Eriksson Enterprises, 1995. 125p.

Krause, Carol. *How Healthy Is Your Family Tree, a Complete Guide to Tracing Your Family's Medical and Behavioral Tree.* New York, NY: Simon & Schuster, 1995. 167p.

MacSorley, M.E. *Genealogical Sources in the United States of America.* Basingstoke, England: Author, 1995. 112p.

Miller, Ilene Chandler. *Preserving Family Keepsakes, Do's and Don'ts.* Yorba Linda, CA: Shumway Family History Services, 1995. 170p.

Pengra, Nancy. *Family Histories: An Easy, Step-by-step Guide to Capturing Your Family's Precious Memories Now, before They're Lost.* St. Paul, MN: Family Histories, 1995. 144p.

Polking, Kirk. *Writing Family Histories and Memoirs.* Cincinnati, OH: Betterway Books, 1995. 250p.

Richards, Tom. *Was Your Grandfather a Railwayman?: A Directory of Records Relating to Staff Employed by Railways in the Following Countries with Details on Material and Repositories: United Kingdom, Australia, Canada, Eire, India, New Zealand, South Africa, United States of America.* 3rd. ed. Birmingham, England: Author, 1995. 101p.

Ritchie, Donald A. *Doing Oral History.* NY: Twayne, 1995. 272p.

Roberts, Gary Boyd. *Ancestors of American Presidents.* Santa Clara, CA: Carl Boyer, 1995. 456p.

The Sourcebook of County Court Records: A National Guide to Civil, Criminal and Probate Records at the County and Municipal Levels within the State Court System. 2nd ed. Tempe, AZ: BRP Publications, 1995. 539p.

Vannoy, Rosamond H. *Your Ancestral Trail, Genealogy for Beginners.* Conover, WI: Author, 1995, 27p.

Wright, Raymond S. *The Genealogist's Handbook: Modern Methods for Researching Family History.* Chicago, IL: American Library Association, 1995. 191p.

African Americans

Braxton Secret, Jeanette. *Guide to Tracing Your African American Civil War Ancestor.* San Pablo, CA: Author, 1995. Unpgd.

Byers, Paula Kay. *African American Genealogical Sourcebook.* Detroit, MI: Gale Research, 1995. 244p.

Cook, Chris. *The Making of Modern Africa: A Guide to Archives.* NY: Facts on File, 1995. 224p.

Curtis, Nancy C. *Black Heritage Sites, an African-American Odyssey and Finder's Guide.* Chicago, IL: American Library Association, 1995. 575p.

DuPree, Sherry Sherrod. *The African American Holiness Pentecostal Movement*. Hamden, CT: Garland, 1995. 365p.

Fears, Mary L. Jackson. *Slave Ancestral Research: It's Something Else*. Bowie, MD: Heritage Books, 1995. 269p.

Hardaway, Roger D. *A Narrative Bibliography of the African American Frontier, Blacks in the Rocky Mountain West, 1535–1912*. Lewiston, NY: Edwin Mellen Press, 1995. 242p.

Henritz, Barbara K. *Bibliographic Checklist of African American Newspapers*. Baltimore, MD: Genealogical Pub. Co., 1995. 206p.

Hodges, Graham, Susan Hawkes Cook and Alan Edward Brown. *Black Loyalist Directory, African Americans in Exile after the American Revolution*. Hamden, CT: Garland, 1995. 384p.

Hoobler, Dorothy and Thomas Hoobler. *African American Family Album*. New York, NY: Oxford University Press, 1995. 128p.

Lawson, Jacqueline A. *An Index of African Americans Identified in Selected Records of the Bureau of Refugees, Freedmen, and Abandoned Lands*. Bowie, MD: Heritage Books, 1995. 99p.

Manat, G. P. *Guide to Books on Black Americans*. Commack, NY: Nova Science Publishers, 1995. 319p.

Olden, Anthony. *Libraries in Africa*. Lanham, MD: Scarecrow Press, 1995. 170p.

Proceedings of the Pan African Conference on the Preservation and Conservation of Library and Archival Materials, Nairobi, Kenya, 21-25 June 1993. The Hague, Netherlands: IFLA, 1995. 220p.

Schubert, Frank N. *On the Trail of the Buffalo Soldier: Biographies of African Amerians in the United States Army, 1866–1917*. Wilmington, DE: Scholarly Resources, 1995. 520p.

Smith, Gloria L. *Beginning Black Indian History and Genealogy, the Cherokees*. Tucson, AZ: Author, 1995. 53p.

Special Collections Department, Emory University Library. *Manuscript Sources for African-American History: A Descriptive List of Holdings in the Special Collections Department*. Rev. ed. Atlanta, GA: The Library, 1995. 51p.

Woods, Isabelle M. *African American Funeral Programs, the Fort-Holman Collection*. Bossier City, LA: Author, 1995. 2 vols.

Asian Americans

Byers, Paula K. *Asian American Genealogical Sourcebook*. Detroit, MI: Gale Research, 1995. 280p.

Coming Man: 19th Century American Perceptions of the Chinese. Seattle, WA: University of Washington Press, 1995. 178p.

Nishimura, Arthur Jiro. *Japanese Emigration in the Pre-World War II Era (1868–1937), A Reconceptualization of the History*. Thesis (M.A.), University of Washington, 1995. 64p.

Pacific Islander Americans, an Annotated Bibliography in the Social Sciences. Laie, HI: Institute for Polynesian Studies, Brigham Young University-Hawaii, 1995. 91p.

Reference Library of Asian America. Detroit, MI: Gale Research, 1995. 3 vols.

Salyer, Lucy E. *Laws Harsh as Tigers, Chinese Immigrants and the Shaping of Modern Immigration Law*. Chapel Hill, NC: University of North Carolina Press, 1995. 338p.

Baptists

Leondard, Bill J. *Dictionary of Baptists in America*. Downers Grove, IL: InterVarsity Press, 1995. 144p.

Bibliography

Bataille, Gretchen M., Miguel Carranza and Laurie Lisa. *Ethnic Studies in the United States, a Guide to Research.* Hamden, CT: Garland, 1995. 183p.

Blazek, Ron and Anna H. Perrault. *United States History, a Selective Guide to Information Sources.* Englewood, CO: Libraries Unlimited, 1995. 411p.

Clegg, Michael B. and Curt B. Witcher. *Periodical Source Index, 1994. Annual Volume.* Ft. Wayne, IN: Allen County Public Library Foundation, 1995. 1,111p.

Gerhan, David R. *Bibliography of American Demographic History: The Literature from 1984-1994.* Westport, CT: Greenwood, 1995. 339p.

Guide to Microforms in Print, 1995, Author-Title. New Providence, NJ: Bowker, 1995. 1,700p.

Guide to Microforms in Print, 1995, Supplement. New Providence, NJ: Bowker, 1995. 150p.

Lipfert, Nathan R. *Guide to Log-books and Sea Journals, 1764–1938, in the Collections of Maine Maritime Museum.* Bath, ME: Maine Maritime Museum Library, 1995. 134p.

Norton, Mary Beth. *American Historical Association's Guide to Historical Literature.* 3rd. ed. NY: Oxford University Press, 1995. 2 vols.

Periodical Shelf List. Portland, OR: Genealogical Forum of Oregon, 1995. 91p.

Subject Guide to Microforms in Print, 1995. New Providence, NJ: Bowker, 1995. 1,450p.

Wood, Virginia Steele. *Handbooks for Foreign Genealogical Research, a Guide to Published Sources in English.* Washington, DC: Library of Congress, 1995. 23p.

Biography

Biographical Dictionary of American Newspaper Columnists. Westport, CT: Greenwood Press, 1995. 411p.

Biographical Dictionary of American Sports. Westport, CT: Greenwood Press, 1995. 811p.

Biography and Genealogy Master Index: 1991–1995 Cumulation. Detroit, MI: Gale Research, 1995. 3 vols.

Blackwell Dictionary of Evangelical Biography, 1730–1860. Oxford, England: Blackwell, 1995. 2 vols.

Dewey, Donald. *Biographical History of Baseball.* NY: Carroll & Graf, 1995. 533p.

Falk, Byron A. *Personal Name Index to The New York Times Index, 1975–1993, Supplement.* Verdi, NV: Roxbury Data Interface, 1995. Unpgd.

Index to Marquis Who's Who Publications, 1995. Chicago, IL: Marquis Who's Who, 1995. 535p.

Miller, Randall M. *Book of American Diaries.* NY: Avon Books, 1995. 522p.

National Law Enforcement Officers Memorial Fund. *Roll Call of Fallen (Police) Officers.* Author, 1995. 223p.

Neubauer, Joan. *Dear Diary, the Art and Craft of Writing a Creative Journal.* Salt Lake City, UT: Ancestry, 1995. 45p.

Variety Obituaries, Volume 15, 1993–1994. Hamden, CT: Garland, 1995. 350p.

Vazzana, Eugene Michael. *Silent Film Necrology: Births and Deaths of over 9,000 Performers, Directors, Producers, and Other Filmmakers of the Silent Era, through 1993.* Jefferson, NC: McFarland, 1995. 367p.

Winslow, Donald J. *Life-Writing, a Glossary of Terms in Biography, Autobiography and Related Forms.* Honolulu, HI: University of Hawaii Press, 1995. 88p.

Cemeteries

Strangstad, Lynette. *A Graveyard Preservation Primer.* Walnut Creek, CA: AltaMira Press, 1995. 126p.

Census

A Key to the United States 1880 Federal Census: Identifying Enumeration District Numbers and Microfilm Numbers of the National Archives and the Family History Library. 3rd. ed. Bountiful, UT: AGLL Publishing, 1995. 86p.

Computers

Clifford, Karen. *Genealogy and Computers for the Advanced Researcher, Putting It All Together.* Baltimore, MD: Clearfield, 1995. 347p.

Clunies, Sandra MacLean. *Computer Creativity for Family Reunions.* Boston, MA: New England Historic Genealogical Society, 1995. 62p.

Crowe, Elizabeth Powell. *Genealogy Online, Researching Your Roots.* New York, NY: McGraw-Hill, 1995. 280p.

Eastman, Richard. *Your Roots, Total Genealogy Planning on Your Computer.* Emeryville, CA: Ziff-Davis Press, 1995. 229p.

Huguenots

Finnell, Arthur Louis. *Register of Qualified Huguenot Ancestors of the National Huguenot Society.* 4th ed. Bloomington, MN: National Huguenot Society, 1995. 337p.

Smiles, Samuel. *The Huguenots, Their Settlement, Churches, and Industries in England and Ireland.* Baltimore, MD: Clearfield, 1868, 1995. 448p.

Jewish

Death Books from Auschwitz. Munich, Germany: K. G. Saur, 1995. 3 vols.

Hoobler, Dorothy and Thomas Hoobler. *Jewish American Family Album.* New York, NY: Oxford University Press, 1995. 128p.

Jacobson, Matthew Frye. *Special Sorrows: The Diasporic Immigration of Irish, Polish and Jewish Immigrants in the United States.* Cambridge, MA: Harvard University Press, 1995. 321p.

Kahn, Bruce E. *Jewish Genealogy on the Information Super Highway.* Version 6. Rochester, NY: Author, 1995. 78p.

Lilenthral, Edward T. *Preserving Memory: The Struggle to Create America's Holocaust Museum.* NY: Viking, 1995. 336p.

Mokotoff, Gary. *How to Document Victims and Locate Survivors of the Holocaust.* Teaneck, NJ: Avotaynu, 1995. 194p.

————. *WOWW Companion, a Guide to the Communities Surrounding Central and Eastern European Towns.* Teaneck, NJ: Avotaynu, 1995. 208p.

Rottenberg, Dan. *Finding Our Fathers, a Guidebook to Jewish Genealogy.* Baltimore, MD: Genealogical Publishing Co., 1995. 401p.

Sack, Sallyann Amdur. *A Guide to Jewish Genealogical Research in Israel.* Rev. ed. Teaneck, NJ: Avotaynu, 1995. 229p.

Land Records

Carter, Fran. *Searching American Land and Deed Records.* Bountiful, UT: American Genealogical Lending Library, 1995. 54p.

Libraries and Archives

Allen, James B. *Hearts Turned to the Fathers: A History of the Genealogical Society of Utah, 1894–1994.* Provo, UT: Brigham Young University Studies, 1995. 392p.

American Library Directory, 1995-96. 48th. ed. NY: R.R. Bowker, 1995. 2 vols.

Barclay, John. *The Seventy-Year Ebb and Flow of Chinese Library and Information Services.* Lanham, MD: Scarecrow Press, 1995. 351p.

Bartowski, Gloria A. *Fundamentals of Managing Local Government Archival Records.* Albany, NY: State Archives and Records Administration, Local Government Records Services, 1995. 21p.

Briggs, Martha T. *Guide to the Pullman Company Archives.* Chicago, IL: Newberry Library, 1995. 794p.

A Directory of History of Medicine Collections. 5th. ed. Bethesda, MD: National Library of Medicine, 1995. 91p.

Frick, Elizabeth. *History, Illustrated Search Strategy and Sources.* 2nd. ed. Ann Arbor, MI: Pierian Press, 1995. 197p.

Genealogical and Historical Societies in the United States. 1995–1996 ed. Indianapolis, IN: Ye Olde Genealogie Shoppe, 1995. 64p.

Guide to Federal Records in the National Archives of the United States. Rev. 1995. Washington, DC: National Archives and Records Administration, 1995. Unpgd.

A Guide to History Libraries and Collections. 10th. ed. London: University of London Library, 1995. 39p.

Guide to Records in the National Archives, Pacific Sierra Region. Washington, DC: National Archives and Records Administration, Pacific Sierra Region, 1995. 85p.

Guide to Records in the National Archives, Pacific Southwest Region. Washington, DC: National Archives and Records Administration, Pacific Southwest Region, 1995. 48p.

A Guide to the Major Collections in the Department of Special Collections. 3rd. ed. Glasgow, Scotland: University of Glasgow Library, 1995. 36p.

Harris, Michael H. *History of Libraries of the Western World.* Lanham, MD: Scarecrow Press, 1995. 309p.

Historical Consciousness in the Early Republic: The Origins of State Historical Societies, Museums and Collections, 1791–1861. Chapel Hill, NC: North Caroliniana Society, 1995. 262p.

Information about Electronic Records in the National Archives for Prospective Researchers. Rev. ed. College Park, MD: Center For Electronic Records, National Archives at College Park, 1995. 12p.

Lilenthral, Edward T. *Preserving Memory: The Struggle to Create America's Holocaust Museum.* NY: Viking, 1995. 336p.

McPhail, David R. *A Strategy for United States Genealogical Research Using the Family History Library in Salt Lake City.* Bountiful, UT: Thomsen's Genealogical Center, 1995. Unpgd.

Minchew, Kay Lanning. *Archival Programs for Local Governments.* Albany, NY: National Association of Government Archives and Records Administrators, 1995. 19p.

Morris, Carla D. and Steven R. Morris. *How to Index Your Local Newspaper Using WordPerfect or Microsoft Word for Windows.* Englewood, CO: Libraries Unlimited, 1995. 167p.

Newberry Library. *Sources Indexed in the Genealogical Index of the Newberry Library.* Chicago: Newberry Library, 1995. 2 vols.

New England Historic Genealogical Society. *150 Years Exploring Our Heritage, Sesquicentennial Commemorative, the New England Historic Genealogical Society, 1845–1995.* Boston, MA: Author, 1995. 187p.

Olden, Anthony. *Libraries in Africa.* Lanham, MD: Scarecrow Press, 1995. 170p.

Paul, Karen Dawley. *Guide to Research Collections of Former United States Senators, 1789-1995: A Listing of Archival Repositories Housing the Papers of Former Senators, Related Collections and Oral History Interviews.* Washington, DC: GPO, 1995. 743p.

Phillips, Faye. *Local History Collections in Libraries.* Englewood, CO: Libraries Unlimited, 1995. 164p.

Schutz, John A. *A Noble Pursuit, the Sesquicentennial History of the New England Historic Genealogical Society, 1845–1995.* Boston, MA: New England Historic Genealogical Society, 1995. 281p.

Swartzburg, Susan G. *Preserving Library Materials.* Scarecrow, 1995. 514p.

World Guide to Libraries. 12th. ed. Munich, Germany: K. G. Saur, 1995. 2 vols.

Mennonites

Davis, Richard Warren. *Emigrants, Refugees and Prisoners, an Aid to Mennonite Family Research.* Provo, UT: Author, 1995. Unpgd.

Methodists

Dickerson, Dennis C. *Religion, Race and Region, Research Notes on A.M.E. Church History.* Nashville, TN: AMEC Sunday School Union, 1995. 144p.

Turner, Kristen D. *A Guide to Materials on Women in the United Methodist Church Archives.* Madison, NJ: U.S. Methodist Church. Commission on Archives and History, 1995. 180p.

U.S. Methodist Church. Commission on Archives and History. *Mission Agency Histories, History of the Missionary Agencies in the United Methodist Tradition, 1819–Present.* Madison, NJ: Author, 1995. 43p.

————. *Missionary Files: Volume 1, Part 1, Methodist Episcopal Church Missionary Correspondence, 1846–1912.* Madison, NJ: Author, 1995. 53p.

Migration

Anderson, Robert Charles. *The Great Migration Begins, Immigrants to New England, 1620–1633.* Boston, MA: New England Historic Genealogical Society, 1995. 3 vols.

Dawsey, Cyrus B. And James M. Dawsey. *The Confederados: Old South Immigrants in Brazil.* Tuscaloosa, AL: University of Alabama Press, 1995. 273p.

Guide to the Microfilm Edition of Records of the Immigration and Naturalization Service. Bethesda, MD: University Publications of America, 1995. 27p.

Jacobson, Matthew Frye. *Special Sorrows: The Diasporic Immigration of Irish, Polish and Jewish Immigrants in the United States.* Cambridge, MA: Harvard University Press, 1995. 321p.

Nugent, Walter T. K. *Crossings: The Great Transatlantic Migrations, 1870–1914.* Bloomington, IN: Indiana University Press, 1995. 234p.

Sato, Tsunezo. *Hawai Imin Sato Tsunezo Shokan, Kindai Nihonjin Kaigai Imin Shiryo.* Tokyo: Keio Tsushin, 1995. 313p.

The Settling of North America: The Atlas of the Great Migrations into North America from the Ice Age to Present. NY: Macmillan, 1995. 208p.

Weatherford, Doris. *Foreign and Female: Immigrant Women in America, 1840–1930.* NY: Facts on File, 1995. 416p.

Younis, Adele L. *The Coming of the Arabic People to the United States.* Staten Island, NY: Center for Migration Studies, 1995. 350p.

Military

Barbuto, Domenica M. and Martha Kreisel. *Guide to Civil War Books, an Annotated Selection of Modern Works on the War between the States.* Chicago, IL: American Library Association, 1995. 221p.

Blewett, Daniel K. *American Military History: A Guide to Reference and Information Science.* Englewood, CO: Libraries Unlimited, 1996. 295p.

Gillett, Mary C. *The Army Medical Department, 1865–1917*. Washington, DC: Center of Military History, U.S. Army, 1995. 517p.

Groene, Bertram Hawthorne. *Tracing Your Civil War Ancestor*. 4th ed. Winston-Salem, NC: John F. Blair, 1995. 130p.

Grossnick, Roy A. *Dictionary of American Naval Aviation Squadrons*. Washington, DC: Naval Historical Center, 1995. Unpgd.

Guide to Civil War Collections. Columbia, MO: Western Historical Manuscript Collection, 1995. 86p.

Guide to Records Relating to United States Military Participation in World War II. Washington, DC: National Archives and Records Administration, 1995. Unpgd.

Hodges, Graham, Susan Hawkes Cook and Alan Edward Brown. *Black Loyalist Directory, African Americans in Exile after the American Revolution*. Hamden, CT: Garland, 1995. 384p.

Hughes, Mark. *Bivouac of the Dead*. Bowie, MD: Heritage Books, 1995. 330p.

Lang, George, Raymond L. Collins and Gerard White. *Medal of Honor Recipients, 1863–1994*. NY: Facts on File, 1995. 2 vols.

Larson, Carl V. *The Women of the Mormon Battalion*. Logan, UT: Author, 1995. 130p.

McCawley, Patrick. *Records of the Confederate Historian*. Columbia, SC: South Carolina Archives, 1995. 14p.

Reamy, Martha. *Index to the Role of Honor*. Baltimore, MD: Genealogical Pub. Co., 1995. 1,164p.

Records Management in the U.S. Army Corps of Engineers. Washington, DC: National Archives and Records Administration, 1995. 87p.

Schweitzer, George Keene. *War of 1812 Genealogy*. Knoxville, TN: Author, 1995. 78p.

Seagrave, Ronald R. *Civil War Books, Confederate and Union*. Fredericksburg, VA: Sergeant Kirkland's Museum and Historical Society, 1995. 748p.

Searching for Your Civil War Ancestors at the Buffalo and Erie County Public Library. Buffalo, NY: Special Collections Department, Buffalo and Erie County Public Library, 1995. 11p.

The Sergeants Major of the Army. Washington, DC: Center of Military History, U.S. Army, 1995. 180p.

Shrader, Charles Reginald. *Reference Guide to United States Military History: 1945 to the Present*. NY: Facts on File, 1995. 336p.

White, Virgil D. *Index to Revolutionary War Service Records*. Waynesboro, TN: National Historical Publishing Co., 1995. 4 vols.

Mormons

Allen, James B. *Hearts Turned to the Fathers: A History of the Genealogical Society of Utah, 1894–1994*. Provo, UT: Brigham Young University Studies, 1995. 392p.

Larson, Carl V. *The Women of the Mormon Battalion*. Logan, UT: Author, 1995. 130p.

Mormon Americana: A Guide to Sources and Collections in the United States. Provo, UT: Brigham Young University Studies, 1995. 695p.

Stewards of the Promise, the Heritage of the Latter-day Saints on the Hawaiian Islands of Maui, Molokai, and Lanai. Kahului, HI: Kahului Hawaii Stake, 1995. 112p.

Native Americans

Armstrong, K. B. and Bob Curry. *Chickasaw Rolls: Annuity Rolls of 1857–1860 and the 1855 Chickasaw District Roll of 1856*. Bowie, MD: Heritage Books, 1995. 258p.

Byers, Paula Kay. *Native American Genealogical Sourcebook.* Detroit, MI: Gale Research, 1995. 219p.

Capes Altom, Mila. *Journey into the Past.* 3rd. ed. Iowa Park, TX: White Wolf Reports, 1995. 46p.

Douthat, James L. *1832 Creek Census, Parsons-Abbott.* Signal Mountain, TN: Institute of Historic Research, 1995. 95p.

Eason, Alice Grant. *The Finding Aid and Subject Index for the Sac and Fox Oral History Project.* Stroud, OK: Sac and Fox National Public Library, 1995. 43p.

Gormley, Myra Vanderpool. *Cherokee Connections: An Introduction to Genealogical Sources Pertaining to Cherokee Ancestors.* Tacoma, WA: Family Historian Books, 1995. 56p.

Haithcock, Richard L. *Occaneechi, Saponi and Tutelo of the Saponi Nation, the Piedmont Catawaba.* Author, 1995. Unpgd.

Johnson, Steven F. *Ninnouock, the Algonkian People of New England.* Marlborough, MA: Bliss Pub. Co., 1995. 282p.

Library of Congress. Prints and Graphics Division. *Indians of North America, a Guide to LOTS (Collections) .* Washington, DC: Author, 1995. Unpgd.

McMillan, Nancy. *Illusive Indians, a Basic Guide to Indian Ancestors.* Gulf Breeze, FL: Author, 1995. 60p.

Miller, Jay, et. al. *Writings in Indian History, 1985–1990.* Norman, OK: University of Oklahoma Press, 1995. 216p.

Smith, Gloria L. *Beginning Black Indian History and Genealogy, the Cherokees.* Tucson, AZ: Author, 1995. 53p.

Statistical Record of Native North Americans. 2nd. ed. Detroit, MI: Gale, 1995. 1,272p.

Watson, Ian M. *Catawba Indian Genealogy.* Geneseo, NY: Geneseo Foundation, State University of New York at Geneseo, 1995. 113p.

White, Phillip M. *American Indian Studies, a Bibliographic Guide.* Englewood, CO: Libraries Unlimited, 1995. 163p.

New England

Anderson, Robert Charles. *The Great Migration Begins, Immigrants to New England, 1620–1633.* Boston, MA: New England Historic Genealogical Society, 1995. 3 vols.

Angelo, Ray. *County Location of New England Place Names.* Cambridge, MA: New England Botanical Club, 1995. 77p.

Bibliographies of New England History. Hanover, NH: University Press of New England, 1995. 299p.

Emery, Eric B. *New England Captives in Canada and the Ransom Missions of Phineas Stevens, 1749, 1751 and 1752.* Thesis (M.A.), University of Vermont, 1995. 115p.

Erling, Maria Elizabeth. *Crafting an Urban Piety, New England's Swedish Immigrants and Their Religious Culture from 1880 to 1915.* Dissertation (T.D.), Harvard University, 1995, 274p.

Holmes, Madelyn. *Lives of Women Public Schoolteachers, Scenes from American Educational History.* NY: Garland, 1995. 249p.

New England Archivists Handbook and Directory, 1995–96. Lexington, MA: New England Archivists, 1995. 46p.

New England Historic Genealogical Society. *150 Years Exploring Our Heritage, Sesquicentennial Commemorative, the New England Historic Genealogical Society, 1845–1995.* Boston, MA: Author, 1995. 187p.

New England Historical and Genealogical Register, Index of Persons, Volumes 51–148. Boston, MA: New England Historic Genealogical Society, 1995. 4 vols.

Nipmuc Place Names of New England. Thompson, CT: Nipmuc Indian Association of Connecticut, 1995. 41p.

Roser, Susan E. *Mayflower Increasings.* 2nd. ed. Baltimore, MD: Genealogical Publishing, 1995. 179p.

Sanborn, Melinde Lutz. *Second Supplement to Torrey's New England Marriages prior to 1700.* Baltimore, MD: Genealogical Pub. Co., 1995. 106p.

Schutz, John A. *A Noble Pursuit, the Sesquicentennial History of the New England Historic Genealogical Society, 1845–1995.* Boston, MA: New England Historic Genealogical Society, 1995. 281p.

Search for the Passengers of the Mary & John, 1630. Toledo, OH: Burton W. Spear, 1995. 83p.

Newspapers

Carter Walker, Fran. *Searching for American Newspapers for Genealogical Research.* Bradenton, FL: Author, 1995. 76p.

Pentecostals

Jones, Charles Edwin. *Charismatic Movement: A Guide to the Study of Neo-Pentecostalism, with an Emphasis on Anglo-American Sources.* Metuchen, NJ: Scarecrow Press, 1995. 1,220p.

Presbyterians

Gleeson, Kristin. *A Guide to Women's Archival Resources in the Presbyterian Historical Society.* Philadelphia, PA: Presbyterian Historical Society, 1995. 183p.

Roman Catholics

The Archives of the Congregation of the Immaculate Heart of Mary, 1862–1967. Rome: Institut Historique Belge de Rome, 1995. 2 vols.

Humling, Virginia. *U.S. Catholic Sources, a Diocesan Research Guide.* Salt Lake City, UT: Ancestry, 1995. 105p.

Thiel, Mark G. *Index to the Catholic Directories for the United States with Appended Countries, 1817, 1822, 1833–.* Milwaukee, WI: Marquette University, 1995. 54p.

Societies

Association of Professional Genealogists. *1995–96 APG Directory of Professional Genealogists.* Washington, DC: Author, 1995. 145p.

Davenport, Robert R. *Hereditary Society Blue Book.* Beverly Hills, CA: Eastwood Publishing, 1995. 319p.

Spanish Americans

Archivo General de Indias. Madrid, Spain: Ministerio de Cultura, Dirección General del Libro, Archivos, y Bibliotecas, 1995. 328p.

Encisco, Carmen Edna. *Hispanic Americans in Congress, 1822–1995.* Washington, DC: GPO, 1995. 136p.

Herrera Saucedo, George Edward. *An Introduction to Hispanic Genealogical Research, a Manual.* Los Angeles, CA: Author, 1995. 68p.

Hispanic American Genealogical Sourcebook. Detroit, MI: Gale Research, 1995. 224p.

Hoobler, Dorothy and Thomas Hoobler. *Cuban American Family Album*. Oxford, England: Oxford University Press, 1995. 128p.

Indice Biografico de España, Portugal e Iberoamérica. 2nd ed. Munich, Germany: K. G. Saur, 1995. 7 vols.

Sanchez Alonso, Blanco. *Las Causas de la Emigración Española, 1880–1930*. Madrid, Spain: Alianza Editorial, 1995. 325p.

Wold, Lillian Ramos Navarro. *Family Origins*. Fullerton, CA: SHHAR Press, 1995. 92p.

Surnames

Anderson, William C. *The Scottish Nation, or the Surnames, Family Literature, Honours and Biographical History of the People of Scotland. Volume C*. Bowie, MD: Heritage Books, 1901, 1995. 235p.

———. *The Scottish Nation, or the Surnames, Family Literature, Honours and Biographical History of the People of Scotland. Volume D-F*. Bowie, MD: Heritage Books, 1901, 1995. 274p.

Dunkling, Leslie. *Guinness Book of Names*. 7th. ed. NY: Facts on File, 1995. 256p.

Jones, George F. *German American Names*. 2nd ed. Baltimore, MD: Genealogical Publishing Co., 1995. 320p.

Lawson, Edwin D. *More Names and Naming, an Annotated Bibliography*. Westport, CT: Greenwood Press, 1995. 298p.

Matheson, Robert E. *Official Varieties of Synonyms of Surnames and Christian Names in Ireland for the Guidance of Registration Officers and the Public Searching the Indexes of Births, Deaths and Marriages*. Bowie, MD: Heritage Books, 1901, 1995. 94p.

Ptak, Diane Snyder. *Surnames: Determining Origins with Biographical and Ethnic References*. Albany, NY: Author, 1995. 28p.

Reaney, P. H. *A Dictionary of English Surnames*. 3rd ed. Oxford, England: Oxford University Press, 1995. 509p.

Rogers, Colin D. *The Surname Detective, Investigating Surname Distribution in England, 1086-Present Day*. Manchester, England: Manchester University Press, 1995. 260p.

Rose, Christine. *Nicknames Past and Present*. 2nd ed. San Jose, CA: Rose Family Association, 1995. 41p.

Wold, Lillian Ramos Navarro. *Family Origins*. Fullerton, CA: SHHAR Press, 1995. 92p.

Women

Cullen DuPont, Kathryn. *Encyclopedia of Women's History in America*. NY: Facts on File, 1995. 336p.

Gleeson, Kristin. *A Guide to Women's Archival Resources in the Presbyterian Historical Society*. Philadelphia, PA: Presbyterian Historical Society, 1995. 183p.

Holmes, Madelyn. *Lives of Women Public Schoolteachers, Scenes from American Educational History*. NY: Garland, 1995. 249p.

King, Jennifer. *Guide to Women's History Resources at the American Heritage Center*. 2nd. ed. Laramie, WY: American Heritage Center, University of Wyoming, 1995. 61p.

Larson, Carl V. *The Women of the Mormon Battalion*. Logan, UT: Author, 1995. 130p.

North American Women Artists of the Twentieth Century: A Biographical Dictionary. NY: Garland, 1995. 612p.

Turner, Kristen D. *A Guide to Materials on Women in the United Methodist Church Archives*. Madison, NJ: U.S. Methodist Church. Commission on Archives and History, 1995. 180p.

Weatherford, Doris. *Foreign and Female: Immigrant Women in America, 1840–1930*. NY: Facts on File, 1995. 416p.

International

Archival Legislation, 1981–1994: Albania-Kenya. Munich, Germany: K. G. Saur, 1995. 324p.

Biger, Gideon. *Encyclopedia of International Boundaries.* NY: Facts on File, 1995. 496p.

MacKenzie, George P. *Further Analysis of the International Survey of Archival Development.* Tunis, Tunisia: International Council on Archives, 1995. 19p.

The National Register of Archives, an International Perspective, Essays in Celebration of the Fiftieth Anniversary of the NRA. London: Institute of Historical Research, University of London, 1995. 103p.

Roper, Michael. *The Present State of Archival Development World-Wide.* Tunis, Tunisia: International Council on Archives, 1995. 36p.

Wood, Virginia Steele. *Handbooks for Foreign Genealogical Research, a Guide to Published Sources in English.* Washington, DC: Library of Congress, 1995. 23p.

Asia

Byers, Paula Kay. *Asian American Genealogical Sourcebook.* Detroit, MI: Gale Research, 1995. 280p.

Pacific Islander Americans, an Annotated Bibliography in the Social Sciences. Laie, HI: Institute for Polynesian Studies, Brigham Young University-Hawaii, 1995. 91p.

Australia

National Library of Australia. *Our Multicultural Heritage, 1788–1945, an Annotated Guide to the Collections of the National Library of Australia.* Canberra, Australia: Author, 1995. 192p.

The National Register of Archives, an International Perspective, Essays in Celebration of the Fiftieth Anniversary of the NRA. London: Institute of Historical Research, University of London, 1995. 103p.

Brunei

Horton, A. V. M. *Brunei, a Biographical Dictionary (1888–1995).* Bordesley: Author, 1995. 159p.

Bulgaria

Jordan, Sonja K. *Preservation Activities in Bulgaria: The State of Affairs and Possibilities for Cooperation Report.* Washington, DC: Commission on Preservation and Access, 1995. 11p.

Canada

Bond, Mary. *Reference Sources for Canadian Genealogy.* Ottawa, Ontario: National Library of Canada, 1995. 101p.

Briggs, Elizabeth. *Access to Ancestry: A Genealogical Resources Manual for Canadians Tracing Their Heritage*. Winnipeg, Manitoba: Westgarth, 1995. 166p.

Craig, Barbara Lazenby. *A Guide to the Fonds d'Archives and Collections in the Holdings of the York University Archives*. Toronto, Ontario: ECW Press, 1995.

Gilchrist, J. Brian. *Genealogy and Local History to 1900, a Bibliography Selected from the Catalogue of the Canadian Institute for Historical Microreproductions*. Ottawa: Canadian Institute for Historical Microreproductions, 1995. Unpgd.

Guide to the Holdings of the Archives of the Ecclesiastical Province of Canada. Toronto: Anglican Church of Canada General Synod Archives, 1995. 352p.

Hryniuk, Stella M. *The Land They Left Behind, Canada's Ukrainians in the Homeland*. Winnipeg: Watson & Dwyer, 1995. 108p.

Tracing Your Ancestors. London: British Tourist Authority, 1995. 21p.

Walker, Dan. *The Marriage Registers of Upper Canada, Canada West*. Delhi, ON: Norsim Research and Publishing, 1995. Unpgd.

Canada - Alberta

Alberta, Formerly the Northwest Territories, Index to Registration of Births, Marriages, and Deaths, 1870–1905. Edmonton, Alberta: Alberta Genealogical Society, 1995. Unpgd.

Canada - British Columbia

Archival Holdings of the British Columbia Archives and Records Service as Listed on the Archives Association of British Columbia Archival Union List. Vancouver, BC: Archives Association of British Columbia, 1995. 391p.

Cemetery Recording Instruction Booklet. 3rd. ed. Richmond, British Columbia: British Columbia Genealogical Society, 1995. Unpgd.

Canada - New Brunswick

Paulsen, Kenneth Stuart. *New Brunswick Vital Records, Finding Aid*. Rev. ed. Boston, MA: New England Historic Genealogical Society, 1995. 30p.

Canada - Ontario

Palmer, Joseph W. *A Guide to Local History Resources in Public Libraries of the Province of Ontario Together with the Results of a Survey of Public Libraries Served by the Southern Ontario Library Service*. Buffalo, NY: School of Information and Library Studies, SUNY Buffalo, 1995. 128p.

Canada - Quebec

Archives Nationales du Québec. Centre Regional de la Mauricie Bois Francs. *Inventaire des Contrats de Mariage Déposés aux Archives Nationales de Trois-Rivières, 1647–1918*. Trois-Rivières, Quebec: Author, 1995. Unpgd.

DuLong, John P. *French-Canadian Genealogical Research*. Palm Harbor, FL: LISI Press, 1995. 71p.

Guide des Archives, Barreau du Québec. Montreal, Quebec: Service de la Gestion de l'Information, Barreau du Québec, 1995. Unpgd.

Ribordy, Geneviève. *Les Prénoms de Nos Ancêtres, Etude d'Histoire Sociale*. Sillery, Quebec: Septention, 1995. 181p.

China

Barclay, John. *The Seventy-Year Ebb and Flow of Chinese Library and Information Services.* Lanham, MD: Scarecrow Press, 1995. 351p.

Coming Man: 19th Century American Perceptions of the Chinese. Seattle, WA: University of Washington Press, 1995. 178p.

Salyer, Lucy E. *Laws Harsh as Tigers, Chinese Immigrants and the Shaping of Modern Immigration Law.* Chapel Hill, NC: University of North Carolina Press, 1995. 338p.

Cuba

Hoobler, Dorothy and Thomas Hoobler. *Cuban American Family Album.* Oxford, England: Oxford University Press, 1995. 128p.

Sanchez Johnson, Mayra F. *Research Guide for Cuba.* Salt Lake City, UT: Cuban Genealogical Society, 1995. 43p.

Czech Republic

Baca, Leo. *Czech Immigration Passenger Lists.* Richardson, TX: Author, 1995. 260p.

Egypt

Willis, Charles Armine. *The Upper Nile Province Handbook, a Report on the Peoples and Government in the Southern Sudan, 1931.* Oxford, England: Oxford University Press, 1995. 476p.

England and Wales

Best Days of Your Life? Archive Sources for the History of Schools: A Beginner's Guide. Derby, England: Derbyshire Record Office, 1995. 13p.

Breed, Geoffrey R. *My Ancestors Were Baptists: How Can I Find Out More About Them?.* 3rd. ed. London: Society of Genealogists, 1995. 97p.

Burgess, John. *Family History and the Church Records of North West England, a Survey of Some Archives of the Denominations of Cumberland, Westmorland, and Lancashire, North of the Sands and Including the Lake District, Together with the Extracts, Information and History for the Uses of Family History Research.* Carlisle, England: Author, 1995. Unpgd.

Carlberg, Nancy Ellen. *Beginning English Research.* Anaheim, CA; Carlberg Press, 1995. 212p.

Christensen, Penelope. *How to Use Register Offices for English Certificates.* Silverton Terrace, British Columbia. Author, 1995. 33p.

Cornwall Record Office. *Guide to Sources at the Cornwall Record Office.* Truro, Cornwall: Cornwall County Council, 1995. 79p.

Crockford's Clerical Directory for 1865, Being a Biographical and Statistical Book of Reference for Facts Relating to the Clergy and the Church. 3rd. ed. Edinburgh: Peter Bell, 1995. 866p.

Dark, Arthur. *Civil Registration.* Gerrards Cross, England: Hillingdon Family History Society, 1995. 20p.

———. *English and Welsh Census Returns, 1841–1891.* Gerrards Cross, England: Hillingdon Family History Society, 1995. 20p.

———. *Military and Naval Records.* Gerrards Cross, England: Hillingdon Family History Society, 1995. 20p.

———. *Parish Officers, Records and Surveys.* Gerrards Cross, England: Hillingdon Family History Society, 1995. 20p.

————. *Parish Registers*. Gerrards Cross, England: Hillingdon Family History Society, 1995. 24p.

————. *Tudor and Stuart Sources*. Gerrards Cross, England: Hillingdon Family History Society, 1995. 20p.

————. *Useful Civil Records*. Gerrards Cross, England: Hillingdon Family History Society, 1995. 20p.

————. *Wills and Administrations*. Gerrards Cross, England: Hillingdon Family History Society, 1995. 20p.

Essex Record Office. *Essex Family History, a Genealogist's Guide to the Essex Record Office*. 4th ed. Chelmsford, Essex: Author, 1995. 167p.

Foster, Janet. *British Archives: A Guide to Archive Resources in the United Kingdom*. 3rd. ed. NY: Macmillan, 1995. 627p.

Gloucestershire Record Office. *Handlist of the Contents of the Gloucestershire Record Office*. 3rd ed. Gloucester, England: Gloucestershire County Council, 1995. 317p.

Goulden, R. J. *Kent Town Guides, 1763–1900, a Bibliography of Locally Published Kent Town Guides, Together with Accounts of the Printing, Publishing and Production of Town Guides in Certain Towns in Kent*. London: British Library, 1995. 134p.

Griffiths, Steven. *East Grinstead (Archival Sources)*. Local History Mini Guide No. 3. West Sussex, England: West Sussex County Library Service, 1995. 8p.

A Guide to History Libraries and Collections. 10th. ed. London: University of London Library, 1995. 39p.

A Guide to the Location of Dorset Nonconformist and Roman Catholic Registers. Dorset, England: Dorset County Archives Service, 1995. 30p.

A Handlist of Basic Sources for Family History in the Lancashire Record Office. Preston, England: Lancashire Record Office, 1995. 209p.

An Introduction to the Society and Its Services. Surrey, England: East Surrey Family History Society, 1995. 29p.

Johnson, Anne E. *A Student's Guide to British American Genealogy*. Phoenix, AZ: Oryx Press, 1995. 208p.

Larn, Richard. *Shipwreck Index of the British Isles*. London: Lloyd's Register of Shipping, 1995. Unpgd.

Lloyd, Annie. *How to Plan a Research Trip to Wales*. Culver City, CA: Author, 1995. 100p.

Park, Keith. *Family History Knowledge*. 3rd. ed. Studio City, CA: Players Press, 1995. Unpgd.

Pelling, George. *Beginning Your Family History*. 6th. ed. Birmingham, England: Federation of Family History Societies, 1995. 88p.

Pinhorn, Malcolm. *Historical, Archaeological and Kindred Societies in Great Britain, a Geographical List and Local History Studies Librarians in Great Britain, a Geographical List*. Calbourne, Isle of Wight: Author, 1995. 50p.

Reaney, P. H. *A Dictionary of English Surnames*. 3rd ed. Oxford, England: Oxford University Press, 1995. 509p.

Richards, Tom. *Was Your Grandfather a Railwayman?: A Directory of Records Relating to Staff Employed by Railways in the Following Countries with Details on Material and Repositories: United Kingdom, Australia, Canada, Eire, India, New Zealand, South Africa, United States of America*. 3rd. ed. Birmingham, England: Author, 1995. 101p.

Rogers, Colin D. *The Surname Detective, Investigating Surname Distribution in England, 1086-Present Day*. Manchester, England: Manchester University Press, 1995. 260p.

Thurston, Anne. *Records of the Colonial Office, Dominions Office, Commonwealth Relations Office and Commonwealth Office*. London: Her Majesty's Stationery Office, 1995. 479p.

Tracing Your Ancestors. London: British Tourist Authority, 1995. 21p.

Victorians in Derbyshire: A Beginner's Guide. Derby, England: Derbyshire County Council, 1995. 8p.

Finland

Vincent, Timothy Laitila. *Finnish Genealogical Research*. New Brighton, MN: Sampo Pub., 1995. 191p.

France

Direction des Archives de France. *Archives Contemporaines et Histoire: Journées d'Etude de la Direction des Archives de France, Vincennes, 18-29 Novembre 1994*. Paris: Archives Nationales, 1995. 126p.

Guide des Fonds Patrimoniaux des Bibliothèques d'Alsace. Strasbourg, France: BNUS, Cordial, 1995. 288p.

Guide du Lecteur des Archives de la Marine, Etat des Repertoires et Inventaires, Eléments de Bibliographie. 3rd. ed. Vincennes: Service Historique de la Marine, 1995. 85p.

La Recherche Historique en Archives du Moyen Age. Paris, France: Ophrys, 1995. 223p.

Thiebaud, Jean Marie. *Pratique de la Généalogie: Guide Universel de Recherche*. Besançon, France: Cetre, 1995. 322p.

Germany

Brandt, Edward R. *Germanic Genealogy*. St. Paul, MN: Germanic Genealogical Society, 1995. 370p.

Braunche, Ernst Otto. *Die Karlsruher Ratsprotokolle des 18. Jahrhunderts*. Karlsruhe, Germany: Stadtarchiv Karlsruhe, 1995. Unpgd.

Emigration and Settlement Patterns of German Communities in North America. Indianapolis, IN: Max Kade German American Center, Indiana University, 1995. 380p.

Germanic Genealogy: A Guide to Worldwide Sources and Migration Patterns. St. Paul, MN: Germanic Genealogical Society, 1995. 370p.

Hacker, Werner. *Eighteenth Century Register of Emigrants from Southwest Germany to American and Other Countries*. Apollo, PA: Closson Press, 1995. Unpgd.

Haller, Charles R. *Distinguished German Americans*. Bowie, MD: Heritage Books, 1995. 303p.

Handbuchlein fur Archivpfleger und Archivordner der Evangelischen Kirche im Rheinland. 2nd ed. Dusseldorf, Germany: Archiv der Evangelischen Kirche im Rheinland, 1995. 480p.

Jones, George F. *German American Names*. 2nd ed. Baltimore, MD: Genealogical Publishing Co., 1995. 320p.

La Cultura Tedesca in Italia: 1750–1850. Bologna, Italy: Patron, 1995. 417p.

Manning, Barbara. *Genealogical Abstracts from Newspapers of the German Reformed Church, 1840–1843*. Bowie, MD: Heritage Books, 1995. 344p.

Palen, Margaret Krug. *Genealogical Guide to Tracing Ancestors in Germany*. Bowie, MD: Heritage Books, 1995. 156p.

People in Transit: German Migrations in Comparative Perspective, 1820–1930. Washington, DC: German Historical Institute, 1995. 433p.

Schweitzer, George Keene. *German Genealogical Research*. Knoxville, TN: Author, 1995. 283p.

Taschenbuch Fur Familiengeschichtsforschung. Neustadt An Der Aisch, Germany: Degener, 1995. 640p.

Honduras

Maldonado, Carlos W. *Indice de Documentos del Archivo Nacional.* Tegucigalpa, Honduras: Archivo Nacional, 1995. 87p.

———. *Indice de Impresos del Siglo XIX.* Tegucigalpa, Honduras: Archivo Nacional, 1995. 168p.

——— and Francisco Javier Ponce. *Inventario de Diarios y Periódicos del Siglo XIX.* Tegucigalpa, Honduras: Archivo Nacional de Honduras, 1995. 28p.

India

Aggarwal, J. C. *Modern History of Jammu and Kashmir, Including Select Documents and Comprehensive Reference Bibliography Covering All Aspects of Jammu and Kashmir, 1844–1994.* New Delhi: Concept Pub. Co., 1995. 2 vols.

Wani, G. A. *Kashmir, History and Politics, 1846–1994, a Select Annotated Bibliography.* 2nd ed. Srinagar, India: Tariq Enterprises, 1995. 230p.

Ireland

Betit, Kyle J. and Dwight Radford. *Ireland, a Genealogical Guide for North Americans.* 3rd ed. Salt Lake City, UT: The Irish at Home and Abroad, 1995. 62p.

Foster, Janet. *British Archives: A Guide to Archive Resources in the United Kingdom.* 3rd. ed. NY: Macmillan, 1995. 627p.

Gillespie, Raymond. *Cavan, Essays on the History of an Irish County.* Blackrock, Ireland: Irish Academic Press, 1995. 240p.

Hollett, Dave. *Passage to the New World: Packet Ships and Irish Famine Emigrants, 1845-51.* Abergavenny: P. M. Heaton, 1995. 232p.

Hoobler, Dorothy and Thomas Hoobler. *Irish American Family Album.* New York, NY: Oxford University Press, 1995. 127p.

Ireland. General Register Office. *Registering the People: 150 Years of Civil Registration.* Dublin, Ireland: Department of Health, 1995. 23p.

Irish Passenger Lists, 1803–1806, Lists of Passengers Sailing from Ireland to America: Extracted from the Hardwicke Papers. Baltimore, MD: Genealogical Pub. Co., 1995. 154p.

Irish Women and Irish Migration. London, England: Leicester University Press, 1995. 238p.

Jacobson, Matthew Frye. *Special Sorrows: The Diasporic Immigration of Irish, Polish and Jewish Immigrants in the United States.* Cambridge, MA: Harvard University Press, 1995. 321p.

Lewis, Samuel. *A Topographical Dictionary of Ireland.* Baltimore, MD: Genealogical Publishing Co., 1837, 1995. 2 vols.

Matheson, Robert E. *Official Varieties of Synonyms of Surnames and Christian Names in Ireland for the Guidance of Registration Officers and the Public Searching the Indexes of Births, Deaths and Marriages.* Bowie, MD: Heritage Books, 1901, 1995. 94p.

Israel

Igud Ha-arkhiyonaim Be-Yisrael. Vaadah le-mivnim, Tsiyud, Shimurve-Shikum. *Madrikh le-Ahzakat Reshumot Be-Arkhiyon.* Haifa, Israel: Author, 1995. 70p.

Israel. Ganzaka Ha-Medinah. *Biur Homer Arkhiyoni Ketsad? Madrikh Le-Viur Homer Arkhiyoni Be-Mosdot Ha-Medinah Uva-Rashuyot Ha-Mekomiyot.* Jerusalem: Misrad Rosh Ha-Memshalah, Arkhiyon Ha-Medinah, 1995. 66p.

Lilenthral, Edward T. *Preserving Memory: The Struggle to Create America's Holocaust Museum.* NY: Viking, 1995. 336p.

Mokotoff, Gary. *How to Document Victims and Locate Survivors of the Holocaust*. Teaneck, NJ: Avotaynu, 1995. 194p.

Sack, Sallyann Amdur. *A Guide to Jewish Genealogical Research in Israel*. Rev. ed. Teaneck, NJ: Avotaynu, 1995. 229p.

Italy

Cole, Trafford Robertson. *Italian Genealogical Records: How to Use Italian Civil, Ecclesiastical and Other Records in Family History Research*. Salt Lake City, UT: Ancestry, 1995. 251p.

Franzina, Emilio. *Gli Italiani al Nuovo Mondo: l'Emigrazione Italiana in America, 1492–1942*. Milan, Italy: A. Mondadori, 1995. 644p.

Glazier, Ira A. and P. William Filby. *Italians to America, Lists of Passengers Arriving at United States Ports, 1880–1899. Volume 5. Passengers Arriving at New York, November 1890–December 1891*. Wilmington, DE: Scholarly Resources, 1995. 670p.

Hoobler, Dorothy and Thomas Hoobler. *Italian American Family Album*. New York, NY: Oxford University Press, 1995. 130p.

La Cultura Tedesca in Italia: 1750–1850. Bologna, Italy: Patron, 1995. 417p.

Marchione, Margherita. *Americans of Italian Heritage*. Lanham, MD: University Press of America, 1995. 234p.

Japan

Nishimura, Arthur Jiro. *Japanese Emigration in the Pre-World War II Era (1868–1937), a Reconceptualization of the History*. Thesis (M.A.), University of Washington, 1995. 64p.

Sato, Bunmei. *Koseki Ga Tsukuru Sabetsu*. Tokyo: Gendai Shokan, 1995. 254p.

Sato, Tsunezo. *Hawai Imin Sato Tsunezo Shokan, Kindai Nihonjin Kaigai Imin Shiryo*. Tokyo: Keio Tsushin, 1995. 313p.

Latin America

Fundación MAPFRE América. *Claves Operativas para la Historia de Iberoamérica: Proyectos y Actividades de la Fundación MAPFRE America y del Instituto Historico Tavera*. Madrid, Spain: The Foundation, 1995. 448p.

Herrera Saucedo, George Edward. *An Introduction to Hispanic Genealogical Research, a Manual*. Los Angeles, CA: Author, 1995. 68p.

Hispanic American Genealogical Sourcebook. Detroit, MI: Gale Research, 1995. 224p.

Indice Biografico de España, Portugal e Iberoamérica. 2nd ed. Munich, Germany: K. G. Saur, 1995. 7 vols.

Mendez Venegas, Eladio. *Emigrantes a América*. Mérida, Spain: Editora Regional de Extremadura, 1995. 159p.

Sanchez Alonso, Blanco. *Las Causas de la Emigración Española, 1880–1930*. Madrid, Spain: Alianza Editorial, 1995. 325p.

Lithuania

Address List of Roman Catholic Churches in Lithuania: A Guide for Family History Researchers. New Milford, CT: Language and Lineage Press, 1995. 60p.

Researching Lithuanian Ancestral Towns. Chicago, IL: Balzekas Museum of Lithuanian Culture, Immigration History Department, 1995. 12p.

Mexico

Castro A., José Luis. *Bosquejo Histórico de Tuxtla Gutiérrez*. Tuxtla Gutiérrez, Chiapas: EDYSIS, 1995. 31p.

Catálogo del Fondo Colonial Coahuila-Texas, 1675–1821. Saltillo, Coahuila, Mexico: Instituto Estatal de Documentación, Universidad Autónoma del Noreste, 1995. 235p.

Fondos del Siglo XVIII, 1703–1713. Colima, Colima, Mexico: Archivo Histórico del Municipio de Colima, 1995. 56p.

Garmendia Leal, Guillermo. *Origen de los Fundadores de Texas, Nuevo México, Coahuila y Nuevo León*. Monterrey, Mexico: Author, 1995. 4 vols.

Hernández García, David. *Guía del Archivo de Testimonios Familiares y Documentos Históricos*. Torreón, Coahuila, Mexico: Universidad Iberoaméricana, 1995. 51p.

Seminario sobre Bibliografia Histórica Regional. Monterrey, Mexico: Universidad Autónoma de Nuevo León, Centro de Información de Historia Regional, 1995. 170p.

Studies in Brownsville and Matamoros History. Brownsville, TX: University of Texas at Brownsville, 1995. 332p.

Vázquez, Josefina Zoraida. *Guía de Protocolos, Archivo General de Notarías de la Ciudad de México, Año de 1846*. Mexico: El Colegio de México, 1995. 327p.

———. *Guía de Protocolos, Archivo General de Notarías de la Ciudad de México, Año de 1849*. Mexico City, Mexico: Colegio de México, 1995. 327p.

Namibia

National Archives, Namibia. *List of Archivalia in the National Archives, Namibia*. Rev. ed. Windhoek, Author, 1995. 27p.

Netherlands

Brinks, Herbert J. *Dutch American Voices: Letters from the United States, 1850–1930*. Ithaca, NY: Cornell, 1995. 480p.

The National Register of Archives, an International Perspective, Essays in Celebration of the Fiftieth Anniversary of the NRA. London: Institute of Historical Research, University of London, 1995. 103p.

New Zealand

Auckland Institute and Museum Library. *Nga Pou Arahi. A Tribal Inventory of Manuscripts Relating to Maori Treasures, Language, Genealogy, Songs, History, Customs and Proverbs*. Auckland, NZ: Author, 1995. 311p.

Nicaragua

Pérez Alonso, Manuel Ignacio. *Fuentes Documentales para la Historia de Nicaragua en Archivos y Bibliotecas del Extranjero*. Managua, Nicaragua: Imprenta UCA, 1995. 30p.

Norway

Slater, Sandra J. *Guide to Norwegian Bygdeboker*. Grand Forks, ND: Special Collections Department, University of North Dakota Library, 1995. 81p.

Paraguay

Pusineri Scala, Carlos Alberto. *Archivo Nacional de Asunción, Bibliotecas, Colecciones y Museos del Paraguay*. Asunción, Paraguay: Imprenta Nacional, 1995. 83p.

Whigham, Thomas. *A Guide to Collections on Paraguay in the United States*. Westport, CT: Greenwood Press, 1995. 114p.

Poland

Jacobson, Matthew Frye. *Special Sorrows: The Diasporic Immigration of Irish, Polish and Jewish Immigrants in the United States*. Cambridge, MA: Harvard University Press, 1995. 321p.

Polish Genealogical Research at the Buffalo and Erie County Public Library. Buffalo, NY: Special Collections Department, Buffalo and Erie County Public Library, 1995. Unpgd.

Stogowska, Anna Maria. *Archiwum Panstwowe w Plocku*. Plock, Poland: Author, 1995. 61p.

Portugal

Indice Biografico de España, Portugal e Iberoamérica. 2nd ed. Munich, Germany: K. G. Saur, 1995. 7 vols.

Russia

Dvorianskie Rody Rossiiskoi Imperii, Families of the Nobility of the Russian Empire. Saint Petersburg, Russia: IPK Vesti, 1995. 262p.

Istoriia Russkoi Pravoslavnoi Tserkvi v Dokumentakh Federalnykh Arkhivov Rossii, Arkhivov Moskvy I Sankt-Peterburga: Annotirovannyi Spavochnik Ukazatel. Moscow, Russia: Izd. Novospasskogo Monastyria, 1995. 397p.

Scotland

Anderson, William C. *The Scottish Nation, or the Surnames, Family Literature, Honours and Biographical History of the People of Scotland. Volume C*. Bowie, MD: Heritage Books, 1901, 1995. 235p.

————. *The Scottish Nation, or the Surnames, Family Literature, Honours and Biographical History of the People of Scotland. Volume D-F*. Bowie, MD: Heritage Books, 1901, 1995. 274p.

Ayrshire Sound Archive Catalogue (Oral Histories). Ayr, Scotland: Ayrshire Federation of Historical Societies, 1995. Unpgd.

Cory, Kathleen B. *Tracing Your Scottish Ancestry*. Baltimore, MD: Genealogical Pub. Co., 1995. 195p.

Dobson, David. *Original Scots Colonists of Early America, 1612–1783*. Baltimore, MD: Genealogical Publishing Co., 1989, 1995. 370p.

————. *The Scots Overseas, Emigrants and Adventurers from Moray and Banff*. St. Andrews, Scotland: Author, 1995. unpgd.

Foster, Janet. *British Archives: A Guide to Archive Resources in the United Kingdom*. 3rd. ed. NY: Macmillan, 1995. 627p.

A Guide to the Major Collections in the Department of Special Collections. 3rd. ed. Glasgow, Scotland: University of Glasgow Library, 1995. 36p.

A Jacobite Source List, List of Documents in the Scottish Record Office Relating to the Jacobites. Edinburgh: Scottish Record Office, 1995. 86p.

The National Register of Archives, an International Perspective, Essays in Celebration of the Fifieth Anniversary of the NRA. London: Institute of Historical Research, University of London, 1995. 103p.

Sources for Family History in Ayrshire. Troon, Scotland: Troon and District Family History Society, 1995. 48p.

Whyte, Donald. *The Scots Overseas: A Selected Bibliography*. Aberdeen, Scotland: Scottish Association of Family History Societies, 1995. 78p.

Slovakia

Sedliakova, Alzbeta. *Historigrafia na Slovensku, 1990–1994, Vyberova Bibliografia*. Bratislva, Slovakia: Historicky ustav Slovenskej Akademie Vied, 1995. 192p.

Velinkonja, Joseph. *Who's Who of Slovene Descent in the United States, 1995*. Rev. ed. NY: Society for Slovene Studies, Columbia University, 1995. 144p.

South Africa

Alphabetical Guide to Biographical Data Recorded in Published Sources. Pretoria: State Archives Service, 1995. 172p.

Beater, J. L. *Inventory of the Archives of the Magistrate and Commissioner, Ixopo*. Pretoria, South Africa: State Archives Service, 1995. 74p.

Index to the Cemeteries Included in the Alphabetical Guides to Gravestones in Smaller Cemeteries in South Africa, Vols. I-XXVIII. 5th. ed. Pretoria: State Archives Service, 1995. 42p.

The National Register of Archives, an International Perspective, Essays in Celebration of the Fifieth Anniversary of the NRA. London: Institute of Historical Research, University of London, 1995. 103p.

Spain

Actas de las V Jornadas de Archivos Aragoneses, Situación y Perspectiva de los Archivos de la Administración Local, los Archivos Militares y los Archivos Policiales. Zaragoza, Spain: Gobierno de Aragón, Departamento de Educación y Cultura, 1995. 424p.

Archivo General de Indias. Madrid, Spain: Ministerio de Cultura, Dirección General del Libro, Archivos, y Bibliotecas, 1995. 328p.

Archivo General de Navarra, 1274–1321. Donostia, Spain: Eusko Ikaskuntza, 1995. Unpgd.

Asociación de Archiveros de la Iglesia en España. *Memoria Ecclesiae VI. Ordenes Monasticas y Archivos de la Iglesia, Santoral Hispano-Mozarabe en España*. Oviedo, Spain: Author, 1995. 563p.

Colección Documental del Archivo Municipal de Bergara. Donostia, Spain: Eusko Ikaskuntza, 1995. Unpgd.

Encisco, Carmen Edna. *Hispanic Americans in Congress, 1822–1995*. Washington, DC: GPO, 1995. 136p.

Fluvia y Escorsa, Armando de. *A la Recerca dels Avantpassats: Manual de Genealogía*. Barcelona, Spain: Curial, 1995. 237p.

Guía del Arxius Historicos de Catalunya. Barcelona, Spain: Generalidad de Catalunya, 1995. 274p.

Gutiérrez Alonso, Carmen. *Fuentes Documentales para la Historia de Torrelavega, el Archivo Municipal de Torrelavega, Inventario de la Documentación Histórica*. Santander, Spain: Fundación Marcelino Botin, 1995. 302p.

Herrera Saucedo, George Edward. *An Introduction to Hispanic Genealogical Research, a Manual*. Los Angeles, CA: Author, 1995. 68p.

Hispanic American Genealogical Sourcebook. Detroit, MI: Gale Research, 1995. 224p.

Historical Themes and Identity. New York: Garland, 1995. 550p.

Indice Biografico de España, Portugal e Iberoamérica. 2nd ed. Munich, Germany: K. G. Saur, 1995. 7 vols.

Inventario de los Archivos Municipales de Sotobanado y Priorato, Bascones de Ojeda, Calahorra de Boedo. Palencia, Spain: Diputación Provincial de Palencia, 1995. 175p.

Le Royaume d'Espagne, Dictionnaire Historique et Généalogique. Paris: CEDRE, 1995. Unpgd.

Lopez, Carmelo Luis. *Catálogo del Archivo Municipal de Piedrahita, Siglo XVI.* Avila, Spain: Ediciones de la Obra Cultural de la Caja de Ahorros de Avila, 1995. Unpgd.

———. *Catálogo del Archivo Municipal de Piedrahita, Siglo XVI.* Avila, Spain: Diputación Provincial de Avila, 1995. Unpgd.

Méndez Venegas, Eladio. *Emigrantes a América.* Mérida, Spain: Editora Regional de Extremadura, 1995. 159p.

Museo de la Casa de la Moneda. *El Archivo de la Casa de la Moneda de Madrid (Archivo Histórico Nacional).* Madrid: Author, 1995. 708p.

The National Register of Archives, an International Perspective, Essays in Celebration of the Fifieth Anniversary of the NRA. London: Institute of Historical Research, University of London, 1995. 103p.

Ortiz Real, Javier. *Fuentes Documentales para la Historia de Torrelavega, Archivos Nacionales.* Santander, Spain: Fundación Marcelino Botin, 1995. 356p.

Ravina, Martín, Manuel. *Inventario de los Fondos de Beneficencia, Archivo Historico Provincial de Cadiz.* Cadiz, Spain: Universidad de Cádiz, 1995. 326p.

Ruiz Franco, Maria del Rosario. *Historia Contemporanea de Andalucia.* Bibliografias de Historia de España, No. 5. Madrid: Centro de Información y Documentación Científica, 1995. 199p.

Sánchez Alonso, Blanco. *Las Causas de la Emigración Española, 1880–1930.* Madrid, Spain: Alianza Editorial, 1995. 325p.

Serrano González, Reyes. *Archivo Histórico Provincial de Teruel, Guía del Investigador.* Zaragoza, Spain: Gobierno de Aragón, Departamento de Educación y Cultura, 1995. 119p.

Wold, Lillian Ramos Navarro. *Family Origins.* Fullerton, CA: SHHAR Press, 1995. 92p.

Yague Ferrer, Maria Isabel. *Jaca: Documentos Municipales, 971–1324, Introducción y Concordancia Lematizada.* Zaragoza, Spain: Universidad de Zaragoza, 1995. 533p.

Sweden

Applequist, Jan. *Arkivvard, en Handbok.* Stockholm, Sweden: Fritze, 1995. 117p.

Erling, Maria Elizabeth. *Crafting an Urban Piety, New England's Swedish Immigrants and Their Religious Culture from 1880 to 1915.* Dissertation (Ph.D.), Harvard University, 1995, 274p.

Johansson, Carl Erik. *Cradled in Sweden.* Rev. ed. Logan, UT: Everton Pub., 1995. 345p.

The National Register of Archives, an International Perspective, Essays in Celebration of the Fifieth Anniversary of the NRA. London: Institute of Historical Research, University of London, 1995. 103p.

Olsson, Nils William. *Swedish Passenger Arrivals in the United States, 1820–1850.* Stockholm: Kungl Biblioteket, 1995. 628p.

Pladsen, Phyllis J. *Swedish Genealogical Dictionary.* 3rd ed. White Bear Lake, MN: Pladsen Sveria Press, 1995. 150p.

Switzerland

Gratz, Delbert L. *Was Isch Dini Nahme? What Is Your Name?* Morgantown, PA: Masthof Press, 1995. 36p.

Turkey

Basbakanlik Merkez Teskilati: Tarihce Ve Mevzuat. Ankara, Turkey: Genel Mudurlugu, 1995.
2 vols.

West Indies

Palmer, Ransford W. *Pilgrims from the Sun: West Indian Migration to America.* NY: Twayne,
1995. 101p.

GENEALOGICAL SOURCES BY STATE

Alabama

Brewer, W. *Alabama, Her History, Resources, War Record, and Public Men, from 1540 to 1872*. Baltimore, MD: Clearfield, 1872, 1995. 712p.

Hageness, MariLee Beatty. *Alabama Divorces, 1818–1868, State Legislature*. Author, 1995. 25p.

Kelsey, Michael. *Marriage and Death Notices from the South Western Baptist Newspaper*. Bowie, MD: Heritage Books, 1995. 223p.

———. Nancy Graff Floyd and Ginny Guinn Parsons. *Miscellaneous Alabama Newspaper Abstracts, Vol. 1*. Bowie, MD: Heritage Books, 1995. 256p.

Thomas, Mary Martha. *Stepping Out of the Shadows: Alabama Women, 1819–1990*. Tuscaloosa, AL: University of Alabama Press, 1995. 237p.

Wilson, Mary Jane Short. *Alabama Blue Book and Social Register, 1929 Index*. Birmingham, AL: Author, 1995. 37p.

Athens

Hageness, MariLee Beatty. *Membership, Round Island Baptist Church, Limestone County, Alabama*. Author, 1995. 10p.

Baldwin County

Hageness, MariLee Beatty. *Marriages of Baldwin County, Alabama, 1810–1836, Arranged Alphabetically by Surnames of Bride and Groom*. Author, 1995. 6p.

———. *1907 Confederate Soldiers Census, Baldwin County, Alabama*. Author, 1995. 8p.

Barbour County

Hathaway, Warrine Sheppard. *Barbour County, Alabama, Marriage Licenses, 1838–1930*. Dothan, AL: Author, 1995. 326p.

Bessemer

Ward, Fred. *Cedar Hill Cemetery, Bessemer, Alabama*. Bessemer, AL: Author, 1995. 150p.

Bibb County

Hageness, MariLee Beatty. *Bibb County, Alabama, Unrecorded Marriages*. Author, 1995. 8p.
———. *1907 Confederate Soldier's Census, Bibb County, Alabama*. Anniston, AL: Author, 1995. 13p.

Birmingham

Birmingham Public Library. *Genealogical Research in the Tutwiler Collection of Southern History and Literature*. Birmingham, AL: Author, 1995. 59p.

Blount County

Hudson, Lottie Painter. *Blount County, Alabama, Marriages, 1892–1910*. Author, 1995. 143p.

Butler County

Middleton, Barbara Perdue. *Butler County Tract Book, 1817–1860*. Greenville, AL: Butler County Historical and Genealogical Society, 1995. Unpgd.

Calhoun County

Bishop, Dorothy Clifton. *Calhoun County, Alabama, Selected Abstracts of Deed Records D-2, E-2, F-2, G-2, H-2, I-2, J-2, K-2, K-2, 1871–1880*. Anniston, AL: Annie Calhoun Book Shop, 1995. 42p.

Chambers County

Hageness, MariLee Beatty. *Chambers County, Alabama, Marriages, Marriage Consenters, Ministers Credentials, Marriage Locations Arranged Alphabetically by Surname of Bride and Groom*. Anniston, AL: Author, 1995. Unpgd.
Lebanon Presbyterian Church, Established 1843 in Chambers County, Alabama, History, Early Records, People, the Cemetery, the Trust Fund. Birmingham, AL: J. M. Spence, 1995. 173p.

Cherokee County

Sprayberry, Gary Shane. *Cherokee County, Alabama, during the Civil War*. Thesis (M.A.), Jacksonville State University, 1995. 112p.

Chilton County

Roberts, Ben. *Yours, Mine and Theirs*. Clarton, AL: Mail Specialist, 1995. 173p.

Clarke County

Hageness, MariLee Beatty. *Probate Book A, 1813–1828, Clarke County, Alabama*. Author, 1995. 19p.

Colbert County

Hageness, MariLee Beatty. *1907 Confederate Soldiers Census, Colbert County, Alabama*. Author, 1995. 10p.

Conecuh County

Brooks, Mary McCoulskey. *1850 Census, Alabama, Conecuh County*. San Angelo, TX: M. M. Books, 1995. Unpgd.

Coosa County

Brooks, Mary McCoulskey. *1850 Census, Alabama, Coosa County*. San Angelo, TX: M. M. Books, 1995. Unpgd.

Covington County

Hidle, Joan Hallford. *Tracking Your Roots, Tombstone Inscriptions of Covington County, Alabama*. Montgomery, AL: L. R. Franklin, 1995. 232p.

Dale County

Brooks, Mary McCoulskey. *1850 Census, Alabama, Dale County*. San Angelo, TX: M. M. Books, 1995. Unpgd.

Hathaway, Warrine Sheppard. *Dale County, Alabama, Marriage Records, 1885–1930*. Dothan, AL: Author, 1995. 223p.

De Kalb County

Hageness, MariLee Beatty. *General Index to Probate Records B, 1905–1927, DeKalb County, Alabama*. Author, 1995. 33p.

———. *Index to Insane Register 2, July 1951–September 1959, DeKalb County, Alabama*. Author, 1995. 12p.

———. *1907 Confederate Soldiers Census, De Kalb County, Alabama*. Author, 1995. 12p.

Etowah County

Hageness, MariLee Beatty. *1907 Confederate Soldiers Census, Etowah County, Alabama*. Author, 1995. 12p.

Pruitt, Carolyn Miller. *Marriages of Etowah County, Alabama, prior to 1900*. Glencoe, AL: Author, 1995. Unpgd.

Henry County

Hageness, MariLee Beatty. *1907 Confederate Soldiers Census, Henry County, Alabama*. Author, 1995. 20p.

Huntsville

Maple Hill Cemetery, Phase One. Huntsville, AL: Huntsville-Madison County Historical Society, 1995. 167p.

Macon County

Martin, William T., III. *Cubahatchee Baptist Church of Christ Church Book, 1838–1850, Macon County, Alabama*. 2nd ed. Miami, FL: Author, 1995. 113p.

Marshall County

Taylor, Betty Jean. *The Democrat Deaths, 1880–1899, Marshall County, Alabama*. Guntersville, AL: Author, 1995. 37p.

———. *Marshall County, Alabama, Marriages, 1874–1876*. Guntersville, AL: Author, 1995. 28p.

Perry County

Hageness, MariLee Beatty. *1907 Confederate Soldier's Census, Perry County, Alabama*. Anniston, AL: Author, 1995. 13p.

Pike County

Senn, Susie K. *The 1860 Federal Slave Schedule for Pike County, Alabama.* Brundidge, AL: Author, 1995. 53p.

Sumter County

Hester, Gwendolyn L. *1855 Census, Sumter County, Alabama.* Dallas, TX: Author, 1995. 64p.

Talladega County

Hageness, MariLee Beatty. *Index to Estate Filing Cases (Loose Packets), 1832–1994, Office of Probate Judge, Talladega County, Alabama.* Author, 1995. Unpgd.
———. *Index to Will Books, Talladega County.* Anniston, AL: Author, 1995. Unpgd.

Tallapoosa County

Hageness, MariLee Beatty. *Index to the Orphan's Court Minutes, Tallapoosa County.* Anniston, AL: Author, 1995. Unpgd.

Wilcox County

Hageness, MariLee Beatty. *Will Book 2, 1841–1850, Wilcox County, Alabama.* Anniston, AL: Author, 1995. 43p.

Alaska

Alaska at War, 1941–1945, the Forgotten War Remembered. Anchorage, AK: Alaska at War Symposium, 1995. 455p.

Falk, Marvin W. *Alaska.* Santa Barbara, CA: ABC-CLIO, 1995. 219p.

Ferrell, Ed. *Biographies of Alaska-Yukon Pioneers, 1850–1950. Vol. 2.* Bowie, MD: Heritage Books, 1995. 371p.

Gold Rush Centennial Photographs, 1893–1916, a Catalog of Selected Gold Rush Views at the Alaska State Library. Juneau, AK: Alaska Historical Collections, Alaska State Library, 1995. 15p.

Postnikov, Aleksei Vladimirovich. *The Mapping of Russian America, a History of Russian American Contacts in Cartography.* Milwaukee, WI: Golda Meir Library, University of Wisconsin, 1995. 35p.

Price, Robert E. *Bibliography of Literature on Alaska Native History from 1741 to 1867.* Juneau, AK: Alaska Siberia Research Center, 1995. 53p.

When Our Words Return, Writing, Hearing and Remembering Oral Traditions of Alaska and the Yukon. Logan, UT: Utah State University Press, 1995. 244p.

Bristol Bay

Dumond, Don E. *Paugvik, a Nineteenth Century Native Village on Bristol Bay, Alaska*. Chicago, IL: Field Museum of Natural History, 1995. 109p.

Juneau

Juneau Douglas Finns of Southeast Alaska. Portland, OR: Finnish American Historical Society of the West, 1995. 33p.

Kokrines

Albert, Phillip. *The History of Kokrines and Ruby along the Yukon River, a Project*. Thesis (M.A.), University of Alaska at Fairbanks, 1995. 198p.

Ruby

Albert, Phillip. *The History of Kokrines and Ruby along the Yukon River, a Project*. Thesis (M.A.), University of Alaska at Fairbanks, 1995. 198p.

Seward

Capra, Doug. *A Handful of Pebbles, Stories from Seward History*. Seward, AK: Yankee-Sourdough, 1995. 55p.

Sitka

DeArmond, R. N. *From Sitka's Past*. Sitka, AK: Sitka Historical Society, 1995. 260p.

Talkeetna

Sheldon, Roberta. *The Heritage of Talkeetna*. Talkeetna, AL: Talkeetna Editions, 1995. 185p.

Arizona

Cady, John H. *Arizona's Yesterday*. Tucson, AZ: Adobe Corral, 1995. 120p.

Guide to Records in the National Archives, Pacific Southwest Region. Washington, DC: National Archives and Records Administration, Pacific Southwest Region, 1995. 48p.

Herrera Saucedo, George Edward. *An Introduction to Hispanic Genealogical Research, a Manual*. Los Angeles, CA: Author, 1995. 68p.

Marsh, Carole. *The Arizona Library Book, a Surprising Guide to the Unusual Special Collections in Libraries across Our State, for Students, Teachers, Writers and Publishers*. Atlanta, GA: Gallopade Pub., 1995. 36p.

Mormon Americana: A Guide to Sources and Collections in the United States. Provo, UT: Brigham Young University Studies, 1995. 695p.

Verdier, Mary L. *Pathway to Adoption, an Arizona Guide.* Phoenix, AZ: Emerald Press, 1995. 376p.

Wilson, Alan. *Navajo Place Names, an Observer's Guide.* Guilford, CT: Norton Pub., 1995. 81p.

Camp Verde

Clear Creek Cemetery Inscriptions, Camp Verde, Arizona. 1995. 41p.

Flagstaff

Flagstaff City - Coconino County Public Library. *Selected Genealogical Sources.* Flagstaff, AZ: The Library, 1995. 182p.

Mesa

Mesa, Arizona, City Cemetery Markers as of November, 1992. Mesa, AZ: Mesa, Arizona Central Stake, 1995. 473p.

Sedona

Index of Sedona Obituaries, Year 1994. Sedona, AZ: Sedona Genealogy Club, 1995. 4p.

Tempe

Double Butte Cemetery, Tempe, Arizona. Phoenix, AZ: Family History Society of Arizona, 1995. 243p.

Yuma

The Arizona Sentinel Newspaper Death Notices and Obituaries, 1872–1899. Yuma, AZ: Genealogical Society of Yuma, Arizona, 1995. 12p.

Arkansas

Dougan, Michael B. *Arkansas History: An Annotated Bibliography.* Westport, CT: Greenwood Press, 1995. 365p.

Hart, Julie C. *Public Libraries of Arkansas.* Little Rock, AR: Arkansas State Library, 1995. 36p.

Lester, Gary W. *Fayetteville, Arkansas, National Cemetery.* Braggs, OK: Green Leaf Creek Publications, 1995. 90p.

————. *Fort Smith, Arkansas, National Cemetery.* Braggs, OK: Green Leaf Creek Publications, 1995. 163p.

McLane, Bobbie Jones. *1850 Census of Central Arkansas: Hot Spring, Jefferson, Montgomery, Perry, Prairie, Pulaski, Saline, Scott, and Yell Counties.* Conway, AR: Arkansas Research, 1995. 107p.

————. *1850 Census of Eastern Arkansas: Arkansas, Chicot, Crittenden, Desha, Greene, Mississippi, Monroe, Phillips, Poinsett, and St. Francis Counties.* Conway, AR: Arkansas Research, 1995. 100p.

————. *1850 Census of North Central Arkansas: Conway, Fulton, Independence, Izard, Jackson, Lawrence, Marion, Randolph, Searcy, Van Buren, and White Counties.* Conway, AR: Arkansas Research, 1995. 139p.

————. *1850 Census of Northwest Arkansas: Benton, Carroll, Crawford, Franklin, Johnson, Madison, Newton, Pope and Washington Counties.* Conway, AR: Arkansas Research, 1995. 158p.

————. *1850 Census of Southern Arkansas: Ashley, Bradley, Clark, Dallas, Drew, Hempstead, Lafayette, Ouachita, Pike, Polk, Sevier, and Union Counties.* Conway, AR: Arkansas Research, 1995. 158p.

Ashley County
1870 Federal Census of Ashley County, Arkansas. Crossett, AR: Ashley County Genealogical Society, 1995. 160p.

Benton County
Easley, Barbara P. *Obituaries of Benton County, Arkansas. Vol. 3, 1905–1909.* Bowie, MD: Heritage Books, 1995. 513p.

————. *Obituaries of Benton County, Arkansas. Vol. 4, 1910–1913.* Bowie, MD: Heritage Books, 1995. 553p.

————. *Obituaries of Benton County, Arkansas. Vol. 5, 1914–1918.* Bowie, MD: Heritage Books, 1995. 533p.

Conway County
Ballard, James, Alta Ballard, C. L. Boyd, and Lina Boyd. *Cemeteries of the Appleton Area of Pope County, Arkansas, plus Cedar Creek Area of Conway County, Arkansas.* Dover, AR: C. L. Boyd, 1995. 132p.

Crawford County
Abstracts from Crawford County, Arkansas, Newspapers, Van Buren Press, Roll #2, April 20, 1869-December 26, 1871. 1995. 353p.

Hawkins, George Julian. *Funeral Records of Crawford County, Arkansas.* Cane Hill, AR: ARC Press of Cane Hill, 1995. Unpgd.

Cross County
Curtner, Muzette. *Cross County, Arkansas, Marriage Record Index, February 1, 1863 to December 31, 1942.* Parkin, AR: J. McNeil, 1995. 278p.

Crossett
Crossett Sawmill Interviews, Recollections of Years, 1860–1948. Crossett, AR: Ashley County Genealogical Society, 1995. Unpgd.

Fayetteville

Cemetery Locator and Map Guide. Fayetteville, AR: Grace Keith Genealogy Collection, Fayetteville Public Library, 1995. 31p.

Fayetteville, Arkansas, National Cemetery. Conway, AR: Arkansas Research, 1995. 90p.

Obituaries, Northwest Arkansas Times, Fayetteville, Arkansas, 1 January 1990-31 December 1994. Fayetteville, AR: L. Miller, 1995. 195p.

Fort Smith

Fort Smith, Arkansas, National Cemetery. Conway, AR: Arkansas Research, 1995. 163p.

Hempstead County

Hempstead County, Arkansas, United States Census of 1830, 1840, 1850 and Alphabetical Listings of Head of Household Taxes for the Years of 1828, 1829, 1830, 1831, 1832, 1839, 1841, 1842, 1847, 1848, 1849. Hope, AR: Hempstead County Genealogical Society, 1995. 137p.

Izard County

Cemeteries of Izard County, Arkansas. Freeman, MO: Hayden, 1995. 142p.

Lonoke County

Lonoke County Marriage Index, Books A thru U, Vol. 1, from 8 May 1873 to 17 July 1921. Sherwood, AR: Dwight Shubert, 1995. Unpgd.

Martinet, Tom C. *Lonoke County, Arkansas, Cemetery Inscriptions*. Cabot, AR: Author, 1995. 6 vols.

Madison County

Gone But Not Forgotten, Madison County, Arkansas, Cemeteries Annotated, Illustrated, Indexed. Huntsville, AR: Madison County Genealogical and Historical Society, 1995. 199p.

Marriage Records of Madison County, Arkansas, Books I & J, from 27 February 1913 to 9 June 1927, also Included Are 8 Marriages from 1859–1899, Which Were Rerecorded. Springdale, AR: H. H. Creek, 1995. Unpgd.

Marion County

Stradley, Lois Sullivan. *Local and Personal, Mountain Echo, May 21, 1921 through December 29, 1921, Marion County, Arkansas*. Yakima, WA: Author, 1995. 97p.

Nevada County

Nevada County, Arkansas, United States Census of 1880. Hope, AR: Hempstead County Genealogical Society, 1995. 163p.

Pope County

Ballard, James. *Cemeteries of the Bakers Creek, Linker Mountain, Morgan Road, and North New Hope Communities of Pope County, Arkansas, Area*. Author, 1995. 109p.

————. *Cemeteries of the Middle Fork and North Fork Area of Pope County, Arkansas, plus Southeast Edge of Newton County, Arkansas*. Author, 1995. 106p.

Ballard, James, Alta Ballard, C. L. Boyd, and Lina Boyd. *Cemeteries of the Appleton Area of Pope County, Arkansas, plus Cedar Creek Area of Conway County, Arkansas*. Dover, AR: C. L. Boyd, 1995. 132p.

————. *Cemetries of the Hatley Gravel Hill and Moreland Communities of Pope County, Arkansas.* Dover, AR: C. L. Boyd, 1995. 147p.

————. *Walnut Grove Cemetery, Hector, Pope County, Arkansas.* Dover, AR: C. L. Boyd, 1995. 133p.

Randolph County

Knotts, Burton Ray. *Randolph County, Arkansas, Marriages.* Conway, AR: Arkansas Research, 1995. Unpgd.

Randolph County, Arkansas, Marriages, 1821–1893. Conway, AR: Arkansas Research, 1995. 156p.

Warren

Oakland Cemetery of Warren, Arkansas. Crossett, AR: Nowlin Print Co., 1995. 171p.

Washington County

Smith, Ted J. *Slavery in Washington County, Arkansas, 1828–1860.* Thesis (M.A.), University of Arkansas, Fayetteville, 1995. 99p.

California

Biennial Report of the Adjutant General of the State of California, 1885–1886, Roster of the National Guard, 1886 (Includes Rewards). Pomona, CA: Pomona Valley Genealogical Society, 1995. 32p.

Breithaupt, Richard Hoag, Jr. *Sons of the Revolution in the State of California, Centennial Register, 1893–1993.* Universal City, CA: California Sons of the Revolution, 1995. 1,319p.

California Library Directory, 1995: Listings for Public, Academic, Special, State Agency and County Law Library. Sacramento, CA: Library Development Service Bureau, California State Library, 1995. 322p.

California Mortality Schedules, 1850, 1860, 1870, 1880. Citrus Heights, CA: Root Cellar, Sacramento Genealogical Society, 1995. Unpgd.

Guide to Records in the National Archives, Pacific Sierra Region. Washington, DC: National Archives and Records Administration, Pacific Sierra Region, 1995. 85p.

Herrera Saucedo, George Edward. *An Introduction to Hispanic Genealogical Research, a Manual.* Los Angeles, CA: Author, 1995. 68p.

Hicks, Randall. *Adopting in California, How to Adopt within One Year.* Rev. ed. Sun City, CA: WordSlinger Press, 1995. 150p.

Index to Naturalization in the United States District Court for the Northern District of California, 1852–1859. Washington, DC: National Archives and Records Administration, 1995. 9p.

Jackson, Robert H. and Edward Castillo. *Indians, Franciscans, and Spanish Colonization, the Impact of the Mission System on California Indians.* Albuquerque, NM: University of New Mexico Press, 1995. 214p.

Lloyd, Glenda Gardner. *California Mortality Schedules, 1850, 1860, 1870, 1880.* Citrus Heights, CA: Root Cellar, Sacramento Genealogical Society, 1995. Unpgd.

McLaughlin, Glen. *The Mapping of California as an Island, an Illustrated Checklist.* Saratoga, CA: California Map Society, 1995. 134p.

Mormon Americana: A Guide to Sources and Collections in the United States. Provo, UT: Brigham Young University Studies, 1995. 695p.

Niles, Reg. *California Bibliography of Adoption and Child Welfare.* NY: Adoption Bibliography Center, 1995. 70p.

Butte County

Corley, Marilyn. *Declarations of Intention to Become a Citizen of the United States, 1843–1929, Butte County, California.* Magalia, CA: Author, 1995. 268p.

Calico

Baltazar, Alan R. *Calico and Calico Mining District, 1881–1907.* Barstow, CA: Author, 1995. 72p.

Costa Mesa County

Freedman, Bernard. *Death Notices, Contra Costa County, California, 1935–1937.* Concord, CA; Author, 1995. Unpgd.

Donner

Ficklin, Marilou West. *Early Truckee Records, a Genealogy Reference for the Historic Truckee-Donner Region of California.* Author, 1995. 104p.

Fort Jones

Luttrell, Richard L. *Fort Jones Cemetery District, Record of Graves of Fort Jones, Siskiyou County, California.* Fort Jones, CA: Fort Jones Cemetery District, 1995. Unpgd.

Fresno

Greer, Rebecca F. *Armenian Cemeteries, Ararat and Masis Ararat Cemeteries, Fresno, Fresno County, California.* Fresno, CA: Fresno Genealogical Society, 1995. 180p.

Kern County

Mayfield, J. Hoyle. *The Great Register (Voter Registration), Kern County, California, a Partial Substitute for 1890 Census.* Bakersfield, CA: Kern County Genealogy Society, 1995. 72p.

Kings County

Athey, Robert L. *They Shall Not Be Forgotten, Pioneers of Kings County, California.* Hanford, CA: Author, 1995. 3 vols.

Lake Elsinore

Elsinore Valley Cemetery, 1880–1994. Lake Elsinore, CA: Lake Elsinore Genealogical Society, 1995. 173p.

Los Angeles

African Americans in Los Angeles and Los Angeles Township, Extracts from United States Censuses. Los Angeles, CA; California African American Genealogical Society, 1995. Unpgd.

Hayashi, Brian Masau. *For the Sake of Our Japanese Brethren, Assimilation, Nationalism, and Protestantism among the Japanese of Los Angeles, 1895–1942.* Stanford, CA: Stanford University Press, 1995. 217p.

Mendocino County

Births, Deaths and Marriages on California's Mendocino Coast. Bowie, MD: Heritage Books, 1995. 324p.

Sverko, Eleanor Feodora. *Early Portuguese Families of the Town of Mendocino: A Mendocino County History, California, United States of America.* Mendocino, CA: Author, 1995. 614p.

Orange County

Milkovich, Barbara Ann. *Townbuilders of Orange County, a Study of Four Southern California Cities, 1857–1931.* Dissertation (Ph.D.), University of California, Riverside, 1995. 149p.

Palm Springs

1894–1995, 100+ Years of History: Palm Springs Cemetery District: Desert Memorial Park, Welwood Murray Cemetery: Internments through February 15, 1995. Palm Springs, CA: Palm Springs Genealogical Society, 1995. 143p.

San Lucas

Gildersleeve, Matthew James. *San Lucas, the History of a California Cattle Town.* Thesis (M.A.), University of San Diego, 1995. 100p.

San Luis Obispo

100 Years Ago, 1896, Excerpts from the San Luis Obispo Morning Tribune and Breeze. San Luis Obispo, CA: W. N. Tognazzini, 1995. 166p.

Parsons, Gerard L. *Port San Luis, Trials and Tribulations, 1855 to 1995.* San Luis Obispo, CA: Author, 1995. 47p.

St. Stephens Episcopal Church Records, San Luis Obispo, California. Atascadero, CA: San Luis Obispo County Genealogical Society, 1995. 73p.

Santa Cruz

Edwards, Patricia D. *Santa Cruz County, California, Probate Records.* Santa Cruz, CA: Genealogical Society of Santa Cruz County, 1995. 94p.

Santa Cruz Evening News Local News Index, 1925–October 1928. Santa Cruz, CA: Friends of the Santa Cruz Public Libraries, 1995. 212p.

Siskiyou County

Meamber, Donald L. *Shasta Valley Cemetery District, Siskiyou County, California.* Yreka, CA: Genealogical Society of Siskiyou County, 1995. 91p.

Sonoma County

1890 Census Sonoma County, California, Reconstructed. Santa Rosa, CA: Sonoma County Genealogical Society, 1995. 301p.

Sutter County

Coping with Disaster, Voices from the 1955 Flood. Yuba City, CA: Community Memorial Museum of Sutter County, 1995. 138p.

Truckee

Ficklin, Marilou West. *Early Truckee Records, a Genealogy Reference for the Historic Truckee-Donner Region of California.* Author, 1995. 104p.

Colorado

Bibliography of Genealogical Reference Materials, a Listing of Genealogical Reference Materials, Books, Microfilm, Fiche, Video, CD-ROM, Vertical Files. Littleton, CO: Bemis Public Library, 1995. 121p.

Hardaway, Roger D. *A Narrative Bibliography of the African American Frontier, Blacks in the Rocky Mountain West, 1535–1912.* Lewiston, NY: Edwin Mellen Press, 1995. 242p.

Index and Abstract of Obituaries for Individuals with Ties to the State of Ohio, Published in Colorado Newspapers. Denver, CO: Colorado Chapter, Ohio Genealogical Society, 1995. Unpgd.

Mining Index to Henderson, Hollister and Canfield Histories. Denver, CO: Western History Department, Denver Public Library, 1995. 114p.

Obituaries With Colorado Connections. Denver, CO: Jeffrey, 1995. 194p.

Plains and Peaks Regional Library Service System. *Colorado History Resources.* Colorado Springs, CO: Author, 1995. Unpgd.

Sherard, Gerald E. *Pre-1963 Colorado Mining Fatalities.* Lakewood, CO: Author, 1995. 300p.

Black Hawk

Granruth, Alan. *Abstract of the 1870 United States Census for Black Hawk, Gilpin County, Colorado.* Author, 1995. 28p.

Boulder County

Bailey, Delores Sylvia. *Boulder County Miners, a Tribute to Those Who Left Their Mark in Colorado History.* Boulder, CO: Author, 1995. Unpgd.

Caribou

Tripp, Betty J. *The Pioneers of Caribou, a Silver Ghost Town.* Livonia, MI: Author, 1995. 113p.

Central City

Granruth, Alan. *Abstract of the 1870 United States Census for Central City, Gilpin County, Colorado*. Author, 1995. Unpgd.

Cheyenne County

The War Years and the Veterans of Cheyenne-Kiowa County, Colorado. Dallas, TX: Curtis Media, 1995. 111p.

Colorado Springs

Here Lies Colorado Springs, Historical Figures Buried in Evergreen and Fairview Cemeteries. Colorado Springs, CO: City of Colorado Springs, 1995. 182p.

Denver

Clement, John Chandler. *Index of Denver, Colorado, Newspaper Obituaries and Funeral Notices, 1 January through 31 December 1994*. Denver, CO: Author, 1995. 177p.

Gilpin County

Granruth, Alan. *Bald Mountain Cemetery, Gilpin County, Colorado*. Author, 1995. Unpgd.

Huerfano County

Maes, Arthur F. *Colorado, Huerfano County, Cisneros and Maes Creek Cemeteries*. Colorado Springs, CO: Author, 1995. 18p.

Riffe, Noreen I. *Huerfano County, Colorado, 1885 Census*. Pueblo, CO: Southeastern Colorado Genealogical Society, 1995. Unpgd.

Kiowa County

The War Years and the Veterans of Cheyenne-Kiowa County, Colorado. Dallas, TX: Curtis Media, 1995. 111p.

Lake County

Griswold, Don. *History of Leadville and Lake County, Colorado, from Mountain Solitude to Metropolis*. Denver, CO: Colorado Historical Society, 1995. Unpgd.

Las Animas County

Las Animas County, Colorado Cemeteries. Pueblo, CO: Southeastern Colorado Genealogical Society, 1995. Unpgd.

Littleton

First Presbyterian Church of Littleton, Colorado: An Indexed Every Name Abstract of Original Records, Baptisms, Marriages, Deaths, Membership, 1883–1982, Including History of the Congregation, 1883–1995. Littleton, CO: Columbine Genealogical and Historical Society, 1995. 435p.

Littleton, Colorado, Church Records. Littleton, CO: Columbine Genealogical and Historical Society, 1995. Unpgd.

Pueblo County

Bureau of Land Management Homestead Records, Pueblo County, Colorado, Range, Township and Section Map. Pueblo, CO: Southeastern Colorado Genealogical Society, 1995. 135p.

Pueblo County, Colorado, 1885 Census. 1995. Unpgd.

Routt County

History of West Routt County, Colorado. Hurst, TX: Curtis Media, 1995. 303p.

Washington County

Oestman, Patricia Ann. *Washington County Cemeteries.* Wray, CO: Author, 1995. 228p.

Connecticut

Brown, Mary H. *Erasure of Criminal Records.* Hartford, CT: Connecticut General Assembly, Office of Legislative Research, 1995. 5p.

Finding Aid to World War II Service Records. Hartford, CT: History and Genealogy Unit, Connecticut State Library, 1995. 6p.

Manwaring, Charles William. *A Digest of the Early Connecticut Probate Records.* Baltimore, MD: Genealogical Publishing Co., 1904–1906, 1995. 3 vols.

Morrison, Betty Jean. *Connecting to Connecticut.* East Hartford, CT: Connecticut Society of Genealogists, Inc., 1995. 342p.

Nipmuc Place Names of New England. Thompson, CT: Nipmuc Indian Association of Connecticut, 1995. 41p.

Rossano, Geoffrey. *Connecticut's Historic National Guard Armories.* Hartford, CT: Connecticut Historical Commision, 1995. 2 vols.

State of Connecticut Register and Manual. Hartford, CT: Secretary of the State, 1995. 930p.

Barkhamsted

White, Lorraine Cook. *The Barbour Collection of Connecticut Town Records. Volume 2.* Baltimore, MD: Genealogical Publishing Co., 1995. 282p.

Berlin

White, Lorraine Cook. *The Barbour Collection of Connecticut Town Records. Volume 2.* Baltimore, MD: Genealogical Publishing Co., 1995. 282p.

Bethany

White, Lorraine Cook. *The Barbour Collection of Connecticut Town Records. Volume 2.* Baltimore, MD: Genealogical Publishing Co., 1995. 282p.

Bethlehem
White, Lorraine Cook. *The Barbour Collection of Connecticut Town Records. Volume 2.* Baltimore, MD: Genealogical Publishing Co., 1995. 282p.

Bloomfield
White, Lorraine Cook. *The Barbour Collection of Connecticut Town Records. Volume 2.* Baltimore, MD: Genealogical Publishing Co., 1995. 282p.

Bozrah
White, Lorraine Cook. *The Barbour Collection of Connecticut Town Records. Volume 2.* Baltimore, MD: Genealogical Publishing Co., 1995. 282p.

Branford
White, Lorraine Cook. *The Barbour Collection of Connecticut Town Records. Volume 3.* Baltimore, MD: Genealogical Publishing Co., 1995. 326p.

Bridgeport
White, Lorraine Cook. *The Barbour Collection of Connecticut Town Records. Volume 3.* Baltimore, MD: Genealogical Publishing Co., 1995. 326p.

Brookfield
Guide and Index to the Genealogical Records, St. Paul's Episcopal Church, Brookfield, Connecticut. Brookfield, CT: The Church, 1995. 20p.

Hartford
Cohen, Edward Allen. *Jewish Cemeteries of Hartford, Connecticut, the Cohen/Goldfarb Collection.* Bowie, MD: Heritage Books, 1995. Unpgd.

Meriden
Beloff, Marvin. *We'll Build a Museum, the American Silver Museum Story, Meriden, Connecticut, United States of America.* Author, 1995. 178p.

New Haven
Smalley, Martha Lund. *Guide to Archives and Manuscript Collections at the Yale Divinity School Library.* New Haven, CT: Yale Divinity School Library, 1995. 63p.

North Grosvenor Dale
Baptisms of St. Joseph Catholic Church, North Grosvenordale, Connecticut, 1872–1900. Pawtucket, RI: American French Genealogical Society, 1995. 2 vols.

Stamford
Marcus, Ronald. *Stamford, Connecticut: A Bibliography.* Stamford, CT: Stamford Historical Society, 1995. 284p.

Willington
Lillibridge, David. *Record of Marriages.* Willington, CT: I. B. Weigold, 1995. 21p.

Wilton

Corrigan, Jeanne Owens. *The Wilton Library, the First Hundred Years*. Wilton, CT: Wilton Library Association, 1995. 85p.

Delaware

Directory of Historical Records in Delaware. Dover, DE: Delaware Historical Records Advisory Board, 1995. 27p.

New Sweden in America. Newark, DE: University of Delaware Press, 1995. 366p.

Preisler, Julian H. *Jewish Cemeteries of the Delmarva Peninsula, a Burial Index for Delaware and Maryland's Eastern Shore*. Westminster, MD: Family Line Pub., 1995. 123p.

Richards, Mary Fallon. *Delaware Genealogical Abstracts from Newspapers. Volume 1. Deaths from the Delaware Gazette, 1854–1859, 1861–1864*. Wilmington, DE: Delaware Genealogical Society, 1995. 316p.

Kent County

De Valinger, Leon. *Calendar of Kent County, Delaware, Probate Records, 1680–1800*. Westminster, MD: Family Line Publications, 1995. 691p.

Sussex County

Moore, Marguerite R. *Index of Sussex County, Delaware, Wills, 1800–1851*. Westminster, MD: Family Line Publications, 1995. 28p.

District of Columbia

Bergheim, Laura. *The Look-it-up Guide to Washington Libraries and Archives*. Osprey, FL: Beacham Pub., 1995. 377p.

Guide to Archives and Historical Collections in the Washington Metropolitan Area. Washington, DC: German Historical Institute, 1995. 133p.

Guide to Inventories and Finding Aids at the German Historical Institute, Washington, DC. Washington, DC: The Institute, 1995. 101p.

Guide to Washington National Records Center Services. Washington, DC: National Archives and Records Administration, 1995. 18p.

Smithsonian Institution Archival, Manuscript and Special Collection Resources. 3rd. ed. Washington, DC: Smithsonian Institution, 1995. 31p.

Warner, Robert M. *Diary of a Dream: A History of the National Archives Independence Movement, 1980–1985*. Metuchen, NJ: Scarecrow Press, 1995. 211p.

Florida

Colburn, David R. and Jane L. Landers. *The African American Heritage of Florida*. Gainesville, FL: University Press of Florida, 1995. 392p.

Florida Almanac: 1995–1996. 10th. ed. Gretna, LA: Pelican Publishing Co., 1995. 432p.

Florida Biographical Directory: People of All Times and Places Who Have Been Important to the History and Life of the State. NY: Somerset Publishers, 1995. 396p.

Hartman, David W., and David Coles. *Biographical Rosters of Florida's Confederate and Union Soldiers, 1861–1865*. Wilmington, DE: Broadfoot Pub. Co., 1995. 6 vols.

Index to Florida City Directories at the State Library of Florida. Tallahassee, FL: Florida Division of Library and Information Services, 1995. 46p.

Lantz, Raymond C. *Seminole Indians of Florida, 1875–1879*. Bowie, MD: Heritage Books, 1995. 428p.

Morris, Allen Covington. *Florida Place Names*. Sarasota, FL: Pineapple Press, 1995. 291p.

Servies, James A. and Lana D. Servies. *A Bibliography of Florida, Volume 2, 1846–1880*. Pensacola, FL: King & Queen Books, 1995. 488p.

Warda, Mark. *How to Change Your Name in Florida*. 3rd ed. Clearwater, FL: Sphinx, 1995. 105p.

Clay County
Deaton, Bonita Thomas. *The Magnolia Unionists, Southern Claims from Clay County, Florida*. Thesis (M.A.), University of North Florida, 1995. 153p.

Flagler County
Holland, Mary Ketus Dean. *First Families of Flagler*. Flagler County, FL: Author, 1995. 218p.

Hillsborough County
Early Settlers of Hillsborough County, Florida, Abstracted from Old Records in the Historical Museum of the Hillsborough County Historical Commission Located in the Courthouse, Tampa, Florida. Tampa, FL: The Commission, 1995. 112p.

Lee County

Demarchi, Gordon. *The Lee County Courthouse through the Years*. Fort Myers, FL: Lee County Board of Commissioners, 1995. 70p.

Miami

Weiss, Susan R. *Miami Bibliography*. Miami, FL: Historical Association of Southern Florida, 1995. 153p.

Polk County

Ruster, William J. *History of the Polk County Court System, 1861–1995*. Bartow, FL: Associated Publications Corp., 1995. 454p.

Santa Rosa County

Marriages, Santa Rosa County, Florida, 1869–1906. Fort Walton Beach, FL: Genealogical Society of Okaloosa County, 1995. 123p.

Tampa

Mohlman, Geoffrey. *Bibliography of Resources Concerning the African American Presence in Tampa, 1513–1995*. Thesis (M.A.), University of South Florida, 1995. 384p.

Georgia

Austin, Jeannette Holland. *30,638 Burials in Georgia*. Baltimore, MD: Gateway Press, 1995. 708p.

Boltzius, J. M. and I. C. Gronau. *Detailed Reports on the Salzburger Emigrants Who Settled in America, Vol. 18, 1744–1745*. Rockport, ME: Picton Press, 1995. 256p.

Brandenburg, John David. *Index to Georgia's 1867- Returns of Qualified Voters and Registration Oath Books (White)*. Atlanta, GA: Author, 1995. 532p.

Brooke, Ted O. *Georgia County Cemetery Bibliography*. Cumming, GA: Author, 1995. 16p.

Holley, Thomas Earl. *Company K, Ramsey Volunteer, the Sixteenth Georgia Infantry Regiment, Army of Northern Virginia, Confederate States of America, the Officers, the Battles, and a Genealogy of Its Soldiers*. Thomson, GA: Author, 1995. 363p.

Roster of Confederate Graves. Atlanta, GA: Georgia Division, United Daughters of the Confederacy, 1995. 7 vols.

Schweitzer, George Keene. *Georgia Genealogical Research*. Knoxville, TN: Author, 1995. 242p.

Sifakis, Stewart. *Compendium of the Confederate Armies Series: South Carolina and Georgia*. NY: Facts on File, 1995. 320p.

Special Collections Department, Emory University Library. *Manuscript Sources for African-American History: A Descriptive List of Holdings in the Special Collections Department.* Rev. Atlanta, GA: The Library, 1995. 51p.

United Daughters of the Confederacy. Georgia Division. Membership Roster, A-Z, November 1895-July 15, 1995. Atlanta, GA: The Division, 1995. Unpgd.

Warnock, Robert Holcomb. *Georgia Sources for Family History.* Atlanta, GA: Georgia Genealogical Society, 1995. 107p.

Warren, Mary Bondurant. *Georgia Military Records.* Author, 1995. 153p.

Windham, Marilyn Neisler. *Marriages, Deaths and etc. from the Butler (Georgia) Herald, 1876- 1896.* Warner Robins, GA: Central Georgia Genealogical Society, 1995. 226p.

Atlanta

Special Collections Department. Emory University Libraries. *Manuscript Sources for African American History, a Descriptive List of Holdings in the Special Collections Department.* Rev. Atltanta, GA: Author, 1995. 51p.

Augusta

Rowland, Arthur Ray. *Index to City Directories of Augusta, Georgia, 1841–1879.* Augusta, GA; Augusta Genealogical Society, 1995. 475p.

Bartow County

Bartow County, Georgia, Heritage Book. Cartersville, GA: Bartow County Genealogical Society, 1995. Unpgd.

Brooks County

Evans, Tad. *Brooks County, Georgia, Newspaper Clippings.* Savannah, GA: Author, 1995. Unpgd.

Bulloch County

Historical Records: New Hope United Methodist Church, Statesboro District, South Georgia Conference, 1842–1995. Statesboro, GA: New Hope Methodist Church, 1995. 168p.

Butler

Windham, Marilyn Neisler. *Marriages, Deaths, and etc. from the Butler (Georgia) Herald, 1876- 1896.* Warner Robins, GA: Central Georgia Genealogical Society, 1995. 226p.

Carroll County

Hageness, MariLee Beatty. *Index to Will Book A, 1852–1896, Carroll County, Georgia.* Author, 1995. 6p.

Clay County

Tatum, Max L. *Clay County, Georgia, Marriage Records.* Albany, GA: Author, 1995. 246p.

Cobb County

Cobb County, Georgia, Index to White Marriages, 1865–1937, and Index to Colored Marriages, 1865–1966. Marietta, GA: Cobb County Genealogical Society, 1995. 173p.

Columbia County

Sheahan, John J., Jr. *Military Markers and Data: Cemeteries Located in Columbia County, Georgia.* Author, 1995. 47p.

Cowetta County

Hageness, MariLee Beatty. *Letters of Guardianship, Book A, 1856–1879, Coweta County, Georgia.* Anniston, AL: Author, 1995. 34p.

Crawford County

Hageness, MariLee Beatty. *Index to Wills, 1835–1948, Crawford County, Georgia.* Anniston, AL: Author, 1995. 11p.

Dodge County

Saunders, Chester. *Cemeteries of Dodge County, Georgia, 1827–1989.* Warner Robbins, GA: Central Georgia Genealogical Society, 1995. 431p.

Elbert County

Hageness MariLee Beatty. *Early Inhabitants of Elbert County, Georgia.* Anniston, AL: Author, 1995. 39p.

Holloman, Ann C. *Elbert County, Georgia, Marriages, 1914–1949, Books H, I, J, K or White Persons (Alphabetically Separated by Bride and Groom).* Albany, GA: Author, 1995. Unpgd.

Fayette County

Austin, Jeannette Holland. *Fayette County, Georgia, Probate Records, 1824–1871.* Roswell, GA: Wolfe, 1995. 383p.

Floyd County

Kinney, Shirley F. *Floyd County, Georgia, Records: Vital Statistics, 1930–1940.* 2nd. ed. Rome, GA: SFK Genealogy, 1995. 128p.

Fort Valley

Hay, Guelda L. *Oaklawn Cemetery Fort Valley, Georgia, 1850–1993.* Warner Robins, GA: Central Georgia Genealogical Society, 1995. 177p.

Franklin County

Warren, Mary Bondurant. *Finding Aid for Franklin County, Georgia, Records.* Author, 1995. 18p.

———. *Franklin County, Georgia, Records: Court of Ordinary Minutes, Wafford Settlement, Bounty Land Warrants, 1800 Tax Book.* Author, 1995. 123p.

Gilmer County

Poteet Pitts, Jennie Vee. *Gilmer County, Georgia, Marriage Records, 1835 through 1960 Recorded in Volumes One through Eight.* Louisville, TN: V. H. Jones, 1995. 241p.

Greene County

Smith, Herschel W., Mrs. *Marriage Records of Greene County, Georgia (1787–1875) and Oglethorpe County, Georgia (1795–1852).* Baltimore, MD: Clearfield, 1995. 210p.

Henry County

Henry County, Georgia Obituaries, 1908–1929. Roswell, GA: W. H. Wolfe Associates, 1995. 386p.

Turner, Freda R. *1870 Census, Henry County, Georgia.* Roswell, GA: W. H. Wolfe Associates, 1995. 247p.

———. *Henry County, Georgia, 1821–1894, Marriage, Colored/Freedman Record of Sales, Inventory and Wills.* Roswell, GA: W. H. Wolfe Associates, 1995. 365p.

Jackson County

Hageness, MariLee Beatty. *Index to Minutes of Ordinary, 1796–1814, Jackson County, Georgia.* Author, 1995. 5p.

———. *Index to Miscellaneous Estates Book, 1796–1813, Jackson County, Georgia.* Anniston, AL: Author, 1995. 23p.

Jasper County

Warren, Mary Bondurant. *Randolph-Jasper County, Georgia, Records, Marriage Book A, 1811-1820, Court of Ordinary, 1807–1817.* Author, 1995. 79p.

Jones County

Hageness, MariLee Beatty. *Index, Ordinary Minutes, 1808–1814, Jones County, Georgia.* Author, 1995. 5p.

———. *Index to Will Books A thru D, Jones County, Georgia.* Author, 1995. 9p.

Lincoln County

Sheahan, John J., Jr. *Military Markers and Data: Cemeteries Located in Lincoln County, Georgia.* Author, 1995. 40p.

Linton

Culberson, Nancy B. *Darien Baptist Church Records, 1794–1862.* Milledgeville, GA: Boyd Pub. Co., 1995. 200p.

McDuffie County

Sheahan, John J., Jr. *Military Markers and Data: Cemeteries Located in McDuffie County, Georgia.* Author, 1995. 23p.

Macon County

Hay, Guelda L. *Cemeteries of Macon County, Georgia, 1836–1994.* Warner Robins, GA: Central Georgia Genealogical Society, 1995. 309p.

Monroe County

Hageness, MariLee Beatty. *Index to Will Book A & B, 1824–1860, Monroe County, Georgia.* Author, 1995. 6p.

Morgan County

Hageness, MariLee Beatty. *Name Index to Will Books, 1808–1860, Morgan County, Georgia.* Author, 1995. 9p.

Oglethorpe County

Cemeteries of Oglethorpe County, Georgia. Lexington, GA: Historic Oglethorpe County Inc., 1995. 305p.

Hageness, MariLee Beatty. *Revolutionary Soldiers, Widows and Orphans Drawing Land Lots in Oglethorpe County, Georgia, 3 February 1804. Ordinary's Office.* Author, 1995. 29p.

———. *A Testator's Index to Wills of Oglethorpe County, Georgia, 1794–1866.* Author, 1995. 12p.

Paulding County

Cemeteries of Paulding County, Georgia. Roswell, GA: W. H. Wolfe Associates, 1995. 281p.

Richter, Sue Bright. *1850 Federal Census, Paulding County, Georgia.* Madison, AL: Author, 1995. 206p.

———. *1870 Federal Census, Paulding County, Georgia.* Madison, AL: Author, 1995. 172p.

———. *Marriages, 1833–1899, of Paulding County, Georgia.* Madison, AL: Author, 1995. 149p.

Pickens County

Teague, Gene E., and Miranda E. Reece. *Cemeteries of Pickens County, Georgia.* Roswell, GA: W. H. Wolfe Associates, 1995. 401p.

Putnam County

Hageness, MariLee Beatty. *Members, Crooked Creek Primitive Baptist Church, Putnam County, Georgia.* Author, 1995. 12p.

Randolph County

Hageness, MariLee Beatty. *Index to Will Book B, Randolph County, Georgia.* Author, 1995. 6p.

Warren, Mary Bondurant. *Randolph-Jasper County, Georgia, Records, Marriage Book A, 1811-1820, Court of Ordinary, 1807–1817.* Author, 1995. 79p.

Richmond County

Sheahan, John J., Jr. *Military Markers and Data: Cemeteries Located in Richmond County, Georgia.* Author, 1995. 188p.

Screven County

Hageness, MariLee Beatty. *Index to Will Book I, 1810–1929, Screven County, Georgia.* Author, 1995. 8p.

Stewart County

Hageness, MariLee Beatty. *Some Wills and Estates, Stewart County, Georgia, Record Group 228-2–1, Georgia Department of Archives, Atlanta, Georgia.* Author, 1995. 20p.

Taylor County

Bethel Primitive Baptist Church, Taylor County, Georgia, the First 100 Years, 15 June 1838 to 14 August 1938. Warner Robbins, GA: Chronicles of Southern Heritage, 1995. 488p.

Warren County

Hageness, MariLee Beatty. *Abstracts of Will Book A, 1794–1810, Warren County, Georgia.* Anniston, AL: Author, 1995. 18p.

———. Index to Miscellaneous Estates, Inferior Court Minutes, 1794–1818, Warren County, Georgia. Author, 1995. 14p.

The Records of the Church at Williams Creek. Powder Springs, GA; Church of Christ, 1995. 176p.

Wilkes County

Sheahan, John J., Jr. *Military Markers and Data: Cemeteries Located in Wilkes County, Georgia.* Author, 1995. 40p.

Hawaii

Arakaki, Makoto. *Uchinanchu at Heart, the Persistence of Okinawan Identity in Hawaii.* Thesis (M.A.), University of California at Los Angeles, 1995. 76p.

Dictionary of Hawaiian Legal Land Terms. Honolulu, HI: University of Hawaii, 1995. 177p.

Fujii, Jocelyn K. *In the Lee of Hualalai, Historic Kaupulehu.* Kailua Kona, HI: Kaupulehu Makai Venture, 1995. 123p.

Guide to Records in the National Archives, Pacific Sierra Region. Washington, DC: National Archives and Records Administration, Pacific Sierra Region, 1995. 85p.

Iowa Pearl Harbor Survivors Book. Honolulu, HI: Pearl Harbor Survivors Association, 1995. 110p.

Kanahele, George S. *Waikiki, 100 BC to 1900 AD, an Untold Story.* Honolulu, HI: Queen Emma Foundation, 1995. 185p.

Moffat, Riley Moore. *Surveying the Mahele: Mapping the Hawaiian Land Revolution.* Honolulu, HI: Editions Unlimited, 1995. Unpgd.

Pacific Islander Americans, an Annotated Bibliography in the Social Sciences. Laie, HI: Institute For Polynesian Studies, Brigham Young University-Hawaii, 1995. 91p.

Saiki, Patsy Sumie. *Hawai no Nikkei Josei, Saisho no 100-nen. Japanese Women in Hawaii, the First 100 Years.* Tokyo: Shuei Shobo, 1995. 249p.

Sato, Tsunezo. *Hawai Imin Sato Tsunezo Shokan, Kindai Nihonjin Kaigai Imin Shiryo.* Tokyo: Keio Tsushin, 1995. 313p.

Spirit of Moiliili, Celebrating 50 Years, 1945–1995. Honolulu, HI: Moiliili Community Center, 1995. 23p.

Stewards of the Promise, the Heritage of the Latter-day Saints on the Hawaiian Islands of Maui, Molokai, and Lanai. Kahului, HI: Kahului Hawaii Stake, 1995. 112p.

Taminzoku Shakai ni Okeru Ibunka Koryu to Shakai Kozo no Hen'yo ni Kansuru Kenkyukai. *1920 Nendai Hawai Nikkeijin no Amerika-ka no Shoso.* Kyoto, Japan: Doshisha Daigaku Jinbun Kagaku Kenkyujo, 1995. 193p.

Where Pearls Flourished, Mo'olelo O Manana, the Story of Pearl City. Pearl City, HI: Pearl City High School Cultural Heritage Learning Center, 1995. 140p.

Idaho

Boise State University. Albertsons Library. *Checklist of Idaho Publications.* Boise, ID: Author, 1995. 253p.

Idaho Oral History Center. *Directory of Oral History Collections in Idaho.* Boise, ID: Idaho State Historical Society, 1995. 58p.

Mormon Americana: A Guide to Sources and Collections in the United States. Provo, UT: Brigham Young University Studies, 1995. 695p.

Boise

Friends of the Boise Public Library. *A Light in the Window of Idaho, Boise's Public Library, 1895–1995.* Boise, ID: Author, 1995. 143p.

Franklin County

Sorge, Martin K. *Lest We Forget, the Story of the Men and Women from Franklin County, Idaho, Who Served in the Second World War, 1939–1946.* Preston, ID: Author, 1995. 646p.

Jordan

Fretwell Johnson, Hazel R. Danner. *They Came to Jordan.* Filer, ID: Print Shoppe, 1995. 203p.

Lincoln County

100 Years Together, a Tribute to Lincoln County, Idaho's Centennial, 1895–1995. Shoshone, ID: Lincoln County Centennial Committee, 1995. 112p.

Nezperce

A Collection of Nezperce History and Memories, Nezperce, Idaho, 1895–1995. Nezperce, ID: Nezperce Centennial Committee, 1995. 508p.

Pocatello

Kissane, Leedice McAnelly. *Pocatello Memories, More Columns from the Idaho State Journal.* Pocatello, ID: Idaho State University Press, 1995. 185p.

Illinois

Births, Marriages and Deaths, 1900–1910, as Published in Paddock Publications, Arlington Heights, Illinois. Northwest Suburban Council of Genealogists, 1995. Unpgd.

Births, Marriages and Deaths, 1911–1915, as Published in Paddock Publications, Arlington Heights, Illinois. Northwest Suburban Council of Genealogists, 1995. Unpgd.

Larson, Carl V. *The Women of the Mormon Battalion.* Logan, UT: Author, 1995. 130p.

Mormon Americana: A Guide to Sources and Collections in the United States. Provo, UT: Brigham Young University Studies, 1995. 695p.

Quad City Heritage League Resource Guide: A Guide to Quad City Area Organizations Dedicated to Preserving the History and Heritage of the Quad Cities. Moline, IL: Quad City Heritage League, 1995. Unpgd.

Schlabach, LaVern. *Illinois Directory of Amish Communities and History of the Arthur Community, Ava Illinois Community, Pleasant Hills Community and Macomb Community since 1995.* 2nd. ed. Tuscola, IL: Author, 1995. 372p.

Whitney, Ellen M. *Illinois History: An Annotated Bibliography.* Westport, CT: Greenwood Press, 1995. 603p.

Ash Grove

Ash Grove Township Cemeteries. Watseka, IL: Iroquois County Genealogical Society, 1995. Unpgd.

Aurora

Chase, Wayne. *Early Burial Records from Sacred Heart Church, Aurora, Illinois, Also Known Then as the French Church.* Aurora, IL: Author, 1995. 6p.

Saint Paul's Lutheran Cemetery, Aurora, Illinois. Aurora, IL: A. Hansen, 1995. 2 vols.

Bond County

Hawley, Carlos. *1900 United States Census of Bond County, Illinois.* Greenville, IL: Bond County Genealogical Society, 1995. 305p.

———. *1910 United States Census of Bond County, Illinois.* Greenville, IL: Bond County Genealogical Society, 1995. 328p.

———. *1920 United States Census of Bond County, Illinois.* Greenville, IL: Bond County Genealogical Society, 1995. 311p.

Brown County

Pictorial History of Brown County, Illinois. Astoria, IL: Stevens Publishing, 1995. 900p.

Winters, Lisa. *1860 United States Census, Brown County, Illinois.* Decatur, IL: Author, 1995. 250p.

Cache
Sands Genealogists. *Cemeteries of Cache Township, Including Lower Cache, Johnson County, Illinois*. Vienna, IL: Jack K. Sistler, 1995. 111p.

Carbondale
Davis, Patricia S. *Index to Louise Morehouse's Death Records for Carbondale, Illinois, 1877–1952*. Marion, IL: Author, 1995. 155p.

Chicago
Abstracts of Funeral Programs, Patricia Liddell Researchers' Collection. Chicago, IL: Patricia Liddell Researchers, 1995. 48p.

Bohemian National Cemetery, Chicago, Illinois. Chicago, IL: Chicago Genealogical Society, 1995. Unpgd.

Novak, Joe. *Obituary Dates from the Denni Hlastel, 1930–1939*. Chicago, IL: Chicago Genealogical Society, 1995. 105p.

———. *Obituary Dates from the Denni Hlastel, 1940–1949*. Chicago, IL: Chicago Genealogical Society, 1995. 130p.

Cook County
Births, Marriages and Deaths, as Published in Paddock Publications, Arlington Heights, Illinois. Mt. Prospect, IL: Northwest Suburban Council of Genealogists, 1995. 84p.

Cumberland County
Cemetery Index·of Cumberland County, Illinois. Toledo, IL: Cumberland County Historical Society, 1995. Unpgd.

Cumberland County Interment List. Toledo, IL: Cumberland County Historical Society, 1995. Unpgd.

DuPage County
Births, Marriages and Deaths, as Published in Paddock Publications, Arlington Heights, Illinois. Mt. Prospect, IL: Northwest Suburban Council of Genealogists, 1995. 84p.

Effingham County
Delinquent Tax Records, 1845–1855, Effingham County, Illinois. Effingham, IL: Effingham County Genealogical Society, 1995. 83p.

Franklin County
Johnson, Janice. *Franklin County, Illinois, Land Records, Book C*. West Frankfort, IL: Author, 1995. 79p.

———. *Union Funeral Home Records, Books One thru Four, 1919–1924*. West Frankfort, IL: Author, 1995. 174p.

Pulliam, Carla. *Early Franklin County, Illinois, Birth Records*. Benton, IL: Author, 1995. 143p.

Hamilton County
Obituaries of Hamilton County, Illinois, 1926–1931. McLeansboro, IL: Hamilton County Historical Society, 1995. 473p.

Hardin County

Reynolds, Marion Lavender. *Hardin County, Illinois, Deaths, 1884–1919, and Notes from the Pleasant Hill Church Register*. Harrisburg, IL: Author, 1995. 177p.

Harrisburg

Schmook, Rebecca. *Obituaries, Harrisburg, Illinois, Newspapers, 1862–1916*. Harrisburg, IL: Saline County Genealogical Society, 1995. 173p.

Iroquois County

Ash Grove Township Cemeteries. Watseka, IL: Iroquois County Genealogical Society, 1995. Unpgd.

Johnson County

Davis, Patricia S. *Index to Parker's History (Cemeteries) of Johnson County, Illinois*. Marion, IL: Author, 1995. 153p.

Honea, Barbara May. *A History of Johnson County, Illinois, Index*. Amarillo, TX: Author, 1995. 209p.

Sands Genealogists. *Johnson County Commissioner's Records Book B*. Vienna, IL: Jack K. Sistler, 1995. 94p.

Lake County

Lake County, Illinois, Map of 1873: Landowner's Index. Libertyville, IL: Lake County, Illinois Genealogical Society, 1995. 49p.

1900 Census, Lake County, Illinois, Vol. 8, Waukegan Township. Mundelein, IL: Lake County Genealogical Society, 1995. 253p.

Lake Forest

Lake Forest Cemetery Burial Book. Lake Forest, IL: Lake Forest/Lake Bluff Historical Society, 1995. 112p.

Lawrence County

Lawrence County, Illinois, 175th Anniversary, 1821–1996. Paducah, KY: Turner Publishing, 1995. 352p.

McLean County

Naturalization Abstracts, McLean County, Illinois, 1853–1955, with Hidden Surname Index. Normal, IL: McLean County Genealogical Society, 1995. 7 vols.

Macoupin County

Bradley, Littleton P. *Index to Macoupin County Memories, a Pictorial History of Macoupin County, Illinois*. Ferguson, MO: Author, 1995. 8p.

Madison County

Wasser, Elsie M. *1855 Census, Madison County, Illinois*. Author, 1995. 124p.

Marion County

History and Families, Marion County, Illinois. Paducah, KY: Turner Publishing, 1995. 304p.

Marissa
Jones, Elda McCormick. *64 Years of Funeral Home Records*. Marissa, IL: Marissa Historical and Genealogical Society, 1995. 113p.

Milford
Milford Township Cemeteries. Watseka, IL: Iroquois County Genealogical Society, 1995. Unpgd.

Morrisonville
St. Maurice Parish, Morrisonville, Illinois, Quasiquincentennial Edition, 1870–1995. Mt. Vernon, IN: Windmill Publications, 1995. 194p.

Murphysboro
Thieme Funeral Home Records, 1924–1942, Murphysboro, Illinois, 5 November 1924–13 May 1929, and Springfield, Missouri, 5 July 1929-5 January 1942. Springfield, MO: Ozarks Genealogical Society, 1995. 150p.

Ogle County
Jacobs, Leonard J. *Early Ogle County*. Oregon, IL: Author, 1995. Unpgd.

Onarga
Onarga Mortality Records: A Collection of Records. Elgin, IL: P. D. Goff, 1995. 223p.

Palatine
Murray, Joan England. *Palatine in 1929: A Biographical Directory of Those Residents Living in the Village of Palatine, Cook County, Illinois, in 1929*. Palatine, IL: Palatine Historical Society, 1995. 196p.

Peoria County
Forgotten Residents of Peoria State Hospital. Peoria, IL: Peoria County Genealogical Society, 1995. 190p.
Lutheran Cemetery Gravestone Inscriptions. Peoria, IL: Peoria County Genealogical Society, 1995. 610p.
Princeville Township Cemeteries. Peoria, IL: Peoria County Genealogical Society, 1995. 106p.
Obituaries, Miscellaneous Peoria Area Newspapers, 1953–1975. Peoria, IL: Peoria County Genealogical Society, 1995. 199p.
Peoria Township Columbariums. Peoria, IL: Peoria County Genealogical Society, 1995. 19p.

Pike County
Ivarson, Darlene. *Biographies of the Villages of Pike County*. AmeriCorps Rural Development Team, 1995. Unpgd.
Pike County, Illinois, Schools, 1823–1995, History and Pictures. Mt. Vernon, IN: Windmill Publications, 1995. 415p.

Pope County
Allen, Ricky T. *Pope County, Illinois, Early Census Records, 1818–1850*. Golconda, IL: Author, 1995. 289p.

Randolph County

Crowder, Lola Frazer. *County, Illinois, Death, 1877 through 1889*. Author, 1995. 148p.

———. *Randolph, County, Illinois, Marriages, 1807 through 1850*. Author, 1995. 31p.

Rockford

Records of Court Street Methodist Episcopal Church, Rockford, Illinois, 1854–1925. Rockford, IL: Kishwaukee Genealogists, 1995. 428p.

Willwood Burial Park. Rockford, IL: North Central Illinois Genealogical Society, 1995. 323p.

Rock Island

Index for the Memorial Park Cemetery Burials, April 1926-April 1982, 30th Street and Blackhawk Road, Rock Island, Illinois. Rock Island, IL: Blackhawk Genealogical Society, 1995. 89p.

The Memorial Park Cemetery, 30th Street and Blackhawk Road, Rock Island, Illinois, 61201, Burials, April 1926-April 1982, Sexton's Books One and Two (Earliest Death Date, 1878–Reprinted). Rock Island, IL: Blackhawk Genealogical Society, 1995. 402p.

Sangamon County

Sangamon County Deed and Miscellaneous Record Index, 1822–1832. Springfield, IL: Sangamon County Genealogical Society, 1995. 94p.

Stockland

Sugar Creek Chapel Cemetery. Watseka, IL: Iroquois County Genealogical Society, 1995. 54p.

Udina

Ghrist, John Russell. *Junction 20, the Story of Udina*. Dundee, IL: JRG Communications, 1995. 278p.

Union County

Union County, Illinois, Probate Records, 1818–1845. Anna, IL: Reppert Publications, 1995. 95p.

Vermillion County

1880 Federal Population Census. Vermillion County, Illinois. Danville, IL: Illiana Genealogical and Historical Society, 1995. 3 vols.

Vermillion County, Illinois, 1920 Census Index. Danville, IL: Illiana Genealogical and Historical Society, 1995. 267p.

Virden

Bradley, Littleton P. *Virden, Illinois, 1920 Federal Census*. Ferguson, MO: Author, 1995. 175p.

Warren

Matl, Fran H. *Warren, Illinois, Elmwood Cemetery Inscriptions, Elmwood Cemetery Interments, St. Ann Cemetery Inscriptions, Church Histories*. Shullsburg, WI: Author, 1995. 139p.

Warren Cemetery Tombstone Inscriptions and Burial Records, Warren Township, Lake County, Illinois. Libertyville, IL: Lake County Genealogical Society, 1995. 208p.

White County

Davis, Patricia S. *Index to Harriet Vaught's Early Land Grants of White County, Illinois, 1814–1854, and Probate Index, 1818–1976.* Marion, IL: Author, 1995. 128p.

―――. *White County, Illinois, Marriages, 1816–1865.* Marion, IL: Author, 1995. 171p.

Williamson County

Lind, Helen Sutt. *Those Left Behind, Cemeteries in the Crab Orchard National Wildlife Refuge, Williamson County, Illinois.* Johnson City, IL: Author, 1995. 90p.

Wilmette

Wilmette Memorial. Wilmette, IL: C. L. Whitehand, 1995. 2 vols.

Winnebago County

Winnebago History Writers. *We Remember People of Our Past. Volume IV, Based on Area Obituaries of Burritt, Seward, and Winnebago Townships, Southwestern Winnebago County, Illinois.* Winnebago, IL: Author, 1995. 294p.

Indiana

African American Resources at the Indiana State Library and Historical Building. Indianapolis, IN: Indiana State Library, 1995. 11p.

Midwest Area Chinese American Resource Guide. Greencastle, IN: Chinese American Librarians Association, 1995. 95p.

Mikesell, Shirley Keller. *Early Settlers of Indiana's Gore, 1803–1820.* Bowie, MD: Heritage Books, 1995. 405p.

Rudolph, L. C. *Hoosier Faiths: A History of Indiana Churches and Religious Groups.* Bloomington, IN: Indiana University Press, 1995. 710p.

Bartholomew County

Stultz, Carolyne J. *Marriage Supplements of Bartholomew County, Indiana, 1882–1920.* Danville, IN: Author, 1995. 2 vols.

Blackford County

World War II, Blackford County Remembers. Blackford County, IN: Blackford County Historical Society, 1995. 84p.

Cass County

1850 Census, Cass County, Indiana. Mt. Vernon, IN: Windmill Publications, 1995. 195p.

Clark County
Pleasant Ridge Cemetery, 1995. Borden, IN: Paul E. & A. Coffman, 1995. 63p.

Dearborn County
Harper, Lois. *Delayed Birth Records at Dearborn County, Indiana*. Apollo, PA: Closson Press, 1995. 67p.

De Kalb County
Harter, Fayne E. *Birth Records of De Kalb County, Indiana, 1891–1993*. Ft. Wayne, IN: Author, 1995. 309p.
———. *Death Records of De Kalb County, Indiana, 1891–1993*. Ft. Wayne, IN: Author, 1995. 240p.

Dubois County
Dubois County, Indiana Cemeteries and Inscriptions. Jasper, IN: Dubois County Genealogical Society, 1995. Unpgd.

Elkhart
Skwiercz, Andrew L. *Index to the Records of the Dale White Funeral Home, Elkhart, Indiana, 1929–1993*. Elkhart, IN: Elkhart County Genealogical Society, 1995. 105p.

Elkhart County
Johnson, Patricia K. *Subject Index to the Michiana Searcher, Volumes 1–226, 1969–1994, Quarterly of Elkhart County Geneaological Society, Elkhart County, Indiana*. Elkhart, IN: Elkhart County Genealogical Society, 1995. 18p.

Elwood
Simmons, Ranny J. *St. Joseph Cemetery Records, 1891–1991, Elwood, Indiana*. Elwood, IN: Author, 1995. 110p.

Floyd County
Mt. Eden Cemetery. Borden, IN: Paul E. & A. Coffman, 1995. 15p.

Fort Wayne
A User's Guide to the Fort Wayne Holdings: The Indiana Jewish Historical Society. Fort Wayne, IN: Indiana Jewish Genealogical Society, 1995. 45p.

Grant County
Kirkpatrick, Ralph D. *Back Creek Friends Cemetery Burial Records*. Bowie, MD: Heritage Books, 1995. 130p.

Hamilton County
Mattingly, John R. *Spencer Cemetery (Adams Township) Hamilton County, Indiana*. Frankfort, IN: Author, 1995. Unpgd.

Hammond
Oak Hill Cemetery Reading. South Holland, IN: South Suburban Genealogical and Historical Society, 1995. 266p.

Howard County

Sheagley, Patricia Sue Bingaman. *1880 Census Index for Howard County, Indiana*. Kokomo, IN: Kokomo-Howard County Public Library, Genealogy Department, 1995. 197p.

Jackson County

1850 Jackson County, Indiana, U.S. Federal Census. Danville, IN: Stultz Computer Services, 1995. 213p.

Johnson, Jonette K. *Jackson County, Indiana, Obituaries 1886–1890*. Bowie, MD: Heritage Books, 1995. 187p.

Jay County

Schindler, Gloria. *J. L. Baird Funeral Home Records, Jay County, Indiana*. Author, 1995. Unpgd.

Jefferson County

Geraets, Gertrude. *Index to a History of Jefferson County, Indiana*. Author, 1995. Unpgd.

Jennings County

Hurley, Phyllis. *The Way They Were, Jennings County, Indiana, Based on Research of Old Newspapers*. Author, 1995. 96p.

Knox County

Caballero, Conrad A. *1880 Census, Knox County, Indiana*. Vincennes, IN: Northwest Territory Genealogical Society, 1995. 516p.

Lafayette

Zook, Haroldyne Schultz. *Knights of Pythias-I.O.O.F. Cemetery, Lafayette Township, Madison County, Indiana*. 70p.

Lake County

Ross Township and Winfield Township Cemeteries, Lake County, Indiana. Valparaiso, IN: Northwest Indiana Genealogical Society, 1995. Unpgd.

Lawrence County

History of Lawrence County, Indiana, 1818–1995. Paducah, KY: Turner Publishing, 1995. 264p.

Richmond, Edna King. *Huron Baptist Church Records, 1883–1892, Lawrence County, Indiana, Spice Valley Township (Formerly Beaver Creek Baptist Church)*. Author, 1995. 33p.

Lawrence County, Indiana, Cemeteries. Bedford, IN: Jay Wilson, 1995. 2 vols.

Madison County

U.S. Bureau of the Census. *1830–1840 U.S. Census, Madison County, Indiana*. Wichita, KS: S. K. Publications, 1995. Unpgd.

Marion County

Obituary Index, 1967–1993, Marion, Indiana, Newspapers. Marion, IN: Marion Public Library, 1995. 7 vols.

Martin County

Martin County, Death Index, 1882–1989. Loogootee, IN: Martin County Genealogical Society, 1995. 180p.

Morgan County

McGuire, Donald H. *An Abstract of Births, Deaths, Marriages, etc. from the Martinsville Republican, Morgan County, Indiana (1888–1890)*. Mooresville, IN: Author, 1995. 225p.

Ohio County

Dorrell, Dillon R. *Burials in Ohio County, April 1, 1985 to January 1, 1995*. Rising Sun, IN: Ohio County Historical Society, 1995. 21p.

Owen County

Combined Marriage Books, Owen County, Indiana, 1819–1850: A Merged Index to the First Three Marriage Records. Owen County, IN: Owen County Historical and Genealogical Society, 1995. 71p.

Perry County

Lest We Forget about Rural Schools of Perry County. Perry County, IN: Perry County Retired Teachers' Association, 1995. 205p.

Manley, Kris. *Perry County, Indiana, Wills, Divorces, St. Augustine Baptismals*. Chrisney, IN: Newspaper Abstracts, 1995. 221p.

Pike County

Ooley, Lynne Walters. *Copies of Press Dispatch Obituaries, Pike County, Indiana*. Winslow, IA: Author, 1995. Unpgd.

Portage

Calvary Cemetery, 2701 Willowdale Road, Portage, Indiana, 1914–1995, Portage Township, Porter County, Indiana. Valparaiso, IN: Northwest Indiana Genealogical Society, 1995. 363p.

Portage Township Cemeteries. Valparaiso, IN: Northwest Indiana Genealogical Society, 1995. Unpgd.

Saint John

Payonk, Joseph L. *Liber Defunctorum, St. John Evangelical Church, St. John, Indiana, Index of Death and Burial Records*. 1995. 67p.

Saint Joseph County

Eisen, David. *Vital Statistics Index to Saint Joseph County, Indiana, Newspapers, 1831–1912*. South Bend, IN: Northern Indiana Historical Society, 1995. 2 vols.

Salem

Harlen, Willie. *St. Patrick Cemetery and the Catholic Church in Salem, Indiana*. Evansville, IN: Evansville Bindery, 1995. 201p.

Sellersburg

St. Paul United Church of Christ Records and History, 1891–1995. Sellerburg, IN: Church, 1995. 2 vols.

Spencer County

Patmore, Sharon. *Spencer County, Indiana, Miscellaneous Records #2.* Chrisney, IN: Newspaper Abstracts, 1995. 227p.

Tipton County

Henry, Marietta F. *Tipton County, Indiana, Marriage Records, Data, 1871–1905.* Kokomo, IN: Selby Pub., 1995. 464p.

Wabash County

Wabash County, Indiana, Marriages, 1835–1899. Warsaw, IN: Scheuer Publications, 1995. 194p.

Warren

Harris, Lillie Alberson. *H. Brown and Son, Warren, Indiana, Funeral Home Records, 1891–1990.* Warren, IN: Bergman, Glancy, H. Brown and Son, 1995. 2 vols.
———. *Ira Brown Funeral Director, Warren, Indiana, Journal and Coffin Records.* Warren, IN: Bergman, Glancy, H. Brown and Son, 1995. 37p.

Washington County

Burns, Clara Marie. *Affidavits and Consents for Persons Making Application for Marriage License in Washington County, Indiana, Years 1844–1877.* Evansville Bindery, 1995. 539p.

Wayne County

Dean, Arnold L. *Early Naturalization Records, Wayne County, Indiana, prior to 1906.* Richmond, IN: Author, 1995. Unpgd.
———. *Early Wayne County, Indiana, Probate and Will Index, Probate prior to 1855, Wills Prior to 1860.* Richmond, IN: Author, 1995. Unpgd.

Iowa

Celebrate Iowa's History of Diversity. Des Moines, IA: The Commission, 1995. 63p.
Frontier Genealogy: Special Sources and Techniques for Tracing Your Pioneer Ancestors. Topeka, KS; Topeka Genealogical Society, 1995. 76p.

Kelly, Anne C. *Iowa History and Culture, a Bibliography of Materials Published from 1987 through 1991.* Iowa City, IA: State Historical Society of Iowa, 1995. 29p.

Mormon Americana: A Guide to Sources and Collections in the United States. Provo, UT: Brigham Young University Studies, 1995. 695p.

Penkake, Marie C. *Privacy in Adoption, Iowa's History, an Historical Study of the Information Policy Relative to the Issue of Sealed Adoption Records in Iowa.* Thesis (M.A.), Drake University, 1995. 143p.

Quad City Heritage League Resource Guide: A Guide to Quad City Area Organizations Dedicated to Preserving the History and Heritage of the Quad Cities. Moline, IL: Quad City Heritage League, 1995. Unpgd.

Ruth, Amy. *Newspapers in Iowa History: A Bibliography and Research Guide.* Thesis (M.A.), University of Iowa, 1995. 87p.

Bear Grove

Foresman, Sherry. *Cemetery Records, Bear Grove Township, Guthrie County, Iowa.* Menlo, IA: Author, 1995. Unpgd.

Calhoun County

Calhoun County Pioneer History: A Sesquicentennial Slice for a County with One Traffic Light. Lohrville, IA: M. O. Black, 1995. 64p.

Carroll County

Greene County, Iowa, History, Index to Greene Section of the Biographical and Historical Record for Green and Carroll Counties, 1887. Des Moines, IA: Iowa Genealogical Society, 1995. 48p.

Cedar County

Cedar County, Iowa, Deaths, Death Record Book 2, October 1897–1909. Des Moines, IA: Iowa Genealogical Society, 1995. 24p.

Dallas County

Dallas County, Iowa, Births. Des Moines, IA: Iowa Genealogical Society, 1995. Unpgd.

Davenport

Scott County, Iowa, Newspapers, Abstracted Names, Davenport Democrat, 1899. Des Moines, IA: Iowa Genealogical Society, 1995. 45p.

Des Moines County

Des Moines County, Iowa, Births, Delayed Birth Index. Des Moines, IA: Iowa Genealogical Society, 1995. Unpgd.

Des Moines County, Iowa, History, Index to Des Moines County Biographic Review, 1905. Des Moines, IA: Iowa Genealogical Society, 1995. 139p.

Dubuque County

Linwood Cemetery Interments, 1868-September 1875, and Linwood Cemetery Association Burials, September 1875–1890. Dubuque, IA: Dubuque County—Key City Genealogical Society, 1995. Unpgd.

Greene County

Greene County, Iowa, History, Index to Greene Section of the Biographical and Historical Record for Green and Carroll Counties, 1887. Des Moines, IA: Iowa Genealogical Society, 1995. 48p.

Guthrie County

Foresman, Sherry. *Guthrie County, Iowa, Records.* Menlo, IA: Author, 1995. Unpgd.

Hamilton County

Hamilton County, Iowa, Newspaper Index to Hamilton County Journal. Des Moines, IA: Iowa Genealogical Society, 1995. Unpgd.

Jasper County

Jasper and Marshall Counties, Iowa, Military, Every Name Index to Honor Roll, Jasper County, 1917–1918–1919, and Marshall County in the World War, 1917–1918. Des Moines, IA: Iowa Genealogical Society, 1995. 30p.

Jefferson County

Baird, Verda Johnson. *Jefferson County, Iowa, 77 Cemeteries, 21,380 Burials, 1839-December 1990, 3,590 Have No Stones.* Fairfield, IA: Author, 1995. 475p.

Jefferson County, Iowa, Census, 1840 Federal Census. Des Moines, IA: Iowa Genealogical Society, 1995. 50p.

Jefferson County, Iowa, Deaths, Mortality Listings of Dr. J. M. Shaffer, 1852–1862. Des Moines, IA: Iowa Genealogical Society, 1995. 17p.

Johnson County

Johnson County, Iowa, Naturalization, Declaration of Intent to Become a Citizen Books, Naturalization Book, 1857–1872, Naturalization Book, 1855–1887. Des Moines, IA: Iowa Genealogical Society, 1995. 32p.

Keokuk County

Keokuk County, Iowa, Deaths Index, 1880–1907. Des Moines, IA: Iowa Genealogical Society, 1995. 49p.

Louisa County

Louisa County, Iowa, History, Every Name Index to Volume 2 of 1913 History of Louisa County. Des Moines, IA: Iowa Genealogical Society, 1995. 96p.

Manti

Jeckel, Nancy K. *Manti, Iowa, a Frontier Settlement in the Lower Nishnabotna River Valley, 1846–1880.* Thesis (M.A.), University of Nebraska at Omaha, 1995. 212p.

Marshall County

Jasper and Marshall Counties, Iowa, Military, Every Name Index to Honor Roll, Jasper County, 1917–1918–1919, and Marshall County in the World War, 1917–1918. Des Moines, IA: Iowa Genealogical Society, 1995. 30p.

Pottawattamie County

Pottawattamie/Shelby Counties, Iowa, Naturalizations, Avoca (Pottawattamie), 1907–1929, Harlan (Shelby), 1854–1930. Des Moines, IA: Iowa Genealogical Society, 1995. 89p.

Ringgold County

Banner, Raymond V. *Ringgold County, Iowa: Bibliography and Resource Guide to History and Genealogy.* Mount Ayr, IA: Author, 1995. 73p.

Scott County

Scott County, Iowa Genealogical Society. *Index of Scott County, Iowa, Probates and Wills, 1835- 1928.* Davenport, IA: Author, 1995. 52p.

Scott County, Iowa, Newspapers, Abstracted Names, Davenport Democrat, 1899. Des Moines, IA: Iowa Genealogical Society, 1995. 45p.

Shelby County

Pottawattamie/Shelby Counties, Iowa, Naturalizations, Avoca (Pottawattamie), 1907–1929, Harlan (Shelby), 1854–1930. Des Moines, IA: Iowa Genealogical Society, 1995. 89p.

Shenandoah

Ingrim, Carol Johnson. *Rose Hill Cemetery, Shenandoah, Page County, Iowa.* Author, 1995. 508p.

Union County

Union County Marriage Index. Clearfield, IA: Rootbound Publishing, 1995. 3 vols.

Wapello County

Wapello County, Iowa, Church, St. Mary's Catholic Baptisms, January 1879-30 December 1885. Des Moines, IA: Iowa Genealogical Society, 1995. 37p.

Webster County

Webster County, Iowa, Marriages, Marriage Index. Des Moines, IA: Iowa Genealogical Society, 1995. Unpgd.

Webster County, Iowa, Newspapers, Dayton Review, 1930. Des Moines, IA: Iowa Genealogical Society, 1995. 53p.

Kansas

Frontier Genealogy: Special Sources and Techniques for Tracing Your Pioneer Ancestors. Topeka, KS: Topeka Genealogical Society, 1995. 76p.

Krehbiel, James W. *Swiss Russian Mennonite Families before 1874*. Elverson, PA: Olde Spring-
    field Shoppe, 1995. 332p.
Land Records and Sources. Topeka, KS: Kansas State Historical Society, 1995. Unpgd.
Ostertag, John and Enid Ostertag. *Weekly Kansas Chief Births, Marriages, Deaths and Other
    News Items and Current Events from 1890 to 1891, Volume 7*. St. Joseph, MO: Author,
    1995. 218p.
Shortridge, James R. *Peopling the Plains: Who Settled Where in Frontier Kansas*. Lawrence,
    KS: University Press of Kansas, 1995. 254p.

Abilene
Early Recollections and Personal Reminiscences of Abilene in 1800s. Abilene, KS: Dickinson
    County Historical Society, 1995. 108p.

Admire
Hodge, Robert A. *Index to the Admire, Kansas Newspapers, 1887–1893*. Emporia, KS: Author,
    1995. Unpgd.

Allen
Hodge, Robert A. *Index to the Allen Weekly Herald, 1854–1897*. Emporia, KS: Author, 1995.
    67p.

Americus
Hodge, Robert A. *Index to the Americus Ledger, 1885–1889*. Emporia, KS: Author, 1995. 67p.

Belle Plaine
Brummett, Barbara Hunt. *Belle Plaine Cemetery, a Record of the Tombstones as of April, 1995*.
    Belle Plaine, KS: Author, 1995. Unpgd.

Brown County
Ostertag, John A. *Township Maps of Brown County, Kansas, 1887*. St. Joseph, MO: Author,
    1995. Unpgd.

Chase County
Hull, Julis McCabe. *Chase County, Kansas, 1994 Obituaries, the Leader-News, Cottonwood
    Falls, Kansas, and Chase County Pioneer, Cottonwood Falls, Kansas*. Dodge City, KS:
    Author, 1995. Unpgd.

Emporia
Hodge, Robert A. *Index to the Emporia Democrat, 1882–1886*. Emporia, KS: Author, 1995.
    94p.

Greenwood County
Hodge, Robert A. *Index to the Fall River Times, Pioneer and Every Pioneer*. Emporia, KS:
    Author, 1995. 17p.

Halstead

Unruh, Mae. *The People of Grace*. Author, 1995. 239p.

Harvey County

Harvey County, Kansas, Marriage License Index, 1872-April 1913. North Newton, KS: Mennonite Library and Archives, Bethel College, 1995. 264p.

Kearny County

Barnes, Betty. *Diggin' Up Bones, Obituaries of Lakin and Hartland Cemeteries, Kearny County, Kansas*. Bowie, MD: Heritage Books, 1995. 2 vols.

Leavenworth County

Leavenworth County, Kansas, Naturalization Records, 1855–1954. Leavenworth, KS: Leavenworth County Genealogical Society, 1995. 81p.

Lyon County

Hodge, Robert A. *Index to Seven Lyon County Newspapers*. Emporia, KS: Author, 1995. Unpgd.
———. *An Index to Volumes 1–10 of the Flint Hills Genealogical Society Newsletter*. Emporia, KS: Author, 1995. Unpgd.

Montgomery County

History and Families, Montgomery County, Kansas. Paducah, KY: Turner, 1995. 352p.

Nemaha County

Ostertag, Enid. *The Corning Gazette of Nemaha County, Kansas, September 1898 to November 1902, Births, Marriages, Deaths, Everyday Events*. Seneca, KS: Nemaha County Genealogical Society, 1995. 218p.

Neosho Rapids

Hodge, Robert A. *Indexes Neosho Rapids, Kansas, Newspapers, 1885–1891*. Emporia, KS: Author, 1995. Unpgd.

Reading

Hodge, Robert A. *An Index to the Reading, Kansas, Advance and the Prohibition Echo, 1893-1895*. Emporia, KS: Author, 1995. 31p.

Sedgewick County

Bennington, Bill. *Sedgewick County, Kansas, Marriages, Books Q through T, January 18, 1913 to September 21, 1917*. Wichita, KS: Midwest Historical and Genealogical Society, 1995. 214p.
———. *Sedgewick County, Kansas, Marriages, Books U through X, September 22, 1917 to August 4, 1920*. Wichita, KS: Midwest Historical and Genealogical Society, 1995. 185p.

Sumner County

Shafer, Melvin D. *Index to Land Patents of Sumner County, Kansas*. Haysville, KS: Author, 1995. 104p.

Kentucky

Kentucky Adjutant General's Office. *Kentucky Soldiers of the War of 1812, with an Added Index*. Baltimore, MD: Clearfield, 1891, 1969, 1995. 436p.

Kentucky Honor Roll of Ancestors. Owensboro, KY: West Central Kentucky Family Research Association, 1995. 278p.

Page, Patsy R. *Directory of Kentucky Dentists, 1904*. Alachua, FL: Page Publications, 1995. 7p.

Sifakis, Stewart. *Compendium of the Confederate Armies Series: Kentucky, Maryland, Missouri, the Confederate Units and the Indian Units*. NY: Facts on File, 1995. 240p.

Sistler, Barbara. *1850 Census, Central Kentucky, Counties of Boyle, Casey, Green, Lincoln, Marion, Mercer, Rockcastle and Taylor*. Nashville, TN: Barbara Sistler & Associates, 1995. 452p.

———. *1850 Census, East Central Kentucky, Counties of Clark, Estill, Fayette, Garrard, Jessamine, Madison, Montgomery and Owsley*. Nashville, TN: Barbara Sistler & Associates, 1995. 563p.

———. *1850 Census, North Central Kentucky, Counties of Anderson, Bullitt, Franklin, Nelson, Shelby, Spencer, Washington and Woodford*. Nashville, TN: Barbara Sistler & Associates, 1995. 574p.

———. *1850 Census, North East Kentucky, Counties of Bath, Bourbon, Fleming, Lewis, Mason and Nicholas*. Nashville, TN: Barbara Sistler & Associates, 1995. 550p.

———. *1850 Census, West Central Kentucky, Counties of Breckenridge, Butler, Edmonson, Grayson, Hancock, Hardin, Hart, LaRue and Meade*. Nashville, TN: Barbara Sistler & Associates, 1995. 486p.

Sprague, Stuart. *Kentucky Black Genealogy*. Clearfield, KY: Author, 1995. Unpgd.

Adair County

England, Beverly A. *1900 Census of Adair County, Kentucky*. Columbia, KY: Author, 1995. 395p.

Allen County

Smith, David C. *Minutes of the Trammel Fork Baptist Church, 1819–1994, Allen County, Kentucky*. Pembroke, KY: Author, 1995. 339p.

Bath County

Nagle, Eric C. *Local Vital Records from Newspapers of Bath County, Kentucky, 1884–1910*. Dayton, OH: Ford and Nagle, 1995. 178p.

Bourbon County

Bourbon County, Kentucky, Court Orders, 1786–1793, an Every Name Index. Miami Beach, FL: T. L. C. Genealogy, 1995. 90p.

Bracken County

Leming, John E. *Bracken County, Kentucky, Obituaries*. Brooksville, KY: Bracken County Historical Society, 1995. Unpgd.

Caldwell County

Jerome, Brenda Joyce. *Caldwell County, Kentucky, Will Book B, 1835–1889*. Newburgh, IN: Author, 1995. 142p.

Calloway County

Brown, Elizabeth. *Calloway County, Kentucky, Vital Statistics, 1874–1878*. Melber, KY: Simmons Historical Publications, 1995. 73p.

Simmons, Don. *Calloway County, Kentucky, Newspaper Genealogical Abstracts, Volume 6*. Melber, KY: Simmons Historical Publications, 1995. 72p.

Stilley, Van A. *Calloway County, Kentucky, Census of 1850*. Melber, KY: Simmons Historical Publications, 1995. 78p.

Willis, Laura. *Calloway County, Kentucky, Wills and Administrations*. Melber, KY: Simmons Historical Publications, 1995. 95p.

Carlisle County

Graves, Ran. *History and Memories of Carlisle County*. Carlisle County, KY: Chamber of Commerce, 1995. 92p.

Clark County

Clark, Thomas Dionysius. *Clark County, Kentucky, a History*. Winchester, KY: Clark County Historical Society, 1995. 445p.

Clinton County

Gorin, Sandra Kaye Laughery. *Clear Fork Baptist Church of Clinton (Formerly Cumberland) County, Kentucky, 1802–1902*. Glasgow, KY: Gorin Genealogical Pub., 1995. 240p.

Edmonson County

Rajewich, Kathleen. *Population Census of Edmonson County, Kentucky*. Brownsville, KY: Author, 1995. 2 vols.

Estill County

Wise, William E. *1920 Estill County, Kentucky, Census*. Ravenna, KY: Author, 1995. 166p.

Fleming County

Curotto, Caren D. *Eden's Chapel Graveyard, Fleming County, Kentucky*. Springdale, KY: P. McAlister, 1995. 52p.

Geary County

Samuelsen, W. David. *Geary County, Kansas, 1898–1923, Index to Willbooks*. Salt Lake City, UT: Sampubco, 1995. 9p.

Graves County

Simmons, Don. *Graves County, Kentucky, Newspaper Genealogical Abstracts, Volume 52*. Melber, KY: Simmons Historical Publications, 1995. 72p.

Willis, Laura. *Graves County, Kentucky, Tax Lists, 1834–1835–1837*. Melber, KY: Simmons Historical Publications, 1995. 71p.

———. *Graves County, Kentucky, Tax Lists, 1839 and 1840*. Melber, KY: Simmons Historical Publications, 1995. 49p.

Grayson County

Dennis, Lennie C. *Grayson County, Kentucky, 1900 Federal Census*. Lewisburg, KY: Author, 1995. 274p.

Greenup County

Phillips, Patricia Porter. *Greenup County, Kentucky, Naturalizations, Revolutionary War Pensions, Lunacy Inquests, 1804–1902*. Bowie, MD: Heritage Books, 1995. 182p.

Hart County

Gorin, Sandra Kaye Laughery. *Hart County, Kentucky, Vital Statistics, Death Records*. Glasgow, KY: Gorin Genealogical Pub., 1995. 109p.

———. *Hart County, Kentucky, Vital Statistics, 4,607 Birth Records*. Glasgow, KY: Gorin Genealogical Pub., 1995. 214p.

Hawley, Carlos. *Hart County, Kentucky, 1900 Census*. Greenville, IL: Bond County Genealogical Society, 1995. 338p.

Hickman County

Willis, Laura. *Hickman County, Kentucky, Deeds*. Melber, KY: Simmons Historical Publications, 1995. 3 vols.

———. *Hickman County, Kentucky, Will Books. Volume 2 (1834–1838)*. Melber, KY: Simmons Historical Publications, 1995. 95p.

Hopkins County

Cox, Evelyn M. *Hopkins County, Kentucky, Tax Lists, 1807, Marriages, 1807–1868*. Madisonville, KY: Author, 1995. 99p.

Jefferson County

1850 Census of Louisville Districts 1 and 2, Jefferson County, Kentucky. Louisville, KY: Louisville Genealogical Society, 1995. Unpgd.

Lancaster

Arnold, Cecil Benjamin. *Cemetery Records of Lancaster, Kentucky, 1857–1994*. Lancaster, KY: Author, 1995. 323p.

Laurel County

Marriage Book AA, Laurel County, Kentucky, 1826–1853. Rev. London, KY: Laurel County Historical Society, 1995. 33p.

Lawrence County

Lawrence County, Kentucky, Cemeteries. Paintsville, KY: T. M. C. Printing, 1995. 118p.

Muncy, Opal Mae Hughes. *Lawrence County, Kentucky, Marriage Register, Volume Number 8 and 9, 1883–1887*. Louisa, KY: Author, 1995. 90p.

Letcher County

Johnson, Wilma Parker. *1870 U.S. Census, Letcher County, Kentucky*. Whitesburg, KY: Letcher County Historical and Genealogical Society, 1995. 166p.

———. *1880 U.S. Census, Letcher County, Kentucky*. Whitesburg, KY: Letcher County Historical and Genealogical Society, 1995. 270p.

Logan County

Logan County, Kentucky, Union Soldiers, 1861–1865. Russellville, KY: Logan County Genealogical Society, 1995. Unpgd.

Simmons, Don and Laura Willis. *Logan County, Kentucky, Census and Tax Lists, 1820 and 1830*. Melber, KY: Simmons Historical Publications, 1995. 140p.

Louisville

Crowder, Lola Frazer. *Early Louisville, Kentucky, Newspaper Abstracts, 1806–1828*. Galveston, TX: Frontier Press, 1995. 283p.

Madison County

Madison County, a Portrait of the Past. Marceline, MO: Heritage House, 1995. 128p.

Mason County

Heflin, Donald L. *Maysville Cemetery, Maysville, Mason County, Kentucky*. Georgetown, KY: 1995. 176p.

Mason County, Kentucky, County Clerk Court Orders, 1789–1800, an Every Name Index. Miami Beach, FL: T. L. C. Genealogy, 1995. 127p.

Maysville

Heflin, Donald L. *Maysville Cemetery, Maysville, Mason County, Kentucky*. Georgetown, KY: Author, 1995. 176p.

Mercer County

Webb, Donna Jean. *1910 Federal Census, Mercer County, Kentucky*. Lexington, KY: Author, 1995. 249p.

Muhlenberg County

Carver, Gayle R. *Muhlenberg County, Kentucky, Marriages as Recorded in Marriage Books 51 through 100 Covering the Years 1921–1960*. Russelville, KY: A. B. Willhite, 1995. 303p.

Nelson County

Nelson County, Kentucky, Record of Wills, 1784–1851, Inclusive. 1995. 12p.

Nicholas County

Heflin, Donald L. *An Index to the Nicholas County, Kentucky, Cemeteries in the Book, The History of Nicholas County*. Georgetown, KY: Author, 1995. 171p.

Owsley County

Smith, Robert L. *Owsley County, Kentucky, Marriages, 1843–1929*. 2nd ed. Cincinnati, OH: Author, 1995. 210p.

Pendleton County

Nagle, Eric C. *County Birth and Death Records of Pendleton County, Kentucky*. Author, 1995. 192p.

Pike

Atkins, Oscar Thomas. *Pike County, Kentucky, 1840, Taken in Part from the Federal Census of Pike County, Kentucky, for 1840 and from Tax Lists, other Census Records, Marriage Records, and from the Library and Files of the Compiler*. Williamson, WV: Author, 1995. 32p.

Robertson County

Nagle, Eric C. *Monument Inscriptions of Robertson County, Kentucky*. Dayton, OH: Ford and Nagle, Historians and Genealogists, 1995. 100p.

Rockcastle County

Bonham, Jeanne Snodgrass. *Rockcastle County, Kentucky, 1880 Federal Census. Rockcastle County, Kentucky, Tenth Census of the United States Schedule No. 1, Population*. Greenwood, IN: High Grass Pub., 1995. 174p.

Scott County

Egbert, Charles. *Kith, Kin, Wee Kirk*. Sadieville, KY: Author, 1995. 6 vols.

Spencer County

Burgin, Edna Montgomery. *Spencer County, Kentucky, Cemeteries, Then and Now*. Louisville, KY: Author, 1995. 99p.

Taylor County

Wilson, DeWayne. *Taylor County, Kentucky, Vital Statistics, Births, 1852-59, 1861, 1874-79, 1893-94, 1901, 1903, 1904*. Campbellsville, KY: Author, 1995. 182p.

Trigg County

Simmons, Don. *Trigg County, Kentucky, Land Surveys South of Walker's Line in Stewart County, Tennessee (30 March 1825–28 April 1827)*. Melber, KY: Simmons Historical Publications, 1995. 96p.

Taylor, Pete. *Trigg County, Kentucky, Bible Records*. Melber, KY: Simmons Historical Publications, 1995. 73p.

———. *Trigg County, Kentucky, Newspaper Abstracts, Volume 25*. Melber, KY: Simmons Historical Publications, 1995. 73p.

Willis, Laura. *Trigg County, Kentucky, Census and Tax List of 1840*. Melber, KY: Simmons Historical Publications, 1995. 53p.

Trimble County

Trimble County Historical Society. *1900 Trimble County, Kentucky, Census*. Pendleton, KY: Trimble County Historical Society, 1995. 175p.

Union County

Heady, Peyton. *Union County Death Records, 1951–1988*. Morganfield, KY: Author, 1995. Unpgd.

Heffington, Ruth. *Abstracts from Will Books A-Y, 1811–1914, Union County, Kentucky*. Morganfield, KY: Union County Historical Society, 1995. 188p.

Uniontown

Heady, Peyton. *Register of St. John's Protestant Episcopal Church, Uniontown, Kentucky*. Author, 1995. 50p.

Washington County

Sanders, Fay Sea. *Washington County, Kentucky, Marriages, 1792–1825*. Louisville, KY: Author, 1995. 98p.

Webster County

McBroom, Jane. *Webster County, Kentucky, Newspaper Abstracts. Volume 1*. Melber, KY: Simmons Historical Publications, 1995. 76p.

Woodford County

Hurst, Melvin E. *Versailles Cemetery, Woodford County, Kentucky*. Lexington, KY: Fayette County Genealogical Society, 1995. 187p.

Louisiana

Adoption in Louisiana, a Guide. Baton Rouge, LA: Louisiana Department of Social Services, 1995. 40p.

Burns, Loretta Elliott. *1911 Louisiana Census, Confederate Veterans or Widows*. Pasadena, TX: C & L Printing, 1995. 98p.

DeVille, Winston. *Mississippi Valley Melange: A Collection of Notes and Documents for the Genealogy and History of the Province of Louisiana and the Territory of Orleans*. Ville Platte, LA: Mississippi Valley Melange, 1995. Unpgd.

Foret, Michael James. *Louisiana Indian Studies, a Selected Bibliography*. Lafayette, LA: Center for Louisiana Studies, University of Southwestern Louisiana, 1995. 284p.

Gautreau, Henry W. *1830s Pre-emption Entries on the Backlands of New River, Louisiana, in Conflict with the Houmas Land Claim*. Gonzales, LA: East Ascension Genealogical and Historical Society, 1995. 81p.

Goins, Charles Robert. *Historical Atlas of Louisiana*. Norman, OK: University of Oklahoma Press, 1995. 200p.

Guide to the Non-Public Records of the Louisiana State Archives. Baton Rouge, LA: Louisiana State Archives and Records Service, 1995. 146p.

Louisiana Almanac: 1995–1996. 14th. ed. Gretna, LA: Pelican Publishing Co., 1995. 624p.

McManus, Jane Parker. *Lest We Forget, Cemetery Inscriptions of Vernon Parish, Louisiana.* Rev. ed. Pineville, LA: Parker Enterprises, 1995. Unpgd.

Roux, Vincent M. and Kenneth D. Roux. *Louisiana's Households of Free People of Color Residing Outside of Orleans Parish and the City of New Orleans in 1810 and 1820.* San Francisco, CA: Author, 1995. 72p.

Sifakis, Stewart. *Compendium of the Confederate Armies Series: Louisiana.* NY: Facts on File, 1995. 160p.

Smith, Virginia Rogers. *Searching For Your Louisiana Ancestors.* Baton Rouge, LA: Author, 1995. 29p.

Lafourche Parish

Westerman, Audrey B. *First Land Owners and 1810 Annotated Census of Lafourche Interior Parish, Louisiana (Lafourche & Terrebonne).* Houma, LA: Terrebonne Genealogical Society, 1995. Unpgd.

Livingston Parish

Livingston Parish, Louisiana, the 1910 Federal Census and the 1911 School Census. Livingston, LA: Edward Livingston Historical Association, 1995. 262p.

New Orleans

Index (1983–1994), the Historic New Orleans Collection Newsletter Quarterly. New Orleans, LA: Historic New Orleans Collection, 1995. 24p.

Ponchatoula

Perrin, James Morris. *Ponchatoula Historical Records.* Hammond, LA: Author, 1995. Unpgd.

Saint Helena Parish

Williams, Ernest Russ. *Genealogical and Historical Abstracts of Legal Records of Saint Helena Parish, Louisiana, 1804–1870, Successions (Probates and Wills), 1804–1854, Tax Assessments Rolls, 1823, 1824, 1826, Marriages, 1811–1870.* Monroe, LA: Williams Genealogical and Historical Pub., 1995. 339p.

St. Landry Parish

Calendar of St. Landry Parish, Louisiana, Civil Records. Baton Rouge, LA: La Comite des Archives de la Louisiane, 1995. Unpgd.

Shreveport

Brock, Eric J. *The Jewish Cemeteries of Shreveport, Louisiana.* Shreveport, LA: J & W Enterprises, 1995. 59p.

Terrebonne Parish

Westerman, Audrey B. *First Land Owners and 1810 Annotated Census of Lafourche Interior Parish, Louisiana (Lafourche & Terrebonne).* Houma, LA: Terrebonne Genealogical Society, 1995. Unpgd.

Maine

Cemetery Inscriptions and Odd Information of Various Towns in the State of Maine in the Counties of Lincoln, Oxford, Penobscot, Somerset, Waldo. Sarasota, FL: Aceto Bookman, 1995. 139p.

Emery, Eric B. *New England Captives in Canada and the Ransom Missions of Phineas Stevens, 1749, 1751 and 1752*. Thesis (M.A.), University of Vermont, 1995. 115p.

Lipfert, Nathan R. *Guide to Log-books and Sea Journal, 1764–1938, in the Collections of Maine Maritime Museum*. Bath, ME: Maine Maritime Museum Library, 1995. 134p.

Mundy, James H. *Hard Times, Hard Men: Maine and the Irish, 1830–1860*. Dissertation (Ph.D.), University of Maine, 1995. 242p.

United States. Census Office. *1790 Census of Maine*. Camden, ME: Picton Press, 1995. 124p.

Young, Elizabeth Keene and Benjamin Lewis Keene. *Marriage Notices from the Maine Farmer, 1833–1852*. Bowie, MD: Heritage Books, 1995. 487p.

Bradford

Corliss, Stephen L. *Twelfth Census of the United States, Bradford Town, 1900*. Author, 1995. 22p.

Calais

First Congregational Church Calais, Maine, Records, 1825–1925. Calais, ME: The Church, 1995. 100p.

Hallowell

Haskell, Jessica J. *Hallowell, Maine History, Tax List, 1850 Census, Marriage Intentions, Family History from Newspaper Columns by Jessica J. Haskell Published in Daily Eastern Argus, 1916–1917*. Sarasota, FL: Aceto Bookman, 1995. 50p.

Jay

Moulton, Virginia Plaisted. *A History of Jay, Maine, from Its Settlement as Phips, Canada*. Camden, ME: Penobscot Press, 1995. 1,013p.

Lee

Crocker, Kay Stevens. *Alphabetical List of Families Buried in Lee, Maine, Cemeteries*. Lee, ME: Author, 1995. 75p.

Lisbon

Groves, Marlene Alma Hinckley. *Vital Records of Lisbon, Maine, prior to 1892*. Camden, ME: Picton Press, 1995. 502p.

Mexico

Labonte, Youville. *Marriages of St. John, Rumford, Maine (1866–1939) and of St. Theresa, Mexico, Maine (1927–1939)*. Auburn, ME: Author, 1995. 113p.

Northport

Mosher, Elizabeth M. *Vital Records of Northport, Waldo County, Maine, prior to 1892*. Camden, ME: Picton Press, 1995. 189p.

Orrington

Swett, David Livingstone. *Vital Records of Orrington, Penobscot County, Maine, prior to 1892*. Camden, ME: Picton Press, 1995. 447p.

Porter

Flewelling, Ann. *Vital Records of Porter, Maine*. Author, 1995. 27p.

Portland

Booth, Glenn Gordon. Thesis (M.A.), University of Maine, 1995. 97p.

Rumford

Labonte, Youville. *Marriages of St. John, Rumford, Maine (1866–1939) and of St. Theresa, Mexico, Maine (1927–1939)*. Auburn, ME: Author, 1995. 113p.

Sanford

Boyle, Frederick. *Sanford, Later Families of Sanford-Springvale, Maine*. Peter E. Randall, 1995. 557p.

Southport

Orchard, Ronald D. *Southport Cemeteries*. West Southport, ME: Author, 1995. 44p.

Thomaston

Sullivan, Steven E. *Vital Records from the Thomaston Recorder of Thomaston, Maine, prior to 1837–1846*. Camden, ME: Picton Press, 1995. 118p.

Troy

Hillman, Ralph E. *Vital Records of Troy, Maine, prior to 1892*. Camden, ME: Picton Press, 1995. 224p.

Unity

Mosher, Elizabeth M. *Vital Records of Unity, Waldo County, Maine, prior to 1892*. Camden, ME: Picton Press, 1995. 314p.

Vassalboro

Vassalboro Cemetery Inscriptions. Vassalboro Historical Society, 1995. 255p.

Waterville

Chenard, Robert E. *Halde Cemetery, Father Doyon Memorial Cemetery, Waterville, Kennebec County, Maine*. 5th. rev. Waterville, ME: Author, 1995. 35p.

York County

Maine Old Cemetery Association. *Cemetery Inscriptions of York County, Maine*. Rockport, ME: Picton Press, 1995. 4 vols.

York Deed Index. Scarborough, ME: Scarborough Historical Society, 1995. 213p.

Maryland

Carothers, Bettie Stirling. *Maryland Oaths of Fidelity*. Westminster, MD: Family Line Pub., 1995. 111p.

Coldham, Peter Wilson. *Settlers of Maryland, 1679–1700*. Baltimore, MD: Genealogical Publishing Co., 1995. 231p.

Directory of Public Libraries in Maryland, 1995-96. Baltimore, MD: Maryland State Department of Education, Division of Library Development and Services, 1995. 116p.

Harper, Irma Sweitzer. *Genealogical Abstracts from Newspapers of Maryland's Eastern Shore, 1835–1850*. St. Michaels, MD: Author, 1995. 146p.

———. *The Omega Connections, Obituaries from Eastern Shore of Maryland Newspapers, 1850–1900, over 10,000 Names Published in Two Volumes*. St. Michaels, MD: Author, 1995. 2 vols.

Jourdan, Elise Greenup. *Early Families of Southern Maryland*. Westminster, MD: Family Line Pub., 1995. 326p.

Long, Helen. *Index to Scharf's History of Western Maryland*. Baltimore, MD: Clearfield Co., 1995. 369p.

Maryland Calendar of Wills. Westminster, MD: Family Line Pub., 1995. 288p.

Moxey, Debra Smith. *Abstracts of the Balance Books of the Prerogative Court of Maryland*. Westminster, MD: Family Line Pub., 1995. Unpgd.

Oszakiewski, Robert Andrew. *Maryland Naturalization Abstracts*. Westminster, MD: Family Line Pub., 1995. 2 vols.

Preisler, Julian H. *Jewish Cemeteries of the Delmarva Peninsula, a Burial Index for Delaware and Maryland's Eastern Shore*. Westminster, MD: Family Line Pub., 1995. 123p.

Sifakis, Stewart. *Compendium of the Confederate Armies Series: Kentucky, Maryland, Missouri, the Confederate Units and the Indian Units*. NY: Facts on File, 1995. 240p.

Skinner, V. L. *Abstracts of the Administration Accounts of the Prerogative Court*. Westminster, MD: Family Line Pub., 1995. 215p.

Soderberg, Susan Cooke. *Lest We Forget, a Guide to Civil War Monuments in Maryland*. Shippensburg, PA: White Mane, 1995. 195p.

Baltimore

Baltimore's Past: A Directory of Historical Sources. Baltimore, MD: History Press, 1995. 255p.

Hoopes, Emil Erick. *A Record of Interments at the Friends Burial Ground, Baltimore, Maryland (est. 1681).* Baltimore, MD: Clearfield, 1995. 66p.

O'Neill, Francis P. *Index of Obituaries and Marriages in the (Baltimore) Sun, 1871–1875.* Westminster, MD: Family Line Pub., 1995. 2 vols.

Peden, Henry C. *Presbyterian Records of Baltimore City, Maryland, 1765–1840.* Westminster, MD: Family Line Pub., 1995. 326p.

Records of the First Reformed Church of Baltimore, 1768–1899. Westminster, MD: Family Line Pub., 1995. 438p.

Wright, F. Edward. *Records of Old Otterbein Church, Baltimore, Maryland, 1785–1881.* Westminster, MD: Family Line Publications, 1995. 212p.

Zimmerman, Elaine Obbink. *Interment Records, 1883–1929, Lorraine Park Cemetery and Mausoleum.* Westminster, MD: Family Line Pub., 1995. 483p.

Carroll County

Zahn, C. T. *Zion Church, the German Church, Manchester, Carroll County, Maryland, Today, Trinity United Church of Christ Records, 1760–1836, Immanuel Lutheran Church Records, 1760–1853.* Westminster, MD: Historical Society of Carroll County, 1995. 131p.

Charles County

Bates, Marlene. *Early Charles County, Maryland, Settlers, 1658–1745.* Westminster, MD: Family Line Pub., 1995. 404p.

Charles County, Maryland, Court Records, 1774–1778, an Every Name Index. Miami Beach, FL: T. L. C. Genealogy, 1995. 124p.

Charles County, Maryland, Land Records, 1765–1775. Miami Beach, FL: T. L. C. Genealogy, 1995. 297p.

Charles County, Maryland, Wills, Administration Accounts, Inventories and Orphan Court Proceedings, 1777–1780. Miami Beach, FL: T. L. C. Genealogy, 1995. 223p.

Dorchester County

Woolston, B. Jean. *Marriage References, Circuit Court, Dorchester County, Maryland, 1780-1867.* Cambridge, MD: Weir Neck Publications, 1995. 252p.

Frederick County

Andersen, Patricia Abelard. *Frederick County, Maryland, Land Records, Liber B Abstracts, 1748–1752.* Gaithersburg, MD: GenLaw Resources, 1995. 100p.

———. *Frederick County, Maryland, Land Records, Liber B Abstracts, 1752–1756.* Gaithersburg, MD: GenLaw Resources, 1995. 120p.

Cavey, Kathleen Tull Burton. *Tombstone and Beyond, Prospect United Methodist Church Cemetery and Marvin Chapel Church Cemetery, Includes Jacob M. Holdcraft's Field Records and Caretaker Records.* Westminster, MD: Family Line Pub., 1995. 94p.

Engelbrecht, Jacob. *The Jacob Engelbrecht Death Ledger of Frederick County, Maryland, 1820- 1890.* Monrovia, MD: Paw Prints, 1995. 354p.

Gordon, Paul. *Never the Like Again.* Frederick, MD: Heritage Partnership, 1995. 337p.

Peden, Henry C., Jr. *Revolutionary Patriots of Frederick County, Maryland, 1775–1783.* Westminster, MD: Family Line Publications, 1995. 412p.

Tull Burton, Kathleen. *Tombstones and Beyond.* Westminster, MD: Family Line Publications, 1995. 94p.

Owings Mills

St. Thomas Parish Deaths and Burials, Owings Mills, Maryland, 1728–1995. Westminster, MD: Family Line Pub., 1995. 122p.

Prince George's County

Baltz, Shirley Vlasak and George E. Baltz. *Prince George's County, Maryland, Marriages and Deaths in Nineteenth Century Newspapers*. Bowie, MD: Heritage Books, 1995. 2 vols.

Bibliographical Resource Guide to Prince George's County, Maryland Historical Literature. 1995. 97p.

Queen Anne's County

Surles, Trish. *Genealogical Data Taken from Obituaries and Marriages in Miscellaneous Maryland Newspapers, Queen Anne's County, 1876 to 1942*. Gambrills, MD: Author, 1995. 93p.

St. Mary's County

Cryer, Leona Alva. *Deaths and Burials in St. Mary's County, Maryland*. Bowie, MD: Heritage Books, 1995. 447p.

Donnelly, Mary Louise. *Colonial Settlers, St. Clement's Bay, 1634–1780, St. Mary's County, Maryland*. Ennis, TX: Author, 1995. 291p.

Massachusetts

Bodge, George Madison. *Soldiers in King Philip's War, Official Lists of the Soldiers of Massachusetts Colony Serving in Philip's War, and Sketches of the Principal Officers, Copies of Ancient Documents and Records Relating to the War*. Baltimore, MD: Clearfield, 1906, 1995. 502p.

City Directories and Related Lists, a Guide to Materials in the Special Collections Department, State Library of Massachusetts. Boston, MA: State Library of Massachusetts, 1995. 85p.

Salisbury, Susan. *Southern Massachusetts Cemetery Collection*. Bowie, MD: Heritage Books, 1995. Unpgd.

Spear, Burton W. *Search for the Passengers of the Mary & John, 1630*. Toledo, OH: Author, 1995. 83p.

Thatcher, Charles M. *Old Cemeteries of Southeastern Massachusetts, a Compilation of Records by Charles M. Thatcher in the Late 1880s*. Middleborough, MA: Middleborough Public Library, 1995. 246p.

Barnstable

Bunnell, Paul Joseph. *Cemetery Inscriptions of the Town of Barnstable, Massachusetts, and Its Villages, 1600–1900, with Corrections and Additions*. Bowie, MD: Heritage Books, 1995. 434p.

Barnstable County

Gibson, Marjorie Hubbell. *Historical and Genealogical Atlas and Guide to Barnstable County, Massachusetts*. Falmouth, MA: Falmouth Genealogical Society, 1995. 40p.

Boston

Harris, Ruth Ann, Donald M. Jacobs and B. Emer O'Keeffe. *The Search for Missing Friends, Irish Immigrant Advertisements Placed in the Boston Pilot. Volume 4, 1857–1860*. Boston, MA: New England Historic Genealogical Society, 1995. 800p.

Page, Patsy R. *Directory of Boston Physicians, 1859*. Alachua, FL: Page Publications, 1995. 8p.

Sarna, Jonathan D. and Ellen Smith. *The Jews of Boston. Essays on the Occasion of the Centenary (1895–1995) of the Combined Jewish Philanthropies of Greater Boston*. Boston, MA: Combined Jewish Philanthropies of Greater Boston, 1995. 353p.

Wyman, Thomas Bellows. *The New North Church, Boston, 1714*. Baltimore, MD: Clearfield Co., 1995. 132p.

Charlestown

Joslyn, Roger D. *Vital Records of Charlestown, Massachusetts, Volume 2, Parts 1 and 2*. Boston, MA: New England Historic Genealogical Society, 1995. 1,231p.

Dukes County

Roosevelt, Tweed. *The Dukes County Intelligencer Index for the Years 1959 through 1994*. Edgartown, MA: Dukes County Historical Society, 1995. 62p.

Fitchburg

Extracts of Death Records from Aubuchon Funeral Parlor, Fitchburg, Massachusetts (1914-1966). Fitchburg, MA: Acadian Cultural Society, 1995. 416p.

Hingham

Gilman, Wayne Clark. *The Hingham Founding Fathers of Old Colony, New Hampshire, Exeter II, the Origins, 1623–1655*. Bowie, MD: Heritage Books, 1995. 174p.

Lowell

Labonte, Youville. *St. Jean Baptiste, Lowell, Massachusetts (1869–1910)*. Auburn, ME: Author, 1995. 146p.

Medway

Medway, Massachusetts, Births, Marriages, and Deaths, 1850–1900. Bowie, MD: Heritage Books, 1995. 193p.

Plymouth

Ness, Beverly. *Genealogical and Local History Resources Available in Plymouth, Massachusetts*. Plymouth, MA: Plymouth Public Library, 1995. 26p.

Worcester

Institute for Asian American Studies. University of Massachusetts at Boston. *Asian Pacific Americans in Worcester*. Boston, MA: Author, 1995. 8p.

O'Keefe, Doris N. *Subject and Personal Name Index to Charles Nutt's History of Worcester and Its People*. Worcester, MA: American Antiquarian Society, 1995. Unpgd.

Michigan

Joki, Mike. *A Directory of Surnames Found in Select Regional History Writings*. L'Anse, MI: Author, 1995. Unpgd.

Listing of Michigan County and Township Addresses. Gaylord, MI: Gaylord Fact Finders Genealogical Society, 1995. 74p.

Michigan, 1870, Census Index. Vol. 6. Lansing, MI: Library of Michigan, 1995. 267p.

Michigan, 1870, Census Index. Vol. 7. Lansing, MI: Library of Michigan, 1995. 328p.

Michigan History Directory: Historical Societies, Agencies and Commissions. 6th. ed. Ann Arbor, MI: Historical Society of Michigan, 1995. 40p.

Sherman, Alonzo Joseph. *Index to Men in Michigan*. Oscoda, MI: Huron Shore Genealogical Society, 1995. 29p.

Allegan County

Castle, Amelia B. *Index to 1873 Allegan County, Michigan, Land Owners*. Dowagiac, MI: Author, 1995. Unpgd.

Alpena

St. Bernard Church Records, Alpena, Michigan, Baptisms, 1864–1894, Marriages, 1870–1894, Funerals, 1870–1925. Alpena, MI: Northeast Michigan Genealogical and Historical Society, 1995. 155p.

Berrien County

Castle, Amelia B. *Index to 1873 Berrien County, Michigan, Land Owners*. Dowagiac, MI: Author, 1995. Unpgd.

Corwin, Nancy. *Early Berrien County, Michigan, Marriages, 1830–1856*. Dowagiac, MI: Author, 1995. 38p.

Big Rapids

Peterson, Norman G. *The Year 1886 at St. Peter's Lutheran Church and in Big Rapids, Michigan, Including the Personal Journal of Rev. Ernst George Franck*. Big Rapids, MI: Morfar's Publishing, 1995. 36p.

Branch County

Branch County, Michigan, State Censuses for 1854 & 1874, a Project of the Branch County Genealogical Society. Coldwater, MI: The Society, 1995. 2 vols.

Byron

Byron Township Birth Records, Kent County, Michigan, 1908 thru 1952. Byron Center, MI: Township Clerk, 1995. Unpgd.

Byron Township Death Records, Kent County, Michigan, 1900 thru 1956. Byron Center, MI: Township Clerk, 1995. 33p.

Cass County

Corwin, Nancy. *Early Marriages, Cass County, Michigan, 1830–1858.* Dowagiac, MI: Author, 1995. 39p.

Detroit

Ibbotson, Patricia. *Reports of City Physicians, 1860–1869, Detroit, Wayne County, Michigan.* Detroit, MI: Detroit Society of Genealogical Research, 1995. 135p.

Record of Juvenile Inmates of the Home for the Friendless, 1862–1868, Detroit, Michigan. Detroit, MI: Detroit Society for Genealogical Research, 1995. 90p.

Woodmere Cemetery, Detroit, Michigan, the First Twenty Years. Lincoln Park, MI: Downriver Genealogical Society, 1995. Unpgd.

Duplain

Duplain Cemetery, Colony Road, Duplain Township, Clinton County. Elsie, MI: Elsie Historical Society, 1995. 24p.

Riverside Cemetery, Elsie, Michigan, Located in Section 10 of Duplain Township, Clinton County. Elsie, MI: Elsie Historical Society, 1995. 70p.

Eaton County

Carr, Julie. *Obituaries, Lansing State Journal, East Lansing Town Courier, Book Four, Eaton County Obituaries.* Lansing, MI: Author, 1995. Unpgd.

Elba

Ford Cemetery, Gratiot County, Michigan, Located 2 Miles North of Elsie, Michigan. Elsie, MI: Elsie Historical Society, 1995. 69p.

Elsie

Elsie Village Cemetery, Clinton County, Michigan. Elsie, MI: Elsie Historical Society, 1995. 16p.

Erie

1876 Township Plat Map, Includes Index, and 1880 Federal Census Index, Includes Census of Erie Township, Monroe County, Michigan. Monroe, MI: Genealogical Society of Monroe County, Michigan, 1995. 124p.

Fairfield

Fairfield Township Cemetery, 1991, (Other Records Included) Located along Vincent Road between Riley and Juddville Roads. Elsie, MI: Elsie Historical Society, 1995. 26p.

Fruitland

Burns, Matthew W. *State Censuses of Fruitland Township, Muskegon County, Michigan.* Muskegon, MI: Author, 1995. Unpgd.

———. *U.S. Censuses of Fruitland Township, Muskegon County, Michigan.* Muskegon, MI: Author, 1995. Unpgd.

Genesee County

Perry, Merle. *Genesee County, Michigan, Cemeteries.* Flint, MI: Michael F. Taylor, 1995. Unpgd.

Grand Rapids

Women in Grand Rapids History, a Guide to Resources in the Local History Department of the Grand Rapids Public Library. Grand Rapids, MI: Greater Grand Rapids Women's History Council, 1995. 39p.

Greenbush

Greenbush Cemetery, Hyde Road, Greenbush Township, Clinton County, Michigan. Elsie, MI: Elsie Historical Society, 1995. 57p.

Independence

Oakland County, Michigan, Independence Township Cemeteries. Birmingham, MI: Oakland County Genealogical Society, 1995. 309p.

Iosco County

Donaldson, James. *Index to the Diary of James Olin Whittemore, Tawas City, Michigan, 1866–1967, and the Reminiscence of Melissa Starkweather Whittemore, 1921.* Detroit, MI: Oscoda, Au Sable Historical Archive, 1995. 26p.

———. *Iosco's Boys in Blue, a Genealogical and Biographical Roster of Resident Civil War Soldiers, Sailors and Veterans, Iosco County, Michigan.* Newly rev. and enlarged. Detroit, MI: Author, 1995. 91p.

Sherman, Alonzo Joseph. *Biographic Index of Iosco County Michigan.* Oscoda, MI: Huron Shore Genealogical Society, 1995. 2 vols.

Kalamazoo County

Corwin, Nancy. *Index to the 1873 Land Owners, Kalamazoo County, Michigan.* Dowagiac, MI: Author, 1995. Unpgd.

Kalkaska County

Corwin, Nancy. *Land Owners, Kalkaska County, Michigan.* Dowagiac, MI: Author, 1995. 22p.

Leelanau County

Player, Margaret. *Cemetery Records of Solon Township and Elmwood Township, Leelanau County, Michigan.* Traverse City, MI: Grand Traverse Area Genealogical Society, 1995. 53p.

Livingston County

1870 Federal Census and Mortality Schedule, Livingston County, Michigan. Howell, MI: Livingston County Genealogical Society, 1995. 342p.

Luce County

Mattson, Minnie Ida. *History of Luce County from Its Earliest Recorded Beginning*. Luce County, MI: Luce County Historical Society, 1995. 400p.

Missaukee County

Corwin, Nancy. *Land Owners, Missaukee County, Michigan*. Dowagiac, MI: Author, 1995. Unpgd.

Muskegon County

Kolb, David J. *A World War Chronicle*. Muskegon, MI: The Muskegon Chronicle, 1995. 51p.

Riley, Ronald J. *Muskegon County Marriage Record*. Muskegon, MI: Author, 1995. Unpgd.

Oakland County

Davis, Joean. *Oakland County, Michigan, Groveland Township Hadley Cemetery, 1820–1994*. Holly, MI: Author, 1995. 20p.

Michigan, Oakland County Genealogical Society Surname Directory. Volume 5, 1995. Birmingham, MI: Oakland County Genealogical Society, 1995. Unpgd.

Otsego County

Marrs, Donna M. *1890 Federal Census Index to Schedules Enumerating Union Veterans and Widows of Union Veterans of the Civil War, Ostego County, Michigan*. Gaylord, MI: Gaylord Fact Finders Genealogical Society, 1995. 5p.

Matelski, K. A. *Otsego County, Michigan, Index of Families, 1875-Present*. Colorado Springs, CO: Author, 1995. 2 vols.

Muzyl, Marleah. *Cemetery Inscriptions, Otsego County, Michigan, 1994*. Gaylord, MI: Gaylord Fact Finders, 1995. 158p.

Ovid

Maple Grove Cemetery, Ovid, Michigan. Elsie, MI: Elsie Historical Society, 1995. 105p.

South Ovid Cemetery, Park's Road, Ovid Township, Clinton County, Michigan. Elsie, MI: Elsie Historical Society, 1995. 12p.

Saint Joseph County

Corwin, Nancy. *Land Owners, 1872, St. Joseph County, Michigan*. Dowagiac, MI: Author, 1995. 31p.

Shiawassee County

Middlebury Township Cemetery, Shiawassee County, Michigan. Elsie, MI: Elsie Historical Society, 1995. 21p.

Summerfield

Muszynski, Shirley. *Death Records, Summerfield Township, Monroe County, Michigan, November 12, 1897 to April 6, 1952, with Index*. Eries, MI: Author, 1995. 93p.

————. *Death Records, Village of Petersburg, Summerfield Township, Monroe County, Michigan, September 28, 1897 to June 18, 1966, with Index*. Eries, MI: Author, 1995. 52p.

Tallmadge

Boersma, Henry. *Restoration of the Unknown Elmwood Cemetery, Section 7, Tallmadge Township, Ottawa County, Michigan.* Marne, MI: Author, 1995. 45p.

Boersma, Loekie. *Tallmadge Township Records, Ottawa County, Michigan, 1838–1882.* Marne, MI: Author, 1995. 204p.

Tawas City

Reorganized Church of Jesus Christ of Latter Day Saints of Tawas City, Michigan (Iosco County) Ledger of Records, 1905–1945. Oscoda, MI: Huron Shore Genealogical Society, 1995. 25p.

Van Buren County

Benson, Toni I. *Van Buren County Poorhouse/Infirmary Records, an Abstract of the Births, Deaths, Burials and General Register.* Decatur, MI: F-AMI-LEE Pub., 1995. 2 vols.

1880 Van Buren County, Michigan, Federal Census Index. Decatur, MI: Glyndwr Resources, 1995. 164p.

Victor

Blood Cemetery, Located on Jason Road about One-half Mile West of Meridian Road, Victor Township, Clinton County, Michigan. Elsie, MI: Elsie Historical Society, 1995. 6p.

Stilson Cemetery, Located about 1/4 Mile South of Price Road on Saint Clair Road, Victor Township, Clinton County, Michigan. Elsie, MI: Elsie Historical Society, 1995. 11p.

Volina

Burton, Conrad and Ann Burton. *Little Fish Lake Cemetery, Southeast Corner of Section 35, Volina Township, Cass County, Michigan, Gravestone Readings.* Decatur, MI: Author, 1995. 31p.

Minnesota

Amundson, Richard C. *A Search for Place, the History of the Minnesota Judicial Center.* St. Paul, MN: Minnesota Court of Appeals, 1995. 123p.

Combined Index to Histories of Chatfield, Chosen Valley, Oronoco, Pleasant Grove and Viola in Olmsted County, Minnesota. Rochester, MN: Olmsted County Genealogical Society, 1995. 234p.

Doering, Anita Taylor. *Guide to Local History and Genealogy Resources: Sources in the Winding Rivers Library System, Wisconsin, Selected Sources in Houston, Olmsted and Winona Counties, Minnesota.* La Crosse, WI: La Crosse Public Library, 1995. Unpgd.

Green, Stina B. *Minnesota's Mining Accidents, 1900–1920, and Mining Deaths, 1889–1990.* Roseville, MN: Park Genealogical Books, 1995. 46p.

Minnesota's Adoption Laws. St. Paul, MN: Minnesota Department of Human Services, 1995. 20p.

Becker County

Peterzen, Conrad. *Becker County, Minnesota, Naturalization Records, 1822–1947.* Chisholm, MN: Range Genealogical Society, 1995. 129p.

Duluth

Bakeman, Mary. *Every Name Index to Recollections of Early Days in Duluth.* Brooklyn Park, MN: Park Genealogical Books, 1995. 14p.

Kandiyohi County

Alphabetical Index to Kandiyohi County, Minnesota, Cemetery Transcriptions. Willmar, MN: Heritage Searchers of Kandiyohi County, 1995. 191p.

Kensington

Belgum, James. *Nora Lutheran Church, Rural Kensington, Minnesota, 125th Anniversary, 1870–1995, a History of Nora Lutheran Church, Its Members and the Community, Nora Township, Pope County, Minnesota.* Glencoe, MN: Author, 1995. 132p.

Kittson County

Peterzen, Conrad. *Kittson County, Minnesota, Naturalization Records, 1881–1955.* Chisholm, MN: Range Genealogical Society, 1995. 117p.

Lake County

Peterzen, Conrad. *Lake County, Minnesota, Naturalization Records, 1891–1952.* Chisholm, MN: Range Genealogical Society, 1995. 102p.

Norman County

Peterzen, Conrad. *Norman County, Minnesota, Naturalization Records, 1882–1949.* Chisholm, MN: Range Genealogical Society, 1995. 137p.

Olmsted County

Index to the 1868 Plat Map, Olmsted County, Minnesota. Rochester, MN: Olmsted County Genealogical Society, 1995. 68p.

Index to the 1896 Plat Map, Olmsted County, Minnesota. Rochester, MN: Olmsted County Genealogical Society, 1995. 125p.

Index to the 1914 Plat Map, Olmsted County, Minnesota. Rochester, MN: Olmsted County Genealogical Society, 1995. 100p.

Polk County

Peterzen, Conrad. *Polk County, Minnesota, Naturalization Records, 1870–1957.* Chisholm, MN: Range Genealogical Society, 1995. 2 vols.

St. Paul

Bakeman, Mary Hawker. *Calvary Cemetery, St. Paul, Minnesota*. Roseville, MN: Park Genealogical Books, 1995. 72p.

Stockholm

Stockholm Township, Wright County, Minnesota, Cemeteries. Brooklyn Park, MN: Park Genealogical Books, 1995. 30p.

Traverse County

Peterzen, Conrad. *Traverse County, Minnesota, Naturalization Records, 1881–1945*. Chisholm, MN: Range Genealogical Society, 1995. 56p.

Walker

Walker on Leech Lake, the First 100 Years, 1896–1996. Walker, MN: Walker Centennial Book Committee, 1995. 240p.

Wilkin County

Peterzen, Conrad. *Wilkin County, Minnesota, Naturalization Records, 1884–1945*. Chisholm, MN: Range Genealogical Society, 1995. 37p.

Mississippi

DeVille, Winston. *Mississippi Land Papers and Secret Militia Rolls of 1799, Anglo-American Settlers in the Spanish Gulf South*. Ville Platte, LA: Smith Publications, 1995. 42p.

General Index to the Interview Collection. Hattiesburg, MS: Mississippi Oral History Program, University of Southern Mississippi, 1995. 220p.

Jenkins, William Lester. *Mississippi Conference Appointments of the Former Methodist Episcopal Church, Methodist Episcopal Church South, Methodist Church and United Methodist Church, 1799–1995*. Jackson, MS: Author, 1995. 283p.

Page, Patsy R. *Directory of Mississippi Physicians, 1886*. Alachua, FL: Page Publications, 1995. 32p.

Sifakis, Stewart. *Compendium of the Confederate Armies Series: Mississippi*. NY: Facts on File, 1995. 160p.

Strickland, Jean and Patricia N. Edwards. *Residents of the Mississippi Territory, Miscellaneous Books 2A and 2B*. Moss Point, MS: Ben Strickland, 1995. 41p.

Terry, Brenda. *Slaves*. Bowie, MD: Heritage Books, 1995. Unpgd.

University of Southern Mississippi. Mississippi Oral History Program. *General Index to the Interview Collection*. Hattiesburg, MS: Author, 1995. 220p.

Attala County

Meredith, James. *Yockanookany, History of Attala County, Mississippi, 1833–1917*. 2nd ed.
    Jackson, MS: Meredith Pub., 1995. 208p.

Calhoun City

Lee, Carol. *Early Records of Calhoun City, Mississippi, Baptist Church*. Carrollton, MS: Pio-
    neer Pub., 1995. 83p.

Carroll County

Bibus, Ethel. *Carroll County, Mississippi, Cemetery Records*. Carrollton, MS: Pioneer Pub.
    Co., 1995. 310p.

Claiborne County

Brown, Ann Beckerson. *St. Joseph Parish, Clairborne-Jefferson Counties, Mississippi*. Port
    Gibson, MS: Clairborne-Jefferson Genealogical Society, 1995. 145p.
Terry, Brenda. *Slaves I, Claiborne County, Mississippi*. Bowie, MD: Heritage Books, 1995.
    207p.

Clarke County

Kemper, Glennie W. *Confederate Pension Record Book, Clarke County, Mississippi*. Merid-
    ian, MS: Lauderdale County Department of Archives and History, 1995. Unpgd.
Strickland, Jean. *Records of Clarke County, Mississippi, WPA Source Materials, Dead Ab-
    stracts, 1834–1854*. Moss Point, MS: Author, 1995. 254p.

DeSoto County

Logan, R. F. B. *R. F. B. Logan's Day Book, 1904 to 1906*. Hernando, MS: Genealogical Society
    of DeSoto County, 1995. 119p.
Roster of Confederate Veterans. Hernando, MS: Genealogical Society of DeSoto County, 1995.
    64p.

Jasper County

Strickland, Jean. *Records of Jasper County, Mississippi. WPA Source Materials, Will Abstracts,
    1855–1914*. Moss Point, MS: Author, 1995. 197p.

Jefferson County

Brown, Ann Beckerson. *Jefferson County, Mississippi, Cemeteries, etc.*. Lorman, MS: Anebec
    & Co., 1995. 2 vols.
———. *St. Joseph Parish, Clairborne-Jefferson Counties, Mississippi*. Port Gibson, MS:
    Clairborne-Jefferson Genealogical Society, 1995. 145p.

Port Gibson

Salassi, Walter L. *Wintergreen Cemetery, Port Gibson, Claiborne County, Mississippi*. Shreve-
    port, LA: J & W Enterprises, 1995. 131p.

Tallahatchie County

Wiltshire, Betty Couch. *Tallahatchie County, Mississippi, Will and Probate Records*. Carrollton,
    MS: Pioneer Pub. Co., 1995. 162p.

Tunica County

Logan, R. F. B. *R. F. B. Logan's Day Book 1904 to 1906*. Hernando, MS: Genealogical Society of DeSoto County, 1995. 119p.

Wayne County

Wayne County, Mississippi, White Marriage Records, 1879–1892. Waynesboro, MS: Wayne County Genealogy Organization, 1995. 87p.

Missouri

Concannon, Marie. *Grand Army of the Republic, Missouri Division, Index to Death Rolls, 1882–1940: Taken from the Proceedings of the Annual Encampments*. Columbia, MO: State Historical Society of Missouri, 1995. 184p.

Eakin, Joanne Chiles. *Confederate Records from the United Daughters of the Confederacy Files. Volume 1, Ab-By*. Independence, MO: Author, 1995. 26p.

Eddlemon, Sherida K. *Genealogical Abstracts from Missouri Church Records and Other Religious Sources*. Bowie, MD: Heritage Books, 1995. 179p..

———. *Missouri Birth and Death Records*. Bowie, MD: Heritage Books, 1995. 437p.

———. *Missouri Genealogical Gleanings, 1840 and Beyond. Volume 2*. Bowie, MD: Heritage Books, 1995. Unpgd.

Frontier Genealogy: Special Sources and Techniques For Tracing Your Pioneer Ancestors. Topeka, KS: Topeka Genealogical Society, 1995. 76p.

Kot, Elizabeth Gorrell. *Missouri Cemetery Inscription Sources, Print and Microfilm*. Vallejo, CA: Indices Pub., 1995. 842p.

Larson, Carl V. *The Women of the Mormon Battalion*. Logan, UT: Author, 1995. 130p.

Mormon Americana: A Guide to Sources and Collections in the United States. Provo, UT: Brigham Young University Studies, 1995. 695p.

Sherarer, Gary W. *The Civil War and Slavery in Missouri: A Bibliographic Guide to Secondary Sources and Selected Primary Sources*. Angwin, CA: Author, 1995. 28p.

Sifakis, Stewart. *Compendium of the Confederate Armies Series: Kentucky, Maryland, Missouri, the Confederate Units and the Indian Units*. NY: Facts on File, 1995. 240p.

Andrew County

Woodruff, Audrey Lee. *Andrew County, Missouri, Marriage Records, 1841–1856, and Early Settlers*. Russellville, KY: A. B. Willhite, 1995. 68p.

Barry County

Lamp, Lisa. *Barry County, Missouri, Marriage Book ABC, 1837–1876*. Monett, MO: Author, 1995. 156p.

Calloway County

Calloway County, Missouri, Augusta Presbyterian Church, Shamrock, Missouri, 1846–1953, Admissions, Dismissals, Baptisms, Burials in the Augusta Cemetery. Shelbyville, MO: Wilham Genealogical Research and Pub., 1995. 118p.

Cole County

Turpin, Tom. *Naturalizations, Cole County, Missouri.* Jefferson City, MO: Mid-Missouri Genealogical Society, Inc., 1995. 47p.

DeSoto

Maness, Charlotte M. *Old Settlers Reunions: DeSoto, Jefferson County, Missouri, September 1891 thru 1941.* Author, 1995. 170p.

Douglas County

Coffman, Brenda Sutherland. *Gone But Not Forgotten, Cemetery Survey of the Eastern District, Douglas County, Missouri.* Flagstaff, AZ: L. Sutherland, 1995. 342p.

Gasconade County

Blattner, Teresa. *Gasconade County, Missouri, Marriage Records, Books A-C, 1821–1873.* Bowie, MD: Heritage Books, 1995. 153p.

Grandview

History of Grandview, Missouri, 1844–1994. Grandview, MO: Grandview Historical Society, 1995. 282p.

Grape Grove

McKemy, Al. *Cemeteries of Grape Grove Township, Ray County, Missouri.* Hardin, MO: Author, 1995. 98p.

Harrison County

History of Harrison County Churches. Bethany, MO: Harrison County Genealogical Society, 1995. 352p.

Iron County

Past and Present, a History of Iron County, Missouri, 1857–1994. Marceline, MO: Heritage House Pub., 1995. 436p.

Jackson County

Marriage Records of Jackson County, Missouri, 1827–1881. Independence, MO: Jackson County Genealogical Society, 1995. Unpgd.

Mayer, Patricia Morrison. *Lee's Summit City Cemetery, 3rd Street and 291 Hiway, Lee's Summit, Missouri 64064, Prairie Township, Burials, 1864 through July 1995.* Lone Jack, MO: Author, 1995. 311p.

Jefferson County

Maness, Charlotte M. *Fink Funeral Home Records: Jefferson County, Missouri.* Author, 1995. 148p.

———. *Old Settlers Reunions: DeSoto, Jefferson County, Missouri, September 1891 thru 1941.* Author, 1995. 170p.

Kansas City

Steen, Esther Laughlin. *Linwood Presbyterian Church, 1890–1975.* 1995. 182p.

Lafayette County

Brunetti, Marty Helm. *Lafayette County, Missouri, Cemeteries Locations and How to Find Them.* Odessa, MO: Author, 1995. 49p.

Lincoln County

Mortality Census, Lincoln County, Missouri, 1850–1860–1870–1880. St. Charles, MO: St. Charles County Genealogical Society, 1995. 15p.

Madison County

Bartels, Carolyn M. *Madison County, Missouri, Marriages.* Shawnee Mission, KS: Author, 1995. Unpgd.

Marion County

Wilham, Kathleen. *Marion County, Missouri, Hannibal Tri-Weekly Messenger Abstracts, 3 October 1855–4 December 1858.* Shelbyville, MO: Author, 1995. 100p.

Milan

Hall, Juanita Bowman. *Riggen Funeral Home, Register of Funerals, 1933–1981.* Unionville, MO: Author, 1995. 112p.
———. *Schoene Funeral Home, Milan, Missouri, Register of Funerals, 1891–1964.* Unionville, MO: Author, 1995. 297p.

Mississippi County

Mississippi County Genealogical Society. *1900 Census, Mississippi County, Missouri.* Ozark, MO: Dogwood Pub. Co., 1995. Unpgd.

Moniteau County

Recordings of Willow Fork and Moreau Township Cemeteries. California, MO: Moniteau County Historical Society, 1995. 227p.

Odessa

Missouri Ledger, a History of Odessa, Lafayette County, Missouri, July 1990. Blairstown, MO: Small Farm Enterprise, 1995. 34p.

Osage County

Gentges, Margaret H. *Births, Baptisms in Osage County, Missouri, prior to the 1880 Federal Census of Children and Spouses of the Immigrant Families.* Great Falls, VA: Author, 1995. 121p.

————. *Immigrants to Osage County, Missouri, and Their Immigrant Ships.* 2nd ed. Great Falls, VA: Author, 1995. 128p.

Ozark County

Looney, Janice Soutee. *Ozark County, Missouri, 1880 Federal Census.* Walnut Grove, MO: Author, 1995. 135p.

Perry County

St. Maurus Catholic Church at Biehle, Perry County, Missouri, Baptisms, Marriages and Burials, Beginning with the 1870 Founding of the Church. Perryville, MO: Perry County Historical Society, 1995. 102p.

Saint Louis

St. Louis Jewish Community Archives, Guide to Archival Collections. St. Louis, MO: The Archives, 1995. 63p.

Sedalia

Obituaries Sedalia, Pettis County, Missouri: Published in the Sedalia Democrat, January 1, 1995 thru December 31, 1995. Sedalia, MO: Daughters of the American Revolution, Genealogical Records Committee, 1995. 254p.

Springfield

Lester, Gary W. *Springfield, Missouri, National Cemetery.* Braggs, OK: Green Leaf Creek Publications, 1995. 225p.

Thieme Funeral Home Records, 1924–1942, Murphysboro, Illinois, 5 November 1924–13 May 1929, and Springfield, Missouri, 5 July 1929-5 January 1942. Springfield, MO: Ozarks Genealogical Society, 1995. 150p.

Sullivan County

Swisher, Annabelle Hoerrman. *Milan Standard Obituary Notices.* Milan, MO: General John Sullivan Chapter, DAR, 1995. 134p.

Montana

Hardaway, Roger D. *A Narrative Bibliography of the African American Frontier, Blacks in the Rocky Mountain West, 1535–1912.* Lewiston, NY: Edwin Mellen Press, 1995. 242p.

Nebraska

Frontier Genealogy: Special Sources and Techniques for Tracing Your Pioneer Ancestors. Topeka, KS: Topeka Genealogical Society, 1995. 76p.

Nebraska Library List, Includes All Public, Academic, Special and Institutional and Educational Service Units in Nebraska. Lincoln, NE: Nebraska Library Commission, 1995. 51p.

Perkey, Elton. *Perkey's Nebraska Place Names.* Rev. ed. 1995. 226p.

Tate, Michael L. *Nebraska History: An Annotated Bibliography.* Westport, CT: Greenwood Press, 1995. 549p.

Antelope County

The War Years and the People of Antelope County, Nebraska. Dallas, TX: Curtis Media, 1995. 167p.

Beatrice

Beatrice Cemetery Association, Beatrice, Nebraska: Old Beatrice Cemetery, Evergreen Home Cemetery, Evergreen Memorial Park Cemetery. Lincoln, NE: Nebraska State Genealogical Society, 1995. 2 vols.

Hall County

Jackson, Vonna J. *Marriages, Hall County, Nebraska.* Grand Island, NE: Prairie Pioneer Genealogical Society, 1995. Unpgd.

Holstein

Plambeck, Jan. *Burials, 1900 to Present, and Cemetery Index, St. Paul's Lutheran Church, Holsten, Adams County, Nebraska.* Lincoln, NE: Nebraska State Genealogical Society, 1995. 15p.

Lancaster County

Lancaster County, Nebraska, District Court Records Intention to Naturalize, 1867–1944. Lincoln, NE: Lincoln Lancaster County Genealogical Society, 1995. 176p.

Pickrell

Pleasant View Church Cemetery, Pickrell, Nebraska, Gage County. Lincoln, NE: E. & R. De Vries, 1995. 15p.

Richardson County

Richardson County, Nebraska, District Court Records Intention to Naturalize, 1857–1952. Lincoln, NE: Ellen De Vries, 1995. 20p.

Sarpy County
Sarpy County, Nebraska, District Court Records Intention to Naturalize, 1856–1915. Lincoln, NE: Ellen De Vries, 1995. 13p.

Talmage
Grant Evergreen Cemetery, Talmage, Nebraska, Nemaha County. Lincoln, NE: E. & R. De Vries, 1995. 16p.

York County
York County, Nebraska, District Court Records Intention to Naturalize, 1870–1929. Lincoln, NE: Ellen De Vries, 1995. 27p.

Nevada

Compiled Service Records of Volunteer Union Soldiers Who Served in Organizations from the Territory and State of Nevada. Washington, DC: National Archives and Records Administration, 1995. 4p.

Crail Rugotzke, Donna. *Dangerous Women, Dangerous Times, Women at the Nevada State Prison, 1890–1930.* Thesis (M.A.), University of Nevada, Las Vegas, 1995. 80p.

Guide to Records in the National Archives, Pacific Sierra Region. Washington, DC: National Archives and Records Administration, Pacific Sierra Region, 1995. 85p.

Guide to Records in the National Archives, Pacific Southwest Region. Washington, DC: National Archives and Records Administration, Pacific Southwest Region, 1995. 48p.

Hardaway, Roger D. *A Narrative Bibliography of the African American Frontier, Blacks in the Rocky Mountain West, 1535–1912.* Lewiston, NY: Edwin Mellen Press, 1995. 242p.

Nevada State Prison Name Inventory to Inmate Case Files, 1863–1950. Carson City, NV: Nevada State Library and Archives, 1995. 99p.

Reed, Ellen. *An Annotated Bibliography of the Nevada Collection at the Clark County Library, and Including an Index and Distribution Finder.* Las Vegas, NV: Clark County Library, 1995. 71p.

Carson City
Ansari, Mary B. *Carson City Place Names, the Names of Old Ormsby County, Nevada.* Reno, NV: Camp Nevada, 1995. 68p.

Reno
Land, Barbara. *A Short History of Reno.* Reno, NV: University of Nevada Press, 1995. 130p.

Virginia City

Francke, Bernadette S. *Inventory Index of the Silver Terrace Cemeteries*. Virginia City, NV: Comstock Historic District Commission, 1995. 34p.

New Hampshire

Batchelder, Jean. *History and Heroes of New Hampshire Aviation*. Spring Hill, FL: Arrow, 1995. Unpgd.

Brown, Jeffrey Ernest. *On the Fringes, Women's Lives and Quaker Theology in Northern New England, 1700–1785*. Thesis (M.A.), University of New Hampshire, 1995. 127p.

Close, Virginia l. *Index to Historical New Hampshire, Volumes 26–35, 1971–1980*. Concord, NH: New Hampshire Historical Society, 1995. 81p.

Dodge, Timothy. *Crime and Punishment in New Hampshire, 1812–1914*. NY: P. Lang, 1995. 406p.

Emery, Eric B. *New England Captives in Canada and the Ransom Missions of Phineas Stevens, 1749, 1751 and 1752*. Thesis (M.A.), University of Vermont, 1995. 115p.

Erwin, Patricia A. *Bridge from the Past to the Future, Preserving New Hampshire's Heritage of Information: Report of the New Hampshire Preservation Initiative Committee to the Citizens of New Hampshire*. Concord, NH: New Hampshire State Library, 1995. 36p.

Gilmore, George C. *Roll of New Hampshire Soldiers at the Battle of Bennington, August 16, 1777, Published with New Hampshire Men at Louisburg, 1745*. Baltimore, MD: Clearfield, 1896, 1995. 63p.

Lanzendorf, Scott. *New Hampshire Militia Officers, 1820–1850, Division, Brigade and Regimental Field and Staff Officers*. Bowie, MD: Heritage Books, 1995. 212p.

———. *New Hampshire Militia Officers, 1820–1850*. Thesis (M.A.), University of New Hampshire, 1995. 85p.

Page, Patsy R. *Directory of New Hampshire Physicians, Attorneys, Dentists, 1884*. Alachua, FL: Page Publications, 1995. 19p.

———. *Directory of New Hampshire Physicians, Attorneys, Dentists, 1894*. Alachua, FL: Page Publications, 1995. 21p.

Rollock, Rich. *New Hampshire Family Histories*. 3rd. ed. Laconia, NH: Family Histories Directory, 1995. 212p.

Scobie, Robert. *Genealogical Abstracts from the New Hampshire Spy, 1786–1793*. Bowie, MD: Heritage Books, 1995. 332p.

Belknap County

Ruell, David. *The Historic Churches of Belknap County, 1791–1940*. Meredith, NH: Lakes Region Planning Commission, 1995. 186p.

Claremont

Boadway, Edgar Atkinson. *A Brief History of the Roman Catholic Church of St. Mary in Claremont, New Hampshire.* Claremont, NH: Letter Man Press, 1995. 67p.

Danbury

Danbury, New Hampshire, 1795–1995, 200 Years of History. Danbury, NH: Bicentennial Committee of Danbury, 1995. 84p.

Dover

Wentworth, William Edgar. *Vital Records from Dover, New Hampshire's First Newspaper, 1790–1829.* New Hampshire Society of Genealogists Special Publication Number 6. Rockport, ME: Picton Press, 1995. 411p.

Dublin

Derby, Samuel Carroll. *Early Dublin, a List of the Revolutionary Soldiers of Dublin, New Hampshire.* 1995. 34p.

Durham

Dodge, Timothy. *Poor Relief in Durham, Lee and Madbury, New Hampshire, 1732–1891.* Bowie, MD: Heritage Books, 1995. 135p.

Exeter

Bell, Charles Henry. *Sketches of an Old New Hampshire Town as It Was a Hundred Years Ago.* Author, 1995. 37p.

Gilman, Wayne Clark. *The Hingham Founding Fathers of Old Colony, New Hampshire, Exeter II, the Origins, 1623–1655.* Bowie, MD: Heritage Books, 1995. 174p.

Jefferson

Corrigan, Robert E. *Jefferson, New Hampshire, before 1996.* Jefferson, NH: Town of Jefferson, 1995. 404p.

Kingston

Arseneault, Judith A. *The Vital Records of Kingston, New Hampshire, 1694–1994.* Baltimore, MD: Clearfield, 1995. 261p.

Laconia

Huse, Warren Daniel. *Laconia.* Dover, NH: Arcadia, 1995. 128p.

Lee

Dodge, Timothy. *Poor Relief in Durham, Lee and Madbury, New Hampshire, 1732–1891.* Bowie, MD: Heritage Books, 1995. 135p.

Lempster

Lempster, New Hampshire, Inhabitants from Incorporation in 1767 through 1900 Federal Census. St. Petersburg, FL: J. W. Stevens, 1995. 135p.

Madbury

Dodge, Timothy. *Poor Relief in Durham, Lee and Madbury, New Hampshire, 1732–1891.* Bowie, MD: Heritage Books, 1995. 135p.

Peterborough

Charpentier, Robert. *Marriages Recorded in the Town Reports of Peterboro, New Hampshire, 1887–1948.* Pawtucket, RI: American French Genealogical Society, 1995. 559p.

Portsmouth

Hackett, Frank Warren. *1645–1656, Portsmouth Records, a Transcript of the First Thirty-five Pages of the Earliest Town Book, Portsmouth, New Hampshire with Notes.* Author, 1995. 76p.

Sandwich

Sandwich, New Hampshire, 1763–1900, a Little World by Itself. Portsmouth, NH: Peter E. Randall, 1995. 359p.

Strafford County

Canney, Robert S. *The Early Marriages of Strafford County, New Hampshire, 1630–1860.* Bowie, MD: Heritage Books, 1995. 2 vols.

Thompson, Lucien. *Revolutionary Pension Declarations, Strafford County, 1820–1932, Comprising Sketches of Soldiers of the Revolution.* 1995. 35p.

Stratford

A History of Stratford, New Hampshire. Rev. ed. Center Stratford, NH: Stratford Historical Society, 1995. 286p.

Unity

Beals, Kathleen C. *Early Families of Unity, New Hampshire, and Cemeteries of Unity, New Hampshire.* Albany, CA: Author, 1995. 235p.

New Jersey

Beck, Clark L. *Revolutionary War Manuscripts in Special Collections and Archives, Rutgers University Libraries.* New Brunswick, NJ: Rutgers University, 1995. 34p.

Cutler, Timothy G. *Bibliography: Sources Related to the French and Indian Wars, 1750–1770.* Blairstown, NJ: New Jersey Frontier Guard, 1995. 23p.

League of Historical Societies of New Jersey Membership Directory. Upper Montclair, NJ: The League, 1995. 12p.

Murrin, Mary R. *New Jersey History, an Annotated and Selected Introductory Bibliography.* Rev. Trenton, NJ: New Jersey Historical Commission, 1995. 24p.

New Jersey in the French and Indian Wars, 1755–1761. Blairstown, NJ: New Jersey Frontier Guard 1756, 1995. 23p.

New Jersey's Women Legislators, 1921–1995. Trenton, NJ: Fitzgerald's New Jersey Legislative Manual, 1995. 80p.

Sheth, Manju. *Asian Indian Immigrant Experience in New Jersey: An Oral History Research Project, 1995.* Author, 1995. 134p.

Sinclair, Donald A. *New Jersey Collective Biographical Sources: A Bibliography.* Metuchen, NJ: Upland Press, 1995. 104p.

Wacker, Peter O., and Paul G. E. Clemens. *Land Use in Early New Jersey: A Historical Geography.* Newark, NJ: New Jersey Historical Society, 1995. 321p.

Atlantic County

Wright, Barbara Epler. *Early Church Records of Atlantic and Cape May Counties, New Jersey.* Westminster, MD: Family Line Pub., 1995. 81p.

Bergen County

Burket, Jerri. *Every Name Index to History of Bergen County, New Jersey.* Englewood, NJ: Bergen Historic Books, 1995. 71p.

———. *Full Name Index to History of Bergen and Passaic Counties, New Jersey.* Englewood, NJ: Bergen Historic Books, 1995. 90p.

Davis, John David. *Bergen County, New Jersey, Deed Records, 1689–1801.* Bowie, MD: Heritage Books, 1995. 412p.

Geismar, Joan H. *Gethsemane Cemetery in Death and Life, a Bergen County Historic Site in an Archaeological Perspective.* Hackensack, NJ: Bergen County Department of Parks, Division of Cultural and Historic Affairs, 1995. 232p.

Bridgeton

Frontline and Homefront, the Story of How World War II Affected the Lives of People Residing in the Area of Cumberland County, New Jersey. Bridgeton, NJ: Bridgeton Evening News, 1995. 104p.

Burlington County

Meldrum, Charlotte D. *Early Church Records of Burlington County, New Jersey. Volume 3.* Westminster, MD: Family Line Publications, 1995. 201p.

Edison

Stelton and Piscatawaytown Graveyards, Burial Records, 1880. Metuchen, NJ: Metuchen Edison Historical Society, 1995. Unpgd.

Hoboken

Askea, Doris Anderson. *1850 Hoboken, New Jersey, Census.* Kernersville, NC: Author, 1995. 70p.

Irvington

Index to the Irvington Local History Photography Collection. Irvington, NJ: Irvington Public Library, 1995. Unpgd.

Middlesex County

Monroe, Barbara J. *Index to History of Union and Middlesex Counties, New Jersey, with Biographical Sketches of Many of Their Pioneers and Prominent Men, Edited by W. Woodord Clayton.* Fort Wayne, IN: Author, 1995. 236p.

Monmouth County

The American Revolution in Monmouth County, New Jersey, an Annotated Bibliography. Freehold, NJ: Monmouth County Historical Association, 1995. 66p.

Morris County

Mitros, David. *Directory of Historic Morris County, New Jersey: A Guide to Historical Resources, Museums, Historical Associations and Archives with an Extensive Bibliography of Local History.* Morristown, NJ: Morris County Heritage Commission, 1995. 71p.

Paterson

Burket, Jerri. *History of the City of Paterson and the County of Passaic, New Jersey, Every Name Index.* Englewood, NJ: Bergen Historic Books, 1995. 132p.

Union County

Monroe, Barbara J. *Index to History of Union and Middlesex Counties, New Jersey, with Biographical Sketches of Many of Their Pioneers and Prominent Men, Edited by W. Woodord Clayton.* Fort Wayne, IN: Author, 1995. 236p.

Warren County

O'Brien, John L. *History of the Year, a Chronological Listing of Events from 1892 to 1915 from the Pages of the Washington Star.* Andover, NJ: Author, 1995. 236p.

Washington

O'Brien, John L. *History of the Year, a Chronological Listing of Events from 1892 to 1915 from the Pages of the Washington Star.* Andover, NJ: Author, 1995. 236p.

New Mexico

Brylinski, Dorothy A. and Ann L. Mossman. *New Mexico Genealogist Comprehensive Index, Volumes 1–33, 1962–1994.* Albuquerque, NM: New Mexico Genealogical Society, 1995. Unpgd.

Cutter, Charles R. *The Legal Culture of Northern Spain, 1700–1810.* Albuquerque, NM: University of New Mexico Press, 1995. 227p.

Directory of Special Libraries and Collections in New Mexico. 3rd. ed. Albuquerque, NM: Special Library Association, Rio Grande Chapter, 1995. 52p.

Garmendia Leal, Guillermo. *Origen de los Fundadores de Texas, Nuevo México, Coahuila y Nuevo León*. Monterrey, Mexico: Author, 1995. 4 vols.

Goulesque, Florence R. J. *Europeans in the American West since 1800: A Bibliography*. Albuquerque, NM: Center for the American West, University of New Mexico, 1995. 81p.

Guide to Records in the National Archives, Pacific Southwest Region. Washington, DC: National Archives and Records Administration, Pacific Southwest Region, 1995. 48p.

Las Cruces

Death Records of Las Cruces, New Mexico, Taken from the Las Cruces Sun News, 1993. Las Cruces, NM: Las Cruces Public Library, 1995. 34p.

Death Records of Las Cruces, New Mexico, Taken from the Las Cruces Sun News, 1994. Las Cruces, NM: Las Cruces Public Library, 1995. 38p.

Lovington

St. Mary's Episcopal Church, Lovington, Lea County, New Mexico, Marriages from Parish Books I & II. 1995. Unpgd.

San Juan County

Wilmer, Anna Lois Tubbs. *Early Marriages in San Juan County, New Mexico*. Author, 1995. 2 vols.

New York

Articles in the New York Genealogical and Biographical Record, 1983–1985, Indexed by Principal Surname or Location. NY: New York Genealogical and Biographical Society, 1995. 17p.

Association Oath Rolls of the British Plantations (New York, Virginia, etc.), AD 1696. Baltimore, MD: Clearfield, 1995. 86p.

Barbour, Hugh. *Quaker Crosscurrents, Three Hundred Years of Friends in the New York Yearly Meetings*. Syracuse, NY: Syracuse University Press, 1995. 432p.

Bowman, Fred Q. *Directory to Collections of New York Vital Records, 1726–1989, with Rare Gazetteer*. Bowie, MD: Heritage Books, 1995. 91p.

Carter, Fran. *New York Genealogical Research Tips*. Walker Publications, 1995. 80p.

Directory of Long Island Libraries and Media Centers, 1995. NY: Library Directory Associates, 1995. Unpgd.

Epperson, Gwenn F. *New Netherlands Roots.* Baltimore, MD: Genealogical Pub. Co., 1995. 147p.

Falk, Byron A. *Personal Name Index to The New York Times Index, 1975–1993, Supplement.* Verdi, NV: Roxbury Data Interface, 1995. Unpgd.

Fowler, Albert W. *Peopling the Adirondacks: A Report of the Adirondack Museum's Survey Describing Documentary Collections Concerning the History of the Diverse Peoples in the Adirondack Region.* Blue Mountain Lake, NY: Adirondack Museum, 1995. 240p.

Guide to Records of the Governor's Office in the New York State Archives. Albany, NY: New York State Archives and Records Administration, 1995. 153p.

Hulsander, Laura Penny. *New York Loyalist Confiscations.* Alexandria, VA: Sleeper Co., 1995. 41p.

Krewson, Margrit Beran. *New Netherland, 1609–1664: A Selective Bibliography.* Washington, DC: Library of Congress, 1995. 92p.

MacWethy, Lou. *Book of Names, Especially Relating to the Early Palatines and the First Settlers of the Mohawk Valley.* Baltimore, MD: Genealogical Publishing Co., 1933, 1995. 209p.

Migration from the Russian Empire, Lists of Passengers Arriving at the Port of New York. Baltimore, MD: Genealogical Pub. Co., 1995. 2 vols.

New Netherland. Council. *Council Minutes, 1655–1656.* Syracuse, NY: Syracuse University Press, 1995. 359p.

Prevost, Toni Jollay. *Indians from New York, a Genealogy Reference.* Bowie, MD: Heritage Books, 1995. 233p.

———. *Indians from New York, in Ontario and Quebec, Canada, a Genealogy Reference.* Bowie, MD: Heritage Books, 1995. 255p.

———. *Indians from New York, in Wisconsin and Elsewhere, a Genealogy Reference.* Bowie, MD: Heritage Books, 1995. 228p.

Rice, Horace R. *Buffalo Ridge Cherokee, a Remnant of a Great Nation Divided.* Bowie, MD: Heritage Books, 1995. 256p.

Roe, Kathleen. *Statewide Access to Historical Records in New York State, Planning for the Future.* Albany, NY: State Archives and Records Administration, 1995. 26p.

Schweitzer, George Keene. *New York Genealogical Research.* Knoxville, TN: Author, 1995. 250p.

Southeastern New York Library Resources Council Documentary Heritage Program: Directory of Repositories, 1995. Highland, NY: The Council, 1995. 35p.

Albany

Ptak, Diane Snyder. *Lost and Found, Albany Area Church and Synagogue Vital Records, 1654–1925.* Author, 1995. 10p.

Wing, Judith G. *Bibliography on the Albany, New York, Area: Listings from Capital District Library Catalogs.* Albany, NY: Hudson Mohawk Library Association, 1995. 411p.

Alfred

Sanford, Ilou M. *First Alfred Seventh Day Baptist Church Membership Records, Alfred, New York.* Bowie, MD: Heritage Books, 1995. 106p.

Arden

Smeltzer Stevenot, Marjorie. *Abstracts of Records from the Parish Register of St. John's Church, Greenwood, Arden, Orange County, New York, 1856–1923.* Sloatsburg, NY: Author, 1995. 72p.

Boonville
Pitcher, James S. *From the Files of the Town Historian.* Boonville, NY: Author, 1995. 175p.

Buffalo
Polish Genealogical Research at the Buffalo and Erie County Public Library. Buffalo, NY: Special Collections Department, Buffalo and Erie County Public Library, 1995. Unpgd.
Searching for Family History at the Buffalo and Erie County Public Library. 3rd ed. Buffalo, NY: Special Collections Department, Buffalo and Erie County Public Library, 1995. 21p.
Searching for Your Civil War Ancestors at the Buffalo and Erie County Public Library. Buffalo, NY: Special Collections Department, Buffalo and Erie County Public Library, 1995. 11p.

Cape Vincent
Rogers, A. E. *Town of Cape Vincent, Jefferson County, New York, Cemetery Inscriptions, Includes 1850 Heads of Household.* Syracuse, NY: J & E Bartlett, 1995. 113p.

Chautauqua County
Chautauqua County, New York, Cemetery Inscriptions and County and Town History. Sarasota, FL: Aceto Bookmen, 1995. 281p.

Clinton County
Samuelsen, W. David. *Clinton County, New York, Will Testators Index, 1807–1902.* Salt Lake City, UT: Sampubco, 1995. 34p.

Dutchess County
Doherty, Frank J. *Settlers of the Beekman Patent, Dutchess County, New York, an Historical and Genealogical Study of All of the 18th Century Settlers in the Patent. Volume 3. Burtis to Dakin.* Pleasant Valley, NY: Author, 1995. 1,129p.

Fort Ann
Cemetery Records of the Township of Fort Ann, Washington County, New York. Rev. ed. July 1995. Queensbury, NY: Historical Data Services, 1995. 123p.

Hempstead
Town of Hempstead Archives: Repository Guide. Hempstead, NY: Office of the Presiding Supervisor, Hempstead, New York, 1995. 65p.

Lawyersville
Richard, Lawrence V. *Vital Records of the Lawyersville Reformed Church, Lawyersville, Schoharie County, NY.* Author, 1995. 139p.

Madison County
Houck, Clara Metcalf. *Vital Statistics from Chittenango Newspapers, 1831–1854.* Mount Airy, MD: Pipe Creek Publications, 1995. 172p.
Kellogg, Minne L. *Deaths and Marriages, 1850–1860, from the Files of the Syracuse Chronicle, the Daily Standard and Madison Observer.* Mount Airy, MD: Pipe Creek Publications, 1995. 216p.

Marcellus

Guide to Archival Collections. Marcellus, NY: Town of Marcellus, 1995. 15p.

Masonville

Goerlich, Shirley Boyce. *Masonville, Delaware County, New York, Early Records from the Past.* Bainbridge, NY: RSG Pub., 1995. 209p.

New York

Epperson, Gwenn F. *New Netherland Roots.* Baltimore, MD: Genealogical Pub. Co., 1995. 147p.

Farrell, Charles. *German Reformed Church in New York City, 1758–1805.* Largo, FL: Author, 1995. 229p.

Inskeep, Carolee R. *The New York Foundling Hospital, an Index to Its Federal, State, and Local Census Records (1870–1925).* Baltimore, MD: Clearfield, 1995. 339p.

Krewson, Margrit Beran. *New Netherland, 1609–1664: A Selective Bibliography.* Washington, DC: Library of Congress, 1995. 92p.

Maffi, Mario. *Gateway to the Promised Land: Ethnic Cultures on New York's Lower East Side.* NY: New York University Press, 1995. 343p.

Shea, Anne M. and Marion R. Casey. *The Irish Experience in New York City, a Select Bibliography.* NY: NY Irish History Roundtable, 1995. 130p.

Onondaga County

Kellogg, Minne L. *Deaths and Marriages, 1850–1860, from the Files of the Syracuse Chronicle, the Daily Standard and Madison Observer.* Mount Airy, MD: Pipe Creek Publications, 1995. 216p.

Otsego County

Barber, Gertrude Audrey. *A Collection of Abstracts from Otsego County, New York, Newspaper Obituaries, 1808–1875.* Mount Airy, MD: Pipe Creek Publications, 1995. 318p.

Reamy, Martha. *Early Families of Otsego County, New York.* Mt. Airy, MD: Pipe Creek, 1995. 248p.

Town of Otsego, New York, Abstracts of the 1825 New York State Census. Syracuse, NY: Tree Talks, 1995. Unpgd.

Phelps

Burnisky, David L. *The Personalities of Melvin Hill Cemetery, Phelps, Ontario County, New York.* Bowie, MD: Heritage Books, 1995. 269p.

Pound Ridge

Pessoni, Philip A. *Historical Notes on the Great South Lots 9 & 10 and the Undivided Lands behind Bedford of the Van Cortlandt Manor, 1640–1940: Now Known as the Ward Pound Ridge Reservation.* Boutonville, NY: Author, 1995. 83p.

Rochester

Freundlich, Charlene. *Master Index to Interments, 1871 thru 1883, at Holy Sepulchre Cemetery, Rochester, Monroe County, New York.* Rochester, NY: Author, 1995. 157p.

Saint Lawrence County

Samuelsen, W. David. *Saint Lawrence County, New York, Will Testators Index, 1830–1916.* Salt Lake City, UT: Sampubco, 1995. 119p.

Sennett

Jennings, Laura O. *Records of First Baptist Church of Sennett, Cayuga County, New York, and History of Cayuga County, New York, with Data from Town of Sennett, and 1867 Directory of Individuals, from Cayuga County, 1868 Directory by Hamilton Child.* Sarasota, FL: Aceto Bookmen, 1995. 21p.

Staten Island

Jackson, Ronald David. *African American History in Staten Island, Slave Holding Families and Their Slaves, Raw Notes.* Staten Island, NY: Staten Island Historical Society, 1995. 91p.

Stephentown

Niles, Susan A. *Records, Stephentown Baptist Church, 1795–1816, Stephentown, Rensselaer County, New York.* Author, 1995. 133p.

Syracuse

Kellogg, Minne L. *Deaths and Marriages, 1850–1860, from the Files of the Syracuse Chronicle, the Daily Standard and Madison Observer.* Mount Airy, MD: Pipe Creek Publications, 1995. 216p.

Tompkins County

Martin, Catherine Machan. *Records of Tompkins County, New York: Wills, Intestates, Bibles, Church and Family Records, Wills, 1817-Mid 1839, Liber A thru C, with Added Wills and Notes Concerning Tompkins County, New York, Early Families as Taken from LDS Roll 0853,070.* Durand, MI: Author, 1995. 195p.

Ulster County

Donohue, Donald C. *The Ulster County Genealogical Society's Families of Ulster County.* Hurley, NY: Ulster County Genealogical Society, 1995. 4 vols.

Warren County

Lynch, Thomas J. *1875 Census Index, Warren County, New York.* Saratoga Springs, NY: Author, 1995. 57p.

———. *Warren County, New York, Archival Index.* Saratoga Springs, NY: Author, 1995. 2 vols.

———. *Warren County, New York, Naturalization Papers, 1814–1906.* Saratoga Springs, NY: Author, 1995. 28p.

Washington County

Jackson, Mary Smith. *Death Notices from Washington County, New York, Newspapers, 1799-1880.* Bowie, MD: Heritage Books, 1995. 477p.

———. *Marriage Notices from Washington County, New York, Newspapers, 1799–1880.* Bowie, MD: Heritage Books, 1995. 443p.

Westchester County

Carmichael, David W. *Westchester County Government Publications in the Westchester County Archives*. Elmsford, NY: Westchester County Archives, 1995. 65p.

Hillman, Carol D. M. *Abstracts and Index to Guardianship Letters, Westchester County, New York, 1802–1896*. Spring Glen, NY: KINFO, 1995. 40p.

Pessoni, Philip A. *Historical Notes on the Great South Lots 9 & 10 and the Undivided Lands behind Bedford of the Van Cortlandt Manor, 1640–1940: Now Known as the Ward Pound Ridge Reservation*. Boutonville, NY: Author, 1995. 83p.

Yates County

Bunce, Bonnie M. *Index to History and Directory of Yates County, New York, by Stafford C. Cleveland*. Aurora, CO: Author, 1995. 170p.

North Carolina

Bradley, Stephen E., Jr. *North Carolina Confederate Militia and Home Guard Records*. Virginia Beach, VA: Author, 1995. 2 vols.

Franklin, John Hope. *The Free Negro in North Carolina*. Chapel Hill, NC: University of North Carolina, 1995. Unpgd.

Guide to Research Materials in the North Carolina State Archives State Agency Records. Raleigh, NC: North Carolina Division of Archives and History, Archives Records Section, 1995. 855p.

Haun, Weynette Parks. *North Carolina Revolutionary Army Accounts, Secretary of State's Papers*. Durham, NC: Author, 1995. Unpgd.

Jones, Houston Gwynne. *North Carolina History: An Annotated Bibliography*. Westport, CT: Greenwood Press, 1995. 796p.

Nuckols, Ashley Kay. *Deaths, American Expeditionary Force, WWI, 1917, 1918, North Carolina*. Tazewell, VA: Author, 1995. Unpgd.

Oakley, Crestena Anna Jennings. *The North Carolina Genealogical Society Journal, a Listing of Journal Articles, 1975–1995*. Raleigh, NC: North Carolina Genealogical Society, 1995. 17p.

Page, Patsy R. *Directory of North Carolina Physicians, 1886*. Alachua, FL: Page Publications, 1995. 18p.

Sifakis, Stewart. *Compendium of the Confederate Armies Series: North Carolina*. NY: Facts on File, 1995. 160p.

White, Barnetta McGhee. *Somebody Knows My Name, Marriages of Freed People in North Carolina, County by County*. Athens, GA: Iberian Publishing Co., 1995. 3 vols.

Alamance County

Teague, Bobbie T. *Cane Creek Mother of Meetings*. Snow Camp, NC: North Carolina Friends Historical Society, 1995. 160p.

Anson County

Kendall, Jerry T. *Concord United Methodist Church, Anson County, North Carolina, Church Register, 1884–1994*. Bennettsville, SC: Author, 1995. 73p.

Beaufort

Cloud, Ellen Fulcher. *Abstracts from Miscellaneous Newspapers Published in Beaufort, North Carolina, 1876–1893*. Ocracoke, NC: Live Oak Publications, 1995. 180p.

Bladen County

McKee, Charles F. *Vital Records of Bladen County, North Carolina, 1753–1915*. Gastonia, NC: Author, 1995. 327p.

Brunswick County

Haskett, Delmas, D. *Brunswick County, North Carolina, 1810 & 1820 Federal Censuses*. Wilmington, NC: Old New Hanover Genealogical Society, 1995. 28p.

Burke County

Cemeteries of Burke County. Morganton, NC: Burke County Genealogical Society, 1995. Unpgd.

Catawba County

Sherrill, Elizabeth Bray. *Catawba County, North Carolina, Delayed Birth*. Sherrills Ford, NC: Author, 1995. Unpgd.

Chapel Hill

African Americana in North Carolina and at the University of North Carolina at Chapel Hill. Southern Research Report, No. 6. Chapel Hill, NC: Academic Affairs Library, Center for the Study of the American South, 1995. 253p.

A Guide to the Archives of the University of North Carolina at Chapel Hill. Chapel Hill, NC: University Archives and Records Service, University of North Carolina at Chapel Hill, 1995. 102p.

Chatham County

Willis, Laura and Dorris Dublin. *Chatham County, North Carolina, Early Deeds. Volume One, 1784–1787*. Melber, KY: Simmons Historical Publications, 1995. 96p.

Cherokee County

Nichols, Mary M. *Cherokee County, North Carolina, Delayed Birth Records, 1875–1913*. Hayesville, NC: Author, 1995. 396p.

Currituck County

Currituck County, North Carolina, Cemetery Records. Baltimore, MD: Gateway Press, 1995. 321p.

Dare County
Everton, Camille Bateman. *Cemeteries of Tyrrell County, Eastern Washington County, East Lake, Dare County*. Bowie, MD: Heritage Books, 1995. 238p.

Edenton
Bradley, Stephen E. *Edenton District, North Carolina, Loose Estates Papers, 1756–1806*. Virginia Beach, VA: Author, 1995. Unpgd.

Edgecombe County
Bradley, Stephen E., Jr. *Edgecombe County, North Carolina, Deeds*. Virginia Beach, VA: Author, 1995. 2 vols.

Forsythe County
Brinegar, Geraldine. *Forsythe County, North Carolina, Marriage Bonds and Co-Habitation Records, 1849–1868*. Winston-Salem, NC: Forsythe County Genealogical Society, 1995. 92p.

Franklin County
Bradley, Stephen E. *Franklin County, North Carolina, Court Minutes*. Virginia Beach, VA: Author, 1995. 2 vols.

Gates County
Fouts, Raymond Parker. *Minutes of County Court of Pleas and Quarter Sessions, Gates County, North Carolina, 1787–1793*. Cocoa, FL: GenRec Books, 1995. 154p.
———. *Registration of Slaves to Work in the Great Dismal Swamp, Gates County, North Carolina, 1847–1861*. Cocoa, FL: GenRec Books, 1995. 144p.

Guilford County
Alamance Presbyterian Church Cemetery Census. Greensboro, NC: J. May, 1995. Unpgd.

Haywood County
Medford, Robert Joseph. *The Families of Haywood County, North Carolina, Based on the 1870 Census Records*. Alexander, NC: WorldComm, 1995. 190p.
———. *The Families of Haywood County, North Carolina, Based on the 1880 Census Records*. Alexander, NC: WorldComm, 1995. 283p.

Henderson County
Henderson County, North Carolina Cemeteries. Spartanburg, SC: Reprint Co., 1995. Unpgd.

Hertford County
Powell, David. *1880 Hertford County Census*. Greenville, NC: Liberty Shield Press, 1995. 208p.

Hyde County
Harris, Morgan H. *Hyde Yesterdays, a History of Hyde County*. Wilmington, NC: New Hanover Print, 1995. 349p.

Johnston County

Ross, Elizabeth E. *Family Bible Records*. Rev. ed. Johnston County, NC: Johnston County, North Carolina Genealogical and Historical Society, 1995. 3 vols.

Kings Mountain

Anthony, Elizabeth Camp. *Sandy Plains, Now Patterson Grove, Kings Mountain, North Carolina*. Shelby, NC: Author, 1995. 53p.

Lenoir County

King, Russell. *Road Overseer's Reports, 1824–1862: Lenoir County, North Carolina*. Author, 1995. Unpgd.

McDowell County

Aldridge, Bryan K. *McDowell County, North Carolina, Cemeteries, Volume 2*. Alexander, NC: WorldComm, 1995. 279p.

Williams, Edward P. *McDowell County, North Carolina, Marriages, 1870–1894*. Author, 1995. 58p.

Mecklenburg County

Karchaske, Susan Janelle. *Mecklenburg County, North Carolina, Cemetery Records*. Charlotte, NC: Family History Researchers and Publishers, 1995. 225p.

Ray, Worth Stickley. *The Mecklenburg Signers and Their Neighbors*. Baltimore, MD: Clearfield, 1995. Unpgd.

Nash County

Rackley, Timothy Wiley. *Nash County, North Carolina, Court Minutes, Volume 5, 1804–1807*. Kernersville, NC: Author, 1995. 113p.

———. *Nash County, North Carolina, Voter Registration, 1902–1908*. Kernersville, NC: Author, 1995. 160p.

New Hanover County

Haskett, Delmas D. *New Hanover County, North Carolina, 1870 Federal Census*. Wilmington, NC: Old New Hanover Genealogical Society, 1995. 3 vols.

Ocracoke

Cloud, Ellen Fulcher. *From Whence We Came, the History of the Original Ocracoke Names*. Ocracoke, NC: Live Oak Publications, 1995. 76p.

Onslow County

Onslow County, North Carolina, Voter Registration Records, 1902, 1904, 1906, 1908. Wilmington, NC: Old Hanover Genealogical Society, 1995. 128p.

Orange County

Bennett, William D. *Orange County Records. Deed Book 12, 1805–1807*. Raleigh, NC: Author, 1995. 102p.

Perquimans County

White, Lori Higley. *Abstracts of Deeds, Perquimans County, North Carolina, 1785–1791.* Boise, ID: Author, 1995. Unpgd.

———. *Abstracts of Divisions of Estates, Perquimans, North Carolina, 1741–1804.* Boise, ID: Author, 1995. 37p.

Pitt County

Churchill, Levis Allen. *Pitt County, North Carolina, Families.* Greenville, NC: Author, 1995. 2 vols.

Portsmouth Island

Cloud, Ellen Fulcher. *The Federal Census of Portsmouth Island, North Carolina, 1790–1900.* Ocracoke, NC: Live Oak Publications, 1995. Unpgd.

Raleigh

Neal, Lois S. *Abstracts of Vital Records from Raleigh, North Carolina, Newspapers, 1830–1839, Part 1 & 2.* Raleigh, NC: North Carolina Genealogical Society, 1995. 2 vols.

Rowan County

Federal Census for Rowan County, North Carolina, 1870. Salisbury, NC: Genealogical Society of Rowan County, 1995. 321p.

The Genealogical Society of Rowan County, North Carolina, Member's Pedigree Charts. Salisbury, NC: Genealogical Society of Rowan County, 1995. Unpgd.

Sampson County

A Portrait of Nineteenth Century Sampson County, as Revealed by Sampson County Court Minutes, 1820–1830. Newton Grove, NC: Sampson County Historical Society, 1995. 309p.

Ross, Elizabeth E. *Sampson County Will Abstracts, 1784–1900.* Clayton, NC: Author, 1995. 177p.

Stokes County

Lineback, Harvey. *Marriage Licenses of Stokes County, North Carolina, 1888–1900.* Mayodan, NC: Genealogical Society of Rockingham and Stokes County, North Carolina, 1995. 252p.

Surry County

Leonard, Carol Jean. *Surry County, North Carolina, Deed Abstracts, Volumes G & H, 1795–1800.* Toast, NC: C & L Historical Publications, 1995. 141p.

———. *Surry County, North Carolina, Deed Abstracts, Volume I, 1800–1803.* Toast, NC: C & L Historical Publications, 1995. 128p.

Tyrrell County

Everton, Camille Bateman. *Cemeteries of Tyrrell County, Eastern Washington County, East Lake, Dare County.* Bowie, MD: Heritage Books, 1995. 238p.

Wake County

Haun, Weynette Parks. *Wake County, North Carolina, Court Minutes, 1808–1811, Book VII.* Durham, NC: Author, 1995. 158p.

Washington County

Everton, Camille Bateman. *Cemeteries of Tyrrell County, Eastern Washington County, East Lake, Dare County.* Bowie, MD: Heritage Books, 1995. 238p.

Watauga County

Marriage Register of Watauga County, North Carolina (1873–1954). Boone, NC: Department of History, Appalachian State University, 1995. 227p.

Wilmington

Hutteman, Ann Hewlett. *St. Paul's Evangelical Lutheran Church. Translation of Congregational and Council Minutes, 6 February 1859–4 February 1873, Originals in German.* Wilmington, NC: Author, 1995. 48p.

Reaves, Bill. *Index to the 1977 Manuscript of Wilmington, North Carolina, an Architectural and Historical Portrait.* Wilmington, NC: New Hanover Public Library, 1995. 37p.

———. *Index to the Seventh Volume of the Morning Star, September 23, 1870–March 22, 1871.* Wilmington, NC: North Carolina Room, New Hanover County Public Library and Old New Hanover Genealogical Society, 1995. 79p.

Sammons, Helen Moore. *Marriage and Death Notices from Wilmington, North Carolina, Newspapers, February 1847–December 1850.* Wilmington, NC: North Carolina Room, New Hanover County Public Library and Old New Hanover Genealogical Society, 1995. 248p.

Wilson County

Howell, Joan L. *Wilson County, North Carolina, Cemeteries, Volume 3.* Wilson, NC: Wilson County, North Carolina Genealogical Society, 1995. 316p.

North Dakota

Becker, Ted Joseph. *Catholic Germans from Russia (Krasna, Bessarabia, Russia) in South-Central North Dakota, 1890–1990, Statistical Compendium.* Fargo, ND: Germans from Russia Heritage Collection, North Dakota Institute for Regional Studies, North Dakota State University, 1995. 1,058p.

Skjei, Jane. *The Dakota Territory, 1885 Census, Nelson and Ramsey Counties Index.* Fargo, ND: North Dakota Institute for Regional Studies, North Dakota State University Libraries, 1995. 157p.

———. *Dakota Territory, 1885 Census, Steele and Griggs Counties Index.* Fargo, ND: North Dakota Institute for Regional Studies, North Dakota State University Libraries, 1995. 136p.

Slater, Sandra J. *Guide to Norwegian Bygdeboker.* Grand Forks, ND: Special Collections Department, University of North Dakota Library, 1995. 81p.

Cathay

Meth, Orville H. *God Was There, Germantown Baptist Church, 1884–1972.* 1995. 260p.

Cavalier County

Cemeteries of North Dakota, Cavalier County. Fargo, ND: Red River Valley Genealogical Society, 1995. 148p.

Cemeteries of North Dakota, Cavalier County. (Cemeteries of North Dakota, Vol. 32). Fargo, ND: Red River Valley Genealogical Society, 1995. 179p.

Grant County

Grant County Veterans Memorial, 1995. Carson, ND: Grant County Veterans Memorial, 1995. 75p.

Pierce County

Pierce County of North Dakota Cemetery Tombstone Readings. Minot, ND: Mouse River Loop Genealogical Society, 1995. 142p.

Renville County

Index. Renville County History, 1901–1976. Minot, ND: Mouse River Loop Genealogical Society, 1995. Unpgd.

Zeeland

Abstracted Records of the St. Andrews Lutheran Church, Zeeland, North Dakota. Kansas City, MO: American Family Records Association, 1995. 55p.

Ohio

Bell, Carol Willsey. *Ohio Genealogical Guide.* 6th ed. Youngstown, OH: Bell Books, 1995. 130p.

Index and Abstract of Obituaries for Individuals with Ties to the State of Ohio, Published in Colorado Newspapers. Denver, CO: Colorado Chapter, Ohio Genealogical Society, 1995. Unpgd.

Ohio Adoption Law. Columbus, OH: Ohio CLE Institute, 1995. Unpgd.

The Ohio 2003 Plan: A Statement of Priorities and Preferred Approaches for Historical Records Programs in Ohio. Columbus, OH: Ohio Historical Society, 1995. 27p.

Adamsville

Kreis, R. Douglas. *The Adamsville Register Obituaries, 1889–1939.* Zanesville, OH: Muskigum County Chapter, Ohio Genealogical Society, 1995. 168p.

Adena

Jankowski, Robert S. *Transcriptions of Markers in St. Casimir Cemetery, Adena, Ohio, December 1994-January 1995.* Adena, OH: Author, 1995. 30p.

Athens

Whiteman, Jane. *Every Name Index to the Harris History.* Stuttgart, AR: Author, 1995. Unpgd.

Athens County

Aiken, Nancy. *Guysville Methodist Church Records from the 19th and Early 20th Centuries.* Athens, OH: Athens County Chapter, Ohio Genealogical Society, 1995. 152p.

Bleigh, Mildred A. *Athens County Obituaries, January 1, 1970 thru December 31, 1974.* Athens, OH: Author, 1995. 582p.

Daniel, Robert L. *West Union Street Cemetery, Athens, Ohio.* Athens, OH: Athens County Chapter, Ohio Genealogical Society, 1995. 249p.

Whiteman, Jane. *Three Books in One.* Stuttgart, AR: Author, 1995. Unpgd.

Auglaize County

Auglaize County, Ohio, Abstracts of Obits and Death Mentions. Auglaize County, Ohio: Auglaize County Chapter of the Ohio Genealogical Society, 1995. 2 vols.

Index of Probate Death Records, Volumes I, II, and III, 1867–1898. Auglaize County, Ohio: Auglaize County Chapter of the Ohio Genealogical Society, 1995. 2 vols.

Belmont County

Fry, Charles E. *The Generals of Belmont County, Ohio.* St. Clairsville, OH: Author, 1995, 222p.

Berne

Trinity (Sponagle) Lutheran Church Baptism, Confirmation and Marriage Records (1842–1892), Berne Township, Fairfield County, Ohio. Lancaster, OH: Fairfield County Chapter of the Ohio Genealogical Society, 1995. 111p.

Brown County

Brown, Clermont and Highland Counties, Ohio, Newspaper Extracts, 1814–1899: A Compilation of Genealogical Items of Interest. Denver, CO: C. Spitz, 1995. 246p.

Brunswick

Kraynek, Sharon L. D. *Life and Times in Brunswick, Ohio.* Apollo, PA: Closson Press, 1995. 199p.

Champaign County

Funeral Home Records. Urbana, OH: Champaign County Genealogical Society, 1995. 94p.

Cincinnati

The Bench and Bar of Cincinnati, Commemorating the Building of the New Court House, 1921. Cincinnati, OH: Frost & Jacobs, 1995. 19p.

Grace, Kevin. *A Bibliography of University of Cincinnati Theses and Dissertations on Greater Cincinnati History*. Cincinnati, OH: Archives and Rare Books Room, University of Cincinnati, 1995. 51p.

Herbert, Jeffrey G. *Index of Death Notices Appearing in the Cincinnati Commercial, 1858–1899*. Cincinnati, OH: Hamilton County Chapter, Ohio Genealogical Society, 1995. Unpgd.

Clark County

Early Clark County, Ohio, Families Vital Statistics. Volume 9. Springfield, OH: Friends of the Library, Genealogical Research Group, 1995. 202p.

Clermont County

Brown, Clermont and Highland Counties, Ohio, Newspaper Extracts, 1814–1899: A Compilation of Genealogical Items of Interest. Denver, CO: C. Spitz, 1995. 246p.

Crawford, Richard. *Thunder before the Dawn, Stories of the Early Settlers and Warriors in Clermont County, Ohio*. Rhiannon Publications, 1995. 123p.

Clyde

Cemeteries in Sandusky County, Ohio, McPherson Cemetery, Clyde, Ohio. Fremont, OH: Sandusky County Kin Hunters, 1995. 332p.

Crawford County

1870 Census of Crawford County, Ohio. Galion, OH: Crawford County Chapter, Ohio Genealogical Society, 1995. 435p.

Danville

St. Luke, Danville, Knox County, Ohio, 1829 and Up, Early Members, Baptisms, Marriages, Confirmations, Deaths. Danville, OH: The Church, 1995. 157p.

Darke County

Royer, Donald M. *The Longtown Settlement, Darke County, Ohio, the History of a People from Slavery to Freedom and Independence*. Richmond, IN: Author, 1995. 42p.

Dayton

Dalton, Curt. *An Index to Buildings of Dayton before 1930, an Alphabetical Listing of Sketches and Photographs of Dayton and Montgomery County Buildings, Businesses and Homes Appearing in Local Books and Other Sources*. Dayton, OH: Author, 1995. 80p.

Delphos

McCabe, Thomas. *St. John the Baptist Catholic Church Death and Cemetery Records, 1866-1994*. Delphos, OH: Author, 1995. 31p.

Dunham

Sams, Catherine J. *Dunham Township Cemeteries*. Little Hocking, OH: Author, 1995. 62p.

Fairfield County

Floral Hills Memory Gardens, Pleasant Township, Fairfield County, Ohio. Lancaster, OH: Fairfield County Chapter of the Ohio Genealogical Society, 1995. 159p.

Fulton County

Broglin, Jana Sloan. *Index to Selected Files, Fulton County, Ohio Probate Court.* Fulton Chapter, Ohio Genealogical Society, 1995. 111p.

Germantown

Transcripts of the Records of Emmanuel's Evangelical Lutheran Church, Germantown, Ohio, Including Birth and Baptisms, Marriages, Deaths, and Funerals and Inscriptions on Tombstones Moved in 1896. Dayton, OH: A & R Johnson, 1995. 128p.

Green County

Revolutionary War Veterans of Greene County, Ohio. Xenia, OH: Greene County Chapter, Ohio Genealogical Society, 1995. 262p.

Hancock County

Hancock County, Ohio, Cemetery Inscriptions, Marion Township. Findlay, OH: Hancock County Chapter, OGS, 1995. 79p.

Hancock County, Ohio, Cemetery Inscriptions, Orange and Van Buren Townships. Findlay, OH: Hancock County Chapter, OGS, 1995. 213p.

Hancock County, Ohio, Cemetery Inscriptions, Pleasant Township, Horn Family Plot, McComb Cemetery, Pickens Cemetery. Findlay, OH: Hancock County Chapter, OGS, 1995. 181p.

Hancock County, Ohio, Cemetery Inscriptions, Union Township, Cannonsburg Cemetery, Clymer Cemetery, Tawa/Flick Cemetery, Smith Cemetery. Findlay, OH: Hancock County Chapter, OGS, 1995. 199p.

Marriage Records of Hancock County, Ohio, 1885 thru 1898. Findlay, OH: Hancock County Chapter, OGS, 1995. 185p.

Harrison County

Harrison County Courthouse, Cadiz, Ohio, 1895–1995. Cadiz, OH: Business Services Associates, 1995. 42p.

Henry County

Henry County, Ohio, Marriages. Deshler, OH: Henry County Genealogical Society, 1995. Unpgd.

Highland County

Brown, Clermont and Highland Counties, Ohio, Newspaper Extracts, 1814–1899: A Compilation of Genealogical Items of Interest. Denver, CO: C. Spitz, 1995. 246p.

Holmes County

Ohio Amish Directory, Holmes County and Vicinity. Sugarcreek, OH: Carlisle Printing, 1995. 793p.

Irondale

Irondale, Ohio, Presbyterian Church, Session Records, 1817–1898, including Various Notes and Letters Pertaining to Church History and an Index. Steubenville, OH: First Presbyterian Church of Irondale, 1995. 182p.

Jackson

Transcripts of the Records of Slifer's Reformed Church, Jackson Township, Montgomery County, Ohio, Including Marriages, Baptisms and Births, Deaths and Funerals, and Register of Members with Communion Dates, 1901–1931. Dayton, OH: Anne & Robert Johnson, 1995. 19p.

Jackson County

Ervin, Robert Edgar. *Jackson County, Its History and Its People*. Jackson, OH: Liberty Press, 1995. 237p.

Jefferson County

Annapolis Cemetery, Leas Cemetery, Hill or Heisler Cemetery. Steubenville, OH: Public Library of Steubenville and Jefferson County, 1995. Unpgd.

The Eleventh Census of the United States Special Schedule: Surviving Soldiers, Sailors, Marines and Widows, etc., 1890 Veterans Census of Jefferson County, Ohio. Steubenville, OH: Jefferson County Chapter, Ohio Genealogical Society, 1995. 140p.

Index to Early Marriages of Jefferson County, Ohio, January 1798 thru December 1820. Apollo, PA: Closson Press, 1995. 72p.

Knox County

DeLauder, Richard. *Marriage Records of Knox County, Ohio, 1808–1875*. Mt. Vernon, OH: Knox County Chapter of the Ohio Genealogical Society, 1995. 385p.

Helwig, Richard M. *Ohio Ghost Towns*. Sunbury, OH: Center for Ghost Town Research in Ohio, 1995. 143p.

Lawrence County

Belcher, Gary. *The Distribution of Schools in Lawrence County, Ohio, from 1816 to 1994, a Study in Historical Geography*. Dissertation, Ohio University, 1995. 226p.

Kocher, L. Richard. *A Listing of Entrymen on Lands in Lawrence County, Ohio*. Columbus, OH: Woolkoch Pub., 1995. 78p.

Logan County

Bokescreek and Rushcreek Townships, Logan County, Ohio: Cemetery Records. Bellefontaine, OH: Logan County Genealogical Society, 1995. Unpgd.

Jefferson Township, Logan County, Ohio: Cemetery Records. Bellefontaine, OH: Logan County Genealogical Society, 1995. Unpgd.

Liberty and Monroe Townships, Logan County, Ohio: Cemetery Records. Bellefontaine, OH: Logan County Genealogical Society, 1995. Unpgd.

Moore, James E. *1870, Logan County, Ohio, Census*. Author, 1995. 244p.

Perry and Zane Townships, Logan County, Ohio: Cemetery Records. Bellefontaine, OH: Logan County Genealogical Society, 1995. Unpgd.

Lucas County

Reed, Beverly Todd. *Lucas County Home Infirmary Register. Volume 2. 1882–1901. Lucas County, Ohio*. Toledo, OH: Lucas County Chapter of the Ohio Genealogical Society, 1995. 149p.

Madison

St. Thomas Evangelical German Lutheran Congregation, 1842–1899, Madison Township, Fairfield County, Ohio. Lancaster, OH: Fairfield County Chapter of the Ohio Genealogical Society, 1995. 85p.

Mahoning County

Mahoning County, Ohio, Coroner's Inquests Book #1, 1883–1908. Rev. Mahoning County Chapter of the Ohio Genealogical Society, 1995. 21p.

Marion

Cemeteries of Marion Township, Hocking County, Ohio. Logan, OH: Hocking County Chapter of the Ohio Genealogical Society, 1995. Unpgd.

Marion, Sharon. *News From Marion County, Ohio, 1844–1861*. Bowie, MD: Heritage Books, 1995. 211p.

Medina County

Kraynek, Sharon L. D. *Local Chips and Splinters, Medina County Gazette, 1886–1888, Medina County, Ohio*. Apollo, PA: Closson Press, 1995. 140p.

Meigs County

Obituaries, 1872, 1873, 1876 & 1877, Copied from the Meigs County News, Middleport, 1872, 1873 & 1876 and Meigs County Telegraph, Pomeroy, 1877. Pomeroy, OH: Meigs County Historical Society, 1995. 23p.

Mercer County

1870 Federal Census of Mercer County, Ohio. Celina, OH: Mercer County Chapter of the Ohio Genealogical Society, 1995. 212p.

Mercer County, Ohio, Cemetery Inscriptions. Rev. ed. Celina, OH: Mercer County Chapter of the Ohio Genealogical Society, 1995. 201p.

Millersburg

Guthrie, Don. *Oak Hill Cemetery, Millersburg, Holmes County, Ohio*. Millersburg, OH: Holmes County Chapter, Ohio Genealogical Society, 1995. 107p.

Montgomery County

Montgomery County, Ohio, Cemetery Inscriptions. Volume 4. Harrison Township. Dayton, OH: Harrison County Genealogical Society, 1995. 2 vols.

Morgan County

Census, 1880, Morgan County, Ohio. McConnelsville, OH: Morgan County Chapter, Ohio Genealogical Society, 1995. 352p.

Marriage Records, Morgan County, Ohio, 1904–1912. 1995. 141p.

Morrow County

An Index to the 1880 History of Morrow County, Ohio. Mount Gilead, OH: Morrow County Genealogical Society, 1995. 143p.

Muskingum County

1829 Muskingum County, Ohio, Tax Duplicate. 1995. 52p.

Perry County

Perry County, Ohio, Jackson Township Cemeteries. 7th ed. Junction City, OH: Perry County Chapter of the Ohio Genealogical Society, 1995. 108p.

Perry County, Ohio, Monday Creek Township Cemeteries. Junction City, OH: Perry County Chapter of the Ohio Genealogical Society, 1995. 47p.

Pickaway County

Hearl, Dan R. *Pickaway County, Ohio, Probate Court Marriage Records, Volumes 6–11, 1862-1898.* Pickaway County, OH: Pickaway County Historical Society, 1995. 133p.

Kocher, L. Richard. *A Listing of Entrymen on Lands East of the Scioto River in Pike County, Ohio.* Columbus, OH: Woolkoch Publishing, 1995. 30p.

Pike County

Kocher, L. Richard. *A Listing of Entrymen on Lands East of the Scioto River in Pike County, Ohio.* Columbus, OH: Woolkoch Publishing, 1995. 30p.

Pleasant

Maple Grove Cemetery, Pleasant Township, Fairfield, County, Ohio. Lancaster, OH: Fairfield County Chapter of the Ohio Genealogical Society, 1995. 217p.

Richland County

Hidinger, Nancy Hill. *Richland County, Ohio, Index to the 1870 Federal Population Census.* Mansfield, OH: Richland County Genealogical Society, 1995. 83p.

Ross County

1840 Census of Ross County, Ohio. Chillicothe, OH: Ross County Genealogical Society, 1995. 221p.

Roundhead

Roundhead Township Cemetery Inscriptions. Kenton, OH: Hardin County Chapter, Ohio Genealogical Society, 1995. Unpgd.

Sandusky County

Cemeteries in Sandusky County, Ohio, McPherson Cemetery, Clyde, Ohio. Fremont, OH: Sandusky County Kin Hunters, 1995. 332p.

Scioto County

Kocher, L. Richard. *A Listing of Entrymen on Lands East of the Scioto River in Scioto County, Ohio.* Columbus, OH: Woolkoch Publishing, 1995. 49p.

Snook, J. E. *Genealogical Abstracts of Scioto County, Ohio, Deedbooks A, B, C, 1803–1812.* Scioto County, OH: Scioto County Chapter, Ohio Genealogical Society, 1995. 45p.

Shelby County

Bevans, Lavern. *Shelby County Children's Home, Located at Sidney, Ohio.* Sidney, OH: Shelby
  County Genealogical Society, 1995. Unpgd.

Index of Inmates, Shelby County, Infirmary, Sidney, Ohio, 1866–1883. Sidney, OH: Shelby
  County Genealogical Society, 1995. 26p.

Stark County

Early Marriages of Stark County, Ohio. Volume 3. 1856–1870. Alliance, OH: Alliance Genealogical Society, 1995. 270p.

Steubenville

Stock, Cindy. *Extracts from the Steubenville Western Herald, 1806–1807, Newspaper Including Index.* Steubenville, OH: Public Library of Steubenville and Jefferson County, 1995.
  58p.

Strongsville

*Strongsville Cemetery, Strongsville, Cuyahoga County, Ohio, 44136. 1816–1994, Memories in
  Stone.* Strongsville, OH: Southwest Cuyahoga Chapter, Ohio Genealogical Society, 1995.
  93p.

Tuscarawas County

Tuscarawas County Original Death Records. New Philadelphia, OH: Tuscarawas Genealogical Society, 1995. 3 vols.

Twinsburg

Inscriptions and Index to Locust Grove Cemetery, Twinsburg, Ohio (Summit County). Hudson,
  OH: Hudson Genealogical Study Group, Hudson Library and Historical Society, 1995.
  51p.

Urbana

Funeral Home Records. Urbana, OH: Champaign County Genealogical Society, 1995. 94p.

Vinton County

Vinton County, Ohio, Brides, 1850–1869. 1995. 43p.

Wayne County

Soldiers Relief Records, World War I, 1917–1918, Account Book for 1924–1939. Wooster, OH:
  Wayne County Public Library, 1995. 400p.

Wood County

Probate Death Records, Wood County, Ohio. Bowling Green, OH: Wood County Chapter of
  the Ohio Genealogical Society, 1995. Unpgd.

Wyandot County

Tilton, Edith Garner. *Early Settlers and Landowners of Wyandot County, Ohio.* Upper Sandusky,
  OH: Wyandot Tracers Chapter of the Ohio Genealogical Society, 1995. 45p.

Youngstown

Oak Hill Cemetery Burial Records, Youngstown, Mahoning County, Ohio. Volume 1. 19 December 1878–18 September 1894. Boardman, OH: Mahoning County Chapter of the Ohio Genealogical Society, 1995. 342p.

Zanesville

City of Zanesville Death Records Index. Zanesville, OH: Muskingum County Chapter, Ohio Genealogical Society, 1995. Unpgd.

Oklahoma

Chasteen, Jerri G. *Our People and Where They Rest. an Index to 1,043 Old Cemeteries within the Boundary of the Old Indian Territory.* Pryor, OK: Author, 1995. 391p.

Follett, Paul. *Genealogy and Local History Collections in Oklahoma.* Tulsa, OK: Oklahoma Library Association, 1995. 19p.

Kennedy, Arthur Ward. *They Came from Everywhere and Settled Here, Settlement in Indian Territory, Two Townships in Pottawatomie County and the Seminole Nation around the Turn of the Century through 1930.* 2nd. ed. Konawa, OK: Kennedy Library of Konawa, 1995. Unpgd.

Lester, Gary W. *Cemetery Relocation Records of Grand and Eucha Lakes.* Braggs, OK: Author, 1995. 96p.

———. *Ft. Gibson, Oklahoma, National Cemetery.* Braggs, OK: Green Leaf Creek Publications, 1995. 206p.

Oklahoma Almanac. 45th ed. Oklahoma City, OK: Oklahoma Department of Libraries, 1995. 922p.

Bryan County

Ellis, Wand M. *Bryan County, Oklahoma, Pre-Statehood Marriages, July 1902-November 1907.* Calera, OK: Bryan County Heritage Association, 1995. 216p.

Choctaw County

Cemetery Records, Choctaw County, Oklahoma. Hugo, OK: Choctaw County Genealogical Society, 1995. Unpgd.

Comanche County

Cache Cemetery, Comanche County, Oklahoma. Lawton, OK: Southwest Oklahoma Genealogical Society, 1995. 117p.

Delaware County

Cemeteries and Burial Places of Delaware County, Oklahoma. Grove, OK: Delaware County
	Cemetery Readers, 1995. Unpgd.

Grady County

Jackson, Gwen. *Trails, Rails and School Tales, a History of 125 Schools and Communities of
	Grady County.* Author, 1995. 165p.

Harper County

Pearcy, Deone Kay. *Gardens of Stone: Harper County, Oklahoma, Cemetery, Funeral Home
	and Newspaper Accounts.* Tehachapi, CA: T. P. Productions, 1995. 808p.

McClain County

Rex, Joyce A. *McClain County, Oklahoma (Old Pontotoc County, Chickasaw Nation, Indian
	Territory), Marriages, 1863–1895, plus Matrimonial Miscellany from Early Newspapers,
	Church Records, and Other Sources.* Purcell, OK: McClain County Historical Society, 1995.
	Unpgd.

Minco

Davis, Jean and Nancy Charlton. *Evergreen Cemetery, Minco, Oklahoma.* Minco, OK: Author,
	1995. 98p.

Muskogee County

Lester, Gary W. *Muskogee County Cemetery Guide.* Braggs, OK: Author, 1995. Unpgd.

Noble County

Stadler, Ann. *Rural Cemeteries of Noble County, Oklahoma, 1994, Includes Some Funeral and
	Obituary Records.* Perry, OK: Author, 1995. 318p.

Perry

Stadler, Ann. *Grace Hill Cemetery, 1893–1994.* Perry, OK: Author, 1995. 399p.

Pocola County

Webb, David M. *Pocola, Ten Miles from Town.* Author, 1995. 278p.

San Bois County

McKim, Sandra. *Permit Register San Bois County, Choctaw Nation, Indian Territory, October
	1888–3 November 1902, Whites in San Bois County with Permission.* San Jose, CA: Au-
	thor, 1995. 242p.

Sequoyah County

1920 Federal Census of Sequoyah County, Oklahoma. Vols 2, 3, 4. Muldrow, OK: Muldrow
	Genealogical Society, 1995. 3 vols.

Skullyville County

McKim Sandra. *Whites in Skullyville County, Choctaw Nation, Permit Register, 1889–Febru-
	ary 19, 1905, Choctaw Volume 222.* Bowie, MD: Heritage Books, 1995. 161p.

Oregon

Compiled Service Records of Volunteer Union Soldiers Who Served in Organizations from the Territory and State of Oregon. Washington, DC: National Archives and Records Administration, 1995. 5p.

Herzberg, Alice Stansfield. *Index to Oregon Newspaper Clippings, 1895–1952.* Medford, OR: Rogue Valley Genealogical Society, 1995. 149p.

Periodical Shelf List. Portland, OR: Genealogical Forum of Oregon, 1995. 91p.

Samuelsen, W. David. *Oregon Naturalization Records Index, Declarations of Intention.* Salt Lake City, UT: Sampubco, 1995. Unpgd.

Deschutes County

Summers, Barbara. *Oregon, 1920, Deschutes County Census with Index.* Bend, OR: Deschutes County Historical Society, 1995. 115p.

Douglas County

Chapman, Carole. *Comstock Cemetery.* Cottage Grove, OR: Cottage Grove Genealogical Society, 1995. 10p.

———. *Register of Funerals in Cottage Grove, Oregon, and Vicinity: 1906 through 1977.* Cottage Grove, OR: Cottage Grove Genealogical Society, 1995. Unpgd.

Eugene

Tofdahl, Gregory. *Oregon Newspaper Death Notices, 1864–1902, an Index to Death Notices Published in Eugene, Lane County, Oregon, Newspapers.* 2nd ed. Springfield, OR: Author, 1995. 139p.

Grants Pass

Obituaries, 1995, Grants Pass Daily Courier, Grants Pass, Oregon. Grants Pass, OR: Grants Pass Genealogical Society, 1995. 246p.

Jackson County

Jackson County, Oregon, Deed Book 1, May 5, 1853 to February 2, 1857. Medford, OR: Rogue Valley Genealogical Society, 1995. 72p.

Lake County

Stephenson, Georgie Ellen Boydstun. *The Growth of Lake County, Oregon.* Wilsonville, OR: BookPartners, 1995. 173p.

Lane County

Chapman, Carole. *Comstock Cemetery.* Cottage Grove, OR: Cottage Grove Genealogical Society, 1995. 10p.

————. *Register of Funerals in Cottage Grove, Oregon, and Vicinity, 1906 through 1977.* Cottage Grove, OR: Cottage Grove Genealogical Society, 1995. Unpgd.

Lebanon

Dunn, Patricia. *Lebanon Pioneer Cemetery, 200 Dodge Street, Lebanon, Oregon, the End of the Trail.* Rev. ed. Lebanon, OR: City of Lebanon, Oregon, 1995. 208p.

Portland

Del Conte, Michele M. *Italian Immigration to Portland, Oregon, 1900–1930.* Dissertation (Ph.D.), Washington State University, 1995. 240p.

Pennsylvania

Burgert, Annette K. *Eighteenth Century Emigrants from Pfungstadt, Hssen-Darnstadt to Pennsylvania.* Myerstown, PA: AKB Publications, 1995. 50p.

Duffin, James M. *Guide to the Mortgages of the General Loan Office of the Province of Pennsylvania, 1724–1756.* Philadelphia, PA: Genealogical Society of Pennsylvania, 1995. 142p.

Guide to Genealogical and Historical Research in Pennsylvania, 1995. Supplement III. Hollidaysburg, PA: Hoenstine Rental Library, 1995. 112p.

Heckethorn, Paul Keith. *Chronological Beginnings of the Christian Church in Western Pennsylvania, 1743–1793.* Apollo, PA: Closson Press, 1995. 54p.

Patriots Index, Members and Ancestors, 1893–1993. Monongahela, PA: Pennsylvania State Society, SAR, 1995. 916p.

Vital Records Disaster Planning. Harrisburg, PA: Pennsylvania Historical and Museum Commission, 1995. 24p.

Woodroofe, Helen Hutchison. *A Genealogist's Guide to Pennsylvania Records.* Special Publication No. 5. Philadelphia, PA: Genealogical Society of Pennsylvania, 1995. 464p.

Beaver County

Lyon, Douglas R. *Green Township Cemetery Inscriptions, Beaver County, Pennsylvania.* Las Vegas, NV: Archives and Chronicles, 1995. 43p.

Berks County

Rice, Phillip A. *Collected Church Records of Berks County, Pennsylvania.* Apollo, PA: Closson Press, 1995. 2 vols.

Bradford

Reamy, Martha. *Quaker Records of Bradford Monthly Meeting.* Westminster, MD: Family Line Pub., 1995. 259p.

Bucks County

Abstracts of Bucks County, Pennsylvania, Wills, 1685–1785. Westminster, MD: Family Line Pub., 1995. 184p.

History of Bucks County, Pennsylvania, by W. W. H. Davis, Surname Index. Doylestown, PA: Bucks County Genealogical Society, 1995. 303p.

California

Smiley, Shawn. *Archaeological Excavation of Tombstones: the Job Johnson Project*. California, PA: California University of Pennsylvania, 1995. 648p.

Cambria County

Warzel, Des. *Cambria County, Pennsylvania, Cemeteries*. Apollo, PA: Closson Press, 1995. Unpgd.

Centre County

Holter, Harvey, Jr. *Index of Centre County, Pennsylvania, Marriage License Docket Books 19–22, Marriage Application and Marriages, 1913–1921*. Author, 1995. 158p.

Rice, Suzanne Walkowiak. *Centre County, Pennsylvania, Records*. Author, 1995. 261p.

Chester County

Martin, Jacob. *Wills of Chester County, Pennsylvania, 1766–1778, Based on the Abstracts of Jacob Martin*. Westminster, MD: Family Line Publications, 1995. 160p.

Reamy, Martha. *Quaker Records of Bradford Monthly Meeting*. Westminster, MD: Family Line Pub., 1995. 259p.

Clarion County

McNamara, Billie Ruth. *Record of Births, Baptisms, Communion Session, Marriages and Deaths in the Mt. Zion Evangelical Lutheran Church*. Knoxville, TN: Author, 1995. 136p.

College

The Cemeteries of College Township, Centre County, Pennsylvania. State College, PA: Centre County Genealogical Society, 1995. 113p.

Dauphin County

Lapp, Elam D. *Amish History of Dauphin County, Pennsylvania, 1978–1995*. Millersburg, PA: Author, 1995. 191p.

Throop, Eugene F. *Pennsylvania Divorces, Dauphin County, 1788–1867, and York County, 1790- 1860*. Bowie, MD: Heritage Books, 1995. 183p.

Wright, F. Edward. *Early Church Records of Dauphin County, Pennsylvania*. Westminster, MD: Family Line Pub., 1995. 140p.

Delaware County

Humphrey, John T. *Pennsylvania Births, Delaware County, 1682–1800*. Washington, DC: Humphrey Publications, 1995. 117p.

Easton

Kieffer, Henry Martyn. *Some of the First Settlers of the Forks of the Delaware and Their Descendants, Being a Translation from the German of the Record of the Book of the First Reformed Church of Easton, Pennsylvania, from 1760 to 1852.* Bowie, MD: Heritage Books, 1902, 1995. 443p.

Erie County

Sons of the American Revolution, Pennsylvania Society, Erie Chapter. *Revolutionary Patriots in Erie County, Pennsylvania.* Gohrs Printing Service, 1995. 158p.

Forks

Forks Church Cemetery (Forks Township, Northampton County, Pennsylvania). Easton, PA: Easton Area Public Library, 1995. Unpgd.

Harford

Index to Harford Township, 1790–1940. Montrose, PA: Susquehanna County Historical Society, 1995. 34p.

Hempfield

Ruff, Paul Miller. *Hempfield Zion Lutheran Church, Hempfield Township, Westmoreland County, Parish Records, 1880–1955.* Greensburg, PA: Author, 1995. 78p.

Indiana County

Warzel, Des. *Indiana County, Pennsylvania, Cemeteries, plus the History of Brush Valley Lutheran Church.* Apollo, PA: Closson Press, 1995. Unpgd.

Jordan

Rice, Phillip A. *Church Records of St. David's Lutheran and Reformed Church at Hebe, Jordan Township, Northumberland County, Pennsylvania (1829–1915).* Apollo, PA: Closson Press, 1995. 74p.

Kittanning

Mechling, Allen R. *History of the Old Kittanning Cemetery, North Jefferson Street, Kittanning, Pennsylvania, 1811–1960.* Apollo, PA: Closson Press, 1995. 113p.

Kutztown

Kern, Lucy. *Resources for Genealogical Research in the Rohrbach Library, Kutztown University.* Kutztown, PA: Author, 1995. 49p.

Lancaster County

Wright, F. Edward. *Abstracts of Lancaster County, Pennsylvania, Wills, 1732–1820.* Westminster, MD: Family Line Pub., 1995. 2 vols.

Xakellis, Martha J. *Grave Undertakings, Clay Township, Volume 3, Gravestone Inscriptions of Old Warwick Township in Lancaster County, Pennsylvania.* Apollo, PA: Closson Press, 1995. 41p.

Lawrence County

Byler, Levi U. *Pennsylvania Amish Directory of the Lawrence County Settlement.* Volant, PA: Author, 1995. 108p.

Cooper, Dwight Edward. *Cemeteries of Lawrence County, Pennsylvania, Clinton Cemetery, New Beaver Boro, Book 12.* New Castle, PA: Author, 1995. 113p.

————. *Mt. Hermon Presbyterian Church Cemetery, Frew Mill Road, Slippery Rock Township, Lawrence County, Pennsylvania.* New Castle, PA: Author, 1995. 70p.

Lebanon

Heilman, Robert A. *Marriage and Death Notices Transcribed from the Pages of the Lebanon Valley Standard.* Bowie, MD: Heritage Books, 1995. 292p.

Wright, F. Edward. *Early Church Records of Lebanon County, Pennsylvania.* Westminster, MD: Family Line Pub., 1995. 511p.

Lehigh County

Roberts, Charles R. *Records of Egypt Reformed Church, Lehigh County, 1734–1834.* Mt. Airy, PA: Pipe Creek Publications, 1905, 1995. 173p.

Martinsburg

Boor, Jim. *Cove Echo, 1872–1874. Martinsburg, Blair County, Pennsylvania Genealogical Abstracts.* New Enterprise, PA: Author, 1995. 8p.

Monroe County

Repsher, Donald R. *Index to Names, History of Monroe County, Robert Brown Keller, Editor, Stroudsburg, Pennsylvania, Monroe Publishing Company, 1927.* Bath, PA: Author, 1995. 41p.

Northampton County

Marriages Registered at the Northampton County Courthouse, 1852–1854. Easton, PA: Jeanne Cheston, 1995. 16p.

Northumberland County

Rice, Phillip A. *Church Records of St. David's Lutheran and Reformed Church at Hebe, Jordan Township, Northumberland County, Pennsylvania (1829–1915).* Apollo, PA: Closson Press, 1995. 74p.

Richardson, William N. *The 1859–1867 Funeral Lists Leichenverzeignissa of Isaac Faust Stiehly, a Pennsylvania-German Reformed Minister of Pennsylvania's Mahantongo Valley.* Sunbury, PA: Northumberland County Historical Society, 1995. 66p.

Philadelphia

Dixon, Ruth Priest. *Index to Seamen's Protection Certificate Applications, Port of Philadelphia, 1796–1823, Record Group 36, Records of the Bureau of Customs, National Archives and Record Administration, Washington, DC.* Baltimore, MD: Clearfield, 1995. 153p.

Gleeson, Kristin. *A Guide to Women's Archival Resources in the Presbyterian Historical Society.* Philadelphia, PA: Presbyterian Historical Society, 1995. 183p.

Humphrey, John T. *Pennsylvania Births, Philadelphia County, 1766–1780*. Washington, DC: Humphrey Publications, 1995. 570p.

Wright, F. Edward. *Abstracts of Philadelphia Wills, 1682–1726*. Westminster, MD: Family Line Pub., 1995. 297p.

Pittsburgh

Pittsburgh City Directory for the Year 1815. Apollo, PA: Closson Press, 1995. 29p.

Robeson

DeTemple, Donald D. *Three Robeson Township Cemeteries, Robeson Township, Berks County, Pennsylvania*. Apollo, PA: Closson Press, 1995. 223p.

Schuylkill County

Crown, H. T. *A Guide to the Molly Maguires*. Pottsville, PA: Mark T. Major, 1995. 149p.

Dellock, Stephen J. *Schuylkill County, Death Records, 1893–1895*. Apollo, PA: Closson Press, 1995. 201p.

Rice, Phillip A. *Schuylkill County, Pennsylvania, Archives*. Apollo, PA: Closson Press, 1995. Unpgd.

Venango County

Hanson, Joan Search. *Venango County, Pennsylvania, Death Book Summary and Index, 1893-1905*. Apollo, PA: Closson Press, 1995. 105p.

Romig, Nancy Byers. *Scrips and Scraps: Scrapbook Abstracts: Venango County and Surrounding Counties*. Apollo, PA: Closson Press, 1995. 318p.

Washington County

Closson, Bob and Mary Closson. *Abstracts of Washington County, Pennsylvania, Will Books 1–5*. Apollo, PA: Closson Press, 1995. 474p.

Weatherly

Records for St. Matthew's Union Church, Packer Township, Carbon County and for Evangelical Lutheran Zion's Church, Weatherly, Carbon County, Pennsylvania. Easton, PA: Easton Area Public Library, 1995. 58p.

Westmoreland County

Westmoreland County History, Organization, Facilities and Services. Laughlinton, PA: League of Women Voters, 1995. 89p.

York County

Dull, Keith A. *Early Families of York County, Pennsylvania. Volume 2*. Westminster, MD: Family Line Publications, 1995. 150p.

Marriages and Deaths from the York Recorder, 1821–1830. Westminster, MD: Family Line Publications, 1995. 83p.

Throop, Eugene F. *Pennsylvania Divorces, Dauphin County, 1788–1867, and York County, 1790- 1860*. Bowie, MD: Heritage Books, 1995. 183p.

Rhode Island

Register of Seaman's Protection Certificates from the Providence, Rhode Island, Customs District, 1796–1870. Baltimore, MD: Clearfield, 1995. 309p.

Taylor, Maureen Alice. *Rhode Island Passenger Lists, Port of Providence, 1798–1808, 1820-1872; Port of Bristol and Warren, 1820–1871, Compiled from United States Custom House Papers.* Baltimore, MD: Genealogical Pub. Co., 1995. 232p.

———. *Runaways, Deserters and Notorious Villians from Rhode Island Newspapers, Volume 1. The Providence Gazette, 1762–1800.* Rockport, ME: Picton Press, 1995. 189p.

Central Falls

Baptisms of Notre-Dame Catholic Church, Central Falls, Rhode Island, 1873–1988, Vol. 1 (A-J) and Vol. 2 (Ju-Z). Pawtucket, RI: American French Genealogical Society, 1995. 2 vols.

Marriages of Notre-Dame Catholic Church, Central Falls, Rhode Island, 1873–1988, Vol. 1 (A-I) and Vol. 2 (J-Z). Pawtucket, RI: American French Genealogical Society, 1995. 2 vols.

South Carolina

Becknell, Mike. *Methodist Church Records at Wofford College.* Jonesville, SC: Author, 1995. 4p.

Broken Fortunes, South Carolina, Soldiers, Sailors, and Citizens Who Died in the Service of Their Country and State in the War for Southern Independence, 1861–1865. Charleston, SC: South Carolina Historical Society, 1995. 413p.

Church Register Johnsonville Circuit, South Carolina, Methodist Episcopal Church South. Hemingway, SC: Three Rivers Historical Society, 1995. 140p.

Hicks, Theresa M. *South Carolina, a Guide For Genealogists.* Rev. ed. Columbia, SC: Columbia Chapter, South Carolina Genealogical Society, 1995. 212p.

Holcomb, Brent. *South Carolina, Marriages, 1800–1820.* Baltimore, MD: Genealogical Pub. Co., 1995. 171p.

Koger, Larry. *Black Slaveowners: Free Black Slavemasters in South Carolina, 1790–1860.* Columbia, SC: University of South Carolina Press, 1995. 286p.

Langdon, Barbara R. *South Carolina, Marriages, 1749–1853, Implied in South Carolina Marriage Settlements*. Aiken, SC: Langdon & Langdon, 1995. 376p.

Lesser, Charles H. *South Carolina Begins: The Records of a Proprietary Colony, 1663–1721*. Columbia, SC: South Carolina Department of Archives and History, 1995. 530p.

McKain, James D. *Index to History of the Presbyterian Church in South Carolina by George Howe, D. D., Volumes 1 and 2*. Columbia, SC: SCMAR, 1995. 88p.

Page, Patsy R. *Directory of South Carolina Physicians, 1886*. Alachua, FL: Page Publications, 1995. 14p.

Rivers, William James. *Roll of the Dead, South Carolina Troops, Confederate States Service*. Columbia, SC: South Carolina Department of Archives and History, 1995. Unpgd.

Sifakis, Stewart. *Compendium of the Confederate Armies Series: South Carolina and Georgia*. NY: Facts on File, 1995. 320p.

Windley, Lathan A. *A Profile of Runaway Slaves in Virginia and South Carolina from 1730 through 1787*. Hamden, CT: Garland, 1995. 219p.

Aiken

Bethany and Sons of Israel Cemeteries. Aiken, SC: Aiken-Barnwell Genealogical Society, 1995. 71p.

Sheahan, John J., Jr. *Military Markers and Data: Cemeteries Located in Aiken County, South Carolina*. Author, 1995. 153p.

Berkley County

Hood, Margaret Keller. *Berkley County, South Carolina, Cemetery Inscriptions*. St. Stephens, SC: Author, 1995. 350p.

Camden

McKain, James D. *Index to Historical Camden, Colonial and Revolutionary and Nineteenth Century*. Columbia, SC: SCMAR, 1995. 81p.

Charleston

Hagy, James William. *City Directories for Charleston, South Carolina, for the Years 1803, 1806, 1807, 1809 and 1813*. Baltimore, MD: Clearfield, 1995. 162p.

Chester County

Guevarra, Mark Bennett. *A Heritage of Service: Families of Chester County, South Carolina, Lawrence County, Mississippi, Wyoming County, New York, and the Philippines*. Houston, TX: Author, 1995. 611p.

Chesterfield County

Pigg, James C. *Chesterfield County, South Carolina, Cemeteries*. Tega Cay, SC: Author, 1995. 6 vols.

Edgefield County

The A B C D's of Edgefield Genealogy, Annotations to Bible Records, Cemeteries of Families, Death Notices. Edgefield, SC: Edgefield Chapter, South Carolina Genealogical Society, 1995. 163p.

Sheahan, John J., Jr. *Military Markers and Data: Cemeteries Located in Edgefield County, South Carolina*. Author, 1995. 38p.

Florence County

Church Register (of) Johnsonville Circuit (of) South Carolina Conference (of) Methodist Episcopal Church South. Hemingway, SC: Three Rivers Historical Society, 1995. 140p.

Georgetown County

Church Register (of) Johnsonville Circuit (of) South Carolina Conference (of) Methodist Episcopal Church South. Hemingway, SC: Three Rivers Historical Society, 1995. 140p.

Wyndham, Melissa J. *The 1860 Census of Georgetown County, South Carolina.* Hemingway, SC: Three Rivers Historical Society, 1995. 89p.

Lancaster County

Lancaster County, South Carolina, Cemetery Data. Lancaster, SC: DD, Inc., 1995. 196p.

Oconee County

Heritage of Oconee County, 1868–1995. Seneca, SC: Blue Ridge Arts Council, 1995. Unpgd.

Orangeburg County

Culler, Daniel Marchant. *Orangeburgh District, 1768–1868, History and Records.* Spartanburg, SC: Reprint Co., 1995. 737p.

Pelzer

Memories of Pelzer, 1881–1950. Bountiful, UT: Family History Pub., 1995. 305p.

Richland County

Blick, David G. *Richland County's Rural African American Schoolhouses, 1895–1954.* Columbia, SC: Historic Columbia Foundation, 1995. 15p.

Spartanburg

Becknell, Mike. *Methodist Church Records at Wofford College.* Jonesville, SC; Author, 1995. 4p.

Union County

Vaughan, Tommy J. *Union County, South Carolina, Marriage Records from Early Newspapers, 1851–1912, Marriage Registers, Deed Books, and Probate Records.* Spartanburg, SC: Pinckney District Chapter, South Carolina Genealogical Society, 1995. 329p.

Williamsburg County

Church Register (of) Johnsonville Circuit (of) South Carolina Conference (of) Methodist Episcopal Church South. Hemingway, SC: Three Rivers Historical Society, 1995. 140p.

Index to Marriage Notices in Williamsburg County, South Carolina, Newspapers, 1897–1994. Hemingway, SC: Three Rivers Historical Society, 1995. 300p.

York County

Langdon, Barbara R. *York County, Marriages, 1770–1869, Implied in York County, South Carolina, Probate Records.* 3rd ed. Aiken, SC: Langdon & Langdon, 1995. 100p.

South Dakota

Historical Listing of South Dakota Legislators, 1862–1995. Pierre, SD: State Legislative Research Council, 1995. 201p.

Krehbiel, James W. *Swiss Russian Mennonite Families before 1874*. Elverson, PA: Olde Springfield Shoppe, 1995. 332p.

Rose, LaVera. *Guide to American Indian Research in South Dakota*. Author, 1995. 93p.

Campbell County

Campbell County, South Dakota, Cemeteries and Burial Sites, 1995. Campbell County, SD: Campbell County Cemetery Board, 1995. 242p.

McIntosh

Petersen, Sandra L. *Index to the Golden Jubilee Book of McIntosh, Morristown, Watauga, South Dakota*. Marceline, MO: Walsworth Pub., 1995. 17p.

Morristown

Petersen, Sandra L. *Index to the Golden Jubilee Book of McIntosh, Morristown, Watauga, South Dakota*. Marceline, MO: Walsworth Pub., 1995. 17p.

Watauga

Petersen, Sandra L. *Index to the Golden Jubilee Book of McIntosh, Morristown, Watauga, South Dakota*. Marceline, MO: Walsworth Pub., 1995. 17p.

Tennessee

Creekmore, Pollyanna. *Tennessee Newspaper Extracts and Abstracts, Marriage, Death and Other Items of Genealogical/Historical Interest*. Knoxville, TN: Clinchdale Press, 1995. Unpgd.

Gospel Advocate, Index to Obituaries and Death Notices in the Gospel Advocate, 1855–1944. Bowling Green, KY: Lehman Avenue Church of Christ, 1995. 126p.

Nikazy, Eddie M. *Forgotten Soldiers, History of the Fourth Tennessee Volunteer Infantry Regiment, (U.S.A.) 1863–1865.* Bowie, MD: Heritage Books, 1995. 160p.

Pruitt, Albert Bruce. *Tennessee Land Entries, John Armstrong's Office.* Author, 1995. 2 vols.

Sifakis, Stewart. *Compendium of the Confederate Armies Series: Tennessee.* NY: Facts on File, 1995. 208p.

Sistler, Byron. *1830 Census, East Tennessee.* Nashville, TN: Author, 1995. 276p.

Sistler, Samuel. *Index to Tennessee Confederate Pension Applications.* Nashville, TN: Author, 1995. 393p.

Tucker, Mabel. *Middle Tennessee Family History.* Author, 1995. Unpgd.

West, Carroll Van. *Tennessee's Historic Landscapes, a Traveler's Guide.* Knoxville, TN: University of Tennessee Press, 1995. 503p.

Anderson County

McGhee, Marshall T. *Coal Mining Towns, Stories and Pictures of Anderson and Campbell Counties.* Jacksboro, TN: Action Printing, 1995. 212p.

Benton County

Smith, Jonathan Kennon. *Tombstone Inscriptions from Black Cemeteries in Benton County, Tennessee.* Author, 1995. 8p.

Bledsoe County

Swift, Barbara Baird. *Bledsoe County Court Letter Book Containing Minutes from January 1847–March 1852.* Pikeville, TN: Bledsoe County Library, 1995. 68p.

———. *Bledsoe County Court Letter Book Containing Minutes from April 1856–March 1860.* Pikeville, TN: Bledsoe County Library, 1995. 52p.

Bradley County

Campbell, Ellen Ann Westerberg. *Union Soldiers' Discharges Found in the Bradley County, Tennessee, Courthouse, Trust Book A, December 1864–May 1869.* Author, 1995. 300p.

Campbell County

McGhee, Marshall L. *Coal Mining Towns, Stories and Pictures of Anderson and Campbell Counties.* Jacksboro, TN: Action Printing, 1995. 212p.

Coffee County

Allen, Tommie. *African-Americans in Coffee County, Tennessee, Transcribed from the 1870, 1880, 1900, 1910 and 1920 Census Records of the 13th Civil District (Tullahoma).* Tullahoma, TN: East Middle School, 1995. Unpgd.

Columbia

Alexander, Virginia Wood. *Riverside United Methodist Church, 1945–1995.* Columbia, TN: Riverside United Methodist Church, 1995. 66p.

Crossville

Boniol, Michael W. *Genealogical and Historical Notes from Crossville, Tennessee, Newspapers.* Crossville, TN: Author, 1995. Unpgd.

Davidson County

Marriage Record Book I, January 2, 1789-December 13, 1837, Davidson County, Tennessee. Greenville, SC: Southern Historical Press, 1995. 166p.

Franklin County

Franklin County, Tennessee, Vital Statistics, 1914 through 1925. Cleveland, TN: Cleveland Public Library, 1995. 37p.

Hamblen County

Contributions of Blacks to Hamblen County, 1796–1996. Morristown, TN: Progressive Business Association, 1995. 383p.

Hamilton County

Douthat, James L. *Hamilton County, Tennessee, Marriage Book 3, September 1874–May 1880.* Signal Mountain, TN: Author, 1995. 78p.

Hardin County

Brown, Albert. *Hardin County, Tennessee, Land Entries, 1820–1837.* Bethel Springs, TN: Author, 1995. 17p.

Henderson County

Smith, Jonathan Kennon. *Tombstone Inscriptions from Black Cemeteries in Henderson County, Tennessee.* Jackson, TN: Author, 1995. 47p.

Henry County

Simmons, Don, and Laura Willis. *Henry County, Tennessee, Wills.* Melber, KY: Simmons Historical Publications, 1995. Unpgd.

Houston County

History of Houston County, Tennessee, History and Families. Paducah, KY: Turner Pub., 1995. 208p.

Pulley, Timothy W. *Obituaries Taken from the Earliest Stewart and Houston County Newspapers, 1876–1942.* Russellville, KY: A. B. Willhite, 1995. 199p.

Jackson

Smith, Jonathan Kennon. *Reported Deaths in Nineteenth Century Jackson, Tennessee, Newspapers.* Author, 1995. 102p.

Jefferson County

McNamara, Billie Ruth. *Jefferson County, Tennessee, List of Free White Males, January 1, 1861.* Knoxville, TN: Author, 1995. 61p.

———. *Miscellaneous Bonds, Administration, 1806–1814, Constables, 1806–1815, Maintenance (Bastardy) 1807–1857, Indentures, 1807–1828, Jefferson County, Tennessee.* Knoxville, TN: Author, 1995. 51p.

Lincoln County

Casey, Joe. *Marriage Records of Lincoln County, Tennessee, 1880–1899*. Tullahoma, TN: Author, 1995. 213p.

Livingston

Livingston Enterprise Obituaries, 1918–1942. Muncie, IN: Overton, 1995. 20p.

Loudon County

Smallen, Tammy L. *1910 Loudon County, Tennessee, Census*. Loudon, TN: Author, 1995. 396p.

Lynchburg

Ferguson, Joan Crutcher. *Abstracts from Early Lynchburg, Moore County, Tennessee, Old Newspapers, 1873–1932*. Wartrace, TN: Author, 1995. 163p.

McMinn County

Sistler, Byron. *1880 Census, McMinn County, Tennessee*. Nashville, TN: Author, 1995. 104p.

McNairy County

The 1890s, a Documentation of McNairy County, Tennessee, 1890–1891. Selmer, TN: N. W. Kennedy, 1995. Unpgd.

Willbook Abstracts of McNairy County, Tennessee. Selmer, TN: N. W. Kennedy, 1995. 69p.

Macon County

Macon County, Tennessee, 1870 and 1880 Census. Lafayette, TN: Macon County Historical Society, 1995. 207, 282p.

Madison County

Smith, Jonathan Kennon. *Genealogical Gleanings from Madison County, Tennessee*. Author, 1995. Unpgd.

———. *Genealogical Gleanings from the Deed Books 10 through 19, 1845–1857, Madison County, Tennessee*. Jackson, TN: Author, 1995. 59p.

———. *Last Will and Testament Abstracts, 1855–1862, Other Selective Public Records of Madison County, Tennessee*. Jackson, TN: Author, 1995. 51p.

———. *My Old Salem Cemetery Tombstone Inscriptions Scrapbook, Madison County, Tennessee*. Author, 1995. 32p.

———. *Tombstone Inscriptions from Black Cemeteries in Madison County, Tennessee*. Jackson, TN: Author, 1995. 207p.

———. *Tombstone Inscriptions from Black Cemeteries in Madison County, Tennessee, a Supplement*. Jackson, TN: Author, 1995. 21p.

Marion County

Marion County, Tennessee, Vital Statistics, 1914 through 1925. Cleveland, TN: Cleveland Public Library, 1995. 30p.

Sistler, Byron. *1880 Census, Marion County, Tennessee*. Nashville, TN: Author, 1995. 85p.

Memphis

Kelly, Aleda Farmer. *The Flame Still Burns, an Updated History of United Methodist Women, Memphis Conference*. Memphis, TN: Author, 1995. 69p.

Monroe County

Hayes, Sallie. *Monroe County, Tennessee, Deed Books*. Signal Mountain, TN: Mountain Press, 1995. Unpgd.

McConkey, Lynn. *Marriage Records of Monroe County, Tennessee, 1838 through 1890*. Vonore, TN: Vonore Historical Society, 1995. 211p.

Montgomery County

Williams, Eleanor S. *Worship along the Warioto, Montgomery County, Tennessee*. Clarksville, TN: Author, 1995. 386p.

Willis, Laura. *Montgomery County, Tennessee, Wills and Administrations*. Melber, KY: Simmons Historical Pubs., 1995. 5 vols.

Polk County

Poteet Pitts, Jennie Vee. *Polk County, Tennessee, Marriages, 1894 through 1970, Recorded in Volumes One through Fourteen*. Louisville, TN: Viola H. Jones, 1995. 224p.

Pulaski

Cosby, James Edward. *Record of Caskets, Bennett-May and Company, 1924–1994*. Pulaski, TN: Author, 1995. 387p.

Putnam County

Patton, Maurine Ensor. *Putnam County, Tennessee, Cemeteries*. Cookeville, TN: Author, 1995. 716p.

Rhea County

Broyles, Bettye J. *Rhea County, Tennessee, Deed Book F*. Dayton, TN: Rhea County Historical and Genealogical Society, 1995. 70p.

———. *Rhea County, Tennessee, Marriage Records of Colored Persons, 1866–1879*. Dayton, TN: Rhea County Historical and Genealogical Society, 1995. 33p.

———. *Rhea County, Tennessee, Scholastic Populations, 1838–1851*. Dayton, TN: Rhea County Historical and Genealogical Society, 1995. 22p.

Roane County

Bailey, Robert L. *Roane County, Tennessee, 1830 & 1840 Censuses and 1830 & 1840 Tax Lists*. Roane County, TN: Roane County Genealogical Society, 1995. 175p.

———. *To Save the County Harmless: Roane County, Tennessee, Bastardy Cases, 1806–1900*. Roane County, TN: Roane County Genealogical Society, 1995. 66p.

Smith County

Partlow, Thomas E. *Smith County, Tennessee, Census of 1910*. Lebanon, TN: Author, 1995. 417p.

———. *Smith County, Tennessee, Census of 1920*. Lebanon, TN: Author, 1995. 387p.

Stewart County

Pulley, Timothy W. *Obituaries Taken from the Earliest Stewart and Houston County Newspapers, 1876–1942*. Russellville, KY: A. B. Willhite, 1995. 199p.

Willis, Laura. *Stewart County, Tennessee, Deeds. Volume 1, 1791–1806*. Melber, KY: Simmons Historical Publications, 1995. 90p.

Sumner County

1870 U.S. Census, Sumner County, Tennessee. Gallatin, TN: Sumner County Archives, 1995. 230p.

Wells, Carol. *Sumner County, Tennessee, Court Minutes, 1787–1805 and 1808–1810*. Bowie, MD: Heritage Books, 1995. 353p.

Trousdale County

Walker, Dorothy. *Trousdale County, Tennessee, Marriage Index, 1905–1950*. Author, 1995. 91p.

Tullahoma

The Citizens Cemetery. Tullahoma, TN: East Middle School, 1995. 90p.

Wilkinson, O. B. *Tullahoma's Maplewood Confederate Cemetery, 1862–1995*. Manchester, TN: Maj. General Benjamin F. Cheatham Camp, 172, Sons of Confederate Veterans, 1995. 64p.

Valley Forge

Merritt, Frank. *Valley Forge Families*. Elizabethton, TN: Author, 1995. 150p.

Wayne County

Wayne County, Tennessee, History and Families. Paducah, KY: Turner Publishing, 1995. 448p.

Weakley County

Willis, Laura. *Weakley County, Tennessee, Register Survey Books, 1784–1857*. Melber, KY: Simmons Historical Publications, 1995. 120p.

White County

Austin Raichart, Deb. *White County Marriages, March, 1921–August, 1957*. Sparta, TN: Author, 1995. 65p.

Clark, Fred L. *Cemeteries of White County, Tennessee*. Quebeck, TN: Author, 1995. 2 vols.

White County, Tennessee, Vital Statistics, 1914 through 1925. Cleveland, TN: Cleveland Public Library, 1995. 29p.

Wilson County

Partlow, Thoms E. *Wilson County, Tennessee, Chancery Court Records, 1842–1892*. Lebanon, TN: Author, 1995. 257p.

———. *Wilson County, Tennessee, Circuit Court Records, 1858–1875*. Lebanon, TN: Author, 1995. 126p.

———. *Wilson County, Tennessee, Genealogical Resource Material, 1827–1869*. Lebanon, TN: Author, 1995. 352p.

———. *Wilson County, Tennessee, Tax Lists, 1830–1832*. Lebanon, TN: Author, 1995. 176p.

Texas

Catalogo del Fondo Colonial Coahuila-Texas, 1675–1821. Saltillo, Coahuila, Mexico: Instituto Estatal de Documentación, Universidad Autónoma del Noreste, 1995. 235p.

Cutter, Charles R. *The Legal Culture of Northern New Spain, 1700–1810*. Albuquerque, NM: University of New Mexico Press, 1995. 227p.

Daughters of the Republic of Texas. *Mapping Texas History: A Select Bibliography of Material Available at the Daughters of the Republic of Texas Library at the Alamo*. San Antonio, TX: Author, 1995. Unpgd.

Daughters of the Republic of Texas Patriot Ancestor Index. Paducah, KY: Turner Pub., 1995. 312p.

Foster, William C. *Spanish Expeditions into Texas, 1689–1789*. Austin, TX: University of Texas Press, 1995. 339p.

Garmendia Leal, Guillermo. *Origen de los Fundadores de Texas, Nuevo México, Coahuila y Nuevo León*. Monterrey, Mexico: Author, 1995. 4 vols.

Garrett, Jenkins. *The Mexican American War of 1846–1848, a Bibliography of the Holdings of the Libraries, University of Texas at Arlington*. College Station, TX: Texas A & M University Press for the University of Texas at Arlington, 1995. 693p.

Gracy, David B. *Too Lightly Esteemed in the Past, Archival Enterprise, Records Management and Preservation Administration in Texas*. Austin, TX: Author, 1995. 31p.

Gwin, Howell H. *The Texas Gulf Historical and Biographical Record, General Index, Volumes I–XXX, 1965–1994*. Beaumont, TX: Texas Gulf Coast Historical Society, 1995. Unpgd.

Herrera Saucedo, George Edward. *An Introduction to Hispanic Genealogical Research, a Manual*. Los Angeles, CA: Author, 1995. 68p.

Jackson, Jack. *Manuscript Maps Concerning the Gulf Coast, Texas and the Southwest (1519-1836)*. Chicago, IL: Newberry Library, 1995. 90p.

Marsh, Carole. *The Texas Library Book, a Surprising Guide to the Unusual Special Collections in Libraries across Our State*. Atlanta, GA: Gallopade Pub., 1995. 36p.

Mearse, Linda. *Confederate Indigent Families Lists of Texas, 1863–1865. Volume 3. South Texas*. San Marcos, TX: Author, 1995. 58p.

———. *Confederate Indigent Families Lists of Texas, 1863–1865. Volume 4. Central Texas*. San Marcos, TX: Author, 1995. 115p.

———. *Confederate Indigent Families Lists of Texas, 1863–1865. Volume 5. North Texas*. San Marcos, TX: Author, 1995. 86p.

———. *Confederate Indigent Families Lists of Texas, 1863–1865. Volume 6. Northeast Texas*. San Marcos, TX: Author, 1995. 132p.

Milner, Larry S. *From Flint to Fiber Optics: A History of Texas Business, Including a Historiography, a Chronology, and a Bibliography*. Thesis (M.A.), Southwest Texas State University, 1995. 268p.

Sifakis, Stewart. *Compendium of the Confederate Armies Series: Texas*. NY: Facts on File, 1995. 160p.

Snapp, Elizabeth. *Read All About Her!: Texas Women's History, a Working Bibliography*. Denton, TX: Texas Woman's University Press, 1995. 1,070p.

Texas Obsolete County Records Guide. Corpus Christi, TX: Brack Warren, 1995. 47p.

Winegarten, Ruthe. *Black Texas Women: 150 Years of Trial and Triumph*. Austin, TX: University of Texas Press, 1995. 427p.

Anderson County

1890 Tax Records, Anderson County, Texas, and Including the 1890 Marriage Records and the 1890 Census of Union Veterans of the Civil War. Tyler, TX: East Texas Genealogical Society, 1995. 173p.

Appleby

Partin, SheRita Kae. *Gone Home to Bethel, a Directory to the Bethel Cemetery in Appleby, Nacogdoches County, Texas*. Nacogdoches, TX: Partin Pub., 1995. Unpgd.

Baytown

Baytown Genealogical Society 30th Anniversary Celebration, 1995. Baytown, TX: Baytown Genealogical Society, 1995. 67p.

Dennis, Lawrence W. *Ancestor Charts of the Baytown Genealogical Society*. Baytown, TX: Baytown Genealogical Society, 1995. 334p.

Bell County

Gardner, Janet Clayton. *Record of Inmates of County Home, Bell County, Texas, 1913–1969*. Huntersville, TX: Author, 1995. 98p.

Bowie County

Bowie County, Texas, Read Hill Cemetery (Includes Paupers Graves) and Associated Cemeteries, Brooks Cemetery, Glass Hill Cemetery, Gooley Prairie Cemetery, Shipp Cemetery. New Boston, TX: New Boston Genealogical Society, 1995. 84p.

Brownsville

Studies in Brownsville and Matamoros History. Brownsville, TX: University of Texas at Brownsville, 1995. 332p.

Caldwell County

Moody, Mary C. *1890 Caldwell County, Texas, Census, Uniquely Reconstructed and Annotated*. Arlington, TX: Blackstone Pub., 1995. 271p.

Cass County

Cheatham, Belzora. *Whittaker Memorial Cemetery Index: Cass County, Texas*. Chicago, IL: Author, 1995. 15p.

Moody, Mary C. *Every Name Index to the 1880 Cass County, Texas, Federal Census*. Arlington, TX: Blackstone Pub. Co., 1995. 152p.

Chambers County

Shepard, Donna. *Historical Archival Research and Oral History Study of an Area East of the Wallisville Townsite and the Associated African-American Community, Wallisville Lake Project, Chambers County, Texas*. Plano, TX: Geo-Marine, 1995. Unpgd.

Coke County

Copeland, Bonita. *Coke County, Cemeteries, Epitaphs and Dates*. 3rd. ed. Bronte, TX: S & S Printing, 1995. 240p.

Dallas County

Butler, Steven R. *Dallas County, Texas, and the Mexican War, 1846–1848, a History and Roster*. Richardson, TX: Descendants of Mexican War Veterans, 1995. 52p.

Jamieson, Adrienne Bird. *Dallas County, Texas, Minute Book A, 1846–1855, 14th District Court Abstracts*. Dallas, TX: Dallas Genealogical Society, 1995. 217p.

Everman

Everman Cemetery. Everman, TX: Everman Historical Society, 1995. 70p.

Foard County

Curtice, Kathrin Neely. *Burial Records of Womack Manard Funeral Home, Crowell, Foard County, Texas, also Includes Foard City, Margaret, Thalia and Vivian*. Victoria, TX: Daniel Braman Chapter, Daughters of the American Revolution, 1995. Unpgd.

Fredericksburg

Greenwood Cemetery. Fredericksburg, TX: Fredericksburg Genealogical Society, 1995. Unpgd.

Hamilton County

Griffits, Horace. *Hico (Hamilton County) Texas Cemetery Genealogical Reference through December 31, 1994*. Fort Worth, TX: Author, 1995. 68p.

Harris County

Glass, James L. *Africans and African Americans in Harris and Contiguous Counties, 1807–1859, a Preliminary Survey of Ten Counties in Southeast Texas Providing an Alphabetical Index of 589 Individuals Noted in 33 Sources*. Houston, TX: Author, 1995. 31p.

Houston County

Davis, Kathryn Hooper. *1900 Census, Houston County, Texas*. Nacogdoches, TX: Ericson Books, 1995. 386p.

Hunt County

Armstrong, John James. *Hunt County, Texas, Marriages, 1912–1920*. Greenville, TX: Hunt County Genealogical Society, 1995. 218p.

Hutchinson County

Morrison, Cleo McGraw. *Hutchinson County, Texas, Marriage Records, Books I, II, III, & IV*. Borger, TX: Author, 1995. 268p.

Johnson County

Basham, L. Malcolm. *1860 Johnson County, Texas, Federal Census, Including a Statistical Profile of Residents*. Dallas, TX: Author, 1995. 162p.

Kaufman County
Kaufman County, Marriage Records, 1901 thru 1910. Terrell, TX: Kaufman County Genealogical Society, 1995. 188p.

Longview
Forman Funeral Home Book, Longview, Texas. Longview, TX: Gregg County Genealogical Society, 1995. Unpgd.

McLennan County
Makovy, Mary. *The Concord Connection, McLennan County, Texas.* Author, 1995. 26p.

Marshall
Index to Deaths and Burials Recorded in Marshall, Texas, Register of Deaths and Burials, 1880- 1905. Marshall, TX: Harrison County Genealogical Society, 1995. 87p.

Mesquite City
Crossley, Marie. *Mesquite City Cemetery, Dallas County, Texas.* Mesquite, TX: Mesquite Historical and Genealogical Society, 1995. 138p.

Nacogdoches
Partin, SheRita Kae. *Cason and Monk Funeral Home Records.* Nacogdoches, TX: Partin Pub., 1995. Unpgd.

Navarro County
Claunch, Alta Hillman. *1870 Federal Census of Navarro County, Texas.* Dublin, TX: Author, 1995. 136p.

New Braunfels
Fey, Everett Anthony. *New Braunfels, the First Founders.* Austin, TX: Eakin Press, 1995. 2 vols.

Newton County
Claunch, Alta Hillman. *1870 and 1880 Federal Census of Newton County, Texas.* Dublin, TX: Author, 1995. 150p.

Nixon
Griffith, Ofelia Garcia. *Nixon and Its People, the Beginning.* Thesis (M.A.), Texas A & M University, Kingsville, 1995. 115p.

Rains County
Bay, Elaine Nall. *Rains County, Texas, Cemetery Inscriptions.* Honey Grove, TX: Newhouse Pub., 1995. 2 vols.

Real County
Kellner, Marjorie. *Wagons, Ho! A History of Real County, Texas.* Dallas, TX: Curtis Media, 1995. 755p.

Rhineland

Century of Faith, St. Joseph's Catholic Church, Rhineland, Texas, 1895–1995. Rhineland, TX: The Church, 1995. 157p.

San Antonio

De la Teja, Jesus F. *San Antonio de Bexar Community on New Spain's Northern Frontier.* Albuquerque, NM: University of New Mexico Press, 1995. 224p.

Matovina, Timothy M. *Tejano Religion and Ethnicity, San Antonio, 1821–1860.* Austin, TX: University of Texas Press, 1995. 168p.

Record, Karl G. *Family Cemeteries in the San Antonio, Texas, Area.* San Antonio, TX: Author, 1995. 26p.

Van Zandt County

Pippin, Ernestine. *Where They Lie, Civil War Veterans of Van Zandt County with Biographies.* Canton, TX: Van Zandt County Genealogical Society, 1995. 213p.

Wood County

Genealogical Abstracts of Wood County, Texas, Newspapers before 1920. Bowie, MD: Heritage Books, 1995. 340p.

Young County

Loftin, Jack. *Complete Cemetery Census of Young County, Texas, 1837–1995.* Wichita Falls, TX: Author, 1995. 454p.

Utah

Allen, James B. *Hearts Turned to the Fathers: A History of the Genealogical Society of Utah, 1894–1994.* Provo, UT: Brigham Young University Studies, 1995. 392p.

Bartholomew, Rebecca. *Audacious Women: Early British Mormon Immigrants.* Salt Lake City, UT: Signature Books, 1995. 288p.

Gregerson, Gary L. *Utah Roadside History, a Compilation of Monuments, Markers and Historic Sites.* Provo, UT: Griffin Associates, 1995. 235p.

Hardaway, Roger D. *A Narrative Bibliography of the African American Frontier, Blacks in the Rocky Mountain West, 1535–1912.* Lewiston, NY: Edwin Mellen Press, 1995. 242p.

Larson, Carl V. *The Women of the Mormon Battalion.* Logan, UT: Author, 1995. 130p.

Mormon Americana: A Guide to Sources and Collections in the United States. Provo, UT: Brigham Young University Studies, 1995. 695p.

Hyrum

Hyrum 5th Ward Cemetery Committee. *A Monumental Work, a Comprehensive List of Persons Buried in the Hyrum City Cemetery.* Hyrum, UT: Downs Printing, 1995. 717p.

San Juan County

Turk, Toni Richard. *Rooted in San Juan, a Genealogical Study of Burials in San Juan County, Utah, 1879–1995.* Blanding, UT: Author, 1995. 729p.

Vermont

Bartley, Scott A. *Vermont Families in 1791.* Genealogical Society of Vermont, Special Publication Number 1. Rockport, ME: Picton Press, 1995. 311p.

Bistrais, Bob. *Place Names on Vermont's Long Trail.* Thesis (M.A.), University of Vermont, 1995. 125p.

Emery, Eric B. *New England Captives in Canada and the Ransom Missions of Phineas Stevens, 1749, 1751 and 1752.* Thesis (M.A.), University of Vermont, 1995. 115p.

Marsh, Carole. *The Vermont Library Book, a Surprising Guide to the Unusual Special Collections in Libraries across Our State.* Atlanta, GA: Gallopade Pub., 1995. 36p.

Nichols, Joann H. *Index to Known Cemetery Listings in Vermont.* 3rd. ed. Montpelier, VT: Vermont Historical Society, 1995. 69p.

Rollins, Alden M. *Vermont Warnings Out.* Camden, ME: Picton Press, 1995. 448p.

Burlington

Records of Baptisms, Marriages, Burials Solemnized by George Goldthwait Ingersoll, Minister of the First Congregational Society in Burlington, Vermont. Sarasota, FL: Aceto Bookmen, 1995. 33p.

Charleston

Colburn, Richard A. *A Catalog of Charleston, Vermont, Cemeteries.* East Charleston, VT: Author, 1995. 163p.

Dorset

Manual of the Congregational Church of Dorset and East Rupert, Vermont. Sarasota, FL: Aceto Bookmen, 1912, 1995. 58p.

East Rupert

Manual of the Congregational Church of Dorset and East Rupert, Vermont. Sarasota, FL: Aceto Bookmen, 1912, 1995. 58p.

Georgia

Mallett, Peter S. *Georgia, Vermont, Vital Records*. St. Albans, VT: Genealogical Society of
    Vermont, 1995. 305p.

Rutland County

Jenks, Margaret R. *Rutland Cemetery Inscriptions, Rutland County, Vermont*. Sykesville, MD:
    Author, 1995. 381p.

Waterbury

Manual of the Congregational Church, Waterbury, Vermont. Sarasota, FL: Aceto Bookmen,
    1893, 1995. 38p.

Virginia

Alphabetical Rent Roll of Virginia, 1704/05. Houston, TX: Wright Electronic Publishing, 1995.
    Unpgd.
Association Oath Rolls of the British Plantations (New York, Virginia, etc.) AD 1696. Balti-
    more, MD: Clearfield, 1995. 86p.
Chernault, Tracy. *18th and 20th Battalions of Heavy Artillery*. Lynchburg, VA: H. E. Howard,
    1995. 128p.
Daulton, David T. *Adoption Procedures and Forms, a Guide for Virginia Lawyers*.
    Charlottesville, VA: Virginia CLE, 1995. 282p.
Dickinson, Bill. *Diggin' for Roots in Old Virginia*. Baltimore, MD: Clearfield, 1995. 165p.
Driver, Robert J. *2nd Virginia Cavalry*. Lynchburg, VA: H. E. Howard, 1995. 302p.
Eckenrode, H. J. *List of the Colonial Soldiers of Virginia*. Baltimore, MD: Clearfield, 1917,
    1995. 91p.
*Gleanings of Virginia History, an Historical and Genealogical Collection, Largely from Origi-
    nal Sources*. Baltimore, MD: Genealogical Pub. Co., 1995. 443p.
Library of Virginia. *1995 Directory of Virginia Libraries*. Richmond, VA: Author, 1995. 113p.
*1995 Obituaries from the Newspapers of Lynchburg, Altavista, Amherst, Appomattox, Bedford,
    Brookneal and Nelson County*. 1995. 101p.
Nuckols, Ashley Kay. *Deaths, American Expeditionary Force, WWI, 1917, 1918, Virginia*.
    Tazewell, VA: Author, 1995. Unpgd.
Page, Patsy R. *Directory of Virginia Physicians, 1886*. Alachua, FL: Page Publications, 1995.
    35p.
Plunkett, Michael. *Afro-American Sources in Virginia: A Guide to Manuscripts*. Charlottesville,
    VA: University Press of Virginia, 1995. Unpgd.
Riggs, Susan A. *Civil War Research at the Earl Gregg Swem Library, College of William and
    Mary*. Williamsburg, VA: Swem Library, College of William and Mary, 1995. Unpgd.

Schweitzer, George Keene. *Virginia Genealogical Research*. Knoxville, TN: Author, 1995. 216p.

Sifakis, Stewart. *Compendium of the Confederate Armies Series: Virginia*. NY: Facts on File, 1995. 288p.

Virginia State Library. Archives Division. *List of the Colonial Soldiers of Virginia, Special Report of the Department of Archives and History for 1913*. Baltimore, MD: Genealogical Publishing Co., 1995. 91p.

Wardell, Patrick G. *Virginians and West Virginians, 1607–1870. Volume 2*. Bowie, MD: Heritage Books, 1988, 1995. 589p.

Windley, Lathan A. *A Profile of Runaway Slaves in Virginia and South Carolina from 1730 through 1787*. Hamden, CT: Garland, 1995. 219p.

Accomack County

Carey, Mary Frances. *Tombstone Inscriptions of Upper Accomack County, Virginia*. Bowie, MD: Heritage Books, 1995. 372p.

Koger, Celestine G. *1850 Slave Inhabitants Schedule of Accomack County, Virginia*. Bowie, MD: Heritage Books, 1995. 250p.

Virginia Marriages, Early to 1800, a Research Tool. Bountiful, UT: AGLL, Inc. 1995. 1,148p.

Alexandria

Pippenger, Wesley E. *Alexandria, Virginia, Death Records, 1863–1868 (the Gladwin Record) and 1869–1896*. Westminster, MD: Family Line Pub., 1995. 337p.

Ring, Constance. *Alexandria, Virginia, Town Lots, 1749–1801, Together with Proceedings of the Board of Trustees, 1749–1780*. Westminster, MD: Family Line Publications, 1995. 218p.

Alleghany County

Arritt, Gay. *Historical Sketches*. Covington, VA: Alleghany Historical Society, 1995. 208p.

Amelia County

Amelia County, Virginia, Marriages, 1735–1810. Indianapolis, IN: The Researchers, 1995. 28p.

Amherst County

McLeRoy, William R. *More Passages, a New History of Amherst County, Virginia*. Bowie, MD: Heritage Books, 1995. 167p.

Augusta County

Burton, Charles T. *Augusta County, Virginia, Birth Dates, Real and Assumed of Minor Children*. Author, 1995. 78p.

Joyner, Peggy S. *St. John's Church Register, German Reformed and Lutheran, Augusta County, Virginia (1748), 1786–1872*. Portsmouth, VA: Author, 1995. 158p.

Botetourt County

Burton, Charles T. *Botetourt County, Virginia Death Records*. Roanoke, VA: V. W. Fowler, 1995. 364p.

Rifle, Conrad. *German Baptist Brethren, Dunkers of the Lion Hill Church, 6 Miles North of Fincastle, in Boutetcourt County, Virginia*. Clinton, OH: Author, 1995. 59p.

Campbell County

Bibliography of Genealogy and Local History Collections of the Campbell County Public Library. Rustburg, VA: Campbell County Public Library, 1995. 82p.

Caroline County

Collins, Herbert Ridgeway. *Caroline County, Virginia, Death Records (1919–1994) from the Caroline Progress, a Weekly Newspaper Published in Bowling Green, Virginia*. Westminster, MD: Family Line Pub., 1995. 181p.

Ridgeway, Herbert. *Cemeteries of Caroline County, Virginia. Volume 2*. Private Cemeteries. Westminster, MD: Family Line Pub., 1995. 312p.

Sparacio, Ruth. *Abstracts of Appeals and Land Causes, Caroline County, Virginia, 1787–1794*. McLean, VA: Antient Press, 1995. 110p.

———. *Order Book Abstracts of Caroline County, Virginia, 1784–1785*. McLean, VA: Antient Press, 1995. 111p.

———. *Order Book Abstracts of Caroline County, Virginia, 1785–1786*. McLean, VA: Antient Press, 1995. 112p.

Charlottesville

Murphy, Mary Catherine. *A Collection of Abstracts of Obituaries from Charlottesville, Virginia, Newspapers, 1820–1869, and Abstracts of Marriages from Charlottesville, Virginia, Newspapers, 1820–1859*. Charlottesville, VA; Author, 1995. Unpgd.

Culpepper County

Green, Raleigh Travers. *Genealogical and Historical Notes on Culpepper County, Virginia*. Bowie, MD: Heritage Books, 1995. 280p.

Dinwiddie County

Dinwiddie County, Virginia Surveyor's Platt Book, 1755–1796, and Court Orders, 1789–1791, an Every Name Index. Miami Beach, FL: T. L. C. Genealogy, 1995. 65p.

Essex County

Wright, Sue. *Essex County, Virginia, 1850 U.S. Census*. Arkadelphia, AR: Poplar Grove Press, 1995. 95p.

———. *Essex County, Virginia, 1860 U.S. Census*. Arkadelphia, AR: Poplar Grove Press, 1995. 107p.

Fairfax County

Johnson, William Page, II. *Brothers and Cousins, Confederate Soldiers and Sailors of Fairfax County, Virginia*. Athens, GA: Iberian Publishing, 1995. 249p.

Sparacio, Ruth. *Deed Abstracts of Fairfax County, Virginia, 1792–1793*. McLean, VA: Antient Press, 1995. 127p.

———. *Deed Abstracts of Fairfax County, Virginia, 1793–1795*. McLean, VA: Antient Press, 1995. 127p

Fauquier County

Sparacio, Ruth. *Minute Book Abstracts of Fauquier County, Virginia, 1766–1767*. McLean, VA: Antient Press, 1995. 119p.

———. *Minute Book Abstracts of Fauquier County, Virginia, 1767–1769.* McLean, VA: Antient Press, 1995. 118p.

Floyd County

Booth, Pat. *Beaver Creek Cemetery, Floyd, Virginia.* Author, 1995. 19p.

Fluvanna County

Hailey, Nell. *Fluvanna County, Virginia, Death Records, 1853–1896.* Athens, GA: Iberian Publishing Co., 1995. 296p.

Fort Myer

Fort Myer Buffalo Soldiers. Fort Myer, VA: Fort Myer Military Community, 1995. 12p.

Frederick County

O'Dell, Cecil. *Pioneers of Old Frederick County, Virginia.* Marceline, MO: Walsworth Publishing Co., 1995. 623p.

Fredericksburg

Hodge, Robert A. *Birth Records, Fredericksburg, Virginia, 1853–1896.* Emporia, KS: Author, 1995. Unpgd.

Goochland County

Weisiger, Benjamin B. *Goochland County, Virginia, Wills, 1742–1749.* Athens, GA: Iberian Publishing Co., 1995. 88p.

Grayson County

Bicentennial Heritage, Grayson County, Virginia, 1793–1995. Independence, VA: 1908 Courthouse Foundation, 1995. 401p.

Halifax County

Carrington, Wirt Johnson. *A History of Halifax County, Virginia.* Baltimore, MD: Clearfield, 1924, 1995. 525p.

Hanover County

Yates, Helen Kay. *Family Graveyards in Hanover County, Virginia, 1995.* Mechanicsville, VA: Author, 1995. 125p.

King and Queen County

Fisher, Therese A. *Vital Records of Three Burned Counties, Births, Marriages, and Deaths of King and Queen, King William, and New Kent Counties, Virginia, 1680–1860.* Bowie, MD: Heritage Books, 1995. 135p.

King George County

Lee, Elizabeth Nuckols. *King George County, Virginia, Bureau of Vital Statistics, Death Records, 1853–1896.* Bowie, MD: Heritage Books, 1995. 400p.

————. *King George County, Virginia Marriages*. Athens, GA: Iberian Pub. Co., 1995. Unpgd.
St. Paul's Parish Register (Stafford-King George Counties), 1715–1798. Baltimore, MD: Clearfield, 1995. 78p.

King William County

Fisher, Therese A. *Vital Records of Three Burned Counties, Births, Marriages, and Deaths of King and Queen, King William, and New Kent Counties, Virginia, 1680–1860*. Bowie, MD: Heritage Books, 1995. 135p.
Old King William County Cemeteries. King William County, VA: King William County Historical Society, 1995. 147p.

Lancaster County

Revolutionary Soldiers and Sailors from Lancaster County, Virginia, Muster Rolls and Pay Rolls of the Ninety-Second Regiment of Virginia Militia, Lancaster County, 1812. Westminster, MD: Family Line Pub., 1930, 1995. 74p.
Sparacio, Ruth. *Deed Abstracts of Lancaster County, Virginia, 1701–1706*. McLean, VA: Antient Press, 1995. 120p.
————. *Deed Abstracts of Lancaster County, Virginia, 1706–1710*. McLean, VA: Antient Press, 1995. 124p.
————. *Order Book Abstracts of Lancaster County, Virginia, 1682–1687*. McLean, VA: Antient Press, 1995. 118p.
————. *Order Book Abstracts of Lancaster County, Virginia, 1687–1691*. McLean, VA: Antient Press, 1995. 111p.
————. *Order Book Abstracts of Lancaster County, Virginia, 1691–1695*. McLean, VA: Antient Press, 1995. 110p.

Lee County

Treadway, Mark Douglas. *Lee County, Virginia, 1870 Census*. Monroe, MI: Author, 1995. 131p.

Leesburg

Frain, Elizabeth R. *Union Cemetery, Leesburg, Loudoun County, Virginia, Plats A & B, 1784-1995*. Lovettsville, VA: Willow Bend Books, 1995. 350p.

Louisa County

Hiatt, Marty. *Louisa County, Virginia, 1850 Federal Census*. Athens, GA: Author, 1995. 203p.

Lunenburg County

Evans, June Banks. *Lunenburg County, Virginia, Deed Book 21, 1806–1808*. New Orleans, LA: Bryn Ffyliaid Publications, 1995. 60p.
————. *Lunenburg County, Virginia, Register of Marriages*. New Orleans, LA: Bryn Ffyliaid Publications, 1995. Unpgd.
Lunenburg County, Virginia Court Orders, 1752–1762, an Every Name Index to Orders Book 2 1/2A, 2 1/2B, 3, 4, 5, 6, 7, 8. Miama Beach, FL: T. L. C. Genealogy, 1995. 160p.

Lynchburg

MacLeod, Douglas C. *Index to Obituaries in Lynchburg, Virginia, Newspapers, 1897*. Author, 1995. 43p.

1995 Obituaries from the Newspapers of Lynchburg, Altavista, Amherst, Appomattox, Bedford, Brookneal and Nelson County. 1995. 101p.

Middlesex County

Sparacio, Ruth. *Order Book Abstracts of Middlesex County, Virginia, 1694–1697.* McLean, VA: Antient Press, 1995. 110p.

———. *Order Book Abstracts of Middlesex County, Virginia, 1697–1700.* McLean, VA: Antient Press, 1995. 113p.

Wright, Sue. *Middlesex County, Virginia, 1850 United States Census.* Arkadelphia, AR: Popular Grove Press, 1995. 56p.

———. *Middlesex County, Virginia, 1860 United States Census.* Arkadelphia, AR: Popular Grove Press, 1995. 58p.

Nelson County

1995 Obituaries from the Newspapers of Lynchburg, Altavista, Amherst, Appomattox, Bedford, Brookneal and Nelson County. 1995. 101p.

New Kent County

Evans, June Banks. *New Kent County, Virginia, Deed Book 1, 1864–1872.* New Orleans, LA: Bryn Ffyliaid Publications, 1995. 101p.

Fisher, Therese A. *Vital Records of Three Burned Counties, Births, Marriages, and Deaths of King and Queen, King William, and New Kent Counties, Virginia, 1680–1860.* Bowie, MD: Heritage Books, 1995. 135p.

Vestry Book of Saint Peter's, New Kent County, Virginia, from 1682–1758. Baltimore, MD: Clearfield, 1905, 1995. 242p.

Northampton County

Buck, Dee Ann. *Northampton County, Virginia, Marriages, 1853–1880.* Fairfax, VA: Author, 1995. 120p.

Mihalyka, Jean Merritt. *Marriages, Northampton County, Virginia, 1660/1–1854, Recorded in Bonds, Licenses, Minister Returns, and Other Sources.* Rev. Bowie, MD: Heritage Books, 1995. 177p.

Sparacio, Ruth. *Order Book Abstracts of Northumberland County, Virginia, 1661–1665.* McLean, VA: Antient Press, 1995. 112p

———. *Order Book Abstracts of Northumberland County, Virginia, 1665–1669.* McLean, VA: Antient Press, 1995. 111p

———. *Order Book Abstracts of Northumberland County, Virginia, 1669–1673.* McLean, VA: Antient Press, 1995. 111p

Orange County

Sparacio, Ruth. *Deed Abstracts of Orange County, Virginia, 1795–1797.* McLean, VA: Author, 1995. 127p.

———. *Deed Abstracts of Orange County, Virginia, 1797–1799.* McLean, VA: Author, 1995. 128p.

Page County

Gilreath, Amelia Cleland. *Page County, Virginia, Wills Books, A, B, C and Deed Book A (Abstracted), 1831–1848.* Nokesville, VA: Author, 1995. 237p.

Patrick County

Kirkman, Eunice B. *1870 Census of Patrick County, Virginia.* Stuart, VA: Author, 1995. 242p.

Pittsylvania County

Dodson, Roger C. *Property Lines from the Old Survey Books, Pittsylvania County, Virginia, 1746 to 1840.* Danville, VA: Virginia - North Carolina Genealogical Society, 1995. 170p.

Kendrick, Desmond. *Pittsylvania County, Virginia, Obituaries and Marriages.* Martinsville, VA: Author, 1995. 171p.

Payne, Lucille C. *Pittsylvania County, Virginia, Inventories and Accounts Current, 1770–1797.* Lynchburg, VA: H. E. Howard, Inc., 1995. 196p.

Pound

Belcher, Loretta M. *Burying Grounds of the Pound Area, Pound, Virginia.* Pound, VA: Author, 1995. 253p.

Prince William County

Turner, Ronald Ray. *Prince William County, Virginia, Birth Records, 1912–1917.* Manassas, VA: Author, 1995. 114p.

———. *Prince William County, Virginia, 1900 Census, Alphabetically Arranged.* Manassas, VA: Author, 1995. 303p.

Princess Anne County

Maling, Anne. *Princess Anne County, Virginia, Land and Probate Records, Abstracted from Deed Books One to Eighteen, 1691–1783.* Bowie, MD: Heritage Books, 1995. 118p.

Richmond County

Sparacio, Ruth. *Deed Abstracts of Richmond County, Virginia, 1725–1729.* McLean, VA: Antient Press, 1995. 125p.

———. *Deed Abstracts of Richmond County, Virginia, 1729–1733.* McLean, VA: Antient Press, 1995. 128p.

Roanoke County

Hutcheson, Charlene D. *Marriage Patterns in Cave Springs and Back Creek, Roanoke County, Virginia, 1700s–1850.* Author, 1995. 47p.

Russell County

Adkins, Anita Owens. *Early Deaths of Russell County, Virginia, 1853 to 1896.* Grundy, VA: Author, 1995. 152p.

Colley, Tom. *Russell County, Virginia Deed Book.* Athens, GA: Iberian Pub. Co., 1995. Unpgd.

Shenandoah, County

Buck, Dee Ann. *Shenandoah County, Virginia, Marriages, 1854–1880.* Fairfax, VA: Author, 1995. 284p.

Risdon, Elisabeth. *Shenandoah County, Virginia, Birth Records of Free Born Children, 1853-1871.* Edinburg, VA, 1995. 89p.

Stafford County

St. Paul's Parish Register, (Stafford-King George Counties), 1715–1798. Baltimore, MD: Clearfield, 1995. 78p.

Surry County

Hodges, Dennis. *Surry County, Virginia Free Negro Register*. Richmond, VA: Virginia Genealogical Society, 1995. 339p.

Tazewell County

Nuckols, Ashley Kay. *Obituary Index, Tazewell Republican, Tazewell, Virginia, 1897–1912*. Tazewell, VA; Author, 1995. 39p.

———. *Obituary Index, Tazewell, Virginia, 1913–1931*. Tazewell, VA: Author, 1995. 69p.

———. *Obituary Index, Tazewell, Virginia, Publications, 1932–1949*. Tazewell, VA: Author, 1995. 62p.

———. *Obituary Index, Tazewell, Virginia, Publications, 1950–1964*. Tazewell, VA: Author, 1995. 45p.

———. *Obituary Index, Tazewell, Virginia, Publications, 1965–1980*. Tazewell, VA: Author, 1995. 85p.

Tazewell County Heritage. Tazewell, VA: Tazewell County Historical Society, 1995. Unpgd.

Warren County

Buck, Dee Ann. *Warren County, Virginia, Marriage Registry, 1854–1880*. Fairfax, VA: Author, 1995. 101p.

Washington County

Burton, Charles T. *Surname Index to Publications of the Historical Society of Washington County, Virginia*. Troutville, VA: Author, 1995. 22p.

Summers, Lewis Preston. *History of Southwest Virginia, 1746–1786, Washington County, 1777–1870*. Baltimore, MD: Clearfield, 1903, 1971, 1995. 912p.

West Augusta County

Crumrine, Boyd. *Virginia Court Records in Southwestern Pennsylvania, Records of the District of West Augusta and Ohio and Yohogania Counties, Virginia, 1775–1780*. Baltimore, MD: Clearfield, 1995. 542p.

Westmoreland County

Sparacio, Ruth. *Deed and Will Abstracts of Westmoreland County, Virginia, 1729–1732*. McLean, VA: Antient Press, 1995. 116p.

———. *Deed and Will Abstracts of Westmoreland County, Virginia, 1732–1734*. McLean, VA: Antient Press, 1995. 117p.

———. *Deed and Will Abstracts of Westmoreland County, Virginia, 1734–1736*. McLean, VA: Antient Press, 1995. 118p.

———. *Deed and Will Abstracts of Westmoreland County, Virginia, 1736–1740*. McLean, VA: Antient Press, 1995. 119p.

———. *Deed and Will Abstracts of Westmoreland County, Virginia, 1740–1742*. McLean, VA: Antient Press, 1995. 117p.

———. *Deed and Will Abstracts of Westmoreland County, Virginia, 1742–1745*. McLean, VA: Antient Press, 1995. 117p.

———. *Deed and Will Abstracts of Westmoreland County, Virginia, 1745–1747*. McLean, VA: Antient Press, 1995. 116p.

Yohogania County

Crumrine, Boyd. *Virginia Court Records in Southwestern Pennsylvania, Records of the District of West Augusta and Ohio and Yohogania Counties, Virginia, 1775–1780*. Baltimore, MD: Clearfield, 1995. 542p.

York County

Willis, Anne Romberg. *The Master's Merry, Slave Prosecutions and Punishments in York County, Virginia, 1700 to 1780*. Thesis (M.A.), College of William and Mary, 1995. 288p.

Washington

Seattle

Litz, John R. *The Chinese and Chinese Americans in the Seattle Times, January 1, 1900 to December 31, 1909*. Seattle, WA: Author, 1995. 72p.

Mahoney, Salley Gene. *Index to Clarence B. Bagley's History of Seattle from the Earliest Settlement to the Present Time, 1916, Volumes I and II, Pages 1–882, and Volume III, Pages 1–1,147*. Seattle, WA: Seattle Genealogical Society, 1995. 105p.

West Virginia

A Guide to Pronunciation of Place Names in West Virginia. 5th ed. Morgantown, WV: West Virginia University, Publications Services, 1995. 59p.

Nuckols, Ashley Kay. *Deaths, American Expeditionary Force, WWI, 1917, 1918, West Virginia*. Tazewell, VA: Author, 1995. Unpgd.

Reddy, Anne Waller. *West Virginia Revolutionary Ancestors*. Baltimore, MD: Clearfield, 1995. 92p.

Barbour County

Cochran, Wes. *Barbour County, West Virginia, Marriages, 1892–1935*. Parkersburg, WV: Author, 1995. 233p.

Braxton County

1840–1860 Census, Braxton County, West Virginia, 1870 Census, Braxton County, Washington District, 1880 Census, Braxton County, Birch District. 1995. Unpgd.

Cabell County

Eldridge, Carrie. *Records of the Greenbottom Baptist Church, Cabell County, West Virginia*. Chesapeake, OH: Author, 1995. 145p.

Charleston

Peterson, Rose W. *Spring Hill Cemetery, Charleston, West Virginia*. Nitro, WV: Peterson Quality Associates, 1995. 4 vols.

Clay County

1860 Census, Clay County, West Virginia, 1870 Census, Clay County, Buffalo Township, 1880 Census, Clay County, Buffalo District, Otter District. 1995. Unpgd.

Fayette County

Shuck, Larry Gorden. *Fayette County, West Virginia, Marriages, 1832–1853 and 1865–1903*. Apollo, PA: Closson Press, 1995. 315p.

Gilmer County

Gilmer County, West Virginia, Deaths, 1853–1880. Parkersburg, WV: Wes Cochran, 1995. 35p.

Greenbrier County

Shuck, Larry Gorden. *Greenbrier County Birth Records, 1853–1899*. Athens, GA: Iberian Publishing Co., 1995. 2 vols.

Hampshire County

Horton, Vicki Bidinger. *Hampshire County, West Virginia, Personal Property Tax Lists, 1800-1814*. Romney, WV: Hampshire Review, 1995. 215p.

Pugh, Maud. *Capton Valley, Its Pioneers and Their Descendants, 1689 to 1940*. Baltimore, MD: Clearfield, 1948, 1995. 350p.

Lewis County

Strader, Hartzel G. *Lewis County Birth Records: Births Recorded in the Lewis County Courthouse, West Virginia*. WV: Hacker's Creek Press, 1995. Unpgd.

McDowell County

Hatcher, Thomas C. *The Heritage of McDowell County, West Virginia*. War, WV: McDowell County Historical Society, 1995. Unpgd.

Mercer County

Hays, Sallie. *Mercer County, West Virginia, Marriage Book*. Signal Mountain, TN: Mountain
    Press, 1995. Unpgd.

Mingo County

Atkins, Oscar Thomas. *Mingo County, West Virginia, 1910*. Williamson, WV: Author, 1995.
    377p.

Nicholas County

Blake, James S. *Early Nicholas County, West Virginia, Marriage Bonds (& Records), 1818–
    1864*. Craigsville, WV: Author, 1995. 118p.
Cochran, Wes. *Nicholas County, West Virginia, Marriages*. Parkersburg, WV: Author, 1995.
    Unpgd.

Ohio County

Crumrine, Boyd. *Virginia Court Records in Southwestern Pennsylvania, Records of the Dis-
    trict of West Augusta and Ohio and Yohogania Counties, Virginia, 1775–1780*. Baltimore,
    MD: Clearfield, 1995. 542p.

Pendleton County

Toothman, Rick. *Pendleton County, West Virginia, Deedbook Records, 1788–1813*. Bowie,
    MD: Heritage Books, 1995. 225p.

Preston County

Sisler, Janice Cale. *In Remembrance, Tombstone Readings of Preston County, West Virginia*.
    Bruceton Mills, WV: Author, 1995. Unpgd.

Randolph County

Randolph County, West Virginia, Cemetery Headstone Readings. Ozark, MO: Dogwood Print-
    ing, 1995. Unpgd.
Rowland, Joseph S. *Southern Peace Families and the Barr Descendants of Margaret Scott
    Barr Peace*. Tuscaloosa, AL: Author, 1995. 563p.

Ritchie County

Ritchie County, West Virginia Cemeteries through 1993. Parsons, WV: McClain Print, 1995.
    852p.

Tyler County

Fiber, Wilma. *Cemetery Reading, McElroy District, Tyler County, West Virginia*. Middlebourne,
    WV: Tyler County Heritage and Historical Society, 1995. Unpgd.
Tyler County, West Virginia, Marriages, 1891–1932. Parkersburg, WV: Author, 1995. 226p.

Wayne County

*Wayne County, Virginia/West Virginia, Marriages, 1853–1900, Excluding Civil War Years, 1861-
    1864, Index by Groom and Bride*. Huntington, WV: Kyowva Genealogical Society, 1995.
    256p.

Wetzel County

Neff, Lisa Hassig. *Wetzel County, West Virginia, Marriages, 1894–1902.* New Martinsville, WV: Wetzel County Genealogical Society, 1995. 114p.

Wood County

Cochran, Wes. *Wood County, West Virginia, 1900 Census, Harris District (with Notes).* Parkersburg, WV: Author, 1995. 59p.

Wyoming County

Wyoming County Heritage, Wyoming County, West Virginia, 1995. Pineville, WV: Wyoming County Genealogical Society, 1995. 202p.

Wisconsin

Doering, Anita Taylor. *Guide to Local History and Genealogy Resources: Sources in the Winding Rivers Library System, Wisconsin, Selected Sources in Houston, Olmsted and Winona Counties, Minnesota.* La Crosse, WI: La Crosse Public Library, 1995. Unpgd.

Hall, Sylvia. *Farewell to the Homeland, European Immigration to NE Wisconsin, 1840 to 1900.* 3rd. ed. Green Bay, WI: Brown County Historical Society, 1995. 153p.

Koltyk, Jo Ann. *New Pioneers in the Heartland, Hmong Life in Wisconsin.* Thesis (M.A.), University of Wisconsin at Madison, 1995. 471p.

Wisconsin Council for Local History: 1995 Roster. Madison, WI: The Council, 1995. 60p.

Wisconsin Society, Children of the American Revolution. *History of the Wisconsin Society, Children of the American Revolution, 1895–1995: Pride of the Past, Promise of the Future.* Madison, WI: The Society, 1995. 262p.

Eau Claire County

Genealogical Research Society of Eau Claire. *Brides of Eau Claire County, Wisconsin, 1854-1928, an Index Based on Records from the Eau Claire County Courthouse.* Eau Claire, WI: Author, 1995. 301p.

———. *Grooms of Eau Claire County, Wisconsin, 1854–1928, an Index Based on Records from the Eau Claire County Courthouse.* Eau Claire, WI: Author, 1995. 301p.

Granville

Town of Granville, Irish and St. Michael's Cemetery. Milwaukee, WI: Milwaukee County Genealogical Society, 1995. 142p.

Lafayette

White Oak Cemetery, Lafayette Township, Walworth County. Delavan, WI: Walworth County
Genealogical Society, 1995. 13p.

Lafayette County

Lemanski, Cheryl D. *Some Lafayette County, Wisconsin, Deaths, 1849–1907.* Fennimore, WI:
Author, 1995. 160p.

Matl, Fran H. *Lafayette County, Wisconsin, Index of Births, 1921-October 1992.* Shullsburg,
WI: Author, 1995. 397p.

Milwaukee

Baehr, Carl. *Milwaukee Streets: The Stories Behind Their Names.* Milwaukee, WI: Cream City
Press, 1995. 317p.

Guide to Genealogical Collections in the Milwaukee Metropolitan Area. Milwaukee, WI: Library Council of Metropolitan Milwaukee, 1995. 185p.

Racine County

A Family Album of Racine County, 1900–1950. Racine, WI: Journal Times, 1995. 127p.

Rock County

Demrow, Kay. *Grove Cemetery, Center Township, Rock County, Wisconsin, the History and
the People.* Janesville, WI: Author, 1995. 365p.

Warn, Eileen. *Luther Valley Cemetery.* Janesville, WI: Rock County Genealogical Society,
1995. Unpgd.

Walworth County

Hollinger, Dorothy. *Index to the 1837 Atlas of Walworth County, Wisconsin.* Delavan, WI:
Walworth County Genealogical Society, 1995. 102p.

Wyoming

King, Jennifer. *Guide to Women's History Resources at the American Heritage Center.* 2nd. ed.
Laramie, WY: American Heritage Center, University of Wyoming, 1995. 61p.

Albany County

Mason, Mary Kay. *World War II and Albany County, Wyoming.* Hurst, TX: Curtis Media, 1995.
120p.

Piedmont

Tippets, Susan Thomas. *Piedmont, Uinta County, Wyoming, Ghost Town*. Author, 1995. 109p.

Sweetwater County

Garceau, Dorothy Claire. *The Important Things of Life, Women, Work and Family in Sweetwater County, Wyoming, 1880–1929*. Dissertation (Ph.D.), Brown University, 1995. 389p.

ISBN 0-8420-2661-4

90000>